COLLECTED WORKS OF ERASMUS

VOLUME 5

THE CORRESPONDENCE OF
ERASMUS

LETTERS 594 TO 841

1517 TO 1518

translated by R.A.B. Mynors and D.F.S. Thomson

annotated by Peter G. Bietenholz

University of Toronto Press

Toronto / Buffalo / London

The research and publication costs of the
Collected Works of Erasmus are supported by the
Social Sciences and Humanities Research Council of Canada
(and previously by the Canada Council).
The publication costs are also assisted by
University of Toronto Press.

Library of Congress Cataloging in Publication Data (Revised)
Erasmus, Desiderius, d. 1536.
The correspondence of Erasmus.
(Collected works of Erasmus, v. 1–   )
v. 5 annotated by P. G. Bietenholz.
Translation of Opus espistolarum Des. Erasmi Roterdami.
Includes bibliographical references.
CONTENTS: [1] Letters 1 to 141, 1484–1500. –
[2] Letters 142 to 297, 1501–1514. – [etc.] –
[5] Letters 594 to 841, 1517–1518.
1. Erasmus, Desiderius, d. 1536 – Correspondence.
I. Title.
PA8511.A5E55 1974   199'.492   72-97422
ISBN 0-8020-1981-1 (v. 1)
ISBN 0-8020-5429-3 (v. 5)

Collected Works of Erasmus

The aim of the Collected Works of Erasmus
is to make available an accurate, readable English text
of Erasmus' correspondence and his
other principal writings. The edition is planned
and directed by an Editorial Board, an Executive Committee,
and an Advisory Committee.

Contents

Illustrations

Preface

This volume covers the first ten months of Erasmus' residence at Louvain, beginning in July 1517 (Ep 596). After a year of intermittent attendance at court and visits to London, Antwerp, and other Netherlandish towns, settling down at Louvain has added to the regularity of his way of life. The seasons begin to form a recognizable pattern. The cold of the winter months (Ep 719), accompanied by a head cold,[1] is rendered more bearable by the beginning of a new calendar year. Friends exchange gifts,[2] and horoscopes for the months ahead are pondered with a mixture of curiosity and scepticism.[3] The great religious feast days of the year are rarely marked in Erasmus' letters,[4] but the arrival of spring calls for a change of air and scene. His trips to Flanders in April 1518[5] and May 1519[6] were primarily holidays. By contrast, one major journey in the service of Erasmus' scholarly calling is a matter of grave concern and meticulous preparation[7] – it is devoted to Erasmus' dominant preoccupation over many months, the re-editing of the New Testament. This volume ends on the eve of his departure by 1 May 1518 for Basel and the workshops of the Froben press.

Time and again Erasmus sees himself cast in the 'last act of the play' or uses similar metaphors derived from the stage[8] to announce the approaching completion of what he considers to be his *magnum opus*. It is through his New Testament that the use he has made of his time and talent will be judged by God and men alike. Frequently he sighs about the unending toil of annotation. The 'midnight oil' keeps burning in his lamp.

* * * * *

1 Epp 665, 720
2 Epp 748, 753, 760, Allen Epp 1056, 1178 introductions
3 Ep 755:32n
4 Ep 691:29n
5 Ep 831:117n
6 Allen Ep 963:1n; cf Ep 1079.
7 Epp 752, 770, 795
8 Epp 756–8

Once the New Testament is in the hands of the public, however, he will be free 'to sing to himself and the Muses.'[9] He may decide to move to Paris[10] or London,[11] where neither friends nor honours will be lacking. Moreover, if he can trust the word of their attendants, a major benefice is waiting for him upon his arrival at the court of either Francis I or Henry VIII. Thus when old age approaches it will find him serene and free from care. But although parts of the New Testament are being printed in Basel, others still await the finishing touches. To relieve himself of the drudgery of textual collation and emendation followed by countless explanatory notes, he tries his hand at the easier-flowing paraphrase of the New Testament (Ep 710) and gives its definitive form to the *Ratio verae theologiae* (Ep 745). After a daily dose of theological argument and unpolished language encountered in Scriptures and commentaries, he will on occasion permit himself a little time in the company of a classical author. It refreshes the mind, refurbishes his style, and may even net some crumbs of scholarship that can be turned over to a modest publisher (Ep 704).

If his residence at Louvain permitted an increased degree of concentration on his scholarly labours, it also caused a number of distractions, some gratifying and some exasperating. Among the former were the establishment of the Collegium Trilingue, Louvain's new college of the three ancient languages, which to the end of this volume progresses without major difficulties (Ep 691), and new and congenial friendships such as the one with the unassuming and scholarly Augustinian Maarten Lips (Ep 750). On the other hand he was finding collegial carousing bothersome.[12] Also the friars in Louvain and elsewhere continued to attack him, and early in 1517 a new critic appeared on the scene: Edward Lee (Ep 765) had arrived earlier in Louvain, recommended by his acquaintance with the best of English friends and patrons, such as Thomas More. For years to come he was to cause Erasmus endless worries and provoke him into moods of rancour and vindictiveness. More immediately, however, it was rather the controversy with Jacques Lefèvre d'Etaples which caused the greatest waste of time and energy and touched off in Erasmus a reaction somewhat out of proportion to the provocation he had suffered.[13]

Although not carefree, Erasmus' position in Louvain was prestigious and secure. He was a member of the theological faculty yet free of regular

* * * * *

9 Epp 731:44, 784:18, 785:10, 809:64, 826:4
10 Epp 723, 778:33n, 810
11 Epp 657, 694, 834
12 Ep 643:37–8
13 Epp 597, 721

academic duties,[14] and he was entitled to receive a regular income that was more than adequate to provide for his modest needs in the College of the Lily.[15] It is true that payment was not always made when due (Ep 621), but the concern shown in some of his letters[16] for supplemental income seems somewhat excessive and indicative, above all, of habits formed in the more difficult days that now lay in the past. The journey to Basel, as a major expense of a special nature, was prepared for with ingenious circumspection.[17]

As never before Erasmus' name now counted among the educated and the powerful. He was overwhelmed with invitations from every corner of Europe.[18] Everywhere he had influential friends, and in Germany especially he had enthusiastic admirers who could now be referred to as Erasmiani or Erasmici even by a critic.[19] They expected him to join in the defence of Johann Reuchlin,[20] and they made sure that he became promptly acquainted with the Ninety-five Theses of friar Martin Luther, whose name he had not yet learnt to remember.[21]

This volume comprises 247 letters. These and some other sources offer evidence of a great many additional letters belonging to the same period, but not known to exist today. Eighty-two such missing letters are mentioned explicitly, and the existence of many more can be surmised. How many others were lost without trace we do not know, nor can we assume that in general it is the more significant ones that have survived. Since the number of letters preserved is one of the highest for any phase of Erasmus' life,[22] we may perhaps suppose that the rate of survival too is unusually high. Two circumstances have worked in favour of posterity. One is the existence of the Deventer Letter-book,[23] into which Erasmus had his amanuenses copy both incoming and outgoing letters. For more than half of the letters contained in this volume it is the only source. The other fortunate factor is Erasmus' belief at the time that the reading public should have access to his correspondence. Of the letters printed in this volume, sixty-five appeared in one or more of the collections of his correspondence published

* * * * *

14 Epp 637:12n, 669–70
15 Epp 621, 800:32n
16 Epp 638, 702, 753–4
17 Epp 772, 793, 823 introductions
18 Ep 809:146ff
19 Ep 769; cf CWE 3 xiii.
20 Epp 610, 694
21 Ep 785:39n
22 See appendix.
23 See Allen I 603–9.

in his lifetime and with his active co-operation; thirty-one letters first appeared in the *Auctarium* of 1518; another thirty in the *Farrago* of 1519; and four more in the *Epistolae ad diversos*, 1521.[24] The preparation of these collections prompted Erasmus to ask several friends for any letters they still had in their possession.[25] Twenty-two letters in this volume were first published elsewhere, but always in Erasmus' lifetime with his direct assistance or at least with his implicit consent. Only two of his own letters, Epp 622 and 713, were published by contemporaries clearly against his wishes. The troubles resulting from unauthorized publication of his letters were bound to increase and contribute later to an abrupt change in Erasmus' willingness to share his copy-books with the public. After the *Epistolae ad diversos* had appeared in 1521, it was not until 1529 that he released another collection of his letters for publication.

It is not easy to discern by what criteria Erasmus selected some of his letters rather than others to be copied into the Deventer Letter-book or even to be printed. Important private concerns, financial transactions for instance, could account for the preservation of some letters in the copy-book only; while a moral lesson, elegance of style, or the rank of a correspondent might explain the publication of others. Either way, consistency seems lacking. The surviving texts, however, reveal a good deal about Erasmus' letter-writing habits. The correspondence is spread out fairly evenly month by month. Occasionally, however, the availability of couriers would cause a flurry of letters to be drafted and copied within a very few days.[26] Bundles of letters might travel either with professional couriers such as the Basel public messenger,[27] with regular travellers such as booksellers,[28] or with casual carriers such as visiting students and humanists.[29] But on many occasions, especially when manuscripts and gifts were to be delivered as well as letters, Erasmus preferred to send one of his own men.[30]

As in preceding volumes, P.S. Allen's critical edition of Erasmus' correspondence has been an invaluable guide in every respect. His text is the basis of the English translation, and his arrangement of the letters normally has been retained, although occasionally with some slight modification in the dates. Only in four cases was the change of date proposed in

* * * * *

24 See CWE 3 347–53.
25 Epp 656, 783, 785
26 Epp 601:64n, 602, 701, 767, 795, 813 introductions
27 Epp 730–2
28 Epp 637:3n, 772, 831
29 Epp 744, 810
30 Epp 594, 653, 772, 820 introductions, 650:10n

this edition significant enough to require reorganization. Thus Allen's Ep 660 is Ep 1013A in CWE, his Ep 692 has become 480A, his Ep 705, 902A, and his Ep 733, 704A. Moreover, new conjectures are proposed for the correspondents addressed in Epp 749 and 792, and also for some issues raised in other letters, especially in relation to the controversy around Johann Reuchlin.[31] A procedure was established in preceding CWE volumes, and has been retained here, that will inform the reader of the date by which each letter first appeared in print. For letters published in contemporary collections of Erasmus' correspondence the introduction cites the earliest such collection to print the letter in question. For letters published elsewhere in Erasmus' lifetime the first edition is cited as well. Where manuscript sources exist these are also cited provided they carry any weight. When no sources are indicated in the introduction the letter was copied into the Deventer Letter-book and was first published in LB. If a manuscript source alone is cited the letter was first published by Allen or before him by another scholar of modern times. These letters, and also the ones coming exclusively from the Deventer Letter-book, cannot be assumed to have circulated widely among Erasmus' contemporaries. Where printed letter collections are described by short titles, a full reference is given among the Works Frequently Cited.

Finally I wish to acknowledge the assistance given me by N. van der Blom, E.J.M. van Eijl, Werner Kaegi, Martin Steinmann, J.B. Trapp, P.M. Swan, Paul F. Grendler, and other scholars whose names could not always be mentioned in the appropriate places. These notes could not have been assembled without the courteous assistance of the staffs of the Library of the University of Saskatchewan, the British Library, the Öffentliche Bibliothek of the University of Basel, and several other libraries. I am particularly grateful to John H. Munro, who generously agreed to check my notes on money matters, correcting some errors and adding the equivalences in gold, silver, or money-of-account. My special gratitude goes to the Warburg Institute, University of London, which provided me with an office close to its stacks and equally close to the congenial common room during a timely year of sabbatical leave.

The index to this volume, prepared by James Farge CSB, contains references to the persons, places, and works mentioned in the volume, following the plan for the correspondence series. When that series of volumes is completed the reader will also be supplied with an index of classical and scriptural references. A Biographical Register will supplement the biographical information found in the annotation to the letters.

* * * * *

31 Ep 694 introduction

The translation is the work of R.A.B. Mynors, who wishes to acknowledge the stimulus and assistance supplied by his colleagues in the enterprise. Finally it should be recalled that the Collected Works of Erasmus could not have been undertaken without the continued support of the Social Sciences and Humanities Research Council of Canada, its generous patron.

PGB

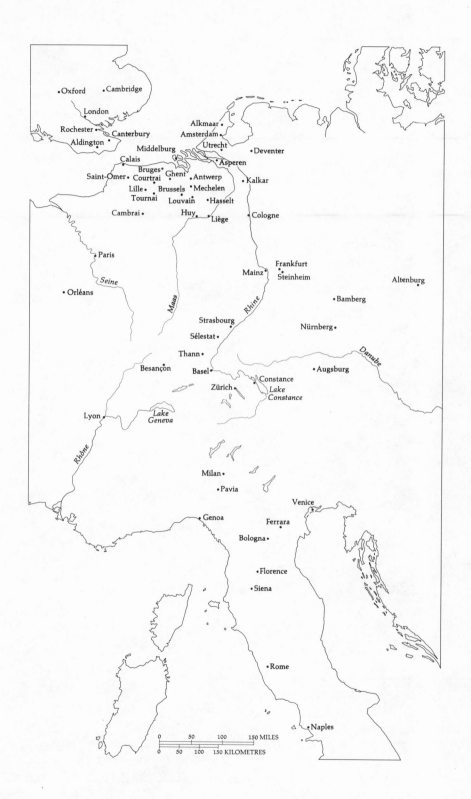

Oxford • • Cambridge

London •

Rochester • • Canterbury
Aldington •

Alkmaar •
Amsterdam •
Utrecht •
Middelburg • • Deventer
Calais • Asperen •
Bruges • Ghent • Kalkar
Saint-Omer • Courtrai • • Antwerp
Lille • Brussels • Mechelen
Tournai • Louvain • Hasselt
Cambrai • Huy • • Liège
• Cologne

Paris •
Seine
Orléans •

Frankfurt •
Mainz • • Steinheim
Altenburg •

Maas
Rhine
• Bamberg

Strasbourg •
Sélestat •
Nürnberg •

Thann •
Besançon • Basel •
Danube
Constance • • Augsburg
Zürich • Lake
Constance

Lyon • Lake
Geneva

Rhône

Milan •
• Pavia

Venice •
Genoa • • Ferrara
Bologna •

• Florence
• Siena

• Rome

• Naples

0   50   100   150 MILES
0   50   100   150 KILOMETRES

THE CORRESPONDENCE OF ERASMUS

LETTERS 594 TO 841

594 / From Beatus Rhenanus   Basel, 8 July 1517

As the principal scholarly consultant and collaborator of Johann Froben's press, Beatus Rhenanus (cf Ep 327 introduction) had found many occasions to be of service to Erasmus, thus earning his friendship and esteem. But since the autumn of 1516 Beatus had ceased to work regularly for the Froben press (cf Epp 460:16–18, 575:47–9), no doubt partly because of personal disagreements with Wolfgang Lachner (cf line 5n). Fearing that without Beatus the press would no longer be able to handle scholarly editions with its former standard of accuracy, Erasmus probably suggested the re-engagement of Beatus when sending the manuscripts mentioned here (cf Ep 597:49–51). The negotiations between Beatus and the press proved difficult (cf Ep 628:2–4), but by the end of the year they had apparently succeeded (cf Ep 732:2). The mutual lack of trust was not entirely overcome, however, and a new quarrel erupted in 1519. Erasmus remained critical of Froben and Lachner; cf Bietenholz *Basle and France* 28, 38–9.

Together with Epp 595 and 598–600 this letter was most likely taken back to Erasmus by his trusted servant, Jacobus Nepos (see Ep 595:11 and n), who had travelled to Basel in May 1517, carrying manuscripts to the printer, among them More's *Utopia* (cf Epp 584:18, 795:12). On his way back Nepos picked up Ep 614 at Mainz (cf Ep 631:4) and probably Ep 615 at Cologne (cf Ep 622:14, 25). On 24–5 August, after his return from a short vacation in Antwerp (cf Ep 622 introduction), Erasmus wrote another series of letters to friends along the Rhine (Epp 625–36), which included his answers to Epp 595, 598–9, and 614; Ep 628 may well be the reply to this letter.

BEATUS RHENANUS TO ERASMUS OF ROTTERDAM, GREETING

On the things you sent I would gladly help the people you speak of, provided it would not embarrass them to deal with me. They will write through their secretary, whom they now use as a corrector of the press, and say what they propose to do. Lachner has gone off to the Strasbourg fair.   5

* * * * *

594

2 things you sent] A group of manuscripts for the Froben press including More's *Utopia* (cf Epp 550 introduction, 584:18–20).

4 secretary] Probably Wolfgang Angst; cf Epp 363 introduction, 575:49n.

5 Strasbourg fair] Held around St John's day, in the second half of June. It gained regional significance only in the sixteenth century; cf P. Dollinger et al *Histoire de l'Alsace* (Toulouse 1970) 154. Wolfgang Lachner (cf Ep 305:198n) owed his considerable success as a bookseller partly to concentrating on the great fairs rather than sending salesmen from town to town or keeping permanent stores in different places, as had been customary in the past. With his strong will and

Beatus Rhenanus
Portrait in Nikolaus Reusner *Icones siue imagines*
Strasbourg 1587
Rare Book Division, The New York Public Library
Astor, Lennox and Tilden Foundations

Ludwig Baer is at Thann, and so this courier will not bring you anything in
the way of a letter from him. We have had a visit here lately from a certain
Clemens Palaeologus from Constantinople, a monk of St Catharine's
monastery on Mount Sinai in Syria. He has been collecting money through
Germany under authorizations from the pope for the repair of his monas-   10
tery, which suffered some damage in former years from the Saracens. He
knows Greek very well, so Bruno and I stammered it with him. During this
time the bishop has often had us to dinner. He always has a high opinion of
you, and expresses it, as he does also in the letter which he has now sent
you. Froben is printing Chrysostom on two presses and the *Elucidatorium*   15
ecclesiasticum of Clichtove of Nieuwpoort on two others. He has written
some notes on the hymns, sequences, canon of the mass, responsories, and
antiphons. Give my greetings to John Smith, our friend from Britain. Best
wishes, my most respected teacher and father.
     Basel, 8 July 1517   20

595 / From Bruno Amerbach   [Basel, c 8–15 July 1517]

Bruno Amerbach (see Ep 331 introduction), the older brother of the well-
known Bonifacius (cf line 15, Ep 408 introduction), spent his short adult life
entirely in the service of the Froben press.

* * * * *

large capital resources he carried great weight in the press of Johann Froben,
his son-in-law and partner, but he continued to operate his book trade with
some degree of independence; cf Grimm *Buchführer* 1366–72.
  6 Baer] Baer taught theology at the University of Basel, but the spring term had
     apparently ended; he held a canonry at Thann and was required to reside there
     for certain periods. Cf Epp 460:15n, 488 introduction.
  8 Palaeologus] He had passed through Chur on his way to Basel, and in the
     autumn of 1518 was again pleading his cause in Switzerland (AK II Epp 583,
     635–6). Two years later Erasmus recommended to Cardinal Wolsey one Chris-
     tophorus Palaeologus, bearer of Ep 1132, who may be the same person.
     Bedouin raids repeatedly compelled the monks to abandon the monastery of
     St Catharine on Mount Sinai for safer places, as they did in 1516; cf H.
     Skrobucha *Sinai* trans G. Hunt (London 1966) 60.
 12 Bruno] Amerbach; see Ep 331 introduction.
 14 letter] Beatus must have been shown a draft of Ep 598.
 15 Froben] See Ep 19 introduction.
 15 Chrysostom] Cf Ep 575:39n.
 15 *Elucidatorium*] First published by H. Estienne, Paris, 19 April 1516, and re-
     printed by Froben in August 1517; cf J.-P. Massaut *Josse Clichtove, l'humanisme
     et la réforme du clergé* (Paris 1968) II 285–335. Josse Clichtove of Nieuwpoort
     (1472–1543), a DD of Paris in 1506, still lived in Paris as a scholar and private
     tutor. Later he became a prominent opponent of Luther.
 18 Smith] Erasmus' student-servant since 1511

An autograph rough draft of this letter is in the Öffentliche Bibliothek of the
University of Basel, MS G II 33a f10; the best edition of the text is in AK II Ep 585.
Erasmus' answer to this letter is Ep 632; for the date see Ep 594 introduction.

You write to all your other friends and neglect me, and me only, and I
should take this very unkindly, if I had not brought this forgetfulness on my
own head – in my own horse and cart, as the saying goes – by still sitting at
home like a hobbling shoemaker after writing and telling you that I should
be off to Rome at Easter. But you must not put down this delay to indolence.   5
My friend Wilhelm Nesen has held me up until the autumn
> What time, in wrath against the race of men,
> Zeus pours torrential rains.
For my friend's sake I tolerate this loss of time, so long as our modern
Callipedes does not leave me in the lurch.   10
    As your man Jacobus is about to return to you, I could not let him
approach you empty-handed; I had rather you accused me of being foolish
than neglectful. In return, when you have a chance to write to us, if you do
not think me worthy of a letter on my own, do at least send me greetings in a
letter to someone else. My brother Bonifacius and Konrad greet you par-   15
ticularly.

596 / [To William Warham?]   [Louvain, c 10 July 1517]

In the Deventer Letter-book this fragment follows the text of Ep 597. It was
scratched through, perhaps with the intention of recopying the letter on a
fresh page. Epp 596 and 597 both convey the news of Erasmus' arrival in
Louvain. Assuming that they were to be carried by the same messenger, John

* * * * *
595
  1 friends] Perhaps answers now lost to Epp 561, 581–2
  3 saying] *Adagia* 1 i 50
  4 writing] Ep 464:11–15
  6 Nesen] Froben's former corrector (cf Ep 329 introduction) was still planning
    the trip in the spring of 1518; cf Ep 816:2. Bruno too had not yet set out for Italy
    in early December 1517 (cf Ep 732A) and it is doubtful that he ever did.
  7 What time] Homer *Iliad* 16.385–6
 10 Callipedes] A man with great projects, but without the energy to carry them
    out; cf *Adagia* 1 vi 43.
 11 Jacobus] Nepos, who had probably entered the service of Erasmus at Antwerp
    in 1516. He had recently been sent to Basel with manuscripts for the Froben
    press (cf Ep 594 introduction). In 1518 he returned to Basel with Erasmus and
    there settled down. See Bierlaire 51–4.
 15 Konrad] Brunner, secretary to the Amerbachs; cf Ep 313:26n.

Palsgrave (cf Ep 607:16n), the first supplies the approximate date and the second the destination, England. That this fragment might be addressed to William Warham, archbishop of Canterbury (cf Ep 188 introduction), is suggested by his invitation in Ep 558:11–17.

It should be noted that the Deventer Letter-book also fails to register the name of Warham in Epp 781 and 893 and omits the name of John Fisher in a series of letters belonging to this period (cf Ep 653 introduction). If there is a reason for this peculiarity it can hardly be important, for the names of both prelates appear in earlier copies of the Deventer Letter-book and also in the letters published by Erasmus himself.

The approximate date is indicated by the arrival of Prince Charles (cf Epp 532:30n, 597:13n) at Middelburg on 5 July (LP II 3453). From Flushing near Middelburg he was finally to set sail for Spain on 8 September. Since Thomas More answered Ep 597 on 16 July, the two letters by Erasmus cannot be dated later than 10 July.

Erasmus' move to Louvain was influenced by his connections with the Burgundian court, of which he was a councillor. On 5 June he was still at Antwerp (Ep 586), but then he followed the court to Ghent (Epp 584:33, 597:3n, 18–20, 621:13) and Bruges (Epp 608:5, 651:8; cf also Ep 619:33–6). It had been suggested to him that he follow Prince Charles to Spain, but he refused (Epp 694:6, 809:146–7; Allen Ep 853:2–3), as subsequently and in similar circumstances he would refuse to tutor Prince Ferdinand (Ep 917 introduction). Erasmus' close relations to the court at this time lend some weight to his later claim that his residence at Louvain (until 1521) corresponded with the wishes of Charles (Allen Ep 1225:27). Uncertain at first whether he should settle down, it seems that he was gradually encouraged to do so by his generally friendly reception; cf Epp 597:28–9, 52–7, 605:9–11, 608:11–12, 625:20–3.

Most reverend Father, my cordial greetings. I have moved to Louvain, waiting to discover what will be the most suitable refuge for the old age which knocks at my door and indeed now presses close upon me. Prince Charles is at Middelburg and will sail from there, they think, for Spain ...

597 / To Thomas More   [Louvain, c 10 July 1517]

For the date cf Ep 596 introduction; the answer to this letter is Ep 601.

In recent years the friendship between Erasmus and Thomas More had been deepened and expanded by More's embassy to the Netherlands in 1515 (cf Ep 332:19n), which led to the writing and publication of *Utopia* (cf CWE 4 preface) and the commissioning of the Metsys portraits (cf Epp 584:8n, 601:56n). The exchange of affectionate and frank letters continued as More was drawn more

APOLOGIA ERASMI
ROTERODAMI
ad eximium virum Iacobum
Fabrum Stapulensem cuius
argumétum verfa pagella de
monftrabit.

THEODORICVSMARTINVS

Erasmus *Apologia ad Iacobum Fabrum Stapulensem* title page
Louvain: Martens 1517
Cambridge University Library

closely into the service of Henry VIII (cf Ep 829:6n). Before long Erasmus'
friendship for More would find expression in his remarkable description of
the future chancellor of England; see Ep 999.

ERASMUS TO HIS FRIEND MORE, GREETING

Nothing from you: I can guess how busy you are. I made do with news from
Tunstall that you were prosperous, or at least safe and sound. I have at last
discovered which of the gentry at court is so much against me. It is a certain
doctor from Paris, a former Carmelite who in hopes of some trumpery   5
position as abbot turned Benedictine, the most abusive man in the world,
but even so he soon became a suffragan – a puppet bishop, if you like – of
Cambrai. This man not merely attacked me violently at court; there is never
a drinking party at which he does not hold forth against Erasmus, being
particularly hot against the *Moria*, saintly character that he is, because he   10
cannot bear any reflections on my lords Christopher and George. And yet
this monstrous fellow has much influence with my lord of Chièvres, whose
lightest word carries the day here, and maybe with the king too, whose
confessor he has recently become after the rejection of Josse Clichtove, who
had been invited to fill the post, and was rejected for no better reason than   15

* * * * *

597
3 Tunstall] Cuthbert Tunstall was in the Netherlands as a member of an English
  embassy (cf Epp 571 introduction, 584:43n). His recent movements can be
  traced as follows: 7 June in Brussels, 9–19 June in Ghent, 2 July in Bruges, 9
  July in Middelburg; cf LP II 3343 passim to 3453 and Ep 663. For Tunstall see Ep
  207:25n.
5 doctor]Jean Briselot of Valenciennes, d 1520 in Hautmont, suffragan bishop
  of Cambrai and prior of the Carmelite house near Valenciennes. In 1507 he was
  given the Benedictine abbey of Saint-Pierre de Hautmont. From 1517 (perhaps
  1515) he is described as confessor to Prince Charles, whom he accompanied to
  Spain.
11 Christopher and George] Mentioned in *Moria* as examples of legendary saints
   who receive immoderate veneration; cf LB IV 450D.
12 Chièvres] Guillaume de Croy, lord of Chièvres, was the principal adviser of
   Prince Charles and opposed an alliance with England against France; see Ep
   532:30n.
13 king] Prince Charles, the future Charles V (see Ep 332:3–4n). After the death of
   his maternal grandfather, Ferdinand of Aragon (23 January 1516), Charles had
   been proclaimed king on 14 May 1516, but he needed to go to Spain to obtain
   the recognition of his insane mother and of the Cortes.
14 Clichtove] Clichtove seems to have declined the position, not because of any
   intrigues on the part of Briselot, but because he wished to remain in Paris. He
   felt afterwards that he had to justify his refusal; see J.-P. Massaut *Josse
   Clichtove, l'humanisme et la réforme du clergé* (Paris 1968) I 10; cf Ep 594:15n.

that he is rather skinny and has scarce ten hairs on his head. Halewijn has made me still more unpopular by translating the *Moria* into French, for now even the theology professors who know only French understand it. I saw as much of Tunstall as I could, and we finished the collations for the New Testament. When that was done, while I was wondering anxiously in what 20 words to express my thanks, he went further and gave me fifty French écus à la couronne, which I was by no means allowed to refuse. Honestly, I do not think our age can show the like of that man. Pieter Gillis is not really fit even now; he suffers frequent relapses and is afraid of something – I know not what but I can guess. I very much hope it will not happen. His wife had a 25 miscarriage about the time I returned from England, from anxiety, I suppose, at the danger to her husband.

I have moved bodily to Louvain, intending to spend several months among the theology faculty, who have given me quite a kind welcome. The chancellor has paid me part of my retainer out of his own pocket – two 30 hundred florins, that is – with the intention of securing a refund by some means or other. I am still hoping for another hundred; but who will produce the cash now they have all departed? The chancellor's parting advice to me was to be optimistic. He intends, I gather, to confer a bishopric on me. So much easier is it for these people to make one a bishop than to pay one the 35 money they have promised to pay.

* * * * *

16 Halewijn] See Ep 641.

19 New Testament] See Ep 864 introduction.

21 fifty French écus à la couronne] From 27 November 1516 officially worth 39s 0d tournois each. Thus this sum amounted to £97 10s 0d tournois = £10 8s 4d sterling = £14 15s 10d gros Flemish. Cf CWE 1 315, 336–7; CWE 2 340 (plate), 327–45; Epp 463:48n, 529:119–20, and 651:7.

23 Gillis] The chief secretary of the town of Antwerp (see Ep 184 introduction) was a close friend of Erasmus and frequently his host. Illness continued to bother him until the spring of 1518 (cf Ep 846 and the index to this volume). He had married Cornelia Sandrien (Sanders, Sandria) in 1514; see Ep 312:93n.

30 chancellor] Jean Le Sauvage (cf Ep 301:38n) had had the money paid out to Erasmus at Ghent, and it was subsequently returned to him when the court finally made payment for most of the pension due to Erasmus (cf Ep 621 introduction). Since Erasmus' appointment as a councillor dated from the beginning of 1516 (cf Epp 370:18n, 392:17n) and nothing had yet been paid, his entire pension for a year and a half, 300 florins, was still owing.

30 two hundred florins] Money-of-account florins (livres d'Artois) worth in total £33 6s 8d gros Flemish = £22 18s 4d sterling = £207 10s 0d tournois = 100 ducats (relative gold values). Cf CWE 1 323, 347.

34 bishopric] Cf Ep 475:1–8.

In hac ſecūda emiſſione obiter relegēdo cōmētarios / caſtigata ſūt nōnulla: aut quia depra
uata / aut quia minus placebāt / ſubſtracta etiā nōnulla aut immutata / ſed hæc paucaꝗ& inſu
per vbi viſum eſt oportunum adiecta nonnulla. Quæ & vniuerſa quæ emittimus / vt omni-
bus prodeſſe ita & ab oībus / grate beneuoleꝗ ſuſcipi pro lectorū animi candore / optamus.

Jacques Lefèvre d'Etaples *Epistola ad Romanos* … (second edition) title page
Paris: H. Estienne 1515
Library of St John's College, Cambridge

My friend Lefèvre has treated me in a very unfriendly fashion in the
latest edition of his apostolic epistles; he clings obstinately to his own
opinion and gets his teeth into some things that had nothing to do with his
point. I touched him on the raw by saying 'He is man.' I shall answer him   40
shortly in an open letter, but with strict control over my temper, so that it is
clearly an argument and not a quarrel. If you wish to know what the point is,
read my notes on the second chapter of Hebrews and his criticisms of the
same passage; you will know which is his second edition from the note by
Lefèvre on the first page of all.   45

* * * * *

37 Lefèvre] Jacques Lefèvre d'Etaples (cf Ep 315 introduction) was still the chief
exponent of Christian humanism in France and a personal friend of Erasmus
from his years in Paris. This is the first indication that Erasmus had seen a
copy of Lefèvre's second edition of the Epistles of Paul, published by H.
Estienne, Paris, with the colophon date of 1515 (cf Ep 480A:23n). When
revising his commentary, Lefèvre had added a lengthy reply to criticism
concerning his interpretation of Heb 2:7 contained in Erasmus' *Annotationes
in Novum Testamentum*. The tone of Lefèvre's reply was not unfriendly, but he
had used words which Erasmus considered a charge of blasphemy. Within
weeks (Epp 731:4, 755:16–17) he composed a rejoinder, his *Apologia ad
Iacobum Fabrum Stapulensem*, dated 5 August 1517 (first ed Louvain: Martens
late August 1517; NK 777; Epp 628:12, 637:14–15). A year later he reiterated his
views when revising his *Annotationes* for the second edition of the New
Testament (cf Ep 864 introduction) in fifty-seven articles. Lefèvre did not
pursue the matter further. The issue debated in this unfortunate controversy
was the humanity of Christ. There is an allusion to it in Erasmus' remark 'He is
man' (line 40), and many arguments on both sides are repeated in Epp 680A,
778:199–211, etc. The texts themselves, including the one by Lefèvre, are in LB
IX 17–80 and VI 985–91. Cf A. Renaudet *Humanisme et Renaissance* (Geneva
1958) 211–14; H. Feld 'Der Humanisten-Streit um Hebräer, 2,7 (Psalm, 8,6)'
Archiv für Reformationsgeschichte 61 (1970) 5–35.

44 second edition] The title page of the first edition merely lists the contents:
Contenta. Epistola ad Romanos ... (Paris: H. Estienne 15 December 1512); cf
Harvard College Library *French 16th Century Books* compiled by Ruth Mor-
timer (Cambridge, Mass. 1964) I no. 61. The second edition (see above line
37n) does the same, but at the bottom of the page there is an introductory note
beginning with the words 'In hac secunda emissione ...' This note is no longer
contained in a third edition: *Epistolae Divi Pauli Apostoli cum commentariis ...
Jacobi Fabri Stapulensis* (Paris: F. Regnault 1517). The colophon of the second
edition shows the date 1515, but it must in fact have been published after
Erasmus' *Novum instrumentum* (March 1516), which Lefèvre had used to make
corrections in the second edition of his commentary, often without mentioning Erasmus. He did, however, specifically refer to Erasmus in launching into
the controversy over Heb 2:7. Erasmus and Thomas More thought that
Lefèvre's second edition had been deliberately predated so as to create the
false impression that he owed nothing to Erasmus' New Testament (Epp

I am staying in Louvain with Jean Desmarez, the public orator of the university; but anything you may have directed to Pieter Gillis will not have gone astray. I wrote and told you that your Lucubrations had already been sent to Basel, *Utopia* I mean, and the epigrams and the Lucian. I warned them either not to take the work on or to put all their efforts into doing it 50 well, and with this in mind I sent them a reliable servant of mine, a pretty well-read and painstaking man. I have not yet made up my mind where to settle. I do not care for Spain, to which I am again invited by the cardinal of Toledo. In Germany I do not care for the stoves, nor for the roads beset with robbers. Here there is a lot of mutual recrimination and no advantage to be 55 enjoyed, and I could not stay here very long, however much I might want to. In England I am afraid of riots and terrified of becoming a servant. If you have any immediate advice, let me know, for I simply despair of reaching a state of things in my own country in which I can overcome the malice of monks and theologians. The ruffians gather thicker every day and feel the 60 need of someone to lead them. For one thing we can be thankful: the suffragan aforesaid is off to Spain, and no doubt will end his life there, for he is past seventy. Apart from that, the Dominicans and some of the Carmelites are beginning actually to call on the mob to start throwing

* * * * *

607:14–15, 683:45–6; LB IX 20D–E). If such was the case, Lefèvre's manoeuvre was so inept that it is best explained by his serious illness in the second half of 1516 which at times seems to have impaired his mind; cf Ep 445:45–8; H. Feld 'Humanisten-Streit' 26–9.

46 Desmarez] Secretary to the university and canon of St Peter's church. It was not the first time that Erasmus had enjoyed his hospitality: cf Ep 298 introduction; Allen I 59.

48 I wrote] Ep 584:18–20; cf Ep 594:2.

49 epigrams] The *Epigrammata*; cf Ep 550 introduction.

51 servant] Nepos; cf Ep 595:11n.

53 cardinal] Francisco Ximénes de Cisneros; for the invitation see Ep 582:11n.

54 stoves] Erasmus believed that stoves, as used especially in German territories, were detrimental to his health. He insisted on open fireplaces for his living quarters; cf Epp 389:8, 800:9n; Allen Ep 1248:10n; LB I 716D–17B, X 1623F.

57 England] In the Netherlands Erasmus was bound to hear about the attacks upon foreigners on 'Evil May Day' 1517 which led to a number of executions; cf LP II p 1689. While always willing to enjoy ecclesiastical benefices which would not impede his freedom, Erasmus could no longer bring himself to accept preferment which might involve attendance at a court or duties in an academic institution. He may at times have feared that such were involved in the offer recently made to him by Wolsey (cf Ep 577), although he continued to give it very serious consideration; cf Ep 657 introduction.

63 Dominicans ... Carmelites] For Erasmus' frequent criticisms of these orders and some of their members see the indexes of CWE 5–8.

stones, and nowhere do those pestilent folk flourish more than in my native   65
country; yet no one says a word against them, either at court or in the
hearing of the common people. They are afraid of the lion's teeth, no doubt,
and will certainly suffer from his claws: serve them right, I would say,
except that this would hardly suit true Christian moderation. Towards one
object I will continue to press with determination, to do what I can for the   70
cause of scholarship.

598 / From Christoph von Utenheim   Basel, 13 July 1517

This is clearly the letter mentioned in Ep 594:14. The date given here is that of
the clean copy, whereas Beatus Rhenanus may have seen a first draft a week
earlier. The original texts of this letter and of Erasmus' answer are given in the
Deventer Letter-book. The published versions underwent some stylistic
refinement, presumably by Erasmus himself, but the changes have no
influence upon the English translation. This letter, first published in the
Auctarium, was answered by Ep 625.

Christoph von Utenheim (c 1450–1527), from a noble family of Lower
Alsace, had graduated from Basel and held a canonry there prior to becoming
bishop in 1502. An exponent of Christian humanism, he had shown much
kindness to Erasmus (Epp 412–14) and remained a good friend. He was,
however, ineffectual in his efforts to reform the diocese.

CHRISTOPH, BY THE GRACE OF GOD BISHOP OF BASEL,
TO ERASMUS OF ROTTERDAM,
THE GREATEST SCHOLAR OF OUR GENERATION AND
OUR ESPECIALLY BELOVED IN CHRIST, GREETING
It is impossible to say, most famous Erasmus, how delighted I was to hear   5
from the bearer of your letter that you are in good health. The affection
which I conceived for you last year in Basel means that I cannot fail to
entertain some concern for your well-being, and what lover of good letters
would not say the same? As long as Erasmus suffers from any suspicion of ill
health, no doubt all the Muses would suffer with him; all would fall silent,   10
and the entire republic of letters would thus be in danger. I was not a little
afraid that the change of clime might have a rather bad effect on you. My

* * * * *

598
6 the bearer of your letter] Nepos (cf Ep 594 introduction) may have brought a
  new letter or Utenheim may be replying to one by Erasmus mentioned in Ep
  477:6, but now lost. Erasmus may have repeated the praise of Basel's climate
  already offered in Ep 412:17–18.

own country, indeed, would pray that this might be so, if there were room
for such a prayer, not out of ill will but to encourage you to another taste of
our climate in Basel. Certainly there is nothing I could wish for more than   15
that I might be allowed to see you often face to face and enjoy your most
delightful and most learned conversation. Now, my dear Erasmus, if the
climate of Basel agrees with you better than others, why not live in it, why
not return to Basel? We and all that is ours shall be at your disposal. I write
this to show that when your friends are far from you in person, we must not   20
be thought forgetful in our hearts. Write to me some time and send me your
news, and so farewell and best wishes.

From our city of Basel, 13 July in the year of Our Lord 1517

599 / From Lukas Klett   Basel, 13 July 1517

This letter was published in the *Auctarium* and answered by Ep 626. Klett (cf
Ep 316 introduction) had quite recently been appointed chancellor to the
bishop of Basel in succession to Johannes Fabri (cf Ep 386 introduction); hence
the elaborate signature.

TO THAT MOST BRILLIANT LEADER OF THE
WORLD OF LETTERS, ERASMUS OF ROTTERDAM,
HIS VERY FAMOUS TEACHER, GREETING
How could I allow the man who brought your letter to return empty-handed
to my great and celebrated teacher, dear Erasmus, without bringing you a   5
letter from me, although my hands are full with difficult business of my
master's? – you who have so often shown me such kindness, such generosity. I should be really ungrateful if I did not enshrine this in my heart, if I
offered you no return of thanks. Yet who could thank you adequately,
however grateful? while you behave in such a way towards all men, loading   10
everyone with kindness, that neither singly nor as a body can the lovers of
good literature ever tender you any gift as a fitting recompense? As for me,
in order not to be entirely ungrateful I do the one thing I can: I keep your
memory green with my master, I praise you as is right and proper and laud
you to the skies, and he listens to your praises greedily and sometimes adds   15
to what I have said as though my tribute had been inadequate. I pray
heaven that you may be spared for many years for the benefit of your friends
and the good of humane studies. More at this moment I cannot do. Farewell,
most learned man on earth, and count me among your friends.

* * * * *

599
4 the man who brought your letter] Nepos; cf Ep 594 introduction.

Basel, 13 July 1517   20
Your devoted Lukas Klett, doctor of civil and canon law, chancellor of
the bishop of Basel

600 / From Wolfgang Faber Capito   Basel, 15 July 1517

For Capito see Ep 459 introduction and below line 21n.

WOLFGANG FABRICIUS CAPITO TO
ERASMUS OF ROTTERDAM, GREETING
At last I have ensured by my angry replies to those who speak ill of you,
most learned Erasmus, that no one launches an attack on you in my hearing
or criticizes you, except perhaps certain blockheads I could name, and not   5
many of them, who are devoid of any feeling for civilized behaviour. Of
course, that such people should hate one openly rather than be doubtful
friends is better, if I am not mistaken, for every man of good will; and I for
my part have long been conscious that they do not like me, negligible as I
am, and will in any case be far more ill disposed if I were one day to be so   10
fortunate as to make my way out of their prison-house into the company of
your friends, which means out of the darkness of ignorance into the clear
light of your erudition. And yet I am more tightly bound, in adamantine
chains of ignorance, which even an axe sharp as Vulcan's, that cleaves rocks
at a blow, cannot sever. I cannot cease to smack of the ancient taint of   15
ingrained barbarism as though it were quite new. On the contrary, as long
as I live they need have no fear that my style will really improve, for I still
carry round with me a remnant, though only a small remnant, of my
acquaintance with them, as a sort of reward for my idleness. Yet there is
some risk that I may lay ignorance under an obligation, for I encourage my   20
boys to do better, urging them constantly to read their Erasmus, to learn
him by heart and imitate his works alone, for they alone leave behind in
those who follow them industriously both wisdom and a mastery of style.
    I will answer your letter first. My opponent is now silent; he was more
        * * * * *
    600
    14 'that cleaves ... blow] Capito quotes in Greek from Lucian *Dialogi deorum* 13
       (8).
    21 boys] Capito was professor of theology and at this time rector of the univer-
       sity, but he also taught Hebrew; like other Basel professors he apparently had
       some student-servants living in his house; cf below line 26.
    24 letter] Evidently Erasmus' answer to Ep 561, which Nepos had taken to Basel
       along with other letters; cf Ep 594 introduction.
    24 opponent] Cf Epp 557 and 561.

annoyed with me in many ways than he was with you. My idle remarks on   25
Hebrew are now being copied out by one of my boys; these I have decided
to publish at the next fair but one, since this summer Chrysostom takes up
pretty well all Froben's presses, and various useless bits of business, or
rather obstacles to my finishing, have crept upon me unawares, as so often
happens. These I shall soon be quit of; then I shall resume my intimacy with   30
literature and nothing else and attend to nothing henceforward, after Christ
and my obligations to my friends, except the study of Greek and Latin
authors. Whatever energy I have after that I shall devote to Hebrew and
Chaldean, hoping to get something from them in passing, like a dog
drinking from the Nile as he runs.   35
    I am grateful for your letter. It is a most elegant piece and, to indicate
all its virtues in a single word, purest Erasmus. You not so much commend
your Fabricius, my dear Erasmus, as rouse and inspire him wonderfully to
model his work on the picture you draw of him. For you have a habit of
seeming to intend to praise your friends and really giving them most   40
valuable though concealed advice. That is how you have now depicted not
the man I am but the man you hope I shall be one day. Such utterances I shall
treasure most religiously and they will set the standard for my life in future,
if the powers of heaven grant me a longer span. Farewell, jewel of teachers.
    Basel, 15 July 1517   45

601 / From Thomas More   London, 16 July [1517]

This is More's answer to both Epp 584 and 597. Like most of his early letters to
Erasmus, it was not published in their lifetime in spite of its elaborate style; cf
preface.

THOMAS MORE TO ERASMUS OF ROTTERDAM, GREETING
You made me very anxious, dearest Erasmus, by your latest letters (for I
have had two), which give me to understand that our friend Pieter is not yet
really restored to health and has something else hanging over him as well.

* * * * *

26 Hebrew] *Hebraicarum institutionum libri duo* (Basel: Froben January 1518). For
    critical reaction to the work in Louvain and Paris see Epp 798:15–16, 810:397n.
27 Chrysostom] Basel: Froben July–October 1517; cf Ep 575:39n.
35 runs] Because he fears the crocodiles: *Adagia* I ix 80
36 letter] Ep 541, which had now been published in *Epistolae elegantes* of April
    1517.

    601
 3 Pieter] Gillis; cf Epp 584:10, 597:23–7.

What sort of thing this is you guess rather than know, and I could wish that   5
whatever it is that you guess you had given me a few oracular hints, for even
guesswork is beyond me, and affection being full of fears, I am driven to be
afraid of many things which may be worse than the truth. Another thing too
distresses me, that as though illness and anxiety were not enough, his
wife's miscarriage has now been as it were piled on the top. O how unfair   10
are the changes of mortal life! Success creeps on us slowly step by step;
adversity descends all at once, and it rarely happens that any misfortune
befalls us in isolation. All the same, human affairs are always changing;
some days play the stepmother, but not all; and so I hope that all his troubles
will be repaid by some great unexpected good fortune, and that I may see   15
this very soon is my dearest wish.

As for that black Carmelite, that he should be so much against you
does not surprise me in the least. Two men could not be more unlike: one
ignorant, one very learned; one bad, one very good. But that he should
inveigh against your *Folly* is hardly credible, for he is entirely made up of   20
folly himself. The insolence and ingratitude of the man! Is he so much
ashamed of his imperial mistress, who has given him her charming daughter Self-conceit 'in lasting wedlock bound, to be his wife,' that in her he may
take continual delight, for otherwise he could not endure his own company? Does he not realize also how much this bountiful goddess has lately   25
done for him? When he was recently a candidate for so high an office, was it
not she alone who wheedled their votes out of the electors? She it was who
blinded them by magic arts and 'o'er his eyes a godlike splendour spread,'
who secured his return with acclamation as worthy holder of that important
office by the decisive vote of right honourable men – he being of course 'in   30
head and shoulders godlike,' while his rival was cast out in disgrace, for
that he skinny was and bald, those depressing marks of a wise man. So this
runaway slave with supreme ingratitude now rants at his own mistress; he
has donned the lion's skin of wisdom to conceal the fact that he is only
Folly's ass. Luckily his ears at any rate stick out, and I hope he will one day be   35
dragged by them away from his parade-harness and back to his panniers.

* * * * *

14 stepmother] *Adagia* I viii 64
17 Carmelite] Briselot; cf Ep 597:5–11.
23 Self-conceit] Cf *Moria* (LB IV 411A).
23 'in lasting wedlock ... wife'] Virgil *Aeneid* 1.73
28 'o'er his eyes ... spread'] *Aeneid* 1.591
30 'in head ... godlike'] *Aeneid* 1.589
34 lion's skin] *Adagia* I iii 66

But that good old man on the other hand – I cannot say how much I
wonder what he would be at. Why does a pious and modest man strive so
immodestly for reputation, of which he will not have a shred left if he goes
on like this? How much better is your own policy! When challenged to a   40
fight, you negotiate for peace and make up your mind so to govern your pen
as not to leave the truth defenceless, and yet to mollify your opponent so
that things do not issue in frenzy. This means in fact that you abandon your
triumph when you have won the day and treat the advantage of all lovers of
learning as something more important than your own glory, so that dis-   45
agreement among the Greeks may not strengthen the barbarians, who turn
their dissensions to their own advantage. If Caesar in the olden days had
combined this moderate way of thinking with his lofty spirit, he would
beyond doubt have won more glory by preserving the republic than he got
from all the peoples whom he conquered and subdued. Though personally I   50
think this modesty that you display is more than anything the product of a
great and lofty heart. What can be more exalted than the humility which
despises and derides fame, the very patron goddess of the proud? Yet fame
follows you and dogs your steps everywhere however much you seek to
escape, and you already have your fill and are almost sick of it.   55

The panel which is to record for me the likeness of you and our dear
Pieter I await with indescribable impatience and curse the ill-health that so
long keeps my hopes unfulfilled. My lord cardinal was speaking warmly to
me of you lately and clearly seems to have in mind some great benefaction
for you. That letter of mine which you say you do not wish to be done out of 60
was so carefully put away by my man William that he cannot find it. None
the less, since you so wish, it shall be found wherever it may be, and I will
see that it is sent to you. Farewell. From London, in haste, 16 July

I send you a bundle of letters from the Venetian envoy and his secretary, and also from the bishop of Rochester.   65

* * * * *

37 old man] Lefèvre; cf Ep 597:37 and n.
56 panel] A double portrait of Erasmus and Pieter Gillis had been commissioned
    from the Antwerp painter Quentin Metsys (Ep 616:10) as a gift for Thomas
    More. It had been in preparation since the spring; see Ep 584:8n and the
    reproductions in CWE 4 370–1.
58 cardinal] For Wolsey's apparently vague promises see Epp 577, 597:57,
    694:11n.
61 William] Gonnell, the tutor of More's children (cf Ep 274 introduction). The
    letter was apparently never completed or sent: cf Ep 584:48–9.
64 letters] Epp 574, 590, 559, 591, copied into the Deventer Letter-book in this
    order, following the present letter, and Ep 592; cf Epp 584:49–51, 623:5n.

602 / To Johann Froben   [Louvain, July 1517]

Erasmus' autograph original of this letter is preserved in the Öffentliche
Bibliothek of the University of Basel, MS G II 13a f 51. Epp 602–6 were very
likely dispatched together in the first bundle of mail to be sent to the Upper
Rhine after Erasmus' move to Louvain. They may have been written about the
middle of July, by which time the previous bundle of letters would already
have reached Basel (see Ep 594 introduction), although any replies to them
would not have had time to reach Erasmus.

The work for which Erasmus was offering a publisher's preface was the
Antiquae lectiones by Lodovico Ricchieri (see Ep 469:10n), a voluminous com-
pilation of classical lore published by Aldo Manuzio in February 1516 and
available in Basel after the Frankfurt autumn fair (cf Ep 469:9–11). Froben
reprinted the work in the following winter – all copies I have seen have a
colophon dated 18 March 1517. Meanwhile Josse Bade in Paris had also
decided to reprint the work; his edition is dated 13 June 1517, and by that time
he had no doubt seen Froben's book.

When this letter arrived in Basel Froben fitted his remaining copies with a
new title sheet which contains on the recto the text suggested by Erasmus. A
copy with the original title page, without Erasmus' text, is in Basel (DD IV 5),
and a copy with the new title page is in the British Library (632 l 5).

Ricchieri's work was held in low esteem by some of Erasmus' humanist
friends in Basel (cf Epp 469:10–11, 556:27–32, 575:29–34; Allen Ep 949:11n),
but this view may above all reflect the quarrel between Beatus Rhenanus and
the Froben firm (cf Ep 594 introduction). Froben must at any rate have found it
profitable, for the firm published several editions of an enlarged version.

Bade has reproduced your book, with a preface in which he maintains that
the work now costs half what it did. You may like to reply with a preface on
these lines:

JOHANN FROBEN TO THE FAIR-MINDED READER, GREETING

My policy in printing books has always been to do the public service   5
by the promotion of good literature no less than to secure my own
private profit, and to win for my work the approval of the best judges
rather than that of the majority. Would that all printers were of the
same way of thinking, and pursued their serious calling in a selfless
and serious way! As it is, there are some who think of nothing except   10

* * * * *

602

1 Bade] Josse Bade, a scholar from Brabant, was established in Paris as a printer
   and had published several of Erasmus' works; see Epp 183, 346 introductions.

43.

51

s.d. Badius imitatus est tu(um) opus, addita praefatione, qua testatur, libru(m) duplo minoris ... eni(m) posse. Tu contra potes tali uti praefatione.

Io. Frob. Candido lectori. s.d.

Mihi semp(er) studio fuit in excudendis libris, ut no(n) minus bonis studiis public(e) consulerem, q(uam) privati(m) ... et mea(m) opera(m) optimis probarem, potius q(uam) plurimis. Atq(ue) utina(m) hoc animo sint omnes typographi, et no(n) ... pura sanctaq(ue) tractarent. Nu(n)c fuere qui tantu(m) hoc ag(unt) ut studioru(m) detrimento suo q(uae)stu(m) ... nec alioru(m) ... libros emptori, q(uam) vilitate, hoc fecti paucissi(mi), nos e(ss)e, qui recte de libris iudicemus. Non hac lege ... tabulae, no(n) agri, no(n) vinea, ut maximu(m) sit vendibile quod emi possit minimo. Cu(r) libris minoris sapimus, q(uam) in rebus levioris momenti ... parvo emit. q(uis)q(uis) libru(m) emendatu(m) etiam magno emit. Magno emit, q(uis)q(uis) codicem mendosum etiam minimo emit. Expende tecum optime lector, q(uan)tu(m) impendii detur totius ... dandis exemplaribus. Id nisi a doctis viris p(rae)stari no(n) pot(est), ut hoc opus, no(n) conduatur parvo. Tua igitur no(n) minus ag(itur) q(uam) mea, quod te rogabo. Lector optime, ut nos in excudendis libris synceris studiis, tu(m) in emendis synceru(m) iudiciu(m) respondeat. Bene vale.

Autograph letter, Erasmus to Johann Froben, Epistle 602
Öffentliche Bibliothek, University of Basel, MS G II 13a f 51

to follow their own advantage regardless of any loss to good letters, and who recommend their books to the purchaser by nothing except the low price, relying on the fact that only a very small minority can form a reasoned judgment of a book. Pictures, horses, wines are not valued on the principle that what sells best is what sells for the lowest 15 price. Why should we show less sense over books than over things of less importance? The man who buys an accurately printed book buys it cheap even if he pays a high price for it, and he buys dear who buys a volume full of mistakes, even if he pays very little. Consider, gentle reader, the expense required by the repeated correction of printer's 20 copy. This is work that can be done only by a good scholar, and a good scholar's time is not cheap. It is thus to your advantage no less than my own, dear reader, if I ask you to respond to the honest effort I put into the printing of books with an honest assessment of what you are buying. Farewell. 25
To Master Johann Froben

603 / To Philip of Burgundy [Louvain, July? 1517]

This dedicatory preface was published with Erasmus' *Querela pacis* (Basel: Froben December 1517), which is Erasmus' most substantial appeal for international reconciliation. He later recalled that it was undertaken at the request of Chancellor Le Sauvage (cf Epp 410 introduction, 532:30n), an advocate of friendly relations between the Netherlands and France (see Allen I 19; cf below line 28n). The work also reflects many sceptical conclusions Erasmus had drawn from his recent contacts with princes and politicians, conclusions that were reinforced by the experiences of his friend Thomas More (cf Epp 601:47–50, 628). Cf J.-C. Margolin *Guerre et paix dans la pensée d'Erasme* (Paris 1973).

This preface was probably sent to Froben together with a manuscript of the text. Allen consigned both to the current delivery of mail to Basel (Ep 602 introduction). Had it been sent with the previous one, Erasmus would probably have made specific mention of the *Querela pacis* in Ep 584:18–20. The manuscript could conceivably have travelled with the following bundle in the second half of August (Ep 625 introduction): not until 31 August is there evidence that it had actually been sent (Ep 645:32–5). But by that date

* * * * *

21 copy] *Exemplaria* in the Latin text. Printed books were sometimes corrected by hand before they went on sale, rather than supplied with extra sheets of corrigenda; but the text may refer to extra work undertaken on the 'printer's copy,' since *exemplaria*, like 'copy' in English, can bear either meaning.

Philip of Burgundy
Early sixteenth-century drawing from the Recueil d'Arras
Bibliothèque Municipale, Arras
Photo: Institut Royal du Patrimoine Artistique, Brussels

Erasmus stated that the dedication had been made some time ago and he expected the book to be in circulation soon. Froben did not, however, meet his expectations. The Basel first edition is dated December 1517 (a second edition by Froben was to follow in November 1518). Meanwhile Erasmus was growing impatient. He had the *Querela pacis* copied again on parchment for presentation to Philip, and on 5 October he sent it off (Ep 682). Moreover, another manuscript was given to Dirk Martens in Louvain along with additional texts not supplied to Froben (cf Ep 604:12n). Martens did not miss his chance. The bulk of his edition, *Declamationes aliquot* (NK 2971 and 811), must have been in print by the middle of February (cf Ep 946 introduction), but the last piece is dated 30 March 1518.

Philip (c 1464–1524), natural son of Philip the Good, duke of Burgundy, was admiral of Flanders and governor of Gelderland before his nomination to the see of Utrecht.

ERASMUS OF ROTTERDAM TO THE DISTINGUISHED PRELATE
PHILIP, BISHOP OF UTRECHT, GREETING
My Lord Bishop, distinguished as you are not less by the splendour of your career than by your grand and princely lineage, I would congratulate you on the addition of your new and most honourable office, were I not well aware   5
with what reluctance you have entered on it, and how unwelcome was the pressure exercised by the authority of the high and noble Prince Charles; for whom in any case you must feel such affection as would agree to anything. And it is just this that gives us the surest hope that you will perform your new duties with the utmost credit: does not Plato, that man of exquisite and   10
almost godlike judgment, maintain that none are fit to govern a body politic save those who are brought to do it against their will? Our confidence in you increases further when we remember the qualities of the brother whom you follow and the father from whom you are both sprung. Your brother David, equally scholar and sage, in his long tenure of that position added greatly by   15
his personal distinction to the dignity and splendour of the office itself, grand though it was already. In many ways a great and admirable man, he was a blessing to the commonwealth above all in this, that he thought no

* * * * *

603
5 office] Philip had entered Utrecht on 19 May 1517 (Ep 584:37–40), shortly after his nomination to the see. His earlier career had been that of a soldier: all the more reason for Erasmus to remind him of the virtues of peace, for peace was badly needed at the time in the northern region of the country (cf Ep 628).
10 Plato] *Republic* 7.520D
14 David] Like the addressee, a natural son of Philip the Good, duke of Burgundy, and from 1455 until his death in 1496 bishop of Utrecht

Portrait of David of Burgundy
as St Martin,
by the Master of Delft,
end of the fifteenth century
Rijksmuseum, Amsterdam

object more important than the public peace; and this was another point in
which he recalled your father, Philip, duke of Burgundy, a great man in   20
every way, but above all else distinguished and assured of eternal remem-
brance by his devotion to the peaceful arts. How much more closely should
you take him for a model, who are not only his son but share his name of
Philip! In your wisdom you must have seen clearly long ago what all your
people expect of you. You bear a triple burden on your shoulders, the great   25
examples of your father and your brother, and the destiny (for what else can
I call it?) of our times, which seems to bear us towards war. We have lately
seen with our own eyes how certain persons, more burdensome to their
friends than to their enemies, have left nothing undone to ensure that war
should never have an end; we have seen, again, the difficulty met by others,   30
who sincerely wish well to commonwealth and prince, in securing that we
should accept peace with the French, a thing always to be desired and in
these days essential. This was so monstrous that it roused me at the time to
write a Complaint of Peace everywhere outcast, that by this means I might
either avenge or pacify my all-too-righteous indignation. This little work I   35
send you, as a kind of first-fruits due to our new bishop, that so your
Highness may be more diligent to preserve the peace, however it was
brought into being, if I do not let you forget how much work it cost us.
Farewell.

604 / To Henricus Glareanus   [Louvain, July? 1517]

Published as a preface to Erasmus' *Declamatio de morte* (LB IV 617–24) in
Froben's volume headed by the *Querela pacis* (cf Ep 603 introduction), this
letter is clearly contemporary with the preceding one and like it can be dated
only by inference. At the time he wrote, Erasmus apparently thought that
Glareanus was still in Basel. The latter must, however, have reached Paris by

* * * * *

22 peaceful arts] The reign of Philip the Good was peaceful to a certain degree,
but above all he achieved reconciliation with France at the end of the Hundred
Years' War; cf below line 28n.
28 eyes] The composition of the *Querela pacis* is related to a policy of appease-
ment toward France and of general peace, promoted by Chièvres and Le
Sauvage, which led to the treaties of Noyon (August 1516) and Cambrai
(March 1517); Epp 532:30n, 569:3n. This policy involved major concessions to
France. Erasmus had recently been to court (Ep 596 introduction), and he may
have noticed that controversy about it continued at the very moment that
Prince Charles, Chièvres, and Le Sauvage were preparing to leave for Spain; cf
Elise C. Bagdat *La 'Querela pacis' d'Erasme* (Paris 1924) 1–36; Epp 655:10–11,
694:6–9.

the middle of July (cf Ep 609:22). It is possible that Erasmus wrote this preface
before he had received Epp 581 and 582; otherwise he would have expected
Glareanus to have left Basel. In view of this an earlier date for Epp 603–4 might
be argued. A less charitable explanation is that Erasmus was not anxious for
his letter to reach Glareanus at once (see below line 8n). All we can say,
however, is that Epp 627–8 may very well contain Erasmus' answers to Epp
581–2, in which case the latter could have reached him after he wrote this
preface. For Glareanus, a young and quick-tempered Swiss humanist, see Ep
440 introduction.

ERASMUS OF ROTTERDAM TO HIS FRIEND
HENRICUS GLAREANUS, GREETING

Some years ago, during a stay of several months in Siena for the benefit of
my health, I worked with Alexander, archbishop of St Andrews, a young
man of most promising parts with whom I was then living, at various essay   5
subjects, which the Greeks call *meletai*. I thought no more of these, but have
found one of them preserved by some chance among my papers. It is sent to
you now on the clear understanding that if it does not meet with your
approval, you throw it away as it deserves; but that if you do approve, you
follow my example, set your own young men exercises of the same descrip-   10
tion, and even, if you think fit, see that this essay is added to my other
pieces. I append an essay in praise of the married state, which came to light

* * * * *

604
4 Alexander] Stewart, illegitimate son of James IV of Scotland. Already an
   archbishop, the teenager went to Italy, where Erasmus became his tutor (cf Ep
   216 introduction). They spent the early months of 1509 together in the healthy
   climate of Siena. As a parting present Erasmus was given a ring with an effigy
   which he took to be of the god Terminus. He adopted Terminus as his personal
   emblem, adding the motto 'Cedo nulli.' Since he interpreted these words as a
   memento mori, the topic of the *Declamatio de morte* is related both to his
   appreciation of the gift and to the premature death of Alexander, who was
   slain, together with his father, in the battle of Flodden in 1513; see Ep 325:25n
   and J.K. McConica 'The Riddle of ''Terminus''' *Erasmus in English* 2 (1971) 2–7.
8 not meet] Glareanus was, of course, expected to approve, but Erasmus' defer-
   ence to him was not merely a mark of courtesy. Glareanus had himself
   composed a 'Declamatio mortis contemnendae' and believed that Erasmus
   had promised to publish it. The latter, however, now preferred his own
   declamation to that of his young friend. Glareanus, who had gone to Paris,
   was not consulted when Froben published Erasmus' text and felt deeply
   offended when the volume appeared; cf O.F. Fritzsche *Glarean* (Frauenfeld
   1890) 23–4.
12 married state] The *Encomium matrimonii* (cf ASD I–2 193–7, 400–29) was written
   for Mountjoy when Erasmus was his tutor, probably in Paris. This last sen-

soon afterwards. Best wishes, my dear Glareanus, the glory of your native
Switzerland.

605 / To Johannes Oecolampadius   Louvain, [July? 1517]

Oecolampadius (cf Epp 224:30n, 354:6n) now lived in Weinsberg, but since he
was still a close collaborator of the Froben press it seems likely that this letter
was intended to reach him by way of Basel. If so, it may well have travelled
with the current delivery of mail (Ep 602 introduction). It answers Ep 563, and
nothing suggests that a long delay was incurred in answering. Also Erasmus'
arrival at Louvain is clearly of recent date (cf Ep 596 introduction). This letter
was published by Adriaan Cornelissen van Baerland in his selection from
Erasmus' correspondence for the classroom (see Ep 646 introduction) and
reprinted in Erasmus' *Epistolae ad diversos*.

ERASMUS OF ROTTERDAM TO JOHANNES OECOLAMPADIUS,
MOST UPRIGHT OF THEOLOGIANS, GREETING
It is a common experience that we neglect our blessings while they are at
hand, and when we lose them are tormented by regrets. If our separation
makes you forget the trouble I caused you while we were living together in   5
Basel, I shall have nothing to complain of. But your truly Christian heart, I
know, thinks well of everyone; you put the best face you can on your
friends' faults and treat their trifling merits as something remarkable, while
sitting severely in judgment on yourself. My fortunes carry me now this
way and now that, but it seems that Louvain is to be my headquarters,   10
where I keep my library. But wherever I wander, whether by land or sea, I
carry you, dearest of friends, around with me. I too, for the present, follow
Christ, but afar off, as Peter did in his time of weakness; yet it is something
to follow him even at a distance. St Peter found the profit of it, and I hope it
will profit me too, if only Jesus in his goodness and mercy will deign to turn   15
his eyes upon me. O how I envy you, who in singleness of heart consort

* * * * *

tence of the letter was added only in the Martens edition of *Querela pacis* (cf Ep
603 introduction), where the *Encomium matrimonii* and also the *Encomium
medicinae* (cf Ep 799) appeared for the first time. Froben reprinted the additions as a wedding gift for Anna Schabler and Bruno Amerbach (m September
1518; cf AK II Ep 625) and also appended them to his second edition of the
Querela pacis (November 1518).

605
5 trouble] He assisted Erasmus and Froben in the preparation of the first edition
of the New Testament; cf Ep 373:81–3.
13 afar off] Cf Matt 26:58; Mark 14:54; Luke 22:54.

Johann Brenz
Portrait by an unknown artist in volume 5 of his *Opera*
Tübingen: Georg Gruppenbach 1582
From the original in the possession of
the Württembergische Landesbibliothek, Stuttgart

with the Bridegroom in the secret inner room and think only thoughts of
heaven! You call your present home a cave; I think it a paradise, especially if
you have Brenz as your fellow-student and companion. He gives you all the
advantages of solitude without its tedium. In days of old, religious men,   20
offended by the luxury and wickedness of the majority who called themselves Christians but denied him in their lives, or suffering the cruelty of
the barbarian invasions, sought out the pathless recesses of mountain and
forest. In our time one would be still more happy to escape those men who
under the name of Christ labour to extinguish his teaching.   25
    But what is this, you unnatural wretch? You grudged your own
mother so trifling a gift? Upon my word, you deserve to be given most
generous presents, if you show so much gratitude for things of no value.
You say you are comparing Jerome's version with the Hebrew text, and I am
confident that you do this with judgment; may God give these labours of   30
yours a happy outcome. I wish your index might appear as soon as possible;
I too should find it useful. Such a thing will fire many with the wish to read
Jerome. I cannot quite guess the point of your tragedy; I would only urge
you not to over-task your mental powers and delicate physique with work
of too many kinds. Of Melanchthon I have the highest opinion and great   35
hopes, if only it be Christ's will that that young man should long be spared
to us. He will certainly put my humble self into the shade. Farewell.
    Louvain, 151[8]

606 / To Johann Ruser   [Louvain, July?] 1517

This letter first appeared in the *Farrago* of October 1519, where it is dated
'Basel, 1517.' Erasmus was not in Basel in 1517, but the year, at least, seems
correct. This letter cannot be much earlier than Ep 633, and it probably refers to
the letter, now lost, from Ruser which is mentioned in Ep 612:12. Hence it may
be assigned to the current group (Ep 602 introduction).
    Johann Ruser (cf Ep 302:16n) lived in Sélestat, where he was to die the
following year, but he often worked as a corrector for the Strasbourg printer
Matthias Schürer (cf Ep 224:49n); in fact he dated a letter from Strasbourg, 7
July 1517; see BRE Ep 66.

* * * * *

19 Brenz] The future reformer of Württemberg was assisting Oecolampadius in
   the preparation of an index to the genuine works of Jerome, published by
   Froben in May 1520. See Ep 563:47 and notes.
27 gift] See Ep 563:24–9.
31 index] See above line 19n.
33 tragedy] A play now lost; see Ep 563:50n.
35 Melanchthon] See Epp 454 introduction, 563:56–60.

ERASMUS OF ROTTERDAM TO HIS FRIEND
JOHANN RUSER OF EBERSHEIM, GREETING

When you commend Matthias Schürer to me so warmly, you are wasting
your labour, as the proverb says, for he is a man so much commended to me
already by his outstanding gifts and by the uncommon services he has   5
rendered me, that no one could be more so. There is nothing I would not do
for him. But I have not always something at hand which I can offer to his
press, nor does any and every subject suit him. Moreover, printers among
themselves being much like potters, it is scarcely possible for me to oblige
one without giving offence to another, as I learnt by experience over the   10
reprinting of my *Copia*. For several years Bade had been annoyed with me,
before I was able to detect the cause of his coolness. Not but what his
resentment – excellent fellow that he is – stopped short of all bitterness or
even ill feeling. So let us hear no more of your 'Do not blot him out of the roll
of your friends.' On the day when I allow Schürer's name to be blotted out of   15
my list of friends, I shall be not merely the rudest but the most ungrateful of
men. When the right moment comes, I shall demonstrate, if nothing else,
how warm my feeling is for him.

I wonder very much why the publication of Rodolphus Agricola's
papers is so long postponed. Who pray is this evil genius who grudges our   20
beloved Germany the reputation he will bring her?

But granting that up to this point your letter has been unnecessary, for
your recommendation has added nothing to the good will I already feel for
Schürer, at the same time it has greatly endeared you to me. Your uncommon gifts, which I had somehow guessed long ago from the charm of your   25
conversation and your expression and the look in your eye, were so clearly
reflected in it that I conceived a far greater affection than before for that gay
and charming intelligence of yours, which your unusual modesty makes so
attractive, and for that more than common learning, coupled with an expert
knowledge of both Greek and Latin, but unaccompanied even so by the   30
conceit which goes with it so often. Henceforward, therefore, the name of

* * * * *

606

4 labour] The Latin text, which cannot be translated literally, is 'actum agis,'
'you do what has already been done'; see *Adagia* I iv 70.

9 potters] Who are always fighting amongst themselves; *Adagia* I ii 25

11 *Copia*] Bade had published the first edition of *De copia*, dated 15 July 1512.
Afterwards he had reason to complain about a reprint by Schürer of December
1514, which was clearly authorized by Erasmus; cf Ep 311 introduction. But
this was not his only grievance against Erasmus; cf Ep 472.

19 Agricola's papers] Cf Epp 311:27n, 612:27–31. Rodolphus Agricola, the father
of Dutch humanism, was greatly revered by Erasmus; see Ep 23:58n.

Ruser will be counted not among my humble servants, with which you in your modesty were contented, but among my special friends. Farewell.

[Basel] 1517

607 / To Cuthbert Tunstall   Louvain, 17 July [1517]

For Erasmus' recent and profitable contacts with Tunstall see Ep 597:3n, 18–20. Tunstall's answer to this letter is Ep 663.

ERASMUS TO HIS FRIEND TUNSTALL, GREETING

I have moved bag and baggage to Louvain, although I have not yet found a lodging to my mind, where I can work. Lefèvre d'Etaples has made fresh trouble for me by publishing a new edition of his notes on St Paul, corrected in many places as a result of my comments, and no mention of my name,   5
except in one passage, on the second chapter of Hebrews; and there he is not satisfied with maintaining his own interpretation but attacks mine in a rather unpleasant way, getting his teeth even into several things which had no connection with the point he was making. In a word, he has treated a friend – a dear friend, as he says himself – in a manner not exactly friendly   10
and has shown (to put it no stronger) some human weakness. I shall reply to him, but I shall keep my temper; not so much to prove him wrong – I only discussed his opinion in my own commentary and did not reject it – as to show that I am not so stupid as he makes out. His arithmetic is good, but all the same he has a great deal of void in his make-up.   15

Palsgrave has returned to England. Lee is working very hard at his Greek. I hear that two cardinals have been degraded, to use the language of

* * * * *

607
3 Lefèvre] Cf Ep 597:37n.
13 reject] The rejection was implicit, but obvious; cf LB II 67–8.
14 arithmetic] An ironical reference to his predating the second edition of his *Commentaries*; see Ep 597:44n.
16 Palsgrave] The English scholar John Palsgrave had recently visited Erasmus at Louvain (cf Ep 499:10–11). He took some letters back to England with him, including Epp 596–7; cf Ep 623:2–6.
16 Lee] Cf Ep 765 introduction.
17 cardinals] Alfonso Petrucci, cardinal of Siena, and Bandinello Sauli were arrested on 19 May. A variety of grievances against Leo x had led to a conspiracy against his life in which Petrucci was the leading figure. The two prelates, together with Raffaele Riario, cardinal of San Giorgio, were deprived of all their dignities on 22 June, but only Petrucci was executed after due process. Riario's imprisonment was short. He left the Castello Sant'Angelo on

my friend St Jerome, and he of San Giorgio sentenced to life-imprisonment
– although the kind of punishment inflicted gives one some hope of pardon.
I wish it may now be some help to him in this catastrophe that he has always   20
been such a special supporter of your native England. Best wishes, best of
men.

    Louvain, 17 July

608 / To Pierre Barbier   Louvain, 17 July [1517]

    Barbier (cf Ep 443 introduction) was a member of the household of Chancellor
Le Sauvage and subsequently of Adrian of Utrecht. Weighty financial transactions apart, his correspondence with Erasmus at this time is often enlivened
by jests.
    Probably on 24 June Barbier had left for Spain together with Antoon Sucket
and Jérôme de Busleyden to assist Le Sauvage in preparing for the arrival of
Prince Charles. Travelling overland, they soon caught up with Le Sauvage
(who had left on 19 June) and attended negotiations in Paris. On 12 August,
when Barbier answered this letter, they were near Bordeaux, where Busleyden
was to die of pleurisy on 27 August; cf de Vocht *Busleyden* 93–7; LP II 3375,
3378, 3379, 3468.

ERASMUS TO HIS FRIEND BARBIER, GREETING
News of your success reaches me from afar and through a kind of mist. I feel
myself abandoned since my chief benefactor departed, and you his deputy
– and if your fortune were equal to your desires, you would be first of them
all. It is now about a month since your brother Nicolas met me at Bruges and   5
showed me your letter to him, in which you instructed him, as soon as he
had received the money from the Spaniard, to pay me out of it the balance of

    * * * * *

    24 July after paying the first instalment of an enormous fine of 150,000 ducats.
    The remainder was settled afterwards, and at Christmas 1518 he was publicly
    reinstated with all his rights. See Pastor VII 170–93; A. Schiavo 'Profilo e
    testamento di R. Riario' *Studi Romani* 8 (1960) 414–29; F. Winspeare *La con-*
    giura dei cardinali contro Leone X (Florence 1957).
18 St Jerome] For his use of the term 'regradare' cf *Adversus Iovinianum* 2.28 (PL
    23:339) and *Ad Pammachium* 1.9 (PL 23:386).
21 England] A special messenger was sent to the English court to solicit support,
    and his pleas were supported by Francesco Chierigati; cf LP II 3319, 3341; Ep
    639 introduction; B. Morsolin *Atti, Accademia Olimpica … Vicenza* 3 (1873) 199.

    608
 2 mist] *Adagia* I iii 63
 3 benefactor] Le Sauvage

a hundred francs; besides which, you indicated that the annuity from Courtrai had already been paid in cash. Of what has happened since then, I have heard nothing.   10

I have moved bag and baggage to Louvain. The theologians have received me with the greatest kindness; but I have not yet settled down. I hear that Doctor Adrian has been named cardinal. It seems to me that some black theological planet must now be lord of the ascendant, so much do our Master Doctors rule the roost everywhere: Standish in England, at the   15 prince's court beyond others the man who was lately suffragan of Cambrai, and Adrian in Spain. How wise of the Holy Father to promote into his sacred college only these grave and reverend signiors and Master Doctors! The chancellor is my sheet anchor; and if he were to let me down (which heaven forbid), it would be all over with your poor Erasmus. But I shall find   20 destruction easier to bear – if it were not coupled with derision. When you have an opportunity, mention my name to his lordship. Farewell, my dear Barbier.

* * * * *

8 a hundred francs] Elsewhere (Ep 597:31) Erasmus referred to this sum as 'florins' (livres d'Artois = £16 13s 4d gros Flemish = £11 9s 2d sterling = £103 15s 0d tournois). Cf also CWE 1 323, 347; Epp 522:58n, 613:4–5, and 621 introduction.

13 Adrian] Adrian of Utrecht (see Ep 171:16n) was made a cardinal on 1 July together with thirty others, among them Cajetanus, Egidio of Viterbo, and Campeggi. Some appointments served political ends, but others recognized primarily kinship with, or financial support of, the Medici pope. The way in which Adrian is grouped together with outspoken critics of Erasmus reflects the latter's view of Adrian's training and outlook as a typical Magister Lovaniensis. It does not reflect their personally friendly relations; cf Ep 713:21–2; Allen Ep 969:17–19; K. Schätti *Erasmus von Rotterdam und die römische Kurie* (Basel 1954).

15 Standish] Henry Standish, DD, warden of the Franciscan house in London and a most popular preacher (cf Ep 481:44n). He played a marginal role in the agitation against foreigners in the spring of 1517 when Erasmus hurriedly left London (cf Ep 577) before 'Evil May Day'; cf Ep 597:57n; K. Pickthorn *Early Tudor Government: Henry VIII* (Cambridge 1934) 39, 115. Erasmus, who considered him an ignoramus and his sworn enemy (cf Epp 337:710–18, 777:15–16), probably remembered these events when he reviled Standish in his *Adagia* (cf Ep 829:36n). A willing tool of Henry VIII, Standish was designated bishop of St Asaph in 1518.

16 Cambrai] Briselot; cf Ep 597:5n.

19 chancellor] Le Sauvage had already provided Erasmus with a canonry at Courtrai (Ep 436) and also promised him a bishopric in Sicily (Ep 475: 1–8). Erasmus, whose hints of poverty were hardly exaggerated at this time, continued to set his hopes on him; cf Epp 666:11–12, 694:13–18, Allen Ep 886:37–9; R.H. Bainton *Erasmus of Christendom* (New York 1969) 111.

Lefèvre d'Etaples is having a dispute with me on the second chapter of
Hebrews, and that not without a touch of bad temper; which surprises me   25
very much, since I have kept my own temper under the strictest control, in
spite of provocation. I will not give him tit for tat, but all the same I shall
make it clear that I am not as stupid as he makes out. Farewell once more, O
more than half of my soul.

Louvain, 17 July   30

609 / From Guillaume Budé   [Paris], 17 July [1517]

Budé was a famous Greek scholar and leading advocate of humanism at the
French court (see Ep 403 introduction). Erasmus' reply to this letter is missing.
It may be the one quoted in Ep 810:38–41; cf Ep 744:13n.

BUDÉ TO ERASMUS, GREETING
Early this morning I had sent to Bade's printing-house to ask whether he
had returned from your part of the world, hoping for news of you and of my
new friend Tunstall, and whether he had had my letter. Bade wrote to say
that you had had my letter and had arranged for it to be delivered to   5
Tunstall, and that at that moment a courier was setting off in your direction,
if I wanted to send you anything. At first I began to be annoyed that
Erasmus had sent me not so much as a greeting by Bade, then I decided not
to write. In the end I began to read the draft of the letter I had written to
Tunstall to remind myself what I had said. In it I found I had made a   10
blunder, where it says 'being fired by my father's example, a great respecter
of learning and a very keen collector of books.' The mistake slipped in
because I had added the word 'example' above the line between two other
words, having originally written 'being fired by my father.' So if you should
see my letter and find the same mistake written in it and, what is more, in 15
my own hand, after a moment of mockery at my expense, please put
genitives instead of the ablatives. Let me also inform you that I have written
your friend a very long letter, so that I thought I might make it take the place
of two, since the name Erasmus is mentioned in many passages. I feel

* * * * *

24 Lefèvre] Cf Ep 597:37n.

609
4 letter] Ep 583; for Erasmus' part in establishing their friendly relation cf Ep 571
introduction.
11 blunder] The ablatives *laudatore* and *emacissimo* ought to be replaced by
genitives so as to agree with the genitive *patris*, but Erasmus forgot to do this;
cf Ep 583:414–15 and Allen II 571.

therefore as though I had written to both of you, and you not a word to me,   20
by this courier especially.

The last letter I had from you was brought by Henricus Glareanus, the
Swiss, who is (I take your word for it) a great friend of yours; but I have not
seen him since. That letter began with the words 'You will, I think, have
seen already my annotations on the New Testament, in which I mention my   25
friend Budé,' etc. 'Pray assist me in our common endeavour towards a
purpose which we both have at heart; I have done as much for the moment
as time permitted. So much for my annotations.' What these words mean, I
do not know. There is a letter of mine in print in which I render thanks for
the honour you have done me in your great work. Why you should call my   30
attention to it now, I do not understand. Tell me what help you want from
me, and I will do the best I can, although I am shortly off to the country on
the business of my estates and for two months shall not have the least
respite from the sort of cares that are the enemies of reading and writing.
Dear me, the trouble I have in the management of my affairs, being unac-   35
customed, as you know, to cares of this kind! Poor me, I am tormented, for I
regard as lost every moment not spent in the service of God or of the Muses,
and all the time I am conscious that my ideas, my philosophical notions are
being driven out by this filthy tide of common cares that pours in on me.

Farewell, 17 July   40

I have written this in haste, being summoned to dinner, which is
already on the table.

610 / From Johannes Caesarius   Cologne, 20 July [1517?]

Caesarius (see Ep 374 introduction), an independent humanist teacher at
Cologne, had been honoured by Erasmus, who dedicated to him his translation of Gaza's Greek grammar (Ep 428). This is his reaction, but he also
answers (lines 25ff) another letter by Erasmus, now lost, which raises an
* * * * *
22 letter] To introduce Glareanus. It was apparently written at the beginning of
   May 1516, shortly before Erasmus left Basel, when he had not yet received
   Budé's Ep 403; cf Ep 421:1–3. In the spring of 1516 Erasmus was contemplating
   a new edition of the New Testament (cf Ep 417), hence the remarks that
   puzzled Budé. Presumably the note for Glareanus did not bear a year date, and
   Budé naturally thought that it was written in the spring of 1517 rather than
   1516. Glareanus had long been planning his trip (cf Ep 463:46–8), but had not
   gone until quite recently (Ep 604 introduction). Budé was puzzled and probably irritated too. On his own initiative he had offered to assist Erasmus with
   the New Testament (cf Ep 493 postscript), but Erasmus had declined; cf Ep
   531:596–607.
29 letter] Ep 403 (see lines 52–88) published by Erasmus in 1516

intriguing point about Erasmus' position in the controversy around Reuchlin; see further Ep 694 introduction.

Only internal evidence is available for the year date of this letter, but 1517 seems a satisfactory hypothesis. There is no special problem in relating the entire first paragraph to one work by Erasmus – the one actually dedicated to Caesarius. It appeared in July 1516 and was reprinted in November (cf Ep 428 introduction), so that the dedicatee had had time to read and reread the preface (see lines 16–18). The date of 1517 also permits plausible identifications for the two 'countrymen' of Erasmus mentioned in the postscript. One of them, Georgius Johannis, would actually seem to have taken this letter to Louvain (cf Ep 615:4), and also Ep 611, dated from Cologne on the same day. The fact that this circumstance is not mentioned here may seem strange at first, but Caesarius' postscript was probably written in a hurry. Moreover, the omission of such a reference here explains the beginning of Ep 615.

JOHANNES OF JÜLICH TO MASTER ERASMUS, GREETING
Greeting, dear Erasmus. I now see clearly that you would long ago have acquitted yourself most willingly of your promise to me, provided, as you also wrote on another occasion, it had been clear to you what you should write. For now you do far more for me than I should ever have dared to ask 5 you. So you now give me the clearest proof of the friendship that has grown up between us. I only wish I could show myself an equally good friend to you, as a man who richly deserves all that friendship can offer, that I might somehow deserve to be inscribed in the register of your friends. But you know well what my position is – non-existent or at best very modest. I have, 10 however, one consolation to set against this – that you assess the limits of friendship by sentiments and not possessions. Words can hardly express my delight at the honour paid me by someone of your eminence both as a writer and as a man in one of your works, I mean, when I myself have done you no service such as would be my duty. But it is typical of you, this 15 generosity towards all who wish to learn. I saw and read your preface to the first book of Theodore's grammar; then I read it a second time, and was

* * * * *

610

4 had been clear] Reading *constitisset*
9 somehow deserve] Perhaps by rewarding Erasmus' attention with a monetary gift. It seems likely that Caesarius here refers to the first volume of Gaza's grammar, as he does quite specifically in line 17, rather than to the second volume, about whose dedication Erasmus does not yet seem to have made up his mind (cf Ep 616:6–7), although in the end it too was dedicated to Caesarius: Ep 771.
16 preface] Ep 428

perfectly delighted each time with what I read, as I always am with everything else you write. Everything of yours has the special quality (I speak
quite sincerely) of imparting at the same time both instruction and marvel-   20
lous enjoyment. Such, at least, is my opinion. What others may think, I
leave to the free exercise of each man's judgment. There are some, not
among the multitude, who approve my view. But enough of this; the facts
speak for themselves.

You mention the printing of the pamphlet. I leave that to your judg-   25
ment. All the same, if you had sent it with your letter, I should have
arranged in these last few days (for I wrote to my friend Reuchlin a couple of
days ago, including some mention of you) to entrust it for printing, through
Reuchlin himself, to Thomas Anshelm, whose types I rather like. You must
do whatever you think best, and I will gladly follow. Besides that, you say in   30
your letter that the New Testament is well received in your part of the world
by good men and educated men, although there are some dogs that bark.
This is no surprise: the Author of the New Testament himself could not win
approval except from good men, and perhaps only from those who had a
proper education. Among our theologians too there are some who since   35
reading it have already changed their minds and are better disposed to you
than you would believe possible, considering how zealously they were
opposed to you before; for they used to maintain that you had done them a
great injury. These same men now begin to understand the value of a good
education in Greek and Latin and are most heartily sorry that they lack it,   40
but much more because they despair of acquiring it, partly because they are
ashamed to learn and as it were become schoolboys again, partly as being so
fully occupied with their own nonsense, on which they possess innumer-
able books, that all the time they can find no leisure at all for this purpose.

My master, the illustrious count of Neuenahr, and I speak of you often   45

* * * * *

25 pamphlet] Since it apparently had a bearing on Reuchlin, it may have been an
   appeal in support of him which never got past the planning stage, perhaps
   primarily because of Erasmus' displeasure at the *Epistolae obscurorum virorum*
   (*Letters of Obscure Men*) (cf Epp 622 and 694 introduction). He may, however,
   have referred again to his project in a missing answer to this letter, perhaps
   contemporary with Ep 636; at any rate, on 8 September [1517] Caesarius wrote
   to Reuchlin: 'From our Erasmus I recently received a letter in which he
   mentions you and two little works prepared by him, I think in your honour'
   (RE Ep 244). Five years later Erasmus did finally publish a little work in praise
   of Reuchlin, who had since died, the colloquy *Apotheosis Capnionis*. He may
   have wished to honour an old promise, or he may even have made some use of
   a draft put aside at an earlier time.
29 Anshelm] See Ep 397 introduction.
45 Neuenahr] See Ep 442 introduction.

Ulrich von Hutten
Woodcut by Hans Weiditz, c 1495–c 1537
Kupferstichkabinett, Staatliche Museen, Berlin

enough and most heartily approve your program of bringing humane letters back into the light of day; in which we would gladly work with you, if only such good fortune might come our way. Very best wishes.

Cologne, 20 July

My friend Tielmann and your fellow-countrymen, that excellent per- 50
son Master Georgius and Jacob, who is a really hard-working young man, have received your greetings as you gave me instructions. Nothing could be more welcome to them or more warmly received, and so they told me to return your greetings, not by way of exchange but as a matter of obligation.

611 / From Ulrich von Hutten   Bamberg, 20 July 1517

> After two brief encounters with Erasmus in 1514–15 (see Holborn *Hutten* 65),
> Hutten had left for Italy. He now resumed their contacts with this account. It
> was clearly composed for publication, but Erasmus decided otherwise; for
> Hutten, a Franconian knight, humanist, and brilliant writer, see Ep 365.

FROM ULRICH VON HUTTEN, KNIGHT,
TO ERASMUS OF ROTTERDAM THE THEOLOGIAN, GREETING
If I were to try to give you a continuous narrative, most learned Erasmus, of all that has happened to me since we parted, the longest day would not be long enough; I have had such a series of adventures. But the main points of 5
the story run something like this. On reaching Rome I gave Paolo your greetings, and every time we have met since (though we meet very rarely, for his cardinal keeps him so busy) he has greeted me as a friend. I showed all the learned men in Rome the new and enlarged edition of your *Adagia* printed in Germany, as well as the *Moria* and everything of yours that I had 10
brought on purpose; and this earned me the friendship of many excellent men. But when I had already begun to make myself known, something like

* * * * *

50 Tielmann] Tielmannus Gravius, who matriculated at Cologne in 1496, and from
   1512 was secretary to the Cologne cathedral chapter. He had close ties to
   Archbishop Hermann von Wied. He remained a faithful friend to Erasmus.
51 Georgius] Georgius Johannis of Rotterdam is recorded from 1504 to 1523 as a
   student and teacher in the University of Cologne; cf H. Keussen *Die alte
   Universität Köln* (Cologne 1934) 550.
51 Jacob] Probably Jacobus Ceratinus or Teyng of Hoorn; cf Ep 622:34.

   611
6 Paolo] Bombace, the secretary of Cardinal Lorenzo Pucci. His friendship with
   Erasmus dated from their personal contact in Bombace's native city, Bologna,
   1506–7; cf Ep 210 introduction.
9 *Adagia*] Published by Froben, Basel 1515; cf Ep 269.

a fierce tempest arose, dear Erasmus, which drove me out of the city as far as Bologna. Five Frenchmen of appalling physical strength and ferocity attacked your poor Hutten and almost deprived you of him. However, with   15 the very present help of the Almighty I set about defending myself and drove off the robbers, killing one of them and being wounded myself in the left cheek, which you will say was little in proportion to the danger I was in. This meant that I could not stand the persecution of the French and made my escape; but it was out of Scylla into Charybdis. For a dispute arose in   20 Bologna between the Germans and the Lombards, in which I was nearly killed, and I was told to sum up the case on behalf of the whole German nation before the governor of the city, whose name is Fieschi, a Genoese by birth. Considering the injuries we had suffered and the man's prejudices, my remarks were by no means severe; but all the same I gave great offence. I   25 therefore left for Ferrara where, when I spoke of you, those very good scholars Niccolò Leoniceno, Celio, and a secretary of the duke's who was with you on your journey from England approached me of their own accord; and you cannot think, dear Erasmus, how highly they value you. I myself, because I knew you and called you my teacher, had wonderful kindness   30 from them. Besides them, Antimaco, the professor of Greek, never mentions your name without a complimentary introduction.

I spent a few days there, being invited to visit them in Venice by two Huttens on their way to Syria. The first man who received me there as a

* * * * *

14 Frenchmen] The incident occurred in the spring of 1516 when Hutten had stopped for the night in an inn at Viterbo. It started with Hutten's complaint that he was not being served fast enough and ended with the death of a Frenchman. Hutten soon began to exaggerate his prowess in the brawl and continued to do so in six epigrams devoted to the affair; cf Holborn *Hutten* 81–2; Hutten *Opera* III 280–2.

20 dispute] Early in 1517 quarrels occurred between the two 'nations' of students in Bologna. The Germans were held responsible, and Hutten, their syndic, was called to account; cf Holborn *Hutten* 84–5.

23 Fieschi] Lorenzo Fieschi, d 1519; bishop of Mondovì and papal governor of Bologna

27 Leoniceno] A famous professor and translator of Greek medical texts: cf Ep 216A:21n.

27 Celio] Calcagnini, 1479–1541, a well-known humanist and eloquent supporter of Erasmus in various causes. They had first met at Ferrara in 1508.

27 secretary] Girolamo Sestola, who was sent to England in July 1516 and returned in August; cf A. Frizzi *Memorie per la storia di Ferrara* 2nd ed (Ferrara 1847–8) IV 278; LP II 2117, 2149 and p 1472.

31 Antimaco] Marco Antonio Antimaco, c 1473–1551, an accomplished Greek scholar

34 Huttens] Frowin von Hutten-Stolzenberg zu Hausen, canon at Mainz and

guest was Battista Egnazio, and he gave me as a leaving-present a copy of   35
Horace most elegantly printed on very thin vellum. There appeared at once
Alvise Bragadin, Ermolao Barbaro, nephew of the great Ermolao, and
Angelo Contarini, all of them young nobles of patrician family. They all
embraced me and made me most welcome, and when they had taken me
round the whole city and exhibited me in a complimentary way to their   40
fellow-citizens, they conducted me at length, like some Ulysses to the
palace of Alcinous, to Asulanus' house. There the old man came out to meet
me and received me most courteously, first himself; then he told Gianfrancesco, one of his two sons, to step forward, and then the rest of his
household among whom was a young man who is a Greek and Latin scholar   45
and is used by Egnazio to supervise the transcription of texts; and they
greeted me one after the other. Even Aldo's little boy was brought forward
and told to greet his Hutten with a kiss. Then presents were produced,
Suetonius with those who wrote lives of the Caesars after him and Cicero's
De officiis and Egnazio's new edition of the *Caesars*, and I was given the   50

* * * * *

high official at the court of the archbishop, d 1529, and Ludwig, the younger,
von Hutten-Frankenberg, d 1532. Their party reached Venice on 9 April 1517,
and on 17 June they set sail; cf R. Röhricht *Deutsche Pilgerreisen nach dem
Heiligen Lande* 2nd ed (Innsbruck 1900) 208–11.

35 Egnazio] The scholar Giambattista Egnazio was mentioned to Hutten by
Erasmus; see Ep 588.

36 Horace] There is an Aldine edition, March 1509.

37 Bragadin] Alvise (Angelus) di Andrea Bragadin was the son of a procurator of
St Mark. He joined the Dominican order and was bishop of Vicenza from 17
March 1550 to his death in 1560.

37 Barbaro] c 1493–1556, son of Alvise and nephew of the famous Ermolao
Barbaro (cf Ep 126:150n). The younger Ermolao occupied many offices in the
republic (cf DBI).

38 Contarini] Perhaps Anzolo di Zorzi (Angelo di Giorgio) of the San Silvestro
branch of the Contarini family. Zorzi was married in 1484 and received a
'cavalierato' (an honorary knighthood). Angelo's brother, Giulio di Zorzi, was
a procurator of St Mark and very wealthy. In spite of these connections,
Angelo has apparently failed to leave his mark in history, possibly because he
died young; see Venice, Archivo di Stato, MS 'Arboro dei patritii veneti' (by
Marco Barbaro) II 515.

42 Alcinous] The hospitable king of the Phaeacians in Homer *Odyssey* 7–8

42 Asulanus'] Andrea Torresani of Asola, the father-in-law and partner of Aldo
Manuzio. Gianfrancesco was his older son; see Epp 212, 770.

47 boy] Paolo Manuzio, son of the great Aldo who was Erasmus' host and
employer in Venice; see Ep 207 introduction.

49 Suetonius] Aldine edition of August 1516

49 Cicero's] Aldine edition of June 1517

50 *Caesars*] Cf Ep 588:61n.

CHVONRADO · PEVTINGERO · SEN · PATR · AVGVSTANO ·
· ET · IVRISCONSVLTO · AETATIS · SVAE · ANNO · VIII · SVPRA ·
· LXX · FILII · OB · PIETATIS · OFFICIA · PATRI · FACI⁰ ·
· VNDVM · CVRAVERVNT · SALVT · ANNO · M · D · XLIII ·

Konrad Peutinger
Portrait by Christoph Amberger, 1543
Städtische Kunstsammlungen, Augsburg

choice of anything else I wanted. I call all the gods to witness, dearest
Erasmus, never have I found greater kindness, if I retrace the whole circle of
my wanderings. From Venice I returned to our native Germany, and when I
got to Augsburg I fell in with Peutinger, Jakob Spiegel, and Stab the
mathematician; they introduced me to the emperor, and in a great gather-   55
ing of notables I was given the poet's crown.

So much for my own history; now for other things. I have seen the New
Testament restored by you to its original brilliance – seen it, I say, and read
that honourable mention of me. Now what could move you to make so
much of me? Whatever was there in me that you could think to deserve your   60
tribute? Kindest of men, how fond you seem to be of your Hutten, although
he has never done anything for you to deserve your gratitude! 'I had almost
forgotten,' you say. Why, if you had quite forgotten me, I should have been
forgotten once and for all by the whole of posterity. May the gods preserve
you for our benefit, O leading light of Germany, and see to it that you never   65
take a fancy to be anywhere but in Germany, where you belong. Short-
sighted as our princes are, they will see you, I think, for the splendid, bright
figure you are. As for me, I do not quite know what will happen. The three
men I spoke of invite me to the emperor's court, although many dissuade
me; some want me to join the archbishop of Mainz. Which course to follow I   70
have not yet decided. In a word, so may heaven preserve me and so may you
live a long, long life among us to shed lustre on the Germans as a whole, as
surely as I should prefer to any other condition of life some place where I
could enjoy your society and make something of my gifts, which seem to
win your approval. If you have a plan, expound it. I send this letter to Jakob   75
Spiegel in Augsburg, who says he often has people travelling in your
direction; please reply the same way. Battista also has written a letter,
which comes with this. You can see how he feels about your letter, although
he writes in a more high-flown style.

Farewell, and look after your health, and do not cease to love your   80

* * * * *

54 Peutinger ... Stab] Three members of the court of Maximilian I. For Peutinger
   see Ep 318:3n; for Spiegel see Ep 323:13n; tor Stab see Ep 409:28n.
56 crown] Maximilian's diploma, dated 12 July 1517, is in Hutten Opera I Ep 57;
   the coronation took place on 15 August; cf Holborn Hutten 87–8.
59 mention] Novum instrumentum (Basel 1516) II 555–6 (reprinted in Hutten
   Opera I 103–4). Erasmus removed it after his quarrel with Hutten, and thus it
   is not in LB.
70 archbishop of Mainz] Albert of Brandenburg (see Ep 661), whose service
   Hutten entered a month later
77 written a letter] Ep 588, from Giambattista Egnazio

friend Hutten, that those Obscure Men may burst their sides with spleen. They are now carrying round an immense bull in which we are excommunicated. Bull or bubble, it is all one: what could be more swollen or more ineffective? Farewell once more.

From Bamberg, 20 July 1517, in haste   85
Reuchlin's case is still before the court.

612 / From Matthias Schürer   Strasbourg, 21 July 1517

The Strasbourg printer (see Ep 311 introduction) gives several reasons why Erasmus should send him some of his works for publication. For his success see Ep 693. Erasmus answered the points raised here in Ep 633 to Ruser.

MATTHIAS SCHÜRER TO MASTER ERASMUS OF ROTTERDAM
Greeting. Your messenger brought me your letter safely, laconic as it was, and as I read and reread it I learnt that all goes well with you. This gave me the greatest joy, for I am always glad and thankful to know you are well. About my own health I do not know what to say. For about ten months I   5
have had trouble in my chest, so that I have difficulty in breathing, my windpipe being sometimes so much narrowed and obstructed (though on this point I have always consulted a physician, not without great loss to my pocket), and the trouble is still obstinate and has refused to leave me. But I must hope it will improve, and that one day I shall be restored to my original   10
health. I have sent on letters from Jakob Wimpfeling and Nikolaus Gerbel, from Ruser, and another from a certain lawyer which had been brought from Italy. Besides which, our literary society send their greetings and long

* * * * *

81 Obscure Men] Cf Ep 622 introduction.
81 burst their sides] An echo of Virgil *Eclogues* 7.26
82 bull] A papal brief, dated 15 March 1517, directing that all copies of *Epistolae obscurorum virorum* must be burnt. It was printed in the *Lamentationes* (cf Ep 622 introduction), now in Hutten *Operum supplementum* I 335–7. *Bulla* means 'bubble' as well as (papal) 'bull.'

612
2 laconic] *Adagia* II x 49
11 Wimpfeling] A few pages before the present letter in the Deventer Letter-book Allen found one by Wimpfeling (see Ep 224 introduction) of which only the heading survives: 'To Master Erasmus ... from Jakob Wimpfeling, now old and going blind.'
11 Gerbel] See Ep 342 introduction.
12 Ruser] Probably the letter to which Erasmus replied in Ep 606
13 society] Cf Epp 302, 633:12–13.

passionately and with hungry ears, as they say, to hear good news of you.
Sturm, the secretary of Henry, Count Palatine, has gone to Aachen to see to   15
his master's business there; for he is the head of that church – what we
commonly call the provost. We expect him back about the end of the second
week in September.

You should know that everything here is in a state of turmoil. People
are afraid of war, high prices have invaded the markets, there is hardship   20
and distress everywhere, and we pray for peace more than anything. For the
rest, I commend myself and all my affairs to your good will; if you will guide
and support me, everything will always go well. And so I beg you not to
strike me out of the list of your friends, and to number me among supporters of the humanities; if that is asking too much, I shall be content   25
if sometimes I do not quite slip out of your mind.

I would have dispatched Rodolphus Agricola's work forthwith by this
courier if I had not put aside one piece of it so carefully when I was moving
house that I am not sure where to find it; I have been through the whole
house in search of it. I shall look for it in future with sharper eyes, in hopes   30
of finding it somewhere and sending it to you one day by a safe hand. Take
my word for it, it is so corrupt in most places that it often seems to need an
Oedipus; but your efforts, your intelligence can clear it up, for nothing ever
escapes you, and at length it will see the light well and truly corrected – of
this I am quite confident, and all educated people agree with me. For the   35
present, farewell.

I hope it will not be tedious to bear me in mind one day if you have
some small piece that my press might publish. Do not be concerned about
proof-correction; I have a reader at the moment who is a perfect Grecian.
Farewell once more and very best wishes.   40

In haste, from Strasbourg, 21 July 1517

* * * * *

15 Sturm] See Ep 302:14n.
15 Henry, Count Palatine] The younger son of Elector Philip, Count Palatine,
   Henry (d 1552) was canon of Strasbourg and provost of Aachen; his loyalty to
   Charles v was rewarded with many benefices. He succeeded Philip of Burgundy (cf Ep 603) as bishop of Utrecht and was bishop of Freising at the time of
   his death.
20 markets] On the scarcity of food see P. Dollinger et al *Histoire de l'Alsace*
   (Toulouse 1970) 177.
27 Agricola's] Cf Ep 606:19–21.
33 Oedipus] He solved the riddle of the sphinx; see, for example, Diodorus
   Siculus 4.64.3.

Henry, Count Palatine
Portrait by an unknown artist, dated 1507,
in the Swedish National Portrait Gallery, Gripsholm Castle
Photo: Nationalmuseum, Stockholm

613 / From Nicolas Barbier   Middelburg, 24 July 1517

Unlike his brother Pierre (see Ep 608), Nicolas Barbier is known only from the
correspondence of Erasmus. His presence at Middelburg at this time (cf Ep 596
introduction) suggests a connection with the court.

NICOLAS BARBIER TO MASTER ERASMUS, GREETING
Reverend and most honoured sir, your letter came today. I heard a few days
ago from my brother. He said that through the Sieur de Marques, a man well
known to you I think, he would be sending one hundred common florins
both for your Courtrai annuity and for your stipend from the king. As for   5
the balance, he will take steps with his master to see that you receive
satisfaction. Today I met the Sieur de Marques, who said he had sent the
money of which I speak by the receiver-general of Louvain. Farewell,
honoured sir.
       From Middelburg, 24 July 1517   10

614 / From Heinrich Stromer   Mainz, 24 July 1517

Stromer (see Ep 578 introduction) was physician to Albert of Brandenburg,
archbishop of Mainz (see Ep 661). Erasmus answered this letter with Ep 631.

TO THE MOST LEARNED AND ELOQUENT MASTER
ERASMUS OF ROTTERDAM, GREETING
Most eloquent and learned Master Erasmus, unseemly as it is for the crow to
sing to the swan, I have plucked up my poor courage and resolved to send
you, gifted as you are beyond compare, what I have written in my unedu-   5
cated, barbarous, and illiterate way, relying on your great, indeed limitless,
kindness and scholarship combined. As I send you an inelegant letter in
hopes of a most elegant reply, I behave like those legacy-hunters who give
petty presents to rich old men with one foot in the grave, intending to be

       * * * * *

613
3 Marques] Antoine de Metteneye, sieur of Marques (or Marcke) and canon of St
   Donatian's, Bruges, was a member of Charles' privy council constituted in
   1517 to govern the Netherlands in his absence (cf Ep 621:7 and Henne II 201,
   323, X 389). For the financial transactions see Ep 621 introduction.
6 master] Le Sauvage
8 receiver-general] He is called Adriaan, the treasurer, in Ep 652:4.
   614
4 swan] For a similar saying see *Adagia* III iii 97.

handsomely rewarded. Kind Master Erasmus, your letter to Huttich was   10
delivered to me, he himself being away, and the most reverend the archbishop of Mainz, my very sympathetic master, opened and read it, for he
hoped that the letter which Huttich and I wrote you about the first of
January had reached you (which you say in your letter was never delivered
by the treacherous bearers of it), in which we invited you in the prince's   15
name; for his grace had desired us to write to you. Our kind and good prince
was sorry to hear that my letter never reached you. His highness not only
desires but, as I wrote to you earlier, begs you to pay him a visit sometime;
for he wishes to have you with him daily and to enjoy your society and
friendship, and would be very glad, so far as it lies in his power, to do as   20
much for you as your energy and your wisdom deserve. In particular, if
your leisure conveniently allowed of it, he would like to commission you to
write the histories of the principal saints. Their lives are written in such an
uneducated and barbarous fashion that, even if they do contain some truth,
it looks like pure invention. He thinks that no one could do this better than   25
you, a man of great learning who traverses the ocean of Holy Scripture and
of history, and reads and rereads them. If it should ever come about that you
could do this, God Almighty will reward you, and the bishop my master,
whose desire is always to support, preserve, and advance our most holy
religion, will be grateful and will show his gratitude. In any case, I wish   30
your excellency unshaken prosperity in both mind and body, and beg you,
when you count up your devoted acquaintance, not to forget the name of
your humble friend Stromer. Farewell.

Written in haste, from Mainz, 24 July in the year of the Incarnation
1517   35

Your devoted Heinrich Stromer of Auerbach, doctor of medicine

Let no other eye see my letter, but commit it to the busy god Vulcan.
Countless patients suffering from flux of the bowels and other acute disor-
ders take up so much of my time that I cannot rewrite a letter, as the bearer of
this, your servant, can confirm.   40

* * * * *

10 Huttich] Johann Huttich, the recipient of Ep 550
23 saints] This request was probably inspired by the considerable success of
   Erasmus' life of Jerome, which had been published in the first volume of
   Froben's great edition of Jerome (cf Ep 396 introduction) and was about to be
   reprinted as a separate edition by E. Cervicornus, Cologne, December 1517; cf
   Ep 661:24–6, 36–8.
37 Vulcan] Fortunately Erasmus had this letter copied into the Deventer Letter-
   book regardless of the conventionally modest request that it should be
   burned.
40 servant] Nepos; cf Epp 594 introduction, 631:4.

615 / From Johannes Caesarius   Cologne, 30 July [1517]

The year date is inferred from the return of Martin Gröning; the answer to this letter is Ep 622.

JOHANNES CAESARIUS TO HIS FRIEND ERASMUS, GREETING
Master Georgius, your fellow-countryman, and besides that an excellent man, will soon be coming to see you. He has been to Friesland already, and then Brabant and Holland. I gave him a letter for you rather fuller than this. Martin Gröning (his family hail from Groningen but he himself is from   5
Bremen) arrived here a few days ago from Rome. He is the man who was so much concerned in Reuchlin's case, together with Dr Johann von der Wyck. He also on the pope's instructions translated the *Augenspiegel* out of the vernacular into Latin. I asked him how Reuchlin's affair was going, and he said admirably, and for this his friends had reason to rejoice and his   10
enemies to be cast down. Nor is this very distant, for Hoogstraten and his party when they returned the other day had either lost all their cheerfulness or concealed it brilliantly, which seems to me incredible. For what is the good of all their efforts, unless
>   This yeasty leaven, this wild-figtree root   15
>   Burst through their liver to the light of day?
For the rest, I wish more than anything that you may keep really well.
Farewell, from Cologne, 30 July

* * * * *
615
2 Georgius] For Georgius Johannis and the letter which he carried, cf Ep 610 introduction and 51n.
5 Gröning] Canon at Bremen, d 1521. He had studied in Italy and had probably known Hermann von Neuenahr at Bologna. In 1515 he was in Rome and defended Reuchlin at the curia. On his recent return (cf RE Ep 244) he had brought back to Germany Benigno's *Defensio Reuchlini* (cf Ep 680:28n).
7 Wyck] Of Münster; from 1515 to 1518 Reuchlin's chief agent in Rome. Later he was syndic of Bremen and organizer of the Protestant party. In 1534 he was put to death by the bishop of Münster.
9 Latin] A majority of the pieces contained in the *Augenspiegel* were written in German. A Latin translation was made by Reuchlin's opponents in Cologne for the benefit of the Paris theologians and subsequently the papal judges in Rome. Gröning made a second translation, correcting nearly three hundred errors in the earlier one, and had the satisfaction of seeing it accepted as the basis for the papal inquiry; see RE Epp 201, 206 and J. Benzing in the epilogue of a facsimile edition of the *Augenspiegel* (Munich [1961]).
11 Hoogstraten] Jacob van Hoogstraten, the leader of the Cologne Dominicans opposing Reuchlin; see Ep 333:114–15n.
15 This yeasty ... day] Persius 1.24, 25

616 / To Pieter Gillis   [Louvain, c 1 August 1517]

This letter was published in the *Farrago*. The date can be assigned from line 13. If Erasmus' statements in Epp 731:3–4 and 755:16–17 are correct, his *Apologia ad Fabrum* was written between 20 July and 5 August (cf Ep 597:37n). For Gillis see Ep 597:23n.

ERASMUS OF ROTTERDAM TO PIETER GILLIS, GREETING

Dearest Pieter Gillis, I have so far received a hundred florins from the court, and the balance they promise shortly. If you should find a reliable person, or if Jacobus will be coming this way, send me your eightfold psalter. No one has a copy here, and I need it for the *Apologia* which I am writing against   5
Lefèvre. Give my very special greetings to master physician. I would have sent him his *Grammar*, but the *Apologia* has somewhat deflected me from my plans. Farewell, dear Pieter.

Remember me to your father and your wife. I myself, thank heaven, am in moderately good health. Tell Quentin he really must finish; and when   10
it is done, I will hasten over to consult with you how it can be most easily and safely dispatched to England, and also to square up with Quentin. This wrangle with Lefèvre has already made me lose eight days. Farewell once more: do your best, indeed, to keep as well as possible.

Remember me warmly to Master Nicholas, your headmaster; he chose   15

* * * * *

616

2 hundred florins] Most likely the money-of-account (livre d'Artois) rather than the gold St Philip coin is meant here. If so, a sum of £16 13s 4d gros Flemish = £11 9s 2d sterling = £103 15s 0d tournois = 50 ducats, in relative gold values. Cf Ep 621 introduction and CWE 1 318, 323, 347.

3 shortly] For this promise, and for the payment now received, see Ep 613.

4 Jacobus] Nepos

4 psalter] In Latin, Greek, Hebrew, Arabic, and Syriac, edited by Agostino Giustiniani and published in November 1516. Erasmus criticized it in the *Apologia ad Fabrum* (LB IX 25C–26A); cf Allen Ep 906:481 and the corresponding note in CWE 6.

6 physician] Henricus Afinius, the chief physician of Antwerp. Erasmus considered dedicating to him his translation of the second book of Gaza's grammar; cf Epp 542 introduction, 638:19–20, 771 introduction.

10 Quentin] Metsys, b 1465/6 in Louvain, d 1530 in Antwerp. A master in the Antwerp painters' guild since 1509, he was at this time probably the most respected painter in the region. For the portraits see Epp 601:56n, 654 introduction.

15 Nicholas] Nicolaas van Broeckhoven (Brouchoven, Buscoducensis, Buschendorp) of 's Hertogenbosch, b c 1478, d between 1550 and 1556, was the master of the Latin school at Antwerp. He later joined the Reformers and became the

to lay me under an obligation, so please look about you, in case there is any service I can do him in return. I had entrusted your friend John with the task of buying me a chair in Brussels; I should like to know what happened. 151[8]

617 / From Antonius Clava   Ghent, 3 August [1517]

> The year date is 1517 rather than 1516, as was assumed before Allen. The greetings to friends in Louvain suggest that this is where Erasmus was living and where Clava, a civic official (cf Epp 175:13n, 524 introduction), had hoped to spend his vacation. Erasmus, however, was not in Louvain in late July or early August 1516 (see Ep 441 introduction). Only 1517 therefore remains, since in the autumn of this year Jan of Friesland, who copied this letter into the Deventer Letter-book (cf Allen I 604–5, Allen Ep 637:13n), left the service of Erasmus; 1517 also permits us to recognize Ep 650 as an answer to this letter.

ANTONIUS CLAVA TO ERASMUS OF ROTTERDAM, GREETING
On 31 July a letter reached me from Josse Bade in Paris, enclosing one from Budé to you, which I included in this letter of mine and gave to the man who carries this as soon as I could to be delivered to you. I had intended by this time to come over and see you, in hopes of learning something from you in   5
the way of Greek and enjoying your delightful society for as long as this public holiday would permit. But my plans were interrupted by other business which I neither wanted nor enjoyed but could not escape, so that I have been obliged to stay at home to attend to several things of no interest and subordinate my own wishes to necessity. Nor is it yet clear to me how I   10
could shake off this burden; indeed I very much fear that other business not a little more tedious may also come my way. Such is the lot which has fallen to me; but I think I must bear it patiently, until a happier day dawns, if indeed there is any happier day in store for me. With your usual kindness please let me know how you are and whether you have had this letter, and   15
also whether there is anything I can do for you or arrange to be done. Farewell.

* * * * *

rector of the Latin school at Wesel. He died as pastor of Blankenburg in the Harz.
17 John] Most likely Jan of Friesland (Johannes Phrysius), a young man who seems to have entered the service of Erasmus in the autumn of 1516; cf Ep 637:15–17.

617
2 from Budé] Ep 609

Please give my warmest greetings to that very kind man Jean Desmarez and that capable writer Adriaan Baerland and to my good friend
Rutgerus of Maaseik as well as his most honourable host. Farewell, farewell,   20
our pride and joy.

Ghent, 3 August

618 / From Henricus Glareanus   Paris, 5 August 1517

> Glareanus had recently arrived in Paris (cf Ep 609:22), taking with him
> some younger students who had lived and studied under his supervision in
> Basel and would now do so in Paris. After paying tribute to Erasmus and his
> ideals, he paints a gloomy picture of academic life in Paris: Greek is non-
> existent and scholastic follies abound. He may have exaggerated but his
> disappointment is real; cf Abel Lefranc *Histoire du Collège de France* (Paris 1893)
> 57–63. Subsequently the Collège de France was created to give humanism a
> secure footing; cf Ep 522 introduction.
>
> The answer to this letter is Ep 707.

TO ERASMUS OF ROTTERDAM FROM GLAREANUS, GREETING
If I am wrong, dearest Erasmus, in my special devotion to you and in
singing your praises everywhere, I am wrong, I assure you, with a light
heart. I am devoted to you because you are a true Christian, and praise you
continually because, so far as you could, you have made me one; and at this   5
thought I rejoice greatly. Nor am I ignorant what a great thing it is to call you
a true Christian; for it is the biggest mistake of our generation not to
recognize who the true Christian is, while the multitude give the name of
Christians to men who are unlike nothing so much as Christ, from whom
they take their name. Only consider, my dear Erasmus, how far your friend   10
Glareanus is from burdening your pious ears with otiose epithets, when I
prefer to call you a true Christian instead of most learned or most eloquent.
What name so worthy as the name Christian? And that it should be applied
with truth to someone – what could be finer than that, granted that he may

* * * * *

18 Desmarez] Erasmus' host in Louvain; see Ep 597:46.
19 Baerland] A scholar at Louvain; see Ep 646 introduction.
20 Rutgerus] Rescius (see Ep 546 introduction), who may have visited Louvain
   during the holiday season. Normally he lived in Antwerp, and his host there
   would be the printer Dirk Martens, for whom he worked.

618
5 made me one] He credited Erasmus with his conversion from scholasticism to
   Christian humanism and, perhaps, with a steadying influence on his wild
   temper.

possess all other qualities? Would that the same mind were in all theolo-   15
gians that is in you; that they did as much for others as you do, that they
incited men so much to virtue, that they led the way by their example as
effectively as they outdo all men in their flow of language, that they would
choose like you to be a help to the whole world! You help all men and are a
burden to none, you rouse them and inspire them all. May God Almighty   20
grant you a long life, that for as long as possible you may be a blessing to the
whole world and succour the ignorance of mankind.

But no more of that. I read quite lately, on my arrival in Paris, your
letter to the bishop of Paris. You may wonder how I felt. In a way, I was
delighted at such exceptional praise from a great scholar; in a way I was   25
indignant and cursed myself for not being the man of whom Erasmus had
given such a pretty picture, with, of course, the same indulgent judgment
that he applies to everyone; in another way, I counted myself lucky for
having a picture set before me not of what I was but of what I ought to be.
My chief source of distress was that I despaired not merely of making my   30
dear Erasmus any return in kind, but even more of contriving in the
slightest degree, even in words, to avoid the appearance of ingratitude,
however grateful I might be in my own mind. But I shall have proved myself
quite grateful enough to satisfy you (such is your kindness and your
readiness to think well of people), if I one day became the man whom you   35
have described with more kindness than accuracy. Another man might say
'Accept my thanks, most learned Erasmus, immortal boundless thanks, all
perfectly unlimited.' But I assure you, I have no knowledge of such phrases,
either because I have never learnt to flatter or because you have always
hated such pretences, having no more appetite for glory than Christ or St   40
Paul. And so, dearest father and teacher, since I can make you no return,
and know not how to, I will love you above all others; love you I will, and so
indeed I do. You are enshrined in my heart; the memory of you and life itself
shall be reft from me together.

Budé has received me kindly, Cop has shown me much courtesy, and I   45
have made great friends with Lefèvre d'Etaples, whom I have found the
man you and our special friend Beatus always used to speak of – a really
honourable and courteous person. The bishop for a particular reason I have
not yet approached. I have an income of my own and am beholden to no one

* * * * *

24 letter] Ep 529, to Etienne Poncher
45 Budé] Cf Ep 609:22–3.
45 Cop] Guillaume Cop, royal physician, was a native of Basel and an old friend
   of Erasmus; see Ep 523.
47 Beatus] Rhenanus, who had himself been a student and a colleague of Lefèvre.
49 income] The French king Francis I allowed him a special grant of 150 francs

Letter from Richard Pace to Erasmus, Epistle 619
The letter was written by a secretary; Pace added the heading and date.
British Library MS Harl. 6989 f 27 recto
Courtesy of the British Library Board

for anything. Only, having come to Paris in pursuit of Greek, I have been   50
severely disappointed, for there is no one to give public lectures on any
important Greek author, nor private teaching either, to the best of my
recollection. A thousand gangs of sophisters are brawling round me. In fact,
I was lately at a disputation in the Sorbonne, where I heard enthusiastic
applause – it might have been the theatre of Pompey. I could not restrain my   55
laughter; or rather, restrain it I did, but with great difficulty. But on their
side everyone kept a straight face, for a great contest was there afoot over the
proverbial goat's wool. They were, if you please, not a little indignant with
our first parent Adam for having eaten apples and not pears, and the
contestants, who have a high opinion of themselves, scarcely refrained   60
from abusing him. At length their solemnity as theologians overbore their
passions, and happily Adam escaped unscathed. I went away sickened by
their nonsense. So now I stay at home, making a little music to my pupils
and abandoned to idleness; I enjoy myself with my beloved Horace and
laugh with Democritus at the folly of the world.   65

But I must stop. Almighty God grant I may some day live in your
company once more. Farewell my lodestar, my brightest jewel, and more
than the half of my own soul. My Peter Tschudi and all my pupils, who are
your great admirers, send you their greetings. Do please send me something by way of reply; for nothing can happen to me in this life more   70
enjoyable than a letter from you.

Paris, in the rue Saint-Jacques, 5 August in the year of Christ 1517

619 / From Richard Pace   Constance, 5 August [1517]

The British Library possesses in MS Harl. 6989 f 27 the original letter actually
sent to Erasmus, or at least prepared for dispatch. The heading, the date and

* * * * *

(£150 tournois = £25 16s 8d gros Flemish = £17 15s 2d sterling in relative silver
values) rather than one of the regular scholarships that were given to young
Swiss for political reasons. He also received income from his charges. Cf CWE 1
318.

55 Pompey] The 'great' Cn. Pompeius (d 48 BC) built in Rome the first theatre
constructed entirely of stone; it was renowned for its splendour.

58 goat's wool] Cf Adagia I iii 53: a dispute on the irrelevant question whether a
goat's fur should be called woolly or bristly.

68 Tschudi] See Ep 490:37n.

72 rue Saint-Jacques] This was the axis of the university district, surrounded by
several colleges. Among the many book shops located in it was the Ecu de
Bâle, a meeting place for Swiss expatriates and students and a convenient
mailing address for all of them; see M. Reulos 'Paris au temps d'Erasme'
Scrinium I 79–86; Bietenholz Basle and France 29–34.

postscript, and the Greek (two full sentences and a number of single terms) are all in Pace's own hand. He also corrected numerous errors made by the scribe.

From October 1515 to late in 1517 Richard Pace was engaged in a diplomatic mission to the Swiss and had also to watch over the actions of the inefficient English ambassador to Maximilian I, Sir Robert Wingfield. His task – bound to fail – was to prevent the Swiss from reaching an understanding with France (lines 46–8). This letter was composed after the publication of *Epistolae ad Erasmum* in October 1516 and before Pace's return to England. He left Constance some time before 6 December 1517 (Ep 729:22), probably passed through Basel and Tournai, which was still in English hands (cf Epp 742:9n, 755), and may have visited Antwerp (cf Ep 736:7). In Bruges he was the guest of Mark Lauwerijns, about 20 December. It was probably there that he met Thomas More (cf Epp 740–2). They returned to England, perhaps together, around Christmas; cf Ep 623:23n, LP II 3885.

RICHARD PACE TO HIS FRIEND ERASMUS, GREETING

Some time ago, dearest Erasmus, a collection of letters reached me, written by you and by Budé, Ammonio, More, and other scholars, which had been printed in Louvain. Among them I found a letter from you to Bullock in which you mention letters addressed to you by two cardinals, Grimani and   5
San Giorgio, which you say you never received; and you seem inclined to lay the blame for this on me. But, unless I am quite wrong, I shall very easily clear my name, even if it is you that sit in judgment; for I shall very clearly show that in the matter of getting those letters faithfully delivered to you I did nothing incompatible with our friendship, which I most scrupulously   10
respect and always shall. I admit therefore that those letters were sent to me by our friend Ammonio and duly delivered, when I was in the Swiss camp near Milan. But they arrived at a time when I not only could not send you

* * * * *

619
2 letters] The *Epistolae ad Erasmum* of October 1516. See CWE 3 348.
3 Ammonio] See Ep 623 introduction.
4 Bullock] Henry Bullock. See Ep 456:228–32 and Ep 338; for the lost letters from Cardinals Domenico Grimani and Raffaele Riario (San Giorgio) see also Ep 835 introduction.
13 Milan] From the second half of March Pace was in Lombardy with the Swiss infantry who were in the pay of Maximilian I, while the French cavalry scoured the country (cf LP II pp lxix–lxxvi). Maximilian soon withdrew to Trent, and Pace eventually followed him. The Swiss themselves were divided. Basel was among the cantons adhering to the anti-French alliance, but a majority was already on the side of France; see J. Wegg *Richard Pace* (London 1932) 94–5; J. Dierauer *Geschichte der schweizerischen Eidgenossenschaft* II (Gotha 1920) 550–1.

yours: I could not send any courier to the king, my master, though business
made that urgent. All roads leading into Germany were occupied on all   15
sides by the enemy; and this was done on purpose to intercept both my
dispatches and the money sent to pay the troops. Thus it came about that I
was obliged to keep your letters by me for a number of days, or else they
would clearly be lost through my negligence. But as soon as ever the enemy
were compelled, partly by force and partly by necessity, to leave those parts,   20
I gave the letters for carriage to you to a most worthy character (or so he
seemed) who was setting out direct for Basel and who (I was very glad to
learn) knew you very well by reputation. A month later, however, I was in
Trent, where I learnt that you had left Basel for an unknown destination;
and this you had perhaps done before the arrival of the man to whom I had   25
given your letters for delivery to you. This therefore, I conjecture, was the
reason why those letters were lost, and perhaps the bearer together with the
letters. For to say nothing of the threat of danger from the enemy,
everywhere was full of brigands.

I was often about to write you on this subject, but since that time I   30
could never hear news of your whereabouts, until the fifteenth of this
month, when I got a letter from our friend More, now I suppose more the
Utopian not the Englishman. From it I learnt that you have a very good and
honourable position with your most illustrious prince, his Catholic
Majesty; for you are, I hear, provided with an ample benefice and made a   35
member of the king's privy council. At this I am delighted, but at the same
time very sorry that you should have left my native England and could not
be kept there on any terms, although More writes that a generous offer was
made you by his eminence the cardinal of York. But wherever you may be, I
pray immortal God that all may turn out well for your happiness and   40
prosperity.

Since you wrote to me from Basel, the life I have led has been most
disagreeable and one for which I am quite unfitted; some of the time I have
been involved in warfare (a thing with which the Muses have nothing in
common), in which much more effort has been devoted to pillage than to   45
fighting, and in part I have been most deeply immersed in the business of
princes, in which it has been the chief object of their efforts that nothing

* * * * *

24 Trent] Pace was there 12–23 May 1516; cf LP II 1877, 1931. Erasmus had left
   Basel about 12 May; cf Ep 408.
31 this month] July – an indication that the composition of this letter had taken
   Pace some time.
35 benefice] Cf Ep 436; for Erasmus' appointment to the council cf Ep 370:18n.
39 York] Cf Ep 577, to Cardinal Wolsey.
42 you wrote] Perhaps Ep 350

should go right. The result of all this has, I am sure, reached you by common report, or at least you have understood it clearly in our friend More's new republic of Utopia, where he deals in characteristic fashion with Naples   50
breaking loose and everything else connected with it.

In the same letter that I mentioned before, I laughed out loud at that college which provided, as you say, by solemn resolution that no man should bring the New Testament as restored by your efforts and with so much labour by horse boat waggon or porter within the curtilage of the said   55
college. You call the college steeped in theology, but I would have thought it devoid of all theology, indeed barely human. If they had any piety (which should be especially the mother of theologians) or cultivation or learning, they would not in this evil and ignorant manner abuse and try to uproot and tear in pieces a work so admirable and so learned, and basely condemn   60
something they perhaps have never seen and would not understand if they did, thereby displaying no judgment, but malice as far removed as could be from theology, not to call it barefaced impiety. As for their principle that nothing of the kind should be undertaken except on the authority of a General Council, this view seems to me more ridiculous even than its   65
authors. The very idea that it is unlawful to correct mistakes and put right gross errors in books, unless the authority of a Council so instructs us! If they wish to maintain this in general, why do they absolve men who sin every day without authorization from a synod? For this in my opinion is something more serious than what you have done, since it involves the   70
liberation of the soul itself or its condemnation to perpetual torments; unless perhaps they wish to object that the decrees of a synod order this to be done. If so, I do not myself think it can be repugnant to the decrees of any synod for all books which enshrine or expound the teaching of Christ to be read in pure and corrected texts without mistakes. To tell you briefly my   75
opinion both of the college you speak of and of your edition of the New Testament, if a synod were to be called now, I would rather spend the time in reading your books than in attending it, if that college were given power to discuss and decide everything. Is it possible that men should be able or willing to take counsel to good purpose about the faith of Christ, who object   80
to seeing or reading what he taught free from mistakes? Besides which, look at their own style: Christ himself, I believe, would turn away from the barbarism of what they write and would rather see his faith in danger than

* * * * *

50 Naples] The case of Naples, won by Charles VIII of France in 1495 and lost again within a year, is invoked by More as an example of the foolish nature of princes who will not normally listen to sound advice; cf *Utopia* 86–7, 352.
56 college] Cf Ep 456:11–15.

disfigured by such solecisms. I really wonder, dear Erasmus, why you
spend so much time in your letter on pacifying those donkeys listening to   85
the lyre, unless perhaps the object of your elegant and authoritative letter
was to deter other men of the same kidney (a difficult task) from making
similar fools of themselves. They ought to be satisfied by your story of our
mass-priest and his *mumpsimus* for *sumpsimus*. If, however, you wish to go
further and attack them in print, I have one request to make of you, that you   90
head your letter to them 'To the College of Numbskulls, with my worst
wishes,' and let your first sentence begin 'Off with you to the bottomless pit
of ignorance, you mere useless burden on the earth.'

Your letter from Budé, that most scholarly and civilized person, and
yours to him, in which the two of you discuss a point of interpretation in the   95
preface of Luke the Evangelist, have been in my hands, and I observed your
translation and what he thought of it. To put it briefly, I see no difficulty in
that passage, nothing hard to catch as Budé thinks, but consider that one
should take παρηκολουθηκότι in its ordinary and common meaning, as
when we say ταῦτα παρακολουθεῖ τῷ προσώπῳ, 'these things follow the   100
person'; so that the sense is: 'It seemed good to me, who am later in time and
followed and succeeded them, to write,' etc. Luke means that he followed,
not the eyewitnesses as Budé thinks, but authorities of a later generation,
who followed the actual eyewitnesses. So in this passage I do not accept
either *prosecuto* or *persecuto* or *assecuto*. But in the second passage, which   105
Budé cites from Demosthenes, I agree with him; for otherwise the place
would be meaningless, like the passage in Galen. But one must remember
that Demosthenes in that place is writing Attic Greek. For in the first
passage cited by Budé, the verb παρηκολουθηκώς is also to be taken in its
usual sense, as is clear from this among other things, that he put εἰδώς in   110
front of it. For if Demosthenes witnessed Aeschines' misdemeanours, he
must needs have followed them; not followed in the sense of keeping up
with them intellectually, but been there as an eyewitness. That verb ἐπεχείρησαν placed at the beginning seems to have moved you to render
persecuto strictly. For you write in your note on this passage 'He used   115
ἐπεχείρησαν to make us understand that in these early writers desire

* * * * *

86 lyre] Cf *Adagia* I iv 35.
89 mass-priest] Cf Ep 456:80–3.
93 burden on the earth] Homer *Iliad* 18.104
94 letter from Budé ... and yours to him] Epp 403 and 421, published in *Epistolae
    ad Erasmum*. For the difficulties in interpreting Luke 1:1–4 see Epp 403:89–120,
    421:40–4. In his discussion Pace seems to confuse the issue still further.
115 note] On Luke 1:1 (LB VI 217)

outruns performance.' But on this point likewise I will tell you what I think.
'Επιχειρεῖν does indeed mean to attempt something; but it is not used any
more of those who do something badly or not as well as they might than it is
of those who make a success of what they intend or perform what they   120
promise – the opposite of *conari* in Latin. And so I approve your *aggressi*
rather than the other translator's *conati* in this passage, looking not only to
the proper meaning of the word, but to the actual sense. I do not think Luke
is finding fault with writers of an earlier generation as though they did not
take enough trouble; for he admits that they wrote on the authority of men   125
who were present at the events related and saw them happen, and it is from
them and no one else that a historian can arrive at the truth. Personally I find
the following λόγου much more difficult. Should we refer it to Christ, as
Valla thinks (whom you accuse of quibbling), or to the narrative? For had
Luke meant it to refer to the narrative he ought to have used the plural rather 130
than the singular, in my opinion, because this would have been much
better Greek. Besides which, I do not see why it would not make good sense
to render the passage 'As those men have handed down to us who saw
Christ and ministered to him.' But this I leave to you for further consideration.   135

But my good Richard, hold hard with that pen of yours. Do you not see
what nonsense you are talking, and what a contest you are laying up for
yourself when you, poor creature, try to take on two paladins, each of them
a Hercules? Peace, my good fellow! I challenge no one, I criticize no one, I
measure myself by the length of my own foot; I say what I think, as one   140
friend to another, in hopes that my errors may be corrected in the same
spirit. Farewell.

From Constance, 5 August

I have been too busy to write to you just now with my own hand.
Forgive me if I dictate, and the letter is badly written – badly written not   145
only as regards the handwriting ...

620 / To Germain de Brie   Louvain, [c August 1517]

Brie was a well-to-do priest and member of the Paris humanist circle. This
letter was first published in the *Farrago* of October 1519, where the year date

* * * * *

129 Valla] For Lorenzo Valla's *Annotations* to the New Testament see Epp 182,
554:81n.
129 quibbling] See LB IV 218E. Erasmus does not refer to Pace and makes no use of
his translation.
139 I measure] *Adagia* I vi 89

was given as 1518. However, 1517 is more likely. It is true that More's *Epi-grams*, which had offended Brie (line 31), were not printed before March 1518 (cf Ep 550 introduction). But there is no difficulty in assuming that Brie had seen a manuscript. Publication had been long delayed, and epigrams are easily copied. This letter makes an excellent answer in every respect to Brie's Ep 569 (dated 5 April 1517), and Erasmus would hardly have waited more than a year before sending such a reply; moreover there is no trace yet of the worsening relations with Budé which coincided with a cooling of his interest in a move to France (cf Ep 778). See also line 41n. This letter did not reach Brie, who first read it published in the *Farrago*. He at once wrote a lengthy reply, Ep 1045, which he appended, together with this letter, to his poem *Antimorus* (Paris: P. Vidoue early 1520).

ERASMUS OF ROTTERDAM TO GERMAIN DE BRIE, GREETING

Your letter, my dear Brie, brought me pleasure of more than one kind. To begin with, it refreshed, to my great satisfaction, the memory of those delightful conversations we enjoyed in Venice and thereafter in Padua. And then it tells me that you are not only in good health but advanced in fortune   5
and in reputation; and no news could be more welcome. Thirdly, it clearly shows how successfully you strive to outstrip yourself, with the object, evidently, of achieving a skill in prose equal to the most happy vein of poetry that has been yours from of old. As to the praises you pile on me with both hands, I accept them without difficulty on the understanding that your   10
affection for me is as unlimited as your panegyric, although (to speak true) I read your praise of that distinguished prelate Etienne Poncher and of François Deloynes and Guillaume Budé with very much more pleasure than your praise of me. When you tell me, indeed, how much I owe to the active support of the bishop and to those two literary paladins Deloynes and Budé,   15
I am grateful to you for reminding me at the same time of my obligations to them. But the more copious their praises of me, the more your friends deter me from going to France; how could I dare come, under such a load of panegyric that I should know I was expected to live up to it? France has always attracted me, nor am I unaware how much men in this place look   20
askance at humane studies, ruled as it is by monks falsely so-called and vain

* * * * *

620
4 Venice ... Padua] In 1508, cf Epp 212:2, 569:167.
10 both hands] Cf *Adagia* I ix 16.
12 Poncher ... Deloynes] The first was bishop of Paris; the second a member of its Parlement and a close friend of Budé; see Epp 494 and 529 introductions.

talkers, who easily impose on blustering Paphlagonians and ass-eared
Midases. But up to now my destiny keeps me somehow chained here. The
offers made to me in the name of your most generous king are ample, I
admit. Yet the proffered friendship of such distinguished men carries more   25
weight with me than the royal bounty, since each of you promises individually to add this on behalf of you all. I rejoice with you over and over
again that your own good fortune should be sufficient, in your opinion, for
us both, since you invite me to come and share it.

A vague rumour of uncertain origin has been circulating here to the   30
effect that you have taken offence at the epigrams of Thomas More and are
preparing some sort of pamphlet with teeth in it by way of answer. My most
learned friend, if you will lend an ear at all to your Erasmus, you will do
nothing of the kind. Yet it is not so much for his sake that I would deprecate
such a course as for your own. If you knew More intimately, you would   35
agree that nowhere in the world is there one that more deserves to be your
friend. Why then, you will say, did he do me wrong? He wrote those lines
not against you, whom he did not know, but against some imaginary
Frenchman, and he wrote in wartime. By now it is proper that all memory of
such things should be entirely done away between you, now that intimate   40
peace has been established between your two peoples. It is expedient also
for the cause of humane studies in general that their disciples like the
ancient Cretans should stand side by side, now that the enemies of literature are banding together so unpleasantly. And finally, I am reluctant to see
two men at odds to both of whom I am devoted.   45

You will exclaim at this point, I feel sure, that I am behaving worse

* * * * *

22 Paphlagonians] Proverbial since Cleon in Aristophanes' *Knights*; cf also Lu-
    cian *Alexander* 9.11. The inhabitants of Paphlagonia, on the south coast of the
    Black Sea, had a reputation for being stupid and superstitious.
23 Midases] Persons of dull wit or of extreme suspiciousness (symbolized by the
    length of the ears); cf *Adagia* I iii 67.
24 offers] See Ep 778:33n.
28 fortune] Brie was a nephew of Cardinal Louis d'Amboise, bishop of Albi, and
    held several benefices in southern France. To these was added in 1514 the
    priory of Saint-Jean-de-Duchaco (diocese of Saint-Flour) and a canonry at
    Auxerre. At about this time he was named almoner to Francis I.
41 peace] Taken literally, this might be a reference to Wolsey's perpetual peace
    negotiated between July and October 1518 (cf Ep 964). But does Erasmus have
    a specific event in mind? The two countries were officially at peace since the
    treaty of Saint-Germain (7 August 1514), which was reinforced by a commer-
    cial agreement reached in London (26 July 1517).
43 Cretans] Cf *Adagia* I i 11.

than Diomede in sending three lines, and those ill written, in exchange for such a long and stylish letter; but you will think more kindly of me, I know, if you bear in mind that I am busy on several large volumes and consider how many letters I have to answer single-handed almost every day.   50
Farewell.

Louvain, 151[8]

621 / From Pierre Barbier   Saint-Cybardeaux, 12 August 1517

Barbier's party (Ep 608 introduction) was now on the way from Paris to Bordeaux. The name of Saint-Cybardeaux (near Rouillac, Dept Charente) appears in a document signed by Le Sauvage on the same day (LP II 3575). This letter answers Ep 608 and was answered by Erasmus with Ep 652.

This letter clarifies some financial transactions mentioned elsewhere in the correspondence. Owing to Erasmus in his capacity as a councillor to Prince Charles was the sum of 300 florins, of which 200 had been advanced to him privately by Chancellor Le Sauvage. Subsequently Barbier should have received 150 ducats for Erasmus, but was given only 120. These gold coins (if indeed they were coins and not money-of-account) may have been Venetian, papal, or Hungarian ducats, Florentine florins, Portuguese cruzados, or Spanish excelentes, all worth about 79–80d each (cf CWE 1 313–14, 316, 336–9; Ep 447:844n). Since Barbier equates one ducat with two 'florins,' obviously the florins mentioned here and previously were not St Philip florins or any other gold coin but the money-of-account florin (gulden) consisting of 40d gros Flemish (livre de quarante gros, livre d'Artois; cf CWE 1 314, 316–18, 323, 347). That assumption is supported by Ep 608:8, referring to 'francs' rather than florins. A sum of 150 ducats or of 300 florins would thus have been worth £50 0s 0d gros Flemish = £311 5s 0d tournois = £34 7s 6d sterling, in relative gold values.

Barbier received the sum of 120 ducats (£40 gros Flemish) through an unidentified 'Spaniard' from special funds rather than from the Netherlands treasury (cf Ep 628:58–60). One hundred ducats were used to repay the advance of 200 florins made by Le Sauvage. Another 100 florins were sent to Erasmus through Marques (cf Epp 608:5–10, 613:2–7, 616:2–3). The 20 ducats left in Barbier's hand provided, therefore, only 40 florins. To make the 100 florins over to Erasmus, he had to add the sum received for payment of the Courtrai annuity to Erasmus for the first half of 1517, amounting to 65 florins

* * * * *

47 Diomede] Cf *Adagia* I ii 1; Diomede in Homer arranges an exchange of armour with Glaucus, by which he gives bronze and receives gold.

(cf Epp 436:6n, 608:8–9). Had Barbier received an additional 30 ducats (60 florins) from the court, he could have paid Erasmus in full, or very nearly so. As it was, approximately the amount of the Courtrai annuity remained owing, and as late as 1530 Erasmus blamed Barbier for the unpaid debt (cf Epp 1548, 2404). For an explanation of why the payment of the Courtrai annuity was initially effected through Barbier cf Gorissen *Kortrijkse pensioen* 114–16.

TO THE RIGHT LEARNED MASTER ERASMUS OF ROTTERDAM
Greeting, right learned Master Erasmus. Your letter of 17 July from Louvain reached me a few days ago. You make a pretty mock of me by exalting my tribulations into successes; but this is your way, and I forgive it. But I cannot easily forgive the man who is the cause of your not getting your 5 money. While I was still in Lille I paid over one hundred florins in cash, putting them in the hands of the Sieur de Marques, a member of the king's council. If you have received both for your Courtrai annuity and for the rest of your stipend no more than a hundred florins, the man responsible is the Spaniard who, though he had promised one hundred and fifty ducats, kept 10 truly Punic faith as his countrymen do and paid over barely one hundred and twenty; of which I gave a hundred at once to my master, which he had given instructions to pay to you in Ghent out of his own funds. But meanwhile I beg you, dear Master Erasmus, to be patient a little longer until we get to Spain, where as soon as I have the chance I will remind my master 15 of you and your affairs and do all I can to see that he leaves you more than satisfied.

As for our new cardinals, for fear my letter may not reach you directly I have thought it better to say nothing than to write with any freedom. I am surprised that Lefèvre should have written anything about you or against 20 you with any display of temper. I met him in Paris, and Clichtove too, whose pact of friendship with you I renewed as you had told me to. They both with one accord speak of you in the highest terms and praise all you do as most proper and necessary for the studious Christian. And so I beseech you earnestly in the bowels of Christ not to write against him with any 25 bitterness, for there will be men who, while quite incapable of understanding any of the fruits of your distinguished labours, will perceive that a

* * * * *

621
6 Lille] Cf LP II 3379.
11 Punic faith] *Adagia* I viii 28
12 master] Le Sauvage
18 cardinals] See Ep 608:13n.
21 Clichtove] See Epp 594:15n, 597:14n.

dispute has arisen between two such leading lights. They will therefore
decide that what you have written for the glory of God and the advantage of
all who wish to learn had no purpose but vainglory, and this they will put   30
about with all the irresponsibility of that sort of men.

My distinguished master has told me to send you his greetings, and
adds: 'Once I am in Spain and find there is a suitable vacancy, I shall see to it
that he gets something better than he has had up to now.' At the same time,
about the payment of your stipend, he instructed me to remind him in   35
Spain. I beg you, dear sir, to give my greetings to Doctor Atensis. Farewell.

From Sensebardeau, halfway between Poitiers and Bordeaux, 12
August 1517

Your humble servant Pierre Barbier

622 / To Johannes Caesarius   Antwerp, 16 August 1517

Erasmus' visit to Antwerp in the middle of August is confirmed by Ep 639; for
its purpose cf Ep 654 introduction. This letter is known only from the *Lamentationes obscurorum virorum* (1st ed Cologne: [Quentel c March] 1518; second,
enlarged ed Cologne: Quentel 1 October 1518; Hutten *Operum supplementum* I
323–418). Erasmus, who admitted his authorship of the letter, never claimed
that the text was incomplete or inaccurate; but he made it clear that the
publication was unauthorized (Allen Ep 967:167–9). In the *Spongia* against
Hutten (LB X 1640E–41B) he repeats this assertion and firmly rejects Hutten's
charge of duplicity in his stand on the Reuchlin controversy. In fact, it does not
seem that he ever spoke with approval of the *Epistolae obscurorum virorum* (cf
Ep 636:3–4). It may be doubted, however, whether he would have sent this
letter to Cologne if he had not wished it to circulate there, at least in manuscript.

The *Lamentationes* were a polemical reply by Ortwinus Gratius to the *Epistolae obscurorum virorum*, using the same technique of ridicule. Hence Erasmus was equally outspoken in his disapproval of the *Lamentationes* (cf Ep 830).
All pieces were fictitious except the letter by Erasmus and the papal bull (cf Ep
611:82n).

In view of the biased source from which this letter is known, it might be
possible that some short statement in favour of Reuchlin, analogous to the one
at the end of Erasmus' very similar Ep 636, was suppressed by the editor. A

* * * * *

33 vacancy] See Ep 608:19n.
36 Atensis] Jan Briart; see Ep 670 introduction. The text has 'magistrum nostrum
   de Aeth.'

more substantial omission would probably have been noted by Erasmus and criticized in Ep 967 or elsewhere.

This letter answers Ep 615.

ERASMUS TO HIS FRIEND CAESARIUS, GREETING
I greatly disapproved of the *Epistolae obscurorum virorum*, right from the beginning. The wit might have proved entertaining if it had not set such an offensive precedent. I like humour, provided it stops short of abuse of any individual. But what I resented still more was the mention of my own name,   5
brought into the later edition as though mere nonsense was not enough unless they had invited me too to share the odium of it, and so had undone a great part of the good I had sought with so much toil. Even that did not satisfy them: they must needs produce a second volume like the first, full of the names of people who I know by no means approve that kind of non-   10
sense. What a lot of harm they do, not only to themselves, but to everyone who has the cause of true learning at heart!

Another thing which I resent most of all, if it is true, was told me by my servant Jacobus when he returned from your part of the world: that many people in Cologne have in their possession some sort of pamphlet attacking   15
Pope Julius, and how after death he was shut out of heaven by St Peter. I had heard long ago that a story to this effect was afoot in France, where this ephemeral stuff has always enjoyed excessive freedom. This, I suppose, has now been translated by someone into Latin. I cannot imagine what has come into their heads, to waste time and labour like that. Besides which, I   20
am surprised that some people suspect me as the source of this egregious absurdity; I suppose because the style is perhaps rather better Latin than some. I have of course written a humorous piece, my *Moria*, but not so as to draw blood; I slighted the reputation of no man by name; I attacked men's foibles, but no man's reputation. If what my servant told me is true, for as   25
yet I can hardly credit it, I do beg you, my friend, to do all you can to get this kind of impious stuff suppressed before it can be printed; not that these people deserve to have this service done them, but because it is our public duty to maintain a standard of decency in scholarship, which they bedaub so disgustingly with their so-called humour. As far as I myself am con-   30
cerned, I am sure that no one who knows me will fail to understand that I

* * * * *

622
5 own name] Cf Ep 581:14–16.
14 Jacobus] Nepos; cf Ep 594 introduction.
17 France] See Ep 636:16n; on the famous dialogue *Julius exclusus*, frequently attributed to Erasmus, see Ep 502 introduction.

particularly disliked this sort of rubbish, as unworthy of a scholar and an honourable man.

Give my cordial greetings to Jacob of Hoorn; I enjoyed his letter more than I can say. As for the settlement of the dispute about Reuchlin, I only   35 hope your news is true. A man from Alkmaar told me you had written me another letter, but I have not had it yet. Farewell, most learned Caesarius.

Antwerp, morrow of the Assumption 1517

623 / From Thomas More   London, 19 August [1517]

In his introduction to this letter P.S. Allen presents evidence that Andrea Ammonio died on 17 August 1517. Ammonio was a secretary to King Henry VIII, but he also held a papal appointment (see Epp 218, 338 introductions). His death deprived Erasmus of a very close and trusted friend. It also caused him personal worry and continuing trouble as he tried to recover documents of the most intimate character which had been left with Ammonio for safe keeping; see Epp 517 introduction, 649, 655–6, 772 introduction, 774–5, 822, 828.

This letter was first printed in the *Farrago* with an incorrect year date.

THOMAS MORE TO ERASMUS, GREETING

The belated and long-postponed departure of my friend Palsgrave, who is daily expected to leave, has meant that you should receive my letter and other people's much later than either I desired or you deserved. For I thought that my answer could most conveniently be carried by the man who   5

* * * * *

34 Hoorn] Jacobus Ceratinus (Teyng), d 1530, of Hoorn (North Holland), was now studying at Cologne. After receiving a degree, he proceeded to Paris, Louvain (cf Ep 992 introduction), and Basel. Erasmus thought highly of him and recommended him repeatedly for employment (cf Ep 691:19n), but he remained on the move.
36 your news] Ep 615:9–11 seemed to indicate a victory for the Reuchlinists. In fact, on 2 July 1516 a papal commission had cleared Reuchlin of the charge of heresy, but Hoogstraten and his friends persuaded Leo x to suspend further action. Leo's final pronouncement on 23 June 1520 was influenced by his concern about Luther's success and amounted to a condemnation of Reuchlin; see Geiger *Reuchlin* 319, 451.
37 another letter] Probably Ep 610; cf Ep 615:4.

623
5 answer] Palsgrave returned from Louvain to London between 10 and 15 July (cf Ep 607:16), taking with him Erasmus' Ep 597 to More. More's reply (Ep 601) and other letters sent through More (cf Ep 601:64–5) were delayed for the

had brought me yours. So it proved necessary to add this to my previous letter, to explain the reason for the delay and also to bring you up to date with the news here. If ever we were in trouble before, our distress and danger are at their greatest now, with many deaths on all sides and almost everyone in Oxford and Cambridge and London taking to their beds within 10 a few days and the loss of many of my best and most honourable friends; among them (which I am sorry to think will bring you sorrow too) our dear Andrea Ammonio, who is a very great loss to learning and to all right-thinking men. He saw himself very well protected against the contagion by his modest manner of life, thinking it due to this that, though he rarely met 15 anyone whose whole household had not suffered, the evil has so far attacked none of his own people. Of this he boasted to me himself and to many other men beside, not very many hours before he himself was carried off. For this sweating-sickness is fatal only on the first day.

I and my wife and children are still untouched, and the rest of my 20 household have entirely recovered. But of this I can assure you: one is safer on the battlefield than in the city. It has now begun, I hear, to rage in Calais, at the moment when I am obliged to go there on a mission; as though it was not enough to have lived in the midst of contagion, but I must actually go in search of it. But what can one do? What one's lot brings must be endured. I 25 have prepared my mind to face any outcome. Mind you at least keep well.

In haste, from London, 19 August 15[20]

* * * * *

reason stated here and must have reached Erasmus together with this letter and, presumably, Ep 624. Whether the carrier was Palsgrave or another (cf Ep 655:6) is not known. But Palsgrave did in the end return to Louvain; see Ep 688:26–7.

9 deaths] From an epidemic of 'sweating sickness.' In the light of other evidence More did not exaggerate. The court was not spared; Anne Boleyn had the disease but recovered. Cf LP II p 1744; J.F.D. Shrewsbury *A History of Bubonic Plague in the British Isles* (Cambridge 1970) 161–2. In Oxford four hundred students were stated to have died within a week (Brown II 945); for Cambridge cf perhaps Ep 777:2–3.

13 Ammonio] See introduction.

23 mission] Officially it dealt with disputes between English and French merchants, but it may have involved some political negotiations resulting from Wolsey's desire to counterbalance the Treaty of Cambrai; cf Rogers Ep 42: the royal commission for the ambassadors Robert Wingfield, William Knight, and Thomas More, dated 26 August 1517. More was still in Calais on 20 November (Rogers Ep 55), but after a visit to Bruges (Epp 740–2) he returned to London around Christmas; cf Epp 726:2, 763.

624 / From Johannes Sixtinus   [London] 19 August [1517]

This letter is contemporary with Ep 623. Ep 655 would seem to be the answer to
this letter. Sixtinus, a native of Friesland who lived in London, was a priest
and an old friend of Erasmus (see Ep 112 introduction). A graduate of Siena, he
had close ties with Ammonio.

JOHANNES SIXTINUS TO ERASMUS, GREETING
Although I know that I shall bring you sad news, I thought I ought to write
and tell you what it concerns you to know. Today our friend Andrea
Ammonio was buried, having been carried off by the sweating-sickness to
which many men of great note have succumbed. May God show kindness   5
and mercy to his soul! The day he paid the debt of nature, he and I were to go
into the country together (we had so arranged between us), the prior of
Merton having sent horses for us to ride; but he, having gone I hope to
heaven, has left me here to follow him when God shall so please. It ought to
be a great comfort to us, and a considerable lightening of our grief for his   10
death, that everyone has nothing but praise for his virtues, his learning,
and his admirable qualities. And, to be sure, a longer life might perhaps
have diminished rather than increased his reputation.
    Of that affair of yours I have no certain news; he was taken from us
before he heard. Three days before he died I had a most delightful and very   15
cheerful dinner with him; for that same day he had occasion for my help in
some piece of business and invited me for the day following. But news of
his death, before I had heard he was ill, was brought to me as I was getting
out of bed and before I was dressed, and greatly astonished me. So frail,
fleeting, and changeable are the affairs of men.   20
    Farewell, 19 August

625 / To Christoph von Utenheim   Louvain, [c 23 August] 1517

This letter was first published in the *Auctarium*; it is the answer to Ep 598 and is
clearly contemporary with Epp 626–36, all of which were probably dispatched
together; see the end of this letter and Ep 637:3; cf Ep 594 introduction.

* * * * *

624
 4 Ammonio] See Ep 623 introduction.
 7 prior] William Salyng (or Seiling), d 1520. An Oxford DD he had been prior of
   the canons of St Augustine at Merton, Surrey, since 1502.
14 affair] Perhaps resulting from the negotiations about Erasmus' dispensation;
   see Epp 517, 772 introductions.

TO THE RIGHT HONOURABLE CHRISTOPH,
BISHOP OF BASEL, SOLE GLORY OF OUR NOBILITY
AND CHAMPION OF RELIGION

Greeting, right reverend Father. I can scarcely express as it deserves how
greatly I respect and welcome your long-standing kindness towards me, of   5
which I had full experience long ago in Basel and which I now recognize
once again in your letter. For a long time I have been on the look-out for
some appropriate subject by means of which your goodness to me and my
grateful devotion in return may be put on record together even for posterity,
if what I write has any power; say rather, that posterity may inherit in you   10
the example of a good bishop and in me the pattern of a devoted protégé. Up
to now, however, I have been torn in so many directions by the cares, at one
time of my research and at another of court business (court nonsense,
rather), or again of the attacks of certain theologians I could name, that to
remember my duty was easier than to perform it.   15

At this moment between the theologians and myself profound peace
reigns, except for the continuing protests of a negligible few in monkish
garb, and they yap at a distance, only when I am not there, and especially
when their tongues are loosened by liquor. The court I have torn myself
away from. Louvain is now my sojourn; the climate suits me well enough,   20
and I hope it will prove possible to find contentment for my spirit; not that I
have driven Basel from my mind, but there are reasons which make it
advisable to spend some months here. I have explained the matter in part to
Ludwig Baer. If anything attracts me to your part of the world, it is not so
much the agreeable climate as the great favour shown me by your lordship.   25
For your goodness and kindness to Beatus Rhenanus, a man of rare integrity, I am no less grateful than if they had been directed to myself. What
news there is, you will learn from the letters of other people. Farewell, right
reverend Father.

Louvain, 1517   30

* * * * *

625
13 court business] See Ep 596 introduction.
15 perform] Erasmus did eventually dedicate two treatises to Utenheim. The
    first, however, *De interdicto esu carnium* (1522, LB IX 1197–1214), was given the
    form of a letter to the bishop primarily so as to invoke his protection. The
    second, *De immensa Dei misericordia* (1524, cf Ep 1474), was a genuine token of
    appreciation after a recent visit to Utenheim at Porrentruy.
19 liquor] Horace *Epistles* 1.5.19
20 Louvain] See Ep 596 introduction.
24 Baer] See Ep 627:7–10.
26 Beatus] Cf Ep 594:12–13.

626 / To Lukas Klett   Louvain, 23 August 1517

This letter answers Ep 599. It accompanied Ep 625 and like it was published in the *Auctarium*.

DESIDERIUS ERASMUS OF ROTTERDAM
TO HIS FRIEND LUKAS KLETT,
EMINENT DOCTOR OF CIVIL AND CANON LAW,
GREETING

That you are well, delights me; that you should not only remember me but 5
wish me well, I am grateful; and your honourable post on the staff of a most
admirable prelate is matter for sincere congratulation. I hope your prosperity may long endure, ever increasing, and I pray you to go on as you have
begun, and keep the name of Erasmus alive before your most excellent
master, which is the thing I most wish for. Would that the world held many 10
like him! Farewell.

Louvain, St Bartholomew's eve, 1517

627 / To Ludwig Baer   Louvain, 23 August 1517

Ludwig Baer was professor of theology at Basel and canon of St Peter's (cf Ep
488 introduction). In Ep 582 he had urged Erasmus to return to Basel. That
letter may have been delayed on the way (cf Ep 604 introduction) and this may
be the answer; cf Ep 625 introduction.

ERASMUS TO THE EMINENT THEOLOGIAN LUDWIG BAER,
HIS PATRON, GREETING

That my special patron Baer is well, I am most sincerely glad to hear. I was
not averse from Basel, which is made agreeable to me not less by the
pleasant climate than by the presence of a spirit such as yours. But Prince 5
Charles has been held on the coast for nearly two months now by winds
adverse not so much to him as to us all. Furthermore, Le Sauvage, the
chancellor of Burgundy, who paid out of his own pocket the annuity due to

* * * * *

626
7 prelate] Christoph von Utenheim, bishop of Basel; cf Ep 598.

627
4 Basel] Erasmus had been invited by Utenheim; cf Epp 598:15–19, 625.
6 coast] Cf Ep 596 introduction.
7 us all] Cf Ep 628:25–7.
7 Le Sauvage] Cf Epp 597:32–6, 621 introduction.

me from the emperor's exchequer, which is perfectly empty, bound me by
the most generous promises when he set out for Spain. I wanted to wait a   10
little time to see what would come of it. Not but what things are now in such
a state that, however eager I might have been, to set out on a journey to your
part of the world would not have been safe. For the time being I stay at
Louvain, and am welcomed by all the theologians with the greatest kindness. This I do the more readily since I hear that some Carmelites still have   15
something or other on foot, I know not what; but only a small number. I am
sorry about Lefèvre, who by his unpleasant discussion compelled me to
reply; the tone of his attack is so nasty. You will learn all about it from my
book. I assure you, I would far rather devote a large volume to praising him
than to proving him wrong. Dorp is a most sincere friend. Farewell, best of   20
teachers.

Louvain, St Bartholomew's eve 1517

628 / To Beatus Rhenanus   Louvain, 23 August [1517]

This letter is primarily an answer to Ep 575, although possibly also to Ep 594 (cf
Ep 625 introduction). For Beatus' strained relations with Froben and Lachner
see Ep 594 introduction. A preference for Lachner is also reflected in Ep 629.

ERASMUS TO HIS FRIEND BEATUS, GREETING
What you say of Froben would not surprise me; I know the man. As for
Lachner, I wonder why he should be unwilling to make use of your advice,
especially as I expressly told him to. Not but what the man through whom
they reply to me writes that you will be brought in to advise when they are   5
getting the edition ready. Which authors they print, my dear Beatus, does
not greatly concern me, provided they do their duty by me. If they are
getting tired of me, I have already heard from Asulanus, Aldus' father-in-
law, that whatever his printing-house can do will be most freely at my
service. I wonder very much what has come into Jacques Lefèvre's head,   10
that he should write all this nonsense against me in his discussion of the

* * * * *

13 safe] See Ep 582:29–36.
15 Carmelites] Cf indexes to CWE 5 and 6.
18 my book] Cf Ep 628:12–13.
20 Dorp] See Ep 628:14n.

   628
 4 man] Probably Angst; cf Ep 634.
 6 Which authors] See Epp 575:33–8, 594:15–16.
 8 Asulanus] See Ep 589.

second chapter of Hebrews; but I have replied to him at length. The book
shall be sent you, if it is finished in time, for it is now not far from the end, in
the hands of a Louvain printer. Dorp, with whom I had come near to having
serious trouble, is on intimate terms with me, and this is genuine, I think.   15
With the theologians I get on very well. But something is still brewing
among the Carmelites, who are no doubt jealous of the Preachers for the
publicity Reuchlin gave them.

At court, things are in such a state that the best men prefer to stay
away. Not to mention others, of whom any criticism would be not so much   20
disrespectful as dangerous, the king's confessor is one Briselot, once a
Carmelite, then turned Benedictine for the sake of some twopenny abbey,
and in no time a suffragan of Cambrai and one of those reverend Paris
doctors – a conceited poisonous fellow, and my sworn enemy. He holds
forth at every drinking-party against my humble self. And we have the   25
wind against us, refusing to carry this monster away from here; for the
prince is still stuck on the coast, nor do I see him ever likely to get away. This
man was chosen instead of Josse Clichtove, who had been sent for to take up
the position although he himself did not know the reason of their sending.
But the crowd at court did not take to him, because he has hardly a hair on   30
his head and is as thin as a lath. So they gave him a hundred guilders to go
back to Paris.

There is a mob, the dregs of mankind, called the Black Band. They

* * * * *

12 book] The *Apologia ad Fabrum*, shortly to be published by Martens (cf Ep
597:37). Beatus was sent a copy as soon as the book appeared; cf Ep 730
introduction.
14 Dorp] The Louvain theologian had criticized Erasmus' *Moria* and his work on
the New Testament; see Epp 304, 337, 474:19–20, 509 introduction.
17 Carmelites ... Preachers] Cf Epp 597:63–6, 615.
21 Briselot] Cf Ep 597:5n. Since Briselot was a protégé of Chièvres, the latter
probably was among the 'others' whom Erasmus did not care to mention by
name; cf lines 69–71.
27 prince] Charles; cf Ep 596 introduction.
28 Clichtove] Cf Ep 597:14n.
33 Black Band] The Black Band was formed in 1514 by Duke George of Saxony in a
desperate attempt to establish fully his rule in the recently acquired province
of Friesland (cf Ep 586:294–5). The duke, however, was penniless, and with
the support of Gelderland the Frieslanders resisted him successfully. In 1515
he sold his claims to the government to Prince Charles. Acting on their own or
in the service of Karel van Egmond, duke of Gelderland (cf Ep 584:40–1), the
Black Band ravaged Holland and Friesland together with the duke's own
soldiers. A truce was made on 17 September 1517, but the dismissed soldiers
continued to oppress the civil population; cf Epp 643:31–6, 829:10–12; P.J.
Blok *History of the Peoples of the Netherlands* trans R. Putnam, 2nd ed (New

have seized and ravaged Alkmaar, a flourishing town in Holland, where they treated even women and children with appalling cruelty because they 35 had put up a brave defence. If they had had even six hundred men by way of garrison, they had been safe. And these are the very men who a short while ago were fighting for us against Friesland. The people were afraid this would happen and sent to ask for protection from the prince; their messengers were not admitted, nor were they given permission even to defend 40 themselves at their own cost with their own weapons; indeed they were forbidden under pain of death, having been ravaged by the men of Gelderland, to invade Gelderland in their turn. After this brutal massacre the chief cities, fearing already for their own safety, appealed to the king. They got permission with difficulty to defend themselves at their own expense, but 45 on condition that they supplied the prince with a new subsidy for his journey, on the ground that the old one was now exhausted, although they had paid already what was due in three years' time. As the Hollanders objected to this, the storm was deliberately unleashed on them. Everyone can see it was a trick, but it is not easy to find a remedy, nor safe to speak the 50 truth. The other day some men were thrown into prison on the charge of having said that if all those who surround the prince loved him as sincerely as I do, his towns would not be treated like this. With great difficulty through the intercession of the Lady Margaret they were let out again three weeks later. There is a suspicion that the cunning of these people is respon- 55 sible for the prince's failure to depart, inasmuch as he is afraid that, once he is not there, the towns will refuse to be scorned like this any longer.

I have received three hundred florins, not from the prince's exchequer, which never pays anything to anybody, but out of the spoils of

* * * * *

York 1970) II 216–20. The sack of Alkmaar in July 1517 lasted eight days. On its horrors and consequences see Henne II 189–97. Erasmus' emotional report was obviously written under the impact of these dreadful events. A careful analysis of Erasmus' comments, here and elsewhere, on the wars with Gelderland is undertaken by James D. Tracy *The Politics of Erasmus: A Pacifist Intellectual and his Political Milieu* (Toronto 1978) chap. 4. Tracy finds that many details given by Erasmus have not so far been corroborated from other sources. If his factual accounts are on the whole plausible, his interpretation, according to Tracy, is in line with popular opinion prevailing in Holland and notably unsympathetic to the political dilemmas faced by Charles' government.

39 prince] Charles; called king in line 44
54 Margaret] The aunt of Prince Charles, regent of the Netherlands for her father Maximilian I; cf Ep 332:3–4n.
58 three hundred florins] Cf Ep 621 introduction.

war. The chancellor, however, is lavish with his promises. He went to Spain   60
some time ago. I am not without hopes, for he has with him as chaplain
Barbier, who is devoted to me, and also Busleyden. I have an invitation
from the cardinal of Toledo; but I have no mind to turn Spaniard. The
bishop of Chieti, in hopes of making his fortune, has ruined himself and all
his friends by the expense. And he has been reported to the king in a note   65
written in cypher, of which he as yet knows nothing. Nor was it safe for me
to give him a hint, for fear of compromising those who had told me.

Please see that they get on with the printing of what I sent, and
especially that they make a good job of More's pieces. Chièvres, whose
lightest word is law here now, has made his nephew an abbot, bishop of   70
Cambrai, cardinal and, so they tell me, coadjutor of the archbishop of
Toledo. He is living in Louvain, a young man hardly twenty, with a most
lively mind. The Black Band is blockaded, I hear, in a marsh somewhere,
and will remain so, I suppose, until the prince's demands have been paid.

Farewell, dearest Beatus. If you see no objection, pass on the news to   75
my friends, for it is hard to write to them all.

Louvain, St Bartholomew's eve

No news yet of Glareanus, except that I gather from a letter of Budé's
that he is in Paris.

* * * * *

60 chancellor] For Le Sauvage's promises and for his journey in company of
Barbier and Busleyden see Ep 608 introduction and 19n.
62 invitation] For Ximénes' invitation see Ep 582:11n.
64 Chieti] Gianpietro Carafa, later Pope Paul IV (cf Ep 287:9n), had gone to
Ferdinand the Catholic as special nuncio in 1515 and was now with Prince
Charles, whom he would accompany to Spain. Although he was confirmed in
his former duties and honours, two main reasons seem to account for a certain
disaffection on the part of the new monarch and some of his Burgundian and
Spanish advisers. The nuncio had earlier supported the autonomy of Naples-
Sicily and the succession of Prince Ferdinand in Spain; see C. Bromato [F.
Carrara] *Storia di Paolo IV* (Ravenna 1748–53) I 64–74.
70 nephew] Guillaume de Croy, b c 1498. In 1516 his uncle secured for him the
abbey of Afflighem near Aalst and the bishopric of Cambrai; on 2 April 1517
he was created cardinal. After a severe illness in May (cf Brown II 894), he
settled down in Louvain to resume his studies, under the direction of Adriaan
Cornelissen van Baerland (cf Ep 647:10) and Juan Luis Vives. In December
1517 he succeeded Ximénes as the archbishop of Toledo, becoming thus the
primate and richest prelate of Spain. Without having ever set foot on Spanish
soil, he died on 6 January 1521.
78 Budé's] Cf Ep 609:22.

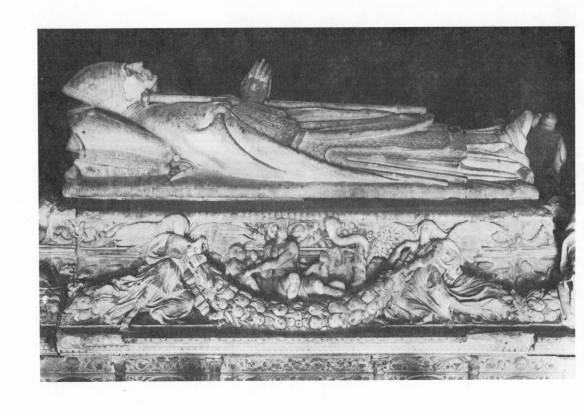

Francisco Ximénes de Cisneros
Tomb sculpture by Bartolomé Ordoñez
Universidad de Alcalá de Henares (Madrid)
Photo: MAS

629 / To Wolfgang Lachner and Johann Froben [Louvain, c 23 August 1517]

This is no doubt the letter mentioned at the end of Ep 634. In spite of the heading, Lachner alone is addressed in the text. Erasmus knew from Ep 581 that he was going to the Frankfurt autumn fair, which normally began between Assumption and Saint Bartholomew's day (15 and 24 August), and it was to Frankfurt that the letters to Basel and copy for publication (lines 2–5) were dispatched via Antwerp (cf Ep 637:3–5). By 21 September, after the end of the fair, Erasmus' copy had safely arrived in Basel (AK II Ep 592 postscript), but Erasmus was still awaiting an acknowledgment in November; cf Ep 704A:16–18.

ERASMUS TO LACHNER AND FROBEN, GREETING

I send you the first book of Theodore revised, and the second in translation. If you still have many copies of the first edition in stock, add a leaf on which you can list the errata, and put the second book with it. I send you what additions have been made in the meantime to my *Proverbs*. I have not yet   5
had speech with Franz since your letter came. And in your letter you do not put a value on the copy I send you. Here I have nothing coming in and heavy

* * * * *

629

2 I send] In response to the request in Ep 575: 7–8. Froben had published an edition of the first book of Theodorus Gaza's Greek grammar in September 1516; for the second book cf Ep 771 introduction. Publisher's stock was normally stored unbound; hence Erasmus' suggestion that both parts of Gaza be included in one volume.

5 *Proverbs*] A new edition of the *Adagia*, containing the fresh material sent with this letter, was published by Froben in the winter of 1517–18; cf Epp 269 introduction, 783: 29n; see below 11n.

6 Franz] Birckmann (cf Ep 258:14n). From 1505 to his death in 1530 his book trade was carried on mainly in Cologne, but he also did business in Antwerp, where he resided for a few years until 1526; cf Grimm *Buchführer* 1523–8.

7 copy] Here and subsequently *exemplaria* means new manuscripts for publication or printed editions with fresh revisions. This letter and the continued correspondence on the matter (cf Epp 581:19–21, 687: 26–30, 704A, 732:2–9, 795:8–14, 801:20–6) show that Erasmus was anxious to find a more businesslike basis for his collaboration with the Froben press. Rather than being given books from time to time, whether or not he had requested them, and occasional cash payments, he desired a specific assessment of the value of his learned labours, to be written off against the equally specific price of only such books as he needed and had ordered. These might be of Froben's own production or purchased from Italian and other publishers. They were to be delivered by Franz Birckmann, who had a close business association with Froben and Lachner. Eventually the Froben firm attempted to meet Erasmus' demands, which were probably quite modest; cf Ep 885 introduction.

expenses. I do not wish to be hard on you, but one good turn deserves another. When Froben sees the printer's copy all ready, he does not give enough thought to the work that went into it; he only looks to see how many 10 printed pages there are. I depend in everything on your friendly spirit, which I have always experienced hitherto.

I had already written to say that the Hermogenes *Rhetoric* which you sent me from Frankfurt has arrived safely. I have seen the works of Gregory Nazianzen in Greek, printed I think by Aldus, not the well-known poems, 15 but the prose works in handy format. Please let me have a copy from the coming fair. Also Strabo in Greek, Aristides in Greek, Plutarch's *Lives* in Greek, and the complete Greek Bible printed by Aldus or Asulanus, his father-in-law, also Wolfgang Faber on the pointing in Hebrew. Work out the price of the books you have bought and also the value of the copy I have 20 sent; and what will come back to you, if you wish to have anything back, I will give to Franz. For as the old maxim has it, between upright men all dealing should be upright.

630 /To Wilhelm Nesen   Louvain, 23 August [1517]

The year date is evident from the reference to Erasmus' *De copia*. The new edition, seen through the press by Nesen, was published by Froben in April 1517 (cf Ep 462). It is clear that Erasmus expected Nesen still to be in Basel, working for Froben, but before the end of 1517 he was to leave for Paris. His presence there is documented for January 1518 (Ep 768) and for June and August (AK II Epp 617, 619). For Nesen see Ep 329 introduction.

* * * * *

8 one good turn] Literally 'hand rubs hand'; *Adagia* I i 33.
11 printed pages] For example, the additions to the *Adagia* sent with this letter, comprised only eleven new adages, but the emendation of the ones already published had taken a great deal of Erasmus' time; cf Ep 704A:9–10 and Phillips 122.
13 Hermogenes] Florence: Giunta 1515
14 seen] Shown to him by Frowick; cf Ep 642.
14 Gregory] The *Orationes lectissimae* (Venice: Aldus April 1516). The *Carmina* had been published by the same firm in 1504.
17 Strabo] Venice: Aldus November 1516
17 Aristides] Florence: Giunta 20 May 1517; the Plutarch by the same firm, 27 August 1517
18 Bible] Cf Ep 770 introduction.
19 Hebrew] No doubt Capito's grammar (cf Ep 600:26), which was, however, not yet published.
22 maxim] A legal formula cited by Cicero *Ad familiares* 7.12.2

ERASMUS TO HIS FRIEND MASTER WILHELM NESEN,
TEACHER OF THE LIBERAL ARTS, GREETING
You made a lovely job of your *Copia*. There is no call to be annoyed with
Budé. He saw fit to make fun like that of a friend. For a friend he is, and a
good scholar and a man of my own way of thinking, and he has had a proper   5
answer from me. Stir up Froben to make an equally handsome and speedy
job of my other things. Beatus' letter, or rather my letter to Beatus, will give
you the rest of my news. Farewell, and remember your old friend.
     Louvain, St Bartholomew's eve
     Greetings to my friend Ludwig, whose progress gives me great plea-   10
sure. Konrad, I see, must still be annoyed with me, for he never writes. Give
him my greetings.

631 / To Heinrich Stromer   Louvain, 24 August 1517

    This letter, first printed in the *Auctarium*, answers Ep 614 and the points raised
    in it. For its journey see Ep 637:3n. Ep 662 is Stromer's reply.

TO THE DISTINGUISHED PHYSICIAN DR HEINRICH STROMER
OF AUERBACH, MY INCOMPARABLE PATRON AND FRIEND
Greeting, most scholarly of physicians. Your letter reached me safely by the
hand of my servant Jacobus, and it was most welcome on many counts, but
especially as evidence that I am well thought of by his Grace and in favour   5
with him, and at the same time that you take a kind of special interest in my
welfare. I had in mind to dedicate to the archbishop an edition of Suetonius
with the other biographies of the Caesars revised by myself, after all the
work that has been done on them, with no small effort; but there were

* * * * *

630
3 annoyed] Nesen had evidently objected to Budé's criticism of Erasmus in Ep
  435:74–92. Other members of the Basel circle were equally inclined to think
  unfavourably of Budé; cf Ep 778:218n.
7 my letter] Ep 628
10 Ludwig] Ludovicus Carinus (Kiel) of Lucerne, who was a fellow student of
  Nesen's at Basel and subsequently his travelling companion; cf Ep 920 introduction; H.G. Wackernagel et al eds *Die Matrikel der Universität Basel* (Basel
  1951–) I 307, 309.
11 Konrad] Brunner; cf Ep 464:22.

631
4 Jacobus] Nepos
5 Grace] Albert of Brandenburg, archbishop of Mainz
7 Suetonius] Cf Ep 586 introduction.

reasons for not doing so. I have not yet felt any practical proof of his   10
goodwill. None the less, when I hear how generously his Grace encourages
scholars of good promise, I think it the duty of every man of learning to join
in the praise of such a leader of men; and I have this further reason for
admiring him, that great prince as he is he yet takes such a lively interest in
theology and sacred causes. If only all men were endowed with such a   15
spirit, how much better, if I mistake not, the complexion of human affairs!
But further, when he encourages me to write lives of the saints, I only wish
that besides his promise to reward me he could give a feeble person like
myself the physical strength adequate to such a task. I have already passed
my fiftieth year, my health is very uncertain, and I am distracted by re-   20
searches of many kinds. If in the future I see any opportunity of a journey in
your direction, I shall most eagerly enjoy a meeting with such an eminent
prelate, and the pleasure of your society. Farewell, most learned Stromer.

Louvain, St Bartholomew's day 1517
Erasmus of Rotterdam   25

632 /To Bruno Amerbach   Louvain, 24 August 1517

This is Erasmus' answer to Ep 595.

ERASMUS TO BRUNO, GREETING

How I envy you, on a visit to Italy at such an auspicious time. If you fear the
climate, at Padua it is very healthy; at Bologna not so, nor in Florence nor in
Rome. Tell Froben he must print Zasius on the origin of laws; the man well
deserves such an honour. Mind you greet Basilius and Bonifacius on my   5
behalf. Brunner, I hear, has won his little kingdom, and I send him my best
wishes; he must work hard to be as good a man as his predecessor. Jerome

* * * * *

10 practical proof] For Erasmus' lack of financial security and dependence upon
   gifts cf Epp 608:19–20, 637–8, 753 introduction, 763:13–14.
12 join] A first hint that Erasmus intended to dedicate another work to the
   archbishop. He did so before long; cf Ep 745.
20 fiftieth] The statement may be reasonably correct; cf Epp 3 introduction, 940.

632
4 Zasius] Udalricus Zasius, the Freiburg professor of law who had been Bruno's
   teacher. His work appeared in 1518; see Epp 303, 862 introductions.
5 Basilius and Bonifacius] Bruno's brothers
6 Brunner] Konrad Brunner began at about this time to lodge and tutor a few
   students. See Ep 313:26n; AK II Ep 609.
7 Jerome] For the success of Erasmus' edition cf Ep 396 introduction.

finds a warm welcome everywhere. This is your good fortune, for my evil
genius never takes a holiday. Farewell, dearest Bruno; wherever you may
be, let me hear where you are.   10
    Louvain, St Bartholomew's day 1517

633 / To Johann Ruser   Louvain, 24 August 1517

As Erasmus indicates, this letter is primarily an answer to Ep 612, from
Schürer. For its journey see Ep 637:3n.

ERASMUS TO HIS LEARNED FRIEND JOHANN RUSER, GREETING
I had written to say that if there were anything in which I might oblige
Schürer, I would most gladly do so; so far am I from having struck him out of
the list of my friends. I know what an open-hearted man he is. I have here
Quintus Curtius, whom I have lately been rereading to clear away the rust   5
that has gathered on my Latin; I have added short notes and corrected a
number of passages, and I propose to add a preface. I would have sent this,
had I been sure it would be welcome. If he likes to send me Agricola's
works, I will do what a friend should, though very busy with other things.
Or if anything else occurs to me, I will let him know. Tell him this as from   10
me, and bid him consider this letter as written to him as much as to you.
Please greet the whole society, Sturm, Wimpfeling, the excellent
Rudolfinger, Gebwiler, doctor Gerbel especially; and make my excuses for
not answering him just now, but I am distracted by a hundred letters that
must be written, besides my load of work. Farewell, my most learned Ruser.   15
    Louvain, St Bartholomew's day 1517

634 / To Wolfgang Angst   Louvain, 24 August 1517

This letter is another indication (cf Ep 594:4n) that Froben's corrector,
Wolfgang Angst, also acted as a secretary. Froben himself had little Latin. It
also casts light on the degree of Erasmus' involvement in the publication of his
letters (cf Epp 886, 1009). For the early editions of Erasmus' correspondence
see CWE 3 346–53.

   * * * * *

633
2 I had written] Ep 606
5 Quintus Curtius] Cf Ep 704.
8 Agricola's works] See Ep 612:27–35.
12 society] Cf Ep 302.

ERASMUS TO WOLFGANG ANGST, GREETING
You will do your best, my excellent Wolfgang, to have the commentary I
have sent carefully printed. As to the letters, I have not sent those which are
to be printed because yet another volume of correspondence is in print, and
I shall correct them both and add some more letters, and send them like that. 5
I should like More's *Utopia* and *Epigrams* to have a letter of commendation
from Beatus Rhenanus by way of preface, and if you think fit they can be put
together in the same volume. If, however, you think it would do any good,
add also a short preface by myself, which I enclose in this letter. Thank my
excellent fellow-godparent for the linen she sent me, and mind you give my 10
greetings to Froben, my beloved fellow-godfather. On other topics I have
written to Wolfgang Lachner, his father-in-law.
Louvain, St Bartholomew's day 1517

635 / To Johann Froben   Louvain, 25 August 1517

This is Erasmus' preface, mentioned in Ep 634, to Froben's edition of More's
Utopia and *Epigrammata*, March 1518. The book was reprinted by Froben in
November–December 1518; cf Allen Ep 904:14–15.

ERASMUS OF ROTTERDAM TO JOHANN FROBEN,
HIS DEAREST FELLOW-GODFATHER, GREETING
Although everything by my friend More has always won my highest ap-
proval, yet before now I used to feel a certain distrust of my own judgment,

* * * * *
634
2 commentary] Probably the printer's copy of Gaza's grammar sent with Ep 629
3 letters] Martens had published the *Epistolae ad Erasmum* in October 1516;
subsequently he published the *Epistolae elegantes* (cf Ep 543:31n) with the
colophon date of April 1517, but the book may not have been ready for the
Frankfurt spring fair, with the result that distribution was postponed to the
autumn fair.
5 send them] Erasmus later did so, although without corrections or new additions (cf Ep 732:36–9). Froben's edition of the *Epistolae elegantes* of January
1518 merely reprints various letters previously published.
8 same volume] This was done (cf Ep 550 introduction). Beatus' letter to
Pirckheimer is BRE Ep 72; Erasmus' preface is Ep 635.
10 fellow-godparent] Gertrud, the oldest daughter of Wolfgang Lachner, married
Johann Froben in 1510. She was the mother of Erasmus or Erasmius Froben,
named after his godfather (see Ep 635:26). *Compater* and *commater*, like the
German *Gevatter* and *Gevatterin*, referred to all persons who accompanied the
baby to the baptismal font. Soon it came to be used in the loose sense of
familiar friend.
12 Lachner] Ep 629

as that of an intimate friend. But when I see the whole learned world with   5
one voice endorsing my assessment and admiring his superhuman gifts
even more emphatically than I do, not because they love him more but
because they see more clearly, I approve my own opinion in good earnest,
and shall have no misgivings in future in saying openly what I think. What
might he not have achieved, with that astonishing natural gift of style, had   10
his great talents been raised in Italy, had all his time been devoted to the
Muses, had he been free to ripen to full bearing and his proper harvest-
time! The *Epigrams* are the fruit of his lighter moments as a very young man,
or even (for many of them) a boy. His native Britain he has never quitted,
save two or three times when on a mission in Flanders on his king's behalf.   15
Beside his duties as a husband and father and the cares of a household,
beside the claims of public office and the flood of litigation, he is distracted
so often by important business of the realm that one might wonder how he
found the time even to think of books.

So I have sent you his *Progymnasmata* and his *Utopia*, that if you think   20
fit they may be launched upon the world and upon future ages with the
benefit of your typography; for your press stands so high that a book can
earn a welcome among the learned for no better reason than that it is known
to issue from the house of Froben. Best wishes to yourself and your excellent
father-in-law, your delightful wife, and your sweet children. And then your   25
little son Erasmus, whom I share with you – he was born into a world of
letters; mind you choose only the best of literature for his upbringing.

Louvain, 25 August 1517

636 /To Hermann von Neuenahr   Louvain, 25 August 1517

This letter follows Ep 622, which deals with the same topics. For Neuenahr,
nobleman, humanist, and canon of Cologne, see Ep 442 introduction.

ERASMUS TO HIS FRIEND THE HONOURABLE COUNT
HERMANN OF NEUENAHR, GREETING
All the learned circle in Basel knows that I have always disapproved of the
so-called *Epistolae obscurorum virorum*, not that I am averse from wit and
humour, but because I cannot approve this precedent they set of hurting   5

* * * * *
635
26 Erasmus] Erasmus' godson, Johann Erasmus or Erasmius Froben, born between his arrival in Basel at the end of August 1514 and 16 October 1515 (cf AK
II Ep 538). In 1522 Erasmus dedicated to the child his *Colloquiorum formulae*. He
was educated at Basel, Freiburg, and Louvain. After his return to Basel in 1534
he joined his stepfather, Johann Herwagen, in the printing business.

other men's reputations, since this is within everyone's reach. I too wrote a
humorous piece once in my *Moria*, but I mentioned no one by name. These
people, whoever they are, not content with that sort of fooling, have added
another book like the first, in which to my surprise they have found it
necessary to mention me many times. If they wish me well, why contrive   10
such unpopularity for me? If ill, why put me on the side opposite to the one
they have attacked in this book? If they continue to publish stuff like this,
they will provoke a ban of silence even on authors of the right sort.

My servant Jacobus told me lately on his return from Cologne that a
pamphlet of some sort was in circulation there, of a humorous description,   15
about Pope Julius. It may well be the same thing of which I heard a story
some time ago, written in Paris by some Spaniard or other and turned into
French; they said it was acted there at the fêtes royales, at which it is
traditional for the students to let themselves go in worthless pieces of this
kind. He added a thing I can hardly credit – that some people even suppose   20
it was made up by me, because (so he says) the Latin is moderately good. I,
however, have neither leisure enough to expend an hour of my time on
nonsense of this kind, nor a mind so irreligious as to poke fun at the Holy
Father, nor am I fool enough to want to unsheath the pen against those who
can reply with the sword. And so I do most seriously beg you, dearest   25
Count, though it is no affair of mine, yet to avoid a scandal which would
involve all scholars equally, if what I hear about a pamphlet of this kind is
true, have it suppressed or, better still, destroyed, or anything else there
may be of the same sort. Two years ago when *The Triumph of Reuchlin* was

* * * * *

636

16 same thing] In Ep 961, Erasmus admits to having himself read such a work,
and he links it with the schism between the pope and France at the time of the
Council of Pisa. That entertainment of this kind was popular in Paris is
documented by two printed editions of a morality play by Pierre Gringore that
was performed on the *mardi gras* of 1512 (when Erasmus was in England). This
play, *Le jeu du prince des sotz*, features Julius II, still alive at the time, as a
principal character under the name of *l'homme obstiné*; see P. Gringore *Œuvres
complètes* (Paris 1858) I 198–286; C. Oulmont *Pierre Gringore* (Paris 1911) 39–40.
Gringore's play does not, however, help to unravel the mystery shrouding the
origins of the *Julius exclusus*; see Epp 502, 664 introductions.

29 *Triumph*] A poem, probably by Hutten, which circulated in manuscript and
was published in 1518; see Hutten *Opera* I 26* and Ep 105, III 413–48; T.W. Best
The Humanist Ulrich von Hutten (Chapel Hill 1969) 47–50. According to Erasmus (*Spongia* LB X 1668) Hutten had shown him the poem at their first meeting
at Mainz in August 1514, and Erasmus had advised him to suppress it. At their
second meeting at Frankfurt in the following year Hutten apparently agreed to
do so (cf Ep 951). Erasmus seems to have had better success with the second
piece, of which nothing is known today.

ready for publication in Germany, I secured its suppression, and the same   30
for another piece called *The Monk*. I support Reuchlin, as a very learned
man, but in such a way as to have no quarrel with Hoogstraten or others of
his party, since the question is nothing to do with me, even though I do not
approve – nor can any truly religious man approve – those virulent personal
attacks, which stem from the spirit of the world and not of Christ. Undoubt-   35
edly, in every place I have visited up to now, every man of good will
supports Reuchlin.

Farewell, best of all patrons of humane studies, and keep your affection for me in repair. If Vinantius is with you, give him my most cordial
greetings.
                                                                                40
Louvain, morrow of St Bartholomew 1517

637 / To Pieter Gillis   Louvain, 28 August [1517]

> The date of this letter, St John's eve, must refer to the eve of the second feast of
> John the Baptist in the Roman calendar, the Beheading, on 29 August. His
> nativity, on 24 June, was prior to the death of Ammonio.

ERASMUS TO HIS FRIEND PIETER GILLIS, GREETING
The death of Ammonio greatly distresses me; but it is More that I wish we
had here safe and sound. I send you the things I want to have taken to Basel;
please entrust them with all diligence to Franz the bookseller, or through
him to some other reliable person. Please inform Master Nicholas that I am   5
ready to accept what he says about the pomegranate, provided we may
  * * * * *

32 Hoogstraten] Jacob van Hoogstraten. See Ep 615:11n.
39 Vinantius] Unidentified. Probably Wijnant, Wijnants, etc, a frequent name; cf
   Ep 722:26. P.S. Allen suggested that the reference might be to Nicolaas van
   Winghe (see Ep 1837), but nothing is known about the latter's presence in
   Cologne, and H. de Vocht rejected the identification; see his MHL 561 note 1.

   637
2 Ammonio ... More] See Ep 623.
3 Basel] Epp 625–35 were probably all sent together with Franz Birckmann, or
   one of his agents, travelling to the Frankfurt fair. On his way there the carrier
   could deliver Ep 631 as he passed through Mainz. He may likewise have taken
   charge of Ep 636, which was to go to Cologne. Cf Ep 629 introduction.
5 Nicholas] Nicolaas van Broeckhoven of 's Hertogenbosch (see Ep 616:15n).
   Erasmus must have sought his advice about the saying 'Hecatae coena,' which
   was to appear among the new adages added to the 1517–18 edition (IV v 11).
   Nicolaas apparently referred him to the old myth in which Hades persuades
   Persephone to eat one seed of a pomegranate. The reference was not used in
   the *Adagia*. For Nicolaas' reaction see Allen VI xix.

identify Proserpine with Hecate. Hecate was very partial to red mullets, and
they were sacred to her, as we learn from Athenaeus book seven (I stumbled
on the passage by chance), for it is a very cheap fish; and also the mullet is
called *trigla* from the number three, which is Hecate's sacred number.   10

I am still staying with Desmarez. The theologians have some plan
afoot for co-opting me into their faculty. Atensis is entirely on my side, and
so is Dorp; but he is more inconstant than any woman. I shall be greatly
pleased with the chairs, when I set eyes on them. I send you two copies of
my *Apologia*; please give one to Master Nicholas. Please arrange for Fries-   15
land to bring me the later series of the *Epistolae obscurorum virorum* but seal
them up so that he does not know what he is carrying. Best wishes to you
and yours, my very special friend.

Louvain, St John's eve

Be sure to remember me warmly to that most scholarly and civilized   20
physician, Henricus of Lier. He sent me a most generous letter to say that
the cups are ready, as I have no doubt they are. I cannot refuse a gift offered
by a friend of his own free will; it remains to consider what service I can do
him in return. So please send them to me by Dirk Martens. Best wishes once
more.   25

* * * * *

8 Athenaeus] 7.325b. Erasmus repeated the reference in his adage. His copy of
   the first Athenaeus edition (Venice: Aldus August 1514), with many marginal
   notes by him, is in Oxford: Bodleian Auct. 1.R. inf. 1.1.

11 Desmarez] See Ep 597:46n.

12 co-opting] Erasmus registered on 30 August 1517 and is styled a 'Sacre
   theologie professor' in the matriculation roll. On 5 September, however, he
   still had not been co-opted into the faculty of theology (Ep 651:25–6), and there
   is no independent proof that he ever was, although he later considered himself
   a member (Epp 694:4–5, 695:20, 707:13–14). He certainly did not belong to the
   restricted number of *regentes*: cf Ep 808:19n; M. Nauwelaerts 'Erasme à Louvain' *Scrinium* I 7.

12 Atensis] Jan Briart of Ath; see Epp 643:9n, 670 introduction.

13 inconstant] Cf Ep 696 introduction.

14 chairs] Cf Ep 616:17–18.

15 *Apologia*] The *Apologia ad Fabrum*, now in print; cf Ep 597:37n.

15 Friesland] Jan of Friesland (Johannes Phrysius) had entered Erasmus' service
   in 1516 and was soon to be sent to England. See Ep 665 introduction; Bierlaire
   51–2.

21 Henricus] Afinius, a physician at Antwerp (cf Ep 542 introduction). For the
   dogged negotiations about his promised gift of silver cups in exchange for a
   dedicatory preface, see Ep 638 and the index.

638 / To Henricus Afinius   [Louvain, late August 1517]

Allen assumed that this letter was contemporary with Ep 637. In view of the
instructions given to Gillis in the postscript of Ep 637 it may, however, be
preferable to date it a few days earlier or later. An earlier date would diminish
the extent of Erasmus' ruse in lines 19–20.

ERASMUS OF ROTTERDAM TO THE DISTINGUISHED PHYSICIAN
HENRICUS AFINIUS OF LIER, GREETING

Your letter, most learned Henricus – and yours it truly was, being as kind as
it was elegant – gave me much pleasure. In this way, at least, I can enjoy my
dear Henricus' society. You say you have had these very valuable silver   5
goblets made. For such generous intentions I am bound to find a warm
welcome. In myself, however, I am filled with mixed feelings. At one
moment it embarrasses me to accept such a present from a man whom my
desire to serve far outruns my performance; at another, I cannot bring
myself to refuse a gift freely offered, for fear I seem to undervalue your   10
kindness or to be unwilling to owe you a debt of gratitude, for to accept an
obligation gladly is as much a sign of affection as to confer one. And so,
since you, kindest of men, have decided to challenge my humble self to a
contest of generosity, I will remember that I have my own part to play: it
must not look as though you had invested your present in someone un-   15
grateful for it. Friesland, the bearer of this, will bring it, whom (as it
happens) I shall be sending, or if he does not come, Dirk the printer.
Farewell, best of friends.

I would have sent Theodore's second book, but it is not fully corrected
yet. I should be glad to know whether you would like to have this dedicated   20
to you, or some other subject in philosophy or medicine; the latter perhaps
would be more appropriate. In any case, I will carefully perform whatever I
understand will give you pleasure. Farewell, most faithful of friends.

* * * * *

638
16 Friesland] See Ep 637:15n.
17 Dirk] Martens
19 corrected yet] The manuscript had been dispatched to Froben together with
    Ep 629. Whether or not the present letter is written after that date, Erasmus can
    hardly have meant to let Afinius have a manuscript copy just to show good
    will. All he wanted was an answer to his question, accompanied, of course, by
    the promised gift; cf Ep 799 introduction.

639 / From Francesco Chierigati   Antwerp [?], 28 August 1517

Francesco Chierigati of Vicenza (d 1539) was a papal diplomat and became
bishop of Teramo in 1522. He was on his way back to Rome after a mission to
England, in the course of which he had quarrelled with Wolsey, and a visit to
Ireland. The letter was perhaps drafted just before Chierigati left Antwerp
(line 13), but dispatched somewhat later, 28 August being the date of the
actual dispatch. Erasmus was in Antwerp on 16 August but did not leave
Louvain between 22 and 27 August (Epp 622, 637:3). B. Morsolin, in *Atti,
Accademia Olimpica ... Vicenza* 3 (1873) 210, prints a letter by Chierigati, dated
from Middelburg on 28 August.

F. CHIERIGATI TO MASTER ERASMUS OF ROTTERDAM, GREETING
Greeting, Erasmus, most learned and erudite of men. When making my
escape from the English sweating-sickness, on my way to Rome I happened
to land in Antwerp, and the moment I arrived I enquired where Erasmus
was living. Some of my friends replied that you were in the town, lodging   5
with one Pieter Gillis, secretary to the town council of Antwerp; and the
news made me so happy that I almost thought myself in the seventh heaven.
Off I went to call at Pieter's house to bring my greetings and pay you a visit,
and to enquire whether you wanted anything from the pope which a friend
could accomplish for you. But alack, some fate played me false, for they told   10
me you had returned to your work in Louvain the day before. This was a
great blow, given my great affection for you; for I longed passionately to
spend all the time I might have in Antwerp, which did not amount to much,
in your sweet and delightful company, which apart from your eminent
scholarship is so entertaining in its mixture of grave and gay. But chance   15
having deprived me of you, I felt I must at least send you my greetings in a
letter, and ask you sometimes to make use of anything a humble friend can
do to help you, who is so keen a supporter of your very rare and almost
superhuman gifts, that to enjoy the affection of Erasmus and be reckoned at
his disposal is the summit of his ambition.   20
    The Venetian envoy and likewise his colleague Sagundino, who have
lately suffered from the sweat, wish to be warmly remembered to you. Our

* * * * *
639
  3 sweating-sickness] The epidemic which killed Ammonio; cf Ep 623.
    Chierigati described it at length; see Brown II 945.
 19 at his disposal] *Adagia* I vii 51
 21 envoy] Sebastiano Giustiniani (cf Ep 559), assisted in his mission to England
    by Niccolò Sagundino (cf Ep 574). Giustiniani and many of his household
    were sick; see LP II 3558; Brown II 950.

friend Ammonio was of the same mind; but alas, he was carried off by the
sweating-sickness in the space of eight hours, and has left me in such a state
of grief and depression that nothing can console me. But what would you?   25
Such is the course of mortal men. Farewell, my most learned, most affectionate Erasmus, and keep my name within your heart.

From Antwerp, 28 August 1517

640 / To [Gianpietro Carafa?]   Louvain, 29 August [1517]

Assuming that Carafa was with Prince Charles in Middelburg (cf Ep 596
introduction), Allen's identification may be accepted. The fact that Carafa was
a Neapolitan would explain line 7, while Erasmus' remarks in Ep 628:64–7
would explain his concern for the bishop's well-being. The gibe at the manners of Carafa's hosts may actually conceal a well-meant warning. The year
date is clear; cf Ep 637:11–13.

Greetings, right reverend Father. I wrote to your Lordship some time ago. If
I do not deserve a letter in reply, at least let me know your state of health, for
the inclemency of the climate where you are now gives me some anxiety,
matching as it does the manners of the natives. Here am I at Louvain, living
all among the theologians, popular with their leaders certainly, and perhaps   5
with them all. If only some friendly power would bring us together in the
shrines of the Muses at Naples! Farewell, O pillar of learning and religion.

Louvain, 29 August
Erasmus of Rotterdam

641 / To Joris van Halewijn   Louvain, 29 August [1517]

Joris, lord of Halewijn and Comines, 1473–1536, was a humanistic author and
a courtier. He took orders in 1519 but failed to become bishop of Tournai. The
year date is confirmed by the references to Louvain. This letter was first
published in the *Auctarium*.

DESIDERIUS ERASMUS OF ROTTERDAM TO HIS FRIEND
THE HONOURABLE JORIS VAN HALEWIJN, GREETING
At last, my dear and honoured Joris, I have scented out (unless I much

* * * * *

640
3 climate] Cf Ep 663.
7 Naples] Cf Ep 756:19–21.

mistake) who it was in Ghent who took offence at my *Moria*. A monk it was,
a black monk, all belly and little else. To begin with, few people understood   5
it until Listrius added his notes; but once Folly began to talk French as well,
thanks to you, she is understood even by these men who cannot understand
their psalter. I should much like to hear my Folly holding forth in French
myself; if you have no copy, do at least indicate where I can get one.

I have moved to Louvain bag and baggage, that is, with all my books.   10
Between me and the theologians reigns the deepest peace and even
friendship – for some talebearers had spread a rumour that we were at war.
They have plans to co-opt me into the faculty. Who would not rate this
higher than an invitation to dine with the gods? Atensis is my especial
supporter. Dorp seems genuinely friendly. One or two of the beggar-boys   15
show their teeth now and again, but only when I am not present. They tell
me that in Antwerp Briselot has been holding forth against me vigorously
with those powerful lungs of his at every drinking-party; but I cannot be
persuaded to believe this of a man of his learning and his character.

Mind you keep well, and preserve yourself in good heart for the   20
benefit of liberal studies and of us all. The monk who brings this seems an
excellent man, and unusually gifted; please help him in anything he needs,
with your usual kindness or to please me.

Louvain, 29 August 151[8]

642 / To Cuthbert Tunstall   Louvain, 30 August [1517]

Cf Ep 643 introduction.

Greeting, most learned Tunstall. I bring you in this letter a treasure of

* * * * *

641
4 Ghent] For Erasmus' recent visit there cf Ep 596 introduction.
6 Listrius] Gerardus Listrius. With the help and inspiration of Erasmus himself
   he had added a commentary to the first Froben edition of the *Moriae encomium*,
   March 1515; cf Epp 495 introduction, 2615.
6 French] Halewijn had translated the *Moria* into French (cf Ep 597:16–17).
   Erasmus later saw the translation and was clearly dissatisfied (cf Epp 739:7–9,
   1013A). It is not now possible to say whether and to what degree Halewijn's
   translation was used in the first printed edition of the *Moria* in French, *De la
   declamation de louenges de follie* (Paris: P. Vidoue for G. Du Pré 2 August 1520),
   but note his renewed interest in the *Moria* in June 1520 (Ep 1115).
15 beggar-boys] Erasmus' critics among the mendicant orders
17 Briselot] Cf Ep 597:4–16.

delights, with which the excellent Frowick regaled me on his return from
Rome. Asulanus has printed both Old and New Testaments in Greek; the
works of Nazianzen he showed me. Strabo has been printed in Greek,
Plutarch's *Lives*, Pindar with the scholia, and many things I forget for the   5
moment. O, if only one could be young again! Andrea Ammonio has died,
after an attack of this dangerous sweating-sickness. More is coming here
with all speed. I am on such good terms with the theologians that they wish
to co-opt me as a member of the faculty, an honour they scarcely confer on
anyone who is not already a doctor of Louvain.   10
    I have answered Lefèvre. As God is my witness, I never in my life did
anything more unwillingly, but it had to be done. I simply cannot think
what he had got into his head. Look after yourself, most faithful of friends.
    Louvain, 30 August
    Erasmus   15

643 / To Cuthbert Tunstall   Louvain, 31 August [1517]

> This letter is an amplified version of Ep 642, which it may have replaced as the
> letter actually sent, for in Ep 663 Tunstall acknowledges receipt of Ep 643 only.

ERASMUS TO HIS FRIEND TUNSTALL, GREETING
This is bitter news I hear, that Andrea Ammonio has died; no Italian ever
yet lived in that England of yours who was either a better scholar or a more
upright man. But I am cheered by the news that More will soon be with us,
and if that happens, I shall get a new lease of life. May Jesus our Saviour   5
preserve the archbishop of Canterbury; as long as all is well with him, I feel
myself secure. I have moved bag and baggage to Louvain. Between me and
the theologians reigns not only the deepest peace but even cordial relations,

* * * * *

642
2 Frowick] Francis Frowick, provincial of the Observant Franciscans in Eng-
    land, had attended a General Chapter of his order in Rome and set out on his
    trip home about 17 June; cf LP II 3370, 3374.
3 Asulanus] Andrea Torresano, the partner of the Venetian printer Aldo Man-
    uzio. For most of the publications here mentioned see Ep 629.
5 Pindar] An annotated edition was published by Zacharias Kallierges, Rome
    1515; cf Ep 832:34.
6 Ammonio ... More] See Ep 623.
8 theologians] Cf Ep 637:11–13.

643
7 secure] Cf 702 introduction.

especially with Atensis, who is the head of the university and its chancellor, and Dorp, who seems my sincere friend. There are moves among them to   10
co-opt me into their number – say rather, into the number of the gods – and they move with great energy. I am still planted on Desmarez, an old friend, but plan to move elsewhere, where I can have more room to spread out my books. This has not yet been possible owing to a minor dispute among themselves, so as not to offend either party, for both are trying to attract me.   15

I send you a copy of my *Apologia* in answer to Lefèvre. I know you will be unhappy on account of us both, but not so much as I am. I cannot sufficiently marvel what that man got into his head. How I hate this destiny of mine, which forced me to undertake such a task! Skim it through, you will not want to read it; it was done in a hurry.   20

Budé in his last letter to me indicates that he is still uncertain whether you had received that long letter; and about that whole business of the offer from the king, which he had undertaken with so much energy, his letters maintain a surprising silence.

Brother Frowick on his return from Rome showed me some works of   25
Gregory Nazianzen newly printed. He added that both Old and New Testaments are to appear from the Aldine press; Strabo in Greek has appeared, besides Plutarch's *Lives*, Pindar together with the scholia, and much else. What riches, if only one could be young again! I count this generation fortunate, even though I cannot include myself.   30

* * * * *

9 chancellor] Jan Briart of Ath was not actually the chancellor, but substituted regularly for his friend Adrian of Utrecht, who was frequently absent. The chancellorship would *ex officio* have fallen to the provost of St Peter's chapter, but in his absence it was exercised by Adrian, who had become dean of the chapter in 1497; cf de Vocht MHL 113–14.

14 dispute] Erasmus had already cast his eye on more suitable quarters in the College of the Lily, but did not want to move before a litigation over the college's regency was settled. Finally on 26 August 1517 an agreement in principle was reached which gave the regency to Jean de Nève of Hondschoote in return for financial compensation for his opponent, Leo Outers, also of Hondschoote, who was formerly regent. Erasmus considered both men his friends and patrons (cf Epp 695:19–20, 714:26–8, 735:9). His position was further complicated by the fact that his temporary host, Jean Desmarez, had opposed Nève, who was actually in control of the college. The agreement of 26 August, however, opened the way for Erasmus to move; cf Ep 651:12–14; de Vocht MHL 180–7.

16 *Apologia*] See Ep 597:37n.

21 letter] See Ep 609:2–4.

22 offer] Budé had conveyed to Erasmus a royal invitation to settle in Paris and assist with the foundation of a humanistic college; see Ep 522; cf Ep 618 introduction.

Three soldiers of the gang that showed more than Turkish ferocity in the destruction of Asperen have paid the penalty, all hanged on the same tree. A man has been arrested who greeted them with a handshake as they were being carried to execution, making no attempt to conceal his relationship with them. How I wish the whole band had been reduced to cinders, so that it really might deserve its name of the Black Band! 35

Look well to your health, my excellent friend. Considering the continual drinking parties, which I find most trying, I myself am pretty well.

Louvain, 31 August

644 / To Richard [Sparcheford] Louvain, 31 August 1517

This letter clearly accompanied Ep 643 and was addressed to an attendant of Tunstall at Middelburg. Richard Sparcheford (d 1560) was Tunstall's chaplain. Along with other preferment he was later named archdeacon of Salop. This letter was published in the *Auctarium*.

DESIDERIUS ERASMUS OF ROTTERDAM TO HIS FRIEND RICHARD, GREETING

I did not write about my John in order to force Tunstall to take him, but in hopes of earning Tunstall's gratitude if the idea should appeal to him. I am most conscious of your kind and helpful feelings towards me, and grateful 5 for them. Press on, dearest Richard: you have a virtuous disposition; match it with studies of the most virtuous kind, on which I see you are now engaged. Farewell.

Louvain, 31 August 1517

* * * * *

32 Asperen] A town fifteen miles south of Utrecht that was sacked by the Black Band (Ep 628:33n) in July 1517 (cf LP II 3472, 3556). Particularly abhorrent was the massacre of schoolboys who had taken refuge in a church (see Henne II 194–5). The sack was still remembered by Erasmus two years later; see Allen Ep 1001:71–72

38 drinking parties] For similar expressions of a lifelong dislike of these cf Epp 83:48–9, 157:8–9, 296:225–6, 597:8–9, and the colloquy 'Diversoria'; see *The Colloquies of Erasmus* trans C.R. Thompson (Chicago 1965) especially 151–2.

644

3 John] Smith, Erasmus' servant-secretary, was looking for a new master in England. Later he found one in the person of Thomas More; cf Ep 820 introduction.

645 / To Gerard Geldenhouwer   Louvain, 31 August 1517

This is a commendatory letter which Geldenhouwer (cf Ep 487) published with his *Epistola ... de triumphali ingressu illustrissimi principis Philippi ... in ditionem suam* (Louvain: Martens [1517]; NK977). Erasmus, who reprinted it in *Epistolae ad diversos*, had clearly composed it at Geldenhouwer's request. Geldenhouwer describes the ceremonial entry into Utrecht of Philip of Burgundy, the new bishop (cf Ep 603:5n), who made him his secretary. His letter is addressed to Jean Desmarez, Erasmus' host, and dated from the bishop's villa near Duurstede, 25 May 1517.

ERASMUS OF ROTTERDAM TO HIS FRIEND GERARD OF NIJMEGEN, GREETING

The inauguration of the right honourable Prince Philip of Burgundy, bishop of Utrecht, your distinguished patron and, if you will admit me, a patron whom I share with you, has been described by you so clearly and so   5
vividly, that I should have seen less had I been an actual spectator of all the ceremonies. What pleased me especially was that you write with the veracity of a true historian, unlike the common run of authors, who in subjects of this kind tend to embroider their facts (for I must not call them fictions). Whether one should count Philip fortunate, I have not yet determined;   10
before this honour was conferred upon him, his personal gifts distinguished him already, and so far was he from desiring it that he would have refused the offer, had he not yielded to his country's call and his affection for Prince Charles. The diocese at least (to whose community I myself belong) is to be congratulated on the acquisition of a prince and prelate who   15
will play both parts as a man of singular wisdom and high personal character. My confidence derives not solely from his own nature, full of the promise of distinction, but also from his father, Duke Philip of Burgundy, the most admirable prince that has fallen to the lot of this happy country for some generations, whether one contemplates his lofty spirit right worthy of   20
a king, his rare affection towards his subjects, his active love of peace, his charm of character, or, in a word, his whole nature, so far removed from any taint of despotism. My hopes are increased by David, his eminent brother,

* * * * *

645
18 Duke Philip of Burgundy] Philip the Good, d 1467; cf Ep 603:22n.
23 David] Cf Ep 603;14n. Erasmus here refers to an incident which he described more fully in the *Ecclesiastes* (LB v 808). Presumably after his appointment to the see of Utrecht, David assembled his entire clergy and subjected them to an examination which, according to Erasmus, most of them failed.

a man very like his father in every way, but who is particularly to be admired because, being himself a man of learning, he strove with all his   25 might to see that ignorant, unlearned persons should not intrude into the sheepfold of the clergy; as we see they still do. I have great hopes therefore that Philip, and he alone, will not only take after the excellent father from whom he is sprung and the excellent brother whom he has succeeded, but will surpass them both and supply you with abundant material for   30 panegyric.

But in this field you must expect competition from me: some time ago I dedicated to him my *Querela pacis*, as the first fruits of my admiration for him. The book is now printing in Basel and will soon find its way to your part of the world. If I find that it gives satisfaction maybe I shall attempt   35 something more adventurous. Farewell, my excellent Gerard, and pray commend me to your distinguished lord bishop.

Louvain, 31 August 1517

646 / To Adriaan Cornelissen van Baerland   [Louvain, 1517?]

This letter is found only in the *Epistolae aliquot selectae ex Erasmicis per Hadrianum Barlandum* (Louvain: Martens December 1520; NK 820). Baerland had undertaken to assemble for Martens a collection of Erasmus' shorter letters suitable for use in schools. Of the pieces it contains, only two are not found in other collections (see Allen III 627–9). This letter could have been written at any time during the presence at Louvain of Baerland's pupil, Cardinal Guillaume de Croy, which lasted until 1520. Allen preferred the date of 1517 in view of the circumstances mentioned in line 3n. For Baerland, a future professor at the Collegium Trilingue, see Ep 492 introduction.

ERASMUS TO HIS FRIEND BAERLAND, GREETING
Your index, indexes rather, make no mention of 'Scythian solitude'; both mine give a false page reference. So I took advice from Plautus, and told my

* * * * *

34 Basel] Cf Ep 603 introduction.

646
2 index] This must be the volume now returned to Baerland, or part of it. Baerland later published an epitome to Erasmus' *Adagia* for use in schools: *In omnes Adagiorum chiliades epitome* (Louvain: Martens June 1521; NK 2844).
2 'Scythian solitude'] *Adagia* III v 94
3 mine] The alphabetical index of the 1515 edition of Erasmus' *Adagia* gives an incorrect page reference for this adage (there is no reference, it seems, in the other index). The subsequent editions of 1517–18 and 1520, by contrast,

servant that, since he did not know the way to the sea, he should choose a
river as his guide; and so the place was found. Your volume is on its way   5
back to you.

How clever you are! I am quite delighted with you, and as soon as I am
quit of my present business, I mean to see more of you at close quarters. You
will, I imagine, give my humble self some share in your society, provided
you are not unfair to my lord the cardinal, the lodestar of our country and   10
the hope of humane studies everywhere. If you do everything you can for
him, in serving one man you will deserve well of us all.

Farewell, and keep it up: throw Erasmus into the shade by all your
efforts, my dear Baerland.

647 / From Adriaan Cornelissen van Baerland   [Louvain, August? 1517]

This letter was written after Erasmus' move to Louvain – hence Baerland's
disappointment at not getting to see him more often – and before October 1517
when the copyist of this letter (Hand B; cf Allen I 605) made his last entry into
the Deventer Letter-book.

This affection of yours for an ignoramus like myself, dear Erasmus, my most
learned teacher, makes me immensely grateful. My devotion to you in
return is something I wish I might have a chance to show; and I shall have, if
you are as willing as you are certainly able to issue orders to your faithful
Baerland, who will never be reluctant to shoulder any burden for Erasmus'   5
sake. But enough by way of preface! Let me come to the thing I wanted out
of you. With his eminence the cardinal I have carried the *De senectute* as far
as the final attack on that stage of life, where Cato holds forth on the
immortality of the soul. At this point you will promote the education of a
most high-born and most promising young man, and lay me also under a   10
great obligation, if you will add to the copy of the book which is brought
you with this by one of my pupils a few notes designed to expound the

* * * * *

indicate the page correctly in both indexes; thus neither of these can have been
on hand when Erasmus wanted to look up his adage.
3 Plautus] *Poenulus* 627–8. Erasmus explains the phrase in *Adagia* II vii 81 as
meaning that if one cannot do something in the simplest way, one must use
any other means that present themselves.
10 my lord the cardinal] Guillaume de Croy; cf Ep 628:70n.

647
7 cardinal] Guillaume de Croy, Baerland's pupil; cf Ep 628:70n.
7 *De senectute*] Cicero's *De senectute* concludes (21.77) with a peroration by Cato
on immortality.

passage in Cicero about the immortality of the soul; for what the commentators on Cicero offer one seems to me mere waste of time. I know that
Lactantius too in his *Institutiones* wrote eloquently at some length, and this   15
may help me on the topic. But I would rather get from Erasmus, that
treasure-house of eloquence and of all recondite learning, the materials I
need to assist his eminence; who does not dislike me, but towards Erasmus
has as warm feelings as a man can have, as you would expect from his
sincere love of the liberal arts.   20

Farewell, most learned Erasmus, sole glory of our age; and as soon as
you have a moment to spare, either today or tomorrow, I beg that you will
do what I ask. You will give me great pleasure and, what is more, you will,
as I say, promote in this way the education of the cardinal, who has
moreover a great affection for you. If my visits are few and far between, the   25
reason is my teaching, which keeps me busy in different ways. If I can ever
work my way out of these trifling occupations, I shall yield in assiduity to
none of those who are dearest to you. Farewell once more, most learned of
teachers.

Written from home   30
Baerland, your highness' most humble servant

648 / To the Reader   [Louvain] 1517

This is a preface published with Erasmus' edition of *The Lives of the Caesars* by
Suetonius in Froben's collection *Historiae Augustae scriptores* (Basel June 1518),
following Ep 586. Since the writing of Ep 586 Erasmus had seen a copy of
Giambattista Egnazio's Suetonius (Venice: Aldus August 1516) and thus had
been prompted to add this second preface to Ep 586. Assuming that a copy of
Egnazio's Suetonius had reached Erasmus shortly before 23 August 1517,
together with Epp 588–9 taken from Venice by Hutten on his return to
Germany (cf Epp 588:61–3, 628:8), Allen concluded that this preface was
probably written in the autumn of 1517. When Erasmus ordered Italian books
from the Frankfurt fair (Ep 629) Suetonius was not included and hence was
presumably available to him at that time. Egnazio's Suetonius also contained
the histories of Aurelius Victor and Eutropius (cf line 12), both of whom were
added to the Froben collection together with Egnazio's notes on them. The
Aldine edition of Suetonius was a companion volume to Egnazio's edition of
Aelius Spartianus and the other five authors normally known as *Historiae
Augustae scriptores* (G. Egnazio *De caesaribus libri III*, etc, Venice: Aldus colophon July 1516). From Erasmus' remarks in lines 11–13 it is clear that he had

* * * * *

15 Lactantius] *Divinae institutiones* 7.8–9

not seen this edition when writing the present letter. Even so, he was clearly
aware of the sharp competition in this field between the rival presses of Aldus
and Froben.

ERASMUS OF ROTTERDAM TO
THE FAIRMINDED READER, GREETING

When I had just finished preparing this edition, there arrived a Suetonius
printed by Aldus, but with the text emended by Battista Egnazio, a man
eminent for both character and learning, two qualities needed equally, in   5
my opinion, by anyone who undertakes to edit or comment on the productions of antiquity. For my part, I bear the death of my friend Aldus with
greater resignation when I see that in this department of restoring the text of
the classics he has a successor capable of overshadowing the dead man's
reputation, distinguished as he was in his own right, if one can use the   10
word 'overshadow' of excellence by excellence outstripped. I only wish
that, having given us Suetonius, Aurelius Victor, and Eutropius, he had
added Aelius Spartianus and the remainder at the same time, in whose
works I have made many restorations. To restore everything was beyond
my powers, without the aid of early codices. Even so, I have emended some   15
corruptions even in Suetonius which had escaped Egnazio's eagle eye; for
instance, in the life of Caesar the dictator, chapter 17, 'Eodem modo
Nouium quaestorem, quod compellari apud se maiorem potestatem passus
esset,' I have deleted *modo* on the evidence of a very ancient codex, for
eodem here is an adverb, so that one must supply *coniecit*.   20

There are other things of the same kind, but too small to deserve listing
in detail. Apart from them, in the life of Otho where Egnazio decides to read
Τί γάρ με δεῖ καὶ τοῖς μακροῖς αὐλοῖς αὐλεῖν; 'Why need I play on the long
pipes?' I disagree with him, because these words or something very like
them have been taken by Beroaldo, following some other scholar, from Dio.   25
Nor do the copies I have seen show any variant here, except that in some
αὐλοῖς has been corrupted to ἀσύλοις. There is no doubt therefore that we
ought to read Τί γάρ μοι καὶ μακροῖς αὐλοῖς; What have the long pipes to do
with me? This point I have treated more fully in my *Adagiorum chiliades*.

* * * * *

648
 7 Aldus] Aldo Manuzio, d 6 February 1515
22 Otho] Chap 7
25 Beroaldo] The reference to Dio (64.7.1) is not by Filippo Beroaldo, but among
    some anonymous additions to his *Commentationes ... in Suetonium* (Venice:
    Ph. Pincius 18 February 1510) f 281 verso, and in reprints thereof. Erasmus
    expressed himself more cautiously in *Adagia* I v 97.

In the Caligula for 'nec dicendi finem factum' I had restored from a   30
very ancient copy 'nec licendi finem factum,' although I afterwards discovered that Budé had corrected this passage in his *De asse*. I thought this
worth a mention to add weight to Budé's correction, although it does not
claim the authority of any ancient codex.

Again, in the life of Augustus, where the reading is Δότε κρότον καὶ   35
πάντες ὑμεῖς μετὰ χαρᾶς τι ποιεῖτε 'Give your applause, and do something
all of you with joy,' on which point Egnazio too has gone astray, I am the
first and only person (unless I am mistaken) to have corrected it, and that too
by following the indications, such as they are, of a very ancient codex. We
should therefore read Δότε κρότον καὶ πάντες ὑμεῖς (or ἡμῖν) μετὰ χαρᾶς   40
κτυπήσατε 'Give your applause, and sound (or give us) a joyful send-off, all
of you.' It is a trochaic line. In an ancient codex κτυπεῖτε appeared to be
written, making it a brachycatalectic trochaic. There is no doubt that these
were the last words of a Greek comedy. There had preceded it in my copy
another similar trochaic, or at any rate a half-line, but the shapes of the   45
letters were so much distorted that I could not guess what had been written.

Further, in the life of Vespasian, where it has ὦ Λάχης, Λάχης,
ὅταν δ'ἀποθάνῃς αὖθις ἐξ ὑπαρχῆς εἰρήσῃ Κήρυλος, if I had any support
from the copies, I would gladly read it like this:

     ὦ Λάχης, Λάχης   50
   ὅταν δ' ἀποθάνῃς αὖθις ἔσσῃ Κήρυλος,
that is,

     O Laches, Laches,
     When dead, you will be Kerylus once more,
so that ὦ Λάχης, Λάχης is the end of the previous line, and then follows a   55
complete iambic trimeter, though I would not fight strongly for this view.

In the comparative material from coins, if there are any differences
between Egnazio, relying on Portis as his authority, and Budé, I was not

* * * * *

30 Caligula] Chap 38.4, corrected in Budé's *De asse*, book 1 (*Opera omnia* II 52),
    and now known to be found in better manuscripts
35 Augustus] Chap 99.1; the correction of the Greek given in the manuscripts
    seems still to be uncertain.
47 Vespasian] Chap 23.2, citing a comedy by Menander; Erasmus' suggestion is
    not accepted by modern editors.
58 Portis] Leonardus de Portis of Vicenza, d 1545, was the author of a book on
    ancient coinage and measures, *De sestertio* ... ed G. Egnazio [Venice: G. de
    Rusconibus 1520?], reprinted by Froben without delay, it seems. Egnazio had
    used this work as early as 1516, but he bitterly resented Erasmus' brief
    reference here as an accusation of plagiarism – cf his letter to Jean Grolier,
    Venice, 5 January 1519 (1518, old style), in M. Goldast *Philologicarum epis-*

anxious to explore them, not having the necessary leisure, nor was it really
part of the task I had set myself. But I have added an index, chiefly devoted   60
to listing expressions that are new or not habitual in earlier authors, and
Greek phrases, that there may be something of profit in the book to persuade the reader to buy it. Nor will this be the only novelty; all the additions
of Egnazio are to be found here, besides several emendations for which I
alone am responsible.   65

Farewell, kind reader, and accept my best wishes for your profitable
use of my labours. 1517

649 / To [Silvestro Gigli]   Louvain, 7 September 1517

This letter must have been addressed to Silvestro Gigli, bishop of Worcester
and English agent in Rome. He had vigorously assisted Andrea Ammonio in
securing for Erasmus the desired papal dispensations (cf Epp 446–7,
521, 566–7), and his friendship might become even more valuable now that
Ammonio was dead. In particular, Erasmus was now trying to ascertain
whether any additional documents of which he had no knowledge had remained in Ammonio's hands; see Ep 623 introduction.

Greeting, right reverend Father. Never, never shall I forget your singular
kindness to me, although I have not yet expressed my thanks in word or
deed. So much have I been distracted, partly by continual changes back and
forth of my abode, partly by the departure of our chancellor, partly by the
emperor's projects, in part too by ill health, but above all by the constant   5
uncertainty which has scarcely allowed me to think of myself, let alone of
others. But you will shortly discover that I am devoted and not ungrateful.
What fresh steps Andrea took in that business of mine since my departure
from England, I do not know. If he has opened anything fresh, I beg you will
press it to a conclusion. I have the New Testament in hand once more. At   10
first it had offended some people by the novelty of it, but it was approved by

* * * * *

tolarum centuria una (Frankfurt 1610) Ep 35 – stating that Erasmus wrote too
much and neglected the study of the evidence on hand. In 1518 Budé too had
heard of Leonardus de Portis' work. He feared that the reputation of his own
De asse might be slighted and challenged Egnazio to publish the work (*Opera
omnia* I 258–9; cf Ep 810:298). Ten years later Erasmus referred again to it, this
time to launch a subtle charge of plagiarism against Budé; see Allen Ep
1840:3–10; M.-M. de la Garanderie 163, 259.

649
3 changes] Cf Ep 596 introduction.
4 departure of our chancellor] Cf Ep 608 introduction.

all those whose approval is most worth having. However, next summer it
will reappear, revised by me in such a way that everyone will like it and that
(if I may be allowed a touch of arrogance) it will win eternal honour for the
name of Leo and the house of Medici, if I am allowed to survive for one more   15
year. When I was last in England, the king treated me with singular good
will, and so after him did his eminence the cardinal of York; both invited
me, making offers that were by no means to be despised. Farewell, my
noble lord bishop, and do not cease to think well of me, the least of your
dependants.   20

Louvain, eve of the Nativity of the Virgin 1517

650 / To Antonius Clava   Louvain, 7 September [1517]

This is the answer to Ep 617.

ERASMUS OF ROTTERDAM TO HIS FRIEND
ANTONIUS CLAVA, GREETING
Budé's letter reached me safely, enclosed in yours, and both gave me great
pleasure. I am ashamed to have to thank you in a department where I owe so
much myself. I could hardly tell you with what kindness the theologians are   5
now pursuing me, especially Doctor Atensis the chancellor, Dorp, and
Vianen. Busleyden has died, of a pleurisy, a sad blow to me; but he almost
deserved this misfortune, for he did not know when he was well off, and
even his brother's example had not taught him to keep clear of Spain. The
Dutchman who brings you this letter regards you with such warm feeling,   10
he depends upon you and guides himself by you to such an extent, that
even if there were nothing else to be said for him, you ought to give him a

* * * * *

15 Leo] Pope Leo x (Giovanni de' Medici); his approval of the new edition was
    expressed in Ep 864.
17 York] Thomas Wolsey
17 both invited] Cf Ep 657 introduction.

650
6 chancellor] Cf Ep 643:9n.
7 Vianen] Willem van Vianen (Gulielmus Johannis Lamberti Vianensis), d 1529,
    was a professor first of philosophy and subsequently of theology, and also
    curate (*plebanus*) of St Peter's.
7 died] Cf Ep 608 introduction.
9 brother's] François de Busleyden, archbishop of Besançon, had died in Toledo
    in 1502 as a cardinal designate.
10 Dutchman] An unidentified servant-messenger (see Bierlaire 51). He also
    carried Ep 651 to Bruges; see Ep 666.

hand when he needs it. You know his business. Give my greetings to
Robert de Keysere and to Clavus the physician, so close to you in name. I
send my best wishes to your good son-in-law and your charming daughter,   15
and especially to your wife. Enclosed is the *Apologia*, which is my answer to
Lefèvre, and a most unwilling one. Greetings to your lady.

Louvain, eve of the Nativity of the BVM

651 / To Mark Lauwerijns   Louvain, 7 September 1517

Mark Lauwerijns, 1488–1546, was a son of Jeroen Lauwerijns, treasurer to
Philip the Handsome. Mark had been canon at St Donatian's in Bruges since
1512, and at this time he was coadjutor to the aged dean (cf line 22). Erasmus
had known Mark and his brothers in Bologna (see Ep 201), and when Erasmus
followed the court to Bruges (see Ep 596 introduction) Mark had shown him
much kindness (line 2).

Mark's elder brother, Matthias (d 1540), succeeded to his father's lordship of
Watervliet and to his office of treasurer. He was often mayor of Bruges and
became a member of the Flanders Council in 1538 (cf line 4). A third brother,
Pieter (line 22), Lord of Leeskens, died young in 1522. See de Vocht CTL II 68.

ERASMUS TO HIS FRIEND MARK, GREETING

I would thank you, most generous of friends, for your singular hospitality to
me, were it not so far from being anything new. Give my congratulations to
your brother Matthias Hydorrhoeus (or squire of Watervliet, if you prefer it
in good Flemish) on his happy return from Spain; his timing indeed was   5
such that I thought he had returned to us before he had set out. My

* * * * *

14 Keysere] A printer at Ghent; see Epp 175, 525 introductions.
14 physician] An unidentified physician of Ghent, a friend of Clava and Robert
   de Keysere (cf Ep 719, 743), whose name was apparently Clavus. Epp 681 and
   788 show that Erasmus wanted Pieter Gillis to consult Clavus. Perhaps he is
   the physician Adrian of Ep 818 who actually attended Gillis and the Doctor
   Adrian mentioned in Ep 755.
14 close ... in name] 'Saluta ... Clavum Clava': Erasmus probably remembered
   Adagia I ii 4, 'Clavum clavo pellere,' one nail drives out another; cf Jerome, Ep
   125:14; PL 22 1080.
16 *Apologia*] Cf Ep 597:37n.

651
4 Matthias] It seems that he accompanied Prince Charles to Spain – cf Epp 717,
   740; L.P. Gachard and C. Piot *Collections des voyages des souverains des Pays-
   Bas* (Brussels 1874–82) II 505 – but while the fleet was still waiting at Middelburg for favourable winds (cf Ep 596 introduction) he may briefly have returned to Bruges; cf introduction.

household exchequer is almost bewitched; beside fifty écus à la couronne
that descended from heaven at Bruges, I was sent soon afterwards at
Louvain a hundred florins from the court, and then another thirty-six
philippi from England. But the trouble is that the money pours out as fast as   10
it pours in.

I have not yet entirely settled down at Louvain, but shall have done so
in four days' time comfortably enough, I think in the College of the Lily,
under a most kindly man and a good scholar, Jean de Nève of Hondschoote.
As for Lefèvre, everyone agrees that I have vanquished him, although, God   15
knows, I myself find this victory most distasteful. I wish anything had
entered his head, rather than to challenge me to combat like this. I do
sincerely like the man; but in this he is so unlike himself, and that towards
me, too, the one man who least deserved such treatment. I am sending you
my *Apologia* as a present. If it should suit you to move here, you will find   20
that the writer of these lines is sincerely yours. Mind you give my greetings
to that worthy man the dean, and your brother Pieter, and our merry
musical friends, not forgetting my dear Ludovicus. I find the theologians
very well disposed towards me, especially the chancellor of the university,
Doctor Atensis, Dorp, and Vianen. They have already made me almost a   25
member of their faculty.

Farewell, my dear Mark, most faithful of friends, most generous of
patrons.

Louvain, eve of the Nativity of the Virgin 1517

* * * * *

7 écus à la couronne] Possibly Tunstall's recent gift (cf Ep 597:21n), or another
sum received from the addressee himself.
9 court] Cf Ep 616:2.
9 thirty-six philippi] Gold St Philip florins of the Hapsburg Low Countries, in
total worth (officially) £7 10s 0d gros Flemish = £5 8s 0d sterling = £47 5s 0d
tournois. We learn nothing about the source of this sum, but cf Ep 712:29; and
also cwe 1 318, 321 (plate), 327, 338–9.
13 College of the Lily] Situated in the present Diest Street, but now demolished.
Erasmus was to live here for four years as a paying guest, occupying a fine
room on the upper floor (cf Epp 735:10, Allen 1347:8–9; M. Nauwelaerts in
Scrinium I 8). For the delay in moving there cf Ep 643:14n.
18 unlike himself] Cf Ep 597:44n.
20 *Apologia*] See Ep 597:37n.
22 dean] Jan Goetgebuer (or Bonivicini), dean of St Donatian's from 1502 to his
death in 1519
22 Pieter] See introduction.
23 Ludovicus] Addressed in Ep 790
24 chancellor] Cf Ep 643:9n.
25 Vianen] See Ep 650:7n.

652 / To Pierre Barbier   [Louvain, c 7 September 1517]

This letter is the answer to Ep 621 and the points it raised. It is contemporary with Epp 650–1.

ERASMUS TO HIS FRIEND BARBIER, GREETING

It was a very great pleasure to learn from your letter that my eminent patron and yourself are well. The money has been faithfully remitted to Louvain by my good lord de la Marques through Adriaan, the treasurer. In this business your brother Nicolas has played the part of a true Barbier, yourself over 5 again. There are some moves on foot among the theologians to co-opt me into their number, though I myself have no such ambitions.

As for Lefèvre, I cannot say how much it grieves me, how I regret this necessity which compels me to answer him. I would rather write a large book in praise of my old friend Lefèvre than this short *Apologia* in support of 10 my own position. You know how I did everything and endured everything in hopes of avoiding a conflict with Dorp; much less would I have wished this to happen with Lefèvre. But when you have read the whole thing, you will decide that he treated the affair in a spirit so unpleasant that it was not open to me to say nothing. I saw that in this way ill-wishers would be given 15 a handle to speak ill of us both; I saw that the fruit of our researches, pursued through so many sleepless nights, went for naught. And I love Lefèvre sincerely, as much as I do anybody. My evil genius thwarts me on every side. 'What power divine' put this into his head? Even so, I keep watch on myself, so as to refrain from personal abuse, for I count it no libel 20 if, while openly refuting his opinion, I cast no aspersions on his private life. My book will reach you with this letter, if I can find someone to whom I can entrust it for transport. When you have read it, I am sure you will be sorry for us both. I had already finished the piece before your letter arrived. Even if it had arrived in very good time, in face of such accusations I could not 25 remain silent, even were my assailant the Holy Father himself.

653 / To [John Fisher]   Antwerp, 8 September 1517

This letter is clearly an answer to Ep 592, hence addressed to Fisher. Fisher's name among others was omitted regularly in the address of letters belonging

* * * * *
652
  2 patron] Le Sauvage
  3 money] Cf Ep 613.
 12 conflict] See Ep 628:14n.
 23 transport] The copy did reach Barbier; see Ep 752:13.

to this period as they were copied into the Deventer Letter-book (cf Epp 667, 784, 824, 889, and Ep 596 introduction). For a possible purpose of Erasmus' visit to Antwerp cf Ep 654.

Epp 653–8 and the gifts to several English correspondents mentioned in them were all carried by Pieter Meghen, called the One-eyed, who had undertaken errands for Erasmus since June 1516 and is mentioned frequently in preceding letters (cf Epp 231:5n, 412:47n; Bierlaire 51). On the progress of his journey to Calais and England cf Epp 667:1, 669:1, 681:12, 688:12, 772 introduction.

Greeting, right reverend Father. I had bitter complaints from Colet that I had sent Reuchlin's book to you, and had not sent him a copy; although he added that he had read it right through before sending it on to you. I am sorry for such a long delay, but you must forgive Colet for his eagerness; I know your kind heart. I had given More leave to show the book to Colet, not   5
to deposit it with him. You say you have no regrets for the effort you have expended on Greek, and heaven knows I am delighted. I only wish I could be at hand for the future. I have opened the subject in a letter to Latimer more than once; he has at length replied, but it is clear from the terms of his reply that he will not be tempted to desert his studies. I send, however, my   10
new version of Theodore's second book, in which a few passages have been emended from a Greek codex. My version, in any case, is fairly straightforward. You must not mind the errors of the servant who copied it, provided the main lines are clear as you read.

With it I send my *Apologia* in answer to Jacques Lefèvre. All the   15
theologians, all those even of his own party, unanimously award the victory to me. But I myself hate the necessity which drove me to compete in this field, and I hate a victory won at the expense of such a good friend. Wise as you are, you will understand both of us, the moment you have read the book, and I am sure you will be sorry for us both, even if my misfortune is   20
lighter to bear, because none of it was my own fault. When you have

* * * * *

653
1 Colet] In Ep 593. The book referred to is Reuchlin's *De arte cabalistica;* cf Ep 500:22.
9 more than once] Two letters by Erasmus, now lost, are replied to by Latimer in Ep 520:3, 14. The suggestion Erasmus made, which was politely declined by the Oxford scholar (see Ep 417 introduction), was that he should tutor Fisher in his Greek studies. In Ep 540 Erasmus had urged Latimer to reconsider, but apparently without success.
11 Theodore's] Theodorus Gaza; see Ep 771 introduction.
15 *Apologia*] See Ep 597:37n.

someone reliable to bring them, let me have back the books relating to the
Reuchlin business, provided you have finished with them. Someone wrote
to me from Cologne that his case is going very well, but I think that case will
never be finished. I only wish it might suit you to visit this country some   25
time. Farewell, and at least let me sometimes have a letter.

Antwerp, 8 September 1517

654 / To Thomas More   Antwerp, 8 September [1517]

This may be dated 1517 because More is in Calais and Erasmus in Antwerp.
Quentin Metsys' diptych of Erasmus and Pieter Gillis was at long last finished,
or nearly so (cf Epp 601:56n, 616:10–12, 669:1n). Erasmus obviously went to
Antwerp because he wanted to see it and, in view of Gillis' prolonged illness,
to help with the arrangements for its safe delivery to More (cf Ep 653 introduction); for More's reaction cf Epp 683–4.

ERASMUS TO HIS FRIEND MORE, GREETING
I send you the pictures, so that you may still have our company after a
fashion, if some chance removes us from the scene. Pieter contributed one
half and I the other – not that either of us would not gladly have paid the
whole, but we wanted it to be a present from us both. Pieter Gillis is still   5
confined by that sickness of his. I am living in Louvain, all among the
reverend doctors, and am in my usual health. I am sorry for you, tied to
Calais as you are. If nothing else is possible, do at least write often, even a
few words. Farewell, my dear More, whom I love best of mortal men.

Antwerp, 8 September   10
Pray mind your health, for our benefit.

655 / To Johannes Sixtinus   Antwerp, 8 September 1517

This letter is a reply to Ep 624, but may also be in answer to another message
from Sixtinus that was taken to the Netherlands by his brother; cf lines 6–7,
Ep 623:5n.

ERASMUS TO HIS FRIEND SIXTINUS, GREETING
O what sad news! But complaints can do no good. I beg you, in the name of

* * * * *

23 Someone wrote] Johannes Caesarius, in Ep 615

654
6 sickness] Cf Ep 597:23n.
8 Calais] Cf Ep 623:23n.

our friendship: let Pietro Ammonio get together all Andrea's letters to me
and mine to him, and either send them to me here or give them to you to
send, and then let any duplicate copies or letters about my dispensation be   5
destroyed, to keep them from falling into hands I should regret. Your
brother I did not see in Louvain, for I was away. Pieter Gillis is laid low with
an unpleasant and prolonged disorder. I find this climate fairly agreeable,
and my fortunes would be in a good way were I willing to become involved
in the business of princes; but I perceive there are such dissensions that it   10
would not be safe to follow either party. So I get on with my researches.
Farewell, my dear Sixtinus, and for my sake look after your health.

 Antwerp, 8 September 1517

656 / To Pietro Ammonio   [Antwerp, c 8 September 1517]

> This letter is contemporary with Ep 655. Pietro Vanni or Vannes of Lucca,
> called Ammonio (d 1563), was a cousin of Andrea Ammonio and had entered
> Wolsey's service as his assistant. After Andrea's death he succeeded him as
> Wolsey's Latin secretary and later served Henry VIII in the same office and as
> an ambassador.

ERASMUS TO HIS FRIEND PIETRO AMMONIO, GREETING
The death of our dear Ammonio distresses me as nothing else could. All
good qualities are lost with him. The man himself I cannot recall from the
dead, but his memory I will certainly not allow to die, 'if aught my pen can
do.' I beg you to collect all his letters to me and mine to him into a single   5

 * * * * *

655
3 Pietro] Cf Ep 656.
5 copies or letters] Kept on file by Andrea Ammonio, or perhaps by Sixtinus in
 his capacity as a witness; cf his postscript to Ep 517.
7 brother] He must have caught up with Erasmus, still at Antwerp, very shortly
 after this letter had been written; cf Ep 668. Johannes' will, made in 1518,
 mentions only one brother, Albertus; cf S. Knight *The Life of Dr John Colet* (2nd
 ed, Oxford 1823) 192–3.
7 laid low] Cf Ep 597:23n.
10 business of princes] Cf Epp 603, 670 introductions.

656
4 'if aught ... do'] An echo of Virgil *Aeneid* 9.446
5 letters] Erasmus wanted them for publication, if they were found suitable. He
 had to make repeated requests for the letters; cf Epp 774–5, 822, 828. Eventually most of the surviving correspondence between Erasmus and Andrea
 Ammonio was published in the *Farrago* of 1519. For an earlier request of the
 same kind cf Ep 186.

bundle and arrange to have them sent to me by a safe hand. Besides which, if there are any papers relating to that business of mine which he conducted at the Holy See, let them please be destroyed or sent to me. Farewell, my dear Pietro, and do not forget that Erasmus is your devoted friend.

657 / To Henry VIII   Antwerp, 9 September 1517

Epp 657 and 658 were no doubt inspired by Erasmus' continued hopes for a permanent position in England, possibly an appointment to a major benefice (cf Epp 597:57n, 649:16–18, 694:9–13, 816). The letters were to accompany an appropriate gift for the king – a recently published volume, perhaps in a handsome binding (cf Ep 658:11–13), containing several pieces, including translations from Plutarch's moral treatises which had originally been published with dedications to Henry VIII and Wolsey (cf Epp 272, 284, 297). An earlier presentation copy, perhaps still in manuscript, had been sent to Wolsey for personal conveyance to the king (cf lines 37–9, 658:25), but Erasmus had never received an explicit response – he assumed because of the king's preoccupation with the war then raging against France (1513). Meanwhile the translations from Plutarch had been reprinted by Martens (Louvain 1 May 1515; NK 3755) and also by Froben, who included the first edition of the *Institutio principis christiani* (spring 1516; cf Ep 393) and the *Panegyricus* for Archduke Philip (cf Ep 179). This was the volume chosen by Erasmus for his gift to the king (all texts are now in LB IV). Charlecote Park in Warwickshire, England, a National Trust property, possesses a copy of the Froben volume containing an inserted leaf of vellum illuminated with the arms of Henry VIII and, on sig. a2, an illuminated border incorporating the Tudor badge of a portcullis, painted over Froben's woodcut border. The existing binding is not the original one. The gift eventually produced the expected reward; see Ep 834 introduction.

The letter to Wolsey appears to be an ad hoc composition, unlike the elaborate epistle to Henry VIII. Probably only the last sentences were added during Erasmus' brief visit to Antwerp at this time, while the bulk of this letter was originally composed as a new dedicatory preface to the third edition of the translations from Plutarch (line 44), although for some reason it was not included in the volume printed by Froben. Thus Epp 657–8 appeared in print only in the *Auctarium* of August 1518.

* * * * *

7 business of mine] The papal dispensations; cf Epp 623 introduction, 655:5.

DESIDERIUS ERASMUS OF ROTTERDAM TO
HIS MOST SERENE HIGHNESS HENRY THE EIGHTH
KING OF ENGLAND, GREETING

Greetings to your serene Highness. Among the manifold natural gifts of a
truly regal and indeed heroic cast, in which you not only recall but even   5
surpass your glorious father Henry seventh of that name, men may well
differ in the praise and admiration they bestow on this or that; I myself
admire them all. But there is one I value above the rest, that, being yourself
so wise in virtue of your rare and penetrating mind, you yet enjoy the
familiar conversation of sage and learned men, and such especially as know   10
not the arts of talking solely to give pleasure. One would think you had read
somewhere – as no doubt you have – that line of Sophocles, 'Converse with
wise men makes a monarch wise.' Above all, amidst all the business of the
realm and indeed of the whole world, scarcely a day passes in which you do
not devote some portion of your time to reading books, enjoying the society   15
of those philosophers of old who flatter least of all men, and of those books
especially from whose perusal you will rise more judicious, a better man
and a better king. So much do you differ from those who think that a
distinguished prince should abhor nothing so much as the study of
philosophy, or, if he must take a book in hand, that he should read nothing   20
but merry tales scarce worthy to be read by women, such things as merely
encourage folly and vice. One would think they were two things diametri-
cally opposed, to be a wise man and to play a monarch's part; whereas in
fact they are so closely connected that, if you take one away, you leave
nothing but the empty name of king, like some cenotaph that displays name   25
and arms to the beholder, and inside is empty. And further, we know that a
judicious and religious prince is wise and watchful and far-sighted for the
common benefit of all, because the office that he holds is public and not
private; and so it is proper that every man should try to assist with these
cares and responsibilities to the utmost of his power. The wider his   30
dominions, the more a monarch has need of this loyal help. A king is
something special in the world of men, and almost like a god; but none the
less he is a man.

For my part, since my writings are for better or worse my only means
of paying kings this due service, I long ago translated from Greek into Latin 35
Plutarch's treatise *How to distinguish flatterer from friend*, and dedicated it to
your Majesty by the means of his eminence my lord cardinal, who stands to

* * * * *

657
12 Sophocles] A fragment, cited in *Adagia* III v 97

Two facing pages in a presentation volume of
Erasmus *Institutio principis christiani* (Basel: Froben 1516)
bound with his *Plutarchi opuscula* (Basel: Froben 1516).
From the library of Charlecote Park, Warwickshire,
a property of the National Trust

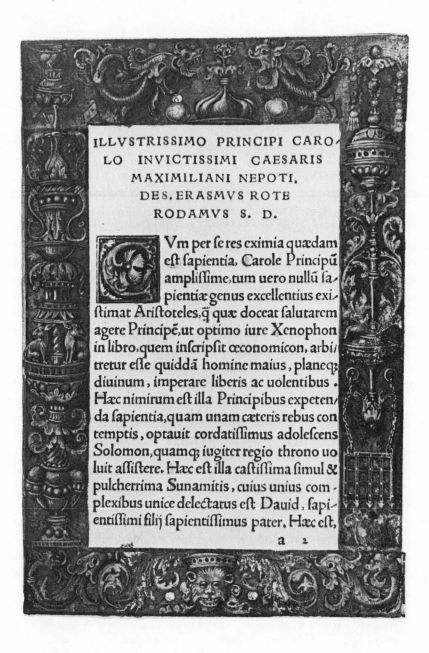

ILLVSTRISSIMO PRINCIPI CARO-
LO INVICTISSIMI CAESARIS
MAXIMILIANI NEPOTI.
DES. ERASMVS ROTE
RODAMVS S. D.

Vm per fe res eximia quædam
eft fapientia, Carole Principū
ampliffime, tum uero nullū fa-
pientiæ genus excellentius exi-
ftimat Ariftoteles,q̄ quæ doceat falutarem
agere Principē, ut optimo iure Xenophon
in libro,quem infcripfit œconomicon, arbi-
tretur effe quiddā homine maius, planeq̃
diuinum, imperare liberis ac uolentibus .
Hæc nimirum eft illa Principibus expeten-
da fapientia,quam unam cæteris rebus con
temptis, optauit cordatiffimus adolefcens
Solomon,quamq̃ iugiter regio throno uo
luit affiftere. Hæc eft illa caftiffima fimul &
pulcherrima Sunamitis, cuius unius com-
plexibus unice delectatus eft Dauid, fapi-
entiffimi filij fapientiffimus pater. Hæc eft,

a 2

LEFT: an inserted leaf of vellum with the arms of Henry VIII
RIGHT: a page of the *Institutio* (f a2 recto)
with the Tudor badge of a portcullis in the lower right-hand corner

you in the governance of your realm as Theseus stood to Hercules or
Achates to Aeneas. Since, however, at that moment you were swept suddenly away into the storms of war by a kind of widespread tempest   40
launched by fate upon the Christian world, you had, I think, too little
leisure for the products of the pen, for there was need to use the sword. And
so I now submit the same work to your Highness, though already published
to the world and printed a third time, and that not without accrued interest;
for I have added a *Panegyricus* in honour of Philip, king of Castile, whose   45
memory I know that you hold sacred, seeing that when he was a young man
and you a boy, you loved him as a brother, and your excellent father had
taken him, not in name alone, as an adopted son.

To these I have added the *Institutio principis christiani*, which I offered
recently for his accession to his Catholic Majesty Prince Charles; not that he   50
stood much in need of my advice, but as in some great tempest a helmsman
of the longest experience is willing to receive advice from anyone, so a
prince called to reign over so many kingdoms ought to despise no man's
counsel zealously offered, and should then choose out of it all what he
judges most worthy to be followed. And what sea ever suffers such up-   55
heaval as the tumults that disorder wide dominions? Who ever saw such
tempests in the ocean as we have seen these few years past in the affairs of
men? And still worse seem to threaten us, unless things can be set to rights
by the wisdom and piety of princes. Lastly, having received a summons to
join the roll of councillors, I thought it right to answer the call of duty from   60
the outset with this offering, and not so much to tender counsel on this
question or on that as to expose in a way the springs of all good counsel to a
prince of great natural gifts but still a youth.

Not that your Majesty needs any such advice; far from it. No, he who
carefully watches your example could draw the model of a perfect prince by   65
drawing you. But here it is: for I knew well, had it no other merits, that a
memorial of two monarchs so very dear to you could not be unwelcome;
further, because these precepts, if their advice is sound, will be more
readily acceptable to kings or to the sons of kings, if they feel that you, the

* * * * *

38 Theseus ... Achates] Celebrated examples of faithful friendship and emulation
45 Philip] The Handsome, of Burgundy, the father of Charles v, d September
   1506. On their way to Spain, Philip and his wife Joanna, were driven to the
   English shore by a gale (12 January 1506). Henry VII used the occasion for a
   display of royal splendour and to forge a treaty of friendship, but also to obtain
   the extradition from the Netherlands of Edmund de la Pole, Earl of Suffolk, the
   last hope of the Yorkists.
49 *Institutio ... christiani*] Cf introduction and Epp 683:49–51, 688:12–14.

most intelligent, most virtuous, most prosperous king alive today, have not   70
rejected them. Lastly, I myself shall to some extent escape the charge of
ingratitude, if I do not cease to bear witness diligently, as and when I can, to
your Majesty's goodness towards me. What do I not owe you, having so
often enjoyed the distinction of kind words from you? Besides which, when
I was last in your country, you invited me on such generous terms, of your   75
own mere motion and with a truly regal affability; for I count this of great
price, that such a humble creature as myself should be favoured by so good
and great a prince with recognition and with friendship. May your Majesty
be long preserved in health and prosperity by the King of Kings, Christ
Jesus our good and gracious Lord, is the prayer of   80

> Your Majesty's most devoted servant,
> Erasmus of Rotterdam.
> Antwerp, morrow of the Nativity of our Lady 1517

658 / To Thomas Wolsey   Antwerp, 9 September 1517

Cf Ep 657 introduction; this letter was published in the *Auctarium*.

TO THE CARDINAL OF YORK
Greeting, most reverend Father in God. I know well with what respect your
Eminence should be approached even by the great, and with what ill
success many men have addressed the powers that be without due form. If I
show confidence, I owe it to your rare, unheard-of affability, of which I have   5
had experience especially during my recent stay in Britain. Outstanding
felicity is usually haunted by envy. But that remarkable affability, which
makes you accessible to all, banishes envy, so that men's admiration for
your great estate is matched by love of your great natural goodness. But I
must not take up with trifles of my own the time of one so fully occupied   10
with important business; so to the point. I am sending to his majesty the
king a book, finished as best I can, containing several pieces that deal with
the way in which a kingdom should be ruled. Philip, king of Castile, under
whose name I have depicted the image of a virtuous prince, was loved as a
brother by his serene highness king Henry eighth of that name, when he   15
was a boy and Philip a man; and the king expressed sorrow at his death in a
letter to me as full of feeling as it was well written. With our Prince Charles,

* * * * *

75 invited] See introduction and Epp 577, 834.

658
6 Britain] Cf Ep 577.
17 letter to me] Ep 206

besides the bonds of kinship, he has such close relations, so intimate a
friendship, and such a brotherly union of sentiments, that their relationship could not be closer. And then you, your Eminence, are to the king, as   20
he rules with unsurpassed felicity the most flourishing kingdom of them all,
what Theseus in the story was to Hercules and Achates to Aeneas; so that it
is not without point that these three great names, so dear to one another,
should be found together within two covers. But the volume which I had
long ago dedicated to the king and offered him by your means, the turmoil   25
of war has not yet, I suppose, left him time to read. Now that peace is at
length restored, I understand that he has returned to the reading for which
he had a not unpromising taste as a boy, and holds converse with books, not
chosen at random, but such especially as will teach him religion and the
wisdom that is fit for a king. For the more virtue he acquires, the greater is   30
his thirst for it. And so I have thought it right to repeat my little offering of
long ago, for what was still unknown did not seem to have been truly
offered. With it is the treatise addressed to you, as small as you yourself are
great.

I have not failed to notice how mean both my gifts are; when offered to   35
such heroic figures what gift would not be mean? But I have put a bold face
on it; I chose to recall your kindness rather than your exalted place, and
decided to refresh your memory of me by the best means I could, letting you
know at the same time the far greater enterprise I have in hand, for at
present I am the slave of the New Testament so completely that I can do   40
nothing else. I am resolved either to die in the attempt or to treat the topic in
such a way that it will earn undying fame and glory both for Pope Leo the
Tenth and for myself. If these words are thought arrogant, I have no
objection, unless I really do what I have promised. To that task this winter
will be devoted, which I shall spend in Louvain, since neither the prince nor   45
the chancellor of Burgundy is here. Meanwhile I urgently would ask your
Eminence first to continue towards my humble self the favour you showed
me at first; and secondly to be so good as to recommend my gift, such as it is,
to his majesty or, if the gift itself does not deserve so much, at least convey to
him my sentiments.   50

* * * * *

18 close relations] Cf Ep 623:23n.
22 Theseus ... Achates] Cf Ep 657:38n.
23 dear] The text of the first printed edition is here preferable to that of the
    Deventer Letter-book, followed by Allen.
33 treatise addressed to you] Plutarch's *De utilitate capienda ex inimicis*; it fills only
    six columns in LB (LB IV 23–30).
46 chancellor] Le Sauvage

His Catholic Majesty has set sail from here successfully; would that equal success may attend on all he does in Spain! In this country I fear the rise of some great revolution, unless the favour of heaven and the piety and religion of princes take thought for human affairs. The death of Ammonio was a severe blow. How many gifts we have lost in that one man! We have   55
also lost Jérôme de Busleyden, who long ago went on a mission to you; these are our first-fruits offered to the Spanish Death, to which already we pay too high a tribute. Best wishes to your eminence, to whom I warmly recommend myself, the least of all your dependants.

Antwerp, 9 September 1517   60

659 / To Jacques Lefèvre d'Etaples   Louvain, 11 September 1517

First printed in the *Auctarium*, this letter was dispatched together with a copy of the *Apologia ad Fabrum* (cf Ep 597:37n, 44n) and taken to Paris by a Sorbonne theologian returning from Louvain; cf Epp 724, 778:322–4, 796.

ERASMUS TO HIS FRIEND LEFÈVRE, GREETING
Those who wish us both well, my dear Lefèvre, are sorry for us both. They are sorry for you, because some god so disastrously put it into your head, without any reason, to make such an unpleasant attack upon me, and to make it in such a way that it was not open to me to remain silent, without   5
admitting the truth of all your accusations in one breath: 'words most unworthy of Christ and of God,' 'words self-destructive from every point of view, and from every aspect exhibiting their own falsity,' 'words which are hostile to the understanding of prophecy,' 'words which support the case of those pestilent Jews and treat Christ with contumely as they do,' 'words   10

* * * * *

51 set sail] Cf Ep 596 introduction.
53 revolution] Cf Ep 628:48–57.
54 Ammonio] Cf Ep 623.
56 Busleyden] Cf Ep 650. In 1509 he had been sent to England to congratulate Henry VIII on his accession to the throne.
57 to which ... a tribute] This clause was added only in the printed edition, no doubt on account of the death in Spain of Jean Le Sauvage.

659
6 accusations] For the quotations that follow cf Lefèvre's second edition of the Epistles of St Paul (1515), ff 226 verso–229 verso. Only the first three citations are taken more or less literally from Lefèvre's text (reprinted in LB IX 67–80); the others are so inaccurate that had he wished to pursue the controversy, Lefèvre might well have accused Erasmus of deliberate misrepresentation; cf Epp 778:130–6, 784:28–33.

Albert of Brandenburg
Drawing by Albrecht Dürer, 1518
Graphische Sammlung Albertina, Vienna

worthy of Bedlam,' 'words which, if obstinately adhered to, would make
me a heretic,' and plenty more of the same kind. One or two shafts of the
sort I might perhaps have overlooked. And they are sorry for me, because,
overwhelmed as I am with other business, and having an intense dislike of
this kind of writing, I have been forced into a decisive contest with a man I   15
particularly like. In the opposite camp, there is rejoicing among those who
wish ill to us and to more liberal studies. They are supplied with arguments
to bring against us both, with means to show that neither of us can be
trusted, with compensations for their own ignorance. As I hope for Christ's
mercy, not only the need to fight but the victory, which all award me with   20
one voice, is hateful to me.

     And so, my dear Lefèvre, by all that you hold sacred, let us make an
end of this impious disputation. 'Better run backward than run quite
astray.' If you wish at all costs to engage in conflict with my poor self, at least
avoid such expressions as it is impossible for me to overlook. We have   25
already given more satisfaction than is good for them to the devotees of
primeval ignorance. I enclose my pamphlet; if you have not yet seen it read
it through carefully. And then take advice from your own better self, and do
not let provocation by other people drive you into a position in which you
may later be very sorry to find yourself. Restrain the language of your   30
supporters as well as yours; I have restrained my own friends so far. Let us
deal with one another in pure and truly Christian sincerity. You will not
find a trace of guile in me.

     Farewell.

     Louvain, 11 September 1517   35

660 / To Gerardus Listrius

     This letter has been assigned a new date and now will be found as Ep 1013A in
     CWE 7.

661 / From Albert of Brandenburg   Steinheim, 13 September 1517

     The correct year date is given in the Deventer Letter-book. In the printed
     editions of this letter (see Ep 745 introduction) the date is given as 1518 in
     correspondence with the date wrongly assigned to Ep 745, which is Erasmus'
     reply. This warm and flattering invitation, written in his own hand, came

     * * * * *

     23 'Better run ... astray'] A line from a lost Greek comedy, quoted by Lucian,
        Lucius or the Ass 18
     31 so far] But cf Ep 663, published by Erasmus in the Auctarium.

from Albert (1490–1545), the younger brother of Joachim I, elector of Brandenburg. He had been archbishop of Magdeburg and administrator of the diocese
of Halberstadt since 1513, and in 1514 was elected archbishop of Mainz. In the
eyes of Erasmus he was an enlightened prelate who had made his court a
centre of humanist learning and had recently become the patron of Hutten (cf
Ep 611:70n). In the spring of 1517, however, the Dominican Johann Tetzel
began to preach on Albert's behalf the famous papal indulgence which called
forth Luther's Ninety-five Theses (31 October 1517). Thereafter Erasmus'
relations with Albert were overshadowed by the Reformation controversies.

ALBERT, ARCHBISHOP OF MAINZ AND OF MAGDEBURG,
PRIMATE OF GERMANY, PRINCE ELECTOR AND
MARGRAVE OF BRANDENBURG, ETC
TO OUR BELOVED DESIDERIUS ERASMUS OF ROTTERDAM,
GREETING IN CHRIST   5
Chancing recently to look into the books you have published, most learned
Erasmus, we marvelled at your superhuman gifts, your universal erudition,
and the powers of expression in which you almost surpass the capacity of
this age and country, and we were taken with a very great desire to see you;
for we thought nothing more in accord with our exalted station, seeing that   10
the goodness of Almighty God has raised us to chief place among the
bishops, than to welcome and encourage the man who not in Germany
alone but through the whole of Europe holds the chief place among men of
letters. If therefore we should happen to depart this life without meeting
you, we should consider ourselves unfortunate, as surely as we number it   15
among our blessings to have been born in an age when so great a man as you
with your learning and your industry are rescuing the Germany we share
from the foul stigma of barbarism; still more, when that divine theology,
which for several centuries now has lost its ancient and true shape and been
distorted into something new and adulterated, is being restored by you to   20
its real splendour and resumes its pristine brilliance. What could be more
desirable in this age of ours than that our texts of the Old Covenant should
be more correct? Now, with you to interpret it, all blemishes are done away,
and all is newly polished. What was more lamentable than our current texts
of the great Jerome, so changed from his true self, so sadly mutilated and cut   25
to pieces? Now, thanks to you, he has returned to the light of day and is as it

* * * * *

661
22 Old] A slip of Albert's pen or an inadvertent admission that he knew Erasmus'
biblical scholarship only from hearsay? Only after the first printed edition was
the text amended to read 'New Testament.'

were raised from the dead. Go forward, beloved Erasmus, glory of Germany! Thus do men scale the sky.

Such being our opinion of you and our feelings towards you, you must not hesitate, if ever you should pass this way, to come and visit us. Happy 30
indeed that day will be, should it ever dawn upon us, when we shall rest our eyes upon your face, devote our ears to your delightful discourse, and quite hang upon your lips! We shall feel ourselves to be no different from those admirers of Livy in the story. May Christ our Saviour grant that we may enjoy in person the society of a man whom we admire at a distance in his 35
books. For thus we hope to see something we have long desired – that some of the Lives of the Saints should be rewritten in better Latin in the style of which you are a master. Farewell, most learned Erasmus; have a care of yourself for our sake, and come and see us.

Farewell once more, from our town of Steinheim on 13 September with 40
our own hand, the year of our Lord 1517.

662 / From Heinrich Stromer   Steinheim, 13 September 1517

This letter answers Ep 631. It accompanied Ep 661.

Greeting. Erasmus, most eloquent and wisest of men, your letter has come, and I have read it and reread it, for it was more welcome than gold and precious gems. Again and again it made me feel your immense kindness, coupled with consummate scholarship; for as your learning and eloquence increase, so does your humility in dealing with a barbarian like me. But to 5
show that I in turn am devoted to you, I have arranged for my most illustrious prince, more truly called your archbishop, to write you a letter in his own hand. I must be brief, overwhelmed as I am with business; but he will invite you at all the greater length himself. Pray believe what he writes, for in his highness there is no differing between tongue and heart. In him, 10
lips and mind are at one. Farewell, O glory of the world and of all men of learning, and keep a kindly thought for one who is so loud in your praises.

In haste, from Steinheim, 13 September in the year of our Lord 1517
Your sincere friend, Heinrich Stromer of Auerbach
* * * * *

28 sky] Virgil *Aeneid* 9.641
34 admirers of Livy] One was said to have travelled all the way from southern Spain to see Livy; see Pliny *Letters* 2.3.8.
37 Saints] See Ep 614:23.
40 Steinheim] On the Main, near Frankfurt, protected by a towering castle

662
7 letter] Ep 661

663 / From Cuthbert Tunstall   Bruges, 14 September [1517]

This letter answers both Epp 607 and 643. It was carefully composed for
publication, and Erasmus duly printed it in the *Auctarium* together with a
suitable answer, Ep 675, in which he rallied to the defence of his opponent,
Lefèvre.

CUTHBERT TUNSTALL TO ERASMUS, GREETING

At long last the king of Spain has set sail for his dominions, and I with my
household am returned from Zeeland barely safe and sound, after such a
severe trouncing from the foul and absolutely pestilential stink of the air in
those parts that many days' fasting has not yet quite driven off the fever that   5
it gave me. Three of my servants, and those the most useful, had fallen ill of
the fever before I left there; and unless on the doctor's advice I had instantly
sent them away for a change of air, I should have buried them all by now.
Even now I would give a lot of money to be sure they are all right. Nor am I
the only sufferer. A great part of the courtiers were sick; thank God the king   10
escaped. Of the councillors in their scarlet, a few at least were attacked; that
island let no one get away unscathed. I think the Styx must be somewhere
handy, the water is so black and so bitter. If you stay at home in the town,
your nostrils are filled with the smoke of your neighbours' peat fires, which
they use in place of wood. These turves are dug from marshy and sour   15
ground, and however long they have been dried in the sun, when burnt
they give off a smoke that goes straight into your vitals and puts chest,
nostrils, head, and everything in peril. I was told by the natives that the
turves in your Holland are cut out of a kinder soil and smell like incense in
comparison. Should you wish to relieve the tedium of the town by taking a   20
walk, a thing I have a habit of doing from time to time, the road itself if
wetted by a drop of rain is stickier than any birdlime and clings to your feet,
for you are forbidden to turn aside into anyone's field or meadow by the
depth of the ditches; and in order to reach eventually the dikes built along
the shore to keep out the sea, which is the only agreeable promenade there   25
is, you are obliged before you get there to cross hundreds of ditches in
which they ret their flax, which stink abominably, far worse than any
cesspool. The smell of an open sewer is nothing to them. On top of that, the

* * * * *

663
2 At long last] On 8 September 1517; cf Ep 596 introduction.
3 Zeeland] The region, especially the island of Walcheren, was infested with
   malaria; cf Epp 640, 716.
12 island] Walcheren, where Middelburg and Flushing are located.

return to the city past the same number of those ditches cancels out all the
refreshment you may have achieved, and sends you home in a fresh fit of   30
the dumps. The whole region is six feet below the level of the sea at high
tide, and unless the dikes prevented it, the monsters of the deep would
break in upon the inhabitants while they are feasting and drinking each
other's health. To escape the ill effects, they say the one and only protection
is to drink by the gallon – a remedy I find worse than any disease, for you   35
know how easily in that kind of contest I throw in the sponge.

But what would I be at, railing like this at an island with such good
harvests and such good harbours, without a word on what could be said in
its praise? I will tell you. Somehow I derive a kind of satisfaction from
getting my own back and voiding against it all the pent-up spleen that   40
tedious country generated. So now I shall suppress its praises to teach it a
lesson. Seriously though, I am thankful to be back at last on solid land where
the air is healthier, and as my shaken state may permit, I shall gradually
crawl back to my own country, leaving my servants here who are still too ill
to travel with me; I pray Almighty God they may one day recover.   45

The *Apologia* you sent containing your reply to Lefèvre has reached
me, together with a letter from you; and a few days before that I had
received another letter in which you indicated that you would reply to him,
but without resentment. In this at least I am glad to see that you have
succeeded; for I had decided to urge you to act like a theologian, that is, a   50
charitable man, in your reply – though he is very far from having done so,
giving judgment in his own case and arrogantly insisting on his own
opinion as though in this question it was not for other men and for posterity
to decide. Not that I have ever thought that on a point of truth or falsehood
you should give way to him, or to any mortal man. The way in which, at the   55
beginning of your *Apologia*, you so modestly invite your crow to give you
back your own plumage, is excellent. I wait with interest to see what excuse
he will put up; but I expect he will brazen it out. I happened to see him in
Italy – a modest man I then thought him, and he was said to have a thorough
knowledge of that cycle of learning which wins its possessors in Paris the   60
honourable title of master. That he had any tincture of Greek I first learnt

* * * * *

35 gallon] Tunstall knew that the abhorrence he professed was shared by Eras-
    mus; cf 643:38n.
36 sponge] *Adagia* I ix 78
47 a letter from you] Ep 643
48 another letter] Ep 607
56 crow] *Adagia* III vi 91
58 brazen it out] *Adagia* I viii 47
59 Italy] No doubt during Lefèvre's second visit to Italy, 1499–1500

HL f

IACOBVS   FABER ,stapulensis.
Barbariem immanem primus, Doctissime FABER,
    Propulsas, artes restituisque bonas.
Te primum celebris vidit lutetia quondam,
    Sed tua te pietas expulit inde procul.

cum priuil.

Jacques Lefèvre d'Etaples
Engraving by Hendrick Hondius the Elder, 1599

from his commentary on the Pauline Epistles. Perhaps he detected by
means of the Greek sources some errors of modern scholars in the field of
Scripture, and thought it worth while to publish his commentary for the
instruction of posterity, to win a reputation as the one-eyed man who sees a   65
little more clearly in the country of the blind. On this point I approve his
intention, were he able to fulfil it; for the prize in this field, as in the sacred
games, is open to any successful competitor. But that he should turn on a
man running in the same race and who looked like leaving him far behind,
and jealously try to trip him up, seems to me far from the conduct of an   70
honest man, let alone of a theologian. In this it may be that he judges the
whole world by the standards of his familiar Paris, where, although he sees
a certain number of capital Greek scholars who are a credit to our generation, he does not see such a supply of men devoted to Greek studies or so
much honour paid to them as might make him hope that ancient standards   75
of Greek scholarship might one day return. And so it might be true that he
was all the more ready to publish, not fearing the judgment of posterity,
whose learning he despaired of. Had he known how those studies are now
flourishing in Italy and Germany and Spain, he might, I think, have taken
Horace's advice and suppressed his book until the ninth year; unless   80
perhaps he has achieved such mastery of both ancient tongues that he is
more ready to challenge criticism than to fear it. Whether he has been thus
successful, let others judge; for I have been unable to see any specimen of
his learning in this field except the Pauline Epistles.

But, after all, anyone can see the reason for this fit of jealousy. By the   85
notes on the New Testament which you have lately published you have not
only opened the Greek sources to this generation of ours; you have gone so
deeply into everything that you have got to the bottom of every commentator worth reading with a completeness that leaves nothing for anyone else
to do. By the brilliance of these studies of yours, like the rising sun that blots   90
out the stars, the other people who hoped for distinction in this field before
you published have been cast into eternal shade. And so he is grieved to see
the modest reputation which he hoped to secure by his book either
snatched from his grasp or cut short. He ought to have realized how lucky
his generation is, in which ancient studies break into new growth, instead   95
of imitating the habit of those who, when they are too weak to keep up the
struggle, are too obstinate to give way. Indeed ambition has much to

* * * * *

62 commentary] Cf Ep 597:37n.
65 one-eyed man] Cf *Adagia* III iv 96.
70 trip] Cf Ep 597:44n.
80 year] Horace *Ars poetica* 388

answer for! He has fallen into a very human failing. Your part, I believe, should be like a true theologian to forgive him. What distresses me is that while you were getting ready your *Apologia* against him, you have   100 sacrificed time when you might have been writing something that would be more use to posterity. And so let the revision and polishing of your notes on the New Testament, which you have promised us and everyone eagerly expects, be a first charge on you. Your great services to pagan literature have won you immortal renown from the light you have thrown on it; devote the   105 rest of your life to the elucidation of Scripture. Thus posterity will know that those studies which lead to salvation meant more to you than those which provide entertainment; for after spending more time on the latter as a young man, by choosing the former in your maturity you showed that you judged them the field in which to grow old.   110

As for the theologians at Louvain, I am delighted to hear they are so fond of you, and if they elect you a member of their order, as you say they will, I advise you not to refuse. Their offer of this distinction and your acceptance of it will form a perpetual pledge of friendship between you.

Your news that Strabo, Pindar, Pausanias, and both Testaments are to   115 be published by Aldus' press in Greek filled me with a joy you would hardly believe. I foresee that in every department of study our posterity will rival the Ancients; and if they have any sense of gratitude, they will have a strong sense of obligation towards those to whose industry the rebirth of these studies is due. Since you will certainly be one of that number, go forward: 120 continue your great services to our successors, who will never allow the name of Erasmus to be forgotten. Farewell.

Bruges, 14 September

Before I sealed this letter I had lost one of my household, whose recovery I would have purchased with all that I possess. God have mercy on   125 his soul. The outcome for the others is still in doubt.

664 / From Thomas Lupset   Paris, 15 September [1517]

This letter of apology follows Lupset's earlier Ep 431, which had apparently not quite succeeded in appeasing Erasmus (cf Ep 690:2). A former student of Erasmus' at Cambridge, Lupset had retained for a time some notebooks in Erasmus' own hand which included a piece on the same topic as the famous

* * * * *

115 Your news] Ep 643:25–30; cf Epp 629, 642. The reference to Pausanias (Venice: Aldus July 1516) was inserted later, when Erasmus prepared this letter for publication.

Julius exclusus now circulating at Cologne (cf Epp 622, 636). However, the notebooks were now safe (lines 31–3; Ep 502), and Erasmus' answer to this letter, Ep 690, is reassuring.

THOMAS LUPSET TO
DESIDERIUS ERASMUS OF ROTTERDAM, GREETING
My letter shall be brief, most respected of teachers, for I am held up by business of various kinds and, to speak somewhat frankly, am uncertain of your feelings towards me. If I thought you would listen to prayers, I would 5
beg you – in any case, I urge you passionately – to get rid now of all your resentment. Whatever I did wrong, put it down to my youth, and forgive it. Please believe, what is the absolute truth, that I must be absolved from blame for letting that pamphlet get out, and that no one alive today is more ready than I to please you. Get out of your head, as the most false of all 10
possible opinions, the suspicion you mentioned that I had estranged many people from you. On this point I call every deity to witness, and may they all forthwith be my undoing if I ever spoke of you in any company, even when you had done me wrong, otherwise than as a grateful pupil should speak of a teacher to whom he is greatly indebted. I approached Master More long 15
ago asking him, since (to speak the truth) I was afraid to write myself, to restore me to your good graces with a letter of recommendation. But as I hear nothing from you, I could easily believe either that he did nothing to urge my suit, or that you are still angry.

Farewell, kindest of masters; and take my word for it that, if you make 20
friends with me, you will not waste your affection, as you say in your letter, on someone who does not want it; but it will be a young man who longs for your good opinion and will love you sincerely in return, which will encourage you to forget my follies. You will please understand that nothing hurts me more than the memory of the way I have behaved up to now. 25

Farewell once again, in haste, from Paris, the morrow of the Exaltation of Holy Cross, from Lombard College; where I shall stay the rest of this month and a few days more, and then fly back to England.

I have finished in these last few days Linacre's book on the preservation of health. I am now concerned with the second edition of More's 30

* * * * *

664
27 Lombard College] Cf Ep 444:43n.
29 Linacre's book] His translation of Galen's *De sanitate tuenda* (Paris: Guillaume Le Rouge 22 August 1517, cf Ep 502). During his studies at Paris Lupset worked as a corrector for several presses.

Utopia, which I hope to finish at the end of this month. Please be so kind as to let me have a note to say whether the papers which on your instructions I left with More have reached you safely.

Your devoted servant and pupil Thomas Lupset

665 / To Antonius Clava   Louvain, 16 September [1517]

Epp 665–9, and perhaps also 675, were dispatched together. The year date is supplied by the references to the *Apologia ad Fabrum* and the movements of Jan of Friesland (cf Ep 616:17n), who now wished to change his master. Erasmus sent him on a trip to Ghent, Bruges, Calais, and England. Everywhere he was to deliver letters which also served to recommend the carrier for employment. Epp 665–9 were the last ones entered into the Deventer Letter-book by hand A (cf Allen 1 604–5). It is therefore likely that hand A is Jan, who copied them before his departure. Epp 665–72 all refer to a head cold that plagued Erasmus; cf Ep 671 introduction.

ERASMUS OF ROTTERDAM TO ANTONIUS CLAVA, GREETING
I have left no stone unturned to keep Friesland here. But fate is against me, and he is off to the nether regions. I too have been sorry, more than once, that I came to Louvain, but I am ashamed of my inconstancy. I sent my *Apologia* by the Dutchman. See whether you can foist him upon those   5
brethren of yours, who are so unlike Jerome. Farewell, kindest of benefactors, you and all yours, and please be sure to give my greetings to de Keysere. I write this half dead with the rheum.

Louvain, eve of St Lambert

* * * * *

31 *Utopia*] Published in Paris by G. de Gourmont, containing G. Budé's letter in praise of *Utopia*, addressed to Lupset and dated 31 July 1517; Erasmus had seen a printed copy by March 1518; cf Ep 785:53.

665
5 Dutchman] Cf Ep 650:10n.
6 brethren] Probably the Brethren of the Common Life (often called Hieronymites), whose house in Ghent was named after St Jerome. Since they had a considerable number of boys to teach and also engaged in the copying of books, they might have had some use for Jan of Friesland. Clearly this reference is to him and not to the Dutchman. Cf R.R. Post *The Modern Devotion* (Leiden 1968) 409–10, 451.
8 Keysere] Cf Ep 650:14.

666 / To [Mark Lauwerijns]   Louvain, 16 September [1517]

The name of the recipient was added correctly in LB. This letter follows Ep 651, carried by the Dutchman (see Ep 650:10n), where the same friends are being greeted.

Greeting, truest of friends. I sent you a letter the other day by the Dutchman. I should not like to enjoy your society if it was inconvenient for you; otherwise, your company would give me great pleasure. I sent you my *Apologia* against Lefèvre by the same messenger. If you cannot come, at least visit me from time to time by letter. I write this nearly dead with the rheum.   5
      Louvain, The College of the Lily, St Lambert's eve
      Take care of your health. Give my cordial greetings to the dean, to Master Ludovicus my host, and to all my other friends. What a barren country this is! Friesland, the bearer of this, a man endowed with as many arts as Mercury himself, has found no position here. So his last hope is   10
Britain; and if Britain had not helped me, I for my own part should still be begging my bread. Farewell once more.

667 / To [John Fisher]   Louvain, 16 September [1517]

This letter follows Ep 653, carried by Pieter Meghen, which was also addressed to Fisher. For the present letter and messenger, Jan of Friesland, cf Ep 665 introduction.

Greeting, right reverend Father. I gave Pieter the One-eyed the second book of Theodore and a letter to take to you. The bearer of this, Jan of Friesland, writes an accurate and legible hand in both Greek and Latin. You were telling me some time ago about a book that you meant to get printed. If this man were to make a copy and compare it with the original, you will retain   5
your own text undamaged. He is making his escape from this very barren

* * * * *

666
8 Ludovicus] Addressed in Ep 790
9 Friesland] See Ep 665 introduction.
667
2 Theodore] Theodorus Gaza: cf Ep 771 introduction.
4 book] Perhaps referring to a projected harmony of the Gospels. In the spring of 1519 Erasmus recalled how impressed he had been with an early draft or summary description of it (see Allen Ep 936:86–8). The project was not realized.

region and seeking more fertile pastures. As I write this, I am sorely afflicted with the rheum and have a touch of fever. Take care of your health, my best of patrons.

Louvain, St Lambert's eve   10

668 / To Johannes Sixtinus   Louvain, 16 September [1517]

This letter was to be delivered by Jan of Friesland; cf Ep 665 introduction.

ERASMUS TO HIS FRIEND SIXTINUS, GREETING

This country is wonderfully barren. Jan of Friesland with all his gifts can find nothing to live on here. I have kept him as best I could for a good many months in hopes that something better would turn up. Now he is trying his sheet-anchor and is off to England. I would have liked him to stay here, if   5
fortune had been kind. Pray help him if you can. I can vouch for his honesty and think well of his scholarship. His manners were somewhat cocksure at first, but ill fortune, I hope, has cured that. I wrote you another letter the other day by Pieter the One-eyed. I spoke with your brother at Antwerp. Pieter Gillis is seriously ill; I am at death's door with the rheum. Farewell.   10
Louvain, St Lambert's eve

669 / To Thomas More   Louvain, 16 September [1517]

More answered this letter with Epp 683 and 688; see also Ep 665 introduction.

I have sent you my true self by one-eyed Pieter, who has gone round by Calais for this purpose. There is no call for you to give him more than ten or a dozen gros for the expenses of his journey; I have taken care of all the rest.

* * * * *

668
5 sheet-anchor] His last chance; *Adagia* I i 24
8 letter] Ep 655, mentioning Sixtinus' brother and delivered by Pieter Meghen; see Ep 653 introduction.

669
1 true self] The Metsys diptych (cf Epp 601:56n, 654). Pieter Meghen had started his journey with some delay (cf Ep 681:12–13), but he found More still at Calais. Erasmus could expect that he would reach there at about the same time as the instructions concerning him given in this letter.
3 dozen gros] The gros or groot was the silver penny of the Burgundian-Hapsburg Low Countries. The English groat, however, was a much larger, more valuable coin, worth 4d sterling (= 5.8d gros Flemish). Always generous, More gave Meghen a noble, probably the angel-noble worth 6s 8d or 8od

How I wish it could be convenient for you to whisk off here! We should both get a new lease of life; for while I was trying to restore Pieter Gillis to health,   5
I myself caught a most accursed rheum, which is such a trouble that it has nearly been the death of me. Atensis approves all my activities without exception. Dorp is on my side in his heart, but is very jealous, not to say mean, where reputation is concerned, and therefore has no praise to spare for anyone else. My dearest More, mind you look after your own health, and   10
mine will recover.

    If you come to Bruges, send for Mark, the dean of St Donatian's, who is my good friend. I have been consulted on the emperor's behalf about questions of some importance. But I will do anything rather than become enmeshed in that kind of business; and how I wish you were at liberty!   15

    Farewell over and over again.

    Louvain, the eve of St Lambert

    I should not like to force this man onto you; but if you need a copyist, he writes accurately and legibly, in both Greek and Latin. Farewell once more.   20

670 / To Jan Briart   [Louvain, c 16 September 1517]

This note is addressed to Jan Briart of Beloeil, near Ath – hence often called Atensis – 1460–1520. A professor of theology since 1506, he was also the university's leading administrator (cf Ep 643:9n). Erasmus' relations with him became increasingly strained until he thought he recognized in Briart his principal opponent at Louvain; cf Epp 930, 946.

    The date of this letter is indicated by a comparison with Ep 669:6, 13–15; its topic, however, is unusual and mysterious. Erasmus is not otherwise known to have been involved in diplomatic negotiations, and his connections with the court of Maximilian I were not significant. In Maximilian's own view the matter of greatest importance for the state at this time would probably have been the appointment of his successor. Although Erasmus avoided saying himself that the matter was of the greatest importance he compared its nature to the duties of Thomas More (cf Ep 669:14–15), who served his king on

* * * * *

sterling (= 116 gros Flemish, or 9s 8d). Cf Ep 683:47n and CWE 1 312, 320–2, 325–6, 336–7, 340–1.
 7 Atensis] See Ep 670 introduction.
 8 Dorp] Cf Ep 696 introduction.
12 Mark] Lauwerijns; cf Ep 651.
14 questions] See Ep 670.
18 this man] Jan of Friesland

embassies and at court (cf Epp 623:23n, 829:6n). Like More, two other humanist friends of Erasmus, Budé and Hutten, attached themselves at just this time to the service of a prince and both were actually to be involved in diplomatic negotiations about the imperial succession (cf Epp 744:2n, 52n, 924). Erasmus considered himself by now a member of the Louvain faculty (cf Ep 637:12n), and the business he was asked to undertake required consultation with the university authorities, but in the first place it must have concerned him personally as he was free to make no reply at all.

No more is heard about this matter in subsequent letters, but a parallel comes to mind when a few years later Gattinara, the chief political adviser of Charles v, approached the University of Louvain on behalf of Erasmus and then prepared to ask him whether he would edit a treatise in support of the emperor's cause as conceived by Gattinara himself (cf Epp 1784A, 1790A). If that approach was actually made, Erasmus seems to have demurred a second time in similar circumstances. Assuming that on this first occasion too he was asked to put his pen in the service of a cause adopted by some of Maximilian's advisers, that cause could conceivably have been the marshalling of support for Johann Reuchlin; cf 694 introduction.

Cordial greeting, dear professor Atensis. A piece of business has been entrusted to me as though by the authority of the emperor, which the man who committed it to me thought was of the greatest importance for the prosperity and safety of the state. I accepted it solely for consideration, on condition that I should none the less be at liberty not to reply. If you ever can   5
find a spare moment, I should be glad to talk it over with you; for this too I have been asked to do. Tell me when you will be at leisure, either today or tomorrow, and I will be there; at the moment I do not leave the house unadvisedly, being in the grip of a rheum. Farewell, most learned professor.   10
Erasmus R.

671 / To [Willem Bollart?]   [Louvain, c 16 September 1517?]

Epp 671–2 and 720 are clearly addressed to the same person. Allen's identification seems plausible in view of another visit to Louvain by Bollart (see Ep 761:43–4). He and Erasmus were old acquaintances, having once been fellow protégés of Hendrik van Bergen. Moreover, Bollart was in the process of acquiring the rich abbey of St Truiden. The date is tentative. The cold from which Erasmus was suffering in Epp 665–70 continued to bother him, if Epp 708 and 720 are to be believed, but the middle of September is suggested by the fact that Epp 671–2 follow Ep 670 in the Deventer Letter-book.

Greeting, very reverend Father. Today, as I was returning home from dinner through the market, on a hint from Desmarez I observed your Reverence passing by; but I did not observe this until you had already passed. This caused me both regret and satisfaction – regret because I had failed to recognize you and pay you due respect; satisfaction at the thought 5 that one who is already so great a prince of the church as yourself was in the town, one with whom I had long ago shared the same roof and the same patron, and for whom I had formed a great attachment through our devotion to the same pursuits. I rejoice with you in your prosperity, and my own position causes me no regrets; I might, had I wished, have been more 10 successful, but this modest station appealed more to my mind. I would have hastened to see you, did not the rheum, the scholar's distemper, confine me to the house. Pray command your old friend Erasmus, and you will find a henchman most ready to do as he is told. Farewell, reverend Father, with the assurance of my devotion. 15

Erasmus, etc

672 / To [Willem Bollart?]   [Louvain, c 16 September 1517]

Greeting. The rheum grows worse; it has entirely taken away my voice and brought on a touch of fever. So I must postpone the pleasure of your Reverence's society until I can enjoy it; for the moment I must do as the state of my health requires. Pray of your kindness forgive what necessity in any case dictates. Farewell. 5

673 / To Antonius of Luxembourg   Louvain, 17 September [1517]

The year date is indicated by the references to the *Apologia ad Fabrum* and More's presence in Calais. Antonius of Luxembourg was steward of the abbey of St Bertin at Saint-Omer and chaplain to the abbot; see Ep 137 introduction.

ERASMUS OF ROTTERDAM TO HIS FRIEND
ANTONIUS OF LUXEMBOURG, GREETING
I hear that the abbot is a little displeased with me, I suppose because certain persons have told him some story of my poking a little fun at monks in my

* * * * *

671
2 Desmarez] See Ep 597:46n.

673
3 abbot] Antoon van Bergen (see Ep 143 introduction). Erasmus resumed his attempts to appease the abbot in Ep 739.

Moria. Yet I cannot believe what I hear; I know the man has too much sense. 5
The subject was in lighter vein, serious comment was not to be expected;
and for all that, nothing in the least offensive was said about monks. That
book gave no offence to the pope, who read it from cover to cover and
approved the author's wit. The prior of the Carthusians has not yet sent
back Reuchlin's letter. If you meet him, please remind him, and give him 10
my greetings. I now have a part in a theological comedy, and it makes
progress of a sort. Certainly the top men are on my side, Atensis and Vianen
and Dorp. But it is not my intention to continue, for the little I get out of it,
producing these performances at my own expense, for fear the theologians
do me some damage. Jacques Lefèvre having provoked me so unpleasantly, 15
I have answered him with some freedom, but this side of abuse; I expect the
book has already reached your part of the world. More, if I mistake not, is
now in Calais on some mission for his king.

Here, one Theodoricus, a bachelor of divinity, is having some kind of
trouble with your abbot. He is a good scholar, amusing and a man of 20
honour. Should any occasion arise for you to forward his business, please
be your kind familiar self. Greet Ghisbert the physician for me, a friend of
long standing, and his wife, although she cannot stand me, at least when I
am on the premises. Give my greetings to kind Gerard and Carolus the
steward. As for you my dear Antonius, take very good care of yourself. 25

Louvain, St Lambert's day

* * * * *

8 pope] Cf Ep 749:16–18.
8 cover to cover] Literally, from head to foot; *Adagia* I ii 37
9 prior] Jean Quonus; the letter is probably the one mentioned in Ep 471:18–25,
   or possibly Ep 562, sent subsequently to the prior.
12 top men] Cf Epp 628:14n, 643:9n, 650:6n.
15 Lefèvre] See Ep 597:37n.
18 Calais] Cf Epp 623:23n, 683:62.
19 Theodoricus] Cf Ep 762 introduction.
22 Ghisbert] He was the town physician of Saint-Omer, who was closely connected with the abbey (see Ep 95:13n). His name was Ghisbert Hessels,
   according to de Vocht *J. de Busleyden* 368.
24 Gerard] Gerard has not been identified. Allen proposed Gérard
   d'Haméricourt (1504–77), a great nephew of Antoon van Bergen, who made
   his profession at St Bertin on 27 May 1519 and was eventually to become abbot
   of St Bertin and bishop of Saint-Omer. However, 'humanissimus dominus
   Gerardus' is hardly the way Erasmus would refer to a boy of thirteen, even if
   Haméricourt's presence at St Bertin at the time could be documented. It would
   rather seem that he was referring to an old friend; cf Ep 792:7.
24 Carolus] Unidentified

674 / From Paschasius Berselius   Liège, 17 September [1517]

The year date must be 1517 because Erasmus is at Louvain and the letter was copied into the Deventer Letter-book by Hand B (cf Ep 647 introduction). This is the earliest preserved letter in the correspondence between Berselius and Erasmus, although it was preceded by one initial exchange of letters, now lost.

Paschasius Berselius, d 1535, probably hailed from Beersel, diocese of Liège. He was a Benedictine at St Laurent's near Liège and enjoyed the confidence of Erard de La Marck. He visited Louvain in the autumn of 1518 and returned in the spring of 1519 to study Greek. On 18 July 1519 he was enrolled in the Collegium Trilingue.

TO ERASMUS FROM BERSELIUS, GREETING

It was impertinent of me, I know, and rash, Erasmus, to have dared to write to you a few days ago. A wretched gnat like me to write to, I will not say a hero, but a deity in the world of letters such as you! It was at least improper for a tiny creature to interrupt with the chatter of its tiny bill a man wholly   5
absorbed in the restoration of sacred literature, and to try to achieve the acquaintance of one for whom so many saintly bishops, eminent monarchs, and brilliant men of letters have not merely approval but respect, venera-tion, and worship. I confess my fault, I know that it has earned me a reproof; but I would beg you to impute it to affection, for Love is blind, and blinds   10
the eyes of lovers. I supposed that errors committed under his influence would be judged by you less severely; and my hopes did not deceive me. Instead of the punishment I feared – a stony silence – you have with your usual generosity given me a richer recompense. For I have received – what I had never thought would happen – your elegant letter, full of friendliness   15
and charm, which arrived on 14 September. What a day for me to mark with a white stone, a more-than-happy day for which I had prayed a thousand prayers! Never did any day dawn more welcome in my whole life than that, no sun shone brighter, no dayspring was more delightful. This day alone knows the full story of the joy that I have taken in your writings. I was   20
beside myself when I had used the knife which you had drawn so skilfully at

* * * * *

674
17 stone] *Adagia* I v 54
21 knife] Perhaps to indicate where the letter should be opened as it was not sealed in the normal fashion. Perhaps the letter was on a small piece of paper, folded only once and glued on the inside, so that the seal could not be affixed over the edge.

the top of the sheet. It ravished my heart, my bowels turned to water, my
mind failed. Never have I felt so sweetly the bewitching magic of affection.
God grant I may have this experience often. I keep your letter carefully, and I
shall regard it as a kind of perpetual pledge of your feelings for me.   25

Our bishop left for France a few days ago, and the date of his return is
uncertain. As soon as he is back in this city or in his own country, I shall be
ready and will take pains to put through the business you told me to open
with him, with all proper activity and vigour.

The young man who brought you this letter from me is a most agree-   30
able and civilized person. He stayed with me for almost a month continuously, during which time he gave me regular lessons in Hebrew; for I had
learnt Greek as well from that all-round scholar Aleandro, shortly before he
left here for Italy. You see, my dear teacher, the efforts I am making. I fear
that while I try to sit on two stools, I may fall between them. But I shall not   35
desist from putting all my strength into it, and maybe unflinching toil will
win the day. I commend my Hebrew teacher to you. He goes to Louvain in
hopes of seeing you, but will soon return to us, bringing, I hope, a letter
from you. For I still long for something I expressed a wish for in my earlier
letter, and which you generously promised in yours; that is, the titles of all   40
the books you have published and those you have on the anvil. If you will
let me have them, you could do nothing I should appreciate more.

Give my greetings to your friends Dorp and Desmarez, for I love them
both passionately, though as yet I know neither of them even by sight.
There is nothing at Louvain in the literary way more perfect than those great   45

*　*　*　*　*

22 ravished my heart] Song of Solomon 4.9
26 bishop] Erard de La Marck (see Ep 738 introduction), who still held the French
see of Chartres (cf Ep 735:6) in addition to the ecclesiastical principality of
Liège. He had several residences in the latter, and his powers were not
restricted, as they were in the city of Liège, by civic government.
30 young man] Two identifications have been suggested: Johannes Cellarius (see
Ep 877) or Robert Wakefield, who came to Louvain in 1518 and held the chair of
Hebrew at the Collegium Trilingue for a short period beginning on 1 August
1519; see Ep 1311 and de Vocht CTL I 379–81.
33 Aleandro] Girolamo Aleandro (cf Ep 256 introduction), Erasmus' close companion at Venice, had been in the service of Erard de La Marck since December
1514. In June 1516 he was sent to Rome to support his master's bid for a
cardinal's hat. His diary bears witness to his friendship with Berselius; cf de
Vocht CTL I 496.
35 two stools] Adagia I vii 29
36 unflinching toil … day] Virgil Georgics I 145, 146
40 titles] For similar requests by others see Ep 492 introduction.

men. Farewell, O glory of scholarship and scholars, and return if you can the affection of your humble son Berselius, who you will find yields to no one in his affection for you.

From my cell in Liège, 17 September

675 / To Cuthbert Tunstall   Louvain [c 17 September] 1517

This answer to Ep 663 was published in the *Auctarium*. Perhaps it was sent together with Ep 666, also destined for Bruges.

ERASMUS OF ROTTERDAM TO THE
HONOURABLE CUTHBERT TUNSTALL, AMBASSADOR OF
HIS MOST SERENE HIGHNESS THE KING OF ENGLAND
TO HIS CATHOLIC MAJESTY, GREETING

Our poor Zeeland owes you a great debt for the honour of such a lively 5
description; but you owe her something in return for having sent you back
half-alive, at any rate. I was sorry to hear of the sickness in your household;
for yourself, I do beg you to mind your health until you are safely back in
England, for fear that while everything else is going as you would wish, that
one thing should not go quite right which matters more than anything else. 10

What you say about my *Apologia* against Lefèvre, although I know it
was written with the most friendly feelings, yet caused me discomfort on
two counts: it revived my old distress, and also I think that on this occasion
you are less than fair to Lefèvre, who is as upright and civilized a man as you
could hardly find in a thousand. The only point in which he was unlike 15
himself was in this savage attack on a friend who did not deserve it. But
what man was ever wise all the time? I only wish it had been possible for me
to spare my adversary. As it is, I am tormented in two different ways: first, I
was obliged to join battle with a friend like him, and now I find some people
prejudiced against Lefèvre, a man of whom I should prefer everyone to have 20
the highest opinion. Besides which, you credit me with qualities to which I
can lay no claim; but this is very kind and very like you, and not my only
experience of your generosity.

I find the theologians in Louvain fair-minded and friendly, and
among them especially Johannes Atensis, chancellor of the university, a 25
man gifted with incomparable learning and exceptionally civilized. The

* * * * *

675
17 wise all the time] *Adagia* II iv 29
25 chancellor] Cf Ep 643:9n.

antiquis, quæ fit via bona, & ambulate in ea, &

State super vias, & audite, & videte, & interrogate de semitis

Invenietis refrigerium animabus vestris. Hieremias 6

·ALARDVS AMSTELREDAMVS

1523.

Apud facrofanctum, religiofumcp Amftelre-
damum, nobile totius Hollandie empo
rium, ad Chriftianæ pietatis & dec⁹,
& augmentū DODO Petrus
Typographus ad caftrum
angelicum pridie pa-
rafceues Chriftianę
excudebat Anno
1523.

Alaard of Amsterdam
Woodcut by Jacob Cornelisz. van Oostsanen, 1523
Rijksmuseum, Amsterdam

standard of scholarship in divinity here is no lower than in Paris, but there is less logic-chopping and less arrogance. Farewell.

Louvain, 1517

676 / To Alaard of Amsterdam   Louvain, [1517]

This is the preface to 'Erudita ... epistola ... Eucherii episcopi Lugdunensis ad Valerianum,' edited and annotated by Erasmus, published together with other material in an edition of Cato *Disticha moralia* (Louvain: Martens 1517; NK 535). The volume opens with a preface signed by Martens and dated 1517, which refers to the death of Jérôme de Busleyden and the foundation of the Collegium Trilingue in much the same terms as Epp 658, 686, 689–90. Allen therefore suggested that the preface in question might have been written for Martens by Erasmus (as Ep 602 was for Froben) and placed the composition of Epp 676–9 at about September or October.

In 432 Eucherius, bishop of Lyon, wrote a letter to his cousin Valerianus, urging him to abandon the pursuit of worldly honour. This is the text which Alaard had sent Erasmus. If it was a printed book, it may have been a copy of *Epistola Valerii episcopi ad propinquum suum ex Greco in Latinum sermonem per magistrum Rodolphum Agricolam traducta* (J. de Breda [Deventer c 1485] British Library). Erasmus identified the letter as that of Eucherius to Valerianus (rather than vice-versa) and also recognized that it was a Latin original rather than a translation from the Greek. He used Alaard's text to prepare his own edition and together with it this preface.

Alaard of Amsterdam (cf Ep 433) had settled at Louvain and earned his livelihood as a private tutor. He had a life-long interest in Rodolphus Agricola, whose collected works he published in 1539.

ERASMUS OF ROTTERDAM TO ALAARD OF AMSTERDAM,
LEARNED TEACHER OF THE LIBERAL ARTS, GREETING
The work you sent me, with its many merits, gave me remarkable pleasure on general grounds, but all the more so because I remember how I read it and enjoyed it as a boy. If you think my opinion of any value, I know no 5 production by any of those Christian authors who have also earned a reputation for eloquence, which can be compared with it in point of style. Everywhere the author shows himself the master-craftsman, in the arrangement, in the continual novelty of the transitions, in the unusual introduction or, so to say, entrance into the subject. No department of the 10 persuasive style is beyond him; he never relapses into the commonplace, but is more ready to press us close with argument, arouse us with direct appeals, satisfy and stimulate us equally by general reflections. What is still

more admirable, although his style is given its variety and structure and
colouring by the Isocratean figures of speech, yet it never becomes artificial   15
or trivial; it has clarity without loss of force, elaboration without obscurity,
novelty without tedious affectation, brilliance with no loss of weight or
power, technical finish and yet a genuinely Christian spirit, urgency and
emphasis and yet consistency all through; it speeds with unvarying energy
right to its target, which is proof of a sound and lively intelligence in the   20
writer. Gennadius, in saying that he had a 'scholastic' style, felt, I suppose,
the lack of more recondite learning. In any case, that the book could not be a
translation made by Rodolphus Agricola is clear enough from the style,
especially since it makes use of several forms of expression which could not
possibly reproduce a Greek original. Gennadius gives the author's name as   25
Eucherius, bishop of Lyon, and proceeds to mention the letter which he
wrote to his kinsman Valerian, how to despise the world and abandon the
study of secular philosophy. I only wish his other works still survived, the
book in which he explained one by one the most obscure chapters of Holy
Scripture, or that in which he summarized the voluminous works of Cas-   30
sian.

     But why deplore the loss of two or three works? I can scarcely refrain
from tears as I read the lists of ancient authors and see what wealth we have
lost. My grief increases when I compare the quality of our losses with what
we now commonly read. And so I cannot but welcome, my dear Alaard, the   35
zeal which you display in bringing into the daylight the works of the
Ancients, especially such as combine true piety with true learning and
eloquence. I only wish that one engaged on so admirable an enterprise may
be encouraged by the favour of the great; though I hear that that venerable
figure, your kinsman Meynard Man, abbot of Egmond, reproduces in this   40
as in all other respects the example of the great prelates of the past. And here

* * * * *

676
15 Isocratean] Cf Ep 677 introduction.
21 Gennadius] A priest of Marseille (fl 490) who had written a continuation of
   Jerome's *Catalogus* of Christian writers. It is normally appended to Jerome's
   work, as it is in Erasmus' own edition of Jerome (Basel: Froben 1516; II 156–62,
   esp 160 verso). Gennadius' chap 63 (or 64) deals with Eucherius. Erasmus'
   knowledge of other works by Eucherius was also gained from Gennadius. The
   epitome of Cassian is in PL 50:867–94.
23 Agricola] Cf Ep 606:19n.
30 Cassian] Johannes Cassianus (c 360–435) founded monasteries in Marseille
   about 415. He had come from the East, and his writings reflect the tradition of
   the desert fathers.
40 Man] See Ep 304:178n.

too is a special debt owed you by France, that she can now add this new glory to her Hilary, her Ausonius, her Paulinus; for the author himself makes it sufficiently clear that he is Paulinus' fellow-countryman. Farewell, and go bravely on as you are going.   45
  Louvain

677 / To the Reader   [Louvain, 1517]

This is a preface to an exhortation ('Paraenesis') by the celebrated Athenian orator Isocrates, also included in the Martens collection of 1517 headed by Cato's *Disticha* (cf Ep 676 introduction). Rodolphus Agricola's translation of this speech was already in print, and so were editions of the Greek text. Despite the correction mentioned in the last line, the text (*Paraenesis ad Demonicum* 49) is not emended in Martens' edition of 1517, nor is there any trace of Erasmus' note concerning the spurious sentence.

ERASMUS TO THE READER
I have collated this treatise afresh with the Greek copies and have found one sentence missing, which in any case I already suspected might be spurious. It has, however, been inserted, with a note, for fear anyone might suppose it omitted by accident, since it appears in current texts. Further, in another   5
passage Rodolphus seems to have read ψυχῆς where the printed Greek copies have τύχης.

678 / To the Reader   [Louvain, 1517]

This is a preface to the *Mimi Publiani*. Erasmus had edited this short collection of precepts taken from Publilius Syrus, together with the precepts of Cato, for Martens in 1514 (NK 534; cf Ep 298), but was now adding this preface in the edition of 1517; see Ep 676 introduction.

ERASMUS OF ROTTERDAM TO THE READER, GREETING
On these pieces I have found brief commentaries, very badly corrupted and far more outlandish than anything on the *Cato*, such that they serve no purpose, either on sea or land, and yet they are most carefully transcribed as

* * * * *

43 Ausonius] Decius Magnus Ausonius, of Bordeaux, c 310–93, the distinguished Latin poet
43 Paulinus] Bishop of Nola, b near Bordeaux 353–4, was a pupil of Ausonius. He is mentioned in Eucherius' *Epistola ad Valerianum* (PL 50:718–19) as a special glory of 'our' France.

though they were something sacred. What a hapless generation that was! 5
Most are iambic senarii, but not eschewing the freedom of Latin comedy.
Should anything different occur, we will provide a note. For the rest,
anyone who wishes to know how monstrous were the errors from which we
have rescued these Mimes may compare them with the text of the copies
that were in common use prior to my edition. Reader, farewell, with my 10
best wishes.

679 / To the Reader [Louvain, 1517]

This is a new preface to the *Institutum hominis christiani*, a short collection of
precepts in Latin verse adapted by Erasmus from an English text by Colet (cf
Ep 298 introduction and Reedijk poem 94). The text reappeared in Martens'
collection of 1517; see Ep 676 introduction.

ERASMUS OF ROTTERDAM TO THE READER, GREETING
Do not forget, gentle reader, that what you have read thus far is the precepts
of the heathen, and so must be read critically. What you will now read is
the sacred words of Christ himself and his Holy Church, which can be
followed in safety, and indeed are the only road to blessedness. Read them 5
therefore as things of great moment, and so farewell.

680 / From Johannes Caesarius Cologne, 22 September [1517]

This letter presents Caesarius' reaction to Erasmus' *Apologia ad Fabrum* (see Ep
597:37n). Some points he raises were made by Erasmus himself in the *Apologia
ad Fabrum* (cf LB IX 58E–F), but more directly in letters such as Ep 652. A similar
letter may have reached Caesarius and other friends in Cologne together with
a copy of the *Apologia*.

JOHANNES CAESARIUS TO ERASMUS, GREETING
I have seen in these last few days a defence against Lefèvre d'Etaples
published over your name – seen it and read it. You cannot think how sorry
I am for you both, not that I am not well aware that this kind of disagreement
between eminent scholars has always existed and that even the most saintly 5
of men have not refrained from it, but because in present circumstances it
seems highly unadvisable. As soon as the barbarians who wage a murder-

* * * * *

680
5 the most saintly of men] He is no doubt thinking of Jerome and Augustine.

ous campaign against you discover that learned men, and such great men as you are in standing and well-founded reputation, are fighting among your-selves, there is no doubt that they will have high hopes of victory over you. Undoubtedly they will be disappointed; their expectation is as vain as it is frivolous. My dear Erasmus, I cannot criticize your principles in this re-spect; but as I read, I was at the same moment full of admiration for the clearness of your mind and full of wonder at what could have moved that worthy, indeed that excellent, man to take in hand a controversy, if con-troversy he must have, against you first of all, whom he knew to be, if not a better man than himself, at least his equal. To declare war on a better man is rash, and even against an equal it is fraught with peril. I know him for a modest man, fair-minded and sympathetic to everyone who is learned and virtuous, since I was for some years his pupil, and I know what sharp and telling attacks he used to make on sophistical philosophers above all, and how at the same time he praised every good scholar and honoured him as he deserved. And so it can only be (and you too express the same feeling) that he is instigated by some evil spirit; and I only wish he had withstood it and chosen rather to encourage your goodwill towards him, that this might increase rather than diminish his reputation.

But enough of that. Our friend Neuenahr has lately had a pamphlet printed that was brought from Rome called *Reuchlin Defended*, a thousand copies and more, two of which are now on their way to you. Besides this I have in hand a Dialectic of sorts, which I collected last summer from good authorities everywhere. I wish you might read it through and polish it up a little. In any case, if you are well, please write back and tell me so by the first courier. Very best wishes.

Cologne, 22 September

* * * * *

20 his pupil] Until 1498, when he received his MA from Paris
28 *Reuchlin Defended*] Giorgio Benigno Salviati (Juraj Dragišić), archbishop of Nazareth, *Defensio praestantissimi viri Ioannis Reuchlin* ([Cologne?] 1517). The work, in form of a dialogue, was composed in 1515. A manuscript had recently been brought from Rome by Martin Gröning (cf Ep 615:5) and personally presented to the emperor Maximilian at Cologne. Erasmus had read the book by 3 November (cf Ep 700:13). Later he also read a rejoinder to it by the Dominican J. van Hoogstraten (*Apologia*, Cologne February 1518) and wrote about it to the author with disapproval (see Ep 1006), but he also deplored that Neuenahr, in turn, felt bound to attack Hoogstraten (cf Ep 808:6–14) and that his own name was being used in the continuing battle (cf Epp 694 introduc-tion, 821:19n). See RE Epp 201, 244, 254–5; Geiger *Reuchlin* 400–4.
30 Dialectic] To be published, together with an *Epistola ad Hermannum comitem Nuenarium* ([Cologne:] E. Cervicornus [1520?])

680A / From Symphorien Champier   [Lyon? September 1517]

The Latin text of this letter is among the preliminary pieces of Allen VI. It was published by Champier in his collection of writings and letters beginning with *Duellum epistolare* ([Lyon] J. Phiroben and J. Divineur for J. F. Deionta 10 October 1519) f g⁵ recto–g⁷ recto.

Symphorien Champier (1472?–1540?) was a physician, polymath, and great admirer of Lefèvre. This letter presents his reaction to Erasmus' *Apologia ad Fabrum* (see Ep 597:37n). To date it more precisely, Allen used another letter in the same collection (f h¹), from Lefèvre, dated 6 October. Lefèvre states that he had received a similar letter from Champier, and that he felt no animosity against Erasmus and would not reply to either Erasmus' or Champier's arguments. There is no evidence that the original of this letter was sent to Erasmus or that he was aware of its existence.

TO ERASMUS, COMPLETEST OF SCHOLARS
IN EVERY DEPARTMENT OF KNOWLEDGE,
FROM SYMPHORIEN CHAMPIER, PHYSICIAN, GREETING

You will perhaps wonder, most learned Erasmus, what should move me to write to you now, who have not hitherto been wont to do so. It has always 5 been my great delight – nor is this less true even now – to turn with nightly and with daily hand your most correct and accomplished works, and often and diligently have I asked our booksellers whether they had any fresh products of your workshop or anything to which you had added either a commentary or at least some touch of brilliance and distinction, for a book 10 has enough and more than enough weight with me, if on its appearance it is distinguished by your name in any capacity. And so while I your footprints trace in this way, I have come across a certain *Apologia* addressed to Jacques, or more truly directed against Jacques Lefèvre d'Etaples, a man who in my opinion has rendered very great services to learning. Since this was your 15 work, I much admired it; but I was grieved and distressed to see two of the leading lights not merely of France but of the whole world, two principal figures in the realm of literature, on a small matter, a question of almost no importance, admitting of a reasonable solution in either sense, fighting so fiercely, so pedantically, and so bitterly, vomiting floods of abuse, spewing 20 out deadly venom, whetting their pens like weapons to draw blood, and menacing like that with ready tusk. Take those *Apologiae* of yours – I mean

* * * * *

680A
7 daily hand] Horace *Ars poetica* 269
12 your footprints trace] Virgil *Eclogues* 2.12

both his and yours, for I have read them and reread them both with a very
sad heart: the more polish, the more subtlety, the more brilliance the
writing displays, the more clearly and inescapably they declare the spite,   25
the passion, and the fury which prompted them. The result is that, while
each of you strives to prove the other wrong, he exposes the sickness, the
black venom in his own mind, and those who ought to give each other
mutual aid and comfort to the advantage of the public impede and damage
one another. Such, remember, is the cunning of that fell arch-enemy of   30
mankind, that with his falsehoods he can raise the smallest spark into a
conflagration, and can use offensive and unbridled language on the part of
eminent men as a means of blackening their reputations. And why? Of
course, that he may erode or utterly root out that charity without which we
are not human beings and without which we have no hope of pleasing God.   35
    Lefèvre in verse six of the eighth Psalm wishes to read with Jerome
'Thou madest him a little lower than God.' You prefer to read 'than the
angels.' Both of them in my opinion can quite correctly be both written and
read; for it is quite clear that if it be understood of any man whatsoever, as
most commentators of that eighth Psalm seem to think, we should read   40
'than the angels.' For man in the order of creatures occupies the tenth place,
being a combination of corporeal and incorporeal, of corruptible substance
and incorruptible, intermediate between the two natures, and a sort of
horizon between light and darkness. Some people give the sense 'than
gods' instead of 'than the angels,' as your friend Reuchlin does in the third   45
book of his *De arte cabalistica*, citing the Hebrew verse, in which beyond
doubt it is far from unsuitable, for we often find God in Scripture taken to
mean angel, as in chapter 32 of Genesis, where the angel addressing Jacob
says 'Thy name shall be called no more Jacob, but Israel; for if thou didst
stand firm against God, how much more shalt thou prevail against men?' –   50
God meaning (so the commentators tell us) the angel who wrestled with
Jacob. If, however, with Paul in the Epistle to the Hebrews we wish it to be
understood of Christ, we are referring either to Christ's whole being as
composite or (as they call it) subordinate, or to the man in him by itself, or to
the humanity or human nature that he assumed. For the subordinate being,   55
Christ himself, that is, we nowhere read to be lower than the angels; for he

* * * * *

36 verse six] Cf Ep 778:203n.
46 *De arte cabalistica*] Haguenau: Thomas Anshelm, March 1517; perhaps a gar-
    bled reference to f 56 recto. At any rate, Reuchlin realized that *elohim* could
    mean both 'God' and 'angel'; cf ff 66 recto, 67 recto, 70 verso.
48 Genesis] 32:28
52 Hebrews] 2:6–7

is the head of the angels and lord of all. For he himself said 'The Father is greater than I,' never 'An angel is greater than I.' And in the Creed of Anastasius we sing 'Equal to the Father, as touching his godhead: and inferior to the Father, as touching his manhood.' Never does it say 'less than   60 the angels,' even as touching his manhood; although his manhood in itself is actually less than the angels.

We therefore consider his humanity only and, as Jacobus a Valentia remarks, whose commentary on the prophet is not without merit, 'Thou madest him a little lower than the angels, by making him the son of man,   65 and able to die and to suffer on behalf of man. In the Hebrew it runs "What is man that thou art mindful of him, or the son of Adam that thou visitest him?" Whence Christ always calls himself the son of man, that is, son of Adam, because from Adam he received flesh, that he might redeem Adam and his descendants.' In any case, as Hugo of St Victor opines on Paul's   70 Epistle to the Hebrews, 'we must not say absolutely that he is less than the angels. But here "He was made a little lower" must be understood in this way: he was made lower in some respects, that is, in respect of the weakness of the flesh and his death and passion, as authority maintains. Nor does it follow that, if he is lower in some respects, he is therefore lower absolutely.'   75 Thus far Hugo.

It might equally well and without incongruity be understood thus: 'Thou madest him lower a little less than the angels,' as though he meant that the very Word of the Father, the very Son of God, equal in all things to the Father, on account of his assumed nature or with his assumed nature, as   80 being the one subordinate being made up of both natures, divine and human, who is called Christ, had been made indeed lower than God, but not so low as an angel; rather, a little lower in the direction of the angels, or better, a little less low than the angels. And perhaps the Greek text gives more support to this opinion, since he himself is lord of both   85

* * * * *

57 said] John 14:28
59 we sing] The words are in the Athanasian Creed, of uncertain authorship, which was sometimes attributed to Pope Anastasius I (399–401).
63 Jacobus] Jaime Pérez (c 1408–90) of Ayora in the territory of Valencia, an Augustinian friar and bishop of Christopolis in Thrace. His commentary on the Psalms was first printed in Valencia in 1484. For the passage quoted see *D. Jacobi Parez de Valentia ... expositiones* (Paris: J. Bade and J. Petit 15 February 1518) f 37 recto (Ps 8:6).
70 Hugo] *Quaestiones in epistolas Pauli* Heb, Quaestio 24 (PL 175:615).
84 Greek text] The quotation is missing in the printed edition, although space is left for it. The two churches are the one on earth and the one in heaven.

churches, intermediate between God and angel, as man is between angel
and those things that are below him.

Since therefore both interpretations can be maintained, and the word
elohim which is found in the manuscripts can be understood both as singular and as plural,   90

Betwixt you both 'tis wrong such strife should rise;
Your praise is earned – let him too have his prize.
Continue therefore both of you, I beg, as you have done to such good effect
already, to advance the cause of learning; and where either falls short, let
the other in a kindly and peaceable spirit supply what is lacking. We cannot 95
all do all things, and what you do not know, veteran though you are, may
possibly be known to a recruit.

Farewell, Erasmus most learned of men, and for your most affectionate
Symphorien spare a little affection in return.

681 / From Pieter Gillis   Antwerp, 27 September 1517

Some points raised in this letter remain obscure, as the letter to which it is a
reply is now lost. It was published in LB, probably from a missing leaf of the
Deventer Letter-book.

TO ERASMUS FROM PIETER GILLIS, GREETING
Cordatus gave me your delightful letter, which did me all the good in the
world. If you are rather late in getting the cloth and the counterpane, the
trouble was that in the mean time no reliable courier presented himself.
When you remind me about those young people, I have not forgotten their   5
sainted parents. About the physician I will do as you tell me; but I cannot
rest till I have tweaked his ear. I am specially sorry that Tunstall has been
sick. As soon as I feel myself a little stronger, I will run over and see you. I

* * * * *

91 Betwixt you] Cf Virgil *Eclogues* 3.108.
92 Your praise] Cf Virgil *Aeneid* 1.461.
92 him too] Reading *huic*
95 We cannot] Virgil *Eclogues* 8.63

681
2 Cordatus] Hadrianus Cordatus, of Wissekerke, d 1538/9 as a canon of Middelburg
6 physician] Afinius; see Epp 637–8.
7 tweaked his ear] *Adagia* I vii 40
7 Tunstall] For his illness see Ep 663; for that of Gillis see Ep 597:23n.

rather agree with what you say about Clavus; but I now begin somehow to
get my strength back. I can thank you in words, my dear Erasmus, but I   10
wish I could make you a proper return, for so generously promising me your
help. The One-eyed has made a prosperous start for England with our
pictures; if More is at Calais, he already has us to look at. Mind you take
special care of your health, dear Erasmus.

Antwerp, 27 September 1517   15

682 / To Gerard Geldenhouwer   Louvain, 5 October [1517]

This letter is answered by Ep 727. Its date is confirmed by the vicissitudes of
the *Querela pacis* (see Ep 603 introduction). It is probable that Ep 603 had not
been sent to Philip of Burgundy previously but reached him for the first time
in the hand-written presentation copy of the *Querela* sent with this letter. It
arrived at an awkward moment, and without having had time to read anything, Philip sent a short reply by the hand of Geldenhouwer (cf Ep 727:3–6),
which by way of a reward promised an invitation for the near future; it
reached Erasmus before 2 November (cf Ep 695:28–30) but is now lost. Erasmus replied about 16 November, but the letter is also lost. In the postscript
he endeavoured to delay the promised invitation, at any rate until the spring
(cf Ep 727:15n). To this letter the bishop replied with Ep 728, referring both to
Ep 603 and to Erasmus' recent letter with the postscript.

ERASMUS TO HIS FRIEND NIJMEGEN, GREETING
That a prince of such distinction should be well disposed towards me gives
me great joy, for this reason among others that it is a pleasure to know that
one who has my heartfelt affection and particular respect feels some affection in return. I am now devoted entirely to the New Testament, which has   5
almost deprived me of my eyesight and my vital force. I hope therefore that
his lordship will not summon me for several months, until this task is
finished. I enclose my *Querela pacis* copied on parchment, a worthless gift if
valued by the worth of him to whom it is offered, but I know his kindness
and rely on your recommendation. Farewell, most learned, most kind-   10
hearted Gerard.

Louvain, in haste, 5 October

* * * * *

9 Clavus] Cf Ep 650:14n.
12 One-eyed] Pieter Meghen; for his orders and the delivery of the diptych see
   Epp 653 and 654 introductions, 683–4.

683 / From Thomas More   Calais, 7 October [1517]

Epp 683–4 were sent together (see Ep 684:8) and express More's joy on receiving the Metsys diptych (see Ep 654 introduction). This letter answers Ep 669.

THOMAS MORE TO DESIDERIUS ERASMUS, GREETING

At last, dearest Erasmus, one-eyed Pieter has brought the portraits of you and our dear Gillis for which I have waited so long, and how delighted I am with them is easier for anyone to gauge from his own feelings than for me to put in words. Here are men whose faces merely sketched in chalk or 5 charcoal might charm anyone who was not wholly dead to all feeling for scholarship and goodness, while I in particular might well be deeply moved by the memory of such dear friends however inadequately recorded; and who can either expound in words or fail to feel in his imagination how I must now be ravished by their pictures, drawn and rendered with such skill 10 that they could easily challenge all the painters of Antiquity? The spectator well might suppose them cast or carved rather than painted, so much do they seem to stand out and project with the proper relief of a man's body. You would hardly believe, my most lovable Erasmus, how my affection for you, which I was convinced would admit of no addition, has been increased 15 by this desire of yours to bind me still closer to you, and how forcibly I exult in the glory of being so highly valued by you; for in this remarkable document you put it on record that there is no one else whose affection you rate so highly. For such is my own interpretation at any rate – conceited it may be, but thus it is: you have sent me this present to remind me of you not 20 merely every day but every hour. You know me well: I am sure I need not expend great efforts in proving to you that, although not free from failings in many other ways, at least I am no Thraso; I am entirely free from vainglory. And yet, to tell the truth, this is the one itch in the way of ambition which I find it impossible to shake off, and which tickles me in a 25 most agreeable manner, when it comes into my head that distant posterity will remember me for my friendship with Erasmus, attested in letters and books and pictures and every other way. If only I had some gift that might make it possible to produce something really distinguished, to prove my-self not unworthy of such warm affection from a man without peer not only 30

* * * * *

683
14 lovable Erasmus] More plays on the name Erasmus and the Greek *erasmios*, 'charming.'
23 Thraso] The soldier in Terence's *Eunuchus*, proverbial for his self-assurance

in his own generation but in future ages! But since it lies so far above my
meagre capacity to do anything that could make the world understand this,
I will at least do all I can to prove myself, on your evidence alone, at any rate
not ungrateful.

I have read your *Apologia* right through with close attention, and its   35
effect on me at least was this: never did I perceive your eloquence more
clearly or admire it less. What ruled out admiration was the feeling that in
such a simple case anyone might shine, not only you who can make the
most difficult case look simple. Really I am quite sorry for the man, who has
been led on by the applause of his local audience and encouraged to choose   40
for the display of his powers to hold forth on the most chaotic problem that
ever was, for the evidence favours now one side and now the other. I hope
that your warning will make him see the light. I admired it all very much,
but especially the witty way in which you rebuke his conceit, in suggesting
that his second edition was prior to your annotations, although it con-   45
troverts notes which we are asked to believe did not yet exist.

I sent your secretary on to England with ten gros for his journey-
money; to Pieter I gave a noble, which was very little indeed for the man
who brought me that picture, but he seemed content. I hope for a prosperous and happy outcome to the book on the education of a prince which you   50
have sent to our prince as a present. Busleyden's death, heaven knows, was
a heavy blow; he was a scholar above the average, a good friend of mine,
and fair and friendly to everybody. As for me, I have to sit here till the

* * * * *

33 all I can] See Ep 684.
35 *Apologia*] Against Lefèvre d'Etaples; see Ep 597:37n.
37 in such a simple case] Ovid *Tristia* 3.11.21
44 witty way] When noticing the incongruence of dates (cf Ep 597:44n) in the
   Apologia, Erasmus suggested that it was probably caused by a simple misprint
   in the date of Lefèvre's book, but he added that the frequent sins of the
   printers offered a convenient cover-up for the shortcomings of the authors; see
   LB IX 20D–E.
47 secretary] Jan of Friesland; see Ep 665 introduction. Both Flemish and English
   coins were current at Calais, England's continental wool staple; but Flemish
   coins were not current in England itself. The silver gros or groats were thus
   probably English coins; cf Ep 669:3n.
48 Pieter] Meghen; see Ep 669:1n.
50 book] A presentation copy of the *Institutio principis christiani* sent to Henry
   VIII; see Epp 653, 657 introductions.
52 friend of mine] More had met Busleyden during his embassy to the Netherlands in 1515. In three of his *Epigrammata* he recalled the refined and hospitable atmosphere of Busleyden's house at Mechelen. For his death see Ep 608
   introduction.

beginning of November so continuously that I with difficulty secured two
days for a trip to Saint-Omer, especially in hopes of seeing the abbot of St   55
Bertin at any rate, whom you described to me long ago. I found him just
what you said; he asked me to dinner and gave me a generous welcome. He
receives all his visitors at some length, and with me he was positively
effusive; but he is a delightful old man and grew young again when he
thought of you. Farewell, dearest Erasmus.   60

Tunstall is back in England. Farewell once more.

From Calais, 7 October

684 / From Thomas More to Pieter Gillis   [Calais] 6–7 October [1517]

In the Deventer Letter-book the date is emended from 'vii octobris' to 'vi
octobris.' Allen preferred the original date since line 8 seems to indicate that
this letter was written immediately after Ep 683. This was, at any rate, the
sequence of More's first drafts. Erasmus published this letter in the *Auctarium*.
It provides impressive evidence of the great importance the artistic taste of the
time attached to accuracy of detail.

THOMAS MORE TO HIS FRIEND
PIETER GILLIS, GREETING
My dearest Pieter, greeting! I want passionately to hear whether you are
getting strong again, which matters no less to me than any of my own
concerns; and so I make careful enquiries and diligently pick up all I can   5
from everybody. A certain number of people have given me a more cheerful
account, either (as I hope) because they know it for a fact, or just to give me
what they knew I wanted. I have written a letter to our friend Erasmus. This
I send you unsealed, and please seal it up yourself, for there is no reason
why anything addressed to him need be sealed when it comes to you. I   10
wrote some verses of a sort on that picture; they are as clumsy as it was
expert, but I have made a copy for you. If you think them worth it, pass them
on to Erasmus; otherwise put them on the fire.

Farewell, this 7 October
Lines written upon the diptych in which Erasmus and Pieter Gillis were   15

* * * * *

54 November] This is a guess by the editors: the Deventer Letter-book gives
   September.
55 abbot] Antoon van Bergen; see Ep 143 introduction.

684
6 more cheerful] Cf Ep 681.

portrayed together by that excellent artist Quentin, in such a fashion that
behind Erasmus, who is beginning his Paraphrase on the Epistle to the
Romans, his books were painted each with its title, while Pieter held a letter
addressed to him in More's hand, which was actually imitated by the
painter.   20

The picture speaks:

    Castor and Pollux were great friends of old:
    Erasmus such and Gillis you behold.
    Far from them, More laments with love so dear
    As scarce a man unto himself could bear.   25
    Yet letters (making naught of envious space)
    Bring near the loved one's mind, and I his face.

Now I, More, speak myself:

    If you have seen these men before,
    Their features will be soon detected.   30
    If not, to make all safe and sure,
    One holds a note to him directed;
    The other writes his name – which yet,
    Though he say naught, you'll soon discover,
    For on the shelf behind are set   35
    Books that are known the wide world over.
    Quentin, who giv'st new art for old,
    Than great Apelles even greater,
    With mingled colours manifold

* * * * *

16 Quentin] Metsys
17 Paraphrase] See Ep 710 introduction.
18 title] These titles and the words written by Erasmus are not, or are no longer,
    visible in the portrait of the Galleria Nazionale d'Arte Antica, Rome, which is
    often assumed to be Metsys' original (see CWE 4 370), but in another version of
    the painting at Hampton Court, whose dimensions correspond with those of
    the Gillis portrait, the following titles can be identified: *Moriae encomium,*
    Novum Testamentum, and the editions of Jerome and Lucian. Likewise the
    opening words of the Paraphrase are clearly discernible, and as they flow from
    Erasmus' pen, Metsys may well have imitated his handwriting too. More titles
    of works and editions by Erasmus can clearly be seen in the portrait of Gillis
    now in the collection of the Earl of Radnor, Longford Castle (see CWE 4 371).
    See M.M. Phillips 'The Mystery of the Metsys Portrait' *Erasmus in English* 7
    (1975) 18–21 and J.B. Trapp et al 'Quentin Metsys, Erasmus, Pieter Gillis, and
    Thomas More' *Burlington Magazine* 120 (1978) 716–25.
22 Castor and Pollux] Cf Ep 706:53ff.
38 Apelles] The most famous painter of ancient Greece

Lending dead shapes the life of nature,   40
If thou canst paint so well such men
As our forefathers scarce beheld 'em,
In our day rarer still – and then
In future they'll be seen more seldom –
This fragile wood why didst thou use   45
Instead of tablets everlasting,
Such as posterity might choose
To keep thy fame and thee from wasting?
In days to come, if someone cares
For liberal arts somewhere on earth,   50
And brutal Mars Minerva spares,
What will these pictures then be worth?

My dear Pieter, marvellously as our Quentin has represented everything,
what a wonderful forger above all else it looks as though he might have
been! He has imitated the address on my letter to you so well that I do not   55
believe I could repeat it myself. And so, unless he wants it for some purpose
of his own, or you are keeping it for your own ends, do please let me have
the letter back: it will double the effect if it is kept handy alongside the
picture. If it has been lost, or you have a use for it, I will see whether I in my
turn can imitate the man who imitates my hand so well.   60

Farewell, you and your charming wife.

685 / From Willibald Pirckheimer   [Nürnberg, October 1517]

This letter is known only from Pirckheimer's autograph rough draft
(Stadtbibliothek Nürnberg, MS PP 330b). An approximate date can be assigned
from the edition of Lucian (line 13n) and from Ep 694, which is Erasmus'
answer.

Greeting, great Erasmus! I have written you several letters this year, but I
suspect you have not had them, since you have not replied; for I am
convinced that, although occupied with more important business, you
would not neglect the laws of friendship to the extent of failing to answer a
friend who approached you first. So do give the man who brings you this   5
one of your delightful letters, not so much for my sake as for your friends, of

* * * * *

46 tablets everlasting] For this suggestion cf Ep 712:40n.

685
1 letters] See Epp 527, 555; a letter from Pirckheimer had been lost two years
earlier; cf Epp 326A, 375.

View of Nürnberg
Manuscript leaf attributed to
Erhard Etzlaub, 1516
Germanisches Nationalmuseum,
Nürnberg

whom your merits have earned you such a good supply; for I am approached by them daily with enquiries: have I any news of the pillar of the literary world, how is the father of learning, what is he engaged on – and I have not a syllable to say in reply. Please let me have news of everything, and for preference direct from you, so that I can satisfy your friends and mine alike in Silesia, Saxony, and Thuringia.

I send you Lucian's *Piscator* together with a letter in defence of Reuchlin, not that I hope I have done anything worth doing, but to show my Erasmus how highly he is valued by his Willibald, although I know that praise from me will not add anything to you, any more than lighting of lamps can add to the brightness of the sun. But I did not want you to be unaware of my feelings towards you and of the singular affection that binds me to you, and I do not believe you will mind if I do the same, though more inadequately, in my other writings, for we see that even the Almighty is often worshipped by quite unworthy people. Please take it in good part, then, if you are praised even incompetently by one who wishes you so well.

Farewell, my excellent Erasmus, and let me ask you once more to steal an odd moment to gratify my longing.

Do not forget to let me have news of your beloved Paul.

686 / To Gilles de Busleyden   Louvain, 19 October [1517]

The year date of this letter must be 1517 as it followed the death of Jérôme de Busleyden (cf Ep 608 introduction) and was published in the *Auctarium* of August 1518. It is addressed to Gilles de Busleyden (c 1465–14 July 1536), the eldest of the Busleyden brothers, lord of Guirsch, etc, first master of the board of accounts in Brussels. He represented the family in the negotiations leading to the establishment of the Collegium Trilingue, endowed by Jérôme's bequest; see Ep 691 introduction.

* * * * *

10 syllable] *Adagia* I vii 3
13 *Piscator*] Translated by Pirckheimer (Nürnberg: F. Peypus, colophon 2 October 1517). The *Epistola apologetica* is in the same volume. It is partially printed in Hutten *Opera* I Ep 64; a complete German translation is in W.P. Eckert and C. von Imhoff *Willibald Pirckheimer* (Cologne 1971) 244–62. It is in this *Epistola* that Pirckheimer had written of Erasmus with high praise; for the reaction see Ep 694:116, and note.
17 lamps] *Adagia* I vii 58
25 Paul] Fulfilling an old and well-known pledge to write a commentary on Romans (cf Ep 747:87–8), Erasmus was then working on his *Paraphrasis ad Romanos* (see Ep 710 introduction).

ERASMUS OF ROTTERDAM TO HIS FRIEND
GILLES DE BUSLEYDEN, GREETING

Greeting, my honoured friend. Since no complaints nor tears can change
the course of fate, I pray that all the tributes due to the posterity and the
immortal memory and fame of your distinguished brother, Jérôme de   5
Busleyden, may meet with the success that has begun to attend on this first
part at least. There has lately arrived here one Matthaeus Adrianus, by race
a Jew but in religion a Christian of long standing, and by profession a
physician, so skilled in the whole of Hebrew literature that in my opinion
our age has no one else to show who could be compared with him. If my   10
judgment in this matter does not carry enough weight with you, this is the
unanimous testimony of everyone I know in Germany or Italy with any skill
in the language. Not only has he a complete knowledge of the language; he
has also deeply explored the recesses of the literature at first hand and has all
the books at his finger-tips. This is the same man whom Luis Vaca lately   15
mentioned to you in Brussels. I have explained to the theologians what sort
of man he is, and I would pledge my word without hesitation that he is the
one man in this generation who was the object of all our prayers. Now that
some favouring deity has freely offered him to us, our duty seems to be to
retain what is offered by every means in our power. I have no axe to grind   20
myself, but I am deeply concerned for the memory of my most generous
benefactor and incomparable friend. I am concerned for the public prosperity of our time, on which I myself to the best of my ability have spent and
still am spending so many sleepless nights. Matthaeus has already been
here for some time, encouraged by Luis, whom I have already mentioned.   25
Give your humble servant instructions, if you think there is anything I can
contribute. Farewell.

Louvain, morrow of St Luke, 151[8]

* * * * *

686
7 Adrianus] He was born in Spain c 1475. He seems to have acquired the degree
of MD in Italy. In compliance with Erasmus' wishes he was appointed professor of Hebrew and began lecturing before 6 December (cf Ep 731:30–1). In
1519, as a result of growing tensions with the theologians (cf Ep 934), Adrianus
left Louvain for Wittenberg; cf de Vocht CTL I 241–56 and passim.
15 finger-tips] *Adagia* II iv 91
15 Vaca] Luis Cabeza de Vaca (c 1465–12 December 1550), former tutor of Prince
Charles; subsequently a member of the Council for the Indies and from 1537
bishop of Palencia.

687 / To Pieter Gillis   [Louvain, c October 1517]

This letter must be roughly contemporary with the preceding one because of
the arrival of Adrianus and the completion of the *Paraphrasis ad Romanos* (cf Ep
710). It was first printed in the *Farrago*.

ERASMUS OF ROTTERDAM TO HIS FRIEND
PIETER GILLIS, GREETING

I wish you could overcome your hot temper; it is very bad for your health
and contributes so little to the dispatch of business that it is actually a great
hindrance. Why need you let it be known that you were angry with the   5
physician? I knew he would produce nothing; he merely enjoyed playing a
part. As it is, if he brazens it out, there will not be the least hope of anything,
and he will begin to be openly hostile. If I had had definite expectations, I
would rather forgo a hundred silver cups than once see you in a passion.
Take my word for it, unless you abstain from two things, disorder of the   10
mind and unseasonable sexual relations, I would rather not confess what I
fear for you, my most dear Pieter. So I beg you most urgently, put your
health in all respects first.

If I wrote about my coming for Christmas, I did this for the physician's
benefit, not meaning it seriously, for fear of arousing vain hopes in you or   15
vain fears in your wife. For I am determined not to leave this place until I
have finished what I have in hand. The paraphrase which I had started in
our pictures is now finished, and has begun to be printed. Jan van Borssele
is here and resident in this college, a most delightful man to live with. I wish .

* * * * *

687
6 physician] Afinius; see Epp 637–8, 681, which were evidently followed by
  another exchange of messages between Erasmus and Gillis. Although he
  clearly wanted the promised silver cups, the funny side of the business was
  not lost on Erasmus.
7 brazens] Cf Ep 663:58n.
11 relations] Late in his thirties, Gillis had married young Cornelia Sandrien
  (Sanders, Sandria) in 1514. Erasmus was inclined to ascribe Gillis' weak health
  in part to his marital relations; cf Ep 597:25–7.
16 wife] Cf Ep 476:34–40, 85–8.
18 pictures] Cf Ep 684:17.
18 Borssele] Jan Becker van Borssele had recently arrived after the death of his
  pupil, François de Busleyden, and lived as a private scholar, supported by
  some income from his benefice and perhaps from tuition; cf de Vocht CTL I
  259–60.

you were free to spend the whole winter with us here and tell the business   20
which so torments you to no purpose to go to the devil. I like More's verses.

There has arrived here a Jew by the name of Matthaeus, who has
exceptional skill in his native language; I have hopes that it may be resolved
to pay him a salary out of Busleyden's benefaction. If you love me, look after
your health, and let everything else take second place. A large element in   25
your sickness depends upon your spirits. If it is convenient, ask Franz to
come and see you, and find out whether he is willing to do what Lachner
proposes or not (but use very friendly language), so that if he would rather
not, I can lay my plans in some other way. For I will not stand their deluding
me without reprisals. If Linacre's Galen has arrived from Paris, please buy   30
it. My best wishes to you and yours, dearest of friends.

151[8]

688 / From Thomas More   Calais, 25 October [1517]

> This letter follows Ep 683, and both answer Ep 669. It was first published in the
> *Farrago*.

THOMAS MORE TO ERASMUS, GREETING

I have had a letter, my dear Erasmus, from Wentford, which I send straight
on to you by the same courier. You will easily discover from it that the man
is what he always was. I will not ask your pardon for opening a letter to you,
for (as you see) though written to you it was addressed to me. I make no   5
doubt that the same mistake has happened and the letter addressed to you
was written to me; but such was my eagerness to read it that I did not choose
to break the seal. If you find anything in it which you feel I should wish to
know (this I at any rate consider unlikely), pray tell me. You have, I
suppose, received the letter in which I reported safe arrival of the picture;   10
for which let me thank you once again – no, dear Erasmus, again a thousand

* * * * *

21 verses] See Ep 684.
26 Franz] Birckmann; see Ep 629:6n, 7n.
30 Galen] Cf Ep 664:29.

688
2 Wentford] Roger Wentford was the headmaster of St Anthony's School in
   London (cf Ep 196 introduction). From the following it would appear that he
   was a rather unexciting correspondent. None of his letters to Erasmus is
   preserved.
5 no doubt] More had guessed correctly; see Ep 772.
10 letter] Ep 683

times. Of your Pieter, since he went to England, I have no news. That was a present worthy of a king, and I only hope that in that quarter it will secure you from the king something worth having. May there be a blessing on the duties entrusted you by the emperor, for nothing goes well for him at the 15 moment; or rather, all is in God's hand. I am sure you are right to wish not to become immersed in the busy nothings of princes, and you show your affection for me in hoping that I may be released from them; for you cannot believe how unwillingly I spend my time on them, nor could anything be more tedious than my present mission. For I am exiled to a small seaside 20 town where place and climate are equally unattractive; and as for the litigation, at home I have a natural distaste for it even when it brings in something, and imagine how tedious it must be here when accompanied by loss. But my lord makes generous promises that the king will make it all up to me. When I get it, I will let you know. Till then, farewell; and I daresay to 25 keep well is all you desire. Give my cordial greetings to Dr Lee, and to my friend Palsgrave if he has returned. Farewell once more.

Calais, 25 October [1520]

689 / To Guillaume Budé   Louvain, 26 October [1517]

First printed in the *Farrago*, this letter appears to be dictated by Erasmus' concern over Budé's silence on matters of considerable importance to him; see Ep 723 introduction.

ERASMUS TO HIS FRIEND BUDÉ, GREETING

What means, my dear Budé, this sudden silence? It is not long since you were overwhelming me not so much with letters as whole volumes. The

* * * * *

12 Pieter] Meghen, who brought the Metsys diptych
15 emperor] More was probably at a loss how to understand Erasmus' cryptic hint contained in Ep 669. So in his first answer, Ep 683, More had refrained from comment, hoping for a clarification.
24 lord] Wolsey had evidently promised to remedy the plight of the English ambassadors who could not terminate their mission (see Ep 623:23n) and were by now spending their own money.
26 Lee] See Ep 765 introduction.
27 Palsgrave] See Ep 623:5n.

689
3 volumes] Some of Budé's letters had run to considerable length, above all Ep 493, although Erasmus' reply was even longer.

prince, the bishop – what a to-do it used to be! And now, not a murmur. I
long to know what monstrous thing is hatching. And then you had encour-   5
aged me to pluck up my courage and write to Deloynes; if my letter gave
offence, a great part of the fault is yours, for he writes nothing himself, nor
do you reply on his behalf.

Tunstall suffered long and severely from the climate of Zeeland; he
caught a fever, and having lost his head servant at Bruges, he left the other   10
two severely ill and retired to his native England. Be sure to write to him
sometimes; believe me, he is the most warm-hearted of men, and no one is
more devoted to you. More is at Calais on a mission for his king. Jérôme de
Busleyden, who had gone to Spain with our chancellor, has died in Gas-
cony; he left a bequest to found a college at Louvain for instruction in the   15
three tongues, Greek, Latin, and Hebrew. A Hebrew teacher has already
appeared, the best scholar living by general repute, by name Matthaeus
Adrianus; they have to get someone for the Greek from elsewhere. Farewell,
and clear my mind of its trouble. Louvain, 26 October

Let me recommend Henricus Glareanus to you most emphatically.   20

690 / To Thomas Lupset   Louvain, 26 October [1517]

> This is the reassuring answer to Lupset's apologetic Ep 664. It confirms the fact
> that most of the missing manuscripts were now safely in Erasmus' hands.

ERASMUS TO HIS FRIEND LUPSET, GREETING
My dear fellow, what made you think I was annoyed with you? Because I
gave you advice in my letter, in such a friendly way? You were more
indignant at my not having written, and have not answered my last letter.
From More I have had a short essay, and one or two things besides. He   5
wrote most affectionately on your behalf, although it was quite unnecessary: I am disposed to be fond of you of my own accord, and shall not

* * * * *

4 to-do] Budé's reports in Epp 522, 568 on the efforts undertaken by Francis I and
   Etienne Poncher, the bishop of Paris (both here referred to in Greek), to bring
   Erasmus to the French capital were not resumed in Ep 609.
4 murmur] Cf Ep 685:10n.
6 Deloynes] See Epp 493:453–73, 531:548–9, 535.
9 Tunstall] See Ep 663.
14 Gascony] See Ep 608 introduction.
18 Adrianus] See Ep 686:7n.

   690
5 From More] See Epp 502, 664 introduction.

willingly take second place. I have not yet had the appendix to my *Copia*
from More; I wish you would try and see that I get it back, if you can. I have
written to Bade to ask you to see that Linacre's version of Galen is sent me,   10
not as a present; I mean to pay for it myself. I wish you could come and visit
me here. Busleyden has founded a college in which there are to be three
first-class teachers of the three tongues. We have the man for Hebrew
already, a brilliant scholar called Matthaeus. Farewell, and give my greetings to your family.   15
    Louvain, 26 October

691 / To Gilles de Busleyden   Louvain, 30 October [1517]

The original of this letter, all in Erasmus' hand, was rediscovered in 1928 and
is now in Brussels, Archives générales du royaume, Archives de l'université
de Louvain (facsimile in de Vocht CTL I 248). The last lines permit one correction in, and one addition to, the text first published by Allen from manuscript
copies.

    The issue raised in this letter and in Epp 686, 699, 778:385–8, 804–5 is the
foundation of the Collegium Trilingue in Louvain. In a will dated 22 June 1517,
Jérôme de Busleyden had directed that a considerable part of his assets be used
to establish and equip an institution for the study of the three classical
languages. Linked to one of the existing colleges, it was to provide for a
professor in each language and for eight to ten scholarships. Erasmus provided much of the inspiration for this generous bequest, and together with
Gilles de Busleyden and the executors of Jérôme's will, he was the driving
force behind its implementation. A bold start was made with the appointment
of a professor of Hebrew, but difficulties arose over the housing of the new
institution. An attempt to set it up in the College of St Donatian failed in view
of the excessive powers of control demanded by the faculty of arts. So an
independent college was established on the Fish Market, in property purchased on 16 April 1519 to accommodate both professors and students. Mean-

* * * * *

8 appendix] The *De pueris instituendis*. A manuscript, apparently incomplete,
   had been handed over to More by Lupset (Ep 502:11). Perhaps because of its
   incompleteness More had retained it when returning the other papers to
   Erasmus. In March 1518 Erasmus asked More to send what he had of it and to
   speak to Lupset about the rest: Ep 785:20–1 (cf J.-C. Margolin's introduction to
   his edition of *De pueris* ASD I-1 4–6). The *De pueris* was not published until
   1529.
10 Bade] Perhaps simultaneously with this letter and Ep 689, which were also
   destined for Paris. For another attempt to get Linacre's book see Ep 687:30–1.
14 Matthaeus] Adrianus; cf Epp 686, 691.

while more difficulties were caused by the opposition of the theologians which, latent at first, soon became outspoken (cf Epp 695:9–10, 934 introduction). Only after lengthy debates involving the council of Brabant did the university accept on 13 March 1520 the establishment of an independent college with the right to appoint its own teachers; see de Vocht CTL I and II passim.

ERASMUS TO BUSLEYDEN, GREETING

The physician has been lingering here for some time, not without considerable expense to himself, having abandoned both his practice and his wife, and winter is coming on. This seems to me a most noble enterprise and worthy of immortality; but it is of the first importance, under what auspices 5 it starts. My own opinion is that one must begin with no common or ordinary teachers, but with distinguished men of high reputation. We now have the chance of one man of a kind we could not get even if we went to Italy for him, and so in my view we should do all we can to secure him. This will be done, if he is promptly assigned a post and a salary is voted him 10 adequate to his merits. To start with, it would be better to withhold the money for the others for the time being, provided the teaching of the three tongues is got under way in dignified and honourable fashion. I have advised the man to discuss the question with you personally. If you are resolved to carry out the bequest, you must settle with him; otherwise, you 15 ought to warn him not to hang about any longer to no purpose.

About inviting a professor of Greek, or if there is any other point on which you would like me to do something, let me know. There is a young man called Rutgerus here who is excellent, and more learned than he gives himself out to be; but, as I say, I should prefer to start with men of 20 established reputation. Farewell, my honoured friend.

Louvain, 30 October

* * * * *

691

2 physician] Adrianus; see Ep 686.
3 wife] In Middelburg which, it was said, he had left in a hurry because of his debts (cf Ep 798:19). His wife and family seem to have followed him to Louvain after a suitable house had been rented on 2 February 1518; see de Vocht CTL I 251.
19 Rutgerus] Rescius, then a corrector in Martens' press. The choice of a Greek professor proved difficult. Among the potential candidates there were also Robert de Keysere (cf Ep 743) and Jacobus Ceratinus (cf Ep 622:34n). Erasmus held Ceratinus in high esteem but would have preferred a native Greek (cf Epp 732A, 805, 836). Finally Rescius was appointed on 1 September 1518; de Vocht CTL I 271–83, 293–4.

Do not let it set you against Doctor Matthaeus, if in Latin he is not equally fluent and polished. He has all he needs for the teaching, and he knows the literature of his own people as well as any man alive; which is the   25 most important thing in this business.

To the honourable Master Gilles de Busleyden, his most esteemed benefactor.

Tomorrow we shall wear no mourning.

692 / From Karel Ofhuys

This letter has been assigned to the year 1516 and is Ep 480A in this edition.

693 / To Matthias Schürer   Louvain, 31 October 1517

ERASMUS TO HIS FRIEND SCHÜRER, GREETING
I send you Quintus Curtius, revised by myself with index and preface. If you like the work, deal with it in a way that will be a credit to us both; if not, give the book back to the man who brings it. Farewell, my dear Schürer, and greet my friends, by which I mean the entire literary society.   5

Louvain, All Saints' eve 1517

I also send you the *Apologia* containing my reply to Lefèvre d'Etaples; I should not like it to be published with any other purpose than to prevent people from thinking there is any hostility in our discussion, though it was he that attacked me in an unfriendly fashion. If you like it, take it; I know I   10 can rely on you.

* * * * *

23 in Latin] He was apparently brought up in a tradition of living colloquial Latin
and continued to speak and write it; cf AK I Epp 476–7 and Hartmann's notes
on them.

25 of his own people] The manuscript reads *suas*, not *sacras*.

29 Tomorrow] The manuscript adds 'Crastino die non lugebimus.' The recently
deceased Jérôme de Busleyden should be remembered with confidence on All
Saints' day (1 November, with liturgical celebrations beginning on the eve).
Jérôme is thus to be remembered among the glorified souls, rather than the
ones in purgatory on All Souls' day, the day following All Saints'.

693

2 preface] Ep 704, dated five days later, presumably when the messenger was
ready to leave. The same messenger probably went on from Strasbourg to
Basel; see Ep 704A introduction.

5 society] Cf Ep 302.

7 *Apologia*] A copy of Martens' edition (see Ep 597:37n) in which Erasmus had
made a few corrections (see Ep 730:26–7). The suggestion was clearly that
Schürer should reprint the work, and he did so without delay; cf Ep 732:21n.

694 / To Willibald Pirckheimer   Louvain, 2 November 1517

This letter is closely related to Epp 700, 701, 703, 713 and possibly others now missing (cf Ep 709:30n). All seem to be called forth by some common stimulus. All express in urgent tones Erasmus' opinion that he himself and other serious scholars should refrain from replying to the polemical attacks of Reuchlin's opponents; rather the authority of the emperor and the church should be invoked to silence them. This cautious and reasonable point, however, is combined with outbursts of abuse against one specific opponent of Reuchlin, Johann Pfefferkorn, a Dominican and a converted Jew. To resolve the apparent contradiction one must consider that none of the present letters was published by Erasmus, who was upset when Reuchlin published Ep 713. Perhaps the abuse heaped upon Pfefferkorn in private was intended to appease and reassure Reuchlin's friends in view of Erasmus' refusal, after much hesitation, further to support their cause in public statements (cf Epp 610:25n, 622, 670 introduction, 680:28n). Erasmus himself had earlier published at once two letters he wrote in 1515 to cardinals Grimani and Riario, each of which contained a final section in defence of Reuchlin (cf Epp 333:112–47, 334:187–218). It should also be noted that the University of Louvain officially supported Pfefferkorn (cf Ep 713:18n).

Erasmus' remarks about the Jews in this group of related letters are unprecedented as far as his earlier correspondence is concerned. In some other letters he took issue with the perils wrought upon Christianity by legal 'Judaism' rather than the Jewish race (cf Epp 164:30, 181:56, 541:149–70n, 710:88), but here, as in Ep 798:24–6, Allen Ep 1006:139–43, the Jews, or at least one individual said to be typical of the rest, are treated with frank contempt, although the ultimate goal in each case is to discourage others from treating the matter polemically and publicly as they would be belabouring the obvious. On Erasmus' attitude towards the Jews see G. Kisch *Erasmus' Stellung zu Juden und Judentum* (Tübingen 1969).

This letter was published in *Billibaldi Pirckheimeri ... opera* (Frankfurt 1610, reprint 1969) 268–9. It answers Ep 685 and is answered in turn by Ep 747. For its journey cf Epp 698, 709.

ERASMUS TO HIS FRIEND WILLIBALD, GREETING
The book and your letter, my honoured friend, have reached me safely; I must send a brief reply, being fully taken up with a great load of work. I am

* * * * *

694
2 book] See Ep 685:13n.

living, after a fashion, and working in Louvain, where I have been co-opted
a member of the faculty of theology, although I am not a doctor of this   5
university. This I preferred to a journey to Spain with Prince Charles, the
more readily as I saw the court divided into so many factions – Spaniards,
Maraños, Chièvres-men, Frenchmen, Imperialists, Neapolitans, Sicilians,
and what not? Last spring, when I visited England on private business, the
king went out of his way to receive me kindly, and so did the cardinal, who 10
is the king's alter ego, so to say. They offered me six hundred florins a year,
besides a splendid house. In returning thanks, I took the middle course
between accepting the conditions offered and rejecting them. Here, although I pay my own expenses, which are considerable, I have resolved to
stay for several months, partly to finish what I have in hand, and partly to   15
see the outcome of the most generous hopes held out to me in the prince's

* * * * *

4 co-opted] See Ep 637:12n.
6 journey to Spain] See Ep 596 introduction.
8 Maraños] Converted Spanish Jews; for the court factions cf Ep 603:28n.
8 Chièvres-men] See Ep 532:30n.
11 They offered] For the first time Erasmus' correspondence here reveals some
   details about the negotiations designed to bring about his settlement in
   England. After somewhat vague offers received in personal conversations
   with Henry VIII and Wolsey (cf Epp 657:73–6, 756:43–4), the terms here
   mentioned may have been specified in an encounter Erasmus had with Lord
   Mountjoy immediately before his departure from England in April 1517. In Ep
   577 Erasmus attempted to have Wolsey confirm them in writing, but this had
   not happened by early September, when Erasmus was writing Epp 657–8.
   From the beginning of 1518 Erasmus' letters return to the matter more frequently (see Epp 756, 761, 775, 784, 786, 794). By early March he had received a
   written statement, but the offer now was for only £20 sterling, according to Ep
   775:24, or £40 sterling, according to Ep 786:40. Mountjoy had evidently promised much more: in both epistles Erasmus states that he had 'been told to hope
   for a hundred' pounds. In this epistle he states the terms of the original
   agreement for the benefice as 600 florins, presumably (writing in Louvain) the
   Flemish money of account also known as livres d'Artois or livres de 40 gros;
   and later, in Ep 816:8, he describes the offer as 'a benefice worth a hundred
   marks' sterling. These two sums are, in fact, approximately the same: for 600
   florins as livres de 40 gros = £100 gros Flemish = £68 15s 0d sterling = 103.1
   marks; and 100 English marks = £66 13s 4d sterling = £97 gros Flemish. When
   he raised the matter again (Allen Ep 886:49–50), he requested an additional
   'hundred marks [= £66 13s 4d], which the king offered me long ago.' If this
   sum were added to the £20 or £40 sterling offered earlier, the amount would be
   comparable to what Erasmus maintained had been the original promise. The
   vagueness of these references may be characteristic of Erasmus' monetary
   affairs; but one must bear in mind that they concerned the estimated value of
   one or more benefices yet to be vacated. Cf CWE 1 347.
16 hopes] Cf Ep 608:19n.

Pope Alexander VI
Fresco by Pinturicchio in the
Borgia apartments of the Vatican, 1492–4
Photo: Fratelli Alinari

name at his departure by the chancellor of Burgundy, Jean Le Sauvage, an excellent scholar and a patron of all learned men. The New Testament, which I rushed into print rather than edited some time ago in Basel, is now being taken to pieces and refashioned, so thoroughly that it will be a new   20 book. It will be finished, I hope, within four months.

I was delighted with your book, and with that warm-hearted defence of Reuchlin, in which you seem to me more eloquent than is your wont; perhaps, as Quintilian suggests, your heart contributed to make you write better, not only your head and your education. But I think nothing more   25 disastrous than to be involved somehow in controversy; and when that happens, there is no disaster worse than conflict with a foul opponent of whom one is ashamed. Who, after all, are the opponents of Reuchlin? A nest of hornets whom the pope himself fears to arouse; so much so that Alexander used to say that he thought it less dangerous to offend some powerful   30 monarch than any one individual among the troops of mendicants, who under the pretext of that humble name ruled Christendom, he said, with a tyrant's rod. Not but what I do not think it fair to ascribe to the whole order what is done by the wickedness of a few.

And then just look at the tool selected by these very far from true   35 champions of true religion: a man utterly uneducated, of the most brazen impudence, whom no amount of misdemeanour could make worse than he is; I would not cast the words 'half a Jew' in his teeth if he did not behave like a Jew and a half. What better instrument could the devil hope to find, the eternal enemy of the Christian religion, than an angel of Satan like him,   40 transformed into an angel of light, who under the most utterly false pretence of defending true religion overthrows everywhere what is the chiefest and best thing in our religion – the public unity of the Christian world? What more improper than that men who deserve immortal memory should have to fight to the death with such a monster, whose name alone would sully the   45 paper I write on? My life upon it, he had no other motive in getting himself dipped in the font than to be able to deliver more dangerous attacks on

* * * * *

20 new book] See Ep 864 introduction.
24 Quintilian] 10.7.15
29 hornets] *Adagia* I i 60
29 Alexander] The source of the saying attributed to Pope Alexander VI is not clear. It probably referred to the Dominican Girolamo Savonarola.
33 order] For Erasmus' continued criticism of some Dominicans see the index to this volume.
35 tool] Johann Pfefferkorn, a converted Jew; the tool in the hands of Reuchlin's Dominican opponents; cf line 77, Ep 487:22n.
41 angel of light] Cf 2 Cor 11:14.

Homo qͧaſi herba ɗies eiꝰ, Sirͧt
flos agri ſic florebit pſ, 102~

I·H

I·P·AN·46

Johann Pfefferkorn
Engraved portrait by Hieronymus Hopfer
(fl early sixteenth century)
Lutherhalle, Wittenberg

Christianity, and by mixing with us to infect the entire folk with his Jewish poison. What harm could he have done, had he remained the Jew he was? Now for the first time he is playing the part of a real Jew, now that he has 50 donned the mask of a Christian; now he lives up to his breeding. The Jews brought false accusations against Christ, but it was Christ alone; this man lets loose his fury against so many upright men of proved integrity and learning. He could render to his fellow Jews no service more welcome than to pretend he is a turncoat and betray the Christian polity to its enemies; a 55 dunderhead in all other respects, only in false inventions fertile. What more acceptable sacrifice could be offered to Satan than to broadcast the seeds of this brand of discord among Christians everywhere?

Whence did Satan get his name among the Hebrews? As the Adversary, of course. Who does Satan's work for him better than the man who, 60 when he sees distinguished figures working for the public good, raises obstacles and protests in their path by nefarious means, and reckons himself born just for this purpose? Why did the Greeks call him the devil? Not from usury, not from adultery, not from theft or any other wickedness, but from calumny. Who is more truly the devil's apostle than the man who has 65 devoted his whole life to a campaign of obloquy, traducing men of highest character before the ignorant mob, and in the most infamous business misusing the name of religion, which is no ordinary devilry, but a trick worthy of the most cunning fiend? He knows that he cannot make himself acceptable to men of learning or character, or easily impose upon them. So 70 he makes a public outcry among the unlearned mob; he chatters away to silly women full of superstition and as St Paul says, 'laden with sins,' and thus secures proper soil for his evil seed. These are the people whom he befogs with resounding titles, to whom he trumpets his defence of the Christian religion and prates of heresies and excommunications; and they 75 are too stupid to detect the prowling wolf that lurks in the sheep's clothing.

How cursed is this 'corn'! How unlike that corn of wheat that fell into the ground and died and brought forth the food of life! This corn is sown by the devil's hand; it is the seed of hemlock, or whatever is more poisonous than that; and unless timely steps are taken, it will infect the unity of 80 Christians with the most virulent venom of discord. For what will happen in the end if this expert in blackmail is allowed to rage in this same way against all who are not of his way of thinking, if scholars are compelled to

* * * * *

65 calumny] Greek *diabolê*, connected with *diabolos*, devil
72 St Paul] 2 Tim 3:6
76 wolf] Cf Matt 7:15.
77 corn of wheat] Cf John 12:24.

publish books in answer to this filthy beast, whose name deserves not to be
mentioned in human society? Take my word for it, my most learned Wil- 85
libald, these beginnings have a wider scope than ordinary men perhaps
realize. We know how small a spark will sometimes start a conflagration.
And so I am surprised that the bishops are not at this point on the watch, to
burn up this hydra in good time and take steps to meet the poison that is so
successful and is spreading everywhere. This foul-mouthed villain cannot 90
be defeated, for he is entirely made up of malignancy and has so many
wicked angels to provide him with new strength when he is tired.

Abuse, then, will never beat him. The only fame he seeks is somehow
or other to be made famous among posterity in every scholar's works. The
horrible fellow reasons somewhat like this: 'I may be anathema to a few 95
upright and learned men; it is enough to me, if I please the crowd. If
however my tricks are detected and my machinations made public, and the
whole Christian world abhors me, I am absolutely certain of glory among
my fellow Jews, who will then understand that when I left them, it was not
with hostile intent.' It is therefore not only dishonourable but a waste of 100
time for the learned to do battle with this man, from whom they can bring
away, win or lose, nothing but discredit. I wish the hangman might suppress this madness. And this is a task for the bishops. It is for that most just
emperor Maximilian, it is for the magistrates of the famous city of Cologne,
not to cherish this poisonous viper for the destruction of the Christian 105
religion, which is certain unless some antidote is provided to match this
great evil. In saying this I indulge no private resentment; he never did me
any harm or, if he has ever raved against me, it leaves me unmoved, and the
whole affair is absolutely nothing to me personally. But I cannot bear to see
the unity of Christian people doomed thus unworthily to be torn asunder 110
by the machinations of one circumcised profane and ignorant ruffian, and
that too with the aid of those who profess themselves pillars of the Christian
faith.

But enough of all this. Lest there should be nothing for me to criticize,
my dear Willibald, in your book, which is otherwise very scholarly, I do not 115
much approve of that list of Reuchlin's supporters. Who is there anywhere

* * * * *

104 Maximilian] Cf perhaps Ep 670. In 1514 Maximilian wrote to Leo x in support
   of Reuchlin, his councillor; see Geiger *Reuchlin* 309–10.
104 Cologne] Cf Ep 821:19n.
116 list] Contained in the *Epistola apologetica* (cf Ep 685:13n). It includes Erasmus,
   of course, but rather than supporters of Reuchlin it lists those contributing to
   the reform of theology according to humanistic principles; cf Pirckheimer's
   reply, Ep 747.

with any tincture of learning or religion who does not support him? Who does not abominate that monster, unless it be someone who does not understand the affair, or who seeks his own advantage at the price of public mischief? And while you wander off into an attack on logicians and philosophers, I should have preferred you to leave out all else and pursue the matter in hand. Farewell, noblest of the learned and most learned of the noble.

Louvain, morrow of All Saints 1517

695 / To Pierre Barbier   Louvain, 2 November 1517

> It is possible that no messenger to Spain was immediately found for this letter and that it finally left together with a copy of Erasmus' *Paraphrasis ad Romanos* (see Ep 710 introduction), which was ready for distribution by the end of November; cf Epp 752, 794:2–4. This letter was printed in the *Auctarium* of 1518 with the omission of four short sentences which appear in the Deventer Letter-book.

ERASMUS TO HIS FRIEND BARBIER, GREETING

I greatly fear, my dear Pierre, that the delights of Spain may make you forget your poor old friends, though I would much rather that happened than for some calamity to produce the same result. I grieve sincerely for the death of Busleyden, and all the more so because before he set out he was so distant with me. As for his bequest to promote the three tongues, I cannot say how heartily I approve. Already by some good fortune there is a Hebrew here who is by far the greatest expert in his native literature, in my own opinion and other people's. Certain theologians are working against this under cover, making other promises in front of him. If this project could only be got under way on a generous scale and with men of note, it is surprising how much credit it would bring to this country.

The lord of Marques had already sent me the money from Zeeland when your letter arrived. Apart from that I have received neither letter nor money. If nothing is sent, I shall bear with the inconvenience somehow, as long as you are flourishing. But if, which heaven forbid, some mischance were to take my friend Barbier from me, I shall be unable to endure such repeated losses. So I beg you most urgently to have a care of your health.

* * * * *

695
6 bequest] See Ep 691 introduction.
7 Hebrew] Adrianus; see Epp 686:7n, 691 introduction.
13 Marques] See Epp 613, 621 introduction.

I am now living in the College of the Lily with a most civilized host, Nève of Hondschoote. I enjoy the full dignity of a doctor and attend 20 assiduously (or nearly so) all the faculty meetings in which they do the same thing over and over again. The New Testament goes on well and should be finished, with God's help, in three months. I have answered Lefèvre, as far as I could without losing my temper. I simply cannot think what came into his head. I have sent him my piece, but not yet had an answer. Some 25 mischief-maker misled the poor innocent man; and I only wish it had been possible for me to overlook it. My case is accepted by all the theologians, especially Atensis and even Dorp himself. The bishop of Utrecht has written to me indicating that he will send for me on his return from Overijssel and will make clear how much he thinks I am worth; but he will sing to deaf 30 ears. The archbishop of Mainz has sent me a letter in his own handwriting, and in the most kindly terms. My Paraphrase on the Epistle to the Romans is now printing, very elegantly. It is only fair that Paul should address the Romans in somewhat better Latin. Atensis likes the work wonderfully.

I beg you in the sacred name of theology, let me know if my excellent 35 benefactor is in good health; he is my one great hope. If he, and he alone, continues to be what he always was, I shall continue to refuse all offers from other quarters. I still live off my own resources, except for three hundred florins or rather more, which I owed to his generosity and the prince's. Nor have I any doubts about his intentions, provided you jog his memory. At 40 least let me have a taste of your Spanish successes by letter, unless you grudge me even that. A most distressing rumour has reached here which was almost too much for me, that Doctor Briselot was no more; but as there is no certainty about it, I suspect it is not true. We had similar news about

* * * * *

20 Nève] See Ep 643:14n.
20 attend] Cf Ep 637:12n.
22 over and over] *Adagia* I iv 70
22 New Testament] See Ep 864 introduction.
25 sent him] See Ep 659.
28 Utrecht] See Ep 682 introduction.
31 Mainz] See Ep 661.
32 Paraphrase] See Ep 710.
36 benefactor] Chancellor Le Sauvage
39 florins] See Ep 621 introduction.
42 distressing] Barbier would understand this ironical expression (cf Epp 794:27–31; also 597:4–16). Still joking, Erasmus refers to Barbier's successes in delightful Spain, where the Burgundian courtiers, like the companions of Ulysses, are transformed into pigs.
43 Briselot] Cf Ep 597:5n.

the learned Doctor Joost, I suppose on the occasion of Busleyden's death. 45
Unless you have suffered among the Spaniards something like what happened to the companions of Ulysses in Circe's palace, commend me warmly
to my special lord and benefactor, the lord chancellor; I intended to write to
him, but that youth with a stammer, a kinsman of your wife's, I think,
barely half an hour before the courier left warned me that my postman was 50
departing.

Farewell, dearest of men and more than half of mine own soul. Give
my greetings to the bishop of Chieti, and to the right reverend Doctor
Marliano. Where Guy Morillon is, I know not, but would gladly know what
he is doing now. 55

Louvain, morrow of All Saints 1517

696 / To Maarten van Dorp [Louvain, c 2 November 1517?]

In the absence of conclusive evidence Allen's tentative date may be retained.
In the Deventer Letter-book this letter stands between Epp 695 and 697. H. de
Vocht (MHL 185) preferred a date prior to 10 October 1517 when the litigation
over the College of the Lily (see Ep 643:14n) was formally ended, assuming
that the letter referred to Dorp's support for the opponents of Jean de Nève,
Erasmus' host at the college. But Nève was according to Erasmus a man of
retentive memory (see Allen Ep 1347:18–19), and new causes for disagreement
between him and Dorp may have arisen. Dorp was in Erasmus' experience a
most difficult man (cf Epp 637, 669, 713). In Ep 838 we hear again that Nève and
Dorp 'do not get on very well.'

ERASMUS TO HIS FRIEND DORP
Although I have never ceased to urge Nève to peace and concord, I spoke to
him, the same day that I had your instructions, about this business, and
spoke so emphatically that he nearly lost his temper with me. There is no
man alive whose nature is more averse from conflict, nor is there anyone 5
who more willingly refrains from meddling in other people's affairs. Nève

* * * * *

45 Joost] Joost Lauwerijns, lord of Terdeghen, d 1527 (cf Ep 1299). He was a
member of Charles' Grand Conseil and probably accompanied the monarch to
Spain; cf Ep 794:92–3; de Vocht *Literae* 184–5.
49 youth] Cf Ep 803. Since Barbier was a chaplain, the reference to his wife must
be another joke.
53 greetings to] Gianpietro Carafa, bishop of Chieti (cf Ep 628:64n); Luigi Marliano, physician to King Charles; see Ep 411:10n.
54 Morillon] A colleague of Barbier in the service of Chancellor Le Sauvage,
Morillon was now in Spain with the court; cf Ep 532 introduction.

is the most civilized character one could find, and the most friendly. I only
wish he had been as fortunate in this regard as in other things. By nature he
richly deserved to be free of vexations of this kind and to devote himself
entirely to humane studies. On this account I held aloof for some time from   10
sharing the same roof with him, and now I would be happier living together
with him if he could be detached from supporting the causes you speak of;
not that he troubles me with them, but we should have more freedom for
scholarly discussion of our common interests. I shall not cease to advise him
to do as I intend to do myself. One thing, my dear Dorp, I do beg of you, to   15
remember how little credit it does you to keep up a quarrel with a man with
whom you have been great friends, especially if the reason is nothing to do
with you. And Nève is the sort of man to remain most faithfully attached to
anyone with whom he has once made friends. Farewell.

697 / To Gerardus Listrius   Louvain, 2 November 1517

> This letter refers to a widespread but quite unsubstantiated rumour accusing
> Listrius (see Ep 495 introduction) of having poisoned Johannes Murmellius of
> Roermond (see Ep 838:3n). Their mutual dislike was notorious, and Murmel-
> lius died suddenly at Deventer on 2 October 1517, only weeks after the
> publication of his *Epigrammata paraenetica*, in which he had attacked Listrius.
> In reply to the rumour Listrius composed his *Carmen apologeticum*, which he
> finally published despite Erasmus' plea not to do so (see Epp 830, 838). For the
> dates of the two publications and all other relevant circumstances see M.E.
> Kronenberg 'Heeft Listrius schuld aan de dood van Murmellius?' *Bijdragen
> voor vaderlandsche geschiedenis en oudheidkunde* VI 9 (1930) 177–214.

ERASMUS TO HIS FRIEND LISTRIUS, GREETING
I read the story of your ordeal, my excellent Listrius, and was heartily sorry.
You must follow the example of St Paul, who through evil report and good
report went on unshaken. Such are the turns of human life, such the web of
tragedy and comedy in which our brief days are spent. If you take my   5
advice, you will not move a step in any direction just now. Take what
pleasure you can in humane studies; this slander was set on foot by villains
and will soon evaporate of its own accord. Everybody knows that you are by
nature utterly incapable of such wickedness. Take my word for it, fortune
will make up for what you suffer by some great advantage. When the   10

* * * * *

697
3 St Paul] 2 Cor 6:8

rumours have died down will be the time to change your abode if you think
fit. If you wish to visit England, I will recommend you in high places; if you
would rather stay here, I will do for you all that a friend should.

My learned friends tell me that one Pfefferkorn, once a damned Jew
and now a most damnable Christian, has published a book in German in   15
which like a mad dog he tears the whole learned world to pieces, and me
with it. A poisonous fellow, unworthy to be pitted against such opponents,
fit only for the hangman. It was indeed worth his while to be dipped in the
font: as a Jew in disguise he could throw peace among Christians into
confusion. Farewell, my dear Listrius, and give my greetings to the excel-   20
lent prior of St Agnes.

Louvain, morrow of All Saints 1517

698 / To Johann [Poppenruyter]   Louvain, 2 November 1517

Erasmus persistently refused to identify more fully the friend for whom the
Enchiridion was written, probably because he did not wish to embarrass him;
see Ep 164 and the beginning of Ep 858.

ERASMUS TO HIS FRIEND JOHANN, GREETING
Please have this letter carried to Nürnberg as soon as you can find someone
to entrust it to, and do not allow our friendship to evaporate. I hear you are
gilded all over by the prince, and congratulate you most sincerely. Except
that I fear you will get the gout from counting out so many thousands. My   5
Enchiridion is read everywhere and is making many people good, or at least,
better than they were. You and I, my dear Johann, must run no risk of being
the only two not to profit from it, considering that one of us wrote it and it

* * * * *

15 book] Probably the *Streydtpuechlyn von der Warheit* [c spring 1517], which
    made a slighting reference to Erasmus without mentioning his name. Erasmus
    had it translated and sent to More for Fisher to read: see Epp 706:3, 713:5, 23–4;
    Geiger *Reuchlin* 383–6.
21 prior] Gerard van Kloster, prior of the Austin house of Sint Agnietenberg near
    Zwolle

698
2 letter] Ep 694. Poppenruyter was a friend of Pirckheimer and a native of
   Nürnberg; cf Ep 709:30n.
4 prince] Charles, who in 1515 appointed Poppenruyter supplier of cannon to
   his court with a salary of £200 gros Flemish. Poppenruyter's foundry at
   Mechelen was huge, famous, and clearly lucrative; see O. Schottenloher in
   Archiv für Reformationsgeschichte 45 (1954) 115.

was written for the other. This servant of mine is German, so treat him as a
German should be treated. Farewell, best of friends. When you come to　10
Louvain, you shall be entertained in college in true collegiate fashion.

Louvain, morrow cf All Saints 1517

699 / To Gilles de Busleyden　　　　　　　　[Louvain, c November 1517]

This letter is clearly subsequent to Ep 691 and prior to Ep 731.

TO THE HONOURABLE GILLES DE BUSLEYDEN,
MY ESTEEMED PATRON AND FRIEND

Greeting. Your kind and courteous reception of the Hebrew scholar would
earn my gratitude, my honoured friend, were it not even more agreeable to
congratulate you on the good fortune that has offered you the very man in　5
every way whom you need for this enterprise; which without doubt will
win undying honour and glory for the whole house of Busleyden and
restore the fabric of learning, now ruinous in many ways. And there will be
no lack in other universities of men who try to imitate this most excellent
foundation. I beg you therefore, for the sake of your admirable brother's　10
memory and the general reputation of the name of Busleyden, and for the
public benefit of all lovers of learning, do not suffer yourself to be diverted
from what you have begun. There are some people perhaps who look
askance at their own good fortune and would rather divert other men from
higher studies than learn anything higher themselves. Personally, I have no　15
axe to grind in all this; I am moved by nothing but thoughts of the general
good. No improvement was ever received with applause so general that two
or three did not protest. All the best men welcome it now, and soon the
welcome will be universal. If all goes as I hope it will, Louvain will seem to
me more and more attractive. There is no community in which I would　20
rather sojourn, and that at my own expense, and I think to have me as a
member will be of some advantage to such a foundation. Nor could I wish
ultimately for any better heir to inherit my own library.

* * * * *

9 servant] Jacobus Nepos
9 as a German should be treated] or 'in brotherly fashion,' with the familiar play
on the two meanings of *germanus*

699
3 Hebrew] Adrianus; cf Ep 686:7n.
15 no axe to grind] Literally 'I neither sow nor reap'; *Adagia* I vi 82
23 library] Erasmus sold it later to Jan Laski; see F. Husner 'Die Bibliothek des
Erasmus' *Gedenkschrift zum 400. Todestag des Erasmus von Rotterdam* (Basel
1936) 228–59.

Matthaeus has not moved here yet. I enclose an epitaph, but only to try
out what you feel about it. I will produce others as soon as I know. Farewell.   25
Lines in the trochaic metre
  Next to first among the leading glories of Busleyden's name,
  Must you thus desert your comrades, ravished in the prime of life?
  Scholars, nobles, court and senate, church and people all demand
  'Where is now our brightest jewel, where our leader, our Jérôme?'   30
  Yet your virtues live for ever, famed among posterity:
  Yours the threefold lively tribute of the triple learned tongues,
  Triple tongues restored that flourish, through the wealth they gained
  from you.
Erasmus R.   35

700 / To Jacopo Bannisio   Louvain, 3 November [1517]

Jacopo Bannisio (d 19 November 1532) was a Dalmatian in the service of
Maximilian I. Since 1509 he had had special responsibility for the affairs of
Flanders and often visited Antwerp, where he held the deanery. In 1521 he
retired to Trent, where he was dean of the cathedral chapter (see DBI).

   He had met Erasmus earlier, but had apparently approached him again in
recent days, as this letter resumes rather than initiates an exchange of ideas
about the Reuchlin controversy. This recent approach (cf perhaps Ep 670)
induced Erasmus to include Bannisio in the group of supporters of Reuchlin to
whom he was now writing closely related letters; see Ep 694. Bannisio's
answer is Ep 709.

Greeting to one who is distinguished on every count. I quarrel with myself
now and again for not having given your kindness a more ready welcome in
Antwerp while it was so accessible; but at that time I had made my escape
from the court of Brussels, having been pestered almost to extinction by the
pitiless courtesy of the Spaniards, with the result that I was then anxious to   5
avoid society in almost any form. But a person like yourself, with your
scholarship and literary gifts and generous disposition, should have been
sought out even at a distance, not by me only but by every man of any
judgment. Should you propose to spend several days in Antwerp, I shall
hasten to your side, to enjoy your conversation and your company for a few   10

* * * * *

24 here] To Louvain. But he did so before long; cf Epp 691:3n, 731:30–1.
25 others] See Ep 804.

700
3 Antwerp] Probably in the spring; cf Epp 566, 586.

Jacopo Bannisio
Portrait medal, with picture on reverse of Bannisio
kneeling before Emperor Maximilian I
Münzkabinett, Kunsthistorisches Museum, Vienna

hours at least, unless my discourtesy has so estranged you that you will now refuse me when I ask it what long ago you offered me of your own accord.

I have read the book which Neuenahr has published at Cologne, and Willibald has sent me his book as well. The struggle, I perceive, is reopening, which I hoped above all else was ended or at any rate put to sleep. I hear   15 that pestilent bit of seed corn which some cunning Satan planted has published a book in which he raves unchecked against the learned world. This is the tool which those grand professors of religion make such wicked use of to undermine peace and concord among Christians. I wish he were an entire Jew – better still if the removal of his foreskin had been followed by   20 the loss of his tongue and both hands. As it is, this angel of Satan transformed into an angel of light is attacking us under our own colours and rendering his colleagues of the circumcision the same service that Zopyrus did to Darius, the father of Xerxes. My life upon it, you would find in his bosom more than one Jew. What more could these curtal wretches hope for,   25 or Satan their leader, than to see the unity of simple Christians rent in twain like this? And what an outrage that scholars, men whose very names I believe will be cherished by posterity, must wrestle with a monster such as this, from whom they can derive nothing, win or lose, but poison, pox, and mischief! Here is that Allecto, queen of the Furies, who blows the signal for   30 battle on her hellish trumpet, Satan's apostle, the devil's spawn, the chosen tool of certain hypocrites, disguised as champion of the faith but really its foe, rascally Jew turned greater rascal as a Christian. Outrageous that his abominable name must appear in the books of scholars, that precious time must be lost in answering one so ignorant and worthless. We need much   35 more some Hercules, who will thrash this Cacus and throw him away, and that right soon. Mischief comes very easy; the fire once kindled ranges widely, and by easy steps the poisonous contagion spreads. Take my word for it, if the emperor puts an end to this monstrosity, he will do a fairer deed than if he were to break the Saracens in open fight. We have here an enemy   40 who advances into the heart of Christianity, and whose advance is all the more dangerous because he attacks us with our own weapons and using our

* * * * *

13 Neuenahr] Cf Ep 680:27–8.
14 Willibald] Pirckheimer's *Epistola apologetica* (cf Ep 694:116n) made reference to Bannisio as well as Erasmus.
16 corn] Cf Ep 694:35n, 77; for Pfefferkorn's book cf Ep 697:15n.
23 Zopyrus] He entered the city of Babylon, claiming to be fleeing from Darius, his master, and then betrayed the Babylonians to him; cf *Adagia* II x 64.
30 Allecto] Cf Virgil *Aeneid* 7.513–14.
36 Cacus] He stole Hercules' cattle and was duly killed by him for his foolish deed.

own troops. If you approve, I will write and urge the emperor, our fountain of justice, to secure the suppression of this frenzy not by any writings of mine, but with the club of Hercules. Farewell, my most learned friend.   45

Erasmus of Rotterdam
Louvain, 3 November

701 / To Johannes Caesarius   Louvain, 3 November [1517]

This letter seems to be an answer to one now lost. It was evidently dispatched together with Ep 703, also addressed to Cologne, and Ep 700, probably also with Ep 694 (cf Ep 709:30n), all of which voice similar abuse of Pfefferkorn and his supporters, often with literal repetitions; cf Ep 694 introduction.

ERASMUS TO HIS FRIEND CAESARIUS, GREETING
It was, I suspect, our one-eyed friend who boasted that he had been dispatched to Rome by me. A year ago, when he happened to be going to Rome, I did burden him with a New Testament, having written to two cardinals, who were to show the book to the pope. I also gave him money for   5
the journey. Thereupon the worthy man wandered about in Switzerland for a couple of months, using my name to beg for money everywhere and carrying my book round with him, as high even as the emperor, who gave him seven gold pieces. The man never gave me a letter from you; but before I had had your last letter, he came to see me in Louvain, saying he was now   10
off to Rome, in case I wanted anything done. So you may drive away vagabonds of this description with a big stick, if you please, and you must give no one anything unless I have written him a letter of recommendation. I hear you have set your cap at a prebend in Liège, and I hope, my dear Caesarius, you may be successful.   15

* * * * *

44 to secure ... writings] Text suggested by Allen to fill an empty line in the Deventer Letter-book; (cf lines 33–5, Ep 703:18–22).

701
2 one-eyed] The Latin term is *luscus*; in Allen Ep 937:1 this term is used in reference to Pieter Meghen, but more frequently Erasmus calls Meghen 'Cyclops' or 'Cocles.' As Meghen had been sent to England at the beginning of September (cf Ep 653 introduction) he cannot well be the man who told Erasmus at about the same time (lines 10–11) that he was off to Rome. There is so far no evidence for Meghen's whereabouts in early 1516, but in the light of Erasmus' remarks here it seems clear that he was not the man who took the New Testament to Rome in February or March 1516; cf Ep 446:74–5.
5 cardinals] Riario and Grimani; see Ep 835 introduction.
10 last letter] Probably Ep 680; the more recent letter seems lost.

That scholars are supporting Reuchlin is a sign of enlightenment. But that they should dispute in writing with that kernel of all mischief, the Furies' trumpeter, the tool of certain well-known theologians in disguise, and Satan's true lieutenant – of this I cannot approve. That man is evil-speaking incarnate; he cannot be brought down by speaking evil in return; 20 he knows not what shame means; to speak a civil word is beyond his ken. And this brazen mountebank supposes it will redound to his credit if he can be pilloried, no matter how, in the works of the learned, for he would rather please the crowd than the best judges. If the world can once understand how crooked he is and can see that under the pretext of defending the 25 Christian faith he is proceeding to overthrow Christianity, this will be very popular among his colleagues of the circumcision, for whom he has done what Zopyrus did for Darius. My life upon it, if he could be opened up, you would find in his bosom not one Jew but a thousand. One must be on one's guard against an angel of Satan transformed into an angel of light. If only the 30 old saying were not so true, that a bad Jew always makes worse Christians! So I could wish that learned men had a higher opinion of themselves than to dispute with a monster so foul that, win or lose, they can get nothing out of it but filth and venom. I marvel that government, the bishops and the emperor himself do not put down such a pestilent fellow. It is very easy to 35 do harm, and the public have no common sense. The least spark can start a wide-ranging fire. What could suit the Jews better (for it is their battles he fights while pretending to oppose them) than for concord among Christians to be rent asunder like this? I would rather, if the New Testament could remain inviolate, see the entire Old Testament done away with than to see 40 the peace of Christendom torn to ribbons for the sake of the Jewish scriptures. If only he were still an entire Jew, and we were showing more caution in admitting the others!

I have now translated the second book of Theodore Gaza, after revising the first, and have sent both to Basel. Greetings to my friends. And so 45 farewell.

Louvain, 3 November

* * * * *

16 scholars] Cf Ep 694:116n.
40 done away with] Carried away perhaps, Erasmus here approaches in a way the position of Reuchlin's opponents. He is prepared to sacrifice even the Old Testament for the sake of preserving the peace of Christendom; they wished to protect Christianity by destroying all of Hebrew literature. There is no evidence that Erasmus ever wished to endorse the tenets of the Marcionite heresy which included a rejection of the Old Testament; cf Ep 798:26–30.
45 Basel] With Ep 629

702 / To Pieter Gillis   Louvain, 3 November [1517]

This letter is followed by Epp 708, 712, 715. Despite its apparently very private
business it was published by Erasmus in the *Farrago*. Erasmus' pleas for
secrecy seem exaggerated at times but usually indicate that the matter on hand
concerns him personally. Ep 706 shows that he had a request for Archbishop
Warham but preferred not to write to him. Instead More was asked to speak to
Warham after his return from Calais, and so probably, according to this letter,
was a certain Nicholas who planned a trip to England. Erasmus' request was
twofold: he desired to arrange for the payment of his pension from Aldington
(cf Ep 823 introduction), but at the same time he desired that the annuity be
redeemed through a single capital payment, as he doubted whether payments
would continue if Warham were to die (cf Ep 643:5–7). As More realized at once,
this second request cast some doubt on Erasmus' professed interest in a
permanent situation in England (cf Ep 706:23–4), and Erasmus dropped the
idea; cf Ep 726.

ERASMUS OF ROTTERDAM TO HIS FRIEND PIETER GILLIS

Greeting, dearest Pieter. I beg you by all that is sacred: learn to face the
chances of our human life with a good courage. I have great hopes of your
father's life; but yet, if anything should happen, see to it that I do not lose
two friends at once. What is the use of grief that can do no good, and may do   5
harm? Tell Nicholas in particular to keep his business dark, and not let out
to anybody whom he is going to see in England or in whose name he was
sent for. Even if he does not go, he must say nothing; let him invent some
reason as far from the truth as possible. You will learn the story from the
secretary's letter, and from what my Jacobus will tell you. Farewell, my best   10
of friends, and quit you like a man – or rather, remember that man is but
mortal and play out your part on the stage of this life. My best wishes to you

* * * * *

702
6 Nicholas] The Nicholas frequently so mentioned in Erasmus' letters to Gillis
  was probably Nicolaas van Broeckhoven of 's Hertogenbosch (see Ep 616:15n),
  who lived in Antwerp and enjoyed Erasmus' intimate confidence (cf Epp
  712:29, 38, 794:18). He may have been planning a trip to England. The name of
  the Bavarian Nikolaus Kratzer has been suggested, but Kratzer's presence in
  England is not, it seems, confirmed before 1519; see Ep 515:3n; Rogers Ep 101;
  LP III 1018–19, 1114, pp 1535, 1537.
10 secretary's] Allen suggested Warham's secretary, Thomas Bedyll; see Ep
   712:9n.
10 Jacobus] Nepos

and yours, and specially to your excellent father. I have written to Bannisio.

Louvain, 3 November

Dearest friend, storm-tossed as you now are, look for some excep-   15
tional fair weather in the future and reserve yourself for that. Farewell once
more. If I can be of any service either in your business or in Nicholas', I will
hasten to your side.

151[6]

703 / To [Hermann von Neuenahr]   Louvain, 4 November [1517]

That this letter was addressed to Neuenahr is confirmed by the contents (cf
Epp 694, 700, 701) and by the reference in Ep 722:24.

Greeting, my honoured friend. The industry and the talent displayed in the
book you have published I appreciated but could not admire. I see you
mention me also by name; I owe you something for your kind thought,
nothing for a kind action. No mortal man hates conflicts of this kind more
than I do. I even dislike my own *Apologia* which I was obliged to write in   5
answer to Lefèvre. As God loves me, it is a shame that learned men who
deserve to be remembered by posterity have to fight with such a monster,
whose name alone would befoul the paper it was written on. And the very
thing he prays for is that he may somehow be pilloried in the writings of the
learned. Why do not men who are genuine Christians keep their claws off   10
that Jewish scab? Everyone with any learning or character agrees that
Reuchlin has been vilely treated. My own policy has always been to overlook things rather than enter into a conflict with all those swarms of hornets,
armed with poison as well as stings, and with an utter rascal, an abominable
monster rather. That would have been the really high-minded line to take.   15
Innocence would not have lacked support. Reuchlin ought to be satisfied
with the approval of all good men. I am surprised that on this point
government and the bishops are asleep, so that they let this poisonous
fellow rage with impunity against men of learning and substance, and that
no Hercules has appeared to thrust this Cacus into some suitable chasm; for   20
that is the way to deal with this species of monster, and not by writing

* * * * *

13 Bannisio] See Ep 700.

703

2 book] See Ep 680:27–8; in Neuenahr's preface Erasmus was mentioned with a
   wealth of extravagant praise.

5 *Apologia*] See Ep 597:37n.

20 Cacus] See Ep 700:36n.

pamphlets. They do not see that from this hellish seed, which Satan, the friend of the Jews, has begun to sow with his own hand, a monstrous jungle will grow up unless timely steps are taken. And so, if you will allow me to give advice even to a man like yourself, I would urge you to use your   25 creative talents, which are worthy of your noble rank, on subjects which will give general satisfaction.

As to the suppression of that pamphlet, my opinion is still what I wrote to you. One must not give a handle to those who try to seize every handle they can find. And then, we must not give offence to one who is a   30 bulwark of humane studies. Nor should we allow an anonymous piece to bring all scholars under suspicion. Let us forget the people who prosper out of public mischief, and let us work for the benefit of our generation and indeed of posterity. The eagle, they say, does not catch flies; still more does it keep its high-born talons from the scorpion and the dung-beetle.   35

But I am remarkably shameless, to try and teach my betters a lesson. Farewell, my friend distinguished not in lineage alone.

Louvain, 4 November

704 / To Duke Ernest of Bavaria   [Louvain] 4 November 1517

This is the preface to an edition of the History of Alexander the Great by the Roman historian Quintus Curtius Rufus. The work – very popular since the Middle Ages, but incompletely preserved (cf lines 21–3) – was sent to the Strasbourg printer Matthias Schürer after the negotiations in Epp 606, 612, 633, 693 and published by Schürer under the date of June 1518 (cf Epp 844 end). Also printed in the Auctarium, this letter reflects Erasmus' criticisms of Greek and Roman historiography and his persistently negative appraisal of Alexander the Great (cf Bietenholz History and Biography 63 and passim). At the same time the letter shows why he believed that authors such as Curtius Rufus were indispensable.

Ernest, the youngest son of Duke Albert IV of Bavaria (see Ep 386 introduction), had left the Ingolstadt humanist circle in February 1517 to assume his duties as administrator of the bishopric of Passau. It is possible that Erasmus still expected him to be at Ingolstadt.

* * * * *

28 pamphlet] The Julius exclusus; see Ep. 636:14–29.
30 one who] Leo x
34 eagle] The adage 'Aquila non captat muscas' permits an allusion to Neuenahr's name in Latin, Nova aquila; cf Adagia III ii 65.
36 teach my betters] Literally 'the sow teaching Minerva'; Adagia I i 40

TO THE MOST NOBLE PRINCE ERNEST, DUKE OF BAVARIA
FROM ERASMUS OF ROTTERDAM, GREETING

Cicero, by common consent the most fertile and inexhaustible source of
eloquence, concedes that the springs of fluency very easily run dry unless
one maintains them by daily practice in reading and composition. And so,   5
illustrious Ernest (illustrious not in lineage alone), what do you suppose can
be my own experience? The merest rivulet of style is all my lot has given me
to draw on, and I have now spent many years upon studies of a kind which
does nothing for the improvement of that style and actually might dry up
even the most generous flow, overspreading even a brilliant faculty of   10
expression with rust and cobwebs. What can do less for the maintenance of
a polished style than the disorderly reading which carries one back and
forth from author to author, and sometimes into such as have no style at all?
And this is how I have had to work, on the New Testament, in casting and
recasting my *Chiliades*, in establishing the works of Jerome.   15

And so, in hopes of correcting at least in part the roughness or poverty
of style acquired in these studies, when I was on my way last spring to
England, I took with me Quintus Curtius as my companion on the journey
by land and sea, for when I read him as a boy long ago, I thought him
wonderfully clear and terse, nor does he seem different when sampled after   20
so long an interval. It is a pity that an author so much worth reading should
have come down to us headless, the first two books being lost and the last
defective and damaged in many places. I smiled, as I read, at the petty
vanity of the Greeks in writing their history, although Curtius seems to
have modified this from time to time; and yet, when they concentrate their   25
powers of mind to draw the picture of a noble and inimitable prince, what
have they presented to us except a frequently outrageous and always fortunate bandit on a worldwide scale? Alexander was dangerous when drunk,
and no less so when drunk with anger and ambition than with wine. The
greater the successes of that rash, unbridled spirit, the greater danger he   30
was to society. To my mind, the Alexander of the Greek historians is a
spectacle no more pleasing than Homer's Achilles; both are shocking examples for a good prince, although we may seem to see some virtues mixed
with so much vice. Was it then really worthwhile to plunge Africa, Europe,
and Asia in bloodshed to please the whims of one unbalanced young man,   35
whose ambition was not to be satisfied by the limits of this entire earth? It

* * * * *

704
3 Cicero] *De oratore* 1.149–50
20 sampled] Cicero *Epistulae ad Atticum* 4.19.1

was a blessing that fortune, too kind to him in other ways, refused to let this scourge live long. I have corrected some passages marked in the course of reading and added a table showing the novel expressions to be found in this author, in order to have a sop to throw at some verbal critics, who bombard   40
me with protests against individual words, declaring that they are found in no respectable author.

The profit to be got out of this, the work I have put into it, I have decided to dedicate to you, to show that I still cherish the memory of a prince to whom I myself owe a great private debt for the most generous   45
offers you made me long ago, and to whom a great public debt is owed by all devotees of humane learning – that learning which you adorn with the illustrious lineage of your ancestors, make attractive by your high character, encourage by your generosity, protect with your authority, in such a way that learning soon would be in the most fortunate case if only other princes   50
would forget their passion for making war and follow your example. Farewell.

4 November 1517

704A / To Wolfgang Lachner   [Louvain, early November? 1517]

In Allen's edition this letter is Ep 733. He thought that it was dispatched together with Ep 734, but his contention that it is 'clearly contemporary' with Ep 732 is questionable. Nichols assigned the letter to October 1517, and he may be closer to the truth. The sequence of letters dealing with the same matter seems clearest if one assumes that this letter followed Epp 629 and 687 but preceded Ep 732, at the end of which it is stated that Erasmus was not writing to Lachner at that time. Epp 726:13–14, 731:45–6, and 732:39–40 mention a messenger who had gone to Basel, clearly some time in November. It can be expected that he carried this letter and probably Epp 693 and 704 for Schürer in Strasbourg. The dispatch of material for Schürer is recalled in Epp 730–2 but not mentioned in this letter.

ERASMUS TO HIS FRIEND LACHNER, GREETING
You remind me of our friendship, but this is quite uncalled-for. It is not my way to withdraw from friendship easily, nor is there any reason why I should want to. I merely wished you had called in a man who knew

* * * * *

45 generous offers] Cf Epp 386:15–38, 392, 394.

704A
4 knew] Reading *nosset* for *noscet* (cf Allen Ep 742:8).

something of this business before setting a value on the copy. Not that I 5
have any wish to squeeze much out of you, but in order that, a definite
principle being once established, you and I might feel ourselves under no
constraint. Whatever you might have decided would have been acceptable
to me. In the *Proverbs* the additional copying-out did not amount to much,
but there was much extra work. These are things that Froben, excellent man 10
that he is and my dear friend, cannot take into account. From Franz I have
still received nothing. Then again, I had written to tell Froben not to take
more from my servant Jacobus than it would be convenient to print. He took
everything, and besides that never answered a word on the subject, any
more than you did. Whatever I have entrusted to you hitherto, I have never 15
allowed anyone else to print, so far as in me lay, nor shall I. At the time of the
last fair, I sent you my translation of the second book of Theodore Gaza, and
my *Apologia*; I suppose they reached you. Please warn your proof-reader to
learn some more Greek and to be ready to listen to men who know more
Greek than he does. You cannot think what harm is done to books by a 20
printer's reader with too good a conceit of himself. Nowadays everyone has
a good word for your press, and this reputation is worth keeping. More's
shorter works I should prefer not to be separated from my dialogues, but to
remain joined with them, as they have been hitherto.

705 / To Bruno Amerbach

This letter has been assigned a different year date and is Ep 902A in this
edition.

* * * * *

5 copy] Copy for print; cf Ep 629:7n. The expert Erasmus has in mind is Beatus
Rhenanus; cf Ep 594 introduction.
9 *Proverbs*] See Ep 629:4–12.
11 Franz] Franz Birckmann; cf Ep 629:6n.
12 I had written] In May 1517; see Ep 595:1n, 11n. The servant was Jacobus
Nepos.
16 anyone else] Cf Ep 732:21n.
17 I sent] Gaza's grammar was sent with Ep 629, but the printing of the *Apologia
ad Fabrum* was not quite finished when Erasmus wrote Ep 628. No doubt a
supply of the newly printed books was sent to the Frankfurt fair by Martens a
few days later; cf Ep 730 introduction.
18 proof-reader] Wolfgang Angst
23 dialogues] From their first appearance in 1506, Erasmus' and More's translations from Lucian had been printed together; cf Ep 187 introduction.

706 / From Thomas More   Calais, 5 November [1517]

This letter was printed in the *Auctarium*.

THOMAS MORE TO HIS FRIEND ERASMUS, GREETING

I had a letter from you today, together with letters for Colet and the bishop
of Rochester, and a pamphlet with them. I will see to it that they are
delivered as soon as possible, so that the pamphlet may not lose the charm
of novelty. As I read your letter, I wondered why you had not written to my   5
lord of Canterbury as well, to deal with your business with him yourself, for
no one else, if I mistake not, carries such weight with him. Though if you
would rather do this through me, and think that someone on the spot can be
more effective than any writing of letters, it will give me more pleasure to
comply than you to command me. But I shall not have the opportunity to   10
complete it as soon as I should wish to complete any business of yours, for it
is the regular practice with us that a man returning from a mission must go
straight to the king and not turn aside to see anyone on the way. Besides
which, my negotiations proceed so slowly that I fear it may be necessary to
stay here longer than I hoped and longer than suits my own interests, unless   15
perhaps I find that there is no hope here which makes it worth while to stay.
But for the time being, if you wish, the business can be done by letter; and I
have no doubt that that will be your wish. I will proceed therefore on the
assumption that this year's annuity is to be deposited with Maruffo and the
bill dispatched to you. But as for commuting your annuity I at least think   20
that nothing should be done, both because there is no one who could
properly commute it except one man who, they tell me, has no funds to do it
from, and because I fear the archbishop will read this as a sign that you have
lost all interest in us. So think again about the commutation; if you decide to
go ahead, you will not find me wanting. Meantime I will myself take steps   25
about payment, and I think it would not come amiss if you put in a letter
too; he perhaps is waiting for that.

I am delighted that the paraphrase is in the press. How I envy Louvain! A great blessing has come its way – how great, as far as I can see, it

* * * * *

706
2 letters] All three are lost; for the book sent for Bishop Fisher see Ep 697:15n.
6 Canterbury] William Warham; for the business see Ep 702 introduction.
19 Maruffo] Raffaele Maruffo, a Genoese merchant and banker in England; see Ep
387:3n.
22 except one man] Richard Master, the rector of Aldington; see Allen I 502n.
28 paraphrase] See Ep 710.

scarcely recognizes. But the man of whom you write, unless I am quite   30
wrong, will never alter. Tunstall just thinks you are too kind-hearted in
continuing to trust him after being deceived so often. Pace is still not back,
nor can I discover when he will return; for that matter, I cannot imagine
what business detains him. At least, as far as I can understand by making
enquiries, for a long time there has been nothing afoot either with the   35
emperor or with the Swiss, yet he is not allowed to pack up and go home,
though he has now been stuck in Constance, I believe, for more than a year.
I am surprised that he has not returned your book. I will write to him about
it to some effect; for there is nothing I would rather achieve, for the cause of
good letters or my own sake, perceiving that you intend to set up a monu-   40
ment to our friendship in that work, which I value above all pyramids and
mausoleums.

Hermans I must leave to you. For Batt I developed such a penchant
long ago from the way you spoke about him that I am almost as keen to see
his memory flourish as my own. Only you must consider how you will   45
couple me with him, for he died when I had scarcely reached man's estate,
or in fact not even that. But you will contrive all this well enough. Mind you,
though: charity begins at home. I insist on a part second only to yours, and

* * * * *

30 the man] Probably Maarten van Dorp; cf Epp 696, 713.
31 Tunstall] Cuthbert Tunstall probably met More at Calais when returning to
England after the exchange; Epp 663, 675.
32 him] Refers to 'the man' (line 30).
32 Pace] For his mission and movements see Ep 619 introduction.
38 book] A manuscript of the first two books of the *Antibarbari*, plus material for
the remainder, entrusted to Pace along with other manuscripts when they met
at Ferrara in 1508. Despite all efforts (cf Epp 732:27, 787:20–2), it was never
recovered. It appears that Erasmus now wished to resume work on the *Antibarbari*. In doing so, he wished to introduce as interlocutors some friends of
more recent years, above all More. Erasmus first published this letter in 1518,
but when it reappeared in the *Epistolae ad diversos* of 1521, the entire section
from 'perceiving' (line 40) to 'immortality' (line 50) had been omitted, clearly
because it no longer corresponded with his plan for the work. Cf ASD I–1
11–12. Meanwhile, in 1519 Erasmus had chosen another way to set up a
monument to More; see Ep 999.
42 mausoleums] The tomb of Mausolus, satrap of Caria, at Halicarnassus. It was
one of the seven wonders of the ancient world; fragments are now in the
British Museum.
43 Hermans] Unlike More, Willem Hermans and Jacob Batt were retained as
interlocutors in the published version of *Antibarbari*.
46 he died] In 1502 when More was 24 or 25
48 at home] Terence *Andria* 635; literally 'I am my own nearest neighbour'

no mistake. I am too fond of talking, as you know, to submit to a walking-on
part, especially in a comedy from which I promise myself immortality.   50

    Farewell, dearest Erasmus. I am glad you liked my poor lines on the
picture. Tunstall thought almost too well of the hendecasyllables, only
moderately of the six-line epigram. But a certain friar I could name even had
the face to pick a hole in it, because I compared the two of you to Castor and
Pollux, and he said you should have been compared to Theseus and Pirith-   55
ous or Pylades and Orestes, who were friends, as you are, and not brothers.
I could not endure the friar, even if he were speaking the truth, and
responded to his well-meant interference with an ill-written epigram:
    Quoth I, of two great friends in brief
    The affection to declare,   60
  'Such friends they are as once of old
    Castor and Pollux were.'
    An owlish brother takes me up,
    Of those who wear the cowl:
  'Who friends and brothers thus confounds,   65
    Sure, he must be an owl!'
  'How so? What can more friendly be
    Than brother is to brother?'
    He laughed at one who did not know
    What's known to every other: 70
  'A large and crowded house is ours,
    Brothers ten score may be;
    In those ten score (my life upon't)
    Two friends you will not see.'

Farewell then once again. From Calais, 5 November, in haste, the courier   75
being in a great hurry, and under pressure, I dare say, from his driver.

707 / To Henricus Glareanus   [Louvain, October–November 1517]

    This answer to Ep 618 is probably contemporary with Ep 689; there are many
    similarities to letters written by Erasmus around the end of October. Allen
    preferred the date of mid-November in view of the printing of the *Paraphrasis
    ad Romanos* (lines 16–18). But Erasmus' reference is vague, and we do not
    know when the printing actually started.

* * * * *

    51 lines] See Ep 684.

ERASMUS TO HIS FRIEND GLAREANUS, GREETING
I must send a brief answer to your letter, the only one I have had, which was
written from Paris on 5 August. I am glad you have moved to France, and
hope all will go well. You will like Paris more when you are more used to it.
This is an elegant town, but financially a dead end. If only your salary from   5
the king would travel with you as far as this, I should much wish you might
move here. Jérôme de Busleyden, whose name you can find among the
Dialogues of Lucian that I have translated, has founded by his will (for he
died on the journey to Spain) a college in Louvain in which the three
tongues are to be taught, for a good stipend, and permanent too. We now   10
have Matthaeus here, who was our friend Wolfgang's teacher and is far the
most learned of Hebrew scholars. We shall also get a Greek of some sort.
You would laugh, if you were here, to see your friend Erasmus daily seated
on high among the grave doctors. Make sure, my learned friend, that at least
you pay me interim visits in the way of frequent letters. I have sent many   15
things to Basel to be printed. Here they are printing my Paraphrase on the
Epistle to the Romans, in which there is much more work than might
appear. I have revised a large part of the New Testament, such a revision as
will make it a new book. Pray let me know in return what your Muse has in
hand. Budé did not know who you were, or so I judge from his letter. The   20
paper on which you had noted down various passages in the New Testament, I have now lost. If the notes still survive in your copy, let me have
another list. Farewell, my sweetest friend, both you and yours.
    Why should I complain of Lefèvre, my dear Glareanus? I do not doubt
that you have already seen my *Apologia*. My life upon it, I never did   25
anything so reluctantly. I love the man sincerely. What evil genius put this
into his head? Farewell once more.

                    * * * * *

707
  8 Lucian] See Ep 205; for Busleyden's death see Ep 608 introduction.
 11 Matthaeus] Adrianus (see Ep 686:7n); he was in Basel in 1513 and gave
    Hebrew lessons to the Amerbach brothers and, at some other time, to
    Wolfgang Faber Capito.
 13 seated] See Ep 637:12n.
 15 many things] See Epp 594:2n, 602–4, 629, 730 introduction.
 16 Paraphrase] See Ep 710.
 18 New Testament] See Ep 864 introduction.
 20 letter] See Ep 609:22.
 25 *Apologia*] See Ep 721 introduction.

708 / To Pieter Gillis   Louvain, 10 November [1517]

> This letter, which is in sequence with Epp 702, 712, 715, was first published in
> the *Farrago*.

ERASMUS TO HIS FRIEND PIETER GILLIS, GREETING
I wish whatever is best to your excellent father. I do beg you most urgently,
dearest Pieter, bear with reason what cannot be altered, and do not let
yourself be overcome with grief which will destroy you, and be a painful
burden to your family and very painful to More and myself. Keep yourself   5
going in your own interest, keep yourself for the benefit of your family,
keep yourself for better things to come. Whether your father lives through
this or not, I know you are much burdened, with business as well as grief.
And so, not to add to your burdens with some of my own, I have sent my
man Jacobus to fetch away what you have of mine; if any of it can be of any   10
use to you, pray pick it out, and let me know what you have kept. I only
wish that the total of all I have could purchase your father's health and
yours. I would have come myself, but I am afraid of the phlegm and entirely
occupied in revising the New Testament. I have had two letters from More.
Look after yourself, and be of good courage. If there is anything in which I   15
can help you, try me, and see whether I truly love you.
        Louvain, St Martin's eve

709 / From Jacopo Bannisio   Antwerp, 12 November 1517

> This is the answer to Ep 700. However, whereas Ep 700 remained unpub-
> lished, Erasmus selected this polite and complimentary letter, together with
> his own reply to it (Ep 716), for publication in the *Farrago* of October 1519. He
> thus managed to give his readers the impression that Bannisio had taken the
> initiative to urge him against participation in the Reuchlin controversy. In
> reality, Bannisio may have done just the opposite; cf Ep 700 introduction.

JACOPO BANNISIO,
COUNSELLOR OF HIS IMPERIAL MAJESTY,
TO ERASMUS OF ROTTERDAM, GREETING
Reverend and most honoured sir, with my humble duty. I was laid very low

        * * * * *

708
 3 bear with reason] Cf *Adagia* I iii 14.
10 Jacobus] Nepos
14 letters] Epp 683, 688

by ill health and not my own master when your most kind letter reached me,   5
and that is why I send a belated answer and not in my own hand. Nor is
there any reason to find fault with yourself for not giving me a more ready
welcome when I came to see you of my own accord here in Antwerp, for you
showed yourself very friendly to me, and all my prayers were answered as
soon as I had seen the man I wanted to see so much. I felt at the time that I   10
had shown some lack of modesty in daring to intrude upon a man who lives
such a studious and well-regulated life, without first taking soundings and
showing more respect, but with a kind of self-confidence bred in those who
live in courts. But you must ascribe this to eagerness, which would have
brought me from the very heart of my native Illyria, and not to principle.   15
Here was a man whom I venerated from afar as a hero for his supreme
learning, and I wanted one day, now that it was permitted, to behold him in
person; and so all delay seemed to me perilous. When I heard therefore that
you were here, had I not hastened to see you, I thought it impossible that
my prayers should be answered. As soon as I am well again, if business   20
permits (since you suggest it), before I leave this part of the world I will visit
you in Louvain, for at this time a man of your eminence ought not to lose
such valuable hours in coming here.

   As for the Jew, or those who on his behalf, pestilential and accursed as
he is, have the face to challenge every learned and right-thinking man, with   25
the sole object of making themselves famous by their infamy, I think it best
to ignore them; with their minds uncircumcised from every righteous
action, they should be left in obscurity in the darkness where they belong.
He who stirs or sets hand to what stinks will have only stink for his pains.

   Your letters for Mainz and for Pirckheimer I will send on. My respect-   30
ful best wishes, and may you long prosper for the benefit and the progress
of all humane studies.

   Antwerp, 12 November 1517

          * * * * *

709
24 Jew] Pfefferkorn
30 Pirckheimer] Another copy of Ep 694 sent to Bannisio with Ep 700, or more
   likely the same copy of Ep 694 that had been sent to Poppenruyter with Ep 698.
   If so, Poppenruyter must have been in close touch with Bannisio who like him
   served the Hapsburgs and who took charge of Epp 701 and 703, both to be
   forwarded to Cologne (see Ep 722:24). No letter to Mainz is known from this
   period.

IN EPISTOLAM PAVLI
Apoſtoli ad Romanos Paraphraſis, p Eraſmum
Roterodamum, ad reuerendiſſimum Cardina‑
lem Grymanum.

Cum gratia τ priuilegio.

Erasmus *Paraphrasis ad Romanos* title page
Louvain: Martens 1517
Courtesy of the British Library Board

710 / To Domenico Grimani   Louvain, 13 November 1517

This is the preface to the *Paraphrasis ad Romanos* (Louvain: D. Martens [November] 1517; NK 846). In the Metsys portrait (cf Ep 684:17–18) Erasmus was shown working on this text, and it was in fact at Antwerp, probably during May and June 1517, that he wrote the paraphrase (cf Allen Ep 1342:935–7). Printing probably began in October (cf Epp 687:18, 719), and by the end of November Erasmus had begun to send out copies (cf Ep 726). He had considered dedicating it to Albert of Brandenburg, but then decided that the paraphrase of Romans ought to be dedicated to someone in Rome (see Ep 745:16–23). He chose Grimani, but did not himself send a copy of the first edition (see Ep 835:5–8), and two years later still had not received word from the cardinal that the dedication was welcome (cf Ep 1017).

The paraphrases of most texts in the New Testament flowed naturally from Erasmus' continued preoccupation with the Greek text and his own Latin translation. He often repeated his desire that the Gospel should be comprehensible to the people. While he left it for others to produce translations into the vernacular, he took it upon himself to make a biblical narrative in smooth Latin which would serve as a guide to easy comprehension as well as to meaningful interpretation. That his first paraphrase should be on Romans is explained by the crucial importance that he and others, including Luther, assigned to the correct understanding of this text. As early as 1514 he had vowed to the Apostle Paul to compose a commentary on Romans (cf Ep 301:20–2), and he had reiterated his promise when annotating Romans 1:1 for the first edition of his New Testament in 1516. However, he then changed his mind (lines 39–53, but cf Allen Ep 894:48–9) and decided to honour his pledge with a paraphrase: Paul would speak colloquially to the contemporary reader; the prolixity and pedantry of a systematic commentary would be avoided, but scholarly standards would be retained in that his work was based on a careful study of the patristic interpretations (cf Allen Ep 1342:929–31). The immediate success of this first paraphrase convinced Erasmus that he had found the right approach (cf Epp 755:4–7, 962). The Louvain first edition was followed by four Froben editions (1518–20), but meanwhile the work had been further disseminated jointly with other paraphrases, first on the remaining Epistles (cf Ep 720:14–16) and subsequently on the Gospels, in dozens of editions and translations.

TO THE MOST REVEREND FATHER IN CHRIST
MY LORD GRIMANI OF VENICE, CARDINAL OF ST MARK'S,
FROM ERASMUS OF ROTTERDAM, GREETING
Those who find it surprising, most reverend Father in God, that Paul the

Apostle, who was a good linguist, should have written to the Romans in   5
Greek rather than Latin, will wonder no more if they remember, first, that at
that date the use of the Greek language was almost as widespread as the
Roman rule, and secondly that the Romans themselves at one time had such
a passion for Greek literature that it was held up to ridicule by the satirists.
Scaevola in Lucilius, mocking Albutius as unusually pro-Greek, greets him   10
with '*Chaere* praetor at Athens,' and in Juvenal some character is indignant
because he cannot stand Rome turned into Greek. Not but what the Apostle's Greek is such that a pure Greek speaker can hardly understand him, on
account of the admixture everywhere of Hebrew idiom. Even had he written in the most perfect and pure Greek, great difficulties for the reader   15
would have remained, because he was writing for men who were still raw
and recently converted to Christianity, and so he touched on some mysteries instead of going into them, and provided indications rather than
explanations, 'serving the time.' Now however that Rome is entirely Christian, so that it is the capital and chief seat of the Christian religion, and Latin   20
is spoken all the world over by everyone who acknowledges the authority of
the Roman pontiff, I thought I should be doing something worth while if I
could make Paul speak to men who are now pure Romans and adult
Christians, not only in the Roman tongue but more intelligibly; if, in fact,
he could talk Latin in such a way that one would not recognize the Hebrew   25
speaking but would recognize the Apostle. He was accustomed to vary his
style, but never lost the apostolic dignity.

I will not set forth here how much this small work has cost me, such as
it is, for I am sure that no one who has not made the experiment himself in
similar subject-matter would find it easy to value or to believe the difficulty   30
of bridging gaps, smoothing rough passages, bringing order out of confusion and simplicity out of complication, untying knots, throwing light on
dark places, and giving Hebrew turns of speech a Roman dress – in fact, of
altering the language of Paul, the heavenly spokesman, and so managing
one's paraphrase that it does not become a *paraphronesis*, a caricature. One   35
must say things differently without saying different things, especially on a
subject which is not only difficult in many ways, but sacred, and very near
the majesty of the Gospel; one works on slippery ground where a fall is very
easy, and yet one cannot fall without grave peril. One thing only I will say,

* * * * *

710
10 Lucilius] Cicero *De finibus* 1.3.9; he should have said, not the Greek *chaere*, but
a proper Roman 'good day to you.'
11 Juvenal] 3.60, 61
19 time] Cf Ep 740:4n.

in honesty rather than arrogance: the labour would not have been greatly   40
increased if I had essayed to publish a full-dress commentary on the epistle.
I shall think, however, that my efforts have been richly rewarded, if I can
feel that as a result Paul has become somewhat more attractive and certainly
more accessible to your Eminence, and through you to the rest of Rome, to
whom it is right that he should be most attractive and most accessible. For I   45
know well how many people have been deterred from reading him hitherto
by the strangeness of the language, and how many more by the difficulty of
disentangling and understanding what he says, wrong though it is that any
inconvenience should deter men from such fruitful reading. It is the distaste
or the despair of such people that I have tried to remedy by this enterprise of   50
mine, so balancing my work that he who rejects any change in the letter of
Holy Writ may use it as a commentary, while he who is free from such
superstition may hear the voice of Paul himself.

Let Rome prepare a welcome, therefore, for the first or at least the
greatest teacher of her religion. Let her embrace the herald of her ancient   55
fame, let her return the love of one who loved a city he had never seen.
Happy indeed the change in the style of her prosperity! Long ago under
imperial despots she offered worship to dumb images; now under Peter
and Paul she presides over the earth. Long ago the handmaid of every
superstition, now she is the great mistress of the true religion. Jove on the   60
Capitol has made way for Christ, who alone is best and greatest; the
emperor for Peter and Paul, immeasurably gifted each of them in his own
way; that solemn famous senate for the College of Cardinals, revered all the
world over. If she is stirred by arch or pyramid, the relics of her ancient
superstition, how can she resist the monuments of revealed religion to be   65
found in the books of those apostles? She marvels at Hadrian's statue or
Domitian's baths; let her embrace instead the most holy epistles of Peter
and Paul. If she loves to read in the works of a Sallust or a Livy the ancient
fables of her early days, how she was exalted from small beginnings to a
world dominion that was soon to fall, guided by vultures, much more ought   70
she to love the writings of apostles and evangelists, in which she can
recognize from what rudiments she rose to a dominion over the church that
shall never fail, guided by Christ. Among the Jews not a trace remains today
of their temple, once so sacred; so too the Capitol of Rome, which foolish
prophets long ago promised should be eternal, has left so few remnants that   75
one cannot even point out where it stood.

* * * * *

66 Hadrian's ... Domitian's] It is unlikely that Erasmus had specific antiquities in
   mind.

If she admires the tongue of Cicero, of which it were hard to say whether it did more good or harm to the republic, why does she not enjoy still more the eloquence of Paul, to which she owes the greatest part of her salvation and religion? She was always greedy for praise, and now she has 80 this great and famous herald of her glory, for what triumph so great as to be praised in the words of an apostle? O Romans, Romans, learn what Paul did for you, and you will understand what the glories are that you must maintain. Listen to his warning voice, lest you fail to know what you must shun. He praises faith, which nowhere else has kept more spotless. He 85 speaks of obedience, which made you early exchange superstition for religion. He grants you affability, whose companion often is credulity; this was the reason why false apostles tempted you into Judaism; but with that ease of manners went prudence, which caused a swift repentance. He marks your proud spirit and therefore warns you so carefully against pride 90 and insolence, calls you from luxury to sobriety of life, from lust to chastity, from brutality to toleration, from strife to concord, from war to peace. Such is your true Roman character, from which it would be disgraceful to descend. Beware lest you, being Rome, degenerate into Babylon.

St Jerome tells us that even in his day there was still evidence of the 95 religious spirit praised by Paul. 'Where else,' he says, 'do such zealous crowds throng round the churches and the martyrs' tombs? Where does the Amen echo like a peal of heavenly thunder, till the idols' empty temples quake? Not that the Romans hold a different faith from all the other churches of Christ, but because in them is greater devotion and the simpli- 100 city that leads to belief!' In truth a splendid tribute from Jerome! But what would he say now, if he could see in that same city all those churches, all those cardinals, those bishops? If he could see all the princes of the world seeking answers from this one infallible oracle of Christ; men gathering in crowds for the sake of religion from the utmost corners of the globe; no man 105 thinking himself truly a Christian until he has seen Rome and the Roman pontiff, as if he were some earthly deity upon whose nod, for yes or no, all human affairs depend; and finally, if he could survey the city of Rome under Leo the Tenth, with the storms of war laid to rest, a flourishing home of literature no less than of religion; the one place that combines so many 110 leaders of the church, so many men distinguished for learning of every kind, so many lights and glories of the world, that Rome seems the earth in little rather than a city? Nor need we pray for anything from the higher

* * * * *

88 Judaism] Cf Ep 694 introduction.
95 Jerome] *Commentarii in epistolam ad Galatas* II (Gal 3:8–9), PL 26:381
107 nod] *Adagia* IV ix 39

powers, except that she may for ever answer to her reputation, that good
fortune in her may for ever be surpassed by piety and majesty outstripped   115
by virtue. And this will come to pass, if she tries with all her might to
express the spirit and the saintly life of Peter and Paul, under whose
patronage and protection she reigns. But nowhere can a more express and
lively image of them be found than in their own writings.

Meanwhile they will more gladly welcome this fragment of Paul,   120
eminent Father, if it is offered to them by the hand of one who, like you, is a
wonderful patron of all learning, and especially of such as is concerned with
knowledge of the tongues; though at the same time you are so conspicuous
for your high character that even among so many great luminaries you
outshine them all, not so as to cast them in the shade but adding to persons   125
gifted and illustrious in their own right a new wealth of light and glory. My
respectful best wishes to your Eminence.

Louvain, 13 November 1517

711 / From Georgius Spalatinus   Altenburg, 13 November 1517

Spalatinus (see Ep 501 introduction), the secretary of Frederick the Wise, held
a canonry in Altenburg, where the Saxon dukes had a large castle. Among his
duties was the assembling of an academic library for the elector's castle and
new university at Wittenberg. This letter, however, did not reach Erasmus
until nearly two years later, when he answered it with Ep 1001. It was first
printed in the *Farrago*.

GEORGIUS SPALATINUS TO
ERASMUS OF ROTTERDAM, GREETING
A letter from you, Erasmus, sole glory of all the native Germany that we
both share, is long awaited, for if mine ever reached you I have no doubt
whatever that you will reply. For I wrote more on a matter of public   5
importance than personally, though to write personally was a great pleasure; for I had long been in search of an occasion to write to you and never
found one until someone appeared who almost compelled me to write, as I
was in any case longing to do. For I became your admirer when I first met
your works, when first I entered the shrine of your many-sided learning and   10

* * * * *

711
4 mine] Ep 501; Erasmus may have answered, but if he did his letter failed to
reach Spalatinus.
8 someone] Martin Luther, who provided Spalatinus with part of the text of Ep
501

Georgius Spalatinus
Portrait by Lucas Cranach the Elder, 1537
Staatliche Kunsthalle Karlsruhe

wide range of style. And so, where and how you are now and what great
work you are building, and what you have on the anvil for our age and for
posterity, are questions I and many others would rather know the answer to
than anything. So I hope you will think you owe it to the position of my
excellent prince, Frederick duke of Saxony, elector of the Holy Roman   15
Empire, to let me have an answer after all this time. For that great prince has
the highest opinion of you, and has all your works in his library, which he
plans to have filled with all the best books. The rest you will hear from my
friend Petrus Alamire. My very best wishes.

In haste, from the castle of Altenburg, 13 November 1517   20

712 / To Pieter Gillis   Louvain, 15 November [1517]

This letter, which is in sequence with Epp 708 and 715, was first published in
the *Farrago*.

ERASMUS OF ROTTERDAM TO HIS FRIEND
PIETER GILLIS, GREETING
Much as I am distressed by your excellent father's death, I think him happy
in the manner of it, for this is the lot to which we are all born, and nothing in
the affairs of men lasts long, much less endures for ever. It is very good news   5
that you are better, and I pray that your recovery may prove lasting.

Although I loaded Jacobus with commissions, I forgot one thing
which needed particular attention. The archbishop of Canterbury writes,
telling me to draw on some friend of mine here for twenty pounds sterling

* * * * *

19 Alamire] Chaplain and composer to Prince Charles; also an informer in English pay. In 1519 he brought Erasmus this letter and also one by Pirckheimer;
   cf LP II 1566–7; R. Eitner *Biographisch-Bibliographisches Quellen-Lexikon der
   Musiker und Musikgelehrten*, 2nd ed (Graz 1959–60).

712
3 father's death] See Ep 715 introduction.
6 are better] For Gillis' health see the index for this volume.
7 Jacobus] Nepos
9 twenty pounds] £20 sterling (= £29 1s 10d gros Flemish = £168 18s 4d tournois,
   in relative silver values) was the amount due to Erasmus as his annuity from
   the Aldington benefice. Warham's letter may have been in response to the
   steps undertaken by Erasmus and More according to Epp 702, 706. Or perhaps
   Erasmus had made an earlier approach to yet another friend with a request
   that he talk to Warham (cf Ep 702:9–10). Erasmus' multiple efforts to secure
   this payment helped to create considerable confusion; see Ep 823 introduction; cf Epp 188, 255 introductions, 467:7n.

and send a receipt, on which he will promptly pay. Since, as I hear, you are   10
not allowed out of the house, I wish you would send for Johannes Crullus,
or some more suitable person if there is one, and have him pay the money
over to you and take my receipt for it; or else entrust the business to me, and
I will make sure that the sum is paid in England to the person nominated by
the man who advanced it. If the archbishop does not pay – but I know very   15
well he will – I will refund it myself. Please stand surety for the sum, if he
demands one; which will be satisfactory and convenient for you, for the
money will remain in your hands. It is important for me that this should be
done as soon as possible. Do you know why? In order that I may decently
ask again as soon as next Easter. So I beg you will do this, which will be a   20
blessing to me, and no inconvenience to anyone.

More is still at Calais, which he finds, it appears, both tedious and
expensive, and the business of a most disagreeable kind. This is how kings
make their friends happy; such a thing it is to be popular with cardinals. It is
the same with Pace; they have now kept him over two years in exile among   25
the Swiss. Let me have his letter. I wish it might be convenient for you to
spend the winter here with me; we shall exchange gossip to our hearts'
content. My paraphrase is now rapidly approaching its end. Thirty-six
philippi, and I think a little more, I left with Nicholas to pay for the blankets,
and left it on the understanding that when he had paid the bill he would   30
repay the balance to you. And I remember writing about this; but no answer
from you. Let me know how we stand.

Do not send Croke his books until I have seen them; he is living at
Cambridge, where he is to teach Greek. Do not let him know you have had
his letter.   35

* * * * *

11 Crullus] A commercial agent at Antwerp; cf Epp 543:28n, 545:3.
20 ask again] An indication that at this time Erasmus was already planning his
    journey to Basel in the spring (cf Ep 732:62) and intended to request another
    payment to meet his travelling expenses; cf Ep 823 introduction.
22 Calais] See Epp 623:23n, 688.
25 Pace] See Ep 706:32–7.
28 paraphrase] See Ep 710 introduction.
29 philippi] See Ep 651:9n.
29 Nicholas] Here and in line 38 probably Nicolaas van Broeckhoven of 's Her-
    togenbosch; see Ep 702:6n.
33 Croke] Richard Croke had recently left Leipzig (cf Ep 415:13–14) and received
    his MA at Cambridge in September. At about the same time he was appointed
    lecturer in Greek (cf Epp 777:3–5, 827). On his way back to England Croke may
    have left his books in Antwerp for shipping, and Erasmus, in his thirst for
    Greek texts, wished to look them over.

The physician is asking for a stay of execution for a fortnight. If you happen to see the man, make him think your relations with me are embarrassed unless he delivers what he promised. Let Doctor Nicholas say the same; surely he heard him forswearing himself. I could have wished the seal had been dispatched earlier; but I know it is not your fault, not being 40 ignorant of the way you conduct your own affairs.

I am enclosing in your letter my receipt and the letter from the archbishop of Canterbury. If Crullus is away, or not enthusiastic, I am sure Franz will not take it amiss. Farewell, most faithful friend.

Louvain, 15 November 151[8] 45

713 / To Johann Reuchlin   Louvain, 15 November [1517]

An eighteenth-century manuscript copy (Öffentliche Bibliothek of the University of Basel MS G² I 15 f 18) provided a better basis for the text than *Illustrium virorum epistolae ... ad Ioannem Reuchlin* (Haguenau 1519); see Ep 300 introduction. At the same time it confirms the essential correctness of the text of this letter published by Reuchlin in 1519. The year must be 1517 because of Adrian's elevation to the college of cardinals (see Ep 608:13n). For Erasmus' recent involvement in the Reuchlin affair see Ep 694 introduction, and for his bitter reaction to the unauthorized publication of this letter see Ep 1041.

ERASMUS TO HIS FRIEND REUCHLIN, GREETING
If you are well, O glory of our modern Germany, I have good reason to be glad. That product of the circumcision, who started as a criminal in the ghetto and is now a greater felon since he became, I will not say a Christian but a Christian ape, is said to have published a book – and that too in his 5 native tongue, for fear his cronies the pimps and the bargemen might not understand him – in which, they tell me, he attacks all the learned world by

* * * * *

36 physician] Afinius; see Ep 637:21n.
40 seal] A seal was being made for Erasmus in Antwerp (cf Epp 736, 754). It is probably the silver one for sealing letters, which was originally mounted on an ivory handle and is preserved from Erasmus' estate. It showed a frontal head bust of the god Terminus and the words 'Cedo nulli' (illustration in CWE 2 150); cf Ep 604:4n.
44 Franz] Birckmann

713
3 product] Pfefferkorn; for his recent *Streydtpuechlyn* see Ep 697:15n. It was probably the piece (line 24) sent to Fisher.
5 Christian ape] Erasmus soon had occasion to regret this expression, or rather the whole letter; see Ep 1041.

name. In my opinion the monster does not in the least deserve to be
mentioned in the writings of the learned. In heaven's name, what a tool
they have chosen, those who behind their masks would overthrow religion!   10
This half-Jew Christian by himself has done more harm to Christendom
than the whole cesspool of Jewry, and clearly, unless I am mistaken, is
playing the same game for his nation that Zopyrus played for Darius,
though this man is much more treacherous. Let us, my dear Reuchlin, forget
these monsters, let us take our joy in Christ, and pursue honourable   15
studies.

My lord of Rochester and Colet are both in splendid health. All good
scholars and all upright men are your friends. I protested to Dorp, asking
why this university has mixed itself up in that business of yours; for they
took advantage of his skill in composition and his simple-mindedness to   20
take a hand in it. He replied that one Adrian was responsible, who has now
become a cardinal, but that heresy was never mentioned, only 'error.' But
what is there that is free from error – not that I see any error there. I had the
piece turned into Latin and sent it to the bishop of Rochester. Farewell.

Louvain, 15 November   25

I would have written more fully, but this messenger was unreliable.

714 / To Gerard Geldenhouwer   Louvain, 16 November [1517]

This letter was published in the *Auctarium*. Geldenhouwer's answer is Ep 727.

ERASMUS OF ROTTERDAM TO NIJMEGEN, CHAPLAIN TO
THE RIGHT REVEREND THE BISHOP OF UTRECHT,
GREETING

I wonder much that you have not written, seeing that I have heard from his

* * * * *

13 Zopyrus] See Ep 700:23n.
17 Rochester] John Fisher
18 Dorp] His relations with Erasmus were now friendly, although not without
   difficult moments (cf Ep 696). Subsequently he would emerge as one of the
   strongest supporters of Hebrew studies in Louvain (see Ep 794:84–5). No
   doubt because he could expect a sympathetic hearing, Erasmus approached
   him with his complaint. This was based on the university's letter to Leo x
   against Reuchlin dated 23 May [1515]. This letter, together with similar appeals to Rome by the university's chancellor, Adrian of Utrecht, and by his
   charge, Prince Charles, was promptly published by Pfefferkorn in his *Defensio
   contra ... obscurorum virorum epistolas*, and in a German translation thereof (see
   Hutten *Operum supplementum* I 149–52). Dorp's answer thus is understand-
   able.

lordship. I cannot think that you are too busy to spare a moment, or so   5
elated by your good fortune that you are tired of your old cronies; though I
could wish it were so. If my *Querela pacis* was well received by your master,
I am delighted, and feel already that the labour I put into it has brought a
great reward, since it is acceptable to the one man whom I should wish to
like it. My paraphrase is hastening to its end; it is a small book, and no one   10
would believe, unless he made the experiment, how much toil it has cost
me. You shall have it as soon as Dirk has finished printing it.

Now here's a comic thing. The other day a man came running up to me
at speed to tell me that the prebend I enjoy at Utrecht has been assessed at
four philippi, if I was prepared to pay in cash. At first I was delighted,   15
dreaming that some new preferment had been given me; but then I began to
wonder what he meant. At length I realized that the mistake arose from an
identity of name. There is, you must know, another Erasmus here, a doctor
of law, a letter to whom I read lately by mistake, supposing it was meant for
me. After that, since the whole thing had nothing to do with me, I suspected   20
it was a hoax, until Barbier cleared up my suspicions.

See to it that your master does not summon me in these winter
months, for I am so deep in the New Testament that I cannot stir a finger-
breadth, and I am resolved in these months to finish it. As to Philip, I can do
no more than urge him to study; if he would live among us, I would try to go   25
rather further. Nowhere in this university is there a better scholar or a better
man, more gay and at the same time more sincere, than my friend Nève, nor
was I ever more contented with my circumstances. Farewell.

Louvain, 16 November

* * * * *

714

5 lordship] Philip of Burgundy, bishop of Utrecht, wrote a letter, now lost; see
  Ep 682 introduction.
10 paraphrase] See Ep 710 introduction.
12 Dirk] Martens
14 Utrecht] Cf Ep 751:12 and note.
18 another Erasmus] Unidentified. The incident with the letter must have occurred before Barbier left for Spain in June 1517; like him, the other Erasmus
  seems to have been connected with the court; cf Ep 727:17–18.
24 Philip] Perhaps Philip (d 1527), the oldest of three natural sons of Philip of
  Burgundy, bishop of Utrecht. Geldenhouwer may have tutored him and in
  1524, after the bishop's death, lived for a time in Philip's house at Antwerp
  (see de Vocht *Literae* Ep 117). When he published this letter in 1518 Erasmus
  replaced the sentence 'if he would ... rather further' with the words 'since we
  have ceased to live in the same house.' Apparently the bishop's son, or
  perhaps some other young Philip of Geldenhouwer's acquaintance, was at
  one point living in the College of the Lily in the company of Erasmus and Jean
  de Nève, but left after a short time without much profit to his studies.

Autograph rough draft, Erasmus to Pieter Gillis, Epistle 715
Copenhagen, Det Kongelige Bibliotek MS G K S 95 fol f238 recto

715 / To Pieter Gillis   Louvain [c 16 November 1517]

This letter was published by Erasmus in the *Epistolae ad diversos* (1521). His autograph rough draft is in the Copenhagen MS (see Allen III 630–4). It seems best to assume that this formal letter of condolences was written shortly after Ep 712, which contains Erasmus' first reaction to the death of Gillis' father.

Nicolaas (Claes) Gillis (c1438–November 1517) was a candlemaker, guild master, and holder of municipal offices in the city of Antwerp.

ERASMUS OF ROTTERDAM TO HIS FRIEND
PIETER GILLIS, GREETING

Nothing in human affairs can last for ever, and this is so true that nothing can even be of long duration; and therefore you must not so much torment yourself, my dear Pieter, over the loss of your father as recognize your good 5 fortune in having a father like him. Cast your eyes, I would beg you, round all the families of your native city, and ask yourself whether you would wish to choose another father, even if some god gave you permission; unless I am much mistaken, you would choose no other than him who has fallen to your lot. And we can account him happy, if ever anyone at all was happy in this 10 life. If long life is a blessing, he had reached his eightieth year, in bodily vigour, his sight still keen, so that he needed neither stick nor spectacles; the first white hairs had scarcely begun to sprinkle his dark head; and, what is the greatest blessing of all, as it is the rarest, his mental powers kept all their force. If it is a part of good fortune to make a wise choice of a wife, he 15 did that twice; and his second marriage was the more blessed in that it brought this excellent father so many children like himself, of whom he lived to see many not only surviving but all of full age and arrived at some honourable station in life.

He himself lived his whole life in the sight of his fellow-citizens, in 20 such a way that no breath of rumour ever sullied the purity of his reputation; and in the same fashion he brought up his children so well that none caused him a moment's shame or regret. Who more upright than your father, more virtuous than your mother? How he loved his wife, how she even revered her husband! And then again, parents however excellent do 25 not always have excellent children. But surely death had no bitterness for

* * * * *

715
17 children] Pieter was Nicolaas' second son. Another brother, Frans, is repeatedly mentioned in Erasmus' correspondence of later years. A third brother, Gillis, d 1534, was canon cantor of Our Lady's in Antwerp; cf de Vocht CTL II 66–7.

him, since he could see himself living on in children so like him. And when
he embraced his darling little grandson, your son Nicolaas, who bore his
own name, he seemed to himself to have escaped death altogether. His
wealth was not great, but it was sufficient and, a great rarity in the days we   30
live in, it was honestly come by. He had chosen a profession which without
dishonesty could supply what he needed to maintain his household and
assist the poor, to whom he was always very generous. He left each of his
children a modest livelihood, even if nothing was added from any other
source. He held several offices in the city, and could have held more, and   35
more important, had he had the ambition. And what he held, he held in
such a way that no complaints were ever heard. Strife in the home was
abhorrent to him, like the plague, and with his fellow-citizens he never had
a dispute of any kind, such was his easy disposition; he would rather forgo
his rights, if he saw that otherwise harmony must suffer.   40

None ever heard him say a foolish, loose, or censorious word. In that
crowded city he had no enemy. After his death many mourned him like a
father, the poor especially. Yet with what courage he endured so many days
of torment, for no death is more painful than that which results from urinary
obstruction. On his death-bed he left his children no commands except to   45
live in harmony and true religion. The disposition of his property was such
that it made no difference who chose one portion rather than another, nor
did anyone appear who said he was owed one farthing. Would you not
rightly seem ungrateful, if you mourned for a father such as this? No, make
the most of his blessed memory, and count him happy to have been carried   50
out of the billows of this life into the harbour of immortality. Do not cease to
reproduce his uprightness of character, as you have done hitherto, and
teach your son, even now, at his tender years, to recall the grandfather
whose name he bears by his purity of life, and his father and uncle by his
learning. Even now let him imbibe the precepts of the Gospel philosophy,   55
for they are the milk of the spirit. Even now let him absorb the seeds of
Greek and Latin, and greet his father with charming prattle in the two
tongues. So may it be your lot, my dear Pieter, with your excellent wife,
Cornelia, to arrive at a blessed old age, and enjoy the honourable happiness
that comes from excellent children. Farewell, my friend without compare.   60

Louvain, 151[8]

* * * * *

28 Nicolaas] Pieter's oldest son, b c 1515; cf Ep 516:2–5.
59 Cornelia] Sandrien (Sanders, Sandria) married Gillis in 1514 (see Ep 312:93n)
   and died in 1526; see Ep 1740 and Erasmus' epitaphs for her in Reedijk poems
   126–7.

716 / To Jacopo Bannisio   Louvain, [November 1517]

This letter clearly answers Ep 709. It was published in the *Farrago* with the date
of 1518, but it appears to have been written earlier. Erasmus evidently assumed that Bannisio's illness had been contracted when he was with Prince
Charles at Middelburg; see Epp 596 introduction, 663.

ERASMUS OF ROTTERDAM TO HIS FRIEND
BANNISIO, GREETING
Honoured sir, I am rightly indignant with Zeeland for sending you back to
us in ill health, but at the same time I am grateful that it has returned you
alive after swallowing up not a few others. You must, I know, be ready to   5
serve the great, but pray never lose sight of your own health. The more
public affairs have need of your wisdom, the more careful you must be to
prolong your power to be of use. I look forward eagerly to your arrival
among us.
      The advice you give me about ignoring mischief-makers and leaving   10
them to the mercy of their complaint is wise and friendly. All they achieve is
the display of their own blend of folly and ignorance. In heaven's name,
look at the dullness, the malevolence, the barbarism of the pamphlets which
they use for weapons. There is no risk that posterity will read such sad stuff,
and an educated man should have the judgment of posterity always before   15
him. Not but what even at this moment no honourable or learned man
approves of their frenzied clamour. But we will speak of all this when we
meet. Farewell, honoured sir.
      Louvain, 151[8]

717 / To Mark Lauwerijns   Louvain, 19 November [1517]

This letter is in sequence with Epp 651, 666, and 740.

ERASMUS TO HIS FRIEND MARK LAUWERIJNS, GREETING
Thank you for a delicious letter, in fact one very like the writer, O most
civilized of men. If the bearer of this had left a little later for your part of the
world, he would have brought with him my Paraphrase of the Epistle to the
Romans, not a large book to look at but a colossal task. It is now printing,   5

                    * * * * *

717
4 Paraphrase] See Ep 710 introduction.

and is almost finished. Together with your letter I received a Flanders noble, a Spanish double ducat, and an English Michael, a generous present in itself but far more welcome for the giver's sake. Though I suspect you misunderstood what I said. I was expressing an opinion about my friend Friesland, to whom I had entrusted my letter to you. He found you not at home. I   10
was surprised at the barrenness of this part of the world, which could not provide a living for a man of so many gifts: musician, prizefighter, swordsman, Latin and Greek scholar, mountebank, scribe, and what you will. My own fortune, slender though it is, I do not much regret: 'Fortune has schooled me now to own defeat, And rue my fate' – or rather, to take in   15
good part whate'er befalls.

     News of your brother Matthias would be most welcome: did he set off for Spain or no, and if he did, how does Spain suit him? How I wish it might be convenient for you to spend these winter months among us here! But I fear you are too much tied up for this to be possible. I have a host who is the   20
most civilized man alive, and as learned as he is civilized. Jan van Borssele is with us, so is Gavere. There is living here a son of the prince of Bergen, a young man of delightful character, with a love of literature beyond what is usual among men of rank. Please give my greetings to the very reverend the dean. Nève cordially returns your greeting.   25

     Farewell. Louvain, 19 November

                    * * * * *

  6 Flanders noble ... Michael] These were all gold coins: the Flemish noble,
     which Maximilian had struck in 1487 in imitation of the English 'ryal' noble;
     the Spanish excelente or ducat; and the English angel-noble, with the figure of
     St Michael on the obverse, trampling on the dragon. Cf CWE 1 312, 316, 319,
     325–6, 329, 336–9; CWE 2 340 (plate); Ep 763.
  9 what I said] In Ep 666, referring to Jan of Friesland
 14 'Fortune ... fate'] Virgil *Aeneid* 4.434
 17 Matthias] See Ep 651 introduction.
 20 host] Jean de Nève
 21 Borssele] Jan Becker; see Ep 687:18n.
 22 Gavere] Joost Vroye of Gavere, d 10 February 1533, a priest. From 1499 he had
     studied and was now teaching at the College of the Lily. Subsequently he
     became a Doctor of Laws and held chairs first in civil and later in canon law. He
     remained a firm supporter of Erasmus.
 22 son] Antoon van Bergen; see Ep 760.
 25 dean] Jan Goetgebuer

718 / To Paschasius Berselius   [Louvain, October–November 1517]

An approximate date can be assigned from the printing of the *Paraphrasis ad Romanos*, mentioned here exactly as in Epp 695, 707. By contrast Epp 714, 717, and 719 state that the printing is almost completed; thus the precise date for this letter suggested by Allen may be questioned.

Greeting. If I write sparingly, my excellent Paschasius, this does not mean that I am less devoted to you or bear you less in mind. If you saw the toilsome researches by which I am distracted, you would agree that even a note like this is of some length. My Paraphrase of the Epistle to the Romans is printing. If he is known to you, give my greetings to the double-canon   5 who knows Greek at St Leonard's and comes, if I remember right, from Hasselt, and also to that very cheerful Dominican divine who extracted a letter from me at Antwerp. Farewell, and please write.

719 / To Antonius Clava   Louvain, 21 November [1517]

ERASMUS TO HIS FRIEND CLAVA, GREETING
I wonder greatly, my dear Clava, how this cold weather is treating you, who are compelled to play your part in public business. For my part, I lead the life of a cuckoo, buried at home, and the theologians grind on in the same old way without me. If the bearer of this had postponed his return by a little,   5
I should have burdened him with a copy of my paraphrase; this very moment the printing is almost finished. I hear Paolo Emilio of Verona on French history is now on sale; he is the most learned and upright man alive. He still lives in Paris. How odd that Lefèvre should not reply, even with a short letter. There was a rumour spread here that he had already answered,   10
but that I was keeping it to myself. This arose, as I discovered later, out of a

* * * * *

718
5 double-canon] An unidentified canon regular – the two words actually mean the same – at the Priory of St Léonard at Liège.
7 cheerful Dominican] Probably the Gaspard of Ep 735:12

719
2 cold] An exceptional cold spell, beginning on 15 November, is mentioned in Jan Reygersberch *Dye cronijcke van Zeelandt* (Antwerp 1551); cf Henne II 214.
7 Emilio] *De rebus gestis Francorum* (Paris: J. Bade [1517?]). The work, still incomplete, had been in the making since 1499. For Emilio see Ep 136:2n.
10 rumour] See Ep 721 introduction.

letter written to me by a certain Jacobus Faber of Deventer, which finally
reached me after prolonged wandering from hand to hand among the friars.
Look after your health, and give my greetings to my friends, especially de
Keysere and the physician.   15
    Louvain, 21 November

720 / To [Willem Bollart?]   [Louvain, end of November 1517]

> For the addressee and the circumstances see Ep 671. The date can be assigned
> from the *Paraphrasis ad Romanos*, now ready for distribution; see Epp 710 and
> 718 introductions.

Greeting, reverend Father. A nasty spiteful rheum has lately deprived me of
the company of your Reverence, and indeed has exiled me from myself for
near a solid month; for exile it seems, the moment I am debarred from my
familiar studies. But now by God's goodness I am restored to myself and
rejoice to think you are likewise restored to me, as one whom long ago,   5
when I was young and you were but a youth, I learnt to love as the friend
and companion of my studies while we campaigned under the same master,
and whom I may respect and admire as my master now, champion alike of
studies and of virtue. Meanwhile I send you my Paraphrase on the Epistle to
the Romans, the latest of my offspring to have seen the light. For engaged as 10
I now am in that most burdensome of all kinds of research, a fresh revision
of the New Testament, I refresh my spirit with this sort of relaxation. When
the feeling that I can no more tries to creep over me, this is my game of skill
or chance, which restores me to my task with powers refreshed. Perchance I
shall do the same for the other Epistles, if I find men's palates not averse   15
from this sort of flavour. For it is astonishing what an element of hazard
there is in these things too: often it happens that the work from which you
expect high praise brings only unpopularity, while in its turn that which
you never thought would be popular is a great source of reputation.
Farewell, most honoured Father, and add the name of Erasmus to the list of   20
your devotees.

    * * * * *

12 Faber] A member of the Brethren of the Common Life who taught in Deventer;
    see Ep 174.
15 Keysere ... physician] See Ep 650.

720
12 New Testament] See Ep 864 introduction.

721 / To Henricus Glareanus   [Louvain, end of November 1517]

This letter was probably dispatched together with Epp 723–5: Adrianus has now moved to Louvain (cf Epp 686:7n, 699:24n), and Erasmus has been reminded of Emilio (cf Ep 719). Erasmus, who had not so far received an answer to Ep 707, goes out of his way (lines 2–3) to write again. His preoccupation, also reflected in Epp 723–4, was with the reaction in Paris to his *Apologia ad Fabrum* (see Ep 597:37n). He had rarely missed an occasion to say how much he regretted this public controversy and he had urged Lefèvre not to continue it (see Ep 659:22–31), although he did not dare to do so too openly lest people might think that he feared him (see Ep 766:22). Yet Erasmus himself initiated three more editions of his *Apologia* (cf Ep 693 and Epp 730, 778 introductions). Meanwhile a growing number of rumours began to reach him to the effect that Lefèvre and his supporters planned retaliation (see Epp 659:28–31, 719, 726, 734:40, 778:73–5), while his own friends in Paris maintained a silence that could mean a conspiracy (cf Epp 689, 723, 767). At least Glareanus, a Swiss who had recently arrived in the French capital and was a close friend, could be expected to provide information; hence Erasmus' pleas for a letter from him in Ep 707 and here. But again, inquiring openly of the Parisians concerning Lefèvre's plans might be interpreted as weakness on Erasmus' part. The rumours were unfounded; Lefèvre planned no reply (cf Ep 680A introduction). Evidence that this might be so was gradually accumulating (see Epp 775, 796, 810:184–8, 849). Finally, in a letter designed for immediate publication, Erasmus could speak of an implicit agreement to abstain from recrimination: Allen Ep 855:57–9.

ERASMUS TO HIS FRIEND HENRICUS GLAREANUS, GREETING
I answered your letter the other day, although I am even busier now than I was in the old days in Basel. If things are as you would wish them, I have reason to be very well satisfied. If only it had been Fortune's will that this post of yours should be here! This university is very prosperous, and their   5
approach to theology is less thorny than elsewhere. Out of a legacy from Jérôme de Busleyden they are setting up a college in which a certain number of young men will be maintained who wish to learn the tongues, and with them three professors to give free public instruction in the three tongues, Greek, Hebrew, and Latin. Matthaeus Adrianus, a very learned Hebraist, is   10
already here. Mind you look after yourself and write to me often. If Paolo Emilio is not already a friend of yours, you must get to know him. Believe me, Glareanus, there is nowhere a better scholar or a better man, or one more devoted to men of goodwill. Farewell once more.

722 / To Hermann von Neuenahr   Louvain, 30 November [1517]

Greeting, my honoured Lord. On St Andrew's eve I received a letter from
you written on St Luke's day; such was the lightning speed of that worthy
courier. To answer it briefly, the friend of whom you write shows a spirit of
which I approve; but how I can be of any use to him, I do not know. I am well
aware of my own inexperience; the desire and intention to help will not be   5
lacking, especially to help a man like him. I am a familiar figure in the
College of the Lily, the principal of which is a man born for humane studies
and a civilized life. There will be room for your friend as a guest, provided
we have something suitable to offer him. Out of a legacy from Busleyden,
who has lately died, they will set up public chairs, with no fees charged, in   10
the three tongues, Greek, Latin, and Hebrew. Matthaeus, whom you know
as a friend of Reuchlin's, is here already, and will lecture for a fixed salary;
he seems to me a man of great learning in his own literature. In the mean
time there was no lack of people to teach Greek.

As for me, I am immersed in work, especially in the revision of the   15
New Testament – I wish I had never touched it. If this is what a scholar's
work is like, much better go on sleeping. But I must play out my part. I hear
you are giving public lectures in your part of the world in Greek and
Hebrew. Happy indeed are those studies, if such men have started to take
them in hand, when they have been so shamelessly befouled by some men I   20
could name; the monkey in the lion's skin, the Greeks would have called it.

The bishop of Utrecht has written to me, indicating that he has it in
mind to send for me, with what prospects I know not; this winter I shall
certainly not shift my snug abode. I sent you a letter recently by Bannisio;
whether it reached you, I do not know. Farewell, my honoured Lord. Best   25
wishes to the excellent Venantius, and also to de Keysere.

* * * * *

722
2 St Luke's day] 18 October
3 friend] Since his name is not given, he was probably not known to Erasmus.
  We do not hear of him afterwards, so he may not have gone to Louvain.
11 Matthaeus] Adrianus (see Ep 691); he had met Reuchlin in Tübingen, 1512; see
  AK I Ep 475.
18 public lectures] Without an academic appointment, it seems
21 the monkey in the lion's skin] A phrase in Greek, echoed from Lucian's
  Philopseudes 5; cf *Adagia* I iii 66.
22 written] Cf Ep 714:5n, 22–4.
24 Bannisio] Ep 703
26 Venantius] Cf Ep 636:39n.

Louvain, St Andrew's day

I know you like de Keysere; let your liking for him grow and bring forth fruit.

723 / To Guillaume Budé   Louvain, 30 November 1517

This letter follows Ep 689 and is dictated by the same concerns – first lest Budé and his circle might have taken offence at some ambiguous phrases in Erasmus' previous letters and at his *Apologia ad Fabrum* (cf Ep 721 introduction), and second that the negotiations about Erasmus' possible move to Paris, suspended by his own dilatory tactics, should not be dropped completely. The letter was published in the *Farrago*. It is answered by Ep 744.

ERASMUS TO HIS FRIEND BUDÉ, GREETING

After the great storms of letters with which you used to overwhelm me, why, pray, this great and sudden silence? If you are entirely absorbed in writing a commentary on the Pandects, I am delighted; but I doubt whether you can be so far in that you have not a moment to tell me in a few words   5
what I want to know. If you do not, I shall infer that you are offended or that your former volubility was all a sham. If I have somehow given you offence, tell me where it hurts, so that I can either put it right or at least be more careful in future. If all that sad business of letters was just a game, I wish to understand it, whatever it is. Farewell, my most learned Budé.   10

Louvain, St Andrew's day 1517

724 / To Jacques Lefèvre d'Etaples   Louvain, 30 November [1517]

See Ep 721 introduction.

ERASMUS TO HIS FRIEND LEFÈVRE, GREETING

I have sent you by one of our theologians the *Apologia* in which I reply to your discussion, or rather, your attack upon me. If you do not like it, you must blame yourself. There were so many points in what you wrote, and so outrageous, that it was neither possible nor proper to overlook them.   5

* * * * *

28 you like] Cf Ep 442:25–9.

723
4 commentary] Cf Ep 493 postscript.

724
2 sent you] With Ep 659

Everyone who has read your piece says and feels just the same. If you reply, I do beg you to remember what befits a man like you, if what you owe to our friendship is not enough to restrain you – and I for my part set a high value on it. Many men, as you can see, are all ready for a mad orgy of personal abuse; let us not give an opening to persons of that kidney. I am willing to 10 learn, and I am willing to be told I am wrong; to be accused of impiety against Christ I do not deserve, and I will not put up with it. Farewell, my esteemed friend, and hold me dear as you are used to do, for you are truly dear to me.

Louvain, St Andrew's day   15

725 / To Jean Pyrrhus d'Angleberme   Louvain, 30 November 1517

This letter was in reply to one now missing, evidently written from Orléans, where Angleberme taught jurisprudence and where his father lived (see Ep 140:38n). In 1517 Jean Pyrrhus published a volume of writings (*Index opus-culorum* Orléans and Paris: J. Hoys), in which he repeatedly praises Reuchlin, Erasmus, and Budé and his circle of friends.

ERASMUS TO HIS FRIEND PYRRHUS, GREETING

Your letter gave me great pleasure. I was delighted to hear that you are flourishing, and that your father is still vigorous. I had no feelings against France, but at that time it was not yet safe for me to talk about moving, nor was it yet sufficiently clear what was being offered me in your part of the 5 world; and somehow that bustle about sending for me, which was so surprising at first, suddenly quieted down. Except that Budé had added to his letter that, as far as that Guillaume was concerned whom they call Petit, he who is now the king's confessor, something had gone wrong. What it was, I do not yet fully understand. You say you are combining humane 10 studies with your other work, and this is good news. Best wishes to you and your excellent father, your delightful wife, and your sweet children. Give my greetings to all my dear friends.

Louvain, St Andrew's day 1517

* * * * *

725
3 father] Pierre d'Angleberme, addressed in Ep 140
4 at that time] In February 1517, before the Treaty of Cambrai (see Ep 603:28n), when Erasmus had received a royal invitation; cf Epp 522–3, 689:4n.
8 Guillaume] 'whom they call Petit ... wrong' is given in Greek; cf Ep 744:24n. For Guillaume Petit see Ep 522:17n.

726 / To Thomas More   Louvain, 30 November [1517]

ERASMUS TO HIS FRIEND MORE, GREETING

Happy man, to be now passing your days (as I suppose) so near the sea! I
send you my paraphrase, and truly it deserves the name. I have not yet had a
chance to see Thomas Linacre's pieces, although I have asked Thomas
Lupset for a copy more than once. Pieter Gillis has lost his father; he is   5
moderately well himself. I am working myself into a lather on books and
letter-writing, in hopes of getting free once for all from this very tedious sort
of labour, so that I can enjoy more agreeable fields thereafter. Nothing has
come from Lefèvre, although I hear he is about to give birth to I know not
what. As far as the man himself goes, I have nothing to fear; only I am afraid   10
that some pupil will be put up to perform, with whom I should think it
beneath me to do battle. I have already written to ask you to take no steps
with the archbishop of Canterbury about the commutation of my annuity. I
have dispatched a man I know from here to Basel, and he will send me
definite news about your books and my own. Farewell, my beloved More.   15
　　　Louvain, St Andrew's day

727 / From Gerard Geldenhouwer   [Vollenhove] 5 December 1517

　　This letter was sent together with Ep 728, and both were published in the
　　Auctarium. This one answers both Epp 682 and 714 and is answered by Ep 759.

　　　* * * * *

726
2 near the sea] That is, ready to return home (see Ep 623:23n). This remark may
　refer to Erasmus' own feelings about the cold in Zeeland and Flanders; see Ep
　719.
3 paraphrase] The term is given in Greek. The prefix 'para' means alongside.
　Erasmus' paraphrase offers a continuous narrative of the biblical text rather
　than a segmented examination in the fashion of a commentary; cf Ep 710
　introduction.
5 Lupset] See Epp 664:29n, 690:10.
5 father] See Ep 715 introduction.
9 I hear] See Ep 721 introduction.
13 commutation] See Ep 702 introduction; the letter here mentioned is not pre-
　served.
14 Basel] See Ep 704A introduction, and for the books referred to Epp 550
　introduction, 603, 634–5, 732.

GERARD OF NIJMEGEN TO THE EMINENT THEOLOGIAN
ERASMUS OF ROTTERDAM, GREETING

Two or three hours before we left the town of Kampen in the direction of
Deventer I received the first of your two letters, when I was very busy
packing; but I showed the bishop my master the small book and your letter.   5
I wrote you a letter in his name, as he had told me to do; but my courage
failed me and I did not dare to write to you, thinking myself unworthy to
write to such a great man. I know your kindly nature and how approachable
you are; but you do not know how poor-spirited I am, and how full of fears
when it comes to writing letters. I can produce a most reliable witness to this   10
in the shape of Borssele, my honest friend from Zeeland.

Your *Querela pacis* gave very great pleasure not only to my lord bishop
but to all the learned members of his council and to Philippus Montius, his
court chamberlain, who are all your keen supporters. I read his lordship the
letter you wrote; he expressed his thanks and laughed at your postscript   15
about dormice and cuckoos. I also read him the letter you wrote to me, and
he was surprised at the benefice given to Erasmus the lawyer, whom he
believes to be in Spain. You may expect from Philip our bishop and your
friend, most learned Erasmus, all that you could expect from the most
friendly of princes. Scarcely a day passes without his speaking of you, and   20
he has it in mind to send for you next Lent when the swallows return and
show by his actions how much he admires you and wishes to encourage
your scholarly work. In the mean time you must write sometimes to his
lordship, and I will not allow your great claims on our bishop to be forgotten
or go for nothing. Nève's frank and open nature I have experienced over and   25
over again. I count you lucky in being blessed with such a host and such
company. Farewell.

St Nicholas' eve 1517

* * * * *

727
3 we left] There is reason to think that Geldenhouwer remembered this detail
incorrectly; see Allen's note.
6 letter in his name] See Ep 682 introduction.
11 Borssele] Jan Becker; see Ep 687:18n.
13 Montius] Not further identified. Ep 759:21 shows that he was not formerly
known to Erasmus, but by the time Erasmus wrote Ep 811 he had met him and
his wife.
15 letter you wrote] To Bishop Philip, accompanying Ep 714. In a postscript
declining Philip's invitation for the time being, Erasmus must have likened
himself to the hibernating dormouse (cf Ep 714:22–3) and the cuckoo 'buried
in his nest'; cf Epp 728, 756:15–16, 758:9.
16 letter you wrote to me] Ep 714, referring to the other Erasmus.

728 / From Philip of Burgundy   Vollenhove, 6 December 1517

This letter was sent together with Ep 727. The bishop's letter is answered by
Ep 758. All were published in the *Auctarium*. For Philip see Ep 603.

PHILIP OF BURGUNDY, BY THE GRACE OF GOD
AND OF THE APOSTOLIC SEE BISHOP OF UTRECHT,
TO ERASMUS OF ROTTERDAM, GREETING
Right learned and well-beloved Erasmus, I have received your letter, which
amid all the cares that weigh so heavily upon me brought me great pleasure.   5
Your *Querela pacis* is a delight not merely to me, to whom it is specially
dedicated, but to all true Christians. I should be sorry to see all your
learning hidden after the fashion of hibernating dormice and cuckoos, and
urge you instead to finish the great works you have in hand for the benefit
and the adornment of our age and the admiration of posterity. With God's   10
help I will endeavour not to fall short of my late excellent brother, David of
pious memory. I write briefly, but as one who takes a great interest in you
and your work. Farewell, good Erasmus, and think well of me, as I know
you do.
      From my castle of Vollenhove, 6 December 1517   15

729 / From Paolo Bombace   Zürich, 6 December 1517

Bombace (see Ep 611:6n) had gone to Switzerland in the company of Antonio
Pucci, the nephew of his Roman master, Cardinal Lorenzo Pucci. For Antonio's mission see Ep 860 introduction.
      This letter probably did not reach Erasmus for some time. He answered it
twice, by Ep 800 (Louvain, 14 March 1518) and Ep 855 (Basel, 26 July 1518). The
second answer repeats the first to a degree, but unlike it also refers to the
postscript of Ep 729. Information contained in this postscript, however, may
already have been used by Erasmus in Ep 803 (Louvain, 26 March 1518).
Various explanations can be suggested for the interval of several months
between the two answers. The simplest is that Erasmus received Ep 729
shortly before 14 March and lost no time in answering it. After his arrival in
Basel he prepared a new edition of his correspondence, the *Auctarium*, and

* * * * *

728
 4 your letter] Accompanying Ep 714
 8 dormice and cuckoos] See Ep 727:15n.
11 David] Cf Epp 603:14–22, 682 introduction.
15 Vollenhove] On the east coast of the Zuyder Zee, north of Kampen

View of Zürich
Painting by Hans Leu the Elder, c 1500
Photo: Schweizerisches Landesmuseum, Zürich

was reminded of Bombace's letter, which he included. Forgetting his first reply, or dissatisfied with it, he wrote a second answer for immediate publication; cf Ep 855 introduction.

PAOLO BOMBACE, SECRETARY OF
THE CARDINAL OF THE SANTI QUATTRO,
TO ERASMUS OF ROTTERDAM, GREETING

If I do not write at great length and inflict on you a wealth of whirling words, as it says in the play, there are several reasons; but the chief is that having 5 earned your gratitude by keeping silence for so long and not interrupting the more important business that fills your time, I wish not to spoil my record now by unseasonable chatter. I do not doubt, however, that when you hear that I am now in Switzerland, you will exclaim 'Great heavens! What doth Bombace among the Switzers? What freak of fortune can have 10 landed him there?' This is the only answer I can give, dear Erasmus: it was my lot (the labours of Hercules without his reputation) that tore me from the charms of Rome, which I had learnt to love more even than my own country, and set me down, a reluctant victim, here. The cardinal of the Santi Quattro, on whose staff I was in Rome, when his nephew (his brother's son) was 15 setting off as nuncio apostolic to the Swiss, instructed me to accompany him, and I was too shy to say him nay, though often murmuring to myself that line of Homer 'Why, hapless wretch, thus leave the light of the sun ...' If it was some misdemeanour on my part, I have now purged it by four unbroken months, and shall spend much longer here, unless some god 20 takes pity on me, deprived of one great, one indescribable solace, the society of our friend Pace, who, as long as he was at Constance, so comforted me with frequent and most friendly letters that I felt myself in Athens.

But why do I tell all this to you, as if you had any time at all for listening 25 to my woes? One comfort I still have, those books of yours that cost you sleepless nights, to which I apply myself steadily, and thus beguile to some extent the tedium of this country. Among the rest I have lately read your *Apologia* against Lefèvre, which you sent to Beatus Rhenanus and he passed

* * * * *

729
2 Santi Quattro] Lorenzo Pucci
5 play] Plautus *Menaechmi* 779
9 Great heavens] Literally, Zeus of marvels: Lucian *Timon* 41
18 Homer] *Odyssey* 11.93
22 Pace] Cf Ep 619 introduction.
29 Rhenanus] See Ep 730 introduction.

it on to me to read. I never saw anything more scholarly. As for Lefèvre, 30
relying on his reputation, but chiefly on your opinion of him, for I had often
heard you praise him very highly, I had always supposed him as sensible as
he is learned; and so I was greatly surprised that he should have been ready
to attack you so wantonly that it is clear he had forgotten not merely the
comity of letters but ordinary standards of behaviour. As regards more 35
advanced studies, I must stick to my last, and would not dare offer any
opinion. But in the fields of Latin and Greek, to judge by what you have
written (his own work I have never opened), he seemed to me quite
laughable, nor did I think him much better in many respects than that
friend of ours who translated *para ten eisodon* 'that is to say, in Hesiod.' But 40
you unmasked him admirably and defended yourself very nicely. I hear he
plans a fresh attack on you; but I do not think he will do so, for I know that a
beaten cock does not usually crow. Whatever his decision, he has met his
match.

As for my long-standing affection and respect for you, I will not go 45
over it again now, for fear I seem to be casting doubt on something that is
quite fixed; any more, goodness knows, than I need congratulate you on the
high reputation of all your writings all the world over (especially in Rome,
where everything is brought to the bar of criticism) and their popularity
with all learned men, so much so that they fall short in no respect of the 50
Ancients, nor does the fact that their author himself is alive stand in their
way. Such congratulations must be a daily and almost ordinary experience,
I do not doubt. And now goodbye, dear Erasmus; may all go well with you,
and do not forget your Bombace.

From Zürich, a town in Switzerland, 6 December 1517 55
The Turkish king has returned to Constantinople after making himself

* * * * *

36 last] Cf *Adagia* I vi 16.
40 friend of ours] He is identified as Giovanni Battista Pio (cf Ep 256:149n) in the
margin of the first printed edition of this letter in the *Auctarium*. Doubtless
having heard the story from Bombace, Richard Pace repeats it in *De fructu* 98–9
(cf Ep 776:4n), without, however, giving Pio's name. The Greek words mean
'near the entrance.'
41 I hear] Cf Ep 721 introduction.
43 beaten cock] Cf *Adagia* II ii 26.
56 Turkish king] Selim I had conquered Syria in August 1516 and Egypt in
January 1517. He was now in Adrianople and could indeed be expected to turn
against the Occident. In fact, he was about to undertake an attack on Rhodes
when he died in September 1520. From the beginning of his pontificate
(1513–21) Leo x had hoped to lead a new crusade against the Turks. His
diplomats in every state had to work continually in support of the plan,
especially after the Treaty of Cambrai (March 1517) had seemed to heighten

master of the whole of Syria and Egypt, and makes great threats and
preparations against the Christians. The pope is therefore demanding help
from the Swiss and summoning all Christian princes to his assistance.
Marcus Musurus, who had lately been appointed archbishop of Monem-   60
vasia, went the way of all flesh this autumn while living in Rome, as our
friend Paleotti had done eight months before. Farewell once more.

730 / To Ludwig Baer   Louvain, 6 December 1517

Erasmus had sent to Basel by way of the Frankfurt autumn fair several copies
of Martens' first edition of his *Apologia ad Fabrum* (see Epp 597:37n, 704A:17n).
One was for Beatus Rhenanus (cf Ep 729:28–30), and another was for the Froben
firm, a clear indication that Erasmus wished to encourage a reprint. A third
copy had gone to Ludwig Baer. As an old friend of Lefèvre, Baer was unhappy
with the controversy, and as a Paris doctor of divinity he found some fault
with Erasmus' theological arguments. He consulted with Wolfgang Faber
Capito, a fellow theologian and editorial adviser to Froben; as a result both
wrote to Erasmus urging him to make revisions, but the carrier of their letters,
the Basel public messenger, only arrived in Louvain on 5 December and
wished to leave again on the morning of 7 December (see lines 2–3, Epp
732:36–42, 734:60). Erasmus managed to have Epp 730–2A ready for him, but
the haste in which he had to write offered an obvious excuse for not making
further changes in the *Apologia*. He did, however, promise reconsideration
(see Ep 732:55), and after a few days' reflection wrote again to Capito (Ep 734).
In his answers Erasmus takes issue with only one point of theology raised by
Baer and Capito, and in this he was clearly right. Whether there were other
specific objections, or whether Baer and Capito had criticized rather the
general tone of the *Apologia*, we do not know, since Erasmus did not preserve
the text of their letters. He did, however, invite them to make further revisions

* * * * *

the chances for success; see Pastor VII 213–38; K.M. Setton 'Pope Leo x and the
Turkish Peril' *Proceedings of the American Philosophical Society* 113 (1969)
367–424; cf below Ep 785.
60 Musurus] Created archbishop in 1516, he died on 9 August 1517; cf Ep 223:5n.
62 Paleotti] There is confirmation of the death of Camillo Paleotti in Rome at
about the time indicated. He was a son of Vincenzo Paleotti, a lawyer of
Bologna, and wrote highly praised poems. Erasmus had met him in 1506. In
addition to the references given in Allen's note, see V. Forcella *Iscrizioni delle
chiese e d'altri edificii di Roma* (Rome 1869–79) VII 83 no 174, where an inscription is recorded giving the date of his death as 1516, that is, probably old style,
before Easter 1517; P. Prodi *Il cardinale Gabriele Paleotti, 1522–1597* 2 vols
(Rome 1959–67) I 36–7

in the text of the *Apologia*, which Froben was going to publish in February 1518.

ERASMUS TO HIS FRIEND BAER, GREETING

The bearer of this came to me at nightfall, with the intention of setting out at first light tomorrow and so I had no time to re-read my *Apologia*; I leave it to your discretion. Although if I guess rightly, you have not read it all, or at least, when you read it, you were thinking of something else. That Christ   5 was not a composite being of two natures is a fact I learnt some thirty years ago. I wonder therefore if I ever said he was composite; indeed all through my argument I maintain the singleness of his substance, nor do I say anywhere that Christ is to be taken as having one of the two, meaning human nature, but that he is to be taken as having one rather than both, as   10 Lefèvre says; by which I mean the divine nature, but a divine which has united the human to itself. You say that the word Christ, that is, a word meaning the substance, is often taken as a word for the two natures. Had I done this, I should not deserve severe criticism; and yet I maintain that in my notes I never went even that far. I wish therefore you would re-read the   15 book at leisure and then discuss it with Wolfgang, and make such changes as your kindness towards me may suggest.

The extraordinary language they are using in Paris causes me no anxiety. You will see a great part of this pedantry sent packing. Cambridge is a changed place. The university there has no use for this frigid hair-   20 splitting, which is more conducive to wrangling than religion. Yet I would rather, so far as in me lies, help them all forward, if they would let me.

Your kind feelings towards me I recognize and welcome, and I have long known them; but I see from your letter that you credit me with little or no skill in theology, expounding as you do at such length in your letter   25 things that I have already set out in my book. I had sent Schürer a corrected

* * * * *

730
8 singleness of his substance] In what follows Erasmus defends himself with specific reference to a passage in his *Apologia* (LB IX 35E–36A) which Baer seems to have misread (cf Ep 734). Erasmus never questioned the traditional doctrine of the two natures. In Ep 111 he had emphasized 'the total incarnation of Christ's divine nature'; see E.W. Kohls *Die Theologie des Erasmus* (Basel 1966) I 103–4. There is, however, a general tendency to make light of dogma, which may have caused Baer more legitimate concern; cf Ep 734:46–50; *Apologia* (LB IX 32–5).
19 Cambridge] See Epp 432, 456:253–63, 457:65–6; but cf also Ep 777:5–7.
26 Schürer] See Ep 693.

copy of my *Apologia* before your letter reached me. In my published letters
there is nothing, I think, to do your reputation any harm, although Pieter
Gillis produced them in the mean time, while I was in England paying court
to my patrons. For my own part, I wish they had not been published; but   30
what can't be cured must be endured.

You are, as I see it, excessively fair to Lefèvre, when you say that I gave
way to ill temper. In the first place, you admit that he had no reason for his
attack on me; and yet do but observe, I ask you, what unpleasant charges he
brings against me so often. Do but compare now how much greater restraint   35
I show in my reply when attacked than he showed in taking the offensive –
unless you call it ill temper to reply at all. I like Lefèvre very much, and hate
my *Apologia*, or rather, the necessity that drove me to it. But it was he who
spared not a thought for the reputation for fair-mindedness which has
always been his great distinction hitherto. In the same way I had no   40
intention of spending much effort on this. I did not undertake to discuss
which was the better reading, or what bearing it has on the substance of
Christ. I merely rebut the charges of impiety, madness, stupidity, and
absurdity which he brings against me in the most unpleasant way all
through his discussion, so that even the keenest supporters of the Lefèvre   45
party are astonished. Farewell, my learned friend, and let there be no break
in your habitual kindness towards me.

Louvain, St Nicholas' day 1517

731 / To Wolfgang Faber Capito   Louvain, 6 December [1517]

Cf Ep 730.

ERASMUS TO HIS FRIEND WOLFGANG CAPITO, GREETING
I could barely find time to write this, much less to re-read the *Apologia*, so
prompt was the courier's departure after he had delivered your letter. After
reading Lefèvre's criticisms I had my *Apologia* finished within a fortnight,

* * * * *

27 letters] *Epistolae elegantes* of April 1517, which contained the earliest known
exchange of letters between Erasmus and Baer (Epp 488, 507). They were
inoffensive, but Baer may have objected to Ep 463:65–8.
29 Gillis ... time] But not without Erasmus' knowledge; cf Ep 546 and CWE 3
348–9.
31 endured] Cf Ep 708:3n.
42 better reading] See Ep 680A:36–8.
43 charges] Cf Ep 659.

731
4 fortnight] See Ep 597:37n.

in which my sole object is to rebut the charges of impiety and blasphemy   5
which someone, I know not who, had inspired him to bring against me.
You say that I set out his opinion in the first place as though I were in favour
of it; but this is enough to prove that I had already rejected what he
attributes to me. Nor was it my business to make clear at that point which
view I prefer; I am concerned with the matter in hand. You say in your letter   10
that I called Christ a composite being. Human though I am, and in humanity 'find nought that does not touch me,' yet I am astonished if there is
anything of the kind in what I said, since I definitely knew the point at issue
before I was five and twenty (that in that substance human nature is united
with divine in such a way that there is nothing composite), and since   15
throughout my discussion I maintain the simplicity of the substance. Unless I am completely mistaken, Baer has not read my *Apologia* or, if he has,
he was half asleep when he read it, or thinking of something else. According to him, I wrote that Christ could be understood as one of the two
natures, meaning the human; on the contrary, in opposition to Lefèvre,   20
who wished Christ to be understood as both, I maintain that he should
preferably be understood as one of the two, meaning the divine, but a
divine with which the human is united. It is superfluous for him to demonstrate that the old writers wrongly used words for substance instead of
words for nature, since I deny that I did so.   25

I send the book with the previous revisions, as I sent it to Schürer, for
Baer writes that the beginning is missing. As for the hair-splitting that goes
on in Paris, I am not prepared to worry overmuch about that. You will soon
see most of it go out of fashion. It is already condemned here, and sent
packing in Cambridge. Matthaeus, your old instructor, has been welcomed   30
here as professor of Hebrew. I wish your Lexicon had appeared. In the
matter of my *Apologia*, let me have your friendly help, as you always do, and
rely on me to do what I can for you in return. I have sent Schürer a copy
similar to yours; you can send your comments to him, if Froben is not
printing it, to be added to the copy I sent him. I sense that Baer is prejudiced   35
in favour of Lefèvre, for he observes that I gave rein to my ill temper against
him, when in fact, though unpleasantly provoked by him, and that without
any reason, I refrained none the less from any abuse. You say truly that the

* * * * *

7 in the first place] In a short *argumentum* prefixed to the *Apologia* in which
   Erasmus summarizes Lefèvre's objections to his published note on Heb 2:7
11 Human] Terence *Heautontimorumenos* 77
30 Matthaeus] Adrianus; cf Ep 707:11n.
31 Lexicon] Of the Hebrew language (cf Ep 459:184–5). It was never completed;
   see Ep 600:26n.

spectacle of Erasmus in controversy with Lefèvre will give some people
pleasure; but what could I do? Was I to go about with such disfiguring slurs   40
upon me, and take no action? The other scoundrels do not much worry me.
But it is kind of you to press the point, for one can very easily do harm. I
have finished a great part of the New Testament; once that is published, I
shall go to sleep, or sing to myself and the Muses, if such is the gratitude to
be expected by those who toil to be of use to the world of letters. I wrote to   45
you the other day by another courier and do not doubt you have had the
letter. Look after your health, most learned Capito.

Louvain, St Nicholas' day

732 / To Beatus Rhenanus   Louvain, 6 December [1517]

This letter is contemporary with Epp 730–1, covering in part the same topics.
Erasmus answers a letter written by Beatus Rhenanus on behalf of the Froben
firm and received on 5 December. Clearly Beatus' services were now available
to the press again; see Ep 594 introduction.

ERASMUS TO HIS FRIEND BEATUS, GREETING
You answer on Lachner's behalf, but without answering the points on
which I most wanted his answer, I mean the valuation of the printer's copy,
so that I may not have much trouble with Franz who, if ever he has much
ready cash for me, makes me poor again instead of rich by always bringing   5
excellent books, so that I do not have to arrange to have them sent. If
Lachner had not valued the copy at more than twenty florins, I should have
been content. It was only the valuation I wanted, so that I might not depend
on Franz.

Again, this was annoying, that at the last fair they sent absolutely   10
nothing of my work, although I was waiting for it here eagerly in vain. I fear
the corrector of the press is either unskilful or idle; and Froben must look to
this forthwith. I cannot discover from anyone's letters if Froben has re-

* * * * *

43 New Testament] See Ep 864 introduction.
44 sing to myself] *Adagia* III v 80
46 the other day] See Ep 704A introduction.

732
3 printer's copy] Cf Ep 629:7n.
4 Franz] Birckmann
5 rich] The text translated is that suggested in Allen's note.
11 nothing of my work] Cf Ep 707:15; nothing had appeared yet.
12 corrector] Wolfgang Angst

ceived my translation of the second book of Theodore and the revision of
the first book. As regards More's *Utopia* and *Epigrams*, the business meant   15
more to me than my own affairs. Though I urged them to produce it, for
some reason they seem to have lost interest. I had it in mind to send my
paraphrase to Basel – a book that will sell, I thought. But when I saw that
nothing whatever came, I suspected that they had too much work, and so I
gave it to this man here. I now send a copy with some revision by me. But it   20
would be uncivil to compete immediately with the productions of this poor
little man here, who has never printed anything that has been printed by
your people except my book on the prince, which he printed secretly at a
time when I was away in England; and I spoke to him sharply on the point. I
try very hard to see that he does not interfere with you Basel printers; he   25
certainly will get no support from me in doing so. Pace writes that my
Antibarbari has been brought to Rome from Marseille. I suspect that Pace
too has altered, though he still keeps a show of our ancient friendship. As to
the *Utopia*, I leave it for you to decide. Desmarez' things can be left out. The
mention of the alphabets in Pieter Gillis' preface need cause you no anxiety.   30
You say nothing about More's *Epigrams*, intending to return to them later,
and end up by saying nothing at all. The *Apologia* with my revisions I have
sent to Schürer at Strasbourg, on the understanding that if he did not like it,
he should send it on to Basel. I also sent him Quintus Curtius, despairing of
finding room in Basel for several things as long as nothing at all appeared.   35
    There is no time at present to correct my *Epistolae*, because the courier

* * * * *

14 Theodore] Gaza; see Ep 629 introduction, 2n.
15 *Utopia* and *Epigrams*] Cf Epp 550 introduction, 634–5, 726:14–15.
18 paraphrase] See Ep 710 introduction.
21 compete] Erasmus claimed repeatedly that he defended the interests of one of
    his publishers against those of another. The fact is that he often did supply
    rival printers with the same texts, but he normally tried to see that editions
    likely to compete on the same markets did not follow one another too closely.
    By sixteenth-century standards his practice was far from inconsiderate. It
    compares favourably with that of some other famous authors of the time; cf
    Epp 575:2–3, 693, 704A:15–16, 730 introduction, 771 introduction, 795. Mar-
    tens reprinted Froben's first edition of the *Institutio principis christiani* in
    August 1516 (NK 830) and sold part of his edition to Gilles de Gourmont in
    Paris, who published it with the date of 7 August 1516 (NK 2952).
27 *Antibarbari*] See Ep 706:38n.
29 Desmarez' things] Two introductory pieces published in the first edition of
    Utopia but no longer found in Froben's of March 1518. On the other hand,
    Froben did reproduce the table with the Utopian alphabet which had been
    omitted in the Paris edition of 1517; see *Utopia* clxxxiv–ix, 18–19, 26–9.
33 Schürer] See Ep 693.
36 *Epistolae*] Cf Ep 634:5n.

who brings this warned me in the evening that he will be off tomorrow
morning. If they can postpone it, I will send a copy with some additions; if
not, that is their affair. I wrote lately to several individuals by the hand of a
man I know I can trust, and I have no doubt that he delivered to Wolfgang   40
Faber. Your last batch of letters reached me on St Nicholas' eve. And so
there was no time to re-read my *Apologia*; and yet I wonder whence they got
the idea that I said Christ was composite, since I avoided that particularly all
through my discussion, and in so many places say things quite inconsistent
with it which quite refuse to admit their opinion. From Baer's letter it is   45
perfectly clear that he has not read my *Apologia* right through; and he is
more inclined to Lefèvre, nor is he quite free from the what-d'ye-call-it
characteristic of theologians. He says I wrote that Christ could be accepted
as one nature, meaning the human, whereas I explained most clearly that he
was better accepted as one nature rather than both, meaning the divine, but   50
a divine which has taken to itself the human. And yet if there is anything of
the sort, which I do not believe, let them change it as they please. There are
theologians here too, and some of them perhaps prejudiced against me;
they would have remarked it, if there were anything of the kind. When I
have re-read it, I will write more definitely.   55

Bombace was always the friend rather than the flatterer; I shall be
much surprised if he has already learnt conceit in Rome. Pace boasts in a
letter to me that you have spoken well of his book on the advantage of
humane learning. He sent a letter in which he defends me against Dorp, but
the sort of letter that I should be ashamed to deliver as coming from him.   60
Commend me warmly to Master Lachner and to Froben, and play the part of
a letter from me. It is possible that I may revisit you next spring. The
archbishop of Mainz has written to me in his own hand a letter full of good
will. But my coming is quite uncertain, and I would rather nothing were
said about it in public. Take good care of yourself, dear Beatus.   65

Louvain, feast of St Nicholas

* * * * *

39 I wrote lately] Cf Ep 704A introduction.
55 I will write] He did: Ep 734.
56 Bombace] Cf Ep 729 introduction, 28–30.
58 book] Cf Ep 776:4n.
59 He sent a letter] Erasmus' controversy with Dorp had ended some time before
   (cf Ep 713:18n); consequently Pace's letter to Dorp embarrassed him, and he
   suppressed it; see Ep 755:3–4, 776:23–4.
63 a letter] Ep 661

732A / To Bruno Amerbach   Louvain, 6 December 1517

The original letter, in Erasmus' own hand, is in the collection (Autographen: Einzelbriefe) of Aargauisches Staatsarchiv in Aarau, Switzerland. It was published, with a photocopy, by A. Hartmann in AK IV (Ep 595A). For the dispatch see Ep 730 introduction.

ERASMUS TO HIS DEAR BRUNO, GREETING
I must say, you are a proper Callippides, preparing for your journey to Italy for two years already! It would have been safer to go just before the winter. Mind you never trust the Italian climate anywhere. In Padua or Venice I find it least dangerous. I wish this was Italy and we could attract you here! At   5
least it has been decided to give Matthaeus the Jew a salary from public funds – part has already been paid to him – so that he will teach Hebrew without fees. A Greek of some sort will be sent for. Other subjects are getting on pretty well. Farewell, my most learned Bruno, and give Basilius my greetings in return.   10
        Louvain, St Nicholas' day 1517
        The edition of Jerome is approved even by the theologians.
        To the learned Master Bruno Amerbach, my especial friend

733 / To Wolfgang Lachner

This letter has been assigned a new date and is Ep 704A in this edition.

734 / To Wolfgang Faber Capito   Louvain, 9 December [1517]

Cf Ep 730 introduction.

ERASMUS TO WOLFGANG CAPITO, GREETING
I think I have detected what has given offence to you and Baer: when replying to a gibe of Lefèvre's that 'I seemed to have taken the name of Christ to be a second nature' (and I maintain I did nothing of the kind), I

        * * * * *

732A
  2 Callipides] This term was used by Bruno in Ep 595 to refer to his delayed
    departure for Italy.
  6 Matthaeus] Adrianus; cf Epp 686:7n, 707:11n.
  8 A Greek] See Ep 691:19n.
  9 Basilius] Amerbach, Bruno's brother; cf Ep 331 introduction.
  12 Jerome] See Ep 396 introduction.

seem, so he thinks, to be saying 'I rather think it more likely that Christ and   5
the name of Christ (to use your own language), though it signifies two
natures, should be taken as one only and not for two, as you would have it,'
or 'one composed of two.' In this I do not make Christ a composite being,
but I pass in review the two latter alternatives as being far from probable.
First of all, it is far from probable that they should be taken as two; and then   10
I add what I mean to appear far less probable, for one composed of two. I
could have expressed both alternatives more conveniently by saying 'for
two united to one another'; but I should by so doing have made more
probable what I mean to appear less probable. Again, I might have said
'made one' (or, as you prefer, 'subsisting') 'out of two'; but by so doing my   15
point would have disappeared. Who would deny that the name of Christ
can be taken to be a substance subsisting out of two natures? But it does not
hold to say 'Of two things one is the more probable; therefore the other is
also probable,' any more than if I were to say 'It is better to marry than to
burn,' it follows that to burn is good, or if I say 'It is better to serve God than   20
Mammon,' therefore to serve Mammon is good.

But if you take offence here too (that is, in the alternative which I
reject) at the word 'composed,' it would be better to delete the third alternative than to add the word 'subsisting.' You can see, I hope, that I meant
nothing of the kind, all the more so since the whole of my argument is   25
directed to a different object. And yet, if anyone had said that Christ was
composite, where was the peril in that? In these high matters, whatever
human speech can utter is mere stammering. Christ is not composite as a
thing is composed of matter and form or a house out of framing and
infilling; but in some way or other he is composite. Things which are put   30
together and joined together are in Latin called 'composite.'

But I have no need of any such defence. I wonder why Baer should say
that I wish Christ to be taken to be either of the two natures or the second of
them (the human nature), when I expressly explained it as one of the two
(meaning the divine). It is no business of mine what Lefèvre said, if he did   35
perchance say anything of the kind. You cannot, I presume, take offence at

* * * * *

734
5 saying] The following quotation is from the first edition of the *Apologia ad
Fabrum*. In the Froben edition of February 1518 Capito and Baer made two
minor changes in this sentence, but in a later edition (*Apologiae omnes*, Froben
1521–2) Erasmus restored the original text, adding only 'but this would be
quite absurd' to 'or one composed of two.' This addition clarifies the text in
accordance with the interpretation here; see LB IX 35F and Ep 730:8n.
23 the third alternative] 'One composed of two.'
34 expressly explained] LB IX 36A; cf Ep 730:8–10.

my saying that both are signified, while one is connoted. Such is my view: to connote something is no more than to mean it in a different or, as your friends would say, secondary sense. I have now written to Lefèvre twice, and he answers not a word; I suppose he has something brewing. I told him, if he does answer, not to forget what is due to his reputation. If however he behaves as discourteously as he has done once already, he will find a certain lack of courtesy on my side too; and perhaps, as Horace puts it,

    seeking to sink his teeth in the soft crumb,

    he'll crash them on a flint.

It is kind of Baer to suggest that I should declare continually that I submit what I write to the judgment of the church. So indeed I do, but to give and take many sureties argues lack of confidence. I suppose no man of good will ever writes in any other spirit than dependence on the judgment of the church; but sometimes it is none too clear where the church is to be found. I shall take care never knowingly to write anything that Christ would disown. Those thorny niceties of which you are thinking – I do not believe the Christian faith depends on them. Not that I undertake to secure that there is never anything with which someone somewhere could find fault; no such success has yet fallen to the lot of anyone, either ancients or moderns.

I wanted you to know my mind; and now I leave the rest to your judgment. I know you are both such good scholars that you will take no false step, and such good friends of mine that you will do only what is for the best. Farewell, my learned Wolfgang.

I wrote a few days ago by the Basel courier. Show this letter, if you think fit, to Baer, and give him my cordial greetings. Louvain, morrow of the Conception of the BVM

735 / To Paschasius Berselius   Louvain, 9 December [1517]

This letter is answered by Ep 748.

ERASMUS TO HIS FRIEND BERSELIUS, GREETING
You send me triplet on triplet piled, and I reply with a single sentence: may

    * * * * *

39 twice] Epp 659, 724; cf Ep 721 introduction.
43 Horace] *Satires* 2.1.77, 78

735
2 triplet on triplet piled] This sentence may refer with slight irony to Ep 674, the Latin text of which is studded with flowery triplets such as 'saintly bishops, eminent monarchs, and brilliant men of letters.' Berselius may well have followed up with a similar letter in reply to Ep 718.

all go as you wish. From your most civilized prince I have no aspirations,
except that, as he is a great man and all sing his praises, I should like first to
be known to him, and then to enjoy his good opinion; especially now that   5
by promoting Aleandro he has set up a kind of rallying point for all lovers of
good literature. If Battista speaks well of me, he does but maintain the spirit
of his brother; I beg you most urgently to greet him warmly on my behalf.
Please remember me quite specially to Doctor Leo, my old and valued
benefactor. I count myself fortunate to have shared rooms with him; some-   10
how everything seems more agreeable when I think of him, the founder and
the host of my place of lodging. Greet Gaspard too; he seemed a learned
man, which in a theologian is nothing new, and (what is rare) courteous
and gay as well. I wonder that we hear no news of Andreas of Hoogstraten.
You tempt me with offices at court, but I shall not compete with you just   15
now. I merely send you a paraphrase, as a token to bind you more closely to
me.

You will forgive me, dear Paschasius, if I write a careless letter to a
friend who deserves better things, but besides the great toil of my researches which overwhelms me at the moment, I am burdened with such   20
bundles of letters from all parts that if I were fit and at leisure this by itself

* * * * *

6 Aleandro] In addition to a salary and several benefices, Erard de La Marck (see
    Ep 738 introduction) had recently given Girolamo Aleandro (see Ep 256 intro-
    duction) the chancellorship of the cathedral chapter of his see of Chartres. The
    nomination was ratified by the chapter on 10 September, but Aleandro appar-
    ently had not left Rome. When Erasmus wrote these lines Aleandro had
    already broken with Erard to join the service of Cardinal Giulio de' Medici; see
    Journal autobiographique du Cardinal Jérôme Aléandre ed H. Omont (Paris 1895)
    17.
7 Battista] Gianbattista Aleandro, a faithful companion to his brother Girolamo,
    who was still at Liège with Erard de La Marck; see Harsin Erard de la Marck
    passim.
9 Leo] Leo Outers of Hondschoote, d 1532, a former student and subsequently
    regent of the College of the Lily (cf Ep 643:14n). He was now living at Liège,
    where he held benefices and would later become chancellor to the bishop; cf
    de Vocht CTL I 92–3.
12 Gaspard] See Ep 718:7n.
14 Hoogstraten] See Epp 299, 381.
15 offices] 'Muneribus aulicis'; perhaps 'courtiers' presents.' From Berselius'
    answer it would appear that Erasmus here referred to the letter he had recently
    received from Berselius which was probably long and full of court gossip, just
    like Ep 748.
16 paraphrase] See Ep 710 introduction.

would be too much for me. I will, however, make it clear to you that the name of Paschasius stands in the list of my more special friends. Farewell.

Louvain, morrow of the Conception of the BVM

736 / To Pieter Gillis   Louvain, [c December] 1517

> This letter, which was printed in the *Farrago*, follows Ep 712, taking up the same topics. Pace may have passed through Antwerp (cf line 7) in late November or early December; see Ep 619 introduction.

ERASMUS TO HIS FRIEND PIETER GILLIS, GREETING
As regards what Jacobus brought me, all is in order, and I have no misgivings about Master Nicholas, but I was surprised that the money was not repaid to you. Your melancholy grieves me; I recalled my own belongings solely in hopes of giving you less to worry about. As for the seal, I am not 5
complaining, only you might send your servant to urge the man on. I wish I had known that Pace would be in your part of the world (for so I gather from his letter); I would have run over to meet him at once. His letter to Dorp did not much attract me, although I have not yet read it right through. What do you suppose Franz and Crullus are offering to do for me, that they should 10
write to the archbishop on my behalf? Or why have they any misgivings, since the money will remain in your hands with you as guarantor? Nor do you run any risk – only of paying back the same sum, if anything should happen. What merry wags they are, and will be charming friends if need arises. Crullus has detected that the archbishop of Canterbury is not the 15
chancellor; otherwise, I suppose, he might even give the money. If they raise difficulties, leave them alone; if they are willing to act, they will do me a great service at no risk to themselves; but there is need of haste. Forget about the physician, my dear Pieter, and play your part in the drama, as I do. His last letter sounded more and more ingratiating; but it will come out 20
all right. Only take care to make life as pleasant as you can, and keep

* * * * *

736
7 from his letter] Three letters were answered by Ep 741.
8 letter to Dorp] Cf Ep 732:59n.
16 chancellor] Warham had resigned the chancellorship in favour of Wolsey late in 1515. Complying with Erasmus' wish in Ep 712, Gillis had now approached Crullus. But rather than advancing the requested amount, Crullus was looking for an excuse. Perhaps the word 'chancellor' was used in the receipt provided by Erasmus; see Ep 823.
19 physician] Afinius

yourself for better days. My own health is pretty good. I send one copy of
the paraphrase with corrections. Best wishes to your dear wife and all the
family.

Louvain, 1517   25

737 / To [Jan van Bergen?]   Louvain, 12 December [1517]

> The identification of the addressee, which was lacking in the Deventer
> Letter-book, has been accepted by Allen and de Vocht (CTL I 260). Erasmus was
> indebted to the Bergen family for support on several occasions, and Jan (see Ep
> 42:21n) was now the head of the family. As a high dignitary he deserved to be
> addressed with deference, and he had a son, Antoon, who had recently begun
> his study in Louvain (cf Epp 717:22–4, 760). Unfortunately the matter is not
> mentioned in Ep 739, addressed to Jan's brother. The year date must be 1517
> because Erasmus is in Louvain and plans to spend the next summer in Basel.

Greeting, my right honoured Lord. I am now more severely distracted by my
toilsome researches than I have ever been, nor have I usually been able to
find time for teaching the young; so far am I just at this moment from being
free to undertake anything of the kind, having reached, as it were, the last
act of my play. Yet in spite of that I should be sorry if your Highness   5
supposed me unwilling to do all I can to please my friends. Whatever I can
do, that I most gladly will. In the party of us who habitually dine together
here, we have among others Doctor Jan van Borssele, a canon of St Peter's,
Middelburg, generally known as a man of high character and a good
scholar, who has had several years' experience in this kind of responsibil- 10
ity, for he has acted as tutor to the nephews of the right reverend Doctor
François de Busleyden, bishop of Besançon, of pious memory. I would
undertake to answer for him at every point. In age and temperament alike
he is ideal for work of this kind. I will gladly be of assistance to him, show
him the way, and be ready with advice and encouragement – sometimes   15
even take a share in the work myself, as long as I am living in Louvain; for

* * * * *

23 with corrections] Cf Ep 732:20.

737
4 last act] *Adagia* I ii 35
8 Borssele] Jan Becker van Borssele had come to Louvain in the autumn (see Epp
687:18–19, 805:20), but is not afterwards mentioned as the tutor of Antoon van
Bergen. Erasmus worked hard to secure him as professor of Latin for the
Collegium Trilingue, but in the end he preferred a lucrative benefice; see Ep
849.
12 Busleyden] Busleyden was archbishop of Besançon 1498–1502, cf Ep 157:67n.

around Easter I shall be obliged to return to Basel for the publication of my work. I have made this bed and I must lie on it, nor shall I be free to return here for six months.

You see how well disposed I am, and how ill situated. What I can do is at your Highness' disposal, nor do I seek for any reward. What little I already possess is enough for a disposition such as mine. Nevertheless I am resolved to devote whatever life remains to me to the common good. My best wishes to one distinguished in so much else besides lineage.

Erasmus of Rotterdam, etc

Louvain, St Lucy's eve

738 / To [Erard de La Marck]   Louvain, 13 December 1517

The recipient may be identified by a comparison with Epp 735 and 746, which is the bishop's answer to this letter.

Erard de La Marck (1472–1538) belonged to a powerful family which owned lands on both sides of the French-Burgundian border. He was elected bishop of Liège in 1505, and in recognition of an alliance between his house and the French crown, Louis XII obtained for him the French see of Chartres in 1507. Maximilian I set out to regain his loyalty when in 1509 he granted him the princely rights pertaining to the see of Liège. This realignment was completed by an alliance with Charles of Spain in 1518 (see Ep 748:29n). It cost Erard the see of Chartres but in 1520 brought him the archbishopric of Valencia and also a cardinalate. As the repeated failure of his previous attempts to secure a cardinalate had caused a measure of disaffection from the Roman curia and as this coincided with the earliest phase of the Lutheran reformation, it had at times been believed that he favoured the German friar (cf Epp 916, 980 introductions). Equally skilful in his political and financial dealings, he was also a patron of the arts and letters. This first approach to him on the part of Erasmus, no more than a polite gesture, soon led to a close and lasting relationship; cf Harsin *Erard de la Marck* passim.

Respectful greeting, my Lord Bishop. If I make bold to address a letter to your Lordship, you must forgive this as the outcome of my admiration for you; if my letter is written with less pains than should be, you will ascribe this to your well-known kindness of heart, of which I have heard much from so many sources, and especially from that champion of all the virtues, 5

* * * * *

18 this bed] Literally 'I have seasoned this dish and I must eat the whole of it';
Adagia 1 i 85.

Erard de La Marck
Portrait by Jan Cornelisz. Vermeyen, c 1530
Rijksmuseum, Amsterdam

Etienne Poncher; if it is short, you will be indulgent to my laborious researches, by which I am at the moment distracted as never before. Rather, for fear you should take offence at the brevity of my letter, I send you with it St Paul, speaking Latin and at somewhat greater length than usual, for it is such solace as this that refreshes me, like an agreeable detour, whenever the 10 feeling tends to come over me that I have done as much research as I can bear. Aleandro's promotion has earned you the gratitude of all men everywhere who care for humane studies. Farewell, and pray enter the name of Erasmus among the least, if you will, of your more humble followers. 15

Louvain, St Lucy's day 1517

739 / To Antoon van Bergen   Louvain, 13 December 1517

This letter was published in the *Farrago*.

TO THE RIGHT REVEREND ANTOON VAN BERGEN,
ABBOT OF ST BERTIN'S, GREETING
Reverend Father, when I was recently in Ghent, I learnt belatedly that your Lordship was there too, and I was just attempting to pay my respects when they told me you had departed. Afterwards I heard from various people 5 something that greatly troubled me – that your Lordship was somewhat displeased with me, I suppose on account of my *Moria*, which a distinguished man, Joris van Halewijn, in spite of my reluctance and my threats, has turned into French; in other words, has made it his book instead of mine, adding, subtracting, and altering at his good pleasure. Let me add 10 that the theme in itself is humorous, and yet I do not attack any sort of men unpleasantly, nor take anyone to task by name except myself. To crown all, this book for better or worse has won the approval of scholars the whole world over; it is approved by bishops, archbishops, kings, cardinals, and

* * * * *

738
6 Poncher] Erasmus had met him in February 1517; see Ep 522:126–7n.
9 St Paul] See Ep 710.
12 Aleandro's] See Ep 735:6n.

739
3 Ghent] In June; cf Epp 596 introduction, 641.
9 into French] See Ep 641:6n.
12 except myself] *Folly* refers twice to 'my Erasmus' (see LB IV 487A, 491C). Erasmus' claim that the work contained no personal attacks is true, in so far as no contemporaries were mentioned by name.

Pope Leo the Tenth himself, who read the whole thing from cover to cover.   15
Even supposing I had written something foolish in it and given offence to
other people, I was confident that your Lordship of all men would support
me, being your usual self; for I have long experience of your liberal mind,
which the genius of liberality itself could not outdo. Indeed, I cannot yet be
induced to credit what certain people have told me on this point. I know   20
that many idle tales are in circulation, and I have now many years' experience of your habitual fairness of mind, in which I have more confidence
than I have in what other people say. I know what a distance separates my
lord of St Bertin from Briselot, although they both begin with B. However
this may be, pray do not relax your affection for my humble self, for no   25
better reason, if you like, than its long standing. Why, if ever I have
deserved the favour of men like yourself, I dare to assert, more in self-
confidence than arrogance, that I most deserve it now. On this point
perhaps posterity will judge more justly when I am gone, although even in
this generation there are those who see the truth.   30

I live in the College of the Lily, of which Theodoricus, the bearer of
this letter, is a member. He is a young man of lively and gifted intelligence,
and of great promise. If, therefore, there is anything in which he needs
assistance from your Lordship, I beg that he may have it. Farewell, best of
patrons.   35

Louvain, St Lucy's day 1517

740 / To Mark Lauwerijns   Louvain, [16 December 1517]

Since Lauwerijns was probably sent a printed copy of the *Paraphrasis ad
Romanos* (see Ep 710 introduction), a common secretarial error in the Latin
month shown in the dates of Epp 740–1 has had to be corrected.

ERASMUS TO HIS FRIEND MARK, GREETING
Your last letter, with so many delightful things in it, gave me as much
pleasure as your present itself. I welcome your attitude towards humane

* * * * *

15 Leo] Cf Ep 749:16–18.
15 cover to cover] Cf Ep 673:8n.
24 Briselot] The assumption is that Antoon knew of Briselot's criticism of Erasmus' *Moriae encomium*; cf Epp 597:4–11; 641:16–18.
31 Theodoricus] See Ep 762 introduction.

740
2 letter] The answer to Ep 717 from Erasmus, in which he thanked Lauwerijns
   for a gift of money and inquired after his brother

studies; but one must 'serve the time,' as no less an authority than St Paul
tells us. I am glad to learn your brother is well. But what is this I hear? He   5
spends his time among Egyptian crows? How they must marvel at this new
swan! I rejoice to know that you like More and Pace; I should like such men
as that, even if they were Scythians. There is no need to trouble yourself
about Friesland; he has gone off heaven knows where. I send you Paul
speaking a new language. Farewell, dearest friend.   10

Louvain, 15 [November]

741 / To Richard Pace   Louvain, [16 December 1517]

> See Ep 740 introduction. Pace probably met More at Bruges and returned to
> England in his company; see Epp 619 introduction, 623:23n.

I had already written twice in answer to two earlier letters from you, and
here comes a third, answering your third, but only a short one, for I am busy
with so much work that I have never known the like. I congratulate you the
more readily on the fortunate leisure you now enjoy; indeed I am almost
jealous, dear friend though you are. A second Hercules indeed, if you have   5
slain such a monster, especially if one can believe you did it single-handed,
and with no Theseus; who is, I hear, a crony of yours, and, to be quite frank,
I am a little jealous; unless you like to call him Hercules and be Theseus
yourself. My paraphrase (*paraphronesis*, if you prefer) you will find in the
hands of Mark, the future dean of St Donatian's; though I suppose this has   10
long been common knowledge. Farewell, my excellent Pace, and if More is

* * * * *

4 'serve the time'] Rom 12:11. Erasmus was now revising his New Testament. In
  the 1516 edition he had adhered to the reading accepted by the Vulgate, 'serve
  the Lord' (*kyrios*), but in future editions he preferred 'time' (*kairos*), that is, the
  right time; see LB VI 631–2.
6 crows] Crows showed Alexander the Great the way to an oasis in the Egyptian
  desert: Quintus Curtius Rufus *History of Alexander* 4.7.15.
7 More and Pace] See Ep 741 introduction.
8 Scythians] Sons of a distant, barbarous country
9 Friesland] Jan of Friesland; see Ep 637:15n.
9 Paul] The *Paraphrasis ad Romanos*; cf Ep 717:3–4.

741
6 monster] Perhaps a reference to Pace's letter to Dorp (see Ep 732:59n). More too
  had earlier written to Dorp in defence of Erasmus (cf Rogers Ep 15); and who
  else but More could be meant by Theseus?
9 *paraphronesis*] Delirium
10 Mark] Lauwerijns; cf Ep 651 introduction.

in your company, give him the warmest greetings from me, to match the warmth of my affection.

Louvain, 15 [November]

742 / To Richard Pace   Louvain, 21 December [1517]

This letter was written shortly after Ep 741.

ERASMUS TO HIS FRIEND PACE, GREETING
Today, being St Thomas' day, I had two letters from you, having already answered three others. All were extremely welcome on two counts, whether as showing your liveliness of mind or because they were full of your affection for me, even though I knew that full well of old. But to give a short   5
answer to so much, wondering at the miracle if it really happened (which was Aristotle's solution for several of his problems): I am sorry about Lefèvre, nor can I yet quite guess what has come into his head. You would not call my modest reaction very bitter, if you knew how I could have attacked him, and that too with the approval of the theologians; the attacks   10
he launched against me you can see for yourself. You say I passed over nothing without a refutation; but this was foresight, not bitterness, and even so I passed over many points deliberately. But there is no reason why you should tell me to keep your opinion to myself; I only wish there were as much agreement between you two as there is between me and Lefèvre. As   15
for our reverend brethren, I scented some time ago that they were up to no good. But some things are so infectious that the only way to get the better of them is to run away; even after a complete victory you cannot leave the field

* * * * *

742
2 two letters] Evidently from Bruges, where Pace was staying with Lauwerijns and probably also More
6 miracle] Perhaps Lefèvre's 'miraculous' knowledge of Erasmus' *Novum instrumentum* prior to the date of its publication; see Ep 597:44n.
9 very bitter] Pace's criticism of Erasmus' *Apologia ad Fabrum* must in part have been similar to that of Baer (cf Ep 730 introduction and lines 32–3). On leaving Constance (see Ep 619 introduction), Pace was bound to pass through Basel, where his *De fructu* (see Ep 776:4n) was published in October. More recently Pace had met Johannes de Molendino, another supporter of Lefèvre (see Epp 755, 806:21). In line 15 'you two' or 'you others' (*inter vos*) probably refers to Molendino and perhaps also to Baer and his friends.
16 brethren] Perhaps the Louvain theologians into whose faculty Erasmus had been co-opted; cf Epp 637:12n, 713:18n, 743:9–10.

without being contaminated by such a plague. So that to challenge them to
public debate is simply 'to bid the horsemen scour the plain.' I hope we   20
shall soon see this brotherly school of thought, and the whole of this
sham-Christian sort of men, ruling the roost with much more circumspection than they are showing now.

As for me, I am now in the last act of my play; what success I have
achieved in earlier ones it is for other men to judge. But I shall not abandon   25
my theme. If More is with you, I wonder that he keeps this more than
Pythagorean silence. I would much have preferred to run over and see you
instead of writing, if my work had left me a spare moment, and if I had been
certain you were there. Give my warmest good wishes to Master Mark. I
send no greetings to More, for he sent me none in your letters, for all there   30
were so many of them. Farewell, my learned friend.

Louvain, St Thomas the Apostle

743 / To Antonius Clava   Louvain, 21 December [1517]

ERASMUS TO THE MOST LEARNED ANTONIUS CLAVA,
COUNCILLOR OF GHENT, HIS RIGHT GOOD FRIEND, GREETING
I would have sent the book before, but no one presented himself to whom I
could entrust it. Now I fear that I am too late in sending it, but here it is all
the same. Take proper care of your health, my dear Clava. Keep up a good   5
fire, especially if you are living in the low-lying place where you usually are.
I congratulate de Keysere on achieving so much Greek. I see what he has in
mind: he has set his cap at the Greek chair in our new college here, which
will be founded in Louvain out of Busleyden's legacy, unless some evil
genius among the theologians prevents it. But what is this I hear about your   10
physician? Has he such a passion for Chrysis, that golden girl? How would

* * * * *

20 horsemen] Cf *Adagia* I viii 82; to encourage a man to do what he is good at, or
   cannot be prevented from doing
27 Pythagorean] Cf *Adagia* IV iii 72: five years of silence were imposed on the
   students of the Pythagorean school.
29 Mark] Lauwerijns

743
7 Keysere] Cf Ep 691 introduction and 19n. After his remark in Ep 530:12–14 it is
   not likely that Erasmus supported his ambition.
11 physician] Perhaps Clavus, mentioned in Ep 650. His fees were apparently not
   the lowest: Chrysis appears in Terence's play *Andria*, but the terms *chrysis* and
   argyris also connote gold and silver coins.

it be if he were content with silver Argyris, if Chrysis eludes him? Mind you do all you can to be able to make a long nose at the medico. Farewell.

Louvain, St Thomas the Apostle

744 / From Guillaume Budé   Paris, 21 December [1517]

This letter answers Epp 689 and 723. It was taken from Paris to Mainz by Hutten and forwarded from there. It did not reach Erasmus until 20 February 1518 (see Ep 778:38–41). Budé kept no record of it (cf lines 59–60, Epp 810:6–14, 896 postscript) and meant what he wrote in the postscript of this letter when he asked Erasmus to suppress it. Erasmus none the less published it, with his answer, in the *Auctarium*, but he felt justified in making some cuts (see lines 40, 88–9, Allen Ep 906:530–2). Towards the end he suppressed some of Budé's uneasy comments about his conflict with Lefèvre. This course of action was unfortunate; bound to irritate Budé, it is also apt to strengthen the impression that Erasmus overreacted in his reply to this letter, Ep 778.

GUILLAUME BUDÉ,
SECRETARY-DESIGNATE OF HIS MAJESTY,
TO HIS FRIEND ERASMUS, GREETING
You have now expressed surprise in two brief notes at my so suddenly falling silent after being so keen on our constantly sending letters to and fro,   5
as though on this point your contribution left nothing to be desired. To take you up on this I am reluctant, or too busy, or perhaps I do not dare to issue a fresh challenge. This much I will say: since that very long letter of yours, I believe I have had only one, the letter you wrote me when you were writing to the king, and apart from that virtually nothing that could deserve to be   10
called a letter. Ever since then, while I have written you two letters in succession, one of them largely in Greek, I have received in return two, or

* * * * *

13 a long nose] The Latin adage is 'medium unguem ostendere' (*Adagia* II iv 68), a gesture of contempt. *Clavus* (nail) and *unguis* (fingernail) both are in Dutch *Nagel*, which was perhaps the physician's name; see M.A. Nauwelaerts in *Commémoration nationale d'Erasme* (Brussels 1970) 166.

744
2 secretary-designate] The first printing, both of this and of Ep 778, had *electus*, which was replaced in the next edition by 'secretary', cf Ep 810:434n.
8 very long letter] Ep 531, followed by Ep 534, contemporary with Ep 533 to Francis I
11 two letters] Epp 568, 609

three at most – I will not call them notes, but scraps of paper cleverly folded
and sealed to look like real letters, and virtually empty inside. If you have
had mine, you cannot be acquitted of a Lethe-drinker's loss of memory   15
when you now demand to be told what has happened in the matter of the
king and the bishop. One of these letters I entrusted to Bade, the other to
some young men who had brought me one letter, or note rather, from you,
and whom I told to wait at my house till I could write a hurried reply; for
they assured me that they would see that it reached you.   20

In this I said that I had been let down by the men who seemed to regard
you as the apple of their eye, and on these grounds I nearly broke off
friendly relations with them. Chief among these was a certain x, so you
must no longer think everyone of that name is your bosom friend; though I
suspect no deeper treachery, only a failure to persevere. For having told me   25
to write to you, presumably on the king's instructions, as long as your
answer was awaited he was constantly urging me. 'What news of Erasmus?'
he would ask, 'What hopes can you hold out for us? For the king speaks of
Erasmus from time to time even without prompting.' When I heard this, to
increase his eagerness I made a suitable reply, hoping no doubt that if your   30
affair went well, it would be better for me too. On this I was criticized by
some people, and some rebuked me to my face, saying I did not understand
that, if your affair should go well, I and everyone else here should actually
be out of credit, as though I suppose you were the only man who could be
sure of success in the literary way, while I all the time confidently and even 35
cheerfully asserted that I was carrying out my orders from the king, in
reliance no doubt on your generosity. But when I turned your letter into
French, as the king had told me to, and showed it to him, he read it through
and said it was no clearer to him what your intentions were; and I replied,

* * * * *

13 three at most] Budé is normally quite specific. In addition to two short letters
    (Epp 689, 723) Erasmus had probably sent an even shorter note accompanying
    a copy of the *Apologia ad Fabrum*; cf lines 74–6.
15 Lethe-drinker's] A classical reminiscence; Lethe was one of the rivers in
    Hades, and shades which drank its waters lost their memory.
16 the king and the bishop] Words written in Greek; cf Ep 689:4n.
22 apple of their eye] *Adagia* v ii 50
24 that name] In Ep 534 Erasmus had given Budé a long list of all his friends by the
    name of William, paying an elaborate compliment to Guillaume Petit, the
    royal confessor (cf Ep 522:17n). Since then he had grown less certain of the
    sympathy of the royal confessor (cf Epp 568, 725). Here Budé confirms his
    suspicions. The following references to Petit and the invitation are all in
    Greek.
32 understand] Reading συνιέναι for συνεῖναι
37 your letter] Ep 533

and so forth. All this time the bishop, who is in truth, I believe, well   40
disposed to you, was never present, for this happened in some place in the
country whither I had gone on purpose. After that he was always in
company, and on a mission to Calais and England. When he returned from
that recently and passed through this city, I went to dinner, where three
tables were laid, there were so many people. I spoke of you, and had your   45
letter in my pocket, but did not show it to him. After dinner Glareanus came
to pay his respects to the bishop. Although I was on my way home and the
bishop had already retired to his private rooms, I came back in order to
introduce him; and I have not refused this Glareanus anything he has
asked, for your sake, since you told me not to. But he is less trouble than I   50
could wish, and I see him only rarely.

Hutten has passed through here. What a cheerful and friendly person
he is, and shows his birth and good breeding. I would have had him to
dinner, had he been ready to fix a day; but I saw him first at Ruzé's, when I
had been invited to dine there and did not know that Hutten was present.   55
Next day he departed, but will return this way, or so he promised. Deloynes
has a letter written some time ago, but was waiting for mine, that we might
write together. Meanwhile I have spent some time in the country, and being
full of business have put off writing to you till now. And now I have written
to you in a hurry in the morning, being about to leave town, and had   60
received your letter in the country. For after dining with the bishop I had
gone into the country, and next day the bishop set off to join the king.

You tell me to write to Tunstall, but I have nothing to write about

* * * * *

40 so forth] The passage here omitted in the printed text was probably a summary
   of Ep 568:28–47.
40 bishop] In September 1517 Etienne Poncher was sent on an embassy to
   England to treat for the surrender of Tournai (cf Ep 780 introduction). For his
   progress cf LP II 3701, 3714, 3723, 3739, 3788. He returned to France In December.
45 your letter] Probably Ep 689
50 you told me] Cf Ep 609:22n.
52 Hutten] On 20 September 1517 Hutten had been sent to Paris by Albert of
   Brandenburg to conclude an agreement for Albert's support of Francis I in the
   next imperial election. The electoral vote of Mainz was to be rewarded by an
   annual pension for Albert, but while Hutten was still in France his master
   changed his mind and joined the supporters of Hapsburg; see Holborn *Hutten*
   90; *Deutsche Reichstagsakten* Jüngere Reihe I (Gotha 1893) 44–5.
54 Ruzé's] The king's *lieutenant-civil* in Paris and a faithful friend of Budé and the
   humanist circle; cf Ep 493:462n.
56 Deloynes] Budé is replying to Ep 689:5–8. Deloynes' letter is not preserved.
61 your letter] Ep 723

unless he first answers my long letter. I should be extremely sorry, and
indeed heartbroken, had anything happened to him. I have also written to   65
Linacre, but have not yet had an answer, assuming of course that he means
to send one; for he had written to me first. I suppose it may be the plague
that has prevented his writing to me. What you say of Busleyden's bequest
or trust is something quite new and unusual, but entirely admirable. A few
weeks ago I lost my brother, a great admirer of your work and a good scholar   70
in Greek as well; he was a priest, and archdeacon of Troyes, which means I
must leave town and go down there.

As for what we have been reading and writing lately, your zeal has
been misplaced, and I would almost say it has done harm. I have read the
passage in Lefèvre's commentary on St Paul's Epistles, as you wished me to   75
do, but I have not yet read your *Apologia*, except in snippets. I know what
people think of the two of you but do not think it necessary to intervene
with my own opinion. With Lefèvre I have not spoken since I wrote to you
about him last year, giving his ill health as his reason for not writing to you;
for so he had told me. I scarcely see him once a year. I wish this dispute   80
between you had never arisen. Our bishop told me that he first heard of it in
England. I hope all the same that, having done battle thus far for the truth,
you can pass the thing over in silence for the future; this is important for
your reputation, which you have built up by all those thoughtful works of
the highest quality. You would not believe how much your supporters   85
regret that this handle for an attack on you should be given to men who
think that your principles may make them uncomfortable; no one is more
sorry than Ruzé. I know how hard it is to control one's pen in full spate, and
so forth; but mind that in your desire to maintain the right by every means
you do not give the impression that you are now careless of your reputation.   90
But you must not take this too hard, as though I were criticizing you; it was a
friend's duty to point this out, for it must not look as though I had done
nothing when a friend was in difficulties. As for your opponent, you do not
insist that I should give my opinion in writing, nor is my friendship with
him such that he is obliged to take my advice; and so I gladly say nothing.   95
You, however, are obliged to abide by my opinion even against your will, if

* * * * *

64 long letter] Ep 583; cf Ep 689:11–12.
66 Linacre] On 10 July [1517]; see G. Budé *Opera omnia* I 248–50.
67 plague] Cf Ep 623.
70 brother] Louis Budé (1470–19 November 1517), archdeacon of Troyes. Budé
     went to Troyes in January to deal with the estate.
75 wished me to do] Cf line 13n.
78 I wrote] Ep 493:495–500.

I preferred to deal with you by the strict letter of the law under the provisions of the Statute of Friendship. So it is fair that you should accept this suggestion with a good grace.

Farewell, from Paris, on Midwinter day.   100

This bundle of letters I advise you to suppress when you have read them, or even throw them on the fire. If you wish me to resume the writing of letters which are fit for publication, set me once again a good example, if you can find the time for these niceties. Farewell once more.

Your sincere friend Budé   105

745 / To Albert of Brandenburg   Louvain, 22 December [1517]

A short *Methodus* was published among the introductory pieces of the *Novum instrumentum* (1516). It reappeared greatly amplified as the *Ratio verae theologiae* in the second edition, the *Novum Testamentum* of March 1519 (see Ep 864 introduction), but was removed from subsequent ones, since meanwhile a long series of separate editions of the text had begun. This letter is a dedicatory epistle for the first separate edition of the *Ratio* (Louvain: D. Martens November 1518; NK 2973; cf Ep 894 introduction). It answered Ep 661, which was also printed in Martens' edition of the *Ratio*. In January and April 1519 Johann Froben, the printer of the New Testament, also published two separate editions of the *Ratio*. This was done without consulting Erasmus, on the advice of Beatus Rhenanus, who also contributed an epistle to Johannes Fabri (BRE Ep 85; cf Epp 89, 91) which took the place of Epp 661 and 745 in the earlier Martens edition. As more separate editions of the *Ratio* were published Erasmus finally replaced the present epistle with a new one, also addressed to Albert (Ep 1365).

The year date of this letter was always thought to be 1518, prior to Allen's edition. The references to Maximilian's presence at the Diet of Augsburg (line 25n) and to Albert's cardinalate (lines 38n, 85n) suggest that the letter could not have been written before the autumn of 1518. However, other evidence suggests 1517: the colophon date of Martens' edition; the date of Ep 661 (confirmed by Ep 695:31), in which Albert does not yet style himself cardinal; Erasmus' toiling over the revision of the New Testament (cf lines 30–5; cf Epp 720, 731, 737, 738, 740, 757); and his change of mind about the dedication of the *Paraphrasis ad Romanos* (lines 16–23), for which he must have been anxious to offer an explanation, and a substitute, at the earliest possible occasion. Allen concluded that the references to Maximilian's presence and to

* * * * *

97 provisions] Including the requirement to give true advice with frankness, and even sternness; see Cicero *De amicitia* 13.44–5.

Albert's cardinalate were added by Erasmus, perhaps on the page proofs of Martens' 1518 edition, after his return from Basel in September 1518. Hence, Allen assigned the year date of 1517 to this letter.

ERASMUS OF ROTTERDAM TO THE
MOST REVEREND ALBERT, CARDINAL ARCHBISHOP OF MAINZ,
GREETING

It was, I suppose, the frank and generous readiness of your nature to think well of others that caused you, most reverend Prelate and most illustrious 5 Prince, to derive from my books a far higher opinion of me than I deserve. And yet I cannot but regard that spirit of yours, though I have no claim upon it, as a gain at least to religion and virtue; I wish those men joy of it who really are what you think I am. Your Eminence may have been wrong hitherto in thinking so highly of my humble self; but in this you are not 10 wrong, that you reckon outstanding goodness coupled with learning to match, wherever it may appear, as deserving of the encouragement and support of princes. I did not doubt that, when we meet, I must lose some of your good opinion of me; but all the same I was most eager to accept with speed the overtures of so eminent a prince, and in order not to arrive quite 15 empty-handed, I had proposed to dedicate to you my Paraphrase on the Epistle to the Romans.

This intention I had communicated by letter to a young man distinguished for learning no less than lineage, Ulrich von Hutten, in this specially notable, that he is included among the principal and more intimate 20 officials of your Eminence. But I soon changed my mind, as it seemed more appropriate that what was written for the Romans should again be addressed to them. In the mean time, as luck would have it, I had no opportunity to meet your Eminence, nor did my enormous labours permit me to prepare a gift worthy of you. For when I last went to Basel, you had gone on a long 25 journey to some other part of your jurisdiction, and again, when I was on my way home, you were attending on the emperor at Augsburg; and although that journey was in many ways ill-omened for me in both going and coming, in nothing was it more unfortunate than in my being deprived

* * * * *

745
16 Paraphrase] See Ep 710 introduction.
25 last went to Basel ... 30 meeting with you] Inserted in 1518 (cf Epp 843, 867 introductions). Maximilian attended the Diet of Augsburg in the autumn of 1518, but in May 1516, when Erasmus had previously returned from Basel, he was in Italy. Also, Albert of Brandenburg received the red hat from the hands of the papal nuncio at Augsburg on 1 August 1518; cf Ep 891.

of a meeting with you. And further, as I toil with all my strength at the New   30
Testament, postponing all other concerns, to make it worthy of Leo the
Tenth to whom it was dedicated, and so continually to give it fresh vigour, I
have grown stale myself; I rescue it from senility and myself grow old; and
while, as you put it, I restore the Testament to its original splendour, I cover
myself with dust and cobwebs. For toil of this kind brings very little   35
pleasure and reputation and much tedium and nuisance; and the nuisance
was almost doubled by the ingratitude of many of those very people for
whose benefit I was toiling at this immense task. At length I have made
some sort of recovery from the labours with which I was burdened and the
illness which had almost snuffed me out, and I begin to remember my   40
obligations and send greeting to your Eminence by way of this letter, since
up to now I could do it in no other way. At the same time, may I offer my
felicitations that the exalted dignity of a cardinal has been added to your
other distinctions, a dignity the more honourable in that it was conferred
upon you by a very upright pontiff and was neither bought nor canvassed   45
for – so little, in fact, that without pressure from the emperor Maximilian
you would obstinately have refused it. I enclose with this letter a little piece
on the principles of the study of theology dedicated to you, not thinking
thereby to pay off my debt, but to bind myself to you more and more by this
token payment.   50
    Your Eminence expressed a wish that I should use my pen to add some
brilliance to the Lives of the Saints. But I have tried by my exertions, such as
they are, to cast a little light upon the Lord of the saints himself; for he who
is the source of all glory is pleased to be glorified after a fashion even by the
pious labours of his people. All the same, I can hardly say how much I   55
welcome your attitude: that you, though young in years and beset with the
not so much sacred as unavoidable cares of administration, should have so
much at heart the Lives of the Saints. You are aware that we possess them
largely in the form of old wives' tales, and transmitted in such a style that no
educated or serious-minded person can read them without disgust; and   60
you are concerned that they should be handed on in more select and more
trustworthy form and in language that is clear and accurate, even if it lacks
literary merit. In your wisdom you perceive, of course, what is perfectly
true, that it contributes not a little to the splendour of the Christian religion
that nothing at all should be sung or read in church that is not able to satisfy   65
the most serious and educated taste, in other words, that is not derived from

* * * * *

34 as you put it] Ep 661:20–4
38 At length ... refused it] See line 25n.
51 expressed a wish] Ep 661:36–8

Holy Writ, or at least the production of exceptional men. As it is, stuff more worthless than Sicilian trash, as the saying goes, and all maunderings of any crazed old man or even old woman have made their way in, and do so daily more and more. But in this matter to accomplish what your Eminence   70 desires I am more willing than able. Beyond sedulous efforts, I can make no promises. There is no lack even in Germany of men who in my opinion are absolutely good enough to meet your pious wishes; after all, you have Hutten, who is a marvel of Latinity, in your own household. In the mean time, I am more disposed to count you fortunate in possessing intentions so   75 worthy of a bishop than in wealth however ample. Happy indeed Christ's people, if they were blessed commonly with such prelates, to whom nothing matters more than the glory of Christ, who reproduce the brilliance of jewels, the glitter of gold, the sheen of silver, the whiteness of linen and scarlet of silk, in a word all Aaron's vestments, in their life and conversa-   80 tion; such men as, even if one took away pallium and crozier, would still be recognized as bishops! In your person Fortune, whom the Ancients pictured as blind, appears to be clear-sighted. The famous glories of your lineage gain a new lustre from the radiance of your disposition. You multiply the dignity of an archbishop by the integrity of your life. The cardinal's   85 hat seems to have gained something in our esteem, since you did not refuse it. What remains save to pray to Our Lord Jesus Christ that he may maintain this mind in you, and you among us in good health, as long as can be?

    Louvain, 22 December 151[8]

746 / From Erard de La Marck   [Huy] 30 December 1517

> This letter was published in the *Auctarium*. It answers Ep 738 and in turn is
> answered by Ep 757. In view of Ep 748:20–1, it is very probable that Erard
> wrote from Huy.

A LETTER FROM ERARD, PRINCE BISHOP OF LIÈGE,
TO ERASMUS OF ROTTERDAM, GREETING
It gave me great pleasure to receive the letter which you sent me by Paschasius, a man devoted to you whom I like very much. I was also much pleased with your Paraphrase on Paul's Epistle to the Romans. I owe you   5

   * * * * *

68 Sicilian trash] Worse than the garrulity of other peoples; cf *Adagia* II iv 10.
80 Aaron's] Cf Exod 28.
85 The cardinal's ... refuse it] See line 25n.

  746
 4 Paschasius] Berselius

therefore undying thanks for writing to me and for the favourable opinion
of me which you express in the same letter. I rejoice in praise from you,
whom all men praise. Hitherto you have been unknown to me personally,
but your name and fame have been most familiar for the past ten years, both
for your high standing as a scholar and for the open and friendly manner of   10
which they tell me. If you would pay me the honour of a visit, I shall
consider that you have done me a welcome service. If however you are
unwilling to come here, I shall arrange to call upon you myself for the
pleasure of your society and conversation. Farewell.

    1517, 30 December   15
    Your sincere friend Erard, etc

747 / From Willibald Pirckheimer   Nürnberg, 31 December 1517

> This letter was first printed in the *Farrago*. It answers various points made in
> Erasmus' Ep 694, especially his criticism of Pirckheimer's latest volume. This
> letter is answered by Ep 856.

WILLIBALD TO ERASMUS, GREETING

You gave great pleasure, my dear sir, not only to me but to many of your
other friends, by letting me know how you are and where you are and what
you are doing. So let me say first how glad we are that you should be held in
esteem by such great kings, but sorry that their affection for you should so   5
long be ineffective, for fine words never made a man rich, and praise in the
last resort always means doing something. I know the ways of princes very
well, for I have spent a long time among them and grown very rich indeed
on their promises; but if I had only those to live on, I should often be obliged
(as they say) to waste good teeth on a bad dinner. But so it generally   10
happens: those who most deserve good fortune have to do without it. Yet
why say, do without it? For often those who are supposed to be ill done by
are the best off of all, even though they have least in the way of coin. Who is
better off than you? For you have not only won a reputation by outward
success, but so excel in goodness and in learning that you seem to combine   15
distinction in this life with immortality even while yet alive.

    But enough of this, or it will look as if I flattered you. I was pleased,
dear Erasmus, that you did not wholly disapprove of my slight pieces; still

* * * * *

7 praise] An echo of a Ciceronian phrase (*Tusculanae disputationes* 4.31.67, etc)
11 visit] To Erard's disappointment, plans for a first meeting did not materialize
    (cf Allen Ep 867:83–4, 185–6), but they did spend a few days together by
    February 1519; Allen Ep 916:4.

more so, that you tell me thus openly and frankly what you do not like, which you surely would not do unless you were fond – indeed, very fond – of me, and wished what I write to be perfect in every way. But you know that no man was ever at a loss for an excuse, and everyone is at his most ingenious when set to defend himself. Must I alone seem dull when it comes to this? No: give my excuses then a kindly hearing. Yet I do not like to put forward the old story: 'I am a very busy man, with many engagements public and private; I wrote in a fit of enthusiasm rather than guided by reason, and published in a hurry what I had written,' for this would invite Cato's rejoinder 'You might have held your tongue.' But hear me.

Most honoured Erasmus, I did not name all the men who are put in my list as a mark of respect. I am by no means unaware that the ignorant are mixed with the learned, right-thinking men with bad, and, what might surprise one more, friends with enemies. But those who were both learned and right-thinking deserved their mention; the right-thinking who are influential though not very good scholars were suitably put forward as a bulwark against the ill-conditioned; the scholars who are not right-thinking or are doubtful allies needed to be aroused or encouraged, and enemies to be filled with suspicion of each other. Nor have I been entirely disappointed, for I made more disturbance than I had at first expected: not only did I confirm the waverers, I actually brought most of them over to our side, so that they have taken up the defence of our cause in both speaking and writing. Besides, certain people who were particularly friendly with our opponents and supported them I have plunged in deep suspicion and no little unpopularity – unless maybe you think it was wrong to have pitched one pack of hornets against another. And what makes me laugh is that these most saintly men are forced to suppress their resentment and put a cheerful face on the discomfort they felt at praise from me, not from love of me, but because they knew I could be both useful to them and the opposite. You know how they always measure everything by their own gain or loss, but always with some respectable excuse.

Then you would have preferred me, where I digress into an attack on the logicians, to have left the rest out and pursued the matter in hand. And I do admit, dear Erasmus, that this was written originally from some rush of spirits rather than from deliberate judgment; but when the inspiration (the fit, I ought to call it) had to some extent cooled off, I reworked a good deal

* * * * *

747

28 Cato's] The Roman statesman, who thus replied to a certain Albinus who, though Roman-born, wrote a history in Greek and apologized in the preface for any mistakes he might have made (Aulus Gellius 11.8)

that was ill digested, made many changes, and deleted and cut out some 55
things altogether. And although I seemed to myself at that moment to be
pursuing the matter in hand (for I wanted to demonstrate that the anti-
Reuchlinists were not only mischievous but thoroughly ignorant barbarians as well, and like Lucian to give a glimpse as though through a lattice of
the distance by which they fall short of real learning), I had none the less 60
decided to abolish that digression entirely; but my friends protested, and so
contrary to my wishes it remained intact. In fact I foretold at the time that it
would seem to contribute more to a display of wit, or rather of erudition,
than to the matter in hand. In fact, though what's done can't be undone, yet
I do not regret what I wrote, for this reason, that it provoked this very 65
friendly advice from you, which gave me far greater pleasure than if you
had said you approved of everything. For it is abundantly clear that you
read me with attention and are not a little concerned for my reputation; and
in this you show yourself a really kind and true friend. How I wish I might
some day be able to repay you adequately! I would do it not so much 70
lavishly as with all my heart, as to the man whom I love and respect more
than anyone alive today.

Of Reuchlin's critics I say nothing, for nothing could be added to what
you have so forcibly and truly written on the subject; and so goodbye to
them. I hear that by means of their idol they have something on foot against 75
me, but whatever it is, I shall not be much moved, for I have lived long
enough in public life to have learnt not only to bear insults and calumnies
with patience but to laugh at them. But do pray listen to what these cursed
rascals have been up to. After attacking Johann Reuchlin on all sides, they
have done what I always feared, and by some fraud, I know not what, have 80
at length aroused the resentment of his own prince against him. I am
desperately afraid that this may plunge him in some major disaster, and
none but God will rescue him from the tyrant's clutches. Only see, dear
Erasmus, the lengths to which iniquity will go, especially in those men who
batten on the sins of the people and think they have the right to lock and 85
unlock the gates of heaven.

* * * * *

59 lattice] Cicero *De oratore* 1.35.162; *Adagia* III i 49
75 idol] The reference is probably to Jacob van Hoogstraten, who was to attack
Pirckheimer's *Epistola apologetica* (cf Ep 685:13n) in his own *Apologia*, published in February 1518 (cf Ep 680:28n; Geiger *Reuchlin* 406). Other opponents
of Reuchlin also took issue with Pirckheimer's epistle.
81 his own prince] Ulrich of Württemberg. It was learnt at the duke's court that
Reuchlin had played some marginal role in Hutten's schemes against the
duke; cf Epp 923, 986, and Geiger *Reuchlin* 459.
85 lock and unlock] Cf Matt 16:19.

Your New Testament is eagerly awaited here, and so are your notes on great Paul. How I do you wrong, when you give us so much, to demand something fresh every day! But it is your fault: you always arouse my appetite, yet never satisfy it – no, it would be truer to say that my greed   90 makes me insatiable. Your *Apologia* I have read with some distress of mind, not because you reply to a false friend in appropriate language, but in the fear that it may give rise to greater disturbance, however much I consider you were rightly obliged for several reasons to react with some violence. But it is sometimes permissible, or rather necessary, to show indignation if we   95 wish to have peace, which we cannot possibly attain to without war.

Farewell, dear Erasmus, my most learned friend; mind you keep well, and love me, as I know you do. Nothing better can happen to me. How I wish I might see you one day face to face! How I wish you would take it into your head to visit me! You will not regret having done so, and you can do it   100 conveniently enough, if you ever think of setting out for Basel. You will experience my affection not in word only but in deed, and if the result is not equal to your deserts, it shall at least be the best I can afford. Farewell once more, glory of the world of letters.

Nürnberg, 31 December 1517   105

748 / From Paschasius Berselius   Liège, 7 January [1518]

First printed in the *Auctarium*, this letter answered Ep 735 and was in turn answered by Ep 756. The date is apparently that of the actual dispatch from Liège. From Erasmus' answer, also dated 7 January, it is clear that he replied at once after having read this letter and probably also Ep 746, which Berselius may have taken with him on his return from Huy to Liège. Erasmus seems to have answered Ep 746 first (see Ep 756:9–10). But it is quite possible that one of the correspondents erred by a day or two when dating his letter.

PASCHASIUS BERSELIUS TO
DESIDERIUS ERASMUS OF ROTTERDAM, GREETING
To be sure, I never could approve the industry (call it greed, rather) of those who freely send their hapless friends small new year presents in hopes of largesse in return. All I did was to send you on one occasion a modest token   5

* * * * *

88 Paul] Cf Epp 685:25, 710 introduction.
91 *Apologia*] against Lefèvre; see Ep 597:37n.

Cæſar reſpond.

Ie le vo9
diray volũ.
tiers, maiz   Publius
premyere.   Sextius
ment ie   Baculus.
ne veueil
oublier

cõment apres toute la deſolation
precedente. ie trouuay le premyer
Centurion Publius Sextius Bacu
lus treffort hõme, ſi fort bleſſe quil
ne ſe pouuoit plus ſoutenir, les aul.
trez eſtoient plus tardifȝ. & les
aulcuns ſe metoient hors de la preſ
ſe pour euiter le trect quant ilȝ ſe
voyoient abandõneȝ de ceulx qui
les deuoient ſuyure. Ie vy pareil

Robert de La Marck (d 1537), son of Robert II de La Marck
Miniature by Jean Clouet
in *Commentaires de la guerre gallique* II (1519)
Bibliothèque Nationale MS Fr. 13429, lxxiii recto

of true affection, and out of my affection you cunningly manufactured a war
between us, that you might win it. For you say that I challenged you by
sending a present, but that so far you do not wish to compete, not refusing
to enter the fray but postponing it to a more convenient season. What, pray,
have you in mind? Surely you are not gathering your forces meanwhile and   10
making ready artillery and engines of war? Do not put yourself out, my
good sir; I issue no challenge, I have no wish to arouse you; moderate your
passion and restrain yourself, for you are too great a man to take the field
against me. What can a mere Paschasius do against Erasmus, a man born for
victory in every sort of literature and of service to his friends? Hold!   15
Enough! I would not have any blood flow on my account; I freely yield. Your
paraphrase is responsible; it made you seem too formidable, and as I cannot
be my own master, I am now with my whole heart your prisoner by the laws
of war.

On 28 December I went to see our most kind prince in the castle at   20
Huy, who gave me a most warm and kindly welcome, as he always does. I
gave him your letter and the paraphrase, because the man to whom you had
entrusted that task had attempted it two or three times in vain. The prince
read what you wrote out loud, raised your present to his lips several times,
and uttered the name Erasmus often with delight. I was instructed to spend   25
that day in the castle. After hearing mass came dinner time. We entered the
prince's hall, which was hung with great lofty tapestries. Shortly after we
were given water to wash our hands. The prince took his seat, and next him
his brother Robert, a keen soldier, as it were the new Achilles of our age.
The third place was taken by his wife, in life Penelope over again, in   30
character Lucretia; the fourth by their daughter, a maiden already of mar-

* * * * *

748
6 a war between us] In his flamboyant manner Berselius here answers Ep
    735:15–17.
21 Huy] A town on the Meuse, about nineteen miles west of Liège
28 water] Plautus *Persa* 769, *Truculentus* 481
29 Robert] Robert II de La Marck de Sedan, d 1536. As the older brother of Erard
    (cf Ep 738 introduction) he was the head of the powerful house. The brothers
    were then preparing for a secret treaty of allegiance to Charles of Spain, to be
    signed at St Truiden on 27 April 1518, but Robert was to revert to the French
    camp in 1521. His wife was Catherine de Croy, niece of Jacques, the duke and
    bishop of Cambrai (see Ep 497). They had a daughter, Philippine, who
    married later Renaud, sieur de Brederode (d 1556), and three sons, Robert,
    sieur de Florange (d 1537), Philippe (d 1545), and Antoine, to whom Erasmus
    dedicated his *Paraphrasis ad Galatas* (see Ep 956). See P. Harsin *Recueil d'études*
    (Liège 1970) 169.

riageable age, and in her looks the picture of Diana. Fifth and sixth sat that
noble lady's two brothers, whom you might well suppose were Leda's
twins. Among this company of gods and goddesses, being specially invited
by Jupiter, I took my place like the beetle, feeding my eyes on gold and   35
precious stones and purple, my ears on sweet music, and my palate on
nectar and ambrosia.

Our hunger spent, tables and feast removed, they sang grace to the
powers above, we rose, and they went to play, some at dice, others at
checkers. I meanwhile was summoned to the prince, where there was much   40
talk about you very much to your credit. He has the highest possible
opinion of you. He wants to see you and give you a warm welcome, as one
might welcome a father or some deity come down from heaven to earth. He
is writing to invite you to visit him. Do not delay; you will give him great
pleasure if you cast off all hesitation. For heaven's sake do not long torment so   45
great a man with the longing to see you. He is different from the prelates
you have seen in Italy, France, England, Scotland, or Germany. All of them
are not to be compared with him, for whether you consider the riches of his
mind, his bodily endowments, or his ample fortune, he leaves all others far
behind. All those to whom you lately told me to send your greetings greet   50
you in return, especially Battista, who loves you just like a father. Do please
give my greetings to your son, my brother, Rutgerus Rescius; I will write to
him when time permits. Farewell, glory of literature. If you have anything
for the prince, you can safely entrust it to the priest who brings this letter.
Farewell once more, from my cell in Liège, 7 January.   55

749 / To Jan [Bijl?] of Louvain   Louvain, 2 January 1518

This letter repeats some of the arguments in defence of the *Moria* offered in Ep
739. It is probably addressed to Jan Bijl (or Bijlkens, in Latin Bilhemius) of
Louvain, who died on 2 November 1540 at Mechelen and is buried there. At
different times he served as the warden of several Franciscan houses, including Mechelen. He is probably the staunch supporter of Erasmus mentioned in
Ep 1044. See de Vocht MHL 224.

Another Franciscan Jan of Louvain ('Joannes de Lovanio, alias Roscampi') is
mentioned in D. Van Wely ed 'Liber recommendationis conventus Werthensis
Ordinis Fratrum Minorum' in *Bijdragen voor de geschiedenis van de Provincie*

* * * * *

33 Leda's twins] Castor and Pollux
38 removed] Virgil *Aeneid* 1.216
51 Battista] Gianbattista Aleandro

der Minderbroeders in de Nederlanden 13 (1962–3) 63. He was a priest and died in
Weert (Limburg) on Easter day 1540, although on Holy Saturday he had
preached a sermon. In his case there is no evidence to suggest a connection
with Erasmus.

We wish to acknowledge the assistance of Professor E.J.M. van Eijl, Louvain, and Father A. Houbeart, the archivist of the Flemish Franciscan province, who supplied the above information and additional references for
Bijl, to be cited in the Biographical Register.

TO THE REVEREND DR JOHANNES OF LOUVAIN,
WARDEN OF MINORITES IN AMSTERDAM

Greeting, reverend Father. Your advice was so kindly, so wise, in a word so
truly Christian, that it could not fail to be welcome. As for the *Moria*, I quiet
the reader's misgivings partly in the preface to the book itself, partly in a   5
letter to Dorp which is now printed at the end of the *Moria*. But what can you
do with the people whom no arguments can pacify, and who in fact condemn with so much noise what they have never read? For no one makes
more crazy uproar than they do. If I had foreseen that they were bound to
take so much offence, maybe I should have had the work suppressed; for I   10
am by inclination such that I should wish to please all men if I can, so far as
one can do that without dishonesty. As things are, regrets are useless, now
the book has been printed a dozen times and more. One thing does astonish
me: why of all people is it only the monks and the theologians who take
offence? Is it because they all recognize themselves in the characters I   15
describe? The Holy Father read the *Moria*, and it made him laugh. He
merely added, 'I am glad to see my friend Erasmus is in the *Moria* too'; and
yet I give no one shorter shrift than popes. Heaven forbid that I should wish
to speak ill of people. But if I took it into my head to describe theologians
and monks as most of them really are, it would then at last have been really   20
clear how lightly they are let off in the *Moria*.

That it is read in schools was news to me. Yet I took care to put nothing
into it that might harm the young. You say you fear that the reading of it will
give them a distaste for the whole of religion; but what this means I do not
fully understand. Is there a risk that they will forthwith take against all   25
religion, if those whose religion is full of superstition are criticized? I only

* * * * *

749
5 preface] Ep 222
6 letter] Ep 337
13 a dozen times] Fifteen editions of the *Moria* are known to have appeared
before the end of 1517.

wish all who nowadays go under the name of religious really deserved to be
so called! I will go further: I wish the secular priests themselves and the
mass of lay folk would follow Christ's true religion in such a way that the
people who now monopolize the name of religious may not look religious at   30
all. The world is full of monastic houses everywhere. Not that I condemn
any kind of religious rule; but just reckon for yourself how few among them
have any tincture of true religion beyond liturgy and ceremonies, who live a
more than worldly life. I myself have never yet blackened any man's
character. My ridicule has been aimed at the widespread and well-known   35
defects of humanity.

In other ways, however, I will be more circumspect in future. Yet if it
proves impossible to content some of these people, I shall console myself
with the example of St Paul, who pursued the right through evil report and
good report. One advantage I do gain without fail: if I cannot win universal   40
approval, I am approved by the best men and the most highly placed. And
those who get their teeth into me while I am alive will maybe praise me
when I am dead. Farewell, excellent Father, and commend me to Christ in
your prayers.

Louvain, 2 January 1518   45

750 / To Maarten Lips   [Louvain, January 1518?]

Maarten Lips (Lypsius) of Brussels (c 1492–1555) was a member of the congregation of Augustinian canons at Sint-Maartensdal in Louvain. He became a
priest in 1518 and distinguished himself as a patristic scholar. He was a
faithful admirer of Erasmus and at about this time began two important
collections of letters by Erasmus and his friends, probably copied in his own
hand: Brussels, Bibliothèque Royale MS 4850–7; and the Codex Horawit-
zianus, published by A. Horawitz in *Sitzungsberichte der kais. Akademie der
Wissenschaften* (Wien, phil.-hist. Klasse 1882) (cf Allen IV xxvii) now in the
Gemeente Bibliotheek Rotterdam (MS 15 c 4). To each letter of the Brussels MS
included in the present volume Lips had added some introductory remarks.
These are printed by Allen in his introductions. The text of this letter is found in
the Brussels MS and was printed in the *Auctarium*.

From Lips' introductory summary to this letter we learn that he himself

* * * * *

27 religious] *Religiosus*, a religious person or a member of a monastic order;
  likewise *religio* can mean religion and a monastic congregation.
33 who live] Removing *qui*, which stands in the manuscript after *his*, to stand
  after *religionis*
39 Paul] Cf 2 Cor 6:8.

copied and transmitted to Erasmus the pamphlet mentioned in line 9. Among
a variety of criticisms it accused Erasmus of an unjustified attack on the
famous twelfth-century scholar Peter Lombard. The point seemed convincing
to Lips, who took it up in a letter of his own to Erasmus. Erasmus was
determined to ignore the pamphlet (cf Ep 765), but he replied to Lips' letter
with the clarifications that follow.

The date is conjectural. Allen chose it because the letter seems closely related
to Ep 765. But Lips states in his introduction that the pamphlet was composed
when Erasmus was staying with Jean Desmarez (cf Epp 597:46, 643:14n); thus
this letter could be as early as July–August 1517.

ERASMUS TO HIS FRIEND MAARTEN, GREETING
Your zeal on my behalf, dear brother, deserves some return without delay,
so let me advise you not to waste valuable time on that kind of nonsense.
You would do better to devote the labour you spent on copying and
perusing all that stuff to reading the works of Jerome. Personally I have   5
neither inclination nor leisure enough to answer all the captious objections
everybody makes. Enough for me if I win approval in the highest quarters,
and from the Holy Father himself, who has sent me a letter of thanks for all
my labours. I have not read the malicious pamphlet you sent me, but I have
heard other scholars reading it. They all thought it absurd, and so did I, who   10
was the target of it. If you take the side of the author, or rather the villain of
the piece, give his rubbish as wide a public as you can, for his object is by
crossing swords with me to become famous; if you take mine, suppress his
worthless stuff – do that indeed if you are truly on his side, for in his hunger
for applause he wants what can only do him harm. Many people need not so   15
much a candid critic as a dose of physic.

Be that as it may, when you too stick at one point about *traductio*, I
could defend myself in various ways, but I will explain in a word what I

* * * * *

750
5 Jerome] Lips later recalls his perusal of Erasmus' edition of Jerome; cf Ep 922.
8 letter of thanks] Ep 519
9 pamphlet] Probably some notes by Edward Lee; see Ep 765.
17 *traductio*] The passage concerned, Matt 1:19, was much discussed by inter-
   preters. The New English Bible has: 'Being a man of principle, and at the same
   time *wanting to save her from exposure,* Joseph desired to have the marriage
   contract set aside quietly.' In the *Novum instrumentum* of 1516 Erasmus translated the crucial words analogously, but in a long note he made a disparaging
   remark about the *Sentences* of Peter Lombard. He also quoted two passages
   (*Sentences* IV, distinction 27; PL 192:911, 913) from which he concluded that
   according to Lombard Joseph did not wish to consummate the marriage by

mean. Let us grant that in this passage 'the conjunction *et* is not merely
explanatory.' I seek no advantage from the fact 'that the object of taking the   20
wife to her new home was that the marriage might be consummated'; see
how elegantly he explains away the mistake. Although *traducere* means to
send away in disgrace, he has made good his escape if 'traductio means
consent to live as man and wife.' This is as if a man had used 'pumpkin' for a
donkey's back and was thought to have escaped censure when someone   25
else explained that he had used 'pumpkin' not for the donkey's back but for
the panniers on the donkey. If anyone makes the quibbling point that
traduci is used here in the popular sense of *deduci*, to be taken to the new
home, how even so can *traductio* mean consent, or *deducta*, the woman
taken home, be equivalent to the woman consenting? Is there no difference   30
between *deductio*, being taken to the matrimonial home, and giving your
consent to being carried off, *abductio*? Or what does such a carrying off
without intercourse contribute to the consummation of a marriage? Lastly,
since the consent which forms a binding union embraces within itself, once
and for all, all the duties which either party to a marriage owes to the other,   35
how does this *traductio* of yours come to be separated from all the other
duties? Consent forms the cement of matrimony, and intercourse consum-
mates it; *traductio* has no place at all. After all, Peter Lombard himself does
not offer this interpretation, but some persons unknown who found the
word difficult and invented this explanation rather than say nothing. Once   40
you see that all this is forced and distorted, let us admit openly that Peter
Lombard thought the verb *traducere*, which he found in St Matthew, meant
the union of the spouses, the more so as there are other places too where he
clearly makes a slip as to the meaning of a word, following Isidore or some
such source.   45
    No, have no more to do with this sort of rubbish, and give yourself the
pleasure of reading good authors, who will make you not only a better

* * * * *

taking the bride into his house. The pamphlet, which Erasmus quotes repeatedly, apparently objected that Lombard spoke of transfer *and* consummation, meaning two separate actions. Erasmus conceded the point, but did not
as a result change the text of his note for the next edition of the *Novum
Testamentum*. He did, however, add to it his answer to the pamphlet's further
point about the bride's consent. The whole discussion here and in the *Novum
Testamentum* (cf LB VI 6D-7B) illustrates the traditional concern for Mary's
virginity, but, as Erasmus recognized, it was irrelevant to the basic problem of
whether Joseph did not wish to 'take home' his pregnant bride or did not wish
to 'see her exposed in public.'
44 Isidore] The seventh-century scholar St Isidore of Seville, most learned in his
    day, but at times ridiculous in the eyes of Renaissance humanists

scholar but a better man. For my part I shall do nothing to make him famous. If he likes to publish his own nonsense, he can have only himself to thank if he is a universal laughing-stock. Farewell in Christ.   50

To Master Maarten of Brussels, most honourable of men and his dear colleague.

751 / To Jan de Hondt   [Louvain, 5 January 1518]

Jan de Hondt of St Paul, Waes, (1486–1571) replaced Pierre Barbier as the canon in possession of the Courtrai prebend which had been conferred upon Erasmus and which he resigned immediately in exchange for an annuity. Hondt was later dean of Courtrai and acquired some other benefices; see Allen IV xxviii; de Vocht CTL III 513–14; Gorissen *Kortrijkse pensioen* 143–4 and passim.

TO THE EXCELLENT JAN SURNAMED DE HONDT,
CANON OF COURTRAI, HIS RIGHT GOOD FRIEND
I have no doubts, honoured sir, that you are at all points the man long ago described to me by Dr Livien van Pottelsberge, sometime receiver-general of Flanders, a man in my opinion both wise and cultivated, through whose   5
recommendation the prebend at Courtrai was ceded to you. My view is confirmed by the judgment of Pierre Barbier, who has entrusted you with the management of his affairs, not unadvisedly, for he is neither foolish nor careless. Nor is there any need for continual giving and taking of security among those who recognize the truth of the old principle that honest   10
dealing should be the rule between honest men. In any case, with respect to a benefice situated in the diocese of Utrecht, you will not find me one to make difficulties; the thing is that I know what agreement I came to with Barbier – what you arranged with him I do not know. This makes it more difficult for me to give you a definite answer on this point, except this: the   15

* * * * *

751
4 Pottelsberge] Lord of Wissekerke, Vinderhoute, etc, d 1531. He was a privy councillor and receiver-general of Flanders and gave generous support to the work of religious orders in Ghent.
10 old principle] Cicero *Epistulae ad familiares* 7.12.2
12 benefice] Apparently one of several benefices belonging to the prebend of Courtrai. It seems that its revenue turned out to be subject to certain deductions which Jan de Hondt tried to pass on to the pension payable to Erasmus (cf Ep 278 for a similar case). Taxation of a benefice in the diocese of Utrecht is also mentioned in Ep 714:14–15, but apparently it concerned another Erasmus.

amount of the annuity having been assessed, and only some part of it being
the income of the benefices, it does not seem fair that, if for one reason or
another the value of the benefices is whittled down, the amount should be
deducted from the total of the annuity that has been assessed once and for
all.   20

My lord the bishop of Utrecht seems uncommonly well disposed
towards me, as he has already shown in several letters. But those people do
not readily open the door to others who will demand similar privileges, nor
did I think it right to use up the good will of so eminent a prelate in a matter
of so little moment. So I rely on your good faith. Whatever Barbier approves   25
will have my agreement: I am expecting to hear from him on this and other
things. While on his journey he sent me the money he had received out of
the annuity, and in this regard I am grateful for his efficiency and your
punctual performance. If anything arises in which I can be of service to you,
you will find me willing and eager to help. Farewell.   30

Louvain, eve of the Epiphany 1518

752 / To Pierre Barbier   Louvain, 6 January 1518

For Barbier see Ep 608.

ERASMUS TO HIS FRIEND BARBIER, GREETING
By the favour of the Muses, were you not acting as deputy for my benefactor, I should have a pretty bone to pick with you, who have had so many
letters from me to provoke you, and yet answer never a word, especially
since you do write to other people. I have left the whole business of my   5
annuity entirely to your good faith; so do not cease to be what you have
always been. After Easter I may perhaps have to go either to Basel or to Italy,
to finish the last act of this comedy of theologians; for in the revision of the
New Testament I have made such progress that I am in sight of harbour in

* * * * *

22 several letters] Cf Ep 682 introduction. Perhaps Jan de Hondt had suggested
that Erasmus approach Bishop Philip of Burgundy to have the deductions
rescinded.
27 While on his journey] See Ep 621 written by Barbier on his way to Spain. The
second payment for 1517 had been due at Christmas but was probably delayed
pending clarification of the matter mentioned above; cf Ep 752:17–19.

752
2 benefactor] Le Sauvage; for Erasmus' hopes cf Ep 621:33–4.
3 many letters] Cf Epp 652, 695.
7 to Basel or to Italy] See Ep 770 introduction.
9 New Testament] See Ep 864 introduction.

the distance. This labour of mine is hateful to me when I call to mind some   10
people's ingratitude; but on the other hand I am encouraged by the ad-
vancement of men of good will. I have sent you the *Apologia* in which I reply
to Lefèvre, and also my paraphrase, and I hear they have reached you. It
surprises me that Lefèvre should not produce so much as a letter to defend
himself or own himself defeated. I have long been hoping for some words of   15
good omen from your part of the world. I should be very glad of some news
of the bishop of Chieti, and also of our delightful friend Guy. But before all
else, please see that my annuity is paid as soon as may be, so that I do not
run short of journey-money; for here everything is expensive, and one
cannot turn an honest penny. Give my greetings particularly to my excellent   20
benefactor, and let me know whether there is any hope of seeing you here
once more. Farewell, dearest of mortals.

Louvain, Epiphany 1518

753 / To Henricus Afinius   Louvain, 6 January 1518

This letter is another attempt on Erasmus' part to obtain the promised silver
cups (cf Ep 687:6n), now as a new year gift. Ep 752 shows Erasmus considering
his financial needs for an anticipated journey; cf Epp 754, 799.

ERASMUS TO HIS FRIEND AFINIUS, GREETING
Most scholarly of physicians and best of friends, the time appointed has so
often run out, and so often leaves me disappointed! Perhaps the stars of this
past year were unfavourable and stood in our way. Now, at any rate, under
the better auspices of the new year, send me the cups you have so often   5
promised, or the friends who now suspect that I was too ready to believe
you will seem to have been right. How can I believe such a thing of a man
like you? You are too serious to wish to make fun of anybody, and I do not
suppose you would think me a proper person to make fun of. So I have sent
Dirk Martens on purpose to fetch them. He is the most reliable of men. You   10
will find me by no means likely to fail in rendering any service, if I have
done little enough to deserve them beforehand. Farewell, and if you sin-

* * * * *

13 have reached you] Cf Epp 652, 695 introduction.
17 Chieti] Gianpietro Carafa; cf Ep 628:64n.
17 Guy] Morillon; cf Ep 695:54n.
18 annuity] Cf Ep 751:27n.

753
3 stars] Cf Ep 755:32n.

cerely return my affection, do not let Dirk, the bearer of this, return empty-
handed, and postpone the happy day no longer, remembering how much of
the value of a kind action is lost by delay. Farewell once more.   15
    Louvain, Epiphany 1518

754 / To Pieter Gillis   [Louvain, c 6 January 1518]

This letter is clearly in sequence with Epp 712, 736, as it deals with the same
topics, yet it was written before 14 January, when Erasmus had heard from
More (cf Ep 763). The letter to Afinius sent with it is therefore very likely Ep
753.

ERASMUS TO PIETER GILLIS, GREETING
I dearly wanted to know what had passed between you and Franz, and you
send not a word in reply. I will accept any excuse, as long as you do not
plead ill health. I should hate you, my dear Pieter, to have such a good   5
excuse. The last act of this drama alone remains. If he should brazen it out, I
will treat the worthless fellow as he deserves. Farewell, and let me have an
answer.
    If you like, you can open my letter to Afinius and seal it up again, so
that you are not left in ignorance of what I have said. If he leads me a dance   10
in future, you will behold a very different scene. Farewell once more, O half
of my better self.
    Still no news of More, for this long time. Send the seal, if it is ready.

755 / To [Johannes de Molendino]   [Louvain, c January 1518]

That Molendino is being addressed follows from line 24 and Ep 780:16–19. He
had taught at Paris in the Collège du Cardinal Lemoine as a colleague of
Lefèvre d'Etaples, but now lived in his native Tournai, where he was a canon
(cf Ep 371). The approximate date is indicated by the state of the controversy
with Lefèvre (see Epp 721 introduction, 752:12–13) and by Molendino's encounter with Pace. If Epp 742 refers to Molendino, this letter could be contemporary with it, cf Ep 742:9n.

* * * * *

754
5 brazen it out] Cf Ep 663:58n.
6 worthless fellow] Possibly Franz Birckmann (cf Epp 736:10, 16n, 823) or more
    likely Afinius (cf Ep 736:19)

Greeting. I am delighted to hear that you and Pace like one another. It is clearly right that, if friends have all things in common, we should also share common friends. The letter which Pace wrote to Dorp on my behalf seemed to me so good that I thought it ought to be suppressed. I am especially pleased that men who are so well thought of should think well of my 5 paraphrase; I only wish I had always laboured in that sort of field. I would rather construct a thousand paraphrases than one critical edition. Mind you though, it is generous of you to praise my efforts in this kind, such as they are, but you would do better to enter the ring yourself. That last letter of yours makes it clear how much you could achieve if only a great part of you 10 were not claimed by business – business not indeed mean in itself, but not worthy of a spirit born for celestial studies.

As for Lefèvre's defence you say that you have told me your opinion at some length in earlier letters, but I must warn you that these have never reached me. My own *Apologia* you call a polished piece of work, but you 15 would think otherwise if you knew it was entirely conceived, begun, and finished within twelve days. You say it has a sting in it. I wish it had been possible for me to avoid stinging altogether, especially against Lefèvre, whom I sincerely like. If this strikes you as having a sting in it which defends itself when forced to it and does not simply hurl back the mon- 20 strous charge of impiety but rejects it without making any similar charges in reply, what language would you use of his defence, which fastens on me the baseless libel of blasphemy against Christ? It is hard to prescribe limits to another man's resentment. Had the name of Molendino been attacked with these weapons, perhaps you would feel differently. But I am astonished at a 25 man who cannot send me so much as a letter to clear himself or to maintain his point, especially as he has been challenged to do this in two or three letters from me.

As for Doctor Adrian, your physician, I congratulate him – yes, I am almost jealous of him – not only because he spends nearly all his time among 30 the stars and is getting on so well with his Greek, as because he has acquired

* * * * *

755
1 Pace] Cf Ep 619 introduction.
2 friends] *Adagia* I i 1
3 letter] See Ep 732:59n.
7 a thousand paraphrases] See Ep 710 introduction; and for the toilsome re-editing of the *Novum Testamentum* see Ep 864 introduction.
9 enter the ring] *Adagia* I ix 83, a favourite phrase
13 Lefèvre's defence] See Ep 597:37n.
29 Adrian] See Ep 650:14n.

the *Therapeutice* with Linacre's help; so much I detected from his prognostics. Mind you greet him warmly from me, and also my special and ever-appreciated benefactor Doctor Sampson, and Eleutherius Audax and his colleague. His name I forget, and as I write have not your letter at hand.   35

756 / To Paschasius Berselius   Louvain, 7 January 1518

Clearly Erasmus' answer to Ep 748, this letter was printed in the *Auctarium*. For the circumstances of this exchange see Ep 748 introduction.

ERASMUS TO HIS FRIEND PASCHASIUS, GREETING

What a man of war you must be, chattering of nothing but battle, mantlets, assault-works, and artillery! Very well, fortify yourself as strongly as you like, I shall attack you with saps and mines if necessary. As it is, I must roll my stone, or rather grind away in this treadmill. But I must congratulate you   5
on your promotion, I see, to demi-god, with leave to attend the banquets of the gods; yet you did your best to give me a share of that most splendid feast by writing such a vivid description that I seem to myself even now to be reclining with you among the gods and goddesses. Joking apart, I have spent the whole of this evening in conversation with the bishop. I should be   10
most reluctant, my dear Paschasius, to torment him with a prolonged

* * * * *

32 *Therapeutice*] An inaccurate reference may have given Erasmus the mistaken impression that Linacre's translation of Galen's *Methodus medendi* was already published and in Adrian's hands. It was not to appear until June 1519. At the same time Erasmus was trying hard to acquire a copy of Linacre's translation of another work by Galen, *De sanitate tuenda* (see Epp 664:29n, 690, 726). This is probably the work of which his friends in Tournai had a copy. In October Erasmus had also seen it and continued to believe that the *Methodus medendi* too was in print; See Allen Ep 868:65–9.

32 prognostics] Apparently he had sent a letter with Erasmus' horoscope promising good luck in 1518 (cf Epp 752:15–16, 753:3–4). For Erasmus' half-hearted attention to astrological forecasts see also Ep 803:10n.

34 Sampson] See Ep 780.

34 Audax] Eleuthère Hardy, canon of Tournai (probably named for St Eleuthère of Tournai, d 531). He is documented as a canon from 1501 to his death in 1525 and from 1503 was in charge of the chapter school, which he maintained at a high academic standard; see de Vocht CTL I 521.

756
5 stone] *Adagia* II iv 40
6 banquets] Virgil *Aeneid* 1.79
10 bishop] Erard de La Marck. The reference is apparently to Erasmus' reading of and replying to Ep 746.

craving for my society; but for one thing, look at the time of year, when none can sail the sea or pass by land, if I may treat you to a touch of poetry. And then my health is such that I can hardly keep well if I bury myself at home, pottering up and down in front of a bright fire, or buried in my nest   15 like a cuckoo. And yet I find this nest worse than a treadmill. I am engaged on the most tedious possible task; but it has now reached a stage at which, as though I were in that pitch-dark tunnel through the mountain which you have to traverse on the road from Naples to Cumae, I can see a spot of light in the distance like a tiny star, which promises a way out, and as I wrestle   20 with the waves, far away I can spy port. Within a month, with Christ's help, I shall make my way out of this labyrinth. If, however, the work were to be interrupted now, I could never force myself to subject my mind to this treadmill again. Proteus is captured; we must tighten his bonds until he returns to his true form and finishes his oracle. The rigours of winter will   25 soon relax, so that I can come flying with the storks and the swallows.

When you rate his lordship above all other prelates, and that in virtues and accomplishments of every kind, I have no quarrel with you, especially since you are not the only one to say so, and it gains credit from his promotion of Aleandro, and from this letter to me, which was full of a new   30 and unprecedented and really noble liberality of mind. Yet the archbishop of Canterbury has been so good to me that I could not hope for anyone more helpful. He by himself would be enough to secure my felicity, if only fortune had placed him here or if there were some bridge joining us to England: so much do I hate that horrible Channel and those still more   35 horrible sailors.

But just as in old days among the Scythians it was not to one's credit to have too many friends (yet I see that Hesiod thinks it equally discreditable to have no friends and many), so perhaps the tribe of poets may think that it is a disgrace to have too many patrons; though I myself desire nothing more   40 than to please good judges, since I cannot please everybody. And such has been my lot, belatedly perhaps, but in good measure. Almost the whole of England thinks well of me. When I was lately there, the king himself soon

* * * * *

19 Cumae] A reminiscence of Erasmus' visit to the famous cavern of the Sibyl near Cumae in the spring of 1509; cf Ep 640; *Adagia* v ii 20.
24 Proteus] *Adagia* ii ii 74; on 'protean' aspects of the New Testament see Bietenholz *History and Biography* 86–8.
30 Aleandro] See Ep 735:6n.
30 this letter] Ep 746
32 Canterbury] William Warham
37 Scythians] *Adagia* iii vi 37; Hesiod *Works and Days* 715

sent for me and made me an offer not to be despised. So did the cardinal of
York. The archbishop of Mainz lately sent me a most friendly letter of   45
invitation, written in his own hand. I have now had a second letter to the
same purpose from Philip, bishop of Utrecht. Then my lord of Basel offered
me the half of his kingdom, but, as I have said, rather belatedly. I now need
a patron, not to make me a star in Fortune's theatre and load me with her
favours, but to restore my bodily health and give me back my vigour of   50
mind. These things were always weak in me, and now age and the constant
effort of study have worn them out. My mind now longs for honourable
repose, and my state of health demands it. The last act of the play remains,
and I wish I may so play my part as to win the approval of Christ, who is the
producer. I never sought for a great position, for it would be too great for my   55
small courage and small physique, and now, even though I sought it, I could
not sustain it. I am determined therefore to defend this freedom of mine
tooth and nail, though I mean to use it, as far as my strength will permit, to
benefit my fellow men, even if for the future I must refrain from the labours
which now overwhelm me and which would be too much even for a   60
younger man. About Lent I shall begin to leave my nest. If his lordship has
no objections, I will put things off until then. Otherwise, I will try to oblige
so great a prince, even at risk to my health.

   You see, my dear Paschasius, how I have made a clean breast of
everything. Farewell. The paraphrase, which you say frightens you, will   65
please you better when you see it at close quarters.

   Louvain, morrow of the Epiphany 1518

757 / To Erard de La Marck   Louvain, 7 January 1518

   This letter, which answers Ep 746, was printed in the *Auctarium*; cf Ep 748
   introduction.

TO THE RIGHT REVEREND ERARD OF AREMBERG,
BISHOP OF LIÈGE
Greeting, right reverend Prelate and illustrious Prince. Allow me to reply
briefly and without formal prologue to your Highness' most kind letter. You
say that you have long known me by reputation and desire to see me face to   5

   * * * * *

45 York] See Ep 694:11n.
45 Mainz] Ep 661
47 Utrecht] Ep 728
47 Basel] Ep 598:14–15

face. Such is the burden laid upon your humble servant by that goddess whom Homer calls Rumour and Virgil Fame, who tells vain tales of others besides myself and inflates everything, so that I can neither disown what she puts into so many men's mouths nor support the character she gives me. I know that nothing is more honourable than 'to stand well with the chiefs of state'; but in the mean time, as I sit at home and take the measure of myself, I see two things. One is, that it is pleasant to have men think well of me whose approval is a great honour and their disapproval a disgrace; the other, that it is equally unpleasant to be unable to satisfy their friendly opinion of oneself or their great expectations, so that I owe the trumpet of Fame no more thanks than the bad lyre-player owes to the man who displays him to a crowded concert-hall glorious in golden robe and gilded lyre in order that the moment he strikes up he may be hissed off the stage. There is nothing in me worth seeing; and if there were, it is all expressed in my published work. That is the best part of me, and what remains would be dear at a farthing.

All the same, on such a kind invitation I would gladly have come running to your Highness. I am deterred first by this more than wintry weather and secondly by my state of health, weak in itself and so much exhausted by the labours on which I am now engaged that I can hardly keep it up, even if I bury myself at home. Such is the effort with which I toil at the renewal of my New Testament that I myself have grown old at my task, and while I rescue the text from age and decay, I have incurred a double ration of them for myself. For I am resolved either, now that I have started, to work on till I die at my task or to make it worthy the attention of Leo the Tenth and of posterity. I have got so far that, though I am still battling on the high seas, the harbour is beginning to appear little by little, and if Christ sends a fair wind, I shall make land before Lent. Then, at a kinder season and in leisure of mind, I shall hasten to visit your Lordship, outstripping the swallows and the storks. But if you do not favour even a short delay, I will throw over everything and come.

But on this subject I have written rather more fully to my good friend Paschasius; whom I count fortunate in many respects, and not least for this,

* * * * *

757
  6 goddess] Homer *Iliad* 2.93; Virgil *Aeneid* 4.173
 10 'to stand ... state'] Horace *Epistles* 1.17.35
 11 measure] *Adagia* I vi 89
 16 lyre-player] [Cicero] *Ad Herennium* 4.47.60
 21 farthing] *Adagia* I viii 9
 33 Lent] Cf Ep 864 introduction.

that he gives satisfaction to a prince as generous as he is powerful; whom
God Almighty preserve as long as possible in health and in all prosperity.   40
    Louvain, morrow of the Epiphany 1518
    Erasmus, your Highness' most devoted servant

758 / To Philip of Burgundy   Louvain, 10 January 1518

    This letter answers Ep 728. It was published in the *Auctarium*.

TO THE MOST NOBLE PRINCE PHILIP OF BURGUNDY,
BISHOP OF UTRECHT, FROM ERASMUS OF ROTTERDAM,
GREETING
Greeting, most noble Prelate and illustrious Prince. Your Highness' letter
was doubly welcome to me, short as it was if one were to count the lines, but   5
of splendid length measured by the kindness in it. But let me be brief, for
we are both fully occupied. It gives me great joy to know that my *Querela*
pacis is approved, first by the judgment of so great a prince, and secondly by
the votes of all truly educated men. I live a cuckoo's life, but such a life that
often there is more treadmill than nest in it. I have gathered cobwebs and   10
old age for myself, while trying continually to restore its novelty to the New
Testament; and in this retired life, I find myself often on the stage of the
world. Such is the perverse malignity of some spectators that I sometimes
grow weary of my enormous task. And then again I am comforted by the
consciousness that I am doing right, and that, if I am not mistaken, this will   15
bring no small advantage to men of good will. Perhaps I was born for this,
and I must not, like the giants of old, fight against the gods; perhaps it was I
made the bed, and if so, it is right that I should lie on it. Since I have made
my entry on this stage, I must play out the play; and now I am almost come
to the last act. And play it out I will, with all the more readiness and all the   20
more attention, with you to encourage and even to applaud me, but above
all with the approval, as I hope, of Christ, for to please him alone is quite
enough.
    I foresee wonderful progress in learning and piety in this country, had

    * * * * *

758
9 educated men] Cf Ep 727:12–14.
9 cuckoo's life] Cf Epp 727:15n, 756:15–16.
12 find myself] Cicero *Verrines* 5.14.35
17 giants of old] An allusion to the Greek myth of the war between the gods and a
    race of giants
18 made the bed] Cf Ep 737:18n.

we only the good fortune of a few benefactors like yourself to raise the flag   25
and summon gifted men to work, to spur them on with rewards and honour
them with the influence they deserve. If it is too much to hope for more men
like yourself, at least we must pray that the powers above may be willing to
keep you among us in good health as long as possible, continually increasing your good will towards us and adding thereto length of years. For your   30
fatherly attitude towards me I can see how much I am indebted. But it is
almost too late for me to try a throw with my lady Fortune and descend into
the arena from which I shrank in horror as a young man. A great position
is a heavy burden, and no less trouble to maintain than it was to get. My
age, my health, my spirits all demand support of an accessible and easy   35
kind that will not spoil the freedom of my studies.

But I am carried beyond the limits proper to a letter. My respectful best
wishes to your Lordship, to whom I and all my labours are devoted.

Louvain, 10 January 1518

759 / To Gerard Geldenhouwer   Louvain, [10 January 1518]

Clearly contemporary with Ep 758, this letter was also published in the
Auctarium. It answers Ep 727.

ERASMUS TO HIS FRIEND NIJMEGEN, GREETING
My learned Gerard, I have always thought it a great and most desirable
thing to win the approval of men in great place, but there is no one I would
rather please than Bishop Philip, who is my own diocesan and a prince of
bishops in every way. Some months ago, I had a letter full of kindness from   5
the archbishop of Mainz, and written in his own hand. The bishop of Liège
has written lately, threatening to visit me here if I refuse to go to him. These
things are very agreeable; but then again I am dissatisfied and crestfallen
when I think how little there is in me that could answer the expectations of
such great men.   10

But what is this? Your letter taught me something quite new. I did not
realize you felt such maiden shyness that you dared not write to me. True, I
have often seen you blushing, but the reason I could never guess. If this is
true, in my judgment you are unfit for court and cowl. So if you mean to

* * * * *

33 arena] Cf Ep 755:9n.

759
6 Mainz] Ep 661
6 Liège] Ep 746

make your fortune, put a bold face on it at once and wipe away these   15
unprofitable blushes.

My work on the New Testament has gone so far that, though I am still
tossing on the deep, I can see harbour in the distance, with its promise of
repose. I send you my paraphrase. If you have not had it yet, show it to your
learned friends and, if you think fit, to the prince himself; but especially to   20
the excellent Philippus Montius, who, you say, is procurator of the court,
for I cannot fail to return his affection most cordially when he invites me to
do so with so much warmth. Please greet him particularly on my behalf.
Nève and Borssele send their greetings. Farewell, dear Nijmegen, sincerest
of friends.   25

Louvain, 151[7]

760 / To Antoon, son of Jan van Bergen   [Louvain, c 13 January 1518]

Antoon, youngest son of Jan, the influential councillor of Margaret of Austria,
was then studying in Louvain (cf Epp 717:22–4, 737). After consultation with
Erasmus (cf Ep 969), it was decided to send him to England. He went in
November 1519 and until 1520 held an appointment at the court of Henry VIII.
He later became governor of Luxembourg and succeeded to his father's titles
and estates. He died in June 1541. For the date of this letter cf Ep 761:23–4.

ERASMUS TO HIS FRIEND ANTOON, GREETING

Your delicious venison was accompanied by an elegant note – a double gift,
one as sweet in the reading as the other in the eating. This of course is
Hesiod's precept: 'Good measure and something more.' Keep it up, my
dear Antoon, pursue your quarry in this kind of forest; renew that ancient   5
glory of princes which has so long been out of fashion and make the glorious
lineage of the house of Bergen still more glorious by adding the humanities,
doubling your distinguished fortune with the distinction of your mind.
Happy indeed is good literature when it begins to please men in great place;
more happy they, if they have deserved respect by true accomplishments   10
personal to themselves. Caesar will teach you the genuine purity of the
Latin language, but mind you do not learn from him this mad ambitious
love of war. Against this you will find an antidote to protect you in my book

* * * * *

19 paraphrase] See Ep 710 introduction.
21 Montius] See Ep 727:13n.

760
4 Hesiod's] *Works and Days* 350

on the Christian prince; and history will mean more to you if you have a
taste of geography first.   15

Every good wish. Ælius is happy to have you as his pupil; make him
happier still. The better scholar you turn out, and the better man, the
happier he will be. As for myself, I can promise you nothing, except that I
am and always shall be most sincerely yours.

761 / To Antoon van Bergen   Louvain, 14 January 1518

Written primarily to advance a cause of importance to the University of
Louvain (see Ep 762 introduction), this letter was published in the *Auctarium*.

DESIDERIUS ERASMUS OF ROTTERDAM TO THE
REVEREND FATHER IN CHRIST ANTOON VAN BERGEN,
LORD ABBOT OF ST BERTIN'S, GREETING
Greeting, reverend Father and my right good Lord. For many reasons I have
long been indebted to your kindness, and now I am even more bound by   5
the kind reception you have given to More, the dearer half of my own soul;
he expresses such satisfaction, in a letter to me, at having seen your Highness. I am not the less grateful for this because in you it is nothing new; at
the same time, devoted as I am to him, I was a little jealous of him because I
could not do the same. My life upon it, this winter has felt longer than a   10
hundred years; all this time I have had to live a cuckoo's life. Though my
time is spent not so much in a nest as in the most odious treadmill you can
imagine. I have put a new face on my New Testament, and with God's help
shall make it seem not unworthy the attention of Leo the Tenth and of
posterity.   15

Although for the moment I am deprived of your society, I do not lack
someone who up to a point can take your place. We have here Antoon, your
brother's son, who recalls and repeats you no less by the mildness of his

* * * * *

14 Christian prince] See Epp 393, 657 introductions.
16 Ælius] Adrian Ælius van Baerland, d c September 1535, a cousin of his more
   famous namesake, Adriaan Cornelissen van Baerland (see Ep 492 introduction). He was to accompany Antoon van Bergen to England as his preceptor
   and secretary. His services to the family were rewarded with a canonry in
   Bergen-op-Zoom, where he was also town priest at the time of his death; see
   de Vocht CTL I 260, II 518–22.

761
6 More] Cf Ep 683:53–7.
11 cuckoo's life] Cf Epp 727:15n, 756:15–16.
17 Antoon] See Ep 760.

character than by his name. May all the Muses hate me if I do not speak the truth, or speak only to please. He is a most gifted young man of whom one   20 can have great hopes, and – what is not common among the well-to-do – he has almost a passion for good literature and loves me for that reason. He comes to see me from time to time and admires my library. Yesterday he sent me two venison pasties, with such an elegant note, so full of courtesy, that the venison was nothing to it. Happy indeed is literature if it begins to   25 please men of such splendid promise! And happy the pedigrees of the nobility if to splendour of lineage they add the honour of a good education!

On this point turns the world's prosperity, that princes should love the best things most. The Holy Father attracts and honours and promotes men of distinguished talent, wherever found. I know and admit that I am   30 nothing, when compared with learned men; and yet because I have a certain reputation for learning acquired from my published work, when I was last in England the king received me with the greatest kindness and offered me a position by no means to be despised. I was welcomed by the cardinal of York, who is not easy and affable to everyone. Twice lately I have   35 heard from the bishop of Utrecht, and since then from the bishop of Liège, threatening to come here if I will not go and visit him. The archbishop of Mainz wrote me a whole letter with his own hand, to show more clearly how warm his feelings towards me are. The bishop of Basel offers me up to the half of his kingdom. I am dreadfully afraid that his Catholic Majesty designs   40 to make me bishop of the Indies. Joking apart, I rejoice that the great ones of the earth should be of this way of thinking, not for my sake but all men's; for if they keep it up, it will go better with all the affairs of men. The abbot of Saint-Amand is here, an old protégé together with me of your excellent brother Hendrik of pious memory.   45

The bearer of this letter is a theologian, no less learned than his colleagues but less arrogant – an upright, humane, and cheerful person. He

* * * * *

33 king] For the following list of attentions recently received cf Ep 756.
36 Liège] Ep 746
40 Catholic Majesty] Cf Epp 475, 621:32–3.
43 abbot] Willem Bollart, or Bollais, of Brussels, d 14 November 1532. He was now in the process of resigning his abbey of Saint-Amand near Tournai, having received the abbey of St Trudo at St Truiden from Antoon van Bergen in 1516. In his youth he had, like Erasmus, belonged to the household of Hendrik van Bergen, bishop of Cambrai (see Ep 49). As an abbot Bollart proved himself a worthy reformer, but he spent his later years increasingly in his town house at Louvain, where he collected a fine library; cf de Vocht *J. de Busleyden* 454–5.
46 theologian] See Ep 762 introduction.

had been given a benefice at Enselede by way of nomination, as they say
nowadays. He has already been in possession for some months, having
come to terms with the man upon whom you had conferred the same   50
benefice, provided he can secure your approval. He would rather devote the
time and effort that would be wasted in litigation to more worthy objects. It
is right to show special favour to this university, partly because it is our
own, partly because in these days it is more flourishing than any other,
partly because you too were once nurtured there and it now shelters two of   55
your nephews. Your Reverence will suffer very little from nominations; you
will comply with one or two now and again; all the more reason for
cheerfully making this concession as a devoted alumnus to your alma mater.
Besides which, Theodoricus is the sort of man, if you knew him thoroughly,
on whom you would most wish to see that benefice of yours conferred. You   60
will acquire a debtor who is neither untrustworthy nor ungrateful. I would
offer to go bail for him myself, were I not so much bound to you already that
further obligation is impossible. He has great hopes from the general
reputation of your generosity, which many have experienced. So I beg you
urgently to let him also have a taste of it.   65

I send you Paul the Apostle speaking in the Roman tongue, and more
intelligibly too than was his wont. A college to teach the three tongues is to
be set up here out of Busleyden's legacy. But there is some opposition from
men who would rather be content with the two languages they have already; faded old parrots, with no hope of learning a new language.   70
Farewell, best of patrons.

Louvain, 14 January 1518, from the College of the Lily

762 / To Antonius of Luxembourg   [Louvain, c 14 January 1518]

Clearly contemporary with Ep 761, this letter offers the fullest account of a
matter mentioned previously. Theodoricus, an unidentified bachelor of
theology (Ep 673:19) and a resident of the College of the Lily (Ep 739:31), was
involved in a contest for a small benefice, perhaps at Enschedé (Overijssel,
thirty miles east of Deventer; cf line 14, Ep 761:48), apparently situated in the
diocese of Utrecht (lines 30–1). Theodoricus had been nominated by the
university, which claimed the right (confirmed by Leo x on 30 January 1518; cf
Ep 916 and Harsin *Erard de la Marck* 230–3, 248) to do so in a few cases in order

* * * * *

48 Enselede] *Enseledense* in the text
58 alumnus] Antoon lived at Louvain between 1486 and 1493.
66 Paul] See Ep 710.
67 college] See Ep 691 introduction.

to provide for promising young scholars. Antoon van Bergen, however, claimed the same right and in this case had already nominated another beneficiary. The two contestants had reached an agreement, but without Antoon's endorsement it was invalid; hence Theodoricus' repeated trips to Saint-Omer. Antonius of Luxembourg was steward of St Bertin; cf Ep 673.

ERASMUS TO HIS FRIEND ANTONIUS OF LUXEMBOURG, GREETING
The bearer of this, Theodoricus by name, a theologian free of theological arrogance, brought me great happiness with the news that you are in good health, and likewise Ghisbert the physician, both of you among my oldest and most faithful friends, and also my lord the abbot, my ancient patron   5
and our common benefactor. We have here a most gifted young man, Antoon van Bergen, who recalls the abbot in charm of character as well as in name. He is really devoted to good literature, unlike the common habit of men of rank, and for the sake of literature is fond of me. Take my word for it, one day he will add new distinction to his splendid lineage by his literary   10
gifts, and will bring honour and glory to literature itself.

But not to delay you unduly, I will explain briefly what I want particularly just now. The bearer of this letter is waging some sort of war with another man about some benefice or other at Ensedale. This is their Helen; but whereas for the other lady they only fought round Troy for ten years, for   15
Helens of this kind one fights on for ever, and this means great damage to the flock and no small profit to the vultures who live by the losses of others. Yet this man's opponent does not refuse to give up his rights, provided he can do it with his lordship's approval, your influence with whom (and it is well deserved) is common knowledge. You for your part perform the duty of   20
a good and faithful friend in thinking that this collation should prevail over nomination and thereby defending the honour of the abbot; but in my opinion this university deserves some support, being the most flourishing of our generation in eminent learning, and all the more because the abbot himself is an alumnus. Nor will he be much troubled by these nominations,   25
once he has complied with two or three. Lastly, Theodoricus himself is an ideal candidate, as learned in theology as some of our high and mighty professors, of frank and upright character, easy and cheerful and well adapted to college life. He has been some months in possession of the benefice, but for the time being the profits are being intercepted by the   30

* * * * *
762
4 Ghisbert] See lines 46, 49 and Ep 673:22n.
7 Antoon] Son of Jan van Bergen and nephew of Antoon, abbot of St Bertin and master of Antonius of Luxembourg; see Ep 760.
14 Ensedale] *Ensedalensi* in the text

bishop of Utrecht. He abhors litigation. His opponent is giving way. All
that remains is that my lord should give his approval to what is in itself a fair
arrangement. Theodoricus would like to owe his benefice entirely to the
abbot, and, believe me, he will not bilk what he owes. And so I beg you
urgently, since a word from you will be enough, to see that he gets what he   35
wants; or if this is not possible, he wants to have the question settled by the
arbitration of some qualified lawyer without the tedious trouble of litigation, including the amount of the annuity that is to satisfy his opponent. I
hope his lordship with his usual kindness will think fit to confer the whole
benefice on him, as a tribute either to his university or to the man's personal   40
gifts. I say nothing of my own interest; but if I carry any weight with you, I
would not refuse to pledge myself also as a debtor in respect of what is
conferred on him. But why should I pledge my own credit, when I have
been long in your debt, and am yours already by right of foreclosure?

I send you Paul speaking in the Roman tongue. I did not like to burden   45
the bearer of this with more books, and I knew that you and the physician
have all things in common. My *Moria* was badly received by some of the
theologians; but the new book is liked by everybody. Give my greetings to
the excellent Ghisbert and his wife, who I trust feels kindly towards me now
I am so far away, and also to Carolus the steward and his bride. And if you   50
fall in with the prior of the Carthusians, greet him kindly and remind him
that he has not yet sent back my copy of Reuchlin's letter. Farewell, Antonius, my best of friends.

763 / To Mark Lauwerijns   Louvain, 14 January 1518

For Lauwerijns see Ep 651 introduction.

ERASMUS TO HIS FRIEND MARK, GREETING
I sent you a letter the other day, if I remember right, by the man by whom
you had sent me three gold pieces; and I also gave him a copy of my

* * * * *

31 Utrecht] Philip of Burgundy. It seems that the benefice was in his diocese so
    that he could claim the revenue for the time of the dispute. If so, Antoon van
    Bergen would seem to have controlled another benefice in the diocese of
    Utrecht, from which the contested one depended.
48 theologians] Cf Ep 739.
50 Carolus] Unidentified; cf Ep 673:24.
51 prior] Jean Quonus; see Ep 673:9n.

    763
 2 letter] Ep 740
 3 three gold pieces] Cf Ep 717:6–7.

paraphrase to take to you. I shall be glad to know whether Pace is with you; I
wrote him a third letter by the same bearer. More writes to me from England   5
that he thinks himself fortunate to have made your acquaintance; he was so
taken with your free and open character and manners. I am now longing for
the end of my work on the New Testament, and when at length I reach it, it
will be a pleasure to recover from such long and tedious labours in the
charm of your society, than which nothing could be more delightful. I have   10
received the kindest letters of invitation from the bishops of Mainz,
Utrecht, and Liège. They offer me their friendship; and that is all they offer.
Meanwhile in the bottom of Simonides' empty money-box the thank-yous
cut a sorry figure. Farewell, my dear Mark, and let us keep our friendship
green.   15
     Louvain, 14 January 1518

764 / To Josse Bade   Louvain, 16 January 1518

    For Bade see Ep 183 introduction and Ep 602:1n.

ERASMUS OF ROTTERDAM TO JOSSE BADE,
SOUND TEACHER OF SOUND LEARNING, GREETING
I had heard nothing previously about the *Parallels*, but am none the less
delighted, nor is there any reason to send any of it here. If Pieter Gillis has it,
that will do; and yet I should be surprised if it has reached him. I should   5
have expected him to send it to me, if for no other reason, so that I could read
what you say about me, unless he is keeping it dark for Dirk's benefit. I have
received no letter from Deloynes except the one you know of in which he

    * * * * *

  5 a third letter] Cf Epp 741–2. Meanwhile Pace had returned to England; see Ep
    619 introduction.
  5 More] Cf Ep 761:7; the letter had arrived after Ep 754 was written.
  11 bishops] Epp 661, 728, 746
  13 Simonides'] *Adagia* II ix 12; *Parabolae* 589C (CWE 23 202). The Greek poet
    Simonides was said to keep a box into which he put the thanks when he had
    done some work without a fee; when he was hard up and went to the
    thank-you box, he never found anything in it worth having. For other indica-
    tions of Erasmus' relative poverty see Ep 631:10n.

  764
  3 *Parallels*] Erasmus' *Parabolae sive similia*, a revised text with vocabulary and a
    preface by Bade himself, addressed to Pieter Gillis and dated 29 November
    1516; cf Epp 312, 434, 472. Erasmus often used this title for the work soon after
    its publication.
  7 Dirk's] Martens, who had published the *Parabolae* in June 1515 (NK 838)
  8 except the one] Ep 494; cf Ep 689.

urges me to write. I am grateful for the tribute you pay me; it is pleasant to
be praised by a man whom others praise; and I will do my best to return the   10
compliment. I am glad to say that Emilio's history has at last arrived here.
But it is surprising that none of Linacre's things appear. I asked Lupset to
send me one volume, but he seems to have behaved with true English
perfidy. Please send again to ask Budé and Deloynes for letters. Best wishes,
dear Bade, kindest of men, to you and yours.   15

    Louvain, 16 January 1518

765 / To Edward Lee   [Louvain, c January 1518]

Edward Lee (c 1482–13 September 1544) was the son of a distinguished
Kentish family. In 1495 he entered Magdalen College, Oxford; in 1512 he
received a prebend in Lincoln, followed by many others, and in 1515 a
degree in theology at Cambridge. He then went to Louvain to study Greek,
matriculating on 25 August 1516 (see de Vocht CTL I 324). In 1520 he returned to
England, undertook several embassies, and was rewarded with the archbishopric of York in 1531. Erasmus often repeated that his conflict with Lee
sprang from the younger man's craving for publicity. He may or may not have
been aware of the inherent danger when he himself came to Louvain and
admitted Lee to friendly intimacy (see Epp 973, 1074). The following events
too are not entirely clear, since Erasmus' own references are far from coherent
and the sequence of his correspondence with a common friend, Maarten Lips,
is for the most part hypothetical. Erasmus was revising the New Testament
(see Ep 864 introduction) and was anxious to receive suggestions. Lee began to
gather critical notes, probably at some time before the winter of 1517–18 (cf
Epp 750 introduction, 886 postscript). Some were in the hands of Jan Briart and
of his secretary (see line 3n) and remained for some time unavailable to
Erasmus. Some were copied by Lips and passed on to Erasmus, who at first
decided to ignore them (cf Allen Epp 843:11–16, 897, and most likely Ep 750).
For a time Erasmus tried to maintain friendly relations with Lee, at least on the
surface. He chose not to name the critic of Ep 750, and this letter may represent
an attempt to appease Lee by consulting him on a point of doctrine, or indeed
to deflect his critical endeavours to the work of Lefèvre. But Lee persevered,
and at the time Erasmus left for Basel in the spring of 1518 their relations were

* * * * *

11 Emilio's] Cf Ep 719:7n.
12 Linacre's things] See Ep 755:32n.
12 Lupset] Cf Ep 690.
13 English perfidy] Cf Allen Ep 1523:203–7.
14 send again] Cf Ep 723 introduction; Budé's Ep 744 had not yet arrived.

hostile. Erasmus decided he could no longer ignore his critic. On the Rhine he composed Ep 843 for speedy publication in Basel, thus carrying the dispute into print, although without mention of Lee's name (cf Allen I 23:15–17). See Emden BRUO, and for the subsequent events see Ep 897 introduction.

The date was assigned in view of the parallels with Ep 766, but the chronological relation between Epp 750 and 765 remains uncertain.

ERASMUS TO HIS FRIEND LEE, GREETING

It has been impossible to make use of your notes, because I could not extract that portion from the hands of the copyist. I send you Lefèvre's new book; the rest of it I like, but one thing surprises me – why he should be willing to carry his argument to this dangerous point, that whoever says that Christ   5
rose from the dead after three days is speaking contrary to the church, to the articles of the faith, and to the whole truth, although this is what the church has been reading all these years. He conducts his case as if he either wished to use the knife himself or it must be used against him. I see nothing to prevent our saying that Christ rose after three days, with the support of the   10
synecdoche, which no one fails to accept, that he rose after the beginning of the third day. But you will see this more clearly for yourself. Nor do I regard μετὰ χεῖρας, in one's hands, and μετὰ τρεῖς ἡμέρας, after three days, as the same construction. Farewell.

Ep 766 / To Henricus Glareanus   Louvain, 18 January 1518

In this letter Erasmus returns to his preoccupation with Lefèvre's intentions (see Ep 721 introduction). The letter was published in the *Auctarium*.

ERASMUS TO GLAREANUS, GREETING

Your two letters brought me redoubled pleasure, my dearest Glareanus. Your father's death you must bear with resignation, especially in view of

* * * * *

765
3 copyist] Possibly Maarten Lips (see Ep 750 introduction), but more probably the secretary of Jan Briart. Briart obtained a copy of Lee's notes at about this time; see *Opuscula* 248; LB IX 125A, 128F.
3 new book] See Ep 766:26n.

766
3 father's death] He was almost ninety, a prosperous farmer and a member of the Glarus council. Henricus' only brother was also living in Glarus, but the settlement of the estate required Henricus' presence. He was in Basel on 23 April and had returned to Paris before 21 June; cf O.F. Fritzsche *Glarean* (Frauenfeld 1890) 1, 22–3; Zwingli *Werke* VII Ep 38.

his great age. I congratulate you on the appointment of which you speak
and pray that it may prove lasting; for these gifts of princes are often only   5
temporary. I am sorry to hear that you are preparing to run away, for I fear
that while you are pursuing things at a distance, what is handy may give
you the slip. Perhaps it would have been better to entrust the business of
the will to your brother. Be sure to let me know when you would like to set
out, and perhaps we can travel together.   10

I am delighted that you are fond of Lefèvre, who in my opinion is a
good scholar, upright and humane, except that he treated me in a way that
was not like him. I know that he was put up to it by other people. But a man
like him should have known better than at anybody's instigation to let fly
like that against the reputation of a man who is sincerely attached to him, as   15
you yourself have been able to discover from the way I always speak of him.
He did little harm to my reputation and no good to his own, which I regret
more than you might think. He has a defence on the stocks, I hear – a step
which I do not recommend, because I am sorry that an opening should be
given to those brutes who match us one against the other with the cunning   20
of a true tyrant, being too tongue-tied to enter the arena themselves. Nor
would I dissuade him from it, lest I seem not to believe in my own case. One
thing you might tell him, as an old friend, and that is, to abstain from
humorous remarks; or he will find that I am not wholly toothless, and in the
end he may be sorry.   25

I liked his book on the three Magdalens. But I should be sorry to bring

* * * * *

4 appointment] See Ep 618:49n.
10 together] Glareanus did not return to Switzerland via Louvain, as Erasmus
  had apparently hoped. Subsequently he seems to have approached Jacopo
  Bannisio as a possible travelling companion; see Ep 700; AK II Ep 611:10–11.
26 book] *De Maria Magdalena et triduo Christi* (Paris: H. Estienne 1517). Like many
  of the Greek Fathers, and later many of the Protestant theologians, Lefèvre
  insisted that the sinner of Luke 7:37, Mary of Bethany, and Mary Magdalen
  were three different women, thus attacking a tradition particularly popular in
  France and incurring censure from the Paris faculty of theology in 1521.
  Lefèvre's second argument was somewhat hair-splitting. He attempted to
  reconcile minor chronological differences in the gospels. By the traditional
  reading of Mark 8:31 and 10:34 (cf Matt 27:63) Christ foretells his resurrection
  $\mu\epsilon\tau\grave{\alpha}$ $\tau\rho\epsilon\hat{\imath}\varsigma$ $\hat{\eta}\mu\acute{\epsilon}\rho\alpha\varsigma$, after three days. But according to tradition supported by
  some scriptural evidence, Christ died on a Friday, probably in the afternoon,
  and was resurrected on the following Sunday by dawn, when Mary Magdalen
  discovered his tomb empty. The usual reconciliation of these texts was to
  understand Christ's prediction to mean 'on the third day.' Lefèvre rejected
  this and instead suggested a far-fetched, very unusual interpretation for $\mu\epsilon\tau\grave{\alpha}$,
  within three days. For John Fisher's reply to Lefèvre's book cf Ep 936.

the argument down to such refinement, that whoever says that Christ rose
after three days must be held to be speaking contrary to the church, to the
articles of the faith, and to the whole truth; such are the Clashing Rocks
between which he gets the thing caught. In the first place, his proof that   30
μετά must mean 'within' is not very well supported: μετὰ χεῖρας, in one's
hands, where μετά is put for κατά. And μεθ᾽ ἡμέραν for καθ᾽ ἡμέραν is a
different shape of phrase from μετὰ τρεῖς ἡμέρας, especially since μετὰ
ἡμέρας ἕξ, μεθ᾽ ἡμέρας ὀκτώ, after six days, after eight days, and similar
expressions are common in the New Testament. Lastly, the synecdoche,   35
which cannot be eliminated from this passage, also dissolves this difficulty:
'He rose again after three days,' that is, after the beginning of the third day.
If whoever says this is contradicting the articles of the faith, and the church
has been reading it in the Gospel all these years without contradiction, I
think it would be wiser to make rather less fuss about it, especially since the   40
synecdoche provides a ready way out. If he can explain the first night by
allegory or by inaccuracy of language, why is he afraid to bring in here the
synecdoche which everyone accepts?

I write this, my dear Glareanus, with friendly feelings towards him,
whatever his may be to me. If it is no trouble, will you speak to him gently   45
about all this, and ask him at the same time, if he answers me, to send me a
copy at the earliest moment, for which I will pay, that I may either acknowledge my mistake or defend myself. For having once been struck such a blow
by him, I ought not to trust him very far. And if he can be put up to it by
rascals, there are rascals everywhere; apart from that, I should not like him   50
to be one jot the less your friend for my sake. I am surprised that Budé has
not written for so long. Farewell, the half of my soul.

Louvain, 18 January 1518, from the College of the Lily

767 / To Guillaume Budé   Louvain, [c 18 January] 1518

This letter is found between Epp 766 and 768 in the Deventer Letter-book and
was clearly dispatched with these and Ep 764, all addressed to Paris. Ep 744
from Budé must have arrived soon thereafter, since it was answered on 22
January by Ep 778.

ERASMUS TO HIS FRIEND BUDÉ, GREETING
I fear I bore you already with these frequent letters, but you have only

* * * * *

29 Clashing Rocks] Between which the Argonauts had to pass when sailing in
   search of the Golden Fleece
51 Budé] Cf Ep 767.

yourself to thank for challenging an Arabian piper. Your quite unexpected
silence surprises me very much. In thinking Henricus Glareanus worthy of
your friendship you lay me under an obligation, no less than if it were me   5
you had done something for. Some thrice-damned rascal has robbed me of
your long letter to Cuthbert Tunstall, plague take him for it. Would you
please get it copied by someone and sent to me, so that I do not lose a great
part of my future fame. Farewell, my most learned and most gifted friend.

    Louvain, 1518   10

768 / To Wilhelm Nesen   Louvain, 18 January 1518

> This letter was subsequently polished and amplified by Erasmus for publica-
> tion in his *Farrago*. It is this text which is given here. Nesen was now in Paris;
> cf Ep 630 introduction.

ERASMUS OF ROTTERDAM TO WILHELM NESEN,
DISTINGUISHED PROFESSOR OF THE LIBERAL ARTS,
GREETING

O happy, happy man, my dear Nesen, to be serving the Muses under
Cyprianus Taleus, a man distinguished not only for learning and integrity   5
but for exceptional wisdom and rare knowledge of the world; since he also
knows Greek, I do not see what one could add to his endowments. In all the
liberal disciplines he has long been so skilled, with no professional arrogance, that I do not know who could be compared with him. And so let me
urge you to make the most of your good fortune. Act like a true German: 10
conquer the French, despoil them, strip them of their liberal learning; you
will leave France no poorer, and you will return to your own country richly
loaded with valuable merchandise. This surely is the point at which to
prove ourselves brave and invincible, and not let it look as though the
Germans were inferior to the French in brains. I beg you particularly to   15

    * * * * *

767
3 piper] Once you got him to play, you could not make him stop; *Adagia* I vii 32.
7 letter] Ep 583; Erasmus wanted it for publication in the *Auctarium*. Complying
   with the request caused Budé some anxiety; see Epp 810:388–9, 501–3,
   819:17–26.

768
5 Taleus] Taleus or Talea is clearly identical with a Cyprianus from Venice
   whose lectures on Pliny Nesen attended at Paris in 1518 (see Zwingli *Werke* VII
   Epp 32, 35). Taleus is mentioned in Ep 903, and is probably also the Cyprianus
   mentioned in Epp 1117, 1713 and described in Ep 2311 as principal of the
   Collège des Lombards in Paris.

approach Doctor Pierre Vitré on my behalf (he lives in the Collège de
Navarre), that I may discover how he is and what he is doing; for it is a long
time since I heard from him. Then let me have any news of Thomas Grey the
Englishman, who has also lost his voice.

Lefèvre's defence, which some say he is getting ready, does not 20
frighten me at all; only it is tiresome to devote valuable time to such
worthless stuff, when I scarcely have the energy for better things. And then
I can see that the enemies of humane studies are zealously trying to match
us one against the other, which is the trick of a true tyrant; for there is
nothing tyrants fear more than agreement among men of good will. What he 25
wants to do is his own affair; for the sake of our old relationship I am very
sorry that by challenging me he has done his own reputation no good. If
anyone stirs him up to provoke me still more unpleasantly, I may not be able
to force myself to show the same moderation. Men who do sacrifice to the
Graces and the Muses, still more those who profess themselves followers of 30
Christ, should have nothing to do with squabbles of this kind. How much
better it is to compete in doing things to help one another! But no one fights
more bitterly than he who is dragged into the fray against his will. I only
wish my sword might remain buried in the scabbard till it rusts away, or if I
must draw it, that I may not be compelled to use it against a friend. I have 35
almost finished the New Testament for the second time, in which I so often
mention Lefèvre much to his credit; unless it is an insult to disagree with
him, while he disagrees with everybody. Do not fail to love and respect the
man; do not like him a hairsbreadth less because he and I have had this
slight difference of opinion. Farewell, my special friend. 40

My servant John Smith sends his greetings. He would write, but was
prevented, not by business, for he has none to occupy him, nor by lack of
leisure, of which he has plenty.

Louvain, 18 January 1518, from the College of the Lily

* * * * *

16 Vitré] See Ep 779.
18 Thomas Grey] An old friend of Erasmus from his student days in Paris (see Ep
    58). He wrote to Erasmus about this time from Paris, apparently promising a
    visit on his way back to England. He was in Louvain in the second half of
    April; cf Epp 777:25–9, 817, 827, 829:30–2.
20 defence] Cf Ep 721 introduction.
34 rusts away] Cf Virgil Georgics 2.220.
41 Smith] Erasmus' student-servant

769 / From Johann Maier von Eck   Ingolstadt, 2 February 1518

This is the first of two letters addressed to Erasmus by the famous theologian Johann Maier von Eck (1486–1543). He was professor of theology and preacher at Ingolstadt and is known chiefly for his unrelenting opposition to Luther. Eck was himself committed to many ideals of Christian humanism and valued the Fathers highly, but since the autumn of 1517 it had become known that he disapproved of Erasmus' New Testament (see *Christoph Scheurl's Briefbuch*, Potsdam 1867–72, Ep 155). Erasmus was probably aware of Eck's reaction when he received this letter. He answered carefully in Ep 844 and published both letters in his *Auctarium*. Moreover, Erasmus' defence was taken up by Udalricus Zasius in his *Apologetica defensio* against Eck (Basel: Froben March 1519).

Whether or not his assurances of friendship were sincere, Eck certainly succeeds here in giving clear expression to some fundamental theological reservations about Erasmus' reading of the New Testament.

JOHANN ECK TO DESIDERIUS ERASMUS OF ROTTERDAM,
GREETING

Such is your reputation, Erasmus most learned of men, for courtesy, such the mildness of your character and the happy balance of your nature, that even uneducated folk may send you quite barbarous letters and be sure of 5 your lively attention. This is the report of you given emphatically by your particular friends, by Wolfgang Faber and Johannes Fabri and Beatus Rhenanus and Sapidus and others too; and it has encouraged my resolve to approach you and make my addresses with an ill-written letter from myself. It is not my intention, however, to devote a whole letter to your praises, as 10 the way of some men is. Not that you do not richly deserve praise; but that you should be praised as you deserve among people at a distance, and your name be handed down in writing to posterity (as I have done more than once in my modest publications, with a proper expression of your eminence in the foreword) is, I think, a better plan than to extol you at length in your 15 presence and to your face, which has a look of flattery about it; although you have no need of tributes from others, bringing forth as you do from the storehouse of your genius the most highly wrought productions with as-

* * * * *

769
7 Faber] Wolfgang Faber Capito; for Sapidus and Fabri see Epp 323, 386 intro-
    ductions.
13 more than once] Cf lines 128–9; Allen's note gives further references to Eck's
    publications.

Johann Maier von Eck
Silver portrait medal with cardinal's hat on reverse
by unknown master, 1529
Photo: Staatliche Münzsammlung München

tonishing fertility that rabbits could not match – productions which to all
posterity will never die. And so your learning earns you a full meed of   20
immortality.

But that I may not seem to have written idly to you, who are, as I say, so
great a man, may I refer to some passages in what you have so brilliantly
written; and I beg you with your naturally fair and supple mind to receive
this in a friendly and charitable spirit, for it comes from one who is your   25
sincere well-wisher. You must be well aware, dear Erasmus, of the high
reputation you enjoy in Germany (I say nothing of the supreme pontiff, of
Italy, France, and England), and of the chorus of praise that extols your
writings, that hails the offspring of your genius and welcomes your distinguished works; so that almost all scholars are convinced Erasmians, except   30
for a few wearers of the cowl and pseudo-theologians. But you know what
carping critics are, how by their zeal for denigrating excellence they try to
earn a shadowy scrap of reputation, like the man who set fire to the temple
at Ephesus; you know precisely how these rascals have not spared the
greatest scholars. And thus you have your critics too, whose wish is to find   35
fault with you and prove you wrong. My own attitude is, as it ought to be,
most friendly; and if I show you a few points, it is with no desire to find
fault, but to give you the occasion to defend yourself and use your all-round
learning and copious powers of expression to make lucid and open and
more mellow anything that might need fuller explanation. In this way your   40
devoted Erasmians will defend you more successfully against the pseudo-
theologians, and you yourself will greatly add to your glory and reputation.

First of all then, to begin at this point, many people are offended at
your having written in your notes on the second chapter of Matthew the
words 'or because the evangelists themselves did not draw evidence of this   45
kind from books, but trusted as men will to memory and made a mistake.'
For in these words you seem to suggest that the evangelists wrote like
ordinary men, in that they wrote this in reliance on their memories and
failed to inspect the written sources, and so for this reason made a mistake.
Listen, dear Erasmus: do you suppose any Christian will patiently endure   50
to be told that the evangelists in their Gospels made mistakes? If the
authority of Holy Scripture at this point is shaky, can any other passage be

* * * * *

33 the man] A certain Herostratus in 356 BC (cf AK II Ep 675:50–1). Eck endeavours
   to use a humanistic style: he calls Erasmus' critics 'Momi' and 'Zoili'; cf *Adagia*
   I v 74; II v 8.
44 Matthew] Cf LB VI 12E–14D. This attack led to a full treatment of the question in
   the 1518–19 edition of the New Testament, as announced in Allen Ep
   844:53–5.

free from the suspicion of error? A conclusion drawn by St Augustine from
an elegant chain of reasoning. Further, you say 'trusted to memory,' as
though they had previously read what they wrote down and stored it in   55
their memories; although they were instructed to take no thought what they
should speak before kings and governors, but that they should be taught all
truth by the Holy Spirit. And 'they did not draw evidence of this kind' you
say 'from books,' as though they put a work together, as we do, from
various written sources and authorities, in the fashion in which books are   60
written nowadays. Heaven forbid that we should suspect this of the Holy
Spirit and of the disciples of Jesus our Saviour, those pillars of our faith who
were informed by more than human wisdom! The Spirit chose men of no
schooling, who could neither read nor write, and made great scholars of
them. Let me beg you, my distinguished friend, to set forth sound doctrine   65
on these points, and pray do not be hard on a man full of such good
intentions and such a keen supporter, who humbly and in all modesty
draws this to your attention.

Let us move onward to another point. When you set yourself to
explain the tenth chapter of Acts, you write in your note as follows: 'None   70
the less, even when the apostles are writing Greek, they reproduce much of
the idiom of their own language,' and further on, 'For the apostles learnt
their Greek, not from the speeches of Demosthenes but from the conversation of ordinary men.' To write like this was less than prudent in you as a
Christian, most people think – if I may say so, dear Erasmus, without   75
offence, for I am a forthright man and do not flatter. What Christian does not
know, or could be ignorant if he wished to be, that the apostles knew divers
kinds of tongues by the gift of the Holy Spirit? On the day of Pentecost,
when they received the grace of the Holy Spirit, the apostles spoke in
various tongues the wonderful works of God. Thus it was not from Greeks   80
but from the Holy Spirit that they learnt their Greek, as Greeks, Romans,
Egyptians, Parthians, and others bore them witness in the second chapter
of Acts. For the gift of tongues is listed among many others also by St Paul.

Of the same sort is what we read in your notes on the third chapter of
Matthew: 'In fact, I wonder that the evangelists misused this word, which   85

* * * * *

53 Augustine] Ep 28. 3
56 instructed] Matt 10:18–20
70 as follows] Cf LB VI 476D–478E. Again Erasmus added his defence in the
   1518–19 edition without changing the two sentences criticized by Eck.
83 Acts] Acts 2:8–11
83 Paul] 1 Cor 12:10
84 your notes] On Matt 4:23; cf LB VI 25E. Erasmus changed his text to read: 'the
   translator of the Evangelist misused ...'

would seem rather one to be avoided' – you speak of the word *therapeuôn*. Why, at this point you seem to set up as the instructor of the evangelists, and to show them what they should have avoided in what they wrote, as though they had not a sufficiently well-meaning and well-instructed preceptor in the Holy Spirit, whose carelessness it was your business to correct   90 so many centuries later! I adduce a few instances, most learned of men, not to attack you but to bring them to your notice.

To conclude, I will pass over much else – for if I find these remarks are acceptable to you, I shall prove an assiduous counsellor – and add something on my own account, admiring and respecting Augustine's eminent   95 learning as I do above everything after the Holy Scriptures and the decrees of Holy Church. I am thus much distressed by the judgment you put forward regarding Augustine in commenting on St John: 'It is quite shameless,' you assert, 'to match one against the other.' For my part, I have a higher opinion of the judgment of Francesco Filelfo, who sums up on the   100 two as follows: 'Augustine shows more penetration, experience, and subtlety in everything philosophical, though Jerome may have more to his credit in elegance of style rather than doctrine.' And at the close of his letter he says: 'If one man could have been made out of these two, nature could have produced nothing nearer to perfection.' And what Filelfo says of them   105 in philosophy is the verdict of all scholars upon Augustine in theology. 'Every man is a good judge of what he knows well,' says the Stragirite; and there is no shortcoming in you which your supporters so much regret as your failure to have read Augustine. Cease therefore, dear Erasmus, to darken by your criticisms a leading light of the church, than which none has   110 been more illustrious since its first pillars. Admit rather that Augustine was a great scholar, steep yourself in his works and turn his pages with all

* * * * *

98 on St John] 21:22; cf LB VI 419A–421B. Erasmus removed the cited words but still maintained that Augustine's Greek was deficient.

100 Filelfo] Francesco Filelfo (1398–1481) was a famous humanist associated for many years with the court of Milan. Eck refers to his letter to Luigi Crotto dated 1449, the last in book 6 of Filelfo's letters. Eck's second citation is literal; the first is a correct but incomplete summary. In his reply Erasmus wrongly accused Eck of interpolation (Allen Ep 844:143–4); he might rather have noted that Eck omitted Filelfo's point that Augustine knew Greek less perfectly than Jerome, and Hebrew not at all.

107 Stragirite] Aristotle in his *Nicomachean Ethics* 1.3.5. The name of Aristotle's birthplace was Stagira, not Stragira. Allen found the same misspelling frequently in Eck's works.

112 all diligence] For the results of Eck's admonition see Bietenholz *History and Biography* 44, 77–9.

Francesco Filelfo
Portrait on parchment by unknown fifteenth-century artist
Municipal Palace of Tolentino, Umbria
Photo: Fratelli Alinari

diligence, and you will regard as quite shameless the man who dares prefer any of the Fathers to Augustine as a scholar.

These few points I wished to bring to your attention, dear Erasmus, 115 most eloquent of living men, or rather, I wanted to give you your cue to develop sound and religious doctrine on them, that those who feel special affection for you as a father for your pre-eminent learning, and respect and revere you, may be able to defend and protect what you write from the poisonous tongues of calumny and detraction, and at the same time to ward 120 off sinister suspicions. As concerns myself, I know well that you not only do not take it amiss but will be grateful to me for sketching rapidly and in passing with the very best intentions, for the benefit of my Erasmus (to whose works I owe no small profit, having been brought up from boyhood on your lesser *Adagia*), these points, some of which are brought against you 125 by your detractors and others might be. Nor do I think that with your honesty and fairness of mind you will be more reluctant to be told this by Eck than when in my commentary on the Dialectic I called you 'the sun of Latin eloquence' and in another place described you as a phoenix among the devotees of polite literature in our generation. Besides which, you must 130 forgive my rough and unpolished style; for like the chameleon which takes the colour of its surroundings, by continual poring over barbarous authors I acquire their barbarism, and they contaminate me. And so my best wishes, dear Erasmus, for your health and wealth, peculiar glory of our age, and pray give Eck a taste of your courtesy, by which I mean, let him have a letter 135 from you. Farewell and prosper.

Ingolstadt, 2 February 1518

Your most devoted servant

770 / From Gianfrancesco Torresani of Asola   [Venice, c February 1518]

This is a preface to the New Testament in the earliest edition of the entire Bible (Septuagint and New Testament) in Greek only, published by the Aldine press, Venice, in February 1518. Since the turn of the century the firm had planned to publish a critical edition of the Bible in Hebrew, Greek, and Latin; now at least the Greek part had materialized. The imminent publication had been announced to Erasmus in August 1517 (cf Epp 629, 643:26–7). More recently, while the revision of his New Testament was making good progress,

* * * * *

125 *Adagia*] The first, slender edition was published when Eck was fourteen.
128 sun ... phoenix] See Allen lines 10n, 113n. Allen found the first phrase in Eck's preface to his *In summulas Petri Hispani explanatio* (Augsburg: J. Miller May 1516).

Erasmus had begun to concern himself with the choice of a publisher. Since November he had expected that he would be away from the Netherlands for the whole summer of 1518 to see the work through the press (cf Epp 712:20n, 753 introduction). But which press? Froben's was an obvious possibility (cf Ep 732 introduction and lines 61–2), but Aldus' was an alternative, and gradually Erasmus seemed to lean towards Italy (cf Epp 752, 775, 781:5–9, 786:15–17, 809:195–6), as disturbing news of a plague in Basel reached him (cf Ep 781:7–8). But having been reassured by friends in Basel (see Epp 801–2), in April Erasmus decided in favour of Froben (cf Epp 809:115–23, 815–17). He set out from Louvain about 1 May (see Ep 843 introduction). It is possible that the arrival of a presentation copy of the Aldine Bible with this handsome dedication influenced Erasmus' decision, since it was doubtful whether the Aldine press would wish to launch another edition of the New Testament in the near future.

FRANCISCUS ASULANUS TO ERASMUS OF ROTTERDAM, GREETING
Nothing, Erasmus, could give me greater pleasure than by my industry and unremitting toil to earn the good will of that class of men, pre-eminent for their experience of affairs and gifts and literary skill, who stand out so far above the generality that all our best judges are moved to spread their fame 5 and daily grow more eager to pay a tribute of praise and glory to their merits. If ever I met with anyone who repaid my good offices in this kind by making me glad and happy, I can at least aver that I gained no small reputation, when I call to mind the days in which I was privileged to do you no small service. For it was Aldus, to whose memory the annals of literature 10 and the plaudits of the learned can never do full justice, who made your name illustrious in Italy and took most careful pains to ensure that devotees of the humanities admire your efforts in the restoration of ancient texts and all our best scholars pay you most lavish tributes as the great authority. And this he did, being a very wise man, not because of the personal familiarity 15 and warm affection that united you, but for the industry and enthusiasm and literary genius which he hoped would combine to make you some day no less a credit to Italy than the ornament and glory of your native Germany and the other provinces of Christendom. Nor was he far wrong, to be sure, in this his hope or expectation. For to say nothing of the immortal glory you 20 have acquired in other countries, there lives among us no man of free birth

* * * * *

770
9 days] 1507–9, during the time when Erasmus was putting the *Adagia* through the Aldine press and living in the house of Gianfrancesco's father, Andrea Torresani; see Epp 211 introduction, 212:3n and 6n.

and liberal education who is not convinced that you have made a great step forward towards renewing the glory of classical literature and bringing back the study of the liberal arts.

Many therefore owe you a debt on this account and devote their minds 25 and thoughts to find some way of making clear the special affection and enthusiasm that they feel for you. And I more than anyone have never had a more heart-felt ambition or a more fervent desire than to make you understand that all my wishes, all my thoughts are concentrated on praising your virtues and securing you an immortal name. To achieve this now to some 30 extent I conceive there can be no better opportunity than for these sacred books reproduced in our typography to be published and supplied for public reading with your name at their head. For I foresee that the reading of them can not only guide a Christian on the right principles but provide him with a high road by which to reach the place where he may combine 35 distinction in every virtue with all that makes life truly noble and sets the seal on human felicity. For here are the accounts written down by those first inspired authors, Matthew, John, Luke, and Mark, of the character, the sayings and doings, and the life of Christ, the founder of our religion and author of our salvation and our liberty. They are followed by a history 40 which sets forth all the achievements everywhere of the hearers and followers of the teaching of Christ, and many epistles written by other men famous for their piety and holiness of life, and in particular by those same followers, to various nations, that they might publish to the whole world and secure a welcome for the name of Christ, which was either unknown or 45 hated, and thus arouse all men to worship him.

If, then, it was the principal merit of the books of Marcus Varro that he found the citizens of Rome foreigners in their own city and wandering like strangers and brought them home, so that they could at length recognize who and where they were, by expounding the laws of religious observance, 50 the code of the priests, the principles of civil government and war, the names, kinds, functions, and causes of all things divine and human, consider what honour and gratitude, what renown and glory we should attribute to the authors of these books! It was they who found the human race torn from its true home and restored it to its proper place, who banished 55 abominable rites, who sapped the proud position of men engaged in continual rapine and whose hands were stained continually with blood, abolished the worship of fictitious deities, and pointed to the one God, to Christ the Son, and to the inspiration of the Holy Spirit. It is they who are

* * * * *

47 Varro ... 52 functions and causes] Adapted from Cicero's tribute in the *Academicus* (1.3.9) to Marcus Varro, the first great antiquary of ancient Rome

the most convenient source from which to draw that virtue which is un- 60
moved in the tempest and radiant in the darkness, when driven from its
place obstinately maintains its ground, shines by its own light, and is never
disfigured by squalor from some alien source so as to lose its loveliness or be
robbed of its grace and beauty. In the possession of this virtue you, my dear
Erasmus, hold a unique position among your countrymen, by which I mean 65
the wisest and most honourable men, and it is above all the example set by
you that fires many people in our time with zeal to recover what they have
lost of their ancient heritage in this respect, and with desire so to excel in
high principles of conduct and in all honourable knowledge that they need
have no fear of fortune's mischief and the malignance of those who wish 70
them ill. Farewell.

771 / To Johannes Caesarius   Louvain, 20 February 1518

> This is the preface to *Theodori Gazae de linguae Graecae institutione liber secun-*
> *dus* (Louvain: Martens [March 1518]; NK 3052). The first book of Erasmus'
> translation of Gaza's Greek grammar had been published by Martens in July
> 1516 and by Froben in November (cf Ep 428). After an interruption (see Ep 616)
> the translation of the second book was completed in August 1517 and dis-
> patched to Froben (with Ep 629). Negotiations were opened about dedicating
> the book to Afinius in return for a valuable gift (see Epp 637–8), and a
> manuscript copy was sent to Fisher to assist him in his study of the Greek
> language (see Ep 653:10–12). Perhaps it was the copy earlier promised to
> Afinius, who had failed to send the expected gift. Fisher also failed to show
> any interest in the work that might have warranted a dedication (see Epp 667,
> 784:44–5). Still worse, Froben, whose edition of the first book was selling
> badly (cf Ep 629:3), did not even acknowledge the receipt of the second, let
> alone promise swift publication (cf Epp 704A, 732). Understandably Erasmus
> felt free to give the work to Martens too (cf Ep 795:17–19), who published it at
> the beginning of March together with a new edition of the revised first book
> (NK 962). Since the first book was dedicated to Caesarius, Erasmus decided to
> do the same with the second.
>
> In the meantime Froben had actually printed the Greek text and Erasmus'
> translation of the second book. The printing was under way in November 1517
> (BRE Ep 69). The Greek was finished in March (cf Ep 801:22–3); the Latin
> translation is dated May 1518. But, as Erasmus had suggested, both texts were

* * * * *

65 countrymen] The following clause is added in view of the unfavourable
characterization of the Hollanders by some classical authors; see *Adagia* III ii
48, IV vi 35.

bound together with the unsold copies of the first book so that the enlarged
work still bears the original colophon of November 1516. This preface was, of
course, not given in Froben's edition but was added to subsequent Basel
reprints.

ERASMUS OF ROTTERDAM TO HIS FRIEND
JOHANNES CAESARIUS, GREETING
My dear Caesarius, you are a most fair-minded man. Is not this, I ask you,
just what the proverb means by 'gathering clouds like the North-easter'?
For I seem to bring work upon myself in my own horse and cart, as they say.   5
I had turned Theodore's first book into Latin in order to lighten the labours
of people who are keen to learn Greek, and at the same time to use it as bait
to attract those who seemed to be deterred by the difficulty of the language.
They took the bait, and now they are driving me on to another stint of hard
work; because I lightened their load, they think it fair to put fresh work on   10
me. I made them a present of the first book, and they demand the second –
and that like people who have a right to it, as though he who asks a man to
breakfast must give him luncheon, dinner, and supper as well. But what can
you do when the public are on your trail? Willy nilly, you must do what they
want. I hope the time will soon come when they are full-grown and active in   15
this department of learning and need my help no longer, but can swim by
themselves without corks. Farewell.
     Louvain, 20 February 1518

772 / To Roger Wentford   Antwerp, 21 February [1518]

Epp 772–7 and another series written a fortnight later, Epp 781–7, 789–92,
were all entrusted to the same messenger going to England. The contents are
often repetitive. During a short visit to Antwerp (cf Ep 789) Erasmus wrote a
number of brief letters designed to help his messenger, John Smith, on his
journey (Ep 773) and with the execution of his business in England. The latter
involved the reclaiming among other papers (cf lines 4–9, Epp 783:32–3,
785:20–1) of such documents concerning the papal dispensations as might be
found among the papers of the late Andrea Ammonio (cf Epp 774–5). He also
sent requests for cash gifts and a horse (cf Ep 785:51n) to facilitate his forthcoming journey (cf Epp 770, 820 introductions).

        * * * * *

771
 4 proverb] *Adagia* i v 62
 5 horse and cart] *Adagia* i i 50
17 without corks] *Adagia* i viii 42

Before Smith could set out, however, Erasmus received two consignments of mail from England, one carried by Franz Birckmann (cf Ep 775), the other by 'one-eyed' Pieter Meghen (cf Ep 653 introduction), who had taken his time, so that his letters were older. He also incurred Erasmus' anger for other reasons (cf Epp 782:5–6, 785:46–7, 786:44–7; but cf Allen Ep 937:1). The newly received letters induced Erasmus to write postscripts to Epp 774–5 and to add more letters to English friends or patrons and to others whom Smith could visit on his way. By 5 March the packet was complete. In the Deventer Letter-book most of these letters were entered by Hand D (cf Allen 1 Appendix VIII). It may be inferred that this was Smith, and that after his departure the copying was completed by Jacobus Nepos (Hand c), who added the postscripts to Epp 774–5, completed Epp 784–5, and copied Epp 777, 786–9.

For Roger Wentford, a schoolmaster in London, see Ep 196 introduction.

ERASMUS TO HIS FRIEND WENTFORD, GREETING

I know that you wrote a letter to More and addressed it to me, and sent the letter meant for me to him, but, my dear Wentford, there was nothing wrong in that: what belongs to either of us is as truly his as mine. You will do me a very great service if you will give my friend John the notes which 5 you say in your letter you have filched from Grocyn; he will either bring them to me himself or will see that I get them. Besides which, if you will send me any of my dialogues of a light-hearted and convivial sort that you may have by you, I shall revise and enlarge them until I think they form a memorial of our friendship that will be worth having; for I shall publish 10 them with a dedication to yourself. Farewell.

Antwerp, eve of St Peter's Chair

773 / To Thomas Parcius   Antwerp, 21 February 1518

Cf Ep 772 introduction; this is the only letter of this consignment sent with Smith that was published by Erasmus. It is in the *Farrago*. The French- or Englishman whom Erasmus believed, perhaps in error, to be the secretary of Calais has not been identified. For suggestions see Allen's note.

* * * * *

772
2 I know] See Ep 688.
5 notes] Perhaps on the New Testament; cf LP II 4267 and Ep 864 introduction. For William Grocyn, a Greek scholar at Oxford who had been living in London since 1514, see Ep 118:26n.
8 dialogues] See Ep 833.
12 Chair] In Antioch (22 February); the feast of St Peter's Chair in Rome was on 18 January.

ERASMUS TO THOMAS PARCIUS,
SECRETARY OF THE TOWN OF CALAIS, GREETING
The bearer of this note, my friend John Smith, is on his way to England for
me on some particular business and will shortly return. May I ask you to
help him to a convenient crossing as soon as possible; and when he returns,   5
send me a letter to say how you are, how things are going with your
financial friends, and any news of your bride. Please give my cordial
greetings, if you have an opportunity, to my lord the deputy governor.
Farewell, my dear Parcius.
      Antwerp, eve of St Peter's Chair 1518   10

774 / To Pietro Ammonio   Antwerp, 22 February [1518]

      Cf Ep 772 introduction.

ERASMUS TO HIS FRIEND PIETRO AMMONIO OF LUCCA, GREETING
I beg you earnestly to hand over to this secretary of mine anything you have
in the way of letters between Ammonio and myself, as well as any copies
that have to do with that business of mine. I do not doubt that you wish to
promote your kinsman's reputation, and I will take care to do what I can to   5
secure him immortality. So I pray you not to delay my servant by doing me
this kindness. If there is anything in which I can be useful to you, you will
discover that I cordially wish you well. Farewell.
      Antwerp, 22 February
      After I had written this, two letters from you reached me together, and   10
they were more welcome than I can say, for they were of a kind to raise my
hopes very high.

775 / To Johannes Sixtinus   Antwerp, 22 February [1518]

      Cf Ep 772 introduction.

ERASMUS TO HIS FRIEND SIXTINUS, GREETING
I beg you urgently to see that my man John gets what I want from Pietro

      * * * * *

      773
    8 deputy governor] Richard Wingfield; see Ep 791.

      774
    4 business] The papal dispensations for Erasmus; cf Epp 624:14n, 655–6.
   12 very high] His hopes were, however, doomed to be disappointed; see Epp
      822, 828; cf Ep 775:17–18. Pietro's two letters are not known to exist.

Ammonio, and that without delay. For the publication of the New Testament obliges me to revisit Basel, or Venice at the least. I brought this calamity on myself, in my own horse and cart, as the saying goes; but I have made my bed, and I must lie on it. The pope and the emperor have a new game on foot: they now use war against the Turks as an excuse, though they have something very different in mind. We have reached the limits of despotism and effrontery. In these parts robbers were beginning to be active right in the middle of the towns, but the authorities at last woke up and have begun to be on the watch. Farewell, most upright of friends and most generous of patrons.

Antwerp, 22 February

I had written thus far when Franz delivered your letter. I have received the money from Maruffo's agents. Franz says that the money was not paid him in cash at your end because the receipt was thought to be of doubtful validity in law. I now send a perfectly valid one. I have written a careful letter to Pietro Ammonio, and am sure he will do his part. What a likeness these Italians have to one another!

Of Lefèvre I hear differing accounts. Some say he is preparing a defence, some say he agrees with me. It is his own affair. If he seeks me out again, he shall have the welcome he is worthy of. Mountjoy is just the same, all either promises or complaints. His grace did not think it beneath his dignity to offer me twenty pounds, while the other man expected me to wait hopefully for a hundred, though I have so often known not only his promises but his solemn oaths prove false. About Pieter Gillis' health I spread no rumours, but I did complain in a letter to More; and I only wish the report was untrue. My dear friend, there is only too much truth in it, and at the sight of the danger he is in, I fear piteously for myself.

* * * * *

775
3 Ammonio] Cf Ep 774.
5 horse and cart] *Adagia* 1 i 50
6 made my bed] *Adagia* 1 i 85
6 pope ... emperor] See Epp 729:56n, 785:22–38, 891.
9 robbers] Cf Ep 829:11n.
15 money] These financial transactions are somewhat clarified by subsequent letters; see Ep 823 introduction.
20 Lefèvre] See Ep 721 introduction.
23 grace] Cardinal Wolsey, who would not confirm the higher amount earlier promised by Mountjoy; see Ep 694:11n.
27 More] Cf Epp 597:25–7, 687:11n.

776 / To Thomas More   Antwerp, 22 February 1518

Cf Ep 772 introduction.

ERASMUS TO HIS FRIEND MORE, GREETING
It is hard to say whether I am more distressed, my dear More, or puzzled,
wondering what can have happened to our friend Pace that he should think
fit to publish this book. I find in it a complete lack of that sound judgment of
which I had thought he had plenty. And I am sorry not only for his own   5
sake, though I am concerned for his reputation no less than for my own, but
for the sake of that England of yours, which I know was expecting from her
offspring a very different specimen of his talents. And then I am sorry for
my own sake too, for he mentions me so often by name; with kindly intent, I
am sure, but in such a way that an enemy could not have done me more   10
harm. The fact that the reader is likely to call up my guarantees for what I
promised on his behalf seems to me less important. In the Muses' name, has
he not bethought him that it is a serious matter to broadcast a friend's name
to the world and to posterity? Has he thought of nothing beyond the
expenditure of ink and paper and midnight oil? What was the point of   15
putting in that nonsense about the roll of my errors and my complaints of
poverty? Does he suppose that what any noisy fellow anywhere drivels over
his cups deserves to be set forth for the world to read?

But these protests are already too late. For what remains, use your
friendship with him to put him on notice not to misuse his pen like this in   20
future. If he translates from the Greek, he will have the support of another

* * * * *

776
4 this book] Richard Pace *De fructu qui ex doctrina percipitur* (Basel: Froben
   October 1517). This treatise in praise of liberal education was written at
   Constance during August and September 1517 while Pace was awaiting new
   instructions (cf Ep 619). Each of the liberal arts makes a speech to illustrate her
   own achievements, but the whole improvisation is studded with anecdotes
   and digressions, and moreover is full of inaccuracies and rash conclusions. For
   Pace's frequent praise of Erasmus cf the index of a modern reprint with
   English translation by Frank Manley and R.S. Sylvester (New York 1967). Two
   references embarrassed Erasmus. He was chosen to exemplify the rule that
   'scholars are a bunch of beggars' (*De fructu* 1967, 22–3; cf Epp 421:140–1,
   631:10n). Further, Pace introduced and insulted an Italian archbishop
   (perhaps a fictitious character invented by Pace) who claimed to have listed
   Erasmus' theological errors for the purpose of taking action against him (*De
   fructu*, 1967, 117–21). *De fructu* was not reprinted until 1967. For more reac-
   tions by Erasmus and others cf the indexes of this edition.
11 I promised] In the preface to *Adagia*: Ep 211:54–7

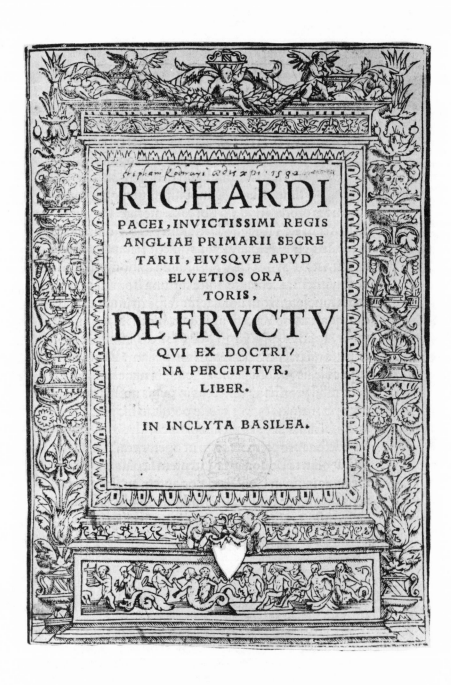

Richard Pace *De fructu qui ex doctrina percipitur* title page
Basel: Froben 1517
Courtesy of the British Library Board

man's judgment and will find no difficulties except the management of his own style. The letter which he wrote to Dorp in support of me I suppressed to spare his own reputation, and I only wish I could suppress his new book.

I have written all this to you, my dear More, without reserve, knowing   25
I could rely on the bearer; I would write in the same vein to him, had I not so often found how much everyone is enamoured of his own productions. And men like him take more kindly to correction face to face. Farewell.

Antwerp, St Peter's Chair 1518

777 / To Henry Bullock   Antwerp [c 22 February 1518]

> This letter appears to have been drafted during Erasmus' visit to Antwerp (cf
> line 31, Ep 772 introduction), but the date given at the end is that of the final
> copy. Bullock was a Cambridge scholar and an old friend of Erasmus; see Ep
> 225:5n.

ERASMUS TO HIS FRIEND BULLOCK, GREETING

First of all, my dear Bullock, I was happy to hear that that accursed pestilence left you alone. I wish Croke joy, and indeed your whole university, of this new honour added to the other excellent endowments in which he excels already. But what is this I hear? Are there even in your part of the   5
world men who enter the lists on Lefèvre's side? What can possibly make them annoyed with me? Is it because I rebut with such clear demonstration the accusation of blasphemy which I share with all catholic writers though Lefèvre launches it at me as though it affected me alone? Why not reserve their fire for the man who attacked me, and attacked me in such a way that it   10
was not open to me to hold my tongue? But let us forget those noisy fellows who condemn or approve just as the fancy takes them things of which they still know nothing. Lefèvre surprises me, first for having taken it into his head to attack me like that and then for not writing me at least a private letter to explain or defend himself. If Standish had assaulted me like that, the   15
beast would have had a very different reception; Lefèvre I answered with the greatest reluctance and passed over many things for the sake of our

* * * * *

23 letter] See Ep 732:59n.

777
2 pestilence] Cf Ep 623:9n.
3 Croke] Cf Ep 712:33–5.
5 even in your part] Cf Epp 730:19–20, 731:29–30; for Pace's criticism of Erasmus'
   Apologia ad Fabrum see Ep 742.
15 Standish] Cf Ep 608:15n.

long-standing friendship. But he and I are not such friends that to please
him I must be an enemy of the dignity of Christ, one who undermines our
understanding of the prophets, and a supporter of the Jews; especially since   20
it was he who first broke the laws of friendship.

I have revised my New Testament by great exertions. For the printing
of it I am now getting ready to set out for Basel or Venice. Such is the fate for
which I was born, my dear Bullock; but it is no good fighting against the
gods. I have had a letter from Grey, but written apparently from Paris.   25
Pieter Gillis entrusted Croke's letter to me to someone, I know not whom;
but whoever he was, he has not delivered it. Please give him my cordial
greetings, as also to the excellent Grey; and tell him about my journey,
though it is not yet certain to which of the two I shall go. Greet all my
friends, Vaughan, Humphrey, Bryan, Watson, and Garret my host, whose   30
praise is in my *Apologia*, though without his name. There is now in Louvain
a teacher of Hebrew who is far the most learned scholar of the age; and there
is also a teacher of Greek. So that is the place to which every one should
hurry who wants to get the three tongues. Farewell, my special friend,
benefactor, and champion.   35

Antwerp, [5 March]

778 / To Guillaume Budé   Louvain, 22 February [1518]

This is the answer to Budé's Ep 744, which had just arrived by way of Mainz.
Without waiting for Budé's reply (Ep 810) Erasmus published this letter in the
Auctarium and in a new edition of the *Apologia ad Fabrum* (Louvain: Martens
[1518]; NK 778). The date and place of dispatch may not be given quite
correctly; cf lines 40–1 and the date of Epp 774–6.

ERASMUS OF ROTTERDAM TO THE
HONOURABLE GUILLAUME BUDÉ, SECRETARY-DESIGNATE
OF THE MOST CHRISTIAN KING OF FRANCE
About that business of mine, my dear Budé, and the proposals for my future
that were being canvassed with Francis the Most Christian King of France, I   5

* * * * *

19 I must be] Cf Ep 659.
23 Basel or Venice] See Ep 770 introduction.
25 Grey] See Ep 768:18n.
27 not delivered] Perhaps untrue; see Ep 712:34–5.
29 all my friends] Cf Ep 456:310–14.
31 *Apologia*] *Apologia ad Fabrum* LB IX 20C
32 Hebrew] Matthaeus Adrianus
33 Greek] Cf Ep 691:19n.

well know and remember what you wrote; you must not think I have been drinking the water of Lethe, as you suggest in your letter. So far was I from worrying about it that, when I noticed that with your usual kindness towards me you were taking energetic and ambitious steps, I wrote to urge you not to let yourself be tormented by the project. Had Fortune hitherto   10
held me enslaved in the service of kings, my present age and state of health, if not my spirit which always abhorred such spheres of activity, would by now be demanding retirement and release. Had I ever thought it right to enter the service of any prince whatever, what better master could I choose than Charles, his Catholic Majesty? Either because he is the greatest   15
monarch of our age, or because whether I will or no he is my sovereign, or because he took the first steps towards making me an unsolicited offer on very generous terms, and has further bound me to him by kindness out of the common; although I thought it both ungrateful and discourteous to meet the favour of so great a prince as Francis with a haughty refusal,   20
especially since I could enjoy that distinction without imperilling my own position. And you had already written that you had abandoned the task you had taken on yourself. It was only that I wanted to know what in the end was the sore place you said you had detected in him who is called Small; for from the very outset the suspicion has been in my mind that his conduct in this   25
business has not been straightforward. The name Guillaume that he shares with my friends is not so much an attraction as an object of suspicion, a mask that covers a 'vain talker' and a Preacher whose purpose, if I mistake not, is to lure me into a trap and make a fool of me.

As for Bishop Poncher, I was longing to know what he was up to, and   30
whether he still maintained the same feelings towards me that he showed here; for they were quite exceptional. Not that I had ambitions to get anything out of him, as he himself can confirm, for he knows what offer he conveyed to me and how I replied; but because I thought it honourable and

* * * * *

778

7 letter] Ep 744:15
9 I wrote] A lost letter (cf Ep 744:13n), or possibly an inaccurate recollection
22 written] Cf Ep 568:56–65.
24 you said] Cf Ep 568:13–14.
24 Small] Guillaume Petit; the crucial words were written in Greek, as were also 'vain talker' and 'Preacher.'
33 offer] During their meeting (cf Ep 738:6n) at Brussels in February 1517 Poncher invited Erasmus to Paris, where he was expected to play a key role in the foundation of a humanistic college. Erasmus never returned to Paris, but Francis I's foundation went ahead and finally became the Collège de France. The terms of Poncher's offer are spelled out in Allen Ep 1434:4–6. Apparently it was complementary to the king's promise conveyed through Ep 522:57–8.

an object of ambition to win the approval of a man so much approved of by 35
all really good men. The eminent counsellor of the Parlement, Deloynes, to
whom I wrote at your instigation, may, I slightly fear, have been offended
somehow by my letter, because I have had no answer. For I must tell you
that for four months nothing in the way of letters has arrived from your part
of the world except this last letter, dated from Paris on midwinter day and 40
sent on from Mainz by our friend Hutten on 20 February.

You say that some people have discouraged you from trying to carry
my business any further on the ground that, if it succeeds, there is some
danger that you will be out of credit; but I confess I could not read this
without laughing. I need hardly ask you, I think, as a sensible and fair- 45
minded man, not to let it count against me if others mistakenly or mock-
ingly or enthusiastically say very grand things about me. You would hardly
believe how unpleasant I find the enthusiasm of such people, which often
lands me with a considerable burden of unpopularity. I cannot make up my
mind whether to pity the bishop's lot or admire his devotion to his country 50
in undertaking a mission that was difficult on so many counts: on a painful
subject, to treat with the English, in winter, and not least when everything
over there is raging with a new kind of pestilence. I am delighted that you
think well of Hutten; to me he has the most delightful nature of anyone I
know. I do hope all is well with Tunstall: when he left here, he was sick and 55
had to leave one of his servants behind, and in England nothing is safe from
the plague. He certainly read your letter several times with great eagerness
and had already detected a point for discussion worthy of you both.

About Lefèvre I do not quite understand what you mean. You say my
supporters find it very disagreeable that an opening should be given to 60
those who think that the task I have set my hand to can do them nothing but
harm; and in that I entirely agree with them. No one, I think, finds it more
disagreeable than I do, and I did not conceal this in my *Apologia*. Nor do I
suppose there are many people who wish well to Lefèvre more sincerely
than myself. I shall never bring myself to do otherwise than dislike my 65
Apologia, and indeed my victory, if things turn out that way. It had to be
written, but it could bring me no credit as my case was so strong, only
unpopularity as it was directed against an old and distinguished friend;

* * * * *

37 I wrote] Ep 535
42 You say] Ep 744:31–4
51 mission] See Ep 744:40n.
53 pestilence] See Ep 623:9n.
54 Hutten] See Ep 744:52n.
55 sick] See Ep 663.
59 You say] Ep 744:85–7

and moreover it could do great harm to both of us and our work, for it does
not escape my notice that this opportunity will be seized on by backbiters   70
who have everything, as the saying goes, except a pretext. You see what an
extraordinary contest this is: the victor repents of his victory and is sorry for
the enemy who is taking the field against him. For I hear that he is preparing
to renew the battle, as though it was not enough to have made a fool of
himself like this once. I begin to find it more likely that Lefèvre is egged on   75
to this by others than that he intended it himself. I knew that in this struggle
the dice were loaded against me: if I lost, I had to admit the accusation of
impiety, and if I won, I should incur the charge of behaving as no man
ought to behave; I should be thought to join battle with an old friend and
one so close to me in the principles on which we work that I could not harm   80
his reputation without doing almost the same amount of damage to my
own. And yet I had to refute him unless I had preferred to imperil, or rather
to betray, the citadel of my beliefs. Besides which, I could see that most
people, who had never read either his attack or my reply, would distort our
confrontation; they would merely express disapproval over their cups of   85
something they had heard somewhere about Erasmus fighting it out with
Lefèvre.

Tell me – you are a very fair-minded man – what would you have had
me do once he had attacked me, making all these atrocious statements in
books that enjoyed world-wide circulation, and had publicly accused me of   90
blasphemy and irreligion? In the first place, as he admits, a friend of his,
secondly quite unprovoked by me; and then again in an affair in which I am
so far from opposing him that I look more like a supporter and am taken to
task in letters from other scholars for not entirely rejecting his opinion,
although that was really no part of the subject which I had then undertaken.   95
I only wish Lefèvre had attacked me with the kind of wild abuse that could
have been overlooked or tolerated with some credit to one's patience. I
would gladly have made the sacrifice to our friendship or to Christian
modesty or to the profit of humane studies. But to admit a charge of
irreligion is forbidden in the first place by religion itself. I thought it better   100
therefore to show some want of reverence to the Graces than to seem one
who undermines and attacks the dignity of Christ; for that was the part for
which he cast me. Not but what in this respect at least I pay some homage to
the Graces, that I refrain from the right of retaliation, though it was ready to
hand. I am content to reject his insulting indictment and bring no charge   105

* * * * *

71 saying] Aristotle *Rhetoric* 1373 a 3
74 renew the battle] See Ep 721 introduction.
93 a supporter] Cf line 203n.

against him in return, and though my adversary moves the criminal law against me, I defend myself with civil process.

And yet there are some people (would you believe it?) who censure my *Apologia* as having sharp teeth; as though when attacked with poisoned arrows, it was my duty mildly to stroke my attacker's hair with soothing 110 remarks to persuade him not to continue these fits of rage. I refute neither opinion, neither in my annotation nor in my *Apologia*, although the view which Lefèvre regards as the only religious one I could reject as irreligious and false, and that too with the approval, I think, of serried ranks of theologians. This was another concession to civilized behaviour. What then 115 are you telling me to do, my good Budé? Do you, like a second Epimetheus, tell me when the business is all over not to start on it? Do you maintain it to be a mistake to carry off Helen, with Troy already fallen? You and I have the same objective, I can see that; but what action you recommend I do not understand, unless maybe you do not distinguish between recommenda- 120 tion and rebuke. But if you are rebuking me, you do it without cause; and if you recommend some different course of action, you are too late. That I am unfortunate, I admit, compelled as I have been to plunge into this contest which I have always abhorred, and into which nothing but this one weapon could have dragged me. That I am wrong, I do not admit; in fact I should 125 have been utterly in the wrong had I suffered in silence under a charge of irreligion, which all the most saintly Fathers always rejected with the greatest vehemence. How I wish, my dear Budé, you had been there to give warning in due time and had restrained my friend Lefèvre from challenging me in such unfriendly fashion! But once he had declared on top of all the 130 other abuse that I 'treat Christ with contumely,' 'undermine the understanding of prophecy,' 'side with the Jews,' 'overthrow in undignified fashion the dignity of Christ,' 'am in opposition to the Spirit,' 'cling fast to the flesh and to the literal meaning,' 'make inconsistent and mutually destructive statements, worthy of Bedlam many times over,' and that too 135 against Christ's glory; once he had presented himself as the champion of the glory of Christ and me as his adversary, and even threatened that I should find myself in jeopardy if I held steadfastly to my opinions, in other words unless I were willing to recant (for these and suchlike are the pleasantries in which that sweet-natured and charming Lefèvre, such an old friend of 140

* * * * *

108 people] Cf Ep 742:9n.

110 soothing remarks] *Adagia* III i 37

116 Epimetheus] He opened Pandora's box filled with all the scourges of mankind, and only remembered the warnings of his brother Prometheus when the harm had been done; cf *Adagia* I i 31.

130 declared] See Ep 659:6n.

mine, indulges at his dearest friend's expense); once he had, as I say,
published this and plenty more like it, as unfriendly as it was untrue,
stuffing the heart of his commentary full of it, and spread it worldwide so
that I was the one person who did not know – tell me, what do you think I
should do? Tell me, I say, for I leave the whole thing to your decision; I   145
accept the law of friendship, I will follow your advice or verdict without
reservation. Will you try to persuade your old friend to say thank you to
Lefèvre for the honour he has done me? Or to pretend that I do not know
what he has written? But no one would believe that, his books are
everywhere; who will believe that I alone am ignorant of something that   150
touches no one but me and that everybody knows? Or to pass the thing over
in silence? Which means that, when accused on a capital charge not before a
single judge but in front of the whole of Christendom, I am to make no reply
to my adversary and admit the whole accusation.

But it is not very honourable, you say, to dispute in public with a   155
friend. But is it, I ask you, honourable to make such attacks on a friend who
does not deserve them? Lefèvre and I are friends; but the man who has
launched an attack like that has ceased to be a friend. Even had I really gone
astray, it was the duty of sincere friendship to cover over a friend's wrong-
doing and put him right in a private letter. Nor should I ever have differed   160
from him in the New Testament, had I not supposed that by so doing no
reflection would be cast on his reputation. Though I myself have never
transgressed the rules of friendship, whatever damage or provocation I
might have suffered; nor, so far as in me lies, shall I ever do so. To lay down
one's life for one's friend is honourable; but for a friend's sake to be counted 165
a blasphemer against Christ is not only absolutely mad but grossly impious.
Suppose Lefèvre were my father or my brother, not my friend: you will not
consider even a father or a brother, I should suppose, worthy of such respect
that for his sake I should be willing to be thought an enemy of Christ. Why,
if Lefèvre had been at the same moment a cardinal and my own brother, I   170
take it that my duty would have been to rebut an intolerable calumny,
especially as I am in all ways free from guilt. Yet I rebut him in such a way as
to leave him in his defeat merely discourteous; irreligious I will not make
him, for I mean as far as I can to secure that no one should think any the
worse of my opponent.   175

Now, when you say that up to now we have fought valiantly for the
truth, and in future the business can easily be covered over, neither of us,
my dear Budé, has fought for the truth, for he made me out to be its

* * * * *

155 you say] Missing in the preserved text of Budé's letter; cf Ep 744 introduction.
176 you say] Ep 744:82–3

adversary, when I was on the same side as he. Nor do I disclose in my
Apologia what I think, for it was not necessary; I merely ward off the   180
weapons directed at me. Nor is there any hope that the affair can be covered
up for the future, since his books are already circulating in Spain, France,
Italy, Germany, and Britain, so it is no longer open to him to suppress what
he has written nor to me to pretend that I have not defended myself. Let him
alter, if he can, the passage in which he tears me to pieces, and I will do my   185
best to suppress the *Apologia* in which I stand up for myself. Do you wish
me to throw away my shield, though he has his sword in hand and is
waving it over my head? It is easy enough to lay down limits for another
man's resentment, easy to be mild and long-suffering in other people's
troubles. Perhaps if you were in my place you would think quite differently;   190
in fact, unless I have got my Budé quite wrong, your attitude would have
been very different – brandishing shield, sword, and spear to some purpose. Only think, my dear Budé, first of all how unpleasant is an accusation
of heresy and irreligion; then notice how often and in what unpleasant
language he lets fly at me, although I have so often mentioned him with   195
great respect; and then will your worship pray deliver your verdict, which
of us two was to be blamed, even if I had given him tit for tat, if I had used
my natural right of retaliation and rebutted his calumnies in the same
language. It would have been fair to lay the blame for the whole trouble at
the door of the man who struck the first blow and aimed it so shrewdly that,   200
if I did not defend myself, I should be leaving Augustine, Ambrose,
Athanasius, Chrysostom, and in a word all the orthodox Fathers, even
Jerome himself, defenceless against the same imputation as myself. For

* * * * *

203 Jerome] In his attack on Erasmus (cf Ep 597:37n) Lefèvre chose as a point of
departure a brief passage from the *Breviarium in Psalmos*, attributed to Jerome
but now considered apocryphal. Ps 8:6 says of the Son of Man: 'For Thou hast
made him a little lower than *elohim.*' The expression is repeated in Heb 2:7.
There it is taken to refer to Christ, and, according to all translations including
the Vulgate and Erasmus' own, *elohim* is identified with the angels. Lefèvre
objected that *elohim* could mean either the angels or God and pointed to the
Breviarium in Psalmos, where the translation 'God' was preferred (PL 26:888).
The other translation, Lefèvre thought, was incompatible with Christ's divine
nature. He may not have been aware of the fact that in his edition of Jerome
(Basel: Froben 1516, 1 f γ verso) Erasmus rejected the authenticity of the
Breviarium, but he ought to have realized that the exegetical tradition was
plainly opposed to his own understanding of the verse in Hebrews. In this
tradition Erasmus included Jerome's commentary on Gal 3:19 (PL 26:391–3).
Although Jerome did not refer to either Ps 8:6 or Heb 2:7, he did in fact
maintain that the angels could act in the place of God. This seemed sufficient
to Erasmus, who had not once claimed that Lefèvre's interpretation was
wrong, only that it was questionable.

Jerome, it is true, in a work of doubtful authenticity, does have a couple of
words which more or less support Lefèvre's view; but elsewhere, and   205
especially in his commentary on Galatians, he is openly on my side. When
the difference of opinion is a slight one, each man is welcome to his own
point of view; friendship should go for something, so should good manners. One should have leave to make mistakes and be corrected, and one
should have leave to disagree even when wrong. I will give no man an   210
opening to find me on this point wanting in common courtesy.

You yourself must remember, my dear Budé, the skirmishing between
us long ago, the characteristic banter you levelled at my 'trivialities,' and
how you overthrew my poor little pieces. So far am I from being moved by
this (though in your humorous way you pretended I was) that my affection   215
for you since has not been one hairsbreadth less. All the same, it is quite
true, as they say, that authors are indulgent to their own productions as
parents are to their children. There were people who urged me to defend my
Copia; I thought their zeal rather a joke and told them to cool down, assuring
them that you and I were of one mind. But Lefèvre's attack is a tragic   220
business, and I am astonished that he should enjoy commotions of this
kind; as he has done in his recent book on the three Magdalens and Christ's
three-day sojourn, as he calls it, in which he lays down the conditions of the
problem so strictly that he makes whoever supposes Christ to have risen
again after three days into an adversary of the Christian faith, the Gospels,   225
and every aspect of the truth. Yet that is how the world-wide church, Latin
and Greek alike, reads this passage in Mark. Nor was that passage ever read
or written with any other meaning, until Lefèvre opened this mystery and
taught us on the authority of Apollonius the grammarian that μετὰ τρεῖς
ἡμέρας means 'in three days,' as though there were any analogy between   230
μετὰ χεῖρας (in my hands) and μετὰ τρεῖς ἡμέρας (after three days). Let him
by all means be the first to have found something no one suspected: it
would have gone better with Christian humility and his own character to
have informed us in more moderate language. Not but what there's another
strange thing, while we are about it: that a man who definitely hates   235

* * * * *

213 long ago] Ep 435:74–94
217 authors] Cf Ep 531:601–2.
218 people] In Allen Ep 906:227, Erasmus specifies that they were German friends.
   One was Nesen (cf Ep 630:3); for other critics of Budé among Erasmus' friends
   cf Ep 869 and Bietenholz *Basle and France* 188–90.
222 book] Cf Ep 766:26n.
229 Apollonius] Apollonius Dyscolus, of Alexandria, second-century grammarian; quoted by Lefèvre in *De Maria Magdalena* (1517) f 44 verso

grammarians (did he not lately pour scorn on Bede for trying to solve a difficult question by appealing to grammar and bringing in a synecdoche?) should himself wish to explain a major difficulty by citing the authority of a single grammarian, without whose assistance the whole of Christendom in both liturgy and scripture would be entirely astray from the truth. Yet why   240
must we have all this sorry business, when a simple synecdoche might have made the whole thing clear, if we understand one who rose after daybreak on the third day to have risen 'after three days'? Lefèvre imagines it to be quite impossible that one who rose on the third day should be said to have risen 'after the third day,' though this could be disentangled by other   245
arguments as well, which there is no need to go into now.

But this is no particular business of mine, and I am more concerned for the risks he runs than for myself. But when I am attacked by name and described in print as 'an adversary of the glory of Christ,' for whose glory, unworthy sinner though I am, I would not shrink from mortal peril or death   250
itself, will you bid me keep silence? Tell me, in the name of all the Graces, which is it that you disapprove of, that I should defend myself at all, or the way in which I do it? If, being the fair-minded man you are, you do not disapprove of my defending myself, you cannot complain of the way I do it either, since I combine self-protection with doing all I can at the same time   255
to help my opponent. Why is it then that you think you must take me to task? Unless you judge it to be my destiny, unlike anyone else, to offer myself to be bullied and trodden on by everybody without reprisal, that hereafter there may be no dogs so cowardly that they dare not bark at Erasmus, no donkey so stupid that it is afraid to bray, no hog that hesitates   260
to squeal at him. Mice defend themselves as best they can with their teeth, bees when hurt ply their stings furiously; must I be the only creature without even the right to use my shield in self-defence, above all in a question touching the faith? Believe me, my dear Budé, he who can patiently endure to be accused of irreligion is religious only on the surface.   265
Look at the thunder and lightning with which Jerome rises in his wrath against Rufinus, who was once his dearest friend, simply because by some metaphorical expression of approval Rufinus had obliged him to share some responsibility for an unpopular view. Look at the temper with which

* * * * *

236 Bede] In *De Maria Magdalena* (1517) ff 35 verso–36 recto, Lefèvre quoted and criticized a text which he attributed to the Venerable Bede (based, it seems, on Bede's sermon II 4; PL 94:152–3). It stated that the difficulty was adequately explained by synecdoche.

261 Mice] Cf *Adagia* II v 31.

267 against Rufinus] Cf Jerome's *Apologia adversus libros Rufini*, PL 23:415–514, and for a fuller discussion Erasmus' Life of Jerome, *Opuscula* 134, 164–7.

he replies threateningly to Augustine because he had dared to pick to pieces   270
his explanation of a single passage. What if he had been soused with the
same vinegar poured on me by Lefèvre? Friend or foe, intentionally or
unintentionally, egged on by others or of his own accord, in joke or earnest,
sober or the reverse, these are questions for him to answer: vinegar it
undoubtedly was. The facts are all too obvious. I only wish we were both in   275
a position to deny them. Not that I am in any way to be compared with
Jerome, in holiness, learning, wisdom, or self-control; and yet you can see
how much more cruelly I have been attacked than he was, and how much
more restrained is my defence.

   'It is hard,' you say, 'to control one's pen in full spate.' That is not the   280
point. If I had said everything that I might have said with perfect justice,
you would understand how far I have reined in my resentment and given
moderation and courtesy full scope. 'It was a friend's duty to point this out,'
you say, 'for it must not look as though I had done nothing when a friend
was in difficulties.' What trouble is this, pray, if I defend myself against   285
palpable malice? Was my future secure, if I had gratefully accepted tributes
of the kind? Did you wish Jacques Lefèvre to be given so much consideration that for his benefit I must endure to be called a blasphemer against
Christ? Certainly, as far as the question at issue goes, I am home and dry,
even in the opinion of less than impartial judges. I only hope that in this   290
department Lefèvre could make out as good a case before the world for his
honesty and fairness of mind as I should wish he might. Those who take his
part with the most friendly feelings explain that he was put up to it, egged
on by I know not whom, by those who have no love for either him or me. As
though that sort of excuse could carry any weight in a man who is a scholar   295
and a thinker, a man of mature years; above all, when the accusation is so
vicious! But I fear that more people will subscribe to the opinion of those
who repeat that these head-in-air tirades stem partly from a supreme
contempt for me and partly from admiration for himself. He had persuaded
himself, they say, that I was only a hack writer: he was philosopher,   300
theologian, hierophant, whose every word was like an oracle. Such a man
could write nothing, in his most careless moments, that would not plunge
me at once in Cimmerian obscurity. He should have remembered that

* * * * *

270 Augustine] Cf Jerome's long Ep 112 (PL 22:916–31), resulting mostly from a
    controversy over the interpretation of Gal 2:11–14; cf Ep 956 end.
271 soused] *Adagia* II iii 52
280 you say] Ep 744:88
284 you say] Ep 744:92–3
289 home and dry] Literally 'my voyage is already in harbour'; *Adagia* I i 46
303 Cimmerian] *Adagia* II vi 34

nothing in warfare is more perilous than complete contempt for the enemy, weak though he may be.   305

Others again suggest that his feelings were hurt because I was bold enough to disagree with him in some passages in my *Annotationes* and like a cuttle-fish he squirted this ink over me by way of reply; repaid me, in other words, with the height of contumely for a service for which he should have been grateful. But surely, if he has leave to differ from Augustine, Ambrose,   310 Jerome, and in a word from all ancient and authoritative opinion, am I not to have leave to differ, even with respect, from Lefèvre? Are these to be the terms on which one writes, that whoever differs from Lefèvre has the Gospels and the sacred texts against him? An honourable mind confronted with evident mistakes might be expected to thank the man who had pointed   315 them out – and pointed them out not only gently and with moderation but with expressions of respect. And yet he does not either apologize or defend himself, even in a personal letter, although I have made the first move two or three times; indeed, he is said to be breathing threats of some kind, exactly as though he were the injured party. How much more straightfor-   320 ward have I been myself! I gave him due notice in writing of my *Apologia* before I began to write it, and when it was finished I sent it to him at once through someone at the Sorbonne, with a covering letter that at the time seemed to meet the case.

Nor do I think there is any danger that it will be thought inconsistent if   325 I now refute Lefèvre, whom I have praised so often. For one thing, it must be considered his fault, not mine, if I were to differ from my former self, now that he himself has begun to be so different. The man who handed him my *Apologia* wrote and told me that when it reached Lefèvre he accused me of disloyalty. If it is a sign of disloyalty to rebut a false accusation with   330 courtesy, what name shall we find for him who attacks a friend out of ambush like this? I only wish he had left me free to be constant to myself and praise him continually more and more. Not that I recant the laudatory things I have said about him; no, nor can I yet alter my opinion of him either; I simply wonder what has happened to the man. And in the end, any   335 man who defends himself must not *ipso facto* be taken as attacking the other party. To repel force with force is any man's right. Only, when the Christian

* * * * *

307 *Annotationes*] See Ep 597:37n, 44n.
308 cuttle-fish] *Adagia* II ii 55
321 notice in writing] Not mentioned elsewhere. Erasmus sent such warnings to common friends (cf Epp 627–8) but only after the composition of the *Apologia ad Fabrum*. Other missing letters to Lefèvre mentioned in the *Apologia* (LB IX 20A) were dated before Erasmus had seen Lefèvre's attack.
323 covering letter] Ep 659

faith is in question, it is actually impious to abandon the cause to one's
opponents. I did not insist on your opinion, perhaps because I saw clearly
that the question was outside your field, perhaps because I knew you were   340
very busy and did not wish to add to your burdens, perhaps in order not to
put you in the most unpleasant position of being arbitrator between two
friends and so obliged to give offence to one of them. I only wish it had been
entirely in my power to secure that no mortal man should be more unfriendly to Lefèvre for my sake or that he should be no more prejudiced   345
against anyone.

    If however, my dear Budé, you are not unwilling to undertake the
hearing of this case although, as I say, it is not entirely within your
bailiwick, go ahead: I do not reject your jurisdiction, provided you inform
yourself thoroughly of the whole course of the affair, which means reading   350
my *Apologia* not idly and 'in snippets,' as you say you have done, but with
proper attention. Otherwise I shall not be afraid to lodge an appeal. 'Appeal
from what and to whom,' you will say, 'when you have entrusted the
decision to me of your own accord?' Appeal from Budé half asleep to Budé
with his wits about him. In any case, I hear that many people everywhere   355
complain of my writing against Lefèvre, but mainly those who never
glanced at his attack on me or my reply to it. If they are indignant because I
defend myself against Lefèvre when forced to do so, why are they not for
preference indignant with him, since he attacked me first and without
excuse? Is it unfriendly to hold a shield for protection over one's vital parts, 360
and yet friendly to attack an old friend with poisoned weapons? If your
object is to reconcile us after our difference of opinion, as far as I am
concerned you will not find it difficult. A man is easily reconciled who was
reluctant to quarrel in the first place. It is easy to pacify someone who has no
wish to be angry, and indeed is not angry at all except with his own destiny.   365
I wish I had been allowed to maintain our friendship unbroken. As it is – the
next best thing – I have many reasons for wishing to make it up again: it is
unseemly in principle to disagree with someone with whom you are linked
by a close relationship, and I should not wish this affair to become a cause of
dissension anywhere, should strong feelings make men take sides, as   370
usually happens. I should much prefer that in accordance with the rights of
friendship we should share our friends mutually, and thus each of us
double his most valuable possession. There are hardly any terms I would
reject. Let him arrange, as I said, to suppress his criticism, and I in turn will
allow my *Apologia* to be done away with; or, if that is too much to hope for,   375
let him exchange cursing for blessing and make all well by recanting his

* * * * *

351 you say] Ep 744:76

attacks. Or at least let him clear himself in a letter to me; or, if that likewise is too much, let him declare that we are now on good terms, no matter what evil genius aroused that earlier storm. He will find me by no means hard to please. There is only one condition I will not accept – if he insists that I   380
suppress my *Apologia* while his attack remains unquestioned.

I had heard of your brother's death in a letter from Bade and feel it strongly for two reasons: because he was your brother and therefore, by the rights of friendship, mine, and because, as you say in your letter, he thought very well of me. Busleyden's benefaction and the Collegium   385
Trilingue is going forward nicely. It is a more splendid affair than I had thought, for more than twenty thousand francs are earmarked for the purpose. Would that this precedent may find plenty to imitate it! Here's a long letter for you, and tedious too, so you must not complain that my letters are mere notes, shorter than the direction written on the other side.   390
Farewell, my most learned Budé.

From Louvain, 22 February

779 / To Pierre Vitré   [Louvain? c 22 February 1518?]

This letter to a former student (see Ep 66) who taught at a college in Paris was printed in the *Farrago*. Allen's tentative date is based on the assumption that before 1517 Erasmus could hardly have been expected to carry weight with Etienne Poncher (cf Ep 522) and that this letter must be later than Ep 528, which answered both Epp 444 and 503 from Vitré. In Ep 768:15–18 Erasmus inquired after Vitré, so this may be the answer to a letter he received in reply to his inquiry. The matter raised in this letter called for another speedy reply from Vitré; this explains the surprise Erasmus expresses at his silence in Ep 817, where he advises Vitré of his forthcoming move to Basel.

ERASMUS TO HIS MOST LEARNED FRIEND PIERRE VITRÉ,
GREETING

It was a happy result, my dear Vitré, that my protest, such as it was, should extract from you such a long and friendly letter. Your feelings towards me over the years I cannot recall without pleasure. I am glad to hear you are in   5
good health. That you should be distracted by so much tedious business I should regret, were it not of a kind in which a truly Christian spirit would gladly be engaged until the day of his death. But I congratulate you on the

* * * * *

385 Collegium Trilingue] See Ep 691 introduction.
389 must not complain] Cf Ep 744:13–14.

manly courage that can support such labours, for your warm heart supplies
what strength of body may be lacking. I must tell you that your last letter   10
never reached me. If you will let me know in what context you want a
recommendation to Etienne Poncher, bishop of Paris, I will do what you
require with speed. Please thank Doctor Beaune, the dean of Tours, most
warmly for his greetings. I should be wicked if I did not like a man who does
so much for the humanities and for virtue, and ungrateful if I did not   15
reciprocate the feelings of one who without prompting offers me his
friendship. Farewell, dearest Vitré.

    151[7]

780 / From Richard Sampson   Tournai, 2 March 1518

This letter was printed in the *Auctarium* together with Erasmus' answer, Ep
806. Sampson (see Ep 388:38n) was a friend from Cambridge times. His
modesty here is exaggerated, since he was well educated and on his way to
high office. For the contest over the see of Tournai see Ep 360. Sampson's
administration on behalf of Cardinal Wolsey ended with the English with-
drawal from Tournai after the Universal Peace of October 1518; cf Ep 964.

RICHARD SAMPSON, COMMISSARY OF THE
MOST REVEREND THE CARDINAL OF YORK AMONG THE NERVII,
TO HIS DEAR ERASMUS, GREETING
If you were familiar with English, or I had any other language in which I
might converse with you in an exchange of letters, dear Erasmus, beyond all   5
dispute most brilliant stylist of our age, I would certainly not send you a
Latin letter; for I well know that there is no one, unless he is either foolhardy
or a master of style, who is not afraid to write in Latin to a man like you who
can be compared with the most eloquent authors of antiquity. Such is the
reverence everyone feels for your exceptional learning; such, too, the extent   10
to which the brilliance of your pen and your more than human and ency-
clopaedic knowledge have conferred on you a kind of majesty peculiar to
yourself.

    * * * * *

779
13 Beaune] Martin de Beaune, d 1527. He was a son of the powerful Jacques de
    Beaune, baron of Semblançay, and of Jeanne Ruzé. In 1513 he became dean,
    and in 1520 archbishop, of Tours; cf DHGE.

780
2 Nervii] In Caesar's time one of the principal tribes of what is now Belgium,
    here standing for the diocese of Tournai

Nor would I on this occasion have written to you in Latin, being an ignoramus and, as far as polite literature is concerned, a complete new- 15 comer, had you not simply driven me to it. For in your last letter to my friend Johannes de Molendino (which he gave me to read three days ago), you told him to give me your greetings and thought fit to describe me as not merely a benefactor but your very special benefactor; which covered me with shame, though in other respects I was delighted with everything. 20 Everyone knows that you are very much *persona grata* (such is your emi-nence as a scholar) with actual kings and princes, and that among them it is the greatest and the best who are your keenest supporters. Pray therefore in future do not embarrass me, who am more insignificant than most men, with so proud a title. You have, if you need them, benefactors or supporters 25 or persons devoted to you not only in positions of great authority but among the most learned of scholars everywhere. If however my assistance, such as it is, can ever be of service to you, please be assured that among all your friends you will find no one more anxious to help than myself. So I should like you to regard me as a friend to the utmost of my power, 30 provided you are kind enough to admit such a minor figure to the list of your friends. Although such is your kindness that I am quite sure you will not despise a man so far inferior to you; for so far are we from being brought up in the same school, as the saying goes, that I am almost uneducated and you are by common consent the leading figure among all men alive today – 35 which I for my part regard as superior to all other distinctions.

Nor can I fail to be devoted to you, being well aware that all my best friends regard you with equal devotion. I enjoy exceptional kindness from the illustrious Lord Mountjoy, and he is, as you know, very much attached to you. I pass over Tunstall, so courteous, so wise, such a good scholar. Pace 40 needs no words from me, for besides his learning he is such a friendly person that one could not hope to find anyone more agreeable and charm-ing, and he beyond others is my friend and benefactor and supporter; for he has at the moment great influence both with the king and with my lord cardinal. It would be wrong not to mention my friend More – everybody's 45 friend, rather, for the quality both of his learning and of his natural wit must be obvious to anyone who is prepared to read his *Utopia* or his other works. I say nothing of his charm in daily life, his courtesy and most amusing conversation, and his outstandingly high character. You see what sort of friends I share with you; but sharing does not mean that you owe them to 50

* * * * *

16 letter] Ep 755:34
40 Pace] See Ep 619 introduction.

me. Not but what you are sufficient all by yourself to absorb all my affection. Farewell.

From Tournai, 2 March 1518

781 / To [William Warham?]   Louvain, 5 March 1518

> This letter is clearly addressed to an English prelate. He cannot be Fisher because of Ep 784. Warham was suggested in LB and has been accepted since, although this letter does not refer to the matters discussed in Ep 782, which would have confirmed the attribution (but cf Allen Ep 892:20–1). Moreover, it ends with the formula TRD (*tua reverendissima dominatio*), which at this period Erasmus mostly employs in letters (except dedicatory epistles) to cardinals, but not to other prelates. He usually addresses Wolsey in this way, but Warham only in Epp 893, 1205. In his struggle for Tournai, Wolsey would have had plausible reasons for presenting a horse to Antoon van Bergen (lines 33–4), but Warham had none, it would seem. On the other hand, the absence of flattery and the references to Ecclesiastes, to the crusade (cf Epp 893, 1228), and especially to Grocyn rather point to Warham. Cf Ep 772 introduction.

Greeting, most reverend Prelate, sole glory and bulwark of my studies. Poets divide their plays into five acts. For me only the fifth act of this comedy remains, and would that I might play it out in such a way as may win the applause of all good men, and above all that Christ, who is the one great producer of the play, may approve. I am off either to Venice or to Basel, 5 either of them a long and dangerous journey, especially through Germany, which besides her long history of robberies is now exposed to the plague; it has already carried off Lachner, the head of the Froben press, and many others. If I go to Italy, I shall need more money for my journey to meet the unexpected accidents which always occur. I have it in mind to enlarge my 10 library with some good books, for new ones are published in Italy every day. I am obliged to attend to the New Testament. It is a complicated business, and, unless I am there, nothing would go right. Wherever in the world I am, I shall be your devoted protégé. If I return safely, I am thinking of moving to England as a secret and remote retreat; and I am confident that 15

* * * * *

781
5 Venice or Basel] See Ep 770 introduction.
8 Lachner] He died on 27 January 1518, but apparently not of the plague (see Epp 801–2; AK II Epp 601–2). Erasmus was well aware of the financial and managerial problems which his death posed for the Froben press; cf Epp 594:5n, 786:16, 794:69–70, 795, 885.

your generosity would add to such resources as I have, for old age approaches daily, and every day I understand better and better the last chapter of Ecclesiastes. If I am not so fortunate as to return, it will be good to be occupied at the hour of death in what is surely a work of piety. Grocyn's disaster distresses me, of course. I could wish for such gifts the fate they   20
deserve, that they should never feel either old age or death. But thus it seemed good to the heavenly powers. We bear around with us this sacred fire, like the Vestals of old, in vessels of clay; and somehow they seem most exposed to the troubles of mortality who most deserve to be immortal.

As to the war against the Turks, I would rather say nothing of the   25
preparations. If I mistake not, the pretext is one thing and the purpose another. From Switzerland I hear that the object is to drive the Spaniards out of Naples. Lorenzo, the pope's nephew, is trying to seize Campania, having married a daughter of the king of Navarre. This does not altogether escape the Swiss, stolid as they are; but everywhere money can do every-   30
thing. In heaven's name, when shall we see an end to these most unChristian quarrels between Christians?

How I wish I now had a horse like the one you once sent through me to the Abbot of St Bertin! Some people are surprised that at my age I can face such a journey; but I wonder more at the bishop of Paris, who is about   35
seventy and undertakes more laborious journeys on business which I think much less important. Please be kind to the bearer of this, who is my servant,

* * * * *

18 Ecclesiastes] Cf 12:7, 8, 12.
20 disaster] He had suffered a stroke and died in June or July 1519.
23 vessels of clay] Cf Ep 784:51.
25 Turks] Cf 729:56n.
28 nephew] Lorenzo de' Medici, 1492–1519, duke of Urbino. The garbled reference is to his marriage (negotiated in January and celebrated on 28 April 1518) to Madeleine de la Tour d'Auvergne, a relative of Francis I and subsequently mother of Catherine de' Medici. Several alternative matches had been discussed, among them one with a daughter of Jean d'Albret, king of Navarre. From this evidence of improved relations between France and Leo X arose the suspicion that Naples rather than the crusade was the goal of the pope's new diplomatic initiative. That similar fears were common in Germany is shown by an anonymous pamphlet (see Hutten *Opera* v 168–75) and by the urgent denials of papal diplomats; see H. Ulmann *Kaiser Maximilian I* (Stuttgart 1891) II 709, 713–15. Like Cardinal Matthäus Schiner, the Basel humanists such as Bonifacius Amerbach were politically opposed to France and to the Franco-Swiss alliance (cf Ep 619:13n and Bietenholz *Basle and France* 105–6).
34 St Bertin] Cf Ep 477:33–4.
35 Paris] Etienne Poncher, b c 1446; for his embassy cf Ep 744:40n.

and send him back soon, so that he does not keep me waiting. And continue
your favour to my humble self. I shall never think myself unfortunate as
long as you are with us. Best wishes to your Grace, to whom I am entirely   40
devoted.

Louvain, 5 March 1518

782 / To [Thomas Bedyll]   [Louvain, c 5 March 1518]

> Cf Ep 772 and for the financial transactions Ep 823 introduction. That War-
> ham's secretary is being addressed is shown by a comparison with Epp 823,
> 892.

Greeting. A plague on that fever which has upset all my business. Franz
returned here bringing no money and no letter. Sixtinus wrote that the
money had been paid in cash against his guarantee. Franz says this is not
so, Potkyn excusing himself because the receipt was not right in law. In
future I shall entrust none of my business to natives of Gelderland or thirsty   5
men with one eye; though I never entrusted anything to either, but it was
done against my orders by Pieter Gillis. But I cannot be angry with him,
partly as an old friend, and partly because he is sick. Anyhow we must go
through with it now we have started.

I suppose your mallow long ago relieved your fever. I am setting off on   10
a long and dangerous journey, but in a pious cause, if I mistake not, in
which one would be content to die, if it must be so. Continue to be what you
always are. Please send me a letter by my servant, the bearer of this, with all
your news in detail, and lend him anything he may need. Farewell.

I badly need one suitable horse that can stand hard work for me to ride;   15
your advice on this too will be welcome. I have thoughts, when this act of
my comedy is finished, of retiring to England. This I should do the more
readily if my generous patron were to produce a small increase in my
resources, such as they are. Do what you can to promote this. Farewell once
more.   20

* * * * *

782
4 Potkyn] William Potkyn, a notary public serving Archbishop Warham. He
  died after 20 October 1538; see *Faculty Office Registers, 1534–49* ed D.S.
  Chambers (Oxford 1966) 92, 152.
5 Gelderland] Johannes Sixtinus; his letter was probably brought back by one-
  eyed Meghen.

783 / To [William Blount, Lord Mountjoy]   [Louvain, c 5 March 1518]

Cf Ep 772 introduction. The married English patron addressed is clearly
Mountjoy, 'best of patrons' (line 1; cf Epp 888, 965) and 'Maecenas of longest
standing' (lines 34–5; cf Ep 829:4–5).

Greeting, best of patrons. I am preparing to set out for either Basel or
Venice. This will be the last act of my comedy. I know it is a very long
journey, but it is even more perilous, and that for several reasons. In
Germany besides the usual robberies there is plague to deter me. Do all you
can, I beg you, my dear benefactor, to secure me a handsome present from   5
the royal bounty; the king will find that the recipient is not ungrateful. And
let it happen soon, so that I do not have to wait for my servant when I am all
ready to set out. I should not dare to trouble you, and should be quite
content with your known feelings towards me, except that everything here
is a matter of ready cash. You will say, 'Then why not run over here   10
yourself?' First because it is essential that I should be there to see this book
through the press. And then circumstances obliged me to stay here longer,
on account of the theologians, who would have stirred up no end of trouble
for me, had I not been here in person. When this act is played out, I have it
in mind to move to England as one of the furthest recesses of the world, and   15
there amuse my old age with easier and more agreeable work. If you regard
me as a dependant who earns his keep, pray show yourself the benefactor
you always were.

　　Richard Pace has caricatured me in his book as a poor starveling,
though anyone might almost take me for a Midas. If this is my reputation,   20
some of it is to be laid at your door. But do not take these remarks of mine
seriously, as long as in all seriousness I can escape these jibes. I receive
invitations on all sides from persons of the greatest eminence, the bishop of
Utrecht, their lordships of Liège and Mainz; but I have little use for hope
deferred. From Spain I am told I may expect something more reliable.   25

　　Do not be afraid to burden the young man who brings this letter with
money. He will deposit it with the bankers on Sixtinus' advice. I need a
convenient horse, but as a dealer in horseflesh you are not usually very
successful; still, give me any help you can. My *Chiliades* are finished in a

* * * * *

783
　1 Basel or Venice] See Ep 770 introduction.
　19 book] See Ep 776:4n.
　23 invitations] See Epp 621:32–3, 661, 728, 746.
　25 Spain] See Ep 608:19n.
　29 *Chiliades*] The *Adagia* (Basel: Froben 1517–18)

new edition, and will appear at the next fair. Farewell, you and your   30
charming wife and your dear children.

Whether I will or no, I must publish two or three books of my letters; if
you possess any, let the bearer have them. I will not publish them except
after any necessary corrections. Farewell again, my Maecenas of longest
standing.   35

784 / To [John Fisher]   [Louvain, c 5 March 1518]

Cf Ep 772 introduction. Fisher's name is not given in the Deventer Letter-book
(see Ep 653 introduction), but the references in lines 10–11, 44–5, 51–2 leave
no doubt that the letter is addressed to him.

Greeting, reverend Father. I am again preparing for a journey, though sore
against my will, in order to see to the printing of my New Testament, newly
revised and now fuller and more accurate. It could not escape my notice that
things would go very badly unless I were there in person. I beg you, of your
piety, if there is anything of which you think I should be aware, to let me   5
know in a letter by the bearer of this, whom I have sent partly for this
purpose and who will return to me without delay. As far as I was able, I have
corrected what needed correction, though I shall never succeed, I imagine,
in satisfying all the Dominicans. If you have finished with what I sent by
Pieter the One-eyed, send it back by the bearer, who is my servant. If you   10
think well to write to Reuchlin, I will see that he gets it. As I am to undertake
a very long journey (for I have to go to Venice, or at least to Basel), I have
need of a suitable horse not afraid of hard work. If you have anything of the
sort to spare, it would be a great service if you would send it with the bearer
of this. This winter has seemed to me to be of enormous length, so much so   15

* * * * *

31 wife ... children] Some years previously Mountjoy had married his third wife,
   Alice (d 1521), daughter of Sir Henry Kebel. He had a daughter and a son by
   his first wife and a son by Alice; see *The Complete Peerage* ed V. Gibbs et al
   (London 1910ff) sv Mountjoy.
33 have them] A similar request was made to More (cf Ep 785); a number of early
   letters to both were published, but only in the *Farrago* of October 1519, not in
   the *Auctarium* of August 1518.

784
9 Dominicans] For other critical statements cf the indexes of this edition.
9 what I sent] Apart from the Gaza manuscript (cf line 44) taken to Fisher along
   with Ep 653, certain pamphlets concerning the Reuchlin affair had been sent to
   him, apparently on one of Meghen's earlier trips; see Ep 653:22–3.
11 Reuchlin] Cf Epp 432, 457.

that partly with boredom and partly with overwork I have almost put an end
to myself. There remains the last act of the play and, I suspect, of life itself.
After that, I intend to go into retirement and sing to myself and the Muses;
for I have no mind to strive for ever with these noisy rascals. I wanted my
work to be some use, so far as my limited talents would allow; and I should   20
not regret my labours if my prayer were answered.

Not a word of answer from Lefèvre, not even in a private letter. But I
hear that he has taken umbrage at my *Apologia*; as though such reverence
was owed to his authority that when attacked like that I had to keep my
mouth shut. And yet I held my righteous anger on a tight rein and made   25
great sacrifices to our friendship or to Christian humility. You know how
Jerome thunders against Rufinus, simply because he had been praised by
him metaphorically. Lefèvre in a published book represents me as 'under-
mining the understanding of prophecy,' 'degrading the glory of Christ with
contumely,' 'siding with blasphemous Jews,' 'saying things unworthy of   30
Christ and of God,' 'clinging fast to the flesh and opposing the spirit,'
'writing things mutually destructive from every point of view, worthy of
Bedlam many times over'; he is the defender of Christ's dignity, and I, if
you please, am his opponent; and am I not to be allowed to answer? Lefèvre
may be a religious and mild-mannered man and an old friend, but these   35
things appear in his books and he admits he wrote them. If they are not
there, let them say I have lost my head; if they are there and much more like
them, it would be a good idea to see whether I deserve any of them. If I do
deserve them, let them show where I went wrong; if I do not, they ought to
keep their indignation for Lefèvre, who made such a bitter and insidious   40
attack on a personal friend, and not for me, who merely defend myself with
my shield and do not go for him with my own weapons, as in common
equity at any rate I had the right to do.

I sent you Theodore's second book before. Now I send it you again in
print, which will make it easier to read; for I know my paraphrase is already   45
in circulation in your part of the world. I was surprised that our one-eyed
friend, by whom I sent it, did not bring back any letter from you. Grocyn's
misfortune, heaven knows, distresses me sincerely, though our relations

* * * * *

18 sing] Cf Ep 731:44.
27 Jerome] See Ep 778:267n.
28 Lefèvre] For his charges against Erasmus cf Ep 659:6n; for criticism of Eras-
    mus' *Apologia ad Fabrum* see Epp 721 introduction, 742:9n.
44 second book] In manuscript; cf Ep 771 introduction. For the *Paraphrasis ad
    Romanos* see Ep 710 introduction.
47 Grocyn's misfortune] See Ep 781:20n, and for a hint of strained relations Ep
    350.

were not all they might be. I wish men of such gifts could be spared death
and old age; but so it seemed good to the powers above. We carry round this   50
treasure in earthen vessels, vessels of glass rather. The problem of the
genealogy of Christ I know to be insoluble, nor does it properly belong to
my undertaking; and I am not really satisfied with what I have collected out
of Annius, who as a scholar, I rather suspect, is rash and pompous, and in
any case a Dominican. And so, if you have discovered anything, please   55
make a note of it, so that my servant, who will pay you his respects if he can,
may bring it back with him when he returns. I gave him for the expenses of
his journey as much as I thought he would need; but if he should run short,
your Lordship's kindness will, I know, be ready to help him. I have dangled
plenty of bait before the king, and plenty before the most reverend his alter   60
ego, and yet that line catches nothing. If it does not work now, I shall risk
neither hook nor bait next time. As I have said, I must play out my part; and
when the play is finished, I have a mind to retire from this accursed world.
The cunning of princes and the effrontery of the Roman curia can go no
further; and it looks as though the state of the common people would soon   65
be such that the tyranny of the Grand Turk would be more bearable. I shall
turn therefore entirely to you, as to a people on the edge of the world, and
perhaps the least infected province of Christianity. If this does not succeed,
at least I shall with a more quiet mind meet death engaged on a religious
work, if I mistake not.   70

785 / To Thomas More   Louvain, 5 March 1518

Cf Ep 772 introduction.

ERASMUS TO HIS FRIEND MORE, GREETING
In the first place, may I ask you to give the bearer of this, my man John, any

* * * * *

51 earthen vessels] Cf 2 Cor 4:7, Ep 781:23.
52 genealogy] Cf Ep 324.
54 Annius] Giovanni Nanni, called Annius of Viterbo, 1432–1502, famous for his
    collection of fragments by ancient writers, many of which were spurious. His
    Antiquitatum variarum auctores (first published in 1498) contained Pseudo-
    Philo's *Liber antiquitatum Biblicarum*, a genuine text of the first century AD
    (critical edition by Guido Kisch, Notre Dame, Ind. 1949; English translation
    by M.R. James, London 1917). It has several chapters on the genealogy of the
    early patriarchs, and Erasmus turned to it when working on the genealogy of
    Christ as given in Luke 3:23–38; cf Epp 324:17, 886 end.
60 bait] Cf Ep 657 introduction. The king's alter ego is Wolsey.
64 effrontery] Cf Epp 775:6–9, 781:28n.

letters of mine or yours which you think suitable for publication after any
necessary changes; for publish I must willy-nilly. Dispatch the young man
so that he returns as soon as possible. If you think Urswick has any feeling   5
against me, perhaps I should not trouble him. If not, give me your help to
get a horse; for I need one badly at this moment, having to set off for Basel or
Venice, mainly to see to the printing of my New Testament. Such, my dear
More, is my destiny. But I will play my part in this last act. After that, I am
almost determined to make music to myself and the Muses, as my age and   10
state of health, which goes downhill day by day, almost demand. Such is
the tyranny here of worthless fellows in disguise. No one here makes any
money except inn-keepers, lawyers, and tax-gatherers. Who can endure a
place where many speak evil, none do good?

Those people in Basel are very apologetic about your *Utopia*, which was   15
delayed for the elegant preface provided by Budé. They have now had it and
have set to work. Lachner, who was then Froben's father-in-law, has died;
but none the less the Froben press will toil away at the product of our
studies. Linacre's *Therapeutice* I have not yet been able to see, there being
some sort of conspiracy against us in Paris. Speak to Lupset politely about   20
the appendix to my *Copia*, and let me have it.

The pope and the princes have several new plays in rehearsal, using as
a pretext a frightful war against the Turks. I am sorry for those Turks! We
Christians must not grow too fierce. Even the wives are affected. All married men will be compelled to bear arms who are under fifty and over   25
twenty-six. In the mean time the pope forbids the wives of those who are
away at the war to give themselves a good time at home; they must not wear

* * * * *

785
3 letters] Cf Ep 783:33n.
5 Urswick] Cf Ep 786:54–7.
10 Muses] Cf Ep 731:44n.
11 downhill] Erasmus refers to the story of Mandrabulus, whose offerings to Juno
were gold the first year, silver the next, and after that, bronze (*Adagia* I ii 58,
citing Lucian).
16 preface] Cf Ep 664:31n. Froben's *Utopia* appeared in March 1518, in time for
the Frankfurt spring fair; see Luther *Werke* (Weimar), Briefwechsel I Ep 60.
17 Lachner] See Ep 781:8n.
19 *Therapeutice*] See Ep 755:32n.
21 appendix] See Ep 690:8n.
22 new plays] The source of the following details has not been traced. We cannot
know how individual preachers explained and embellished the statements
issued from Rome, but some of Erasmus' remarks sound rather like a joke at
the expense of traditional crusading concepts and of More's well-known
devotion to married life; cf Ep 729:56n.

fashionable dress, there must be no silk, gold, or jewelry, they must not
touch rouge or drink wine, and they must fast every other day, in order to
win God's blessing for their husbands engaged in such a bloody war. If any   30
of the men are detained at home by necessary duties, their wives none the
less must observe the same rules as they would have observed if their
husbands had gone. They may sleep in the same room, but it must be in
different beds; nor may they exchange kisses until by the mercy of Christ
this terrible war is successfully concluded. I know this will be intolerable to   35
many wives who do not properly consider the great issues at stake; though I
know that your wife is so sensible and so devoted to the advance of the
Christian religion that she would obey, and gladly too.

I send you Pace's book, the Conclusions on Papal pardons, and the
Proposals for a Crusade against the Turks, as I suspect they may not yet have   40
reached your part of the world. They write to me from Cologne that some
pamphlet has lately been printed about a dispute between Pope Julius and
Peter at the gate of Paradise; the author's name they do not give. The
German presses have gone mad and will be so until their rashness is
controlled by law; and this will do great harm to me, even, who try to be   45
some use to the world. I am quite astonished that neither Franz nor Pieter
the One-eyed should have brought me any letters.

Please allow my servant to sleep one or two nights in your household,
so that he does not find his way to an infected house; and if he needs

* * * * *

37 wife] Alice Middleton
39 Pace's book] See Ep 776:4n.
39 Conclusions] No doubt the famous Ninety-five Theses which Luther had
   posted on the north door of the castle church at Wittenberg on 31 October 1517.
   Erasmus probably sent the first Basel printing of late 1517. It was the first to be
   published as a quarto pamphlet rather than a folio poster and the first to add a
   title: Disputatio ... pro declaratione virtutis indulgentiarum; cf J. Benzing Luther-
   bibliographie (Baden-Baden 1966) No 89; H. Volz M. Luthers Thesenanschlag
   und dessen Vorgeschichte (Weimar 1959) 46–8, 131–8. That Erasmus did not
   mention Luther's name may be an indication that he was not yet familiar with
   it; cf Epp 872, Allen 916:285–91, 933, Allen 967:95–6.
40 Proposals] Cf Leonis decimi consultationes pro expeditione contra Thurcum (issued 12 November 1517) [Augsburg: J. Miller, early 1518] published by A.
   Pucci (see Ep 860 introduction) with an appeal dated from Zürich, 6 December
   1517 (both reprinted in Hutten Opera v).
42 Julius] This is the earliest specific reference to a printed version of the Julius
   exclusus. A Cologne edition was also mentioned by Wilhelm Nesen in June
   1518 (see AK II Ep 617). The earliest editions of this satire are entirely anonymous and difficult to date. For a list see Opuscula 55–64. For Erasmus' desire to
   see anonymous pamphlets suppressed by authority of the law cf Ep 1053.

SANCTISSIMI DOMI
NI NOSTRI PAPAE LEONIS DE:
CIMI, VNA CVM COETV CAR
DINALIVM, CHRISTIANIS:
SIMORVMQVE REGVM,

& principũ oratorum cõsultati:

ones, pro expeditiõe cõtra

Thurcũ. premiſſa tñ

dñi. A. Puccij

apoſtolice ſe

dis legati

exhorta

tione.

Leo x *Consultationes pro expeditione contra Thurcum* title page
Augsburg: J. Miller 1518
Courtesy of the British Library Board

anything, let him have it, though I myself gave him his journey-money.   50
Please take special care to get permission for the export of three horses, even
though perhaps I may not have the luck to find one. Read Budé's letter and
my reply. I have at last seen the Paris print of your *Utopia*, but it is full of
mistakes. It is now in the press at Basel; for I had told them there would be
trouble unless they were more diligent in that business than they are in   55
mine. Farewell, my most sincere friend.

> Louvain, 5 March 1518

786 / To John Colet   [Louvain, c 5 March 1518]

Cf Ep 772 introduction.

TO COLET

Greeting, my respected teacher. I was surprised and sorry that the One-eyed
arrived with no letter from you. He passed on a complaint from you that I
never write. On the contrary, I have, I think, already explained to you why I
write short and seldom, and I am happy to think you have plenty of time,   5
that you should demand frequent long ones. Believe me, my dear Colet, I
am interrupted here by so many letters from bishops, noblemen, scholars,
friends, in Italy, Spain, Germany, France, that, if I had nothing else to do, I
should not be able to cope with this one task. I can return the affection of all
my friends, but reply individually to their letters I cannot.   10
    I was sincerely sorry to hear of Grocyn's illness, whatever his attitude
to me. How unfair it is! Gifts like his should suffer neither old age nor death;
and these troubles afflict all the more those who deserve to be immortal. I
am obliged for the printing of my New Testament and other reasons to go
either to Basel or, what seems more likely, to Venice. For I am put off Basel   15

* * * * *

51 horses] By an act of 1495 – II Henry VII chapter 13; cf *Statutes of the Realm II*
   (London 1816) 578–9 – the export of horses had been restricted. Erasmus
   addressed requests for a horse to Warham, Mountjoy, Fisher (Epp 781–4), and
   indirectly to Urswick (cf line 5; Ep 786:54–7). He also asked Richard Pace to
   help (Ep 787:18–20). John Smith brought back with him one horse donated, it
   would seem, by More himself rather than those approached. It arrived in unfit
   condition but apparently recovered and was still serving Erasmus on his
   return journey from Basel in the autumn; cf Epp 829:2–4, Allen 867:28–30.
52 Read] Ep 744, recently arrived and answered by Ep 778. Presumably copies
   were sent to More with this letter.
53 Paris print] Cf Ep 664:31n.

786
11 Grocyn's] Cf Ep 784:47–8.
15 Venice] See Ep 770 introduction.

partly by the plague and partly by the death of Lachner, at whose expense
the work was mainly published. What, you say, an old man and an invalid
like you undertake such a journey, and that in an age like ours, the most
lawless for many centuries, with robbery so common everywhere? But what
would you? Such is the destiny to which I was born. If I die at my work, it   20
will be at work not wholly bad, if I mistake not. If, after finishing the last act
of this play as I would wish, I am so lucky as to return, I have decided to
spend the remainder of my life with you. This will be my retreat from the
corruption of the whole world. Theologians in disguise hold sway in all the
courts of princes. The Roman curia has abandoned any sense of shame.   25
What could be more shameless than these constant indulgences? And now
they put up war against the Turks as a pretext, when their aim really is to
drive the Spaniards from Naples. For Lorenzo, the nephew, is trying to
claim Campania, having married a daughter of the king of Navarre. If this
turmoil goes any further, the rule of the Turks will be more tolerable than   30
the rule of Christians like them.

But away with useless complaints. I am grateful to you for kindly
opening my business with the king, and I beg that you will put it through.
For I now need a considerable sum for my journey, so that I do not run short
if any of those things happen that beset mortal men. And I have a mind to   35
increase my library. Why is this? I have sounded both the king and his
eminence so many times. Must my nets be always empty? Mountjoy has
nothing for me but affection; which of course is something, but does not
help my journey. He complains, I hear, that I did not accept the terms lately
offered by the king. I was offered forty pounds and told to hope for a   40
hundred. Quite a new procedure – he wished me to hope for something that
they did not dare to promise me; and I have a long experience there of
broken, not so much promises as oaths.

I wonder much that neither Franz nor One-eye returned with any letter
from you. But the one is often full of his own business, and Pieter could not   45
spare the time from his potations; so much so that, when he got to Antwerp,
I could not arrange to meet him on the first day, he was so deep in liquor.
This time I have sent my own servant to your part of the world, who can
bring me more reliable news of everything. Please do not let him return to
me empty-handed, and let him return to me as soon as possible; for this is   50

* * * * *

16 Lachner] See Ep 781:8n.
26 indulgences] See Ep 785:39n.
28 Lorenzo] See Ep 781:28n.
33 with the king] See Epp 657 introduction, 694:11n.
44 One-eye] Pieter Meghen

the one thing that holds up my departure. Bring Tunstall into the business; he is a true friend. Order the money, as Sixtinus advises, to be deposited with Maruffo, and let him give my servant a bill of exchange on which it is possible to get payment anywhere, and at the least possible expense. Doctor Urswick promised me a horse a year ago, and in hopes of that I gave him a 55 New Testament. If I knew that he did not like the idea, I would not press him. If you think fit, write him a couple of lines and let my man take it.

I am delighted to hear you have Folly in person with you, that turbulent man, I mean; I beg you earnestly to give him my very cordial greetings. I love him from the bottom of my heart, and am much indebted to him. He 60 supports me with his prayers, and ministers encouragement and advice in his letters.

If by any chance my servant should need anything, please, with your usual generosity see that he does not go without.

787 / To Richard Pace Louvain, 5 March 1518

Cf Ep 772 introduction.

ERASMUS TO HIS FRIEND PACE, GREETING
You certainly enjoyed yourself in that book of yours, my learned Pace, and made yourself not much more popular with the theologians than I did with my *Moria*. But you immortalized me as disgracefully poor, though I seemed to myself almost a sort of Midas. But some of the odium of this belongs to my 5 patrons, unless you think I am an idle dependant of whom they are right to have had enough. But now, since you have caricatured me in your book, let me have your help in removing this reproach. Prod those benefactors with all of whom, and rightly, you have so much influence. Especially now, when I have an immensely long journey to support, please do what you can 10

* * * * *

53 Maruffo] See Ep 706:19n.
55 Urswick] See Epp 451–2, 785:51n.
58 Folly] Reading *Moriam* for an incomprehensible *Mariam* in the text, this may be a reference to More; although no hint in Ep 785 confirms More's visit or visits with Colet, it is hard to think of another English friend who would match Erasmus' description as well as More. He was continually on the move, frequently wrote in a hurry (cf the end of Epp 502, 513, 601, 706), and said he was praying for Erasmus in Ep 499:38 ('Deum precor' in the Latin text). Cf also Ep 999.

787
2 book] See Ep 776:4n.

Christopher Urswick
Rubbing from a memorial brass
in the parish church of St John, Hackney, England
Victoria and Albert Museum, London

to secure the success of an appeal that is now before the king, whom I have
so often wooed in vain. Bring in, if you need them, Mountjoy and Tunstall.
Colet has been busy on this for some time. What I need is ready money. For
various definite reasons I have not given Dorp your letter. He and I are
getting on pretty well, and the course of things demands that I should have   15
some universities on my side.

That Cyclops told me that you had something ready for me in the way
of a letter. Whatever it is, give it to the bearer of this. I need a horse, a
suitable one, not afraid of hard work, and reasonably tall. I have sent my
servant to hunt for one. Please help him in this department too. I wonder   20
what all this is about my drafts. Those books of yours have now been on the
high seas for nearly five years. This is something like contrary winds! If you
know there is no hope, please do not tantalize me. I sent you the paraphrase, unless I am mistaken, with my *Apologia*. The former gets a favourable vote from all the theologians. The *Apologia* is ill received by some sup- 25
porters of Lefèvre – not that they do not accept my case, but because I dared
to reply to so great a man. If he attacks me again with remarks like those, he
will feel a very different weapon in my armoury; for up to now I have only
used my shield. Bombace feels himself (so he writes) really living among the
Goths, since you left Constance. Farewell, most learned Pace.   30

Louvain, 5 March 1518

788 / To Pieter Gillis   Louvain, 5 March [1518]

The year date must be 1518 because of Gillis' health and Erasmus' preoccupation with the New Testament. This letter was published in the *Farrago*.

ERASMUS TO PIETER GILLIS

If only I really were 'the sounder half of your own soul,' as you think fit to
call me! As it is, my health is not good, and I suffer when my friends are ill;
and yet the New Testament needs so much work that I have no time to be ill
myself. I see no hope, unless first you take a firm grip of yourself and then   5
undertake a journey, either to us here or to Ghent. At Ghent you will find

* * * * *

11 before the king] See Epp 657 introduction, 694:11n.
14 letter] Cf Ep 732:59n.
17 Cyclops] One-eyed Pieter Meghen
18 horse] See 785:51n
21 drafts] For the *Antibarbari*; cf Ep 706:38n.
23 paraphrase] See Ep 710 introduction.
25 supporters] See Ep 742:9n.
29 Bombace] See Ep 729:18–24.

Clavus, a physician with a foul tongue; I will give you a letter of introduction if you wish, so that his bad language, if nothing else, may drive you to
look after your health. Beware of drugs which depress the powers of nature.
Go out for a walk; take Nicholas with you, or some friend like him who is   10
devoted and agreeable. Anything in the way of a dispute must be sent
packing. It is a wise man's part before all else to take thought to prolong his
life. Farewell, and maintain your health; then mine too will improve.
      Louvain, 5 March 151[6]

789 / To Mark Lauwerijns   Louvain, 5 March [1518]

      Cf Ep 772 introduction.

ERASMUS TO MARK LAUWERIJNS
I had intended to visit you before Lent, but I was detained in Antwerp by
various tiresome things. Then the bad weather changed my plans. But I
shall be with you, I hope, in a few days' time. I am sending my servant to
England, and he will return this way shortly when he has dispatched some   5
business. Send your greetings to More and Pace, who are devoted to you.
And please, my dear Mark, do what you can for my servant to help him
reach Calais or Dunkirk easily with his belongings; and so that he is not
obliged to set foot in inns of dubious reputation, either put him up yourself,
or entrust him to my friend Ludovicus. In short, pray treat the young man as   10
befits a servant whom your friend Erasmus finds not unsatisfactory. When
he returns, give him a letter for me; though I expect to be with you before
that. Farewell, my excellent Mark. Give my greetings to the dean and to
your brother Pieter, and my other friends.
      Louvain, 5 March   15

790 / To Ludovicus   [Louvain, c 5 March 1518]

      Cf Ep 772 introduction. This letter is addressed to an unidentified friend. From
      Epp 651, 666, 789 it may be gathered that he lived in Bruges; Allen tried

      * * * * *

      788
      7 Clavus] See Ep 650:14n.
      10 Nicholas] Nicolaas of 's Hertogenbosch; cf Ep 702:6n.

      789
      2 to visit] The plan was carried out before long: see Ep 831:117n.
      10 Ludovicus] Cf Ep 790.
      13 dean] Jan Goetgebuer; see Ep 651; also for Pieter.

unconvincingly to identify him with a former servant-pupil addressed in Ep
167, but cf Bierlaire 48.

ERASMUS TO HIS FRIEND LUDOVICUS, GREETING
If you and your wife are well, I have good reason to be glad. The bearer of
this is my servant, whom I am sending over to England for some particular
business. Please assist him to find a wagon and reliable company, and in
any other way in which he may need your help, for it is important to me that   5
he should return safe and sound as soon as possible. In default of any other
place, take him into your own house, so that he is not obliged to set foot in
inns, which are now under suspicion everywhere. What you spend for his
benefit will be spent for mine. It may be that I shall revisit you shortly.
Meanwhile farewell, dearest Ludovicus, you and your delightful wife and   10
your dear children.

791 / To [Sir Richard Wingfield]   Louvain, 5 March [1518]

> Cf Ep 772 introduction. The addressee's identity is revealed by the reference to
> his father-in-law. Wingfield was deputy of Calais 1513–19; cf Ep 773.

Greeting, honoured sir. Though almost overwhelmed by my literary
labours, I have not forgotten your instructions about a physician. I dared
not recommend the first comer, and I had already almost found the person
we wanted; but in the mean time the man to whom I had entrusted this
business is carried off by the prince, or rather, before the prince himself   5
leaves, by my lord the chancellor of Burgundy.
    The bearer of this is my servant, whom I am sending over to England
on particular business. It will be like your noble self, if you will give him
what help he may need towards a safe and convenient crossing. You have
done so much for me, you will be willing to add this further service.   10
    Farewell, you and your charming wife and your delightful children. I
hope your father-in-law, the comptroller, is in the best of health.
    Louvain, 5 March
    Erasmus of Rotterdam
    * * * * *
    790
9 revisit] See Ep 831:117n.

    791
4 the man] Perhaps Pierre Barbier; cf Ep 608 introduction.
12 comptroller] Sir John Wiltshire, comptroller of Calais 1503–19. His daughter
    and heiress, Bridget, became Sir Richard Wingfield's second wife in about
    1512.

792 / To [Antonius of Luxembourg?]   Louvain, 5 March [1518]

Cf Ep 772 introduction. Identical references to 'humanissimus Gerardus' in Ep 673 and here suggest that both letters may have been addressed to Antonius of Luxembourg. Saint-Omer was not on the direct route Smith would take from Bruges to Calais, but if by any chance he were to cross from Netherlandish Dunkirk (cf Ep 789:8) rather than from English Calais, the official of the powerful abbot Antoon van Bergen might be of use to him. Jean de Nève was from Hondschoote, not far from Dunkirk and Saint-Omer. After More's recent visit to Saint-Omer (cf Ep 683:53–7) Antonius might carry some influence in Calais too. Allen suggested that the letter could be addressed to an official in Dunkirk.

Greeting, my honoured Lord. If you are well, I have good reason to be glad. On particular and necessary business I am sending the bearer of this, my servant to whom I am attached, over to England, and he is due to return shortly. I think he will have no need of your good offices; but if he has, pray provide him with all he may require for a safe and speedy crossing. Any   5 kindness you show him I shall reckon as shown to myself. Give my greetings to that excellent scholar Gerard, my old and special friend. Nève, our commander-in-chief, sends his cordial greetings. Farewell.

    Louvain, 5 March
    Erasmus of Rotterdam   10

793 / To Jean Le Sauvage   Louvain, 6 March [1518]

The purpose of this ornate letter is to request a travel subsidy from Le Sauvage, who had gone to Spain. This is the letter mentioned in Ep 794:80–1. The first two paragraphs are incorporated, almost without change, in Ep 853.

TO THE CHANCELLOR OF BURGUNDY
Greeting, my best of patrons. If I knew that your Highness felt the need of a letter, or gauged the loyalty of your supporters by trivial tributes of the kind, I should in this matter refuse to take refuge in any excuse, however just, although I can truly say that hitherto I have been as heavily burdened   5 by my literary labours as you are by the business of more than one kingdom. That your burden is more glorious I would not deny, but heavier I cannot think it, if for a moment I may compare the elephant and the gnat. As

    * * * * *

793
8 the elephant and the gnat] Cf *Adagia* III i 27.

it is, I know you are cast in a heroic, superhuman mould, and yet there is but
one of you, and you are assailed on every side by the great pressure of   10
affairs; and so I think there is no better way of showing myself truly dutiful
than to forgo the duty of paying my respects. In fact, I should feel I was
doing wrong in every way – to his Catholic Majesty, to whom you stand as
Hercules did to Atlas, and to the whole commonwealth, whose prosperity
you seem sent by the kindness of heaven to promote – were I to interrupt   15
you often with a letter, especially as there would be nothing in it but the
assurance of my devotion. And this devotion I would gladly prove by more
solid evidence, were my powers of mind equal to my zeal; prove it I will,
some day, if the powers above graciously grant me a few more years of life
and health.   20

I count myself happy, and I render thanks to Christ our Saviour, at the
news which I learn in a letter from Barbier, that amid the stormy seas of
anxiety and peril which a heart of steel could scarcely confront, your
Magnificence has enjoyed unbroken good health – whether it is some rare
felicity of nature gives you this strength beyond your years, or you derive it   25
from outstanding devotion to your great prince and to your country, or it is
a gift made through you to us all by the kind providence of a heavenly
power that wishes to help the human race. As I look upon an active old age,
equal to such a burden of affairs, I always seem to see a Massinissa or a Cato,
except that you are their equal in endurance and surpass them in toleration.   30
If only we might one day be blessed with many such, we might hope soon to
see the Christian world blossom with liberal studies, high standards of
conduct, and all the joys of peace.

My New Testament has been made new a second time; the toil of
revision is now finished, and it remains to take equal care in the printing.   35
This is a complicated business and cannot be completed unless I am there in
person to watch over it. If I go to Basel, I shall return here next autumn; but if
to Venice, my return must be postponed till the following spring. Wherever
I go, I will soon see that you know where I am. Age, which grows heavier
daily, has sapped some of my strength, and I hasten towards the last act of   40
my play. Would I might reach my final curtain with the approval of the

* * * * *

14 Hercules] Bearing for a while Atlas' burden, the sky
29 a Massinissa or a Cato] The king of Numidia (d 148 BC), who was allied with
the Romans, and the Roman statesman M. Porcius Cato (d 149 BC) were both
remembered for their energy in old age and their untiring opposition to
Carthage. However, Le Sauvage, who was 63 years old, was to die on 7 June
1518.
38 Wherever I go] See Ep 770 introduction.

producer, who is Christ; I will certainly do what I can to play the last act
better than before. I do not ask for your generosity, nor do I write to put you
in mind of it, knowing full well that of your own accord you will see that
what I must abandon to old age is made good by an increase in resources.   45
Even were there no increase, I should still protest that I owe everything to
you. Farewell, my most honoured Lord.

Louvain, 6 March

794 / To Pierre Barbier   Louvain, 6 March 1518

This letter was dispatched in duplicate. The second copy had a long postscript
of 26 March, printed separately as Ep 803 in Allen and in this edition. The
Auctarium, where this letter was first printed, and subsequent editions ig-
nored the later date of the postscript.

TO BARBIER

Greeting. Yes indeed, if things are as you say, it was the same people that
suppressed the books who suppressed the letters too; for I attached mine
first to the *Apologia* and then to the paraphrase. The canny canon de Hondt
produced and remitted the money for my annuity of his own accord; he is   5
more trustworthy than most people nowadays. That worthy archbishop of
Canterbury did the same, even without my knowledge. If only I knew ten
men like them! They would be more use than the ten Nestors whom
Agamemnon wishes for in Homer.

I have dispatched my man John, the Englishman, to England on other   10
definite business, and also to bring me back a suitable horse. He is due back
about Easter. In the mean time I am preparing for a journey and quite fear
that your contribution to the expenses of it may not find me here. But if
anything arrives, I shall leave reliable friends here, who will keep anything

* * * * *

794
3 letters] Epp 652, and probably 695
4 canny canon] 'Canonicus ille Canius,' a play on de Hondt's name: *canis* is the
   hound.
5 own accord] The second instalment for 1517 (cf Ep 751:27), or more likely a
   prepayment for the following semester, analogous to that for the Aldington
   pension arranged by Archbishop Warham; cf Ep 823 introduction, Allen Ep
   913:2.
9 Homer] *Iliad* 2.372
10 John] Smith; see Ep 772 introduction.
12 Easter] 4 April 1518

safe that is delivered to them: Doctor Jan van Borssele, who is destined for   15
the Latin chair; Jean de Nève of Hondschoote; Pieter Gillis, whose excellent
father has lately died, and he himself is afflicted with a sickness he cannot
shake off; Nicolaas of 's Hertogenbosch, a schoolmaster in Antwerp. His
eminence the cardinal of Cambrai arranged for two or three of your letters to
be delivered to me, one of which Guy Morillon wrote on your behalf. But   20
what do I hear? Does your friend Guy feel himself out in the cold in your
part of the world, a man in the prime of life in such a hot country? He ought
to have his bride with him; she would help to keep him warm. Yet I firmly
believed there were whole regions in your parts where the ground was pure
gold, and there were none of those Indian ants to guard the gold, but   25
anyone was free to dig as much as he liked. I am delighted that the bishop of
Chieti is well, except that I suspect him too of suffering from the cold. I had
heard a most damnable rumour, at which I almost fainted away, about
Briselot, that he had departed for the Elysian Fields, and I was preparing a
suitable lament to commemorate the loss of such a leading light; but your   30
last letter was a douche of cold water and revived me. Joking apart, though, I
was very happy to hear such a good report of my great Maecenas Jean Le
Sauvage, a man, as heaven's my witness, who deserves to live for ever.

Between me and the theologians these are halcyon days, indeed there
is a surprising degree of intimacy. They thank me openly for my Jerome,   35
there are no complaints of my New Testament; in fact the leaders of the
faculty heartily approve. Not a dog barks, except a few friars of some sort at
Cologne, I hear, and Bruges, but in the distance and behind my back.
Many, I am told, are frightened by the rough welcome given to Lefèvre, for
even his own supporters admit he is knocked flat; and yet I did not exert my   40
full strength against him but spared my adversary as far as I could. I wonder
why it is that he does not at least send me a private letter to apologize or
defend himself. I am freely congratulated on the defeat of this Frenchman

* * * * *

15 Borssele] See Ep 737:8n.
17 father] See Ep 715 introduction.
19 Cambrai] Guillaume de Croy; see Ep 628:70n.
23 bride] Elisabeth de Mil, d 1552; see de Vocht CTL III 46, 49–50. For her recent
    marriage to Morillon cf Ep 587.
25 Indian ants] Pliny Historia naturalis 2.3; cf Ep 913.
27 Chieti] Gianpietro Carafa; cf Ep 628:64n.
29 Briselot] Cf Ep 695:43.
31 cold water] This to Erasmus was a stimulus, not a discouragement; see Adagia I
    x 51, III ii 60.
38 Cologne] Cf Ep 821:19n.
38 Bruges] Cf Allen Ep 885:19–20.

Guy Morillon and his family on two outer panels of
Michael Coxie's *Ascension of Christ*

The left-hand panel shows St Guido of Anderlecht leaning on a harrow
and immediately beneath him, kneeling in prayer, Guy Morillon.
Behind Morillon is his son Antoine, and beside him is another son,
Maximilien. The two small children are Jerome and Philip van Winge,
grandchildren of Morillon by his daughter Elisabeth.

The standing figure in the right-hand panel of Coxie's painting
is St Elizabeth of Hungary.
Kneeling, from left to right, are Elisabeth de Mil, wife of Guy Morillon, and their two
daughters, Elisabeth and Marie
Stadsmuseum Leuven, Belgium (Photo: P. Laes)

by Germans, Italians, and English; yet they do not make me any less
unhappy at my victory, which could not earn much glory as his case was so   45
weak, and might earn unpopularity as it was a friend I was defeating in
single combat. Even now I wish him well, but not well enough to be
willingly labelled a blasphemer against Christ, merely to give him satisfaction. And so I pray Almighty God to supply my well-wishers with some
happier reason for congratulating me.   50

My *Apologia* has now been printed four times. Let him remove all
traces of his attack, and I will do what I can to suppress my defence. Let him
put away his offensive weapons, and I lay down my shield. Let him abolish
the poison, and I will cease to use the antidote. But if anyone else had
attacked me in similar language, he would have had a very different recep-   55
tion. I am only human; and when I really have made a mistake, I shall not
only acknowledge my fault but be grateful to the man who points it out and
yield to my pursuer. But when with similar effrontery I am again attacked
with monstrous abuse, I shall not so react that hereafter, as though I were
unarmed and toothless, any donkey may bray at me and any hog grunt. I   60
was the only person whom Lefèvre attacked by name. I have hitherto
attacked nobody, and his is the only attack that I have answered. Some
people say he is preparing to renew the battle, others say no. I want nothing
more than peace, especially with him; not that I fear him, but because I am
genuinely fond of him. If he does renew the attack, that is his look-out; he 65
will have only himself to thank if he gets a rough reception.

The New Testament compels me to go either to Venice or to Basel, I
have not yet decided which. I am deterred from Germany by three things –
the stoves, the robberies, and the plague, which has carried off among
others Lachner, the head of the Froben press; from Italy by the length of the 70
journey and the near prospect of summer. Wherever I go, I will send you
word. I had an idea that in effect I was writing to his lordship the chancellor
every time I write to you; for he must be so immersed in business that I was
afraid to interrupt him. I am overwhelmed here with loving proposals from
all quarters. I have had a letter from the archbishop of Mainz, one or two   75
from the bishop of Utrecht, others from the bishops of Liège and Bayeux.

* * * * *

51 four times] Erasmus had supplied revised copies of Martens' first edition (cf
   Ep 597:37n) to Schürer (cf Ep 693), to Froben (cf Ep 730 introduction), and to
   Martens himself (cf Ep 778 introduction). Thus he expected three additional
   editions to be in print, or nearly so.
63 renew the battle] Cf Ep 721 introduction.
67 Venice or Basel] Cf Ep 770 introduction.
70 Lachner] See Ep 781:8n.
74 from all quarters] See Ep 809:146–53.

They invite me to share bed and board. Invitations come from the king of England and his *fidus Achates* the cardinal of York, and from the king of France. I have so many suitors that it is difficult even to answer all their letters. I have written however to my lord the chancellor, as you told me to; 80 for I think it unsafe not to do as I am told, in view of your hot temper. We are all being taught to speak three tongues here instead of two. Matthaeus, a man of rare skill in his native language, is giving public lessons in Hebrew; as if we had not enough inhebriates here already! Dorp is the leader of the Hebrew party. You will soon see a new Louvain, and they will welcome the 85 very Erasmus at whom so lately they were throwing stones; though my paraphrase is praised throughout by everyone. It is something to have produced even one small book that can find favour with critics so preju- diced and hard to please. I only wish I had confined myself to the sort of fields in which there was not a little more fame to be had, and far less work. 90

But we are driven by fate, my dear Barbier, and fate we must obey. Mind you give my greetings to the lord of Halewijn. Cordial best wishes to Marliano, to Joost, that prince of lawyers, and to Guy Morillon, your bosom friend. Farewell, most faithful friend.

Louvain, 6 March   95

795 / To Johann Froben   Louvain, 12 March 1518

After writing to his patrons and friends in England and Spain, Erasmus continued his preparations for the journey (cf Ep 770 introduction) with Epp 795–8, all addressed to Froben and his collaborators and directed to Frankfurt, where the spring fair was now opening. It is from Frankfurt that Froben sent his reply, Ep 801.

ERASMUS TO FROBEN, HIS DEAR FELLOW-GODFATHER, GREETING

I beg you most urgently, my dear Froben, to bear the common lot of all men with a brave and undaunted spirit like the wise man that you are, especially since our sorrow cannot change the course of fate. What more I can do to 5

* * * * *

80 chancellor] Ep 793
82 Matthaeus] Adrianus; see Ep 691.
87 is praised] See Ep 710 introduction.
91 obey] Adapted from Seneca *Oedipus* 980
92 Halewijn ... Marliano] See Epp 641, 695:53n.
93 Joost] Lauwerijns; cf Ep 695:45n.

795
5 sorrow] At the death of Lachner; cf Ep 781:8n.

make things easier for you, I do not see; but this much I do promise, that anything one sincere friend can do for another I will do, with greater diligence than ever I have shown before. In the matter of the value of the printer's copy for those books I should have spoken much more gently had I not thought the money came from Lachner and was no embarrassment to 10 you. Some time ago I had received from Franz fourteen gold florins for what I had spent on Jacobus, and that was on Lachner's instructions; and then, equally on his instructions, thirty gold florins. Anything I had from him in the way of books I paid for with my own money.

I shall visit you this summer, if the highway robberies permit. I have 15 sent you my *Enchiridion*. If it is no use to you, pass it on to Schürer, who is a good friend. If you can make anything of it, do so. The second book of Theodore has lately been printed by Dirk, for I quite thought it had never reached you, since you never mentioned it in all those letters to me. Farewell, dearest Froben; you can be quite sure that I shall stand by you to 20 my life's end, as I stood with you that day at the font.

Louvain, St Gregory's day 1518

796 / To Beatus Rhenanus   Louvain, 13 March [1518]

This letter is contemporary with Ep 795.

ERASMUS TO HIS FRIEND BEATUS, GREETING
Pace's dreary book, my dear Beatus, fills me with indescribable discomfort and regret. It is just like the proverb: Cinders for gold. I know that every scholar who is a friend of his will be, like me, sincerely sorry; but he

* * * * *

9 printer's copy] See Ep 629:7n.
11 received] Birckmann's first payment was to cover the expenses of Jacobus Nepos, who had travelled to Basel in the spring of 1517 (see Ep 594 introduction), or so Erasmus assumed; the amount seems generous. The second payment was for the printer's copy supplied by him; see Ep 629:7n.
11 gold florins] Possibly Rhenish florins (Rijnsgulden) of the Four Electors, or St Philip florins of the Hapsburg Low Countries, or even Florentine florins. Cf CWE 1 316–18, 321 (plate), 336–9.
16 *Enchiridion*] See Epp 801, 858 introductions.
18 Theodore] See Ep 771 introduction.
21 at the font] See Ep 635:26n.

796
2 book] See Ep 776:4n.
3 proverb] Gold was expected, but cinders were given; cf *Adagia* I ix 30.

meanwhile enjoys his good fortune, he is rich and the favourite of king and   5
cardinal. I have, however, written to tell More to give him friendly warning
not to persevere in this nonsense.

I am sorry for Froben's misfortune and will never fail him as long as I
live. And I recommend my fellow godfather in turn to you, for you can be a
tower of strength to him. My own age and state of health have long been   10
demanding my release from labours of this kind; I pass on the torch to
younger, and indeed happier, men like you.

Tell Bruno to forget all his scruples about a second edition of Jerome. I
assure you, what he is afraid of is a mirage; but I have written to him too
about this. I shall be with you this summer to see the New Testament   15
through the press, provided it is safe to enter Germany, which with all these
robberies is in a worse state than hell itself, for you can neither enter nor
leave. God help us, what tragic work these princes have in hand! The sense
of honour is extinct in public affairs. Despotism has reached its peak. Pope
and kings regard the people not as human beings but as beasts for market.   20

Not a word from Lefèvre, but I hear different things from that quarter.
Some say he has a defence in hand; others say not. The man by whom I sent
my *Apologia* and a covering letter wrote as follows to a friend of his, who
gave me the letter to read: 'I delivered the *Apologia* to Lefèvre and the letter
with it. Lefèvre in my presence maintained that Erasmus is very easily   25
upset; but he need expect no retaliation.' I cannot imagine what has come
over the man, unless beneath that modest and gentle exterior there lurks
some inborn venom. Farewell.

Louvain, morrow of St Gregory

797 / To Johannes Oecolampadius   Louvain, 13 March [1518]

Cf Ep 795 introduction.

ERASMUS TO HIS FRIEND OECOLAMPADIUS, GREETING
How could I have guessed, my dear Oecolampadius, that a man devoted as

* * * * *

6 cardinal] Wolsey
6 More] Ep 776
13 Jerome] See Ep 802:12n.
14 him too] Cf Ep 801 introduction.
19 Pope and kings] Cf Ep 781:28n.
22 The man] See Epp 659, 721 introductions.

you are to heavenly things would be found at Frankfurt in that sink of
human vileness? Now, since you admit to the name of Theseus, you ought
faithfully to play Theseus' part. The Hebrew parallels I added, relying on 5
you, have met with much criticism, especially the references collected out of
Annius which I gave on Luke. I shall be in Basel before May, if the robberies
in Germany permit, to make a fresh edition of the New Testament. I wish
you could be there and throw yourself into it whole-heartedly. For I cannot
think of Gerbel without indignation, whenever I remember the superior 10
and contemptuous way he behaved on this question. We have here one
Matthaeus, the teacher of Wolfgang Capito, who has been hired for a
regular salary from public funds to lecture in Hebrew. The thing is going
very well. Farewell, dear Oecolampadius, and count Erasmus your dear
friend, as he does you.   15
      Louvain, 13 March

798 / To [Wolfgang Faber Capito]   Louvain, 13 March [1518]

      Cf Ep 795 introduction.

Your sincere and characteristic kindness to my humble self is visible at
every point, in your not showing my letter to Baer and in being so much
concerned about my *Apologia*. Here is a tale about Matthaeus that will make
you smile. He had called to see me. I was at that moment busy and feared he

      * * * * *

797
3 Frankfurt] Oecolampadius seems to have written to Erasmus complaining that
   he found no letter at the Frankfurt fair, perhaps in the autumn of 1517.
   Probably in May 1518 he was to return from Weinsberg to Basel, where he had
   been appointed to a benefice, but Erasmus did not know of this when he wrote
   this letter; see E. Staehelin *Das theologische Lebenswerk J. Oekolampads* (Leipzig 1939) 86–7.
4 Theseus] See Ep 373:72–83.
7 Annius] See Ep 784:54n.
10 Gerbel] Erasmus' indignation is probably due to difficulties experienced at the
   time of editing the New Testament, 1516. Nikolaus Gerbel was hired to read
   the proofs; see Epp 417:6n, 421:58–62.
12 Matthaeus] Adrianus; see Ep 691.

798
1 characteristic] Reading *germana*
2 my letter] Ep 730 or Ep 734; see Ep 734:60–1. Clearly Capito had sent a
   conciliatory answer to Epp 730–1, 734 and added a letter for Adrianus.
3 *Apologia*] Cf Ep 734:5n.
3 Matthaeus] Adrianus, Capito's former teacher

would waste my time, so I sent down your letter addressed to him. My   5
servant returned from the hall with the news that he would be grateful for a
few words with me at any rate. 'All right,' I said, and up he came; showed
me the letter; asked me to read it to him – 'he had not brought his spectacles.' I read half a paragraph, then turned to him and said 'Not a very civil
start; you had much better read it yourself.' 'No, no; I want you to know   10
what he says.' I did as I was told, and went on. The severity steadily
increased, and I urged him to read it to himself in private; but he asked me
to go on reading. So on I went, with a grin every now and again. He starts to
defend himself loud and long: it was all perfectly untrue, it was you that
were indebted to him. Whereupon I, for I was extremely busy, begged him   15
to postpone all that to another day. He says he has answered you; threatens
that he will prove wrong everything you have put in your grammar. I think
the man will leave us, as he always does; he made a very stormy departure
from Middelburg because of his debts. Farewell.

I could wish you were more inclined to Greek than to that Hebrew of   20
yours, with no desire to criticize it. I see them as a nation full of most tedious
fabrications, who spread a kind of fog over everything, Talmud, Cabbala,
Tetragrammaton, *Gates of Light*, words, words, words. I would rather have
Christ mixed up with Scotus than with that rubbish of theirs. Italy is full of
Jews, in Spain there are hardly any Christians. I fear this may give that   25
pestilence that was long ago suppressed a chance to rear its ugly head. If
only the church of Christians did not attach so much importance to the Old
Testament! It is a thing of shadows, given us for a time; and now it is almost

* * * * *

8 spectacles] On the comical and satirical effects of eye-glasses at this time see
  J.-C. Margolin 'Des lunettes et des hommes ...' *Annales: Economies, Sociétés,
  Civilisations* 30 (1975) 375–93.
17 grammar] Cf Ep 600:26n.
19 Middelburg] See Epp 686:7n, 691:3n.
23 Tetragrammaton] The four letters YHWH forming the most common name of
  God in the Judaeo-Christian tradition; according to the interpretations placed
  on Exod 3:14–15 it was held to be most mysterious. The various names of God
  are a recurrent topic of Jewish theology; this had been the subject of a recent
  publication of excerpts from the work of Joseph ben Abraham Gikatilla with
  the title *Gates of Light* (Paulus Ricius, trans, *De porta lucis*, Augsburg: J. Miller
  1516). On Erasmus' attitude towards Jewish literature see also Ep 694 introduction.
24 Scotus] John Duns Scotus, the Franciscan theologian of the late thirteenth
  century, is sometimes mentioned by Erasmus as a typical representative of
  scholastic thought.
27 Old Testament] Cf Ep 701:40n.

preferred to the literature of Christianity. Somehow or other we are all the time turning away from Christ, who was enough for us, all by himself.   30 Farewell.

Louvain, 13 March

799 / To Henricus Afinius   Louvain, 13 March 1518

This is the preface to the *Encomium medicinae*, one of Erasmus' early composi-tions (cf Allen I 18:19–21, 233), published in Martens' edition of *Declamationes aliquot* of 30 March 1518 and reprinted by Froben in November (cf Epp 603 introduction, 604:12n).

The tug of war between Afinius, who had promised a gift of silver cups, and Erasmus, who had promised a dedication, had been going on for some time (cf Epp 637–8). The tone of this letter suggests that Erasmus still had not received anything. But instead of the provocative language and threats he had used in Epp 753–4, he now tried a conciliatory approach. No doubt this was a final effort to obtain Afinius' gift before Erasmus' departure for Basel (cf Ep 772 introduction). Nothing is heard about the matter thereafter.

ERASMUS OF ROTTERDAM TO THE
DISTINGUISHED PHYSICIAN HENRICUS AFINIUS OF LIER,
GREETING
I was lately looking through my library, dear Afinius, my learned friend, when there came into my hands a speech I composed long ago, when I was   5 trying my hand at everything, in praise of the art of physic. I thought at once of dedicating a not very good speech to a very good physician, that the attraction of your name at least might recommend it to the suffrages of educated readers. For the time being it shall be a small token of my feelings towards you, until something is available more worthy of our friendship.   10 Farewell.

Louvain, 13 March 1518

800 / To Paolo Bombace   Louvain, 14 March 1518

This letter is probably the first of two answering Ep 729.

ERASMUS TO HIS FRIEND BOMBACE, GREETING
I felt myself reviving on receipt of your letter, Bombace my learned friend, the moment I recognized the handwriting I love so well. What is all this? Sent on a mission, you feel yourself banished? You must play the part of the wily Ulysses, who adapted his part skilfully to audiences so different as   5

Phaeacians and Cyclopes; only steer clear of Calypso and Circe, and I hope you never have any business with Irus. Trebatius froze among the Britons; how much more fortunate you are, who have been able to sweat for a whole winter in the steam-baths of the Swiss. And finally, pray remember that these diplomatic missions, which seem to you so deplorable, are the nurse- 10 ries of bishops and of cardinals. Suppose one day I see my friend Bombace glorious with two-peaked mitre and pastoral staff, or eminent in a red hat? I have often, and vainly, regretted my departure from Rome, nor have I any consolation except the old tag, 'Tis fate that drives us. And now I do not like to return to the city I left, partly for shame at my grey hairs, partly because I 15 feel the burden of advancing years. But nothing in my fate seems to me more intolerable than to have to endure those mischievous divines who take it upon themselves to condemn what they have never read. Yet those are the men for whose benefit I have chiefly toiled; if only they would learn rather than make mischief. It was they, I suppose, who egged on Lefèvre, to 20 his great loss, if he values his reputation.

I knew Richard Pace as a man of absolutely spotless character, upright, liberal minded, as faithful a friend as you could find anywhere, a linguist and a polymath; all the same, I could wish that book on the value of liberal studies had not been published under his name. I know that the good 25 scholars of whom there are not a few in England were looking for a very different specimen of his talents and his learning. If it is meant as a serious work, how can one take it seriously? If it is humorous, where is the humour? Nothing makes sense or hangs together; it is all 'like sick men's dreams ...' And then why need he drag in my poor self so many times, starving in one 30 place, in another hated by the theologians? There is no doubt at all that with

* * * * *

800

7 Irus] A beggar who insults Ulysses in *Odyssey* 18 and challenges him to a fight (in which Irus is soundly beaten). The preceding names also refer to encoun- ters, bitter or sweet, that Ulysses had on his voyage.

7 Trebatius] C. Trebatius Testa, c 80 BC–c 4 AD, a legal adviser to Caesar. He spent the winter 54–3 in the army headquarters at Amiens, and Cicero, writing to him in December (*Ad familiares* 7.10.2), expresses the fear that he will find it very cold.

9 steam-baths] Erasmus loathed the German stoves and subsequently Froben had to put an open fireplace into the room of his house that Erasmus occupied; cf Epp 302:50n, 597:54n.

14 fate] Cf Ep 794:91.

24 book] Cf Ep 776:4n.

29 'like sick men's dreams ...'] Horace *Ars poetica* 7–8, 'like sick men's dreams, all will be empty show.'

the best theologians I get on very well; and I, his starveling, have over three
hundred ducats a year of my own, besides what more I get from the
generosity of my patrons and as the fruit of my own labours; I could have
more if I wished, and any amount more if I were willing to immerse myself   35
even a little in the business of princes. Does he think it so necessary to dash
down on paper whatever comes into his head, without a moment's thought
how he should mention a friend when he writes a book? I certainly treated
him with rather more respect in my *Chiliades*, when he was not yet the great
man he is now. Maybe I shall visit you this spring, unless you have returned   40
to Rome before then; and perhaps I may find you there. Farewell, dear
Bombace, most loyal of friends.

Louvain, 14 March 1518

801 / From Johann Froben   [Frankfurt, second half of March 1518]

Two drafts for this letter, both in the hand of Bruno Amerbach, are in the
Öffentliche Bibliothek of the University of Basel, MS G II 33a ff 17a recto and
17b recto. On f 17b verso is the rough draft for Ep 802. It is clear that both letters
were drafted in and most likely dispatched from Frankfurt. Froben and Bruno
Amerbach had left Basel for the Frankfurt spring fair on about 10 March 1518
(cf AK II Ep 606). The approximate date is confirmed by a comparison with Ep
795, a letter answered here, and with Ep 815.

There can be little doubt that Ep 795 reached Froben in Frankfurt and was
the letter mentioned in Ep 802. Both Epp 801 and 802, however, deal with
Erasmus' fear of the plague at Basel, a matter that had preoccupied him for
some time (cf Ep 770 introduction) but is not raised in the surviving text of Ep
795. Likewise Ep 801 answers an inquiry, not in Ep 795, as to whether Froben
would take on the new edition of the New Testament. It also acknowledges
receipt of the revised *Enchiridion*, which had already been dispatched when

* * * * *

32 three hundred ducats] A modest estimate provided that his emoluments were
paid. The various Italian, papal, Hungarian, Portuguese, and Spanish ducats
were then worth 79d–80d gros Flemish (two florins money-of-account), so
that this sum amounted to £100 gros Flemish = £68 15s 0d sterling = £622 10s
0d tournois (gold values). Erasmus was entitled to 200 florins (= 100 ducats =
£33 13s 4d gros Flemish = £22 18s 4d sterling = £207 10s 0d tournois) annually
from King Charles. His benefices in Courtrai and Aldington produced somewhat more than 300 florins a year. Cf CWE 1 314, 317–18, 336–7; Ep 712:9n.
37 on paper] The phrase comes from Horace *Satires* 1.4.36.
39 *Chiliades*] See the preface of the *Adagia*, Ep 211:50–61.
40 visit you] As it turned out, Bombace had left Switzerland before Erasmus
arrived in Basel; cf Ep 855 introduction.

Erasmus wrote Ep 795. It can thus be assumed that earlier, probably in February, Erasmus had sent Froben and his collaborators a letter (or letters) now lost, but mentioned in Ep 796:14.

Greeting. Your friendly feelings towards me, most learned Erasmus, are much appreciated; heaven send that I may some day be able to respond to them, at least in part. Your saying that you will visit us this coming summer fills me with delight, and I urgently beg you to do so. As for the plague, there is no cause for alarm. There have been some deaths here in 5 these last few months, I admit – a few people – not the plague, but some kind of fever. But now for two months or more there has been no mention even of sickness, so far are we from any deaths.

Your offer of your Testament for a new edition lays me under an obligation I can never repay. I will take pains to see that the book when it 10 comes out is as correct as possible. But I fear this may not be feasible in time for the next Frankfurt fair, partly from shortage of time, and partly because I have nearly four hundred copies of the earlier edition to be sold somehow in the mean time. I will endeavour to put it in circulation at the Easter fair at Frankfurt. Your Suetonius will be finished by this coming August. The 15 *Enchiridion* I will put in train as soon as ever I get home. You will do me a most welcome service if you will send me as soon as you can at my expense your book on the prince for me to reprint. I sold out the earlier edition some time ago.

If you have any offspring newly hatched by your fertile brain, I beg 20 you to share them with me; you will find the recipient of your kindness is not ungrateful. Theodore's second book, which you have lately translated, I have now printed. Our mutual friend Matthias Schürer is very ill; I fear he may not recover. As for the short pieces of yours which I lately printed, take

* * * * *

801

7 fever] This seems confirmed by Zwingli *Werke* VII Ep 31.
13 four hundred] Probably more than twelve hundred had been printed; see Ep 864 introduction.
15 Suetonius] See Ep 648 introduction.
16 *Enchiridion*] See Ep 858 introduction.
18 prince] See Epp 393, 853 introductions.
22 Theodore's second book] See Ep 771 introduction.
23 Schürer] The Strasbourg printer too had gone to Frankfurt (cf AK II Ep 611:23). His health was apparently still poor half a year later at the time when he welcomed Erasmus to Strasbourg (cf Allen Epp 867:23, 883:6–7) and he was to die in the autumn of 1519. Froben and Schürer were competing for Erasmus' business.
24 short pieces] See Ep 629:7n.

as many as you wish from Franz, and I will make it good at the next fair.   25
Other things it will be better to speak of when you are here in person.
Farewell, dearest fellow-godfather, and love me as I know you do.

Your sincere friend Johann Froben

To Master Erasmus of Rotterdam, the universal scholar, and his dear
fellow-godfather   30

802 / From Bruno Amerbach   Frankfurt, [second half of March 1518]

Cf Ep 801 introduction.

Our common friend Johann Froben has shown me your letter to him in
which you say that you will be going to Basel this coming summer; and
when I read this I could not refrain from waving my arms in the air and
jumping for joy. My life upon it, I cannot admit that anybody could look
forward to that more keenly than I do. How popular you will be if you keep   5
your promise! The plague, which you fear may be spreading among us,
certainly need not stop you. For twelve years and more we have not so much
as heard it mentioned.

A certain Eucharius Cervicornus of Cologne has copied some letters of
Jerome from our edition. We have taken him to court in Frankfurt for   10
neglecting and indeed despising privileges from the highest authorities.
He will pay the penalty, if I mistake not, for his rashness. Jean Petit the Paris
printer is a new menace; he threatens to counterfeit the whole work. His
efforts can be suppressed by one note from you.

Farewell, from Frankfurt, late at night   15

* * * * *

802

9 Cervicornus] Eucharius Hirtzhorn, called Cervicornus, enrolled in 1513 in the
University of Cologne. From 1516 to 1547 he owned a press, printing especially humanistic works, located at Cologne and from 1535 to 1538 also at
Marburg. He often worked for the prominent publisher Gottfried Hittorp and
also for Peter Quentel and Johann Gymnich (see Benzing 222). The book here
referred to is Jerome *Epistolae tres*, edited by Erasmus, J. G[ymnich, Cologne
1518], reprinted in 1524 by Konrad Caesar for Hittorp; see *Short-Title
Catalogue of Books Printed in German-Speaking Countries ... in the British
Museum* (London 1962). In December 1517 Cervicornus reprinted under his
own name Erasmus' *Vita Hieronymi*, another portion of the Froben edition of
Jerome of 1516; see *Opuscula* 131.

11 privileges] Privileges by both the Emperor Maximilian and Pope Leo x were
abstracted on the verso of the title page of the Froben edition of 1516.

12 Petit] Bruno's fears had already come to the attention of Erasmus (cf Ep
796:13–15), who now lost little time in warning Petit; see Ep 815.

803 / To Pierre Barbier   Louvain, 26 March [1518]

This is the postscript to the duplicate of Ep 794.

Several days ago I sent off this letter by a youth with a stammer, but, since I
see that some letters do not get through, I am sending the same letter again
by another hand. I congratulate my right reverend benefactor Doctor Marliano; please greet him from me as warmly as possible. He was so good as to
mention me in a letter to our common friend Remaclus, who lately almost   5
killed me with his caresses but is now not fit for such things, being cruelly
afflicted with a severe complaint. Fausto, the immortal poet, has at length
died in Paris; in Rome we have lost M. Musurus the Cretan, a good scholar
and already preferred to a bishopric, in Rome also Paleotti. The astrologers
say there will be such a pestilence this year that only men of upright life will   10
survive, which means very few. Look after yourself.
    If what I hear about the dean of Besançon is true, who is an old friend
of mine, I have good reason to be glad.
    Added by me in Louvain, 26 March. Farewell again, my sheet-anchor.

804 / To Gilles de Busleyden   Louvain, [c 26 March] 1518

This is a formal letter designed for speedy publication in the *Auctarium*,
together with the epitaphs. It is clearly later than Ep 699, since the Latin
epitaph now appears in a revised form and is accompanied by another in

* * * * *

803
1 stammer] Cf Ep 695:49.
3 Marliano] The court physician Luigi Marliano, who in 1517 received the see of
    Tuy in Spain. For his friendship with Remaclus Arduenna cf Ep 411.
7 Fausto] Andrelini; see Ep 810:489n.
8 Musurus ... Paleotti] See Ep 729 postscript.
10 pestilence] Despite his joke, Erasmus took the warning very seriously; cf Epp
    755:32n, 770 introduction, 861, Allen 936:52–5.
12 dean] The dean of Besançon since 1493 was Jean Carondelet (1469–1544), who
    also held benefices in the Netherlands, where he had frequently resided. He
    was a member of the council of Prince Charles and accompanied the monarch
    to Spain in 1517–19. In the latter year he was nominated to the archbishopric
    of Palermo. Erasmus found in him a reliable patron, but there is no other
    evidence in the surviving correspondence that he was an old friend. Possibly
    Erasmus confused the two brothers Jean and Ferry Carondelet. Ferry, who had
    been archdeacon of the Besançon chapter since 1504, had met him at Rome in
    1509; cf Ep 1359, DHGE.

Greek. Since a transcript of the epitaphs was also enclosed in Ep 805, it may be
assumed that the two letters are roughly contemporary; cf Reedijk 326–8.

ERASMUS OF ROTTERDAM TO THE
HONOURABLE MASTER GILLES, TREASURER OF
HIS CATHOLIC MAJESTY, GREETING
How much distinction we have lost in this one man! I can easily guess how
you must feel your brother's death, when the entire society of scholars and   5
all our best men grieve for him as they would for no one else. But to what
purpose are vain lamentations and useless tears? For this end are we all
born. In the epitaphs I have not done justice to his merits, nor to my
intentions. I courted the Muses, but to no purpose; for so many years now
have I been immersed in studies of the kind furthest removed from these   10
more graceful forms of composition. I stand in fear of your very exquisite
taste; but remember that I wrote to please you, lest I might ever seem not to
be doing my duty by the name of Busleyden. If you do not like the lines, I
will keep them by me, in hopes that one of the Muses may one day deign to
visit me; yet I do not doubt that all those who have good literature at heart   15
are ready, each according to his gifts, to woo immortality for this irreplace-
able patron of their studies.

As to the foundation of the college, do not let yourself be seduced from
your first intentions. Believe me, such a thing will be more advantageous
than I can say to every kind of study, and will add no small increase of glory   20
and distinction to the name of Busleyden, which in so many ways is
illustrious in its own right already. Farewell.

Louvain, 1518
[Enclosed in this letter were the drafts of two different epitaphs, one in Greek,
the other in Latin]   25
INSCRIPTION FOR THE PAINTED PICTURE OF THE MOST WORTHY JÉRÔME DE
BUSLEYDEN SOMETIME PROVOST OF AIRE AND COUNCILLOR TO HIS
CATHOLIC MAJESTY & BROTHER TO THE MOST REVEREND FATHER IN GOD
FRANÇOIS LATE ARCHBISHOP OF BESANÇON WHO FOUNDED IN LOUVAIN AT
GREAT EXPENSE A COLLEGE WHEREIN INSTRUCTION MIGHT BE GIVEN   30
PUBLICLY IN THE THREE TONGUES HEBREW AND GREEK AND LATIN

* * * * *

804
18 college] See Ep 691 introduction.
29 François] De Busleyden, d 1502; see Ep 157:67n.

[Greek]
O skilful painter of this outward face,
Thou shouldst have limned the likeness of the mind!
Then had we seen in one small picture's space   35
The lovely choir of virtues all confined.
Religion, piety and wisdom there,
Goodness and noble nurture did combine:
To these and more Jérôme alone was heir,
The light and glory of BUSLEYDEN's line.   40
[Latin]
[As in the draft enclosed in Ep 699, with small verbal changes, and one new
line between lines 4 and 5:]
He who ends his life in honour knows not what it is to die.

805 / To Jan Robijns   Louvain, 26 March 1518

Robijns (cf Ep 178:9n) had been named as one of the executors of the will of
Jérôme de Busleyden. Although he does not seem to have acted in this
capacity, he assisted vigorously in the establishment of the Collegium Trilingue and left it a bequest after his own death in 1532; see de Vocht CTL
18–12 and *J. de Busleyden* 47.

TO THE DEAN OF MECHELEN
Greetings, honoured Mr Dean. Matthaeus plays his part actively, and with
good results. He has as good an audience as one would expect in so new a
subject, and of a very good class of people; it includes some doctors of
divinity. I only wish we had someone who could fill the shoes of the Greek   5
man with equal success. For Borssele, whom you intended for the Latin
chair, is so good a candidate that we could not wish for anyone better. Nor
would it be easy, though one looked everywhere, to find so many outstanding gifts in one individual: such a high character, learning with more
in reserve than appears on the surface, and brains that can learn anything, a 10
wonderfully tenacious memory, and in addition an unexceptionable manner of life.

But how foolish of me to paint you a picture of a person whom you

* * * * *

805
2 Matthaeus] Adrianus
5 Greek] See Ep 691:19n.
6 Borssele] See Ep 737:8n.
10 in reserve] Quintilian 1.4.2

must know better than I do! One thing I would ask, that he should not be
prejudiced by the fact that he is and has been an old, well-known, and   15
devoted dependant of the Busleyden family. You are aware that his resources, such as they are, are too small to support him at Louvain, where he
has already been sitting for some months not without expense, so that he is
obliged to think of supplementing what he has from some other source. It is
important for us all that such a man should be kept in Louvain, so that his   20
light may shine as widely as possible. It is also important for me personally;
for since I am obliged to be away for as much as six or eight months, I had
decided to entrust to him my worldly wealth, that is, my books, not only for
safe keeping but for use, reckoning that all I have is shared with him. And
he will be kept here, if the same arrangement can be made for him as for the   25
Hebrew professor: that he should be assigned a salary worthy of his merits.
Nor do I doubt that, as a wise man, you will understand that his post will
have far heavier duties than the Hebrew chair. The Hebrew man instils the
rudiments into people who know nothing; the Latin man will be obliged to
satisfy the requirements of a number of advanced scholars. As for a house,   30
the necessary steps will be taken when the time comes. My own opinion is
that the chairs should be got under way at once, that the thing may not cool
off in the mean time, and to prevent any evil spirit from upsetting a scheme
that will be so good for us all. Take my word for it, there will always be
enough colleges for theology, and of questionists more than enough   35
everywhere; but this most noble project, unless it goes forward in accordance with Busleyden's intentions, will not be set on foot, so far as I can see,
by anyone else. This one enterprise will recall students everywhere from
muddy pools to the clear springs of Holy Scripture.

On the subject of sending for a Greek, pray tell Borssele what you have   40
in mind, and he in return will give you my opinion. I should not like to
intrude into other men's business, especially since I have no personal axe to
grind; but I am concerned for the public benefit, concerned also for the
memory of that good man Jérôme de Busleyden, which I will not allow to
die, if words of mine have any power at all. I send you some epitaphs,   45
which are not worthy of him, but they are the best I have been able to do, for
I have for some years now been occupied in studies as far removed as
possible from elegant composition, especially in verse. If you think any-

* * * * *

30 house] Cf Ep 691 introduction.
42 axe to grind] *Adagia* I vi 82
45 epitaphs] See Epp 699, 804.

thing should be changed, inform Borssele, and he will write and tell me your
views. Farewell, and Christ have you in his keeping, honoured sir.   50

Louvain, 26 March 1518
Erasmus, your devoted servant

806 / To Richard Sampson   Louvain, [March] 1518

This letter answers Ep 780. It was written before Erasmus' departure for Basel
and published in the *Auctarium* of August 1518.

ERASMUS OF ROTTERDAM TO THE
EXCELLENT RICHARD SAMPSON, DOCTOR OF
CIVIL AND CANON LAW, GREETING

It is, as you say, a great proof of true affinity between us, my most gifted
Richard, that we should have so many friends, distinguished friends, in   5
common, especially since you did not introduce them to me nor I to you.
And so some secret force of fate seems to be at work. Although I should in
any case be hardly human if I did not count you among my chiefest friends,
having had so much pleasure from your company first in Cambridge and
lately in Tournai – for what can be more delightful than your personality? – I   10
should be not merely most inhuman but most ungrateful, did I not write the
name of Sampson in the list of my principal benefactors; for it was you who,
unasked and unsolicited, got me all unexpectedly my Tournai prebend.
That I could not follow it up was not your fault, but the effect of my absence.
And so I think I owe you an undiminished debt of gratitude for this   15
benefaction, for it was not your doing that I do not enjoy it now. His
eminence the cardinal makes very generous promises, but this is no time to
wait upon hope deferred. Though I already possess enough to satisfy my
present spirit and my present use of my time. I am delighted that you think
well of the paraphrase, and also that Johannes de Molendino likes it, for he   20
is a keen critic. He had passed on greetings to you on my account, and now
you must perform the same service for him in turn, and that with special
care. Farewell.

Louvain, 1518

* * * * *

806
9 Cambridge] Both men left Cambridge early in 1514. The Tournai meeting
   probably was in the spring of 1515; see Epp 332:3, 388:38.
13 prebend] See Ep 360:16n.
20 paraphrase] See Ep 710 introduction.
21 critic] Literally 'a good nose': *Adagia* II viii 59. For Molendino cf Ep 755.

807 / To Maarten Lips   [Louvain, spring 1518?]

Lips' introductory remarks to this letter in the Brussels MS (see Ep 750 introduction) confirms that his gift was a purse. The choice would seem to reflect
Erasmus' campaign for travelling funds (see Epp 772 introduction, 793–4) or
his forthcoming departure for Basel. Lips also reveals that the present Erasmus
gave him in return was the Aldine edition of Gregory. This fact perhaps
suggests that the letter was contemporary with Ep 841. Erasmus published it
in *Epistolae ad diversos*.

ERASMUS OF ROTTERDAM TO HIS FRIEND
MAARTEN OF BRUSSELS, GREETING
Can you suppose your present was well chosen, to send a purse to one who
has no money? I have found in my small library a Gregory Nazianzen, an
author praised even by Jerome, who is as pious as he is learned and   5
eloquent. Thinking you would like him, I am sending him round to you, a
quid pro quo if you like, or a token, however inadequate, of my regard for
you. Keep it up: you are in the prime of life and have talents above the
ordinary, both of these things the gift of God, and you must employ them in
sacred study, being very careful to put into practice what you read.   10
Farewell, dearest friend, my son in years, my brother in the priesthood, and
commend me to Christ in your prayers.

  Erasmus, etc
  To Doctor Maarten of Brussels
  151[9]   15

808 / To Johannes Caesarius   Louvain, 5 April 1518

ERASMUS TO HIS FRIEND CAESARIUS, GREETING
I enclose the second book of Theodore, dedicated to you, as I think you
already know. I hear that Busche has returned to your part of the world, and

  * * * * *

807
4 Gregory] *Carmina* in Greek and Latin (Aldus June 1504). The book was trea-
    sured by Lips, and some time ago it turned up in England; cf Horawitz Epp
    72–4 (Ep 750 introduction), Allen IV xxviii.
5 Jerome] *De viris illustribus* 117
11 son in years] Cf Jerome's greeting to Augustine in Ep 105.5.2.

808
2 enclose] Cf Ep 771 introduction.
3 Busche] Hermann von dem Busche; see Ep 830 introduction.

I am delighted; this is much better than that his gifts should be hid somewhere in obscurity. Very soon, if I mistake not, barbarism will be entirely   5
expelled from Cologne too, by the valour of all ranks. I hear that my lord the
count of Neuenahr is doing battle like a very Hercules against those arrogant professors of unlearned learning, but I wish he had somewhat more
honourable opponents. It seems to me to be the depths of misfortune to
struggle with monsters like that, from whom you can win no trophies but   10
the pox. I am sorry too for the order, which contains many excellent men
who by no means approve of their temerity, and say they do not value the
ambitions of two or three of their number so highly that for their sake they
are willing to become universally unpopular.

The man who invented the title *Obscurorum virorum* did civilization a   15
bad turn: if the title had not given away the joke, those letters would still be
read everywhere to this day as though they were written in support of the
Dominicans. Here in Louvain we have a noble doctor of divinity who used
to be their prior in Brussels; and he had bought twenty copies as presents to
his friends a little before the bull was published that condemns the book   20
with all its thunders. At first I wished the book had never come out; but
once it had been published, I wished it had another title. They deserve, of
course, to be attacked far more seriously; but this is a dangerous precedent,
and the most mischievous thing in such frauds always is that, as no one
knows the author, suspicion ranges unchecked, everyone following his   25
own guess or his predilections. There were even people who thought I
wrote the letters, although I did not even know the men's names and could
not have reproduced the style. Farewell, dearest Caesarius.

I was surprised when John Siberch arrived without a letter from you.
Mind you give my greetings to the noble count of Neuenahr.   30

Louvain, Easter Monday 1518

* * * * *

7 doing battle] Against Hoogstraten (cf Ep 680:28n). In May 1518 Neuenahr
published with Cervicornus the *Epistolae trium illustrium virorum*, written in
April (cf Ep 1006). One of the letters was written by Hermann von dem Busche.
11 order] The Dominicans
19 prior] The story is repeated in Allen Ep 2045:171–5. The prior of the Brussels
Dominicans was Jacobus Remigii, DD at Louvain in 1517. On 30 September
1517 he and another Dominican were admitted to the Collegium strictum of
the theological faculty in addition to the regular eight members or regents. De
Vocht noted that the move coincided with Erasmus' being co-opted into the
Collegium largum (see Ep 637:12n) and suggested that it was designed to
counterbalance the latter; de Vocht MHL 190–1.
20 bull] See Ep 611:82n.
29 Siberch] Johann Lair of Siegburg, near Cologne (d 1554). In 1492 he was
admitted to the University of Cologne. Subsequently he married a sister of

809 / To Mark Lauwerijns   Louvain, 5 April 1518

> This letter presents a defence of Erasmus' commitment to Christian humanism
> that is comparable to Ep 296 but less wide in scope. It was evidently designed
> for wide circulation and was printed at the first opportunity in the *Auctarium*.
> Perhaps Erasmus also hoped that it might serve his friends in the Netherlands
> in case he were attacked during his absence in Basel; see Ep 770 introduction.

ERASMUS OF ROTTERDAM TO HIS FRIEND
MARK LAUWERIJNS, GREETING

I must thank you for your letter – your parcel of unmixed affection, I would
call it; such was the language, such the atmosphere of every line. For my
part, I look forward to enjoying your society as much as you do mine, and   5
this, I hope, will still be possible. As for the abuse I get from the detractors
who, after getting their teeth into everyone, are now at length charging me
with infirmity of purpose, I laughed, I must admit, for I am well used to that
sort of nonsense, but it was a partly sardonic laugh. For I myself should find
a good conscience sufficient protection against their calumnies; but who   10
could bear without impatience men's obstinate and perverse ingratitude?
No one has more need of my work than those who clamour so loudly against
my researches, of which they get the benefit; and no one clamours more
furiously and fiercely than those who have never so much as seen the cover
of the book. Try the experiment, my dear Mark, and you will find I am   15
speaking the truth. When you happen on a man of this sort, let him rant
away against my New Testament, and when he has unloaded all his bad
temper and made himself quite hoarse, ask him whether he has read
through the actual book. If he puts a bold face on it and says he has read it,
urge him to produce a passage he disapproves of. You will find no one who   20
can.

   Just consider how Christian it is, how worthy indeed of those who
have taken monastic vows, in front of the uneducated multitude to do

* * * * *

Franz Birckmann's wife and became a travelling book seller. In 1519 he was at
Cambridge, where he set up the first press, printing a number of books in 1521
and 1522, including the unauthorized first edition of Erasmus' *De conscribendis epistolis* (cf Ep 71 introduction). In 1526 he returned to Siegburg, where he
afterwards held a benefice; see O. Treptow et al *John Siberch* (Cambridge
1970).

809
3 letter] An answer to Ep 789
6 possible] Cf lines 193–4, Ep 831:117n.
9 sardonic] *Adagia* III v 1

damage to a man's reputation which they could not repair even if they
wanted to, being perfectly ignorant what it is they are attacking, and not   25
stopping to think of the truth of Paul's words 'Revilers shall not possess the
kingdom of God.' Nor can any sort of obloquy be more criminal than to
accuse a man of heresy, a word they instantly apply to anyone who annoys
them even by a nod of his head.

   And then it is like the custom among the Swiss, where (they say) one   30
of the crowd raises his finger, and they all raise a finger and rush upon the
spoil: the moment any of that crew sets up a squeal of suspicion, they squeal
one and all, appeal to the mob for help, and summon them to start throwing
stones, as though they had forgotten their monastic vows and had vowed to
do nothing more than to befoul the names of honest men with their slimy,   35
venomous tongues, just as the Psalmist puts it: 'They have sharpened their
tongues like serpents, the poison of asps is under their lips.' Thus those
who ought to be preachers of Christian piety are zealous detractors of the
piety of other men; they profess themselves stewards of the mysteries and
prove themselves purveyors of calumny. And (what almost amounts to a   40
portent) although they are tongue-tied in the way of blessing, when it
comes to calumny and innuendo their tongues are loose enough; in other
respects they give the Muses and the Graces a wide berth, but in spreading
filth over the reputations of honest men they think they show their wit and
charm.   45

   On top of that, what they cannot do themselves they hire other men to
do, suborning some worthless Cherylus or third-rate speaker; such is their
passion for making mischief and their thirst for something perfectly easy
and perfectly outrageous. To do good is far from easy, but at the same time it
is our Christian duty; why do they not choose that department to show   50
what great and honourable men they are, if they wish to be anything of the
kind? This sort of men richly deserved to be put on record as a warning to
posterity what outstanding perversity of character and intelligence can lurk

* * * * *

26 Paul's words] 1 Cor 6:10
31 raises his finger] As a sign of victory. Attempts to prevent premature looting
    had begun as early as 1393, when the Sempacherbrief laid down that looting
    was not permitted until the commander had given the sign that the battle was
    won. After his hearing before the Diet of Worms on 18 April 1521, Martin
    Luther stretched out his arm like a victorious warrior (so reported by the
    eye-witness Sixtus Oelhafen; see H. Grisar *Luther* trans E.M. Lamond, Lon-
    don 1914–17, II 65).
36 Psalmist] Ps 139:4 (Vulgate)
47 Cherylus] A court poet of Alexander the Great, proverbial for his lack of
    inspiration; e.g. Horace *Ars poetica* 357

beneath the outward semblance of the Christian religion; and maybe I
could find strength to do this if I were to put some effort into it. But I am 55
dissuaded partly by the self-restraint proper to a Christian and partly by the
unfairness of bringing ill will for the sake of a few malignant individuals on
religious orders as a whole, for I know there are very many in them who
resent these men's effrontery as much as I do. I much prefer to take into
account the men of distinguished piety, learning, and position who express 60
their gratitude for my nightly labours, such as they are, approving my
intentions, I suppose, if I have not achieved my purpose. Otherwise, if I
found those mischief-makers typical of the majority, nothing would have
been easier than to fall asleep and hold my peace, making music for Christ
and myself alone. 65

Then again, they object that my making a new edition proves my
dissatisfaction with the earlier one. Let us pretend that this is true: what
have they to complain of, if I do my best to surpass myself and to do what
Origen did and Jerome did, yes, and what Augustine did? Especially since I
openly announced in the first edition that I would do so if it should prove 70
desirable. At the moment this is not my purpose, but I am trying to do the
same as I have now done for the third time in the publication of my
Proverbs. Besides which, I was sparing of changes in the earlier translation,
in order not to annoy over much those men who are so quick to find fault;
but now, on the advice of good scholars, I have attempted rather more in 75
this direction. Then I support these changed passages by more frequently
naming my authorities, so as to give no scope for rejection to the people
who are hard to convince. Finally, I add some references which in my haste I
formerly overlooked. If anything has slipped in here and there that might
offend learned and pious ears, I do not hesitate to alter it, nor will I deny that 80
I am only mortal.

They are welcome to despise this first edition, if I have not cleared up
in it many passages in which Thomas Aquinas went astray, to say nothing

* * * * *

64 music] Cf Ep 731:44n.
70 in the first edition] Erasmus had made an analogous statement in the *Apologia
ad Fabrum* (LB IX 53E). In the preliminary pieces to the *Novum instrumentum* of
1516 he had in fact invited criticism and offered to make corrections: *Novum
instrumentum* f bbb⁶; cf LB VI f **2 recto and Ep 373:238–40. Some of his letters
spoke more directly of his intention to produce a new edition (Epp 417:7–10,
421:76–8, 446:79–82), but he realized that Froben would need time to sell the
first (cf Ep 801:13–14). His revision was spurred on by his own dissatisfaction
with the proofreaders of the 1516 edition and by the criticisms of others; see
Ep 864 introduction.
73 *Proverbs*] Cf Ep 269:4–5.

of the rest. Let them deny this or disprove it if they can. If it is obvious and
generally accepted, they must admit how much they have stood to profit 85
from my work – work from which Thomas too would have benefited, were
he still alive. Let no one twist what I say into a criticism of him. I make no
comparison between him and myself, though I have explained some points
which had escaped him. What I have said of Thomas, they may consider
said of Lyra, or of Augustine and Hilary for that matter. Let them despise 90
this, once they have admitted that I have expounded countless places which
previously were not understood even by men of more than average learning.

On top of that, why do these gentry condemn something that is not
condemned by the pope, to whom the work is dedicated? I sent it to him, he 95
accepted it and read it, he sent me a letter of thanks and showed his
gratitude by his actions. But these wretches, such is their natural stupidity,
and doubly blinded as they are by a morbid passion for finding fault,
believe, I suppose, that I wished to put out of business the whole of the
version now in common use, which I frequently prefer to the reading of the 100
Greeks. In fact, I have translated only what I found in the Greek manuscripts, indicating in my notes what I approve of and what not. Very well,
let them imagine that I had nothing else in mind and merely translated the
Greek manuscripts so that they might be compared with the current edition
by Latin-speakers who know no Greek: what pray would they have to 105
complain of? As it is, I show in so many places by manifest proof that our
text is corrupt, though without any risk to the faith. I show that Cyprian and
Jerome and Ambrose agree with the Greek copies. And yet they cry out
exactly as though I had committed sacrilege. But what purpose is served,
my dear Mark, by using proofs with people who deliberately close their 110
eyes that they may not see and their ears that they may not hear? All their
objections had been fully met in my *Apologiae*, were they willing to understand; if they are not willing, it will be vain to try and satisfy men who
prefer calumny to instruction.

But my firmness of purpose is now called in question by these strait- 115
laced critics because they have heard that I propose to visit Basel. As though
I were to visit Basel for my own amusement, or had ever done so! I have
edited Jerome, I have edited the New Testament, and much besides; and in
order to do a service to the reading public I have thought nothing of a most

* * * * *

90 Lyra] Nicholas of Lyra (d 1349), a scriptural commentator, elsewhere much
abused by Erasmus
96 letter of thanks] Ep 519, but cf Epp 338:27n, 835 introduction.
112 *Apologiae*] Cf line 70n and the *Ratio verae theologiae* (Ep 745 introduction).

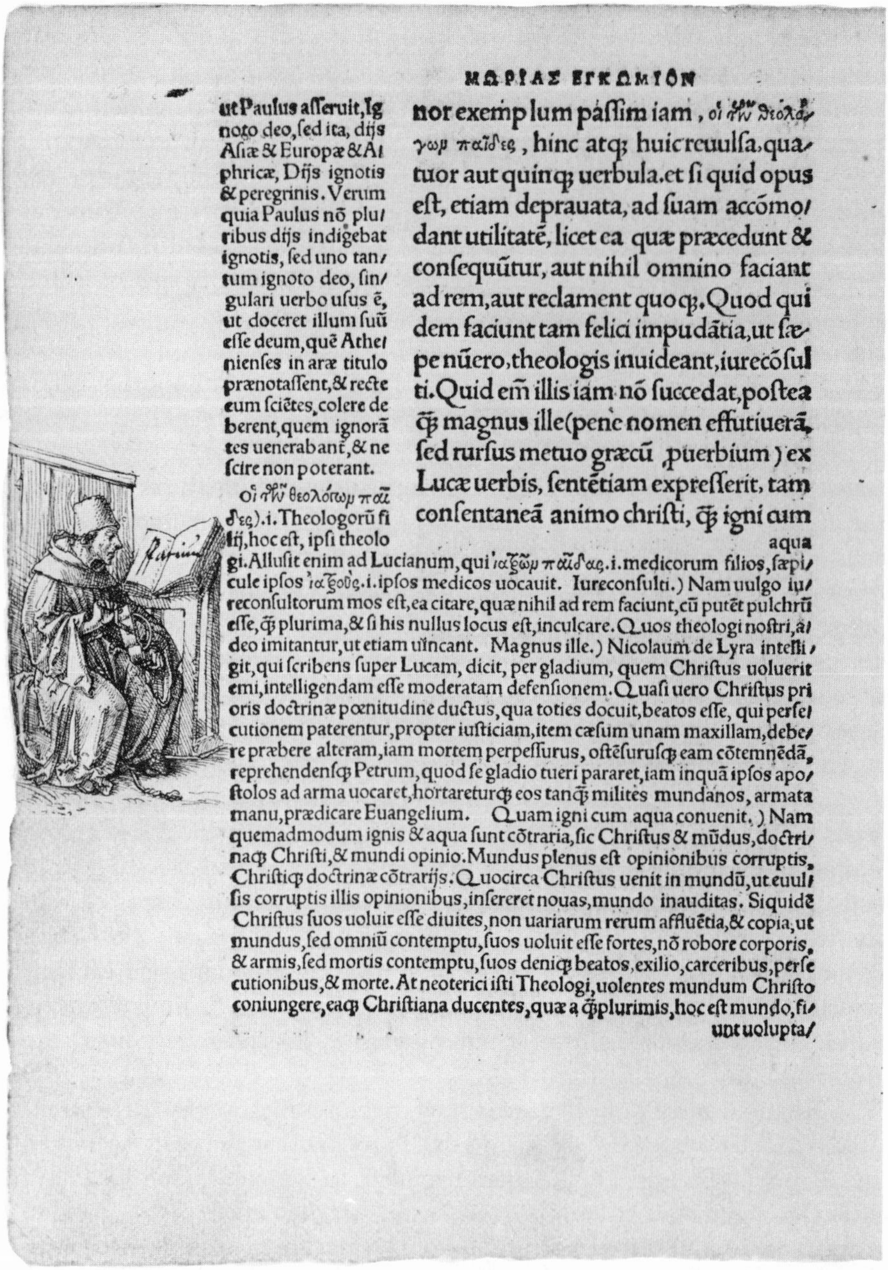

ΜΩΡΙΑΣ ΕΓΚΩΜΙΟΝ

nor exemplum paſſim iam, οἱ τῶν θεολό/
γων παῖδες, hinc atq; huic reuulſa, qua/
tuor aut quinq; uerbula. et ſi quid opus
eſt, etiam deprauata, ad ſuam accõmo/
dant utilitatẽ, licet ea quæ præcedunt &
conſequũtur, aut nihil omnino faciant
ad rem, aut reclament quoq;. Quod qui
dem faciunt tam felici impudãtia, ut ſæ/
pe nũero, theologis inuideant, iurecõſul
ti. Quid em̃ illis iam nõ ſuccedat, poſtea
q̃ magnus ille (pene nomen effutiuerã,
ſed rurſus metuo græcũ ꝓuerbium) ex
Lucæ uerbis, ſentẽtiam expreſſerit, tam
conſentaneã animo chriſti, q̃ igni cum
aqua

ut Paulus aſſeruit, Ig
noto deo, ſed ita, dijs
Aſiæ & Europæ & A/
phricæ, Dijs ignotis
& peregrinis. Verum
quia Paulus nõ plu/
ribus dijs indigebat
ignotis, ſed uno tan/
tum ignoto deo, ſin/
gulari uerbo uſus ẽ,
ut doceret illum ſuũ
eſſe deum, quẽ Athe/
nienſes in aræ titulo
prænotaſſent, & recte
eum ſciẽtes, colere de
berent, quem ignorã
tes uenerabant, & ne
ſcire non poterant.

οἱ τῶν θεολόγων παῖ
δες). i. Theologorũ fi
lij, hoc eſt, ipſi theolo
gi. Alluſit enim ad Lucianum, qui ἰατρῶν παῖδας. i. medicorum filios, ſæpi/
cule ipſos ἰατρούς. i. ipſos medicos uocauit. Iureconſulti.) Nam uulgo iu/
reconſultorum mos eſt, ea citare, quæ nihil ad rem faciunt, cũ putẽt pulchrũ
eſſe, q̃ plurima, & ſi his nullus locus eſt, inculcare. Quos theologi noſtri, a/
deo imitantur, ut etiam uincant. Magnus ille.) Nicolaum de Lyra intelli/
git, qui ſcribens ſuper Lucam, dicit, per gladium, quem Chriſtus uoluerit
emi, intelligendam eſſe moderatam defenſionem. Quaſi uero Chriſtus pri
oris doctrinæ pœnitudine ductus, qua toties docuit, beatos eſſe, qui perſe/
cutionem paterentur, propter iuſticiam, item cæſum unam maxillam, debe/
re præbere alteram, iam mortem perpeſſurus, oſtẽſuruſq; eam cõtemnẽdã,
reprehendenſq; Petrum, quod ſe gladio tueri pararet, iam inquã ipſos apo/
ſtolos ad arma uocaret, hortareturq; eos tanq̃ milites mundanos, armata
manu, prædicare Euangelium. Quam igni cum aqua conuenit.) Nam
quemadmodum ignis & aqua ſunt cõtraria, ſic Chriſtus & mũdus, doctri/
naq; Chriſti, & mundi opinio. Mundus plenus eſt opinionibus corruptis,
Chriſtiq; doctrinæ cõtrarijs. Quocirca Chriſtus uenit in mundũ, ut euul/
ſis corruptis illis opinionibus, insereret nouas, mundo inauditas. Siquidẽ
Chriſtus ſuos uoluit eſſe diuites, non uariarum rerum affluẽtia, & copia, ut
mundus, ſed omniũ contemptu, ſuos uoluit eſſe fortes, nõ robore corporis,
& armis, ſed mortis contemptu, ſuos deniq; beatos, exilio, carceribus, perſe
cutionibus, & morte. At neoterici iſti Theologi, uolentes mundum Chriſto
coniungere, eaq; Chriſtiana ducentes, quæ a q̃plurimis, hoc eſt mundo, fi/
unt uolupta/

Nicholas of Lyra
Satirical portrait of Nicholas playing a hurdy-gurdy (or *lyra rustica*)
by Hans Holbein the Younger
in a copy of Froben's 1515 edition of *Moriae encomium*
Kupferstichkabinett Basel (Inv 1662 166 f T3 verso)

perilous journey, nothing of the expense, nothing at all of the toils in which   120
I have worn out a great part of my health and life itself. 'Infirm of purpose'
indeed! Because I would not rather stay drinking with them than set off for
Basel. They themselves go trotting off to Rome and back, they are here there
and everywhere, land and sea alike – not at their own expense, for poverty is
their profession, but by scraping together all the money they can get from   125
milking widows laden with sins whom they drive out of their minds, or
despoiling some devout sisterhood, or defrauding simple brethren of their
comforts. All this in order to make mischief and sully the good name of men
who do good service to the Christian commonwealth; and they pass, if you
please, for firm and weighty men! And I, because I serve the public good at   130
my own expense and to my own detriment, I am infirm of purpose! Let him
choose himself, say they, a city to dwell in. Why, do they think I live here in
a Scythian wilderness? Do they regard as outside the realm of nature anyone
they do not meet nightly over their wine? My home, in my own opinion, is
wherever I keep my library and such possessions as I have. If the public   135
interest counsels me to change my abode, I should be praised, if I am not
mistaken, for my sense of duty and not condemned for infirmity of purpose.
If I had been allowed to commute the obligation of this journey for three
hundred gold crowns, I would have paid over the cash without reluctance;
as it is, business required it, and I had to go. Never have I moved from one   140
country to another unless driven by the plague, compelled by ill-health, or
for some honourable business reasons. To Italy alone I have journeyed of
my own free will, partly to pay at least one visit to her holy places, partly to
profit from the libraries of that part of the world and make the acquaintance
of its men of learning. If this was infirmity of purpose, I have yet to regret it.   145
     I have now lived here nearly two years without a break. I might have
joined his Catholic Majesty with the most generous prospects. I have been
invited with the promise of mountains of gold by the king of France. I have
been invited on most generous terms by the king of England and his grace
the cardinal of York, and by Francis archbishop of Toledo, who died so   150
lately. I have been invited by the bishops of Paris and Bayeux, by the

* * * * *

126 laden with sins] Cf 2 Tim 3:6.
146 here] In the Netherlands
147 Catholic Majesty] See Epp 596 introduction, 608:19n.
148 mountains of gold] *Adagia* i ix 15
148 France] See Ep 522:52–8.
149 king of England ... cardinal of York] See Ep 694:11n.
150 Toledo] See Epp 582:11n, 597:53–4.
151 Paris] See Ep 778:33n.
151 Bayeux] See Ep 489.

archbishop of Mainz and the bishops of Liège and Utrecht, of Basel and of
Rochester, by the duke of Bavaria and the duke of Saxony. This is not mere
invention, the facts are widely known, the truth is established from many
letters I have had directly from them. All these I have put aside and   155
concentrated solely on the task I had in hand; and I am called infirm of
purpose because, having begun my work with such long nights of toil, I
yearn to finish it. If the virtue of firmness consists in staying as long as
possible in the same place, first prize must go to stocks and stones, and after
them to barnacles and sponges. There is nothing wrong in changing your   160
abode; to change it for a bad reason is wrong, nor is there any virtue in
remaining a long time in the same place, but in living there in honour. They
praise Socrates for spending his life as a virtuous citizen of Athens; they do
not criticize Plato for his travels. John the Baptist never left Judaea. Christ
did but reach its borders. Yet we do not condemn the apostles for infirmity   165
of purpose because they travelled all the world over. No one criticizes
Hilarion's wanderings because Paul never set foot outside his cave.

   Yet why do I cite these examples to men who do not even remain firmly
in the same town? For they are ever switching meadow and manger and
migrating to some place where there is more promise in the smoke and   170
savour from the kitchen chimney. 'Infirm of purpose' they call me because I
have not spent forty-five years in the same town drinking with them – like a
lot of sponges fixed on a rock whose life consists in drinking – sharing their
fornication, their gambling, their mischief-making. Personally I prefer my
infirmity of purpose to their firmness many times over. For I think it far and   175
away more creditable to have lived in many places on such terms that,
wherever you have lived, all the best men hope for your return, than to live
in the same town the kind of life that makes no difference to anyone when it
is over – to say nothing of a life of vice. Suppose ill health obliges one to

* * * * *

152 Mainz] See Ep 661.
152 Liège] See Ep 746.
152 Utrecht] See Ep 682 introduction.
152 Basel] See Ep 598.
153 Rochester] See Epp 577, 592:24–5.
153 Bavaria] See Ep 704:45n.
153 Saxony] See Ep 514. In August 1518 there was talk of Erasmus' visiting the
     University of Leipzig; see *Documenta literaria varii argumenti* J. Heumann ed
     (Altdorf 1758) 233.
167 Hilarion's ... Paul] Paul of Thebes (fl c 300) was the first and Hilarion of Gaza (d
     371) the second anchorite whose biographies were written by Jerome (PL
     23:17–54). In his edition of Jerome Erasmus held that by travelling around
     Hilarion became as famous as Paul did by staying hidden; see his short
     argument to the life of Hilarion, *Hieronymi opera* (Basel 1516) I f 109 verso.

change one's abode: will they not excuse a man who has to think about his   180
health? At the moment they condemn me for putting the public interest
first. But do these men reject my work? Let them do so, provided it is
acceptable to men of character and learning; no one need be wiser than he
wishes, to please me. But as for them, my dear Mark, let us have done with
them; let us love good men in pure Christian charity and put up with bad, if   185
they cannot be mended even by doing them a service. Sooner or later every
thistle finds its donkey. The tough knot will find its match in a tough wedge,
and

> seeking to sink their teeth in the soft crumb,
> they'll crash them on a flint.   190

Personally I have neither leisure nor spirit to do battle with this scum.

I should not like you to run over here if it is inconvenient; otherwise
you will be most welcome. I hope to see you soon, to spend some days with
you and enjoy the pleasure of your society before I leave; though my
absence is not to be a long one. If I go to Basel, I shall be back next autumn; if   195
it is Venice, next spring. I am surprised that you make no mention of my
servant John, whom I sent to England a month ago; for I think he paid you
his respects. Farewell, most trustworthy of friends.

Louvain, Easter Monday 1518

810 / From Guillaume Budé   Paris, 12 April [1518]

This letter answers Ep 778. It was given to Adolf Eichholz for delivery (see Ep
819:2) and reached Pieter Gillis safely in Antwerp (see Epp 846, 849). But on its
way to Erasmus at Basel it went astray and did not reach him until about 1
September, immediately before his departure for Louvain. This he explained
in a brief preliminary reply to Budé, Ep 869. Subsequently he answered at
great length in Ep 906.

This letter was first published in the *Farrago*. It divides into two parts (cf Ep
723 introduction). The first is a critique of Erasmus' conduct with regard to
Lefèvre (cf Ep 597:37n). The second, starting at line 387, encourages Erasmus
to state his terms for a move to Paris. The argument is hairsplitting, but the
tone sincere and even warm. Unfortunately Budé himself raises the possibility

* * * * *

186 every thistle] *Adagia* I x 71
187 tough knot] Cf *Adagia* I ii 5.
189 'seeking ... flint'] Horace *Satires* 2.1.77, 78
196 Venice] See Ep 770 introduction.
197 John] Smith; see Ep 772 introduction.

that he is writing in jest (line 453) and he declines personal responsibility (lines 471–2) for the negotiations with Francis I.

BUDÉ TO ERASMUS, GREETING

Here I am, protesting again! I was complaining that I had had nothing in the way of a letter from you for many months now, nothing at least that I should call a letter, when you sent me one as quarrelsome as it was lengthy, just as though I had roused you rather roughly from a prolonged sleep, which is 5 your prolonged neglect of me. Hutten, whom I and my friends think as well of and like as much as you do, on his way back from attendance on the king passed through here and extracted a hasty letter from me, in which I put down anything that came into my head in either Greek or Latin, and added a word or two, I think, about that *Apologia* of yours, regretting that the 10 publication of it, coupled with what Lefèvre had written, might give the impression that something like a quarrel had broken out between you. I do not remember very clearly what I wrote, and it was the sort of letter of which I do not generally keep a copy. At these few words of mine you have taken offence passionately, and have turned your horns suddenly against the 15 peacemaker, as though I had rashly or eagerly taken up the contest on Lefèvre's behalf, and diverted the greater part of your attack against my unsuspecting self, even though by a kindly expression from time to time you seem to mingle caresses with expostulations.

In the first place, I wish to make this quite clear, that I have not cast 20 myself for the part of peacemaker or arbiter agreed on by the parties in this matter, not from any fear that if I did so you would not leave me unscathed, or that you would be indignant with me if I took such liberties with you, but because I have never had a word on the subject with Lefèvre. I had therefore no reason to desire the role of arbiter in the case, which was not referred to 25 me by the two parties or laid before me on their initiative; though Louis Ruzé, the deputy-prefect of Paris, who is by choice a friend to all good scholars, told me to do so, and when I refused covered me with reproaches. But being sorry to see you, as an old and dear friend, in that position, I thought I ought to say something, if for no other reason, for this at least, that 30 you should not suppose I was asleep when your case and his were being pleaded at length and often before a large audience at the tribunal of public

* * * * *

810
2 complaining] At the beginning of Ep 744
4 sent me one] Ep 778
8 a hasty letter] Ep 744
27 Ruzé] Cf Ep 744:54n.

opinion; with the further point, to tell the truth, that I reckon Lefèvre too
among my friends. You will say I am Pandora's husband over again, trying
– or so you complain – to apply some remedy to a cause which is already lost   35
and explaining when Troy has already fallen that Helen should never have
been carried off. Now, dear brother Prometheus, have you forgotten saying
in your letter 'Lefèvre, who is given honourable mention so often in my
preface, repays me in an odd fashion, which many people at least think
unfair. I too feel that he is treating me more harshly than his usual frank   40
friendliness would suggest. I regret the opening thus afforded,' and so on.
At that point you should give advance warning that you are planning a
defence, and I perhaps should have performed my function. It was you
made me an Epimetheus; for all you cared, I was not to discover that the play
was to be produced until you had already sent someone on the stage to   45
speak the prologue.

   'So what is the object,' you will say, 'of speaking out now? Unless you
wish to give the impression of giving a black mark, or a black-and-white
one, to my *Apologia*; for you nearly always under-value my work on some
pre-conceived principles, misusing (some people think) your confidence in   50
our long-standing friendship.' Pray, dear Erasmus, bite your lip and let me
borrow your patience for a little while, while I upbraid you in my turn. For I
simply must reply to your letter, which was elegantly written and successful
in point of style, but in fairness and sympathy left something to be desired,
as you will not deny if you are now yourself again and have recovered your   55
former spirit – at any rate, as far as my own case is concerned; to think only
of myself for the moment, for from time to time you slap me or box my ears,
and then smoothe me down again with honeyed words, so that I cannot
rightly appeal for help, as though I had made the cause my own like an
incompetent arbitrator, just because I dared put in a word, however briefly,   60
when you were disputing with Lefèvre.

   * * * * *

34 Pandora's husband] Epimetheus. Budé repeats Erasmus' words in Ep
   778:116–18. It follows, as Budé notes, that Erasmus himself is the impetuous
   Prometheus.
37 saying] Perhaps in a letter now lost. In reply (Ep 906 end) Erasmus stated that
   Budé's passage was unclear. He also seemed to question the citation. Budé,
   however, insisted (Ep 915 postscript) that he had copied it from one of
   Erasmus' letters, although he could not say which. He also insisted that he had
   meant to suggest that the citation failed to make reference to the *Apologia ad
   Fabrum* at a time when Erasmus had already decided to reply.
47 you will say] Cf Allen Epp 906: 133–6, 915:130–5.
48 black mark] *Adagia* i v 53
55 will not deny] Cf Ep 896 postscript.
57 slap me or box my ears] Juvenal 13.127, 128

And somehow you have slipped back again to those 'trivialities' and the unfair criticism of your *Copia*, being unable to control your indignation. These are points on which I was wrong, and you forgave me long ago when I apologized; and now, like a man demanding the return of a present, you 65 bring a collateral action against me on the same facts by way of appeal and enter a fresh indictment for an offence which I supposed to be once and for all expunged in good faith from the archives of your memory. Is this necessary? If I say something to you as to an old acquaintance, relying on the privilege of friendship, must you unsheath the flashing blade of your 70 eloquence against me? In order to oblige your rather passionate spirit, must you have the law on me until it is satisfied? Because I cannot write as well as you can, are you confident without more ado that you will win your case? And will you expect all grave and reverend seniors to give you the verdict? Even though, beginner as I am, I may have the right on my side? Even 75 though your ally the goddess of Wisdom may find Justice herself against her? Even though the very facts cry out that you rely not so much on a foundation of equity as on a façade of eloquence?

But 'Tell me,' you say, 'for I leave the whole thing to your decision, I accept the law of friendship: what do you think I should do? Will you try to 80 persuade your old friend to say thank you to Lefèvre for the honour he has done me?' Most certainly not. 'Or to pretend that I do not know what he has written?' Of course I would try to persuade you, if it was open for you to do so. And why? First, because you are Erasmus. Secondly, you are a theologian. Thirdly, you are one of those theologians who have seen active service 85 in the cause of ambition and reputation, and have earned their discharge; you can be quite sure that you have reached a level of distinction that absolves you henceforward from depending on panegyrics from other people. Suppose that Lefèvre, however highly we may value him, should in defence of something of his own go wrong somewhere (as often happens) 90 about something of yours, are you of all people to be afraid that your reputation will instantly be imperilled by this hostile verdict, unless you enter an appearance with a long and carefully thought-out defence? And a defence in such terms! But I will stop there. As though one would suppose a man to admit an accusation without more ado who, when it is levelled 95 against him no matter how, has failed to issue a spirited and indignant reply! So likely, is it not, that in future some grand tribunal of the learned will deprive you unheard of your civic rights and reputation if you fail to reply instantly to any foolish criticism that appears in print!

* * * * *

62 'trivialities'] Cf Epp 435:74–92, 778:212–20; Allen 906:222–8.
79 you say] Ep 778:145–8

'Yes,' you will say, 'but it is no ordinary man and no casual accusation   100
that have forced me against my will to enter the lists. It is Lefèvre, in old
days, and still I suppose, my friend and a scholar of distinction, and the
charge he brings against me is impiety.' I know what tragic passions these
words can arouse. I can see that, once I concede that his intentions in casting
these aspersions on you were as full of outrage as the spirit in which you   105
have accepted them, once I give you free rein to plead your case with a full
and proper display of argument, I shall never get out of you the admission
that you are wrong. But who could recommend or endorse such behaviour?
There you are, with all that reputation, all that glory earned by such a list of
publications, raised to such a pinnacle of distinction by all your achieve-   110
ments in this department of public life; and yet in controversies like this
you seem to put your trust more in disputatiousness and dreary pamphlets
full of argument than in the unspoken verdict of every scholar and every
man of judgment. In this contest it seems to me that you would be victorious
all the sooner if you stood your ground in silence and refused to listen to   115
attacks on what you have written, rather than treating the charges as though
they deserved serious attention and putting together a string of arguments,
as with your great talents you so easily can. As far as I am concerned, I read
with admiration the case you make against Lefèvre and what you say in
your own defence, and I felicitate you on those powers of expression by   120
which I am quite overcome; but when I think of the position you hold, I fear
that in what you write on this you will be thought by the majority of
educated men to have gone too far. At this point, of all absurd things, you
will adduce Jerome as your precedent for this behaviour, who, you will say,
could not endure Rufinus' metaphors, and threatened Augustine because   125
he had ruined the interpretation of a single passage. How can we be sure
that this was not the reason why he was brought before Christ's judgment-
seat and given a whipping? I would rather you offered me the whole of
Jerome as a model, instead of putting forward a sort of blemish in him as an
example. It is like Phidias' Minerva, whose sandal was open to criticism.   130
For Jerome himself was not beyond making mistakes, and even Augustine
admitted that he was often wrong and actually wrote books devoted to
nothing else.

* * * * *

124 Jerome] Cf Ep 778:266–71.
127 judgment-seat] In his famous dream; cf Opuscula 153–4.
130 Phidias'] One of the greatest of Greek sculptors. For the sandal of the goddess
    as the one thing with which one could find fault, cf Adagia I v 74, where,
    however, the goddess is Venus, and not the statue of Minerva (Athene) by
    Phidias.
132 to nothing else] The Retractationes (PL 32:583–656)

I see you stamp your foot in irritation; but it is essential that you endure to the end and give me the whole of your attention while you take in   135
what I say, for in your long letter you played fast and loose with me just as you pleased, as though I had betrayed our friendship and sided with your opponent or used the freedom of a letter to reduce the value of your work. Therefore pray hear me out. You would have been thought, would you, to have abandoned Augustine and Jerome and almost the whole body of   140
orthodox Fathers under the shadow of the guilt you shared with them, had you not come forward as champion of the truth and answered Lefèvre? Suppose the same would be true of you, turned the other way round? Which are we to believe, that you were afraid of being tainted with disgrace in common with so many authorities of the first rank, or that you were really   145
more concerned for their reputation than your own? As though those great men were not quite capable of bringing over our contemporaries or pos- terity to their way of thinking and yours, merely by the force of their own authority; or as though it would have been disgraceful and disastrous for you, had you not defended yourself against accusations which touched   150
them too.

In arguing thus, I speak as though Lefèvre admits or cannot deny that in all this he has been the slave of his own indignation rather than writing what he did as a contribution to a debate which was too passionate, maybe, but undoubtedly was aimed at the defence of truth. On the question at issue   155
between you I do not touch; I know you think it goes beyond my own field or even is too sacred to be exposed to the votes of outsiders. Nor has it entered into the discussion in the immediate controversy which is now brought up for decision. But when you say that to use force to repel force is a principle of our public law, I agree with you if you adopt the civil law as   160
your shield in this case. But remember: that chapter of law or interdict on the use of force has not been adopted by the eternal praetor and supreme judge as part of his code or his edict; and in any case, the civil law to which you appeal demands from the injured party that his self-defence be limited and itself free from all taint of wrong. If you ask for justice in accordance   165
with this principle, I fear I may be unable to exculpate you: you have published such a huge defence, and in such terms too, for fear of not being thought to have got even with a few short pages in his commentary. This I am sure you would never have done had you been willing to take your own indignation as a guide and not your friends, who support you (or so many   170

* * * * *

140 Augustine ... Jerome] Cf Ep 778:201–3.
156 you think] Cf Ep 778:196–9, 339–43.

men think) with more zeal than discretion and do not always see clearly what is best for you.

Be that as it may, of this I am entirely convinced: if some deity were able and willing at this moment to allow you to begin again, so that what has been published could be erased from the memory of men, and if you 175 yourself were willing to keep the decision to yourself and give your friends no share in it, you would inevitably so arrange matters (I put it as concisely as I can) that you would for preference show yourself the winner by your responsible and moderate behaviour, rather than by a sub-acid exchange of verbiage and disputation. Besides, I suppose that Lefèvre in the same way 180 must be sorry for what has happened, being the excellent man he is, as you yourself seem to have recognized elsewhere, when you attribute these events too to Homer's Infatuation, who 'with madness fraught strides o'er the heads of men.' Nor is there anything I should find harder to believe than that he himself should reply to your *Apologia*, though an irresponsible 185 rumour has spread as far as you, or perhaps the over-zealous suspicions of your supporters have imagined that Lefèvre is engaged on something of the sort. I hear, moreover, that he speaks highly of what you write, not with any insincerity or innuendo or secret hostility or through some sudden change of heart, but in good faith and habitually and with the air of one who means 190 what he says, although your *Apologia* may have irritated him perhaps. Who would be surprised if you were to make him unhappy on a point where you are not happy yourself? As I gather from your letter too, in which you seemed to me to make it pretty plain that you entered this contest with reluctance. 195

You see how lavishly I take advantage of the rights of friendship and use the undue freedom of an intimate. I can see already how much you are annoyed with me as you read this, for proving (you think) such a biased judge, though you yourself in your letter call me most impartial, since, having been entrusted by you with the arbitration of this dispute, I have 200 given my ruling against you in this contest, which you have so much at heart; so that it may well prove impossible for you even to appeal to any other judge, having entrusted the arbitration of this matter to me absolutely – not even to that same Budé who does at least pay attention to what you say in your own defence – though you meant to reserve the right to do so. For, 205

* * * * *

183 Infatuation] *Iliad* 19. 93–4. Budé is referring to the *Apologia ad Fabrum* (LB IX 59A).
194 with reluctance] Cf Ep 778:62–3.
199 most impartial] Cf Ep 778:88.
205 meant to reserve] Cf Ep 778:354–5.

say you, you are behaving most unfairly and most unlike yourself. Do not provoke me, then, with your trumped-up charges that I have overthrown what you have written and made light of your *Copia*, to the indignation of your friends. Whether in this I ought to find you lacking in fairness is a question that I may perhaps raise on another occasion, for you must know   210
perfectly well what I think, and have put in writing, about your work.

But to turn after all this to something serious, I should like you to understand that it is still open to me to make up my own mind on this dispute between you. For although you for your part were willing up to a point to leave the matter to my decision, Lefèvre may perhaps be unwilling   215
to run the hazard of such a verdict, for I suspect that he actually believes me to lean towards you; while you hold a different opinion and are not slow in your letter to regard me as a hostile witness, if I may use that lawyers' term. But even if both of you by agreement were to entrust the arbitration of this to me, I should be loath to undertake it. If, however, you do not reject me as   220
an adviser, I should eagerly counsel you for the future to devote yourselves once more to the duties of friendship; and if that cannot happen itself in the near future while your feelings though now at rest are not yet fully purged, at least to bury the past in silence and, if you can manage it, in oblivion. Though great authors give you an honourable precedent, when you and he   225
are writing something in the future, for covering over this minor damage to your reputations with some honourable scar or cunning plaster and giving other scholars to understand that this was more a difference of opinion than personal hostility. When I wrote to you as I did, I wanted not so much to condemn what had happened, which by this time there was no holding and   230
which had passed out of your control; I strove to restrain the increasing tension between you that it might not grow beyond all bounds – although you put a different interpretation on this, being always unfairly suspicious of me. And this is the general feeling among us here about your dispute: good men whose opinion counts are more sorry to see that certain mad fits,   235
which can only harm the interests of good literature, have raised such a commotion between you, than they are ready to condemn one of you and acquit the other; what they wish most is to see you make it up. This perhaps is how the famous dispute between Jerome and Rufinus was finally settled; but that was more obstinate and bitter while it raged. So true is it that all   240

* * * * *

208 *Copia*] Cf Ep 778:212–20.
211 in writing] Especially in the flattering Ep 583, which Erasmus now planned to publish; cf Ep 767:7n.
218 lawyers' term] Cf Corpus iuris civilis *Codex Justinianus* v 43, 2.
229 wrote to you] Ep 744:74–99

men err, and our status as human beings means that even in men otherwise
of the highest standing one finds this fault in plenty: the fatal attractions of
strife creep on over the reason and drive a man into such a state of obstinacy
that he would rather do the most misguided things to defend his reputation
than check the passion that wells up in his mind.   245

For my part, my dear Erasmus, to speak to you now quite frankly,
when I first understood this, I could not help but be sorry both for you and
for Lefèvre. After all the service you have both seen in Pallas' standing
army, each at his allotted post, at a time when all the companies both of
juniors and veterans were already taking the view that the two of you   250
deserved to hold high command, some sinister influence impelled you to
reduce yourselves again very nearly to the ranks. If you two were to go still
further, to let obstinacy have its own way and dispute pigheadedly to the
extent of open strife, I should be afraid that in the opinion of all those men of
worth and influence whose vote carries the day the two of you would finally   255
be cashiered and stripped of your honour and glory. As for him, though a
friend of long standing rather than an acquaintance and bound to me by our
common manner of life and the ideas we share, he must be responsible for
his own conduct. But you, who have now invited me in two letters to take
cognizance of this business, if you wish to be your true self and to win me   260
over to join your party, must of necessity adopt the attitude of one who will
do as he is told, even if you protest inwardly and grind your teeth without a
word. So let us hear no more of that sentence in your letter 'If you were in my
place, my dear Budé, you would think quite, quite differently.'

My view of the question is this. The status of human life in general is   265
such that the more care, and even the more innocence, with which a man
draws up rules for the conduct of his life, the more trouble as a rule he will
find waiting for him from the irrationality of chance; and this chance carries
unhappy mortals to and fro, while Infatuation, the poets' queen of darkness, lurks keen and watchful for every opportunity, which no man can   270
foresee. On top of this, men of our walk of life are for the most part assailed
by the heartless solicitations of Discord, the parent of strife, she who once at
a banquet of the gods is said to have rolled the famous golden apple into
their midst with its inscription 'For the fairest'; and it was she who taught
men – and they took a long time to learn – to be wise after the event, like   275

* * * * *

248 Pallas' standing army] The scholars
255 the two of you] Reading *vos* for Allen's *nos*
259 two letters] Ep 778; for the other letter, now lost, cf above line 37n and Ep
   744:13n.
263 'If ... differently'] Ep 778:190

Epimetheus, whose name you rebuked me with. A celebrated and classical example of this was left to posterity by Homer, greatest of poets, as a kind of antidote to anger and contention. For, as you know, in the twenty-second book of the *Iliad* Achilles regrets that he has obeyed the anger in his heart more obstinately than was right, although Agamemnon has done him a   280
grievous injury; and at length he sees that he is in the wrong, and condemns his own persistence in contention and anger in the words

> May strife from gods and men be done away
> And wrath, that blinds a man, for all his wit;
> Sweeter by far than honey oozing down,   285
> It grows and darkens in men's hearts like smoke.

And so I should like you to make up your mind that, even if Lefèvre has set out to start a controversy, as you have been led to expect by believing baseless rumours, you will give yourself strict orders to keep quiet. Suppose he has decided to be unjust and offensive, against his natural self, in   290
order to oblige the men behind him, would you immediately join in the struggle, in a contest with him that can only disgrace you both? Would you have no thought for the reputation you enjoy and for what is to be expected of a man in your position? And when I lay down a law for you like this, it is no private enactment for you alone: I should wish the same law to bind me   295
too. I know that there are learned men, whose opinion carries weight, who have had the idea of criticizing me in what they write, and I know that some of them have already done so in books they have published; but I have given myself orders once and for all to comply with a resolution, signed sealed and delivered by myself, not to reply to them unless I see my silence   300
being turned to my discredit or likely to do me serious harm. In so doing I act on the advice and instructions of friends, good men and true, whose opinions carry the greatest weight. I no longer enjoy things which have no wit except what they draw from personal spite, nor can a civilized and cultivated mind find any pleasure in the kind of struggle where applause   305
cannot be won without dealing serious wounds. It is of the nature of strife that one's appetite should be aroused by things that have more gall in them than wit. Are you – am even I, though far beneath you – who have long been slaves in the dreary and toilsome service of ambition and at last have won our freedom, are we to give up our liberty and return to the treadmill,   310

* * * * *

276 Epimetheus] Cf Ep 778:116n.
279 *Iliad*] 18.107–10
298 in books] Probably an allusion to Giambattista Egnazio's edition of Suetonius (1516; cf Ep 648 introduction). Egnazio's notes included a sentence which, Budé feared, could be interpreted as a charge of plagiarism; cf Ep 648:58n.

plunging periodically into bitter conflict whenever it pleases some scribbler
to sharpen his itching pen against us? For my part, if I had to choose
between the two, I would rather forswear all devotion to good literature
than be reduced to such mental torment. You are already fixed at the
pinnacle of reputation, and while you cannot now be thrown down from it   315
by anybody, yet if you yourself make a false step, you cannot escape the
eyes that are turned on you. For my part, I am confident that I have immured
myself in such a citadel (either not being at risk or not caring), that anyone
will find it hard to lure me out to do battle in the field. I would rather be
thought the better man for having a soul above such things than for con-   320
ducting a brilliant defence. And you had formed the same resolution, as I
perceive from your letter and from your *Apologia* itself, for you say you have
undertaken this confrontation with deep regret and carried it through with
a heavy heart.

But if I am now to give you my opinion, you must look on me more   325
kindly. What it comes to, is this. Up to now you may be thought to have
defended the truth and your own reputation, and so I and our common
friends are ready to agree; for this is the kind of controversy where defer-
ment and reconsideration are more in place than a decision once and for all;
but if you add one word more, your friends will never forgive you. Do not   330
think I am arguing on Lefèvre's side; it is you I am sorry for, when I urge you
to resume contact with what is honourable and reasonable – or rather, to
resume your own proper nature, to return to yourself and to us, and give
yourself once again to sacred study and research. Much weight must be
given to your friendship with Lefèvre, which you abandon with reluctance,   335
so that you seem more to protest against some unintentional breach of it
than to arraign him with a view to prosecution; much also to that famous
name Erasmus which is now heard in every province of the West; much to
the dignity of the priesthood and to your professional ethic as a theologian.
Your vehemence in dispute ought to grow weaker as you grow older, and   340
this contest is of such a kind that victory may earn you more ill will than
applause.

Nor shall I listen to you at this point if you proceed to turn the blame
off on him who first started this dispute. I am not concerned now with the
merits; it is your case, not his, on which I pronounce. I want you to prove to   345
me that you have a good case out of your own materials entirely, without
adding in his. You must prove your innocence to me by your own moderation and not by hurling charges back at him; for a good man's innocence
should rely on its own force and its own merits and not try to win acceptance
by defending itself against other men's calumnies. I can hear you at this   350
point protesting to heaven and earth that here you are, on trial for impiety,

and I am refusing you a fair trial and the right to plead your cause in your
own way. And yet suppose I had been the judge in such causes lawfully
appointed, and you had applied for leave to defend the suit; granted that I
could not lawfully have refused you leave, I should have prescribed limits to   355
your pleading, in terms of the water-clock. And now just see how much
time you have taken for yourself! I take a certain pleasure in criticizing you
with some spirit, for I have long been jealous of you for obstructing my
ancient lights, and up to now I have disliked always coming off second in
our epistolary arguments. But I fear that you will turn all your wrath against   360
me, and that if you have not yet swallowed all your indignation, or have
swallowed and not yet digested it, you will throw up the remains of it in my
face, and write me one very acid letter. Never mind: I do not refuse to act as
scapegoat and to come forward as Lefèvre's whipping-boy, provided you
really purge your indignation, and at the same time I am cleared of your   365
suspicions in the matter of those trivialities. This will please many people
who think it in the public interest that you should distract your mind from
this controversy, for fear that this subsidiary matter should hold you back or
divert you from some major piece of original work.

I have written all this, dearest of friends, more to show what I feel and   370
to answer your letter than because I supposed you to need advice from me.
Yet this I would gladly do, if I could – bring those who love to speak ill of me
back to a sense of duty and modesty by either suffering or despising their
abuse; but if I cannot achieve that, at least I will not make the mistake of
allowing myself to be diverted by other people's selfishness from main-   375
taining the equanimity on which I am resolved, and from standing my
ground. For it is a natural quality of an abusive and quarrelsome attack that,
if you give way before the force of its approach, it soon becomes aimless and
ridiculous and fades into nothing, as a whirlwind is baffled and loses its
violent force if it encounters no obstacle. At this point I shall play the sow   380
teaching Minerva and tell you to consult your own books. Your Christian
knight, of whom I and everyone think so highly, has taught me that it is
contrary to military discipline for the chosen soldiers of Christ to learn the
use of arms in this kind of skirmishing, and that vicious sparring is no
training for the athletes of Christ, if I may use your own words as evidence   385
against you.

* * * * *

356 water-clock] Cf *Adagia* I iv 73.
366 trivialities] See above line 62n.
381 Minerva] Cf *Adagia* I i 40.
381 Christian knight] Cf *Enchiridion militis christiani*, especially chap 2 (LB V 5–10).
385 your own words] Literally 'sealed tablets' (a phrase from Cicero *Tusculanae*

It is surprising that Tunstall has not answered my letter; I fear he may
have been in poor health still. I have not yet had a copy of my letter to him,
as I wrote to you before, and I suspect it may be lost. If, however, you want
to have it very much, it can be reconstructed from the draft when I have   390
time. Etienne our bishop came here from court for several days; but he was
sent for again and will return shortly, nor is he in town at this moment, but
will be back, they say, tomorrow and set off soon thereafter. I have spoken
with him twice, but not out of earshot of other people. He has a very high
opinion of you, and this excites me greatly, coupled with the way the people   395
at court and the king himself are always talking of you, as he told me. The
king has had a Bishop Giustiniani, a Dominican, sent for from Italy, and
another man, a Hebrew scholar, whose name, I believe, is Ricius; so now he
has a rival to Mithridates, who knows almost all languages, or so those men
say who have seen him. When he himself was talking about them in my   400
presence, and I had said something, as one does, 'What is your opinion,
Budé,' he said, 'about Erasmus? Do you know what his plans are, and
whether he could some day be persuaded to come to France by the recompense he deserves?' 'If you feel,' I said, 'that the king is really serious, I
could readily make further inquiries whether he could be induced to move   405
to Paris and make a settled home there. For if I know him at all, he would not
accept a fat bishopric as the price of setting up to live as a member of the
court.' To cut matters short, as he had no time to write to you, he authorized
me to sound you and encourage you to write to him and tell him what you

* * * * *

disputationes 5.11.33), depositions authenticated by the seals of witnesses,
which when made by one of the parties to a suit could later be used as evidence
against him. So here, Erasmus is refuted by the testimony of his own Enchiridion.

387 my letter] Cf Ep 767:7n.
391 Etienne] Poncher, bishop of Paris
397 Giustiniani] Agostino Giustiniani of Genoa, 1470?–1536, since 1514 bishop of
Nebbio in Corsica. In 1516 he published a Psalterium octaplum, of which
Erasmus was critical (cf Allen Ep 906:481–7). Following the king's invitation
he taught Hebrew at Paris from 1517–22. At first he based his instruction on
Capito's grammar, published by Froben (see Ep 600:26n), but he must have
conveyed to his students that the book left much to be desired. Eventually he
prepared his own grammar, and when Froben declined it, it appeared in 1520
as the first Hebrew publication printed in Paris (cf AK II Epp 619, 643–4). In late
1518 he visited Erasmus in Louvain (cf Ep 906). See Encyclopaedia Judaica
(Jerusalem 1972).
398 Ricius] Paulus Ricius; see Ep 548:16n. It is not known that he went to Paris.
399 Mithridates] Tongue in cheek, Erasmus sometimes repeated the ancient claim
that Mithridates knew more than twenty languages (cf ASD I-2 49, 244). His
equal here is Giustiniani rather than Ricius.

think, so that he can pursue the matter at court. So now, my ever so slightly 410
fastidious friend, consider, take counsel, and decide whether you would
like to be one of us, and let us have no more of this shilly-shally, if I may
quote the comedy. Tell me what salary you would like to grow old among
us; a benefice will soon be added, or so he thinks. If you can be persuaded to
come and join us, your arrival will be welcome, I believe, to many of my 415
countrymen, of whom we now have a fair number who are learned even in
Greek as well as Latin; and you will have Budé with whom sometimes to
spend your lighter moments, and when you have got to know him better
and at close quarters, you can even play mora with him in the dark.

But you must sometime have found favour with the Graces, to enable 420
you after a few days' acquaintance to make a clear-sighted man like him
your admirer and supporter. For the warm reception you get from so many
of my countrymen who have never set eyes on you, you owe to your
exquisite style, and to a kind of spirit in your works which charms and
cheers the reader; for the French themselves feel the want of this in French 425
authors, as though Vulcan's consorts looked the other way when my people
set out in pursuit of style, if they are writing only for French readers, for
natives among us are not usually well thought-of. Observe how unfairly the
Fates have treated me compared with you; for though I have worshipped
Pallas both in Roman and Greek dress not only with devotion but at great 430
expense, and that too without ever feeling even the impulse to assault her
maidenhead, I have hitherto been unable to secure from my service to her
even her aid to make me popular at court, just as I have never managed on
my own account to restore my position at court since I once left it. You were
born under a star that made you popular, and are capable of winning ample 435
rewards as well, if you so wish, from your own people, from strangers, and
even (which is unusual) from my countrymen, unschooled as they are; for
your patroness, Minerva, can win you approval from everyone. And when I
envied you for this, my efforts made no progress if I tried to depreciate and
pick holes in your works, which find a ready market for their learning and 440
their charm alike. This I always thought I did in a circumspect and prudent

* * * * *

413 comedy] Budé uses a phrase familiar from Plautus.
419 mora] Cf *Adagia* I viii 23. One player in the game held up a certain number of
fingers, and the other had to guess rapidly what that number was; a man with
whom one could play this in the dark was proverbially a very honest man.
421 acquaintance] At Brussels in February 1517; cf Ep 522:126–7n.
426 Vulcan's consorts] The Graces; Homer *Iliad* 18.382
434 left it] In 1498, after spending eight months at court at the time of the succession of Charles VIII, but he continued to be involved with the king's business,
especially of late; cf Epp 744:2n, 924.

fashion; but you contend that in letters written to you I openly depreciated your books, on account of one or two remarks I dropped as between friends. Why then, dissatisfied as you are, do you still blame Fortune, who continues to lavish her blessings on you with both hands? Fortunate indeed is   445
that Minerva of yours, of whom we shall soon hear that two of the greatest of all sovereigns are now suitors. And happy am I, who shall soon, I hope, have the pleasure of seeing eloquence held in such high esteem that two most powerful monarchies are bidding against one another to secure you as high master of eloquence for their domains – always assuming that your   450
Prince Charles begins to grudge Francis this distinction, although you deserted his company when he set off for Spain.

   You think I am not serious? There is sound sense in my jests and in what I say. And so, while the thing is warm, summon the senate of your friends, that they may resolve as soon as may be in which place, here or   455
there, you should pass your declining years. If I am the leader of the house and you ask my opinion, I shall not hesitate to give my vote that it will inure to your worldly status and your reputation if you transfer yourself here with all your scholarly materials, to adorn the institution which the king wishes, they say, to set up in this city, and satisfy the desires of those who have   460
definitely formed the wish to see you join us. What you decide on this point you must write to the bishop of Paris, and name a figure for your stipend and for the expenses of your removal, if you think fit. For I think that better than to use me as your agent for the formulation of this offer; he is, I gather, the master-builder of the institution that is to be set up. As he is your strong   465
supporter, he will conclude everything with the prince on your behalf and will watch generously over your interests, so that the thing goes through not only without any criticism of you but to your great profit and advantage. Only be careful to set out your side of the business in full in your letter and explain the whole thing in such a way that he can understand you have been   470
briefed by me. I do not guarantee the result, nor am I eager to assume the responsibility (I shall not claim a large share of the credit for myself when the thing is done, though I did ask to be given the task of telling you), but at the same time I do not see what pitfalls you ought to fear in this business. If you are not content when such a great man makes himself responsible,   475
Crassus himself, if he came to life again, would not be rich enough to satisfy you. Protest now if you must, and lose your temper with me after all this; I

* * * * *

442 you contend] See above line 62n.
452 deserted] See Ep 596 introduction.
467 generously] See Ep 778:33n.

always enjoy bringing you some good news, and it is only reluctantly or by mistake that I report the omens as unfavourable.

At any rate, now if you have any probity, you will not only take in   480
good part whatever I have written in this letter; you will send me a letter on purpose to admit that you owe me the reward for the bearing of good news, whether you mean to accept the offer or whether you will be difficult and send an ambiguous reply, as you did last year even when you were writing to the king. The king himself was surprised at this, when I gave him your   485
letter at Saint-Maur, where he then was, where I have my Saint-Maur estate; and I defended your hesitation as well as I could, using the absence of your patron the chancellor as an excuse, as though you were not really your own master. Your friend Glareanus has been appointed to succeed the late Fausto, and is to have a stipend. So exhaustively does Fortune begin to   490
favour you that she blesses the business of your friends as well. He is already known to the bishop, who approves of him.

My friend Deloynes told me to send you his greetings; he had newly returned from the court when I got your letter. Ruzé thinks very highly of you and has devoted a whole shelf to your books, which he has a habit of   495
picking up when he wishes to annoy me, for I often visit him. Jacques Toussain, a scholar in Greek and Latin and his familiar friend, plans to write to you, at my urging; I tell him not to be shy. Such are the scruples everyone feels in approaching you except me, who am bold as brass. Farewell; and clear your mind of all disagreement and suspicion. Paris, 12 April   500

After this letter was finished I secured my letter to Tunstall after much trouble, but I could not conveniently send it you now because it is not yet copied out. I want to keep a copy of it in case it is lost on the way. So if you want it very much, I will get a copy made. Here's a nice long letter for you,

* * * * *

484 writing to the king] Ep 533
486 Saint-Maur] Saint-Maur-des-Fossés, on the Marne before the gates of Paris
488 chancellor] Le Sauvage was away in Cambrai between 18 February and 17 March 1517, just at the time Erasmus composed Epp 533–5; cf LP II 2940, 2943, 3032.
489 appointed] To the office of poet royal, which Andrelini had held to his death on 25 February 1518. The matter was not easily settled, however. Only in 1519 was an agreement reached by which Glareanus received Andrelini's stipend (though no longer his own scholarship from the king; see Ep 618:49n), but unlike Andrelini he did not have to give public lectures; see O.F. Fritzsche *Glarean* (Frauenfeld 1890) 23.
497 Toussain] Jacques Toussain, d 1547. Student and biographer of Budé and collaborator of Josse Bade. In 1529 he was appointed royal professor of Greek; cf Ep 522 introduction.
501 letter to Tunstall] Cf line 387, Epp 767:7n, 819.

and as badly written as though I had written it out myself. You can no longer   505
accuse me of bad writing, for I use a secretary for your benefit. Farewell once
more.

811 / To Gerard Geldenhouwer   Louvain [1518–19]

Provided the chronological references in Ep 812 are given correctly, the
background to Epp 811–12, 837 can be traced as follows. For some days before
17 April, Bishop Philip of Burgundy had been at a place which was only a few
hours distant from Louvain, perhaps in Mechelen (see Allen IV xxviii). Erasmus had gone there too, and on or about 12 April he had met Geldenhouwer,
the bishop's secretary, and perhaps another official, Philippus Montius,
whom he did not yet know in January 1518 (see Ep 759). On or about 13 April
he returned to Louvain. How he had failed to meet the bishop himself is
explained in Ep 812, to which Ep 837 is a sequel. (The latter, however, seems to
indicate that Erasmus had wished to avoid, rather than meet, the bishop and
that Geldenhouwer was aware of this.) Hence it is possible that Ep 811 was
written immediately after Erasmus' return to Louvain on or about 13 April,
although it does not refer to the circumstances of his departure. The rest of the
letter, however, does not give much support to this assumption, and the
beginning could, in fact, reflect any chance encounter with Geldenhouwer
that Erasmus may have had on returning to Louvain from an outing between
February 1518 and the publication of this letter in the *Farrago* of October 1519.
The date of 1519 was indicated in the *Opus epistolarum* of 1529, perhaps with
good reason.

ERASMUS OF ROTTERDAM TO GERARD OF NIJMEGEN,
CHAPLAIN TO MY LORD OF UTRECHT, GREETING
Most warm-hearted of friends, I happened upon a driver who was quite as
fond of the bottle as my servant, with the result that we reached Louvain
before nine o'clock, not without danger, for the wagon that preceded us   5
overturned.

That part of your letter gave me great pleasure, in which you say that
the very reverend Father Jacob Kalkar, provincial of the Dominicans in your

* * * * *

811
8 Kalkar] The Dominican Jacob Rydder of Kalkar, d 7 May 1529 in Utrecht. In
    1507, after studies in Rostock and Cologne, he became prior of Kalkar and
    subsequently of Utrecht. With the title of bishop of Hebron he was the
    suffragan of three successive bishops of Utrecht, among them Philip of Bur-
    gundy, whom he passed through all stages of ordination at the time of his
    elevation to the see (cf Ep 603:5n); cf NNBW I 541.

part of the world, is a supporter of mine. For I think it is a masterpiece to have won the approval of such a great man as you describe, and I readily believe such a good authority. Only I can scarcely believe that he should lower himself to read my inferior productions. I turned up the passage, and things are just as he says. I do appreciate the fair-mindedness of the man for having discovered how the passage could be mended by writing *or* instead of *and*: 'but against gentiles or renegades.' Not but what the same sense remained if we kept the *and*, for when we say 'This man honours only the learned and the good,' nothing prevents the learned and the good from being different people. But he was quite right to wish to throw a little more light and disperse the darkness of ambiguity.

I remembered the story of the almost complete extinction of the tribe of Benjamin. But in the first place I thought the general statement could stand, even if there were one or two exceptions, just as when St Paul said 'In Adam all sinned' he did not utter a falsehood merely because we believe that the Virgin and Christ were free from sin; although I admit that it would not hold water if a logician were to argue with you according to the letter of the law, as they say. Secondly, it seemed to me that that should not properly be classed as war, but rather as punishment, unless maybe one thinks that when Moses killed so many thousand men on account of the golden calf, he declared war on them. Finally it was enough for me that while we are constantly going to war with one another, they never did so, or very rarely. Exaggeration contributes to conviction, so that one says 'never' for 'hardly ever'; like St Paul, who when he says 'All seek their own' did not think that everybody was like that but wanted it to be understood how few there are who take the Gospel sincerely.

I could wriggle out of it like this; everyone is full of ideas when it comes to defending himself; but I have no wish to disagree with such an excellent man. So in the next edition the passage shall be altered. Mind you give him my most cordial greetings, for he is a man whom I should like to

* * * * *

9 masterpiece] *Adagia* IV ix 55
12 passage] In the adage 'Dulce bellum inexpertis' (IV i 1; LB II 963A; cf Phillips 335) Erasmus set in the 1523 edition: 'The Jews hardly ever warred against each other, but only against gentiles and renegades.' Originally the sentence read: 'The Jews never warred ...' The amendment obviously resulted from the considerations stated in this letter.
20 extinction] Cf Judg 20:14–48. Evidently this passage had been invoked by Jacob to challenge Erasmus' statement.
22 St Paul] Rom 5:12–15; cf 1 Cor 15:22.
28 Moses] Cf Exod 32:28–9.
32 St Paul] Cf Phil 2:21.

know better. I have no other commissions for you at the moment, except to
remain just what you are. Farewell.   40

Give my greetings to Philippus Montius, one of the most agreeable
people I ever met, and his wife. And give my usual message to his lordship.

Louvain, 1519 [?]

812 / To Gerard Geldenhouwer   Louvain, 17 April [1518]

> See Ep 711 introduction. This letter was published in the *Farrago*. The bearer
> was John Smith; cf Epp 820 introduction, 837:5.

TO GERARD GELDENHOUWER, CHAPLAIN TO
MY LORD OF UTRECHT, FROM ERASMUS OF ROTTERDAM,
GREETING

What penalty am I to invoke, my dear Gerard, for the way you have
behaved? I pray that you may soon be afflicted with a good fat benefice. You   5
said, and you were not the only one, that his lordship would be starting in
four or five days' time and not before; I followed the usual custom and
doubled the number, thinking that he would not move before the week was
up, and I had plenty to do here. I could see that his lordship was too busy at
that moment, I foresaw that you would dine late, and I was famished. So I   10
slipped away, assuring you that I would wait at home that day, in case he
should have any commands for me. No message reached me. Next day I ran
across in the morning to Louvain, thinking that as far as meeting his
lordship was concerned it did not make much difference whether I was here
or there. I left a note at home to say that I was ready to come at any hint.   15
Today I had almost made up my mind to come running back, when your old
boon-companion Desmarez informed me that my lord is off today. If this is
true, you must act the part of the eminent benefactor, so that my lord does
not suspect anything other than the truth; or rather, I must lodge a complaint against you, you are the man I have to pick a bone with, for saying   20
things that misled me.

Believe me, my dear Nijmegen, there is not a great man anywhere in
the world whom I would more sincerely wish to please than Bishop Philip,
not only because I live under his jurisdiction, but because he is an outstanding man in every way, and because he thinks well of such gifts as I   25

* * * * *

41 Montius] See Ep 727:13n.

812
20 pick a bone with] *Adagia* 1 i 84
24 jurisdiction] Probably as a native of Rotterdam

have. In fact, there is some silent and secret impulse in my mind which drives me to admire him. In the business of courts I am certainly worth very little; but in the field where I am worth something I shall make it clear how much I look up to and like his highness. I would not wish anyone to believe this unless I prove it by action in the near future. I have not dared interrupt 30 him so often with a letter from me; you must play the part of a letter. If he summons me, I will come at once; if not, I shall take more trouble over preparing my departure, so that I can return all the sooner. I expect to be back before October; and then I shall disentangle myself from these theological thickets and devote my time with a mind clear and at peace to 35 literature and my friends. Nor would I undertake this very perilous journey, did not concern for my reputation make it essential. Wherever I may be in the future, there is one thing I can promise: his lordship will have a humble and devoted servant, and your reverence a true friend. Farewell, my excellent benefactor.   40

Louvain, 17 April 151[4]

813 / To Guillaume Budé   Louvain, 17 April [1518]

Epp 813–17 are all addressed to correspondents in Paris and were dispatched together in a consignment directed to Josse Bade (cf Ep 815:10). Most of these letters are to announce Erasmus' impending departure for Basel; see Ep 770 introduction.

TO BUDÉ

Greeting. I have sent by a courier I did not know a rather tiresome letter, in which I dispose of the arguments used by the people who think it was very rash of me to reply to Lefèvre. I suppose it has reached you, for I had addressed it to Bade. Tunstall makes his excuses in a letter to me for not 5 having sent you an answer, but he is so plunged in business both public and private that up to now he has never been his own master. I am off to Basel to see to my edition of the New Testament. Meanwhile look after yourself, and love me as I know you do.

Louvain, 17 April   10

* * * * *

813
2 letter] Ep 778
6 an answer] To Ep 583

814 / To Jacques Lefèvre d'Etaples   Louvain, 17 April [1518]

See Ep 813 introduction. This letter was printed in the *Auctarium*. It presents another attempt to end the controversy with Lefèvre on terms favouring Erasmus; see Ep 721 introduction.

ERASMUS OF ROTTERDAM TO THE WORTHY
JACQUES LEFÈVRE D'ÉTAPLES

Greeting. Most learned and excellent Jacques Lefèvre, I have declared already in one or two letters how much it grieves me that malicious people should have been presented with this opening to make gossip about us. I 5
foresaw this trouble coming; but as it was not open to me not to reply, I chose what seemed the lesser of two evils. One thing now remains: I beg you in the name of Christian charity, by our common love of sacred study, for the sake of your and my reputation which by the laws of friendship ought to be equally dear to us both, let us with a common purpose remedy 10
this evil in such ways as we can, before the conflagration spreads any further. You know how men are prone to evil and seize on a pretext for discord wherever they can find one. There is hardly a convivial gathering in which argument does not arise, for Lefèvre against Erasmus on one side and for Erasmus against Lefèvre on the other, especially among people who 15
know absolutely nothing about it. Various remarks are in circulation as coming from you: some say that you are preparing a reply, others say that you do not think Erasmus deserves an answer. Again some say that you do not disapprove of me for defending myself; others the opposite, that you blame my rashness. As far as I am concerned, I do not much care whether 20
you reply or no, provided you refrain from those unpleasant remarks, which it is no credit to you to direct against one of your friends, and which it is impossible for me to ignore. In any case, it is painful that you and I should be the reason for the spread of discord among Christians, and that our disagreement should be a cause of glee to men who hate your work as much 25
as mine. I do not suggest that you should recant, though I was attacked in ways I did not deserve. Do just publish some letter which will make it clear that you entered the lists from zeal to pursue the truth, and that in other respects we are personally in agreement. If you would rather not do this, I

* * * * *

814
4 letters] Epp 659, 724
27 publish some letter] Erasmus had advanced the same suggestion when writing to Budé; see Ep 778:377–9.

would rather you published a reply than fostered party discord by your   30
silence, provided you show the moderation suitable to what has always
been your character. No mortal man ever heard me mention the name of
Lefèvre without affection and admiration. I can only say that I cannot think
what induced you to attack me. What I feel is exactly what I say, as Christ is
my witness. Farewell.   35
        Louvain, 17 April 151[7]

815 / To Josse Bade   Louvain, 17 April [1518]

        See Ep 813 introduction.

ERASMUS TO HIS FRIEND BADE, GREETING

How I wish, my dear Bade, you had had a good supply of Greek type! As it
is, I am obliged to go to Basel, at the risk of my life, for the New Testament
cannot be published unless I am there in person. I hear from those excellent
Amerbach brothers that the man they call Jean Petit threatens I know not   5
what – that he will print Jerome's works, despising the papal privilege and
flouting, what is worse, the canons of decent behaviour. He had better be
very careful, or by his plans to damage other people he will bring harm on
himself. I do not doubt that you know the man well, and I beg you to
dissuade him from behaving so badly. Please let Budé and Lefèvre have   10
their letters. Farewell.
        Louvain, 17 April

816 / To Wilhelm Nesen   Louvain, 17 April [1518]

        See Ep 813 introduction.

        * * * * *

815
2 Greek type] In a letter to Nicolas Bérault of 24 February [1520] Budé mentioned
    that Bade had recently acquired a set of Greek type from Germany; see L.
    Delaruelle *Répertoire ... de la correspondance de Guillaume Budé* (Toulouse 1907)
    Ep 60.
5 Amerbach] See Ep 802.
5 Petit] Jean Petit (cf Ep 263:15n), perhaps a relative of Guillaume Petit, the royal
    confessor, was printer and bookseller to the University of Paris. When Bade
    first came to Paris, Jean Petit set him up as a printer, and he continued to
    market many of Bade's editions; cf L. Febvre and H.J. Martin *L'Apparition du
    livre* 2nd ed (Paris 1971) 181–2, 216–17.

ERASMUS TO HIS FRIEND NESEN, GREETING
What business takes you to Rome, especially on the verge of summer? I shall
be at Basel until the winter, if only I have the chance to force my way there.
John Smith is going back to his native England to please his doting mother,
who cannot believe her son is safe and sound unless she sees him in Britain. 5
He will live in Thomas More's household. More himself is entirely absorbed
by the court, being always in attendance on the king, to whom he is now
secretary. Pace is triumphantly successful. The king has sent me a present of
sixty angels, with the offer of a benefice worth a hundred marks; but he says
he will only confer it on me in person.   10
      Glareanus, I think, has already left. If he should happen to be still with
you, give him my cordial greetings. Farewell.
      Louvain, 17 April

817 / To Pierre Vitré   Louvain, 17 April [1518]

      See Ep 813 introduction.

ERASMUS TO HIS FRIEND VITRÉ, GREETING
I am surprised that Thomas Grey should have left your part of the world
without a letter from you to me. He is now with us at Louvain but will soon
return to England. I am taking wing for Basel, to see to the publication of

        * * * * *

      816
    2 Rome] Cf Ep 595:4–5.
    3 force my way] Cf Epp 829:11n, 832:14–16.
    4 England] See Ep 820 introduction. Smith had recently returned from his earlier
      mission to England (see Ep 772 introduction) with letters and news reflected in
      this letter.
    7 court] Cf Ep 829:6n.
    8 Pace] He spent most of 1518 at court; on 12 February he was granted a coat of
      arms; cf LP II 3941, 3985, and passim.
    8 The king] See Ep 834 introduction. He had sent English gold angel-nobles,
      with the figure of the Archangel St Michael on the obverse. This present was
      worth £20 sterling = £29 gros flemish = £183 tournois. Cf CWE 1 312, 336–9;
      CWE 2 340 (plate).
    9 hundred marks] See Ep 694:11n. A mark was two-thirds of a pound sterling
      (13s 4d). This sum was thus worth 200 angel-nobles = £66 13s 4d sterling =
      £96 13s 4d gros Flemish = £610 0s 0d tournois; cf CWE 1 325.
   11 Glareanus] See Ep 766:3n.

      817
    2 surprised] See Ep 779 introduction, and for Grey's movements Ep 768:18n.

some things that cannot be published without me. Look after yourself till 5
we next meet, my dear Pierre. Grey sends his greetings.

Louvain, 17 April

818 / To Pieter Gillis   Louvain, 17 April [1518]

This is a farewell message before Erasmus' departure from Louvain (see Ep 770
introduction), published in the *Auctarium* of August 1518.

ERASMUS OF ROTTERDAM TO HIS FRIEND
PIETER GILLIS, GREETING
In the name of our friendship, than which none could be closer, and for the
sake of your own well-being, which is as dear to me as my own, do all you
can, my dear Pieter, to speed your recovery. On my return, let me find you 5
cheerful and in good heart, for only then shall I feel I have returned safely.
Live carefully until your friend Adrian gets back, in whom I must say I have
much confidence; it is a great thing to have such a friend as one's physician.
Meanwhile, mind you do not lower yourself with too much physic. Above
all, avoid all strong emotion, excessive joy, unrestrained laughter, too much 10
walking, excessive study, anger especially. My dear Pieter, life is what
matters most. Maybe my good advice is tedious; I only hope it may be as
successful as it is heartfelt. I think nothing of my own danger, if I may but
have the good fortune to see you recovered, by which I mean really vigorous
and strong again. Farewell, with your beloved wife and your dear little 15
ones.

Louvain, 17 April 151[7]
Erasmus of Rotterdam

819 / From Guillaume Budé   Paris, 20 April [1518]

This letter was perhaps given to Francesco Giulio Calvo, together with letters,
now lost, by Deloynes and Bérault, and promptly delivered to Erasmus at
Louvain; see Epp 831 introduction, 925, 989, 994, Allen Ep 1002:24–8. As in
some preceding letters, Budé's references to the royal invitation (see Ep
778:33n) are 'coded' in Greek, as they were when this letter was printed in the
Farrago.

* * * * *

818
5 recovery] See Epp 597:23n, 846.
7 Adrian] Perhaps Clavus; see Ep 650:14n.
13 my own danger] See Epp 829:11n, 832:14–16.

FROM GUILLAUME BUDÉ TO ERASMUS, GREETING

I wrote to you a few days ago by way of a student from Cologne, a most cultivated man and, if I mistake not, an honest one; a good long letter it was, in which I said among other things how your prospects look with us, and about the king, and how much people here are again regretting your   5
absence, so that you may decide what to do with yourself when Fortune smiles on you. I do not doubt that the letter reached you, or soon will; the man from Cologne has such an honest face, and he promised he would either give it you himself or in any case make sure it would reach you, for he was particularly anxious to take a letter to you from me. Glareanus first   10
introduced him to me. I want to know what you have in mind about what I write to you on behalf of the king, and how you took my rebukes, and whether you were pacified by my letter or still more annoyed. If the latter, I shall expect a most controversial reply.

Only, when that man from Cologne came to see me, he found me just   15
setting off for my house in the country and not proposing to return for three or four days. I said I had a copy of a very long letter which I was about to send you, as soon as ever I had had a transcript made. When he heard this, he asked if he could do it for me, to which I demurred. Eventually I let him have it on condition that while I was away he should bring back to my house   20
the copy he had made himself; but I found at home on my return not the copy he had made, but the text I had given him to take to you with my own corrections. And so, if you mean to publish my letter to Tunstall, hold it up until you can let me know, and I will send you another copy with corrections. For I fear that in copying it in a hurry he will have made mistakes. So   25
please let me know whether it is necessary to send you another copy. Farewell.

Paris, 20 April

I wrote down the name of the young man from Cologne on a piece of paper which I could not lay hands on when I wrote you this letter; he teaches   30
some boys or young men of good family, who have been studying law at Orléans.

* * * * *

819
2 I wrote] Ep 810, given to Eichholz; see line 15n.
4 I said] Ep 810:393–419
15 that man] Adolf Eichholz (see Ep 866 introduction). His copying of Ep 583 (cf Ep 767:7n) is recalled in Budé's letter to him of 22 February [1520]; cf Budé Opera omnia I 269–70.

820 / To William Gonnell   Louvain, 22 April [1518]

Epp 820–8 and 832–4 probably formed a consignment of letters which John
Smith carried back to his native England (see Ep 832:36, 44; but cf Ep 829
introduction). Smith had been with Erasmus since 1511 but since August 1517
had been looking for a new master in England (cf Ep 644). Complying with the
wishes of his mother, he had now accepted a position in the household of
Thomas More (cf Epp 816, 832:46–8), whom he had recently visited on Erasmus' business (cf Ep 785). In fact, many of the following letters indicate the
results, not always satisfactory to Erasmus, of Smith's previous mission to
England (see Ep 772 introduction). This letter was published in the *Auctarium*.
   William Gonnell was the tutor of More's children. See Ep 274 introduction.

ERASMUS TO HIS FRIEND GONNELL, GREETING
Your present was very welcome, more welcome still such a friendly letter,
and most of all that there should be no change in your feelings although it is
so long since we last met. Tell Clement from me – that young man is full of
promise – not to overwork. I remember how devoted he was to his books. In   5
particular, tell him never, so far as he can, to write at night; and if the
cardinal's business obliges him to write, he must learn to do so standing up.
It would be a pity for such gifts to fail before their time, and I would rather
they were kept for humane studies than expended on business for the
cardinal. Farewell.   10
   Louvain, 22 April 151[7]

821 / To Richard Pace   Louvain, 22 April 1518

See Ep 820 introduction. This letter was published in the *Auctarium*.

ERASMUS TO HIS FRIEND RICHARD PACE, GREETING
How truly splendid is the court of your native Britain, the seat and citadel of
humane studies and of every virtue! I wish you joy, my dear Pace, of such a
prince, and I wish your prince joy, whose kingdom is rendered illustrious
by so many brilliant minds. On both counts I wish your England joy, for,   5

* * * * *

820
4 Clement] John Clement, a young man who had recently advanced from the
   service of Thomas More to that of Cardinal Wolsey, perhaps thus making room
   for More's appointment of Smith; see Ep 388:185n.

821
2 splendid] Cf Ep 834 introduction.

blessed as she is in many other ways, on these grounds she so much excels
all else that no region can be compared with her. At this stage I should like to
spend my whole life in England, where under the favour of princes the
humanities hold sway and the love of honour flourishes, while the painted
mask of false piety and the useless and tedious learning of monks are alike   10
exiled and overthrown. I much regret that Grocyn is no longer with you; but
then again I see many who will be growing on to fill that one man's place.

You have most kindly done my business for me, and in this I gladly
recognize your old feelings for me. How I wish I could hand over to
someone else my present task of editing the New Testament! But I have   15
made my bed, such as it is, and I must lie on it to the end; and I hope this will
do those pseudo-theologians no good. I wish I had taken it into my head to
try and help men rather than monsters. I get on reasonably well with the
theologians in Louvain. Cologne university is torn by unlovely strife. The
paper they write on has teeth in it, and little by little they are already   20
bringing my name in. Those Preachers in their cowls run to and fro,
spreading foul rumours among the common folk and lying brazenly; which
is nice and easy for them before an audience which knows absolutely
nothing about the subject, any more than they do themselves. Dorp seems
to have become a sincere friend. I will try to come back to you before the   25
winter, if only heaven allows me to return. My paraphrase is printed again
in Basel. The *Apologia* in which I try to pacify Lefèvre has lately come out in
Basel with notes, having some time ago been printed in Strasbourg. I pray

* * * * *

11 Grocyn] See Ep 781:20n.
13 my business] An indication that Pace had talked to the king on Erasmus'
   behalf as he had been asked to do in Ep 787:10–12; cf Ep 834 introduction.
16 made my bed] Cf Ep 737:18n.
19 strife] About Reuchlin. Opponents of Reuchlin such as Pfefferkorn, Hoogstraten, and Gratius were closely tied to the faculty of theology, while his defen-
   ders grouped around Neuenahr had close links to the faculty of arts. Both sides
   published their controversial tracts in Cologne, and both invoked the name of
   Erasmus (cf Epp 622, 680, 694:114–16, 722:17–19, 808). His concern was
   heightened by the fact that the *Julius exclusus* was circulating in Cologne (cf
   Epp 636, 703:28–35, 785:41–5, 908, 961). His New Testament too could not fail
   to arouse the suspicion of Reuchlin's critics (cf Ep 794:36–8). The disputes in
   Cologne continued to trouble Erasmus; cf Epp 824, 830, 852, 948, 950.
20 teeth] *Adagia* III vi 87
21 to and fro] *Adagia* I iii 85
26 paraphrase] The *Paraphrasis ad Romanos* (see Ep 710 introduction) was reprinted by Froben in January 1518.
27 *Apologia*] The *Apologia ad Fabrum*; cf Ep 794:51n.

Almighty God that he may long preserve these feelings in you, and you
among us in prosperity. 30
Louvain, 22 April 1518

822 / To Pietro Ammonio   Louvain, 23 April [1518]

See Ep 820 introduction. This letter continues the efforts undertaken in Epp
656, 774.

ERASMUS TO HIS FRIEND PIETRO AMMONIO, GREETING
At long last you have sent me one or two scraps, although I wrote Ammonio
so many long letters. You did not even give my servant the cardinal's letter
to me. If you so much grudge your kinsman his reputation, why ask me to
do what I can to promote it? And in your letter you harp on one or two things 5
I am supposed to have done wrong. To put it shortly, I do not find in you in
this regard the same spirit that was in Ammonio. And then, having sealed
up your own letter, you gave my servant the copy of the dispensation
unsealed. This is not like an Ammonio! Farewell.
Louvain, 23 April 10

823 / To Thomas Bedyll   Louvain, 23 April [1518]

See Ep 820 introduction. This letter resumes the complicated dispute over the
payment of Erasmus' Aldington annuity. Since November 1517 (cf Ep 702
introduction) Erasmus had appealed to several people in an effort to receive as
much cash as possible from his annuity in Aldington in view of the expense he
would incur on his forthcoming trip to Basel or Italy (cf Ep 770 introduction).
Warham promptly authorized payment of one annuity or £20 sterling (cf Ep
712:9n). As Erasmus took this to be a prepayment, specially authorized by
Warham, of the annuity for 1518 (ending Lady Day 1519) and issued his receipt
accordingly (cf Epp 712, 794:6–7, 828:1–2, 892), it is reasonable to assume that
he was then satisfied that the 1517 annuity had already been settled. The
validity of Erasmus' receipt was questioned by the Antwerp bankers, Crullus
and Franz Birckmann, on technical grounds (cf Epp 712, 736:16n), but
Birckmann eventually paid, giving Erasmus a credit note which he could use
on his journey, and apparently also some cash (cf Epp 828, 892). He then went

* * * * *

822
2 Ammonio] Andrea Ammonio
3 cardinal's] See 835 introduction.
8 dispensation] See Ep 828:17n.

to England where Warham's notary Potkyn rejected Erasmus' receipt (Epp 782:3–4, 892). After his return Birckmann visited Erasmus in Louvain on 22 February, explaining that he had not been paid, so Erasmus sent with John Smith another receipt, evidently again for 1518, to Johannes Sixtinus in London (cf lines 10–11, Ep 775:14–17). By that time, however, he had been paid in cash the equivalent of another year's pension by Benedetto de' Fornari, Antwerp agent of Maruffo (cf lines 5–9, Ep 775:14–15), perhaps as a result of steps undertaken by Thomas More (cf Ep 706:17–20). This amount also came from the coffers of Warham, and since they too assumed that the 1517 annuity had been settled earlier, Potkyn and Bedyll, Warham's secretary, now requested a receipt for 1519 (cf lines 14–15, Ep 892). Although Erasmus had earlier acknowledged Maruffo's payment when writing to Sixtinus, who acted for Warham (cf Epp 775:14–15, 828), he now argued that he had not been told about its source (cf lines 8–9, Ep 828:6–10). Secondly, he argued that the money, if it came from Warham, had to be a delayed payment for the 1517 annuity; accordingly he claimed here that the receipt sent to Sixtinus was for 1517, rather than a replacement of the faulty receipt for 1518, as he seems to accept in Ep 828:10–13. So he merely sent another receipt for the 1517 annuity (cf Ep 828:5). Six months later the matter was still not resolved; see Ep 892.

ERASMUS TO HIS FRIEND BEDYLL, GREETING
I was a little hurt that my man John should return from your part of the world without a letter from you. You tell me to send a receipt for my annuity for the year '19; but I think you have not given this sufficient thought. The receipt which you have I had sent, not for the money I had from Maruffo, 5 but for what Franz gave me, definitely against a receipt. I had money from Benedetto de' Fornari to the amount of 166 French livres and 8 sous, but without any document of title, except that they said Raffaele had sent a bill, although they did not show me one. If this was paid in respect of my annuity, it was paid for the year '17 last past, for which I sent Sixtinus a 10 receipt by John, this servant of mine. I also sent another for this current year, '18, in respect of money paid before the due date; for it was paid at the

* * * * *

823
7 Fornari] A member of a great Genoese banking family, perhaps at this time active in the Netherlands. Soon afterwards he was involved in the financing of the election of Charles v; see R. Carande *Carlos V y sus banqueros* (Madrid 1965–7) III 63.
7 amount] £166 8s 0d tournois, the equivalent of £20 sterling, less exchange and banking charges (by the relative silver contents of the two coinages = £19 14s 0d sterling = £28 13s 2d gros Flemish). Cf Ep 467:7n.
8 Raffaele] Maruffo

beginning of the year although the whole sum was not due till the following
Lady Day. If I were to sign an acknowledgment that my claim for '19 has
been met, first I should not be speaking the truth, saying that something has   15
been done which has not been done, and further, I should do myself out of
one year's annuity. Make sure that I find you in good health when I return,
and be the same good friend to me with his grace that you have always
been.

    Louvain, 23 April   20

824 / To [John Fisher]   Louvain, 23 April [1518]

> See Epp 820 introduction, and for the attribution to Fisher Ep 653 introduction
> and line 2.

Greeting, right reverend Father. I salute your truly Christian spirit equally
for your sake and ours, and pray that we may long be allowed to enjoy it. I
was hoping to hear what you thought of Reuchlin's book, but I see that you
are devoted to things of greater moment. At Cologne this devilish struggle
gets more bitter every day. Both sides are using paper with teeth in it. And   5
all this uproar in Christendom is aroused by blackmailers in cowl and
cassock, who wish to pass for preachers of the Gospel message. Farewell.

    Louvain, 23 April

825 / To John Colet   Louvain, 23 April [1518]

> See Ep 820 introduction. This letter was printed in the *Farrago*.

ERASMUS TO JOHN COLET, DEAN OF ST PAUL'S
Greeting, best of patrons. For your kindness towards me I have already

* * * * *

14 Lady Day] 25 March 1519. Erasmus thus thought in accordance with the old
    calendar that the Lady Day instalment was the second for 1518. This was
    correct in so far as the initial instalment of his pension had been payable at
    Michaelmas (29 September) 1513 (cf Ep 255; Allen I 501). It is possible that
    Warham's officials counted the Lady Day instalment as the first for 1519, but
    such a misunderstanding could only reduce the disputed amount by half.
    Erasmus insisted that he stood to lose a whole annuity if he gave in.

    824
3 Reuchlin's book] *De arte cabalistica*; cf Ep 592.
4 Cologne] Cf Ep 821:19–21.

expressed my thanks through Franz, and have given him a receipt in which I
state formally that my claim in respect of money from the king has been met
in full. I am getting ready for a journey, which will be full of danger from the   5
recent acquittal of the robbers and criminals who were banded together,
several thousand of them, to attack anyone at their own sweet will. So cruel
is the so-called clemency of our princes – mercy for godless ruffians and
notorious villains, no mercy on their own citizens. So much dearer to them
are the agents of their oppression than the common people themselves   10
whom they oppress.

I wish you had added a couple of words to explain why I have not
satisfied you in chapter seven; it may be that what I took to refer to the
affections, you preferred to apply to the Mosaic Law. But in that passage St
Paul is so slippery that he looks first one way and then another, so that in   15
explaining all this Origen works himself into a lather. You say you will write
another day; but another day will be too late. Once my work is finished, I
shall hurry to your side, body and soul, especially if there is any good news
for me; and I urge you to go on doing your best to see that there is
something. Farewell.   20

Louvain, 23 April 151[7]

826 / To Henry Bullock   Louvain, 23 April [1518]

See Ep 820 introduction. This letter was first published in the *Auctarium*.
Bullock had been addressed in Ep 777.

ERASMUS TO HIS FRIEND HENRY BULLOCK, GREETING
Such, I now see, is the perversity and ingratitude of men, my dear Bullock,
that I am almost of a mind, once the New Testament has been re-edited, to

* * * * *

825
 3 Franz] Birckmann; see Ep 834 introduction.
 6 robbers] See Ep 829:11n.
13 chapter seven] Of the *Paraphrasis ad Romanos* (cf Allen Ep 891:23–4). See
    Erasmus' paraphrase of Rom 7:17–21 where, consistent with his understand-
    ing of the entire chapter, he stressed a moral interpretation (LB VII 799–800),
    and the note about Origen's difficulties with this passage in the *Novum
    Testamentum* LB VI 598D–E.
17 too late] To make corrections in the *Novum Testamentum*. Erasmus was ready to
    start for Basel to see the new edition through the press; see Ep 770 introduc-
    tion.

make music in future to my own ear and the Muses. Men in motley
garments, especially some of the Preacher and Carmelite gang, are putting   5
their heads together and baying in the distance; to my face, not a word from
anybody. They spread among the public the lies you would expect from
such mountebanks, for all the world as though it were the object of their
vows to befoul the good name of others with their falsehoods, and as if they
had decided to pursue not so much holy mysteries as unholy mischief. I   10
have no time to spare just now; but if they go on like this, they will get the
reception they deserve one day. The news that in your part of the world you
are at daggers drawn in support of Lefèvre or myself grieves me profoundly.
I wrote to the man lately, asking him either to publish some sort of letter to
show that we are now in agreement, if he is ashamed to withdraw, or to   15
write a reply if there is any point he wishes to maintain, provided he
abstains from the friendly, indeed over-friendly, expressions with which
he made game of me before. As things are, I said, his silence makes our
disagreement more serious, for everyone harbours his own suspicions. Of
quarrels there is no end. And if this plague is so closely connected with our   20
studies that we cannot have one without the other, I would rather bid
farewell to all my work. Sleep will be better than scribbling. Farewell, my
learned friend. Give my greetings to all my friends, especially Vaughan and
Humphrey and Bryan.

    Louvain, 23 April 151[7]   25

827 / To Richard Croke   Louvain, 23 April [1518]

    See Ep 820 introduction; for Croke see Ep 227:31n.

ERASMUS TO HIS FRIEND CROKE, GREETING
I congratulate you, my dear Croke, on your splendid professorship, which

    * * * * *

826
  4 make music] Cf Ep 731:44n.
  4 motley garments] Patched together of so many lies; see *Adagia* II iv 58. For
    attacks on and by Dominicans and Carmelites cf the indexes to this edition.
 13 grieves me] Erasmus nevertheless seemed eager for proof that Bullock had
    taken an active part in the controversy on his side. See Ep 890.
 14 lately] Ep 814:26–32
 15 withdraw] *Adagia* I ix 59
 23 friends] At Cambridge. John Vaughan and Humphrey Walkden were fellows
    of Queen's; John Bryan was at King's; cf Epp 262:14n, 276, 283:142n.

827
  2 professorship] See Ep 712:33n.

does as much honour to you as it will bring profit to Cambridge University, for whose well-being I feel a special concern on account of ancient ties of hospitality. I have to report that none of your books has yet reached me. 5 Exceptionally, Franz did show me some letters in Greek revised by you, of which I thought well; but he said they were on their way to someone else. I gave back your Theocritus to Master Thomas Grey. Farewell, dearest Croke.

Louvain, 23 April

828 / To Johannes Sixtinus   Louvain, 23 April [1518]

See Ep 820 introduction, and for the financial transactions see Ep 823 introduction.

Greeting, most learned Sixtinus. I have already given Franz a receipt for the annuity of the year '18, because he intended to pay me in cash, had I not preferred his note for the money in view of the risks of travel. In case the money which I have had from Maruffo's partners was paid on account of my annuity, I enclose the receipt for the year '17; but you will only make use of this 5 if it is clear that the money was paid on that account. For the Italian who gave it me showed me no letter and no bill, nor did he explain on what account it was paid me, only saying it came from Maruffo. So I did not think it was my business to say anything about the payment of my annuity, since nothing definite was said about the reason for the payment. Only I thought 10 you had got it wrong, in thinking that the receipt which bore the year '18 had been sent in respect of the payment from Maruffo, as though I intended to add another dated '19 for the money I had from Franz.

What monster can be more abominable than Pietro Ammonio? How like an Italian! He sends me two or three letters only out of all that large 15 collection, but he does not send me the letter written to me by the cardinal.

* * * * *

5 books] Perhaps the ones mentioned in Ep 712:33–5, or others ordered more recently, perhaps through Franz Birckmann. The Greek letters Birckmann showed Erasmus are not otherwise known.
8 Grey] See Ep 768:18n. At the very time he wrote this letter Erasmus acquired his own edition of Theocritus (see Ep 832:33). Croke's could have been among the books mentioned in Ep 712:33–5.

828
1 Franz] Birckmann
6 Italian] Benedetto de' Fornari
14 Pietro Ammonio] See Epp 774, 822.

And of the copies of my dispensation he has sent only one, to which several clauses have been added in my own hand; and he handed this unsealed to the servant, though the futile stuff he wrote himself was covered with seals. I only wish I may one day get a chance to repay the frightful fellow – so   20 unlike our friend the real Ammonio, unless he simply took us in. Farewell, most learned Sixtinus, and continue your kindness to me, as I know you do.

Louvain, 23 April

829 / To Thomas More   [Louvain, second half of April 1518]

This letter must be roughly contemporary with the consignment of letters carried by John Smith (see Ep 820 introduction), but was given to Thomas Grey, who was then returning to England (cf lines 30–4). From Ep 827 it would appear that Grey left a few days before 23–5 April when the other letters to England were written or copied. Accordingly there was no need for Erasmus to write to More on 23–5 April. But the evidence is slight, and it is possible that Grey might have carried some of the other letters as well.

ERASMUS TO HIS FRIEND MORE, GREETING

Was it really necessary, my dear More, to strip the naked, and lay a further load of obligation on one loaded enough already? John brought the horse, having ruined it on the way. I wonder that Mountjoy, my Maecenas of such long standing, should be so hard to move; but no doubt a wife and a son and   5 heir have aggravated his natural defect. As for your being haled to court, I

* * * * *

17 only one] A copy of Ep 517 with clauses added in Erasmus' hand no longer exists. He may have destroyed it upon receipt at this time. However the original, with autograph subscriptions by Andrea Ammonio and Sixtinus, and another copy were in his possession at the time of his death; see Ep 517 introduction.

829
2 the naked] Cf *Adagia* I iv 76; 'the naked' is More, who had sent a gift in response to Ep 785 (cf Ep 772 introduction). More's gift was probably the horse. In addition, Erasmus was told by John Smith that More had given 12 angels (= £4 os od sterling = £5 16s od gros Flemish = £36 12s od tournois. Cf CWE 1 312, 336–9; Ep 895). This sum, however, had apparently been pledged by Mountjoy, perhaps through More. The confusion led to embarrassment: Erasmus' financial agent probably drew a bill on the wrong person so that it had to be changed (see Allen Ep 885:28–9), and Erasmus was very late in thanking Mountjoy for his gift; see Allen Ep 888:18–20.
5 hard to move] See line 2n; and for Mountjoy's family see Ep 783:31n.
6 to court] More had taken up his duties as privy councillor soon after his return from Calais (cf Epp 623:23n, 816:6–7). The first payment of his councillor's

have one consolation, that you will serve under an excellent king; but certainly you are lost to literature, and to us.

I am setting off on a highly dangerous journey, cursing from time to time those idiot theologians who have driven me to it. It is to be expected 10 that troops who have been disbanded with empty pockets by our dukes will be all the more eager to plunder whom they can. Here is a new form of mercy! Those frightful ruffians were surrounded, so that not one could escape. The duke of Cleves, the duke of Jülich, and the duke of Nassau tried to secure that they should be let go scot free, and unless a trumpet had 15 sounded by accident, no one knows on whose authority, not one would have perished. In the confusion that resulted over a thousand were cut to pieces. Only the bishop of Cologne, who began by saying he was a priest, replied that, if he were responsible, he would treat them in such a way that they would never try anything of the sort again. The common people 20 understand this, and they can do nothing about it.

My man John told me that you had suggested to him that he should

* * * * *

annuity was made on 21 June 1518 and covered the period from Michaelmas 1517, but he is called 'councillor' somewhat earlier, on 26 August. When the court was at Abingdon he wrote at Henry VIII's request his famous letter to the University of Oxford dated 29 March, and on 22 May he wrote, still from the court, to William Gonnell. More's continual attendance upon the king's person is documented by a series of official letters signed by him beginning in July 1519 and continuing for ten years; see E.E. Reynolds *St Thomas More* (New York 1957) 100–1; Rogers Epp 42:29–30, 60, 63; G.R. Elton 'Thomas More, Councillor (1517–1529)' in *St Thomas More: Action and Contemplation* ed Richard S. Sylvester (New Haven 1972) 85–122.

9 journey] See Ep 770 introduction.
11 troops] The Black Band (cf Epp 628:33n, 832:14–30) had crossed the Rhine into Cleves early in 1518. The princes mentioned by Erasmus gathered an army to oppose it, but then permitted the marauders to surrender their weapons and disband. Only one column was annihilated by the *reiters* of Cologne near Verloo at the beginning of April, after it had been engaged in a skirmish with local peasants; cf Henne II 214–15; *Annalen des historischen Vereins für den Niederrhein* V (1858) 70–1.
14 Cleves] John II, 1458–1521
14 Jülich] John III of Cleves (1490–1539), son of John II and subsequently a patron of Erasmus. In 1511–12 he succeeded his father-in-law in the duchy of Jülich, to which Cleves was added after the death of his own father.
14 Nassau] Heinrich III, count of Nassau-Dillenburg, 1483–1538, the uncle of William the Silent. He had been the governor of Holland and Zeeland since 1515; see Ep 147:64n; NNBW.
18 Cologne] Hermann von Wied, 1477–1552; he had been archbishop of Cologne since 1505.
22 John] Smith; see Ep 820 introduction.

join your household. If this is true, I am delighted; for his precious mother
does not think her son can be all right except in England. He has made some
progress with his education, although he is not a literary type; as a person   25
he is as honest and as friendly as you could wish. I know you will do what
you can to keep him from being spoilt by bad company; and you will not
find it difficult to take upon yourself some part of what I have done for him.

Linacre's work I have not yet been able to see in this part of the world,
the French having some conspiracy against us. The bearer of this, Thomas   30
Grey, my enthusiastic admirer but a slightly tedious one, is trying to buy
some land that belonged to his ancestors from Colt, your relative. If you
have no leisure to help him over the business, please at least advise him
what you think he had better do.

When the next edition of my *Proverbs* arrives, mind you read the   35
adage 'Cum Bitho Bacchius,' and also 'Ut fici oculis inherentes.'

830 / To Hermann von dem Busche   Louvain, 23 April 1518

This letter was printed in the *Farrago*. Hermann von dem Busche, 1468–1534,
was a Westphalian knight, humanist, and poet. In Deventer he studied under
Alexander Hegius together with Johannes Murmellius, who became his close
friend. He continued his studies in Heidelberg, Italy, and Cologne and afterwards lived as an itinerant teacher and professor. In 1516–17 he was head of
the school at Wesel, and in a letter of 18 November [1517] (printed by Kronen-
berg; see Ep 697 introduction) he was the first to spread the rumour of
Murmellius' poisoning, without, however, casting suspicion on Gerardus
Listrius (cf Ep 697). He returned to Cologne repeatedly, and Erasmus expected
him to be there when he wrote this letter (cf Ep 808:3). He was a friend of both

* * * * *

29 Linacre's work] See Epp 755:32n, 785:19–20.
31 Grey] See Ep 768:18n.
32 Colt] John Colt, of Netherhall, near Harlow, Essex (d 22 October 1521), the
   father of More's first wife
35 *Proverbs*] The *Adagia*; cf Ep 783:29n.
36 'Cum ... Bacchius'] *Adagia* II v 97; but Erasmus was most likely thinking of II v
   98, to which he added in the 1517–18 edition a malicious story about a
   controversy between Henry Standish and an Italian friar (cf Phillips 361–8). It
   hints at Standish's hatred of the Italian merchants and his popularity with the
   London mob; cf Ep 608:15n.
36 'Ut ... inherentes'] 'Like figs [tumours] which grow in the eye' (and cannot be
   removed without destroying the sight) : *Adagia* II viii 65. In the 1517–18
   edition Erasmus added some bold remarks about wicked princes corrupted by
   dishonest counsellors, especially friars, and also some about the Swiss; cf Epp
   809:31n, 855 beginning.

Hutten and Neuenahr and contributed to both parts of the *Epistolae obscurorum virorum* as well as to other publications in connection with the Reuchlin controversy; cf Holborn *Hutten* 61, 65; D. Reichling *Johannes Murmellius* (Freiburg i. Br. 1880) 11 and passim.

ERASMUS TO HIS FRIEND HERMANN VON DEM BUSCHE,
GREETING

You cannot believe how sorely it grieves me that your disagreement should daily get worse. I am surprised that theologians and professed followers of a strict religious life should stir up trouble of this kind, the outcome of which 5 must be quite uncertain. Those *Lamentationes* – what could be more misguided or unpleasant or ill-written or malignant? I could wish that our eaglet would keep his talons off such frightful stuff, from which he can get nothing but corruption and filth. A man who takes on the Preachers has mob-warfare on his hands. 10

As for Listrius, if what you say is true, I am very sorry that he should have been so foolish. I will write to him and protest; though it will be too late, if the book is already published. Farewell, my learned friend.

Louvain, 23 April 1518

831 / To Jean Grolier   Louvain, 24 April 1518

This is a formal letter to a potential patron, composed with great care and published in the *Auctarium*. For variants between the three drafts in the Deventer Letter-book and for another MS copy see Allen's notes and the *addendum* in Allen IV xxviii.

Jean Grolier (1479–1565) was born in Lyon of a family originally from Verona. He succeeded his father as the treasurer of the duchy of Milan under French occupation and was a famous bibliophile. The suggestion that Erasmus should write to him came from the bookseller Francesco Giulio Calvo (see Ep 581:33n), who was in Louvain at this moment (cf Ep 832:32–3). He held out hopes for a rich reward and later mentioned an answer by Grolier. It seems that the treasurer wrote one, but it had not reached Erasmus in August 1519 and seems now to be lost; see Allen Ep 1002:24–8.

* * * * *

830
3 disagreement] See Ep 821:19n.
6 *Lamentationes*] See Ep 622 introduction.
8 eaglet] Neuenahr; see Ep 808:7n.
11 Listrius] See Ep 838.

ERASMUS OF ROTTERDAM TO THE
RIGHT HONOURABLE JEAN GROLIER, HIS MAJESTY'S
TREASURER IN LOMBARDY, GREETING

The friendship of great men, men like yourself, illustrious Grolier, when it
is freely offered or by some good fortune comes my way, is a thing I always 5
eagerly accept, for to my mind it is the greatest and the most blessed thing
there is; and having once accepted it, it is my delight to preserve the link
without letting go. And yet it is not my way to force myself upon another
man's acquaintance, for such is my natural dislike of all forms of self-
seeking that I could not endure to pursue even that one thing in human 10
affairs which I think worth pursuing, if anything ever is. Tell me, by all the
Graces, what possession could fall to a man's lot that is more honourable,
more secure, or more enjoyable than sincere and truly congenial friends?
Some men measure their felicity by the produce of their estates and their
annual revenue; I count myself truly rich and more fortunate than Croesus 15
himself in the possession of so many friends in many parts of the world of
proved integrity and famous learning and distinguished rank. As long as
the powers above in their kindness allow me to retain these unimpaired, I
cannot fail to think myself blessed with true opulence, let others despise my
modest fortunes if they will. 20

And if a new friend is added to the familiar list, I reckon my fortune
and my property increased by no small gain. Guillaume Budé, with whom I
long ago contracted a friendship of an ordinary kind, has recently been
united with me in a close and sacred bond of intimacy, and has brought
with him to share our relationship two gifted men in Deloynes and Ruzé. 25
May all the Muses hate me if I am not more pleased by this acquisition than
if his Catholic Majesty had made me a bishop. And yet, such being my
attitude, the one thing I secretly desire above all else I cannot bring myself to
pursue. At last, however, the almost invincible modesty of my temperament has been overcome and driven out by the importunity or the persua- 30
sive power of Giulio Calvo; for he insisted in such terms that I should
approach your noble self by letter, and so urged and pressed his point, that
willy-nilly he drove me to obey him and was able to drag his friend Erasmus
wherever he would by the scruff of the neck. And then he painted your

* * * * *

831
15 Croesus] *Adagia* I vi 74
22 Budé] His Ep 819 may just have arrived with Calvo, likewise a letter from
Deloynes; see Ep 819 introduction.
27 bishop] See Ep 475:2–8.
34 scruff of the neck] Cf *Adagia* IV ix 50.

distinguished virtues to me with such rare eloquence that I was fired to   35
follow my captor of my own accord, and even to outrun him. What else
could one expect? With the bright colours furnished him in plenty by your
natural gifts, and with the cunning brushwork of his eloquence, he gave me
no mere outline of you, mind and body, but set before my eyes a lifelike
finished picture, reproducing Grolier full-length like a modern Apelles on   40
the canvas, or more truly in the mirror, so that I should have seen you less
clearly had I gazed upon you in person at close quarters with the most
penetrating eyes. His native fluency was aided by his great devotion to you,
for, as Quintilian reminds us, a great part of eloquence comes from the
heart. She is an active and very powerful deity, the goddess of persuasion,   45
called by the Ancients with good reason 'mistress of minds'; and she is
quite unconquerable and uncontrollable, when supported by desire.

How he swept me away, how he kindled and inflamed me, as he told
his long and yet delightful tale of some new heroic figure, blest alike with
every gift of mind and body, richly endowed with all the Rhamnusian   50
goddess can bestow, deserving our respect and awe by every excellence,
every distinction – and yet with such modest affability of manners that he
alone seemed to be ignorant of his own greatness; such munificent
generosity towards all who have character and learning to recommend them
that one might think he held his fortune in trust for others, not for himself;   55
as though divinely sent for the express purpose of doing good to the whole
field of humane studies and those who pursue them. A true image in this
our age of Maecenas of old, in whose praises so many of the greatest authors
vied with one another, you not only favour learned men, encourage them
and support them, but shed upon the circle of scholarship as much the   60
honour of your company as the material blessings of your patronage. You
choose the gifted objects of your affection; and only that affection seems to
me worth the name that comes by choice. And a clear-sighted choice indeed
it is, but not so clear as to preclude a fair and open mind; nor, yet again, so
open as not to know Homer from Cherylus or Mevius from Maro. Another   65
proof of your outstanding merit, and one that does you great honour, is
this: his most Christian Majesty, well knowing how you unite integrity and
wisdom with no common learning, has set you at the head of great affairs
while your years are yet fresh and green. But far more honourable it is that

* * * * *

44 Quintilian] *Institutio oratoria* 10.7.15
46 Ancients] Pacuvius the tragedian, quoted by Cicero *De oratore* 2.44.187
50 Rhamnusian goddess] Properly Nemesis, as Erasmus knew – cf *Adagia* II vi 38;
    LB II 597F; but he uses the expression here and elsewhere to mean Fortune.
65 Cherylus ... Mevius] Proverbially bad poets (cf Ep 809:47n)

the office of treasurer, unpopular of itself, should have been rendered   70
acceptable and even popular by your fairness and your affability; for during
your tenure of it you have redoubled the glory lately won by your prince on
the field of arms, making the Italians understand, by the way you perform
your duties, that among the French too there are men whom it is no
discredit to obey – who receive the willing and cheerful obedience of those   75
who have learnt to obey nothing save excellence.

As I set down all this, my mind has long been warming to its work, and
my friend Calvo fans the flame, leaving no stone unturned to fill me with
enthusiastic admiration for you, as he produces one book after another to
show what distinguished scholars strive to exalt the name of Grolier by   80
their publications, because they think a work needs no further brilliance or
splendour if it has Grolier's world-famous name shining at its head. Not
that I think outstanding merit needs any advertisement. Moderate accomplishments, maybe, gain from the gifted support of skilful pens; but
although one may help out starlight with a lantern, if one will, the sun at   85
least, wherever he may be, outshines all save himself, darkening as he does
whatever light you may bring forward from another source. It is ourselves
we benefit, when we commend what we write by the popular patronage of
such names as yours. You owe nothing to our books; it is our books that are
in debt to you, for you will secure them an undying name among posterity.   90
Even if it were true that outstanding merit needs the support of literature to
secure immortality, you yourself need not seek elsewhere what you have at
home; for with all your encouragement of literary men, you are at the same
time yourself the most literate of them all. A great spirit indeed, and worthy
of royalty! Happy is France, which you ennoble in so many ways! Happy   95
the Milanese, ancient Insubria, to whom, as in that famous apophthegm of
Plato, you offer the spectacle of the ruler-philosopher, governing public
affairs in such a way that all the time you are the high-priest of intellectual
activity!

Need I waste words, most honoured Grolier? I confess with shame,   100
but truth will out: my mind was filled with longing by all this, promising
itself a great accession of felicity if it should be the good fortune of my

* * * * *

73 field of arms] In the battle of Marignano (13–14 September 1515), which
   re-established the French rule in Lombardy
78 stone unturned] *Adagia* I iv 30
96 the Milanese] Erasmus refers to them here as *Insubria*, the Latin name for that
   part of Cisalpine Gaul, the later Lombardy. Both France (called as usual Gaul)
   and Insubria were added when the letter was revised for publication; the text
   as sent ran 'Happy the commonwealth to whom ...'

humble self to be enrolled among the heralds of your virtues. As I dwelt
upon this, I felt a flattering hope, based on your exceptional generosity; but
as I spat in my bosom and reckoned 'how scanty is the gear I have at home,'   105
it struck me that this was a selfish dream. 'What have my worse-than-
Carian Muses,' I cried, 'worthy the glory of a Grolier? It is not every hand
can model a Jupiter.' But as I was already almost abandoning hope, Calvo
restored my spirits, first building up with all the figures in rhetoric a picture
of your incredible generosity to all men of learning, and then a certain   110
special leaning towards my gifts and my writings, such as they are. Having
persuaded me of this with an oath by all that is sacred, he begins to urge me,
the headstrong fellow that he is, actually to make the first overtures with a
letter. But anything, I thought, would be better than the *bêtise* of seeking the
friendship of a man without peer by way of a careless letter written on the   115
spur of the moment. For at that time what else could I do, wearied as I was
by a journey to Flanders, and so much occupied in the preparations for a
German journey that I thought it was almost more trouble to get ready than
to go? I do assure you, it seemed a question not merely of discourtesy
towards you but even of damage to my reputation.   120

I was successful with my arguments, but none the less Calvo maintained the pressure, taking upon himself the whole risk of the enterprise
and promising to be responsible if anything should go astray; he knew, of
course, that the risk was negligible, relying on your generosity, of which he
had so much experience. To cut it short, he tipped the cart that was already   125
half over, as the old saying goes. I put a bold face on it and summoned up
my courage under Calvo's inspiration for the daring deed. If it should turn
out well, if you are not reluctant to add the name of Erasmus to the list of
your dependants, I will strive to rouse to their full pitch such little gifts as I

* * * * *

105 spat in my bosom] This keeps Nemesis away and is advisable after anything
    that might attract her attentions, such as boasting or unusual good fortune
    (Theocritus 6.39 etc).
105 'how scanty ... home'] Persius 4.52, a favourite quotation
107 Carian Muses] Coarse, unsolicited adulation: *Adagia* I viii 79
117 journey to Flanders] A visit with Mark Lauwerijns at Bruges had been planned
    earlier but was postponed because of Lent (beginning 21 February 1518; Easter
    was on 4 April; cf Ep 789:2). On 5 April Erasmus' departure was imminent (cf
    Ep 809:4–6). The journey probably included a dinner with Antonius Clava at
    Ghent (cf Ep 841). It may have been on his way to Flanders or on his return
    from there that Erasmus failed to meet with Philip of Burgundy on or about 12
    April; cf Ep 811 introduction.
118 German journey] See Ep 770 introduction.
126 old saying] *Adagia* I vi 13

may have and try out every vein, in hopes of being able to rough-hew   130
something on a grander scale and worthy of a great name like yours.
Perhaps what nature will not give me will be supplied by my enthusiasm for
you, and what my own genius lacks your gifts will provide. But if my
forwardness earns your disapproval, cast all the blame for my rashness on
Calvo; you must charge me with nothing, except that I believed the word of   135
a most persuasive man or yielded to one who urged me and knew not what
it was to be defeated. In short, I care not if you reject my letter, provided you
accept my sentiments towards you, of which I have given you some evidence now and will provide fuller proof hereafter. Farewell, most distinguished and most learned of men.   140
        Louvain, 24 April 1518

832 / To Cuthbert Tunstall   Louvain, 24 April 1518

        See Ep 820 introduction.

TO TUNSTALL

Greeting. I have thrown over everything else and am devoting all my efforts
to one end, that the New Testament should come out as soon as possible as I
should wish to see it, fortified also with Leo's approval, that Codrus and his
like may burst with spleen. I am surprised that you should object to *hyemare*   5
(to overwinter), which occurs so often in Caesar, in many other places but
especially at the start of the third book. *Exaltare* (to raise up) I find in
Columella. That old friend of mine is up to his old tricks. From the bill of

* * * * *

832
4 Leo's approval] See Ep 864.
4 Codrus] Virgil *Eclogues* 7.26
5 *hyemare*] See *Novum Testamentum* 1 Cor 16:6 (LB VI 745C–D, 746A). Erasmus
    retained the word in both the 1516 and the 1518–19 editions, but in a note
    newly added to the latter he expressed misgivings about its appropriateness,
    despite Caesar.
6 Caesar] *De bello gallico* 3.1
8 Columella] 3.13.4
8 old tricks] Tunstall supported Erasmus repeatedly with gifts of money (cf Epp
    597:21–2, Allen 1487:1–2). The bill of exchange that he sent later brought
    Erasmus 60 florins money-of-account (= livres d'Artois), which is the exact
    equivalent of the 30 ducats referred to by Erasmus (= £10 0s 0d gros Flemish =
    £6 17s 6d sterling = £62 5s 0d tournois). Cf CWE 1 314, 336–9, 347; Epp 463:49n,
    621 introduction, 886. Erasmus' statement that the only part of the bill of
    exchange that he could understand was 'thirty ducats at the rate of 30 deniers,'
    as published in Allen (Ep 832:10–11), does not make any sense, however, for

exchange I learnt nothing, not understanding a single word. I exchanged
one bill for another on account of attacks by robbers everywhere. All went   10
without a trace of suspicion on either side. But even now I do not understand what they put, except that I read 'thirty ducats at the rate of 30
deniers.'

I am getting ready to start from hour to hour, but hardly see how I can
creep into Germany. Those criminal scum, the Black Band, have lately been   15
disbanded by the clemency of our rulers, which will prove so cruel to us all.
They were kept in a state of siege, there was no way of escape, the farming
people were fired with one ambition, to kill them to a man – and indeed they
deserved to be killed over and over again. A thousand more or less were cut
down, on orders shouted by someone, it is not known who; otherwise it   20
was the intention of the princes to turn this godless band, reeking with
every crime, loose on our lives and fortunes. The slaughter was stopped,
and the survivors given leave to lay down their arms and depart, so as to
make it a serious offence for anyone, country or town, to kill them wherever
they might be found. Could there be a more disastrous policy for the   25
community? Those ruffians will feel that they owe their lives to two or three
princes; the loss of some among their number they will avenge on the lives
of ordinary people. Already there are stories everywhere of the murder of
travellers. This is not disbanding the band, this is rousing against us all a set
of robbers who are ready of their own accord for any outrage. Whichever   30
way I turn, I will let you know.

Giulio Calvo is here, a bookseller from Pavia, a cheerful, scholarly
man. He brought me a Theocritus printed with added commentary, and
Pindar too with notes added by various hands. He gave me also some
fragments of Fronto and Varro and other authors which are very ancient; I   35
will send them to you by my man John, if I am allowed to carry them off, but
I am not perfectly certain that I was not dreaming when he said 'The book is

* * * * *

the ducat was worth 8od gros Flemish. But Allen's rendition 'duchati trenta
della ragione di xxx denari' could very easily be a misprint, or a misreading (by
Allen or the scribe of the Deventer Letter-book) of 'lxxx denari' – that is, the
8od gros that was the current rate.
15 Germany] See Ep 770 introduction.
15 Black Band] See Ep 829:11n.
32 Calvo] See Epp 819, 831 introductions.
33 Theocritus] Probably the edition by Zacharias Kallierges (Rome January 1516);
   cf Ep 827:8n. The same scholar-printer also published a Greek Pindar in 1515;
   cf Ep 642:5n.
35 fragments] Presumably a manuscript
36 John] Smith

yours.' I should be really sorry for poor More's bad luck in being haled to
court, were it not that under such a king and with so many educated
colleagues and acquaintances, one might think it more a shrine of the Muses   40
than a palace. But meanwhile there is no news out of Utopia to make us
laugh, and he, I know, would rather enjoy a joke than ride in a state coach. I
made excuses for you in my last letter to Budé for not writing.

I am sending my John back to England; he has not, I perceive, such a
natural gift for scholarship that he can look to it to better himself, and his   45
mother cannot think her precious son safe anywhere outside England. Yet I
do not feel I am parting from him, since he is moving to join the household
of my beloved More. He is the most sincere person in the world, and I
should like to recommend him to you, in case you perceive that he needs
help to escape being corrupted by bad company. Farewell.   50

    Louvain, 24 April 1518

833 / To Roger [Wentford]   Louvain, 24 April [1518]

This letter follows Ep 772; see Ep 820 introduction.

ERASMUS TO HIS FRIEND ROGER, GREETING
I am grateful to you for adding something out of your own notes. But, by
suppressing the chief dialogue, you seem to be the enemy of your own
reputation; for I was getting ready to dedicate this book, such as it is, to you.
Your letter, though it was very brief, gave me great pleasure. Keep it up.   5
Best wishes.

    Louvain, 24 April

834 / To Henry VIII   Louvain, 25 April 1518

Of all the gifts and messages which John Smith had brought back from

* * * * *

39 court] See Ep 829:6n.
43 Budé] See Epp 778:55–8, 813.

833
2 notes] Perhaps concerning the New Testament; cf Ep 864 introduction.
3 chief dialogue] Of the manuscript, now returned to Erasmus (cf Ep 772),
   containing some drafts for Erasmus' *Colloquia*. The first authorized edition (cf
   Ep 909 introduction) contained no recognizable references to Wentford, nor
   did subsequent ones.

England (cf Epp 820, 823 introductions), Henry's (described in Ep 816) were no doubt the most significant. The purpose of this letter – first published in the *Auctarium* – was twofold. First, it acknowledges a cash gift of 60 angel-nobles (= £20 sterling = £29 gros Flemish = £183 tournois) in response to the dedication of Plutarch (cf Ep 657; Allen I 44:10–15) and the appeals conveyed through Epp 783, 787; the money was remitted through Colet and Franz Birckmann (cf Ep 825). Secondly, Erasmus accepts a renewed invitation to settle in England as the titular holder of a major benefice (cf Ep 694:11n). His intention to go there after his return from Basel was serious. It is often stated, frequently with added praise for the unique patronage of scholarship extended by the English court; cf the indexes to CWE 5, 6 and 7 sv 'England' and Ep 886 introduction.

TO HIS SERENE MAJESTY HENRY VIII KING OF ENGLAND
FROM ERASMUS OF ROTTERDAM, GREETING
Prosperity and undying fame attend your Highness. Your Majesty's present was most acceptable to me in many ways, being generous in itself and the gift of a king, especially a king as much distinguished by his love of   5
excellence as by the wealth of his dominions, so that to win approval from his judgment is more glorious than to be enriched by his generosity. Yet it was welcome for this reason in particular, that it seemed to add a fresh endorsement to your long-standing opinion of me, which has led you so often to bestow not honour only but kindness on my humble self. And as if   10
your goodwill towards humane studies found this insufficient, you now freely offer me a permanent position, and that of no common kind. So far am I from refusing this, that I could wish to serve even without reward under such a prince, in whose presence a man's position and influence are in direct relation to his literary culture and his uprightness of life, whose court   15
is a model of a Christian society, so rich in men of the highest attainments that any university might envy it. I pray God Almighty that it may be his pleasure to continue this mind in you perpetually and to preserve you in health as long as possible for the benefit of your realm, that for many years it may flower and flourish in true blessedness under a most excellent and   20
flourishing prince. I myself am obliged to expend four months on the publication of the New Testament; but when once that business is finished, I shall devote myself entirely to the service of your Majesty. May Christ Jesus, who is the sole guide and defender of princes, preserve you in health and wealth and bring you to ever greater glory.   25
    Louvain, 25 April 1518
    Erasmus of Rotterdam

835 / To Domenico Grimani   Louvain, 26 April 1518

Erasmus had written Epp 333–5 to cardinals Grimani and Riario (of San Giorgio) and to Leo x in an effort to solicit papal sanction of the forthcoming edition of Saint Jerome. Both cardinals sent an answer to Andrea Ammonio, but only Riario's (Ep 340) was finally recovered and published by Erasmus in 1529. Now in this letter, as in Ep 860 (cf Ep 619:11–12), Erasmus expects Ammonio to have received letters by Grimani and another cardinal concerning the dedication of the New Testament to Leo x (cf Ep 384). Perhaps he confused the two editions – a confusion that is all the more likely as he had not seen the answers. In view of Epp 338:27n and 456:218–28 it appears that he wished to create the impression that Leo x had included the New Testament in his sanction of the Jerome edition. His confusion may thus be an inadvertent expression of the same desire.

This letter was first published in the *Auctarium*.

TO HIS EMINENCE CARDINAL GRIMANI
Greeting, my most revered Lord. My Paraphrase of St Paul's Epistle to the Romans, which is dedicated to you, has been in the hands of the public for some time, and is received with applause in learned circles. This is no doubt due to your personality rather than to the work itself. So far I have not sent   5
the volume to your Eminence, partly because I did not much care for the first edition, partly because I know that parcels of any weight do not easily survive so long a journey. Now it has been rather elegantly printed by a press in Basel, and I have decided to risk it, in case the work has not yet reached your Eminence. If I understand that the work is acceptable, and   10
even satisfactory, to the judgment of so great a man, I shall soon address myself to a similar exposition of the other Epistles, for the demands of those who in many places are anxious to learn encourage me to make the effort.

I hear that your Eminence has been so kind as to write to me about my New Testament, of which I had sent a copy still wet from the press from   15
Basel by the hands of some gadabout fellow. But though it was dispatched nearly two years ago, I have not yet been allowed to see your letter, whether this is due to bad faith or my misfortune. A letter from his eminence the cardinal of San Giorgio went so badly astray, having been sent by Am-

* * * * *

835
2 Paraphrase] See Ep 710 introduction.
5 not sent] For a similar failure cf Epp 446:75–7, Allen 939:12–16.
15 New Testament] Perhaps a confusion; see introduction.
16 gadabout fellow] See Ep 701:2n.

monio to Germany, that I have never been able to trace what happened to it.   20
Your letter has perished with Ammonio himself. My respectful best wishes
to your Eminence, to whom I commend myself and my work as to my best of
benefactors. I will shortly write at greater length, when I have the chance of
a more reliable courier.

Louvain, morrow of St Mark, 1518   25

836 / To Johannes Lascaris   Louvain, 26 April 1518

Lascaris (cf Ep 269:55) had been in Rome since 1513, but had left for Paris
before October 1518 (cf Allen Ep 865:57–8). In Paris Glareanus met him
frequently during 1518 and early 1519 (cf Ep 903; Zwingli *Werke* VII Ep 69, 25
March 1519). In 1520 Francis I sent him to Milan, where he established a
college for Greek boys similar to the one he had directed at Rome (cf Zwingli
Werke VII Ep 153). This letter was probably directed to Rome and dispatched
with Ep 835. Erasmus may perhaps have hoped to catch Lascaris himself in
between two masters and to win him for the Collegium Trilingue at Louvain;
cf Epp 691 introduction, 865.

This letter was first printed in the *Auctarium*.

TO JOHANNES LASCARIS, THE GREEK SCHOLAR
Greetings to a man distinguished in many fields. Jérôme de Busleyden, a
learned and influential man and a leading light of this kingdom, who died
recently on a journey into Spain, has bequeathed many thousands of ducats
for the foundation of a new college in Louvain, where the university is at   5
present most flourishing, in which free and public instruction is to be given
in the three tongues, Hebrew, Greek, and Latin, in return for a substantial
salary of about seventy ducats, which can, however, be increased according
to the person appointed. The Hebrew teacher is already in residence, and so

* * * * *

836
8 seventy ducats] Indeed a substantial offer worth 140 florins of account or livres
  d'Artois (= £23 6s 8d gros Flemish = £16 0s 10d sterling = £145 5s 0d tournois
  in relative gold values). Busleyden's will stipulated annual salaries of 72 livres
  d'Artois for the professors (= £12 gros Flemish = £8 5s 0d sterling = £74 14s 0d
  tournois). Matthaeus Adrianus was paid 30 livres d'Artois, probably in addition to free lodgings. Rutgerus Rescius, when first appointed to the Greek
  chair, received 36 livres d'Artois plus board and lodging. Cf de Vocht CTL I 251,
  294; CWE 1 314, 336–9, 347, CWE 2 327–44; Epp 447:844n, 463:48n, 621 introduction. In Allen Ep 854:55 100 gold pieces, undoubtedly ducats, are offered for a
  comparable position in Venice.
9 Hebrew teacher] Matthaeus Adrianus; see Ep 686:7n.

is the Latin. For the Greek chair there are a number of candidates. But my   10
advice has always been that we should secure a native Greek, from whom
his audience could acquire the true pronunciation of Greek at first hand. My
opinion is supported by all those who have the charge of this business, and
they have asked me to invite on their behalf anyone whom I might consider
to be suitable. I therefore beg you, with your habitual kindness towards me   15
or, if you prefer, with your known desire to encourage humane studies, if
you know of anyone who you think might do credit both to you and to
myself, arrange for him to come here as soon as possible. His travelling
expenses, salary, and lodging will be provided. He will find his colleagues
most honourable and civilized men. He can rely on this letter of mine as   20
surely as if we had taken a hundred legal documents to settle the business.
Between honest men honest dealing needs no parchments. Pray do your
best to choose a suitable man, and I will see that he does not regret his
coming here. Farewell, most learned and distinguished friend.
    Louvain, morrow of St Mark 1518   25

837 / To Gerard Geldenhouwer   Louvain, 26 April [1518]

    See Ep 811 introduction.

ERASMUS TO HIS FRIEND NIJMEGEN, GREETING
I beg you most earnestly to make sure my lord understands that my failure
to wait upon him was due to a misunderstanding; do not let him suspect
that I sought to avoid speech with him, when it was the thing I most wished
for. That was my motive in writing the letter which my man John brought   5
for you, hoping that you would pass on the gist to his lordship. I thought I
had couched it in such terms as would clear my own name without putting
any blame on you. I am in all the turmoil of preparing for a journey, where to
I do not yet know, but in any case I am preparing. Be true to yourself, my
dear Gerard. And so farewell.   10
    Louvain, morrow of St Mark

    * * * * *

    10 the Latin] Jan Becker van Borssele, who did not, however, choose to stay in
      Louvain; see Ep 849.
    10 number of candidates] See Ep 691:19n.

     837
    5 John] Smith, carrying Ep 812
    8 journey] See Ep 770 introduction.

838 / To Gerardus Listrius   [Louvain, c 26 April 1518]

This letter was written in accordance with the intention stated in Ep 830:12.
Listrius had prepared to defend himself against a slanderous rumour that he
had caused Johannes Murmellius to die of poison (see Ep 697 introduction).
Erasmus was so concerned that he wrote twice (cf line 2) to Listrius, but failed
to stop him. Only the second letter is known. It may have been dispatched
with Ep 837, which was copied on the same page of the Deventer Letter-book.

ERASMUS TO HIS FRIEND LISTRIUS, GREETING
I sent you a letter yesterday by a man who is twice a canon, and a black
canon at that. Now I send another by Goswin. If your attack on Murmellius
is not published yet, I urge you and beg you to suppress it, for Busche is
threatening something in the way of a counterblast. I should hate to see so   5
much satisfaction given to those accursed enemies of humane studies. It is
not yet clear by which route I shall make my way into Germany; for I want to
revisit Basel if I can. Your friend Herman I have not yet seen. Nève is
resentful because Goswin asked Dorp to take charge of a young man with
letters of introduction to himself, for those two do not get on very well. And   10
in fact Dorp's behaviour was very uncivil, not to say dishonest. Farewell.
    I shall return to you, God willing, next winter.

839 / To Cornelis Batt   Louvain, 29 April [1518]

Cornelis, the son of Erasmus' old friend Jacob Batt, was an assistant teacher
and private tutor at Groningen. A year earlier he had written to Erasmus in

* * * * *

838
2 twice a canon] An unidentified canon regular of St Augustine (in black garb);
    cf Ep 718:5–7.
3 Goswin] Goswin of Halen near Roermond (c 1468–1530), a member of the
    Brethren of the Common Life and head of the brethren's house at Groningen.
    For the purpose of his trip to Louvain cf lines 8–10.
3 Murmellius] Johannes Murmellius of Roermond (1480–2 October 1517). Like
    Goswin he was a pupil of Agricola and Hegius. A prolific writer of humanistic
    text books and verse, he was headmaster at Alkmaar from 1513 until the city
    was sacked by the Black Band (cf Ep 829:11n) in June 1517. While looking for a
    new position he died suddenly at Deventer; cf NNBW.
8 if I can] See Ep 832:14–31.
8 Herman] Perhaps Hermannus Stuvius (Stüve), a teacher at the school of
    Zwolle which was headed by Listrius; cf D. Reichling *Johannes Murmellius*
    (Freiburg i. Br. 1880; reprint Nieuwkoop 1963) 107 and passim.
11 uncivil] Cf Ep 696 introduction.

search of a more satisfactory position (see Ep 573). This letter was published in the *Farrago*.

ERASMUS OF ROTTERDAM TO CORNELIS BATT, GREETING
Your feelings towards me, my dear boy, are gladly and gratefully received, and I will do my best to show you that the memory of your dear father and my affection for him are by no means dead. Only make it your business to see that in both life and learning you are worthy of so excellent and scholarly 5
a man. I am now off to Basel, at the call of business. If you can endure to remain where you are, stay until I get back; for I shall return, God willing, in October. Otherwise you should consult Jean of Hondschoote, regent of the College of the Lily at Louvain, and if he approves go to Bruges and talk with Dr Mark Lauwerijns, the coadjutor, as they call him nowadays, of the dean 10
of St Donatian's, to whom I will write a line about you today. Mind you give my greetings to that excellent and liberal-minded man, Father Goswin. I hope you are devoting time to Greek and to reading good authors. You will find enclosed in this letter a gold Flemish noble, as a small token of my good wishes for the time being. Farewell, dear Cornelis. 15
Louvain, 29 April, 151[7]

840 / To Mark Lauwerijns   Louvain, 29 April [1518]

This is the letter promised in Ep 839:10–11. It was published in the *Farrago*.

ERASMUS TO HIS FRIEND MARK, GREETING
I have had a letter from Cornelis, the son of my old and dear friend, Batt. The young man is a good linguist and quite well read, but a cripple. He has a great longing for this part of the world, for he is now under-master at Groningen. If by any chance he comes to see you, consider whether he can 5
be any use to you; if not, send him back to Louvain. I should not like you to do anything to please me against your better judgment. Farewell. I will write another time at greater length.
Louvain, 29 April

* * * * *

839
6 Basel] See Ep 770 introduction.
8 Hondschoote] Jean de Nève
11 a line] Ep 840
12 Goswin] See Ep 838:3n.

841 / To Antonius Clava   Louvain, 29 April [1518]

This letter was published in the *Farrago* of October 1519. Erasmus' imminent journey is most likely the one in 1518 to Basel (see Ep 770 introduction), since it will permit easy replacement of the Herodotus. The note implies that Erasmus is under an obligation after a recent meeting with Clava. He had probably spent a night with him during his journey to Flanders; cf Ep 831:117n.

ERASMUS OF ROTTERDAM TO HIS FRIEND
ANTONIUS CLAVA, GREETING

You seemed the other day to be wishing for a Herodotus in Greek. I am sending one to you as a present, for I shall easily find another in the course of my present journey. Farewell. I hardly like to send greetings to Robert de   5
Keysere, who abandoned us so haughtily at supper the other day.

Louvain, 29 April 151[7]

* * * * *

841
3 Herodotus] Allen has identified both the copy given to Clava and the one subsequently purchased to replace it as being the Aldine edition of September 1502. Clava bequeathed his to Levinus Ammonius, and in 1922 it was in a private American collection. The other copy, bound together with an Aldine Pausanias of July 1516, belonged subsequently to Jan Laski and Daniel Hein-sius. It is now in the British Library (c 45 k 6); cf Allen IV xxviii and Allen Ep 885:5–8.
6 abandoned] A recent incident or a jocular reminiscence? Cf Ep 175:8–10.

THE CORRESPONDENCE OF ERASMUS

BY YEARS

This table shows the number of letters in Allen's edition written and received by Erasmus each year from 1494 to 1536 and the number of pages occupied by each year's correspondence in that edition. For the period from 1484 to 1493 Allen includes 35 letters (totalling 58 pages), 29 written by Erasmus and 6 written to him; few of these can be dated precisely.

year	pages	letters from Erasmus	letters to Erasmus	total
1494	13	4	3	7
1495	14	4	2	6
1496	7	2	0	2
1497	30	17	0	17
1498	27	19	1	20
1499	51	27	5	32
1500	39	21	2	23
1501	26	24	2	26
1502	4	5	0	5
1503	14	5	1	6
1504	11	3	0	3
1505	9	4	1	5
1506	20	19	1	20
1507	7	3	1	4
1508	7	3	1	4
1509	5	0	3	3
1510	0	0	0	0
1511	45	20	17	37
1512	22	11	5	16
1513	28	16	0	16
1514	68	22	14	36
1515	136	26	36	62
1516	245	46	80	126
1517	357	141	101	242
1518	282	135	25	160
1519	315	111	37	148
1520	284	101	24	125
1521	171	62	12	74
1522	160	45	35	80
1523	214	45	30	75
1524	243	92	38	130
1525	245	90	35	125
1526	203	77	42	119
1527	330	89	65	154
1528	264	105	52	157
1529	311	103	61	164
1530	194	94	81	175
1531	308	106	67	173
1532	209	78	81	159
1533	203	78	66	144
1534	111	42	50	92
1535	206	35	59	94
1536	90	24	37	61

TABLE OF CORRESPONDENTS

WORKS FREQUENTLY CITED

SHORT TITLE FORMS

INDEX

TABLE OF CORRESPONDENTS

WORKS FREQUENTLY CITED

This list provides bibliographical information for works referred to in short-title form in the headnotes and footnotes to Epp 594–841. For Erasmus' writings see the short-title list, pages 433–6. Editions of his letters are included in the list below.

AK	Alfred Hartmann and B.R. Jenny eds *Die Amerbachkorrespondenz* (Basel 1942–)
Allen	P.S. Allen, H.M. Allen, and H.W. Garrod eds *Opus epistolarum Des. Erasmi Roterodami* (Oxford 1906–58) 11 vols and index
ASD	*Opera Omnia Desiderii Erasmi Roterodami* (Amsterdam 1969–)
Auctarium	*Auctarium selectarum aliquot epistolarum Erasmi Roterodami ad eruditos et horum ad illum* (Basel: Froben August 1518)
Benzing	Joseph Benzing *Die Buchdrucker des 16. und 17. Jahrhunderts im deutschen Sprachgebiet* (Wiesbaden 1963)
Bierlaire	Franz Bierlaire *La familia d'Erasme* (Paris 1968)
Bietenholz *Basle and France*	P.G. Bietenholz *Basle and France in the Sixteenth Century* (Geneva-Toronto 1971)
Bietenholz *History and Biography*	P.G. Bietenholz *History and Biography in the Work of Erasmus of Rotterdam* (Geneva 1966)
BRE	A. Horawitz and K. Hartfelder eds *Briefwechsel des Beatus Rhenanus* (Leipzig 1886; repr 1966)
Brown	Rawdon Brown et al eds *Calendar of State Papers and MSS relating to English Affairs existing in ... Northern Italy 1202–1668* (London 1864–1935) 23 vols
Budé *Opera omnia*	Guillaume Budé *Opera omnia* (Basel 1557; repr 1966) 3 vols
CWE	*Collected Works of Erasmus* (Toronto 1974–)
DBI	*Dizionario biografico degli Italiani* ed A.M. Ghisalberti et al (Rome 1960–)
DHGE	*Dictionnaire d'histoire et de géographie ecclésiastiques* ed A. Baudrillart et al (Paris 1912–)
Emden BRUC	A.B. Emden *Biographical Register of the University of Cambridge to AD 1500* (Cambridge 1963)
Emden BRUO	A.B. Emden *Biographical Register of the University of Oxford to AD 1500* (Oxford 1957–9) 3 vols; *Biographical Register of the University of Oxford, AD 1501 to 1540* (Oxford 1974)
Epistolae ad diversos	*Epistolae D. Erasmi Roterodami ad diversos et aliquot aliorum ad illum* (Basel: Froben 31 August 1521)
Epistolae ad Erasmum	*Epistolae aliquot illustrium virorum ad Erasmum Roterodamum et huius ad illos* (Louvain: Martens October 1516)

Epistolae elegantes (1517)	*Aliquot epistolae sanequam elegantes Erasmi Roterodami et ad hunc aliorum eruditissimorum hominum* (Louvain: Martens April 1517)
Epistolae elegantes (1518)	*Aliquot epistolae sanequam elegantes Erasmi Roterodami et ad hunc aliorum eruditissimorum hominum* (Basel: Froben January 1518)
Farrago	*Farrago nova epistolarum Des. Erasmi Roterodami ad alios et aliorum ad hunc: admixtis quibusdam quas scripsit etiam adolescens* (Basel: Froben October 1519)
M.-M. de la Garanderie	Marie-Madeleine de la Garanderie ed and trans *La Correspondance d'Erasme et de Guillaume Budé* (Paris 1967)
Geiger *Reuchlin*	Ludwig Geiger *Johann Reuchlin* (Leipzig 1871; reprint 1964)
Gorissen *Kortrijkse pensioen*	P. Gorissen 'Het Kortrijkse pensioen van Erasmus' *De Leiegouw* 13 (1971) 107–51
Grimm *Buchführer*	H. Grimm 'Die Buchführer des deutschen Kultur- bereichs und ihre Niederlassungsorte in der Zeitspanne 1490 bis um 1550' *Archiv für Geschichte des Buchwesens* 7 (1965–6) 1153–1772
Harsin *Erard de la Marck*	Paul Harsin *Etude critique sur l'histoire de la principauté de Liège* II: *Le règne d'Erard de la Marck 1505–1538* (Liège 1955)
Henne	Alexandre Henne *Histoire du règne de Charles-Quint en Belgique* (Brussels-Leipzig 1858–60) 10 vols
Holborn *Hutten*	Hajo Holborn *Ulrich von Hutten and the German Reformation* trans R.H. Bainton (Harper Torchbooks, New York 1966)
Hutten *Opera*	E. Böcking ed *Ulrichi Hutteni opera* (Leipzig 1859–61; repr 1963) 5 vols
Hutten *Operum supplementum*	E. Böcking ed *Ulrichi Hutteni operum supplementum* (Leipzig 1869–71) 2 vols
LB	J. Leclerc ed *Desiderii Erasmi Roterodami opera omnia* (Leiden 1703–6) 10 vols
LP	*Letters and Papers, Foreign and Domestic, of the Reign of Henry VIII* ed J.S. Brewer, J. Gairdner, R.H. Brodie (London 1862–1932) 36 vols
Luther *Werke* (Weimar)	*D. Martin Luther Werke: Kritische Gesamtausgabe* (Weimar 1883–)
Nichols	F.M. Nichols ed and trans *The Epistles of Erasmus from his Earliest Letters to his Fifty-First Year* 2nd ed (New York 1962) 3 vols
NK	W. Nijhoff and M.E. Kronenberg eds *Nederlandsche Bibliographie van 1500 tot 1540* (The Hague 1923–71)
NNBW	*Nieuw Nederlandsch Biografisch Woordenboek* ed P.C. Molhuysen et al, 2nd ed (Amsterdam 1974) 10 vols and Register

Opuscula	W.K. Ferguson ed *Erasmi opuscula: A Supplement to the Opera omnia* (The Hague 1933)
Pastor	Ludwig von Pastor *The History of the Popes, from the Close of the Middle Ages* ed and trans R.F. Kerr et al, 3rd ed (London 1938–53) 40 vols
Phillips	Margaret Mann Phillips *The 'Adages' of Erasmus* (Cambridge 1964)
PL	J.P. Migne ed *Patrologiae cursus completus ... series latina* (Paris 1844–1902) 221 vols
RE	L. Geiger ed *Johann Reuchlins Briefwechsel* (Tübingen 1875; repr 1962)
Reedijk	C. Reedijk ed *Poems of Desiderius Erasmus* (Leiden 1956)
Rogers	Elizabeth Frances Rogers ed *The Correspondence of Sir Thomas More* (Princeton 1947)
Scrinium	*Scrinium Erasmianum: Mélanges historiques publiés ... à l'occasion du cinquième centenaire de la naissance d'Erasme* ed J. Coppens (Leiden 1969) 2 vols
Utopia	The Yale Edition of the Complete Works of St Thomas More vol 4 *Utopia* ed E. Surtz SJ and J.H. Hexter (New Haven 1965)
de Vocht CTL	Henry de Vocht *History of the Foundation and the Rise of the Collegium Trilingue Lovaniense 1517–1550* Humanistica lovaniensia 10–13 (Louvain 1951–5) 4 vols
de Vocht *Busleyden*	Henry de Vocht *Jérôme de Busleyden* Humanistica lovaniensia 9 (Turnhout 1950)
de Vocht *Literae*	Henry de Vocht *Literae virorum eruditorum ad Franciscum Craneveldium 1522–1528* Humanistica lovaniensia 1 (Louvain 1928)
de Vocht MHL	Henry de Vocht *Monumenta humanistica lovaniensia* Humanistica lovaniensia 4 (Louvain 1934)
Zwingli *Werke*	*Huldreich Zwinglis Sämtliche Werke* ed E. Egli et al, Corpus Reformatorum vols 88–101 (Berlin-Zürich 1905–)

SHORT TITLE FORMS FOR ERASMUS' WORKS

Acta contra Lutherum: Acta academiae Lovaniensis contra Lutherum

Adagia: Adagiorum chiliades 1508 (Adagiorum collectanea for the primitive form, when required)

Admonitio adversus mendacium: Admonitio adversus mendacium et obtrectationem

Annotationes de haereticis: Annotationes in leges pontificias et caesareas de haereticis

Annotationes in Novum Testamentum

Antibarbari

Apologia ad Fabrum: Apologia ad Iacobum Fabrum Stapulensem

Apologia ad Caranzam: Apologia ad Sanctium Caranzam

Apologia adversus Petrum Sutorem: Apologia adversus debacchationes Petri Sutoris

Apologia adversus monachos: Apologia adversus monachos quosdam hispanos

Apologia adversus rhapsodias Alberti Pii

Apologia contra Latomi dialogum: Apologia contra Iacobi Latomi dialogum de tribus linguis

Apologia contra Stunicam: Apologia contra Lopidem Stunicam

Apologia de 'In principio erat sermo'

Apologia de laude matrimonii: Apologia pro declamatione de laude matrimonii

Apologia de loco 'omnes quidem': Apologia de loco 'Omnes quidem resurgemus'

Apologiae duae

Apologiae omnes

Apologia invectivis Lei: Apologia qua respondet duabus invectivis Eduardi Lei

Apologia monasticae religionis

Apophthegmata

Argumenta: Argumenta in omnes epistolas apostolicas nova

Axiomata pro causa Lutheri: Axiomata pro causa Martini Lutheri

Carmina

Catalogus lucubrationum

Cato

Christiani hominis institutum

Ciceronianus: Dialogus Ciceronianus

Colloquia

Compendium rhetorices

Compendium vitae

Conflictus: Conflictus Thaliae et barbariei

De bello turcico: Consultatio de bello turcico

De civilitate: De civilitate morum puerilium

De conscribendis epistolis

De constructione: De constructione octo partium orationis

De contemptu mundi

De copia: De duplici copia verborum ac rerum

Declamatio de morte

Declamationes
Declamatiuncula
Declamatiunculae
Declarationes ad censuras Lutetiae: Declarationes ad censuras Lutetiae vulgatas
De concordia: De sarcienda ecclesiae concordia
De immensa Dei misericordia: Concio de immensa Dei misericordia
De libero arbitrio: De libero arbitrio diatribe
De praeparatione: De praeparatione ad mortem
De pronuntiatione: De recta latini graecique sermonis pronuntiatione
De pueris instituendis: De pueris statim ac liberaliter instituendis
De puero Iesu: Concio de puero Iesu
De puritate tabernaculi
De ratione studii
Detectio praestigiarum: Detectio praestigiarum cuiusdam libelli germanice scripti
De tedio Iesu: Disputatiuncula de tedio, pavore, tristicia Iesu
Dilutio: Dilutio eorum quae Iodocus Clithoveus scripsit adversus declamationem
    suasoriam matrimonii

Ecclesiastes: Ecclesiastes sive de ratione concionandi
Enchiridion: Enchiridion militis christiani
Encomium matrimonii
Encomium medicinae: Declamatio in laudem artis medicae
Epigrammata
Epistola ad fratres Inferioris Germaniae: Responsio ad fratres Germaniae Inferioris
    ad epistolam apologeticam incerto autore proditam
Epistola consolatoria: Epistola consolatoria in adversis
Epistola contra pseudevangelicos: Epistola contra quosdam qui se falso iactant
    evangelicos
Epistola de apologia Cursii: Epistola de apologia Petri Cursii
Epistola de esu carnium: Epistola apologetica ad Christophorum episcopum
    Basiliensem de interdicto esu carnium
Epistola de modestia: Epistola de modestia profitendi linguas
Exomologesis: Exomologesis sive modus confitendi
Explanatio symboli: Explanatio symboli apostolorum sive catechismus

Formula: Conficiendarum epistolarum formula

Gaza: Theodori Gazae grammaticae institutionis libri duo

Hyperaspistes

Institutio christiani matrimonii
Institutio principis christiani

Julius exclusus: Dialogus Julius exclusus e coelis

Liber quo respondet annotationibus Lei: Liber quo respondet annotationibus
    Eduardi Lei

Lingua
Liturgia Virginis Matris: Virginis Matris apud Lauretum cultae liturgia
Lucubrationes
Lucubratiunculae

Methodus
Modus orandi Deum
Moria: Moriae encomium, or Moria

Novum instrumentum
Novum Testamentum

Obsecratio ad Virginem Mariam: Obsecratio sive oratio ad Virginem Mariam in
    rebus adversis
Oratio de pace: Oratio de pace et discordia
Oratio de virtute: Oratio de virtute amplectenda
Oratio funebris: Oratio funebris Berthae de Heyen

Paean Virgini Matri: Paean Virgini Matri dicendus
Panegyricus: Panegyricus ad Philippum Austriae ducem
Parabolae: Parabolae sive similia
Paraclesis
Paraphrasis in Elegantias Vallae: Paraphrasis in Elegantias Laurentii Vallae
Paraphrasis in Novum Testamentum
Paraphrasis in Matthaeum: Paraphrasis in Matthaeum, etc.
Peregrinatio apostolorum: Peregrinatio apostolorum Petri et Pauli
Precatio ad Virginis filium Iesum
Precatio dominica
Precationes
Precatio pro pace ecclesiae: Precatio ad Iesum pro pace ecclesiae
Progymnasmata: Progymnasmata quaedam primae adolescentiae Erasmi
Psalmi: Psalmi (Enarrationes sive commentarii in psalmos)
Purgatio adversus epistolam Lutheri: Purgatio adversus epistolam non sobriam
    Lutheri

Querela pacis

Ratio verae theologiae
Responsio ad annotationes Lei: Responsio ad annotationes Eduardi Lei
Responsio ad annotationem Stunicae: Responsio ad annotationem Iacobi Lopis
    Stunicae
Responsio ad collationes: Responsio ad collationes cuiusdam iuvenis gerontodidas-
    cali
Responsio ad disputationem de divortio: Responsio ad disputationem cuiusdam
    Phimostomi de divortio
Responsio ad epistolam Pii: Responsio ad epistolam paraeneticam Alberti Pii
Responsio adversus febricitantis libellum: Responsio adversus febricitantis cuius-
    dam libellum

Spongia: Spongia adversus aspergines Hutteni
Supputatio: Supputatio calumniarum Natalis Bedae
Syntaxis (De constructione)

Vidua christiana
Virginis et martyris comparatio
Vita Hieronymi: Vita diui Hieronymi Stridonensis

Index

This book

was designed by

ANTJE LINGNER

based on the series design by

ALLAN FLEMING

and was printed by

University

of Toronto

Press